D1320827

THE PRIVATE LIFE OF CHAIRMAN MAO

THE
PRIVATE
LIFE OF
CHAIRMAN
MAO

The memoirs of Mao's personal physician
Dr. Li Zhisui

Translated by Professor Tai Hung-chao

With the editorial assistance of Anne F. Thurston

Foreword by Professor Andrew J. Nathan,
Columbia University

Chatto & Windus
LONDON

First published in 1994

1 3 5 7 9 10 8 6 4 2

Copyright © 1994 by Dr Li Zhisui
Map of China copyright © 1994 by David Lindroth Inc.
Map of Zhongnanhai copyright © 1994 by Anita Karl and Jim Kemp

First published in the United Kingdom in 1994 by
Chatto & Windus Limited
Random House, 20 Vauxhall Bridge Road
London SW1V 2SA

Random House Australia (Pty) Limited
20 Alfred Street, Milsons Point, Sydney
New South Wales 2061, Australia

Random House New Zealand Limited
18 Poland Road, Glenfield
Auckland 10, New Zealand

Random House South Africa (Pty) Limited
PO Box 337, Bergvlei, South Africa

Random House UK Limited Reg. No. 954009

A CIP catalogue record for this book
is available from the British Library

ISBN 0 7011 4018 6

Printed and bound in Great Britain by
Clays Ltd, St Ives plc

In remembrance of my
beloved wife,
Lillian Wu

FOREWORD

BY ANDREW J. NATHAN

No other leader in history held as much power over so many people for so long as Mao Zedong, and none inflicted such a catastrophe on his nation. Mao's lust for control and fear of betrayal kept his court and his country in turmoil. His vision and his intrigues drove China through the Great Leap Forward and its terrible consequences, the great famine and the Cultural Revolution, with deaths in the tens of millions.

Nor has any other dictator been as intimately observed as Mao is in this memoir by the man who served as his personal physician for twenty-two years. Suetonius's *Lives of the Twelve Caesars* shows the deranging effects of absolute power in the gluttony, lechery, greed, sadism, incest, torture, and commission of multiple murders by Tiberius, Caligula, and Nero, but the author did not know his subjects personally. Procopius's *Secret History* is a scandalous attack on the Roman emperor Justinian and his wife, Theodora, devoid of sympathy or understanding. Albert Speer knew Hitler well, but their common interests were limited to public works and war. Stalin's daughter seldom saw her father. The diaries of Napoleon's and Hitler's personal physicians are merely clinical.

Personal memoirs about great democratic leaders, like Moran's *Churchill* and Herndon's *Lincoln,* tell us less about history than the biographies of dictators do, because democratic leaders have less room to impose their personalities on events. As for the Chinese tradition, the "basic annals" of each reign record the rituals, portents, alliances,

memorials, and enfeoffments that made up each emperor's performance of his role, but they rarely reveal the personalities beneath the
robes. Even Chinese fictionalized accounts of historical rulers, like the
Romance of the Three Kingdoms, deal with types rather than characters. The combination of access and insight makes *The Private Life of
Chairman Mao* unique.

The real Mao could hardly have been more different from the
benevolent sage-king portrayed in the authorized memoirs and poster
portraits that circulate in China today. To be sure, on first meeting he
could be charming, sympathetic, and casual, setting his visitor at ease
to talk freely. But he drew on psychological reserves of anger and
contempt to control his followers, manipulating his moods with frightening effect. Relying on the Confucian unwillingness of those around
him to confront their superior, he humiliated subordinates and rivals.
He undertook self-criticism only to goad others to flatter him, surrounding himself with a culture of abasement.

Emulating the first Tang emperor, Mao bound men and women
to him by discovering their weaknesses. Dr. Zhisui Li came from an
upper-class family, was trained at an American-sponsored school in
Suzhou, and had an early and trivial involvement with the Guomindang. These potentially dangerous facts enslaved him to Mao. Corruption existed within Mao's entourage and Mao knew it, but he
needed people who could cut corners. Fish cannot live in pure water,
Mao liked to say. He enjoyed swimming in polluted water and walking
through fields of night soil.

Mao's retainers remained on permanent probation, whatever
their backgrounds. Old comrades were sent into internal exile, in some
cases to their deaths, although Mao's role in these tragedies was indi-
rect. In one scene we see Mao sitting on a stage behind a curtain
listening, unseen, as two of his closest colleagues are attacked at a mass
meeting. Mao controlled his top colleagues' medical care, denying
some of them treatment for cancer, because he was convinced that
cancer could not be cured and he wanted them to work for their
remaining time. Having lost children, a brother, and a wife to war and
revolution, he seldom seemed moved by the suffering of lovers, children, and friends any more than he flinched from imposing misery on
millions of the faceless "masses" in pursuit of his economic and political schemes. He understood human suffering chiefly as a way to control people. In politics and personal life alike, he discarded those for
whom he had no present use, just as coolly calling them back when he
wanted them, if they were still alive.

Dr. Li usually found Mao with a book of Chinese history in his hand. He loved the traditional stories of strategy and deception. He was an expert in when to wait, feint, and withdraw, and how to attack obliquely. He liked to "lure snakes out of their holes," encouraging others to show their hands so he could turn against them. His closest colleagues could seldom sense whether he agreed with them or was waiting to pounce. Dr. Li says Mao was a marvelous actor. He could sentence a retainer to exile with a story so convincing that the victim backed out bowing in gratitude.

Imperial power allowed the ultimate luxury, simplicity. Mao spent much of his time in bed or lounging by the side of a private pool, not dressing for days at a time. He ate oily food, rinsed his mouth with tea, and slept with country girls. During a 1958 tour of Henan, Mao's party was followed everywhere by a truckload of watermelons. Mao liked cloth shoes; if he had to wear leather ones for a diplomatic function, he let someone else break them in. He did not bathe, preferring a rubdown with hot towels, although this made it hard for Dr. Li to stop the spread of venereal infections among his female companions. He slept on a specially made huge wooden bed that was carried on his private train, set up in his villas, airlifted to Moscow.

He exercised sovereignty over clock and calendar. The court worked to Mao's rhythm, and many of its activities took place after midnight. It was not unusual to be summoned to Mao's chambers at two or three in the morning. He traveled frequently, convening meetings of the nation's leaders wherever he was. He sought to triumph over death through Daoist methods of sex. He followed no schedule except on May Day and National Day and on the rare occasions when he received foreign visitors. Then he had to dress, taking barbiturates to control his anxiety.

Women were served to order like food. While puritanism was promoted in his name, Mao's sex life was a central project of his court. A special room was set aside in the Great Hall of the People for his refreshment during high-level party meetings. Party and army political departments, guardians of the nation's morality, recruited young women of sterling proletarian background and excellent physical appearance, supposedly to engage in ballroom dancing with the leader, actually for possible service in his bed. Honored by the opportunity, some of those chosen introduced their sisters.

Each province's party secretary built Mao a villa. He moved from place to place partly because of security concerns, partly out of paranoia. "It's not good for me to stay in one place too long," he told Dr. Li. All rail traffic stopped and stations were closed as his special train went through. Security officers posing as food vendors lent the stations an air of normalcy for his benefit. During the Great Leap, peasants were mobilized to tend transplanted crops along miles of tracks, creating the impression of a bumper harvest when the harvest was a disaster. Mao's favorite villa was located on a small island in the Pearl River, where he enjoyed privacy in the middle of the busy city of Guangzhou. Special food grown in a labor camp near Beijing was airlifted to him and tried by tasters before he ate it. Guards cooled his room with tubs of ice.

Absolute power affected Mao's mental and physical health, his human relations, and, through these, his country and the world. He spent months in bed, ill with worry. But when the political struggle was going his way, he might fill up with cheerful energy that kept him from sleeping. Dr. Li dosed him constantly with barbiturates so he could rest. Political stress sometimes made him impotent, at other times stimulated his libido. As tens of millions starved to death during the Great Leap Forward and the Chairman lost face before the party, he temporarily gave up meat. But he needed more women. One of them told Dr. Li that the Great Helmsman was great in everything, even in bed.

Politics in a dictatorship begins in the personality of the dictator. Mao established a regime like no other, an ensemble of economic, social, and political institutions that grew from his effort to build a unique form of socialism in a country that was poor, backward, and vulnerable.

Facing the hostility of the West, Mao aligned with Moscow. But his admiration for the West was one reason he chose the American-trained Dr. Li as his physician, and was a subject of many of their conversations. He told Dr. Li that America's intentions toward China had always been benign. But he held his allies the Russians in contempt. Mao aimed to surpass the primitive Russian model with Chinese-style socialism, raise his country to the level of the advanced Western world, and by this achievement join the pantheon of Marxism-Leninism. The Great Leap Forward was his effort to create a model of socialism better than that of his northern neighbors, and the Cultural Revolution was his attempt to sustain the experiment in the face of its failure.

In a vast, continental country with a huge and poor population, Mao sought economic growth through mass mobilization, trying to substitute ideological fervor for material rewards. He froze the people's standard of living at subsistence levels in order to build a massive, wasteful industrial structure. In doing so, he ignored realities that contradicted his vision. A farmer's son from rural Hunan, he allowed himself to be deluded by vast Potemkin fields at the start of the Great Leap Forward. As Dr. Li says, why should Mao have doubted that the communist paradise had arrived when he himself was living in it? He thought there was more to learn about leadership from the pages of Chinese history than from textbooks of modern engineering. While people starved, he imagined that they had more than they could eat.

The ideology that bore Mao's name promoted self-denial, defined a person's value in terms of political virtue, and dehumanized the class enemy. A system of work units, class labels, household registrations, and mass movements fixed each citizen in an organizational cage, within which people exercised political terror over themselves and each other. A pervading bureaucracy governed the economy, politics, ideology, culture, people's private lives, and even many of their private thoughts. The apparatus led the people in singing the praises of the regime that had expropriated them. Mao toppled the party machinery when it proved insufficiently responsive to his fantasies of speed but rebuilt it when he needed it to stop factional violence.

At the top, thirty to forty men made all the major decisions. Their power was personal, fluid, and dependent on their relations with Mao. Dr. Li describes the system of Central Committee organs, political and confidential secretaries, bodyguards, kitchens, car pools, and clinics that served the leaders. An underground tunnel complex allowed the leaders to move secretly from their headquarters in Zhongnanhai to buildings elsewhere in Beijing. Mao's closest retainers bugged his premises, trying to keep better records of his decisions, but found themselves cashiered for spying on him.

Set up to serve and protect the leaders, the structures of power isolated them, Mao more than the others. Mao's comrades gradually ceded to him the Forbidden City swimming pool, the dance parties, and the best Beidaihe beach. The saga of his swim in three great rivers, over the objections of his security men, symbolized his solitary struggle against the bureaucracy, his fear that the revolution might bog down, and his challenge to comrades he thought were betraying his radical aims.

At the Eighth Party Congress in 1956, Mao's colleagues attempted to rein him in, taking advantage of de-Stalinization in the Soviet Union to write his guiding thought out of the party constitution, pledge the party against the cult of personality, and criticize Mao's attempts to force the premature birth of communism. Mao claimed falsely to Dr. Li that he had not been consulted about these decisions. Forces abroad also threatened his control. The new Soviet leader, Khrushchev, wanted an accommodation with the West. Dr. Li portrays the bitter last meeting between the two by the side of Mao's swimming pool, which marked the start of an open split with the Soviets and the onset of China's long period of isolation.

Mao held fast to three ultimate tools of power: ideology, the army, and his spider's position at the center of the party's factional web. He summoned up the epochal Great Leap Forward with a whistle-stop farm tour that passed a message over the heads of the economic planners to the basic-level cadres. At the Lushan plenum in 1959, when the other leaders tried to rein Mao in, he threatened to raise a new army and take to the hills. The others surrendered.

After the famine began, Mao retreated to a secondary position of power. As the other party leaders restored the economy, he brooded that they were "zombies" and complained about their failure to consult him. He patiently ensnared them in a debate over classic operas and enmeshed them in confusion over the issue of rural corruption. When his colleagues were vulnerable enough, he launched the Cultural Revolution.

Millions of victims later, Mao stood victorious at the Ninth Party Congress of 1969, his rivals dead or in internal exile, the nation singing his praises and waving his red book before his ubiquitous poster. By his side stood the abject Lin Biao, the sole survivor from the old ruling group. Mao's dream of development had failed, but his power was absolute in the country he had ruined. Lin Biao's coup attempt two years later disappointed Mao so badly that Dr. Li traces his final decline from then. He used his final energies to engineer the opening to the West, which later made possible Deng Xiaoping's reforms.

Psychological pathologies flourished in the atmosphere of court politics. The more complete Mao's control, the greater his fear of others' attempts to control him. Their anxiety to please made them more suspect. He thought his villas were poisoned and panicked when he heard wild animals scratching inside the roof of one. Mao spied on the other leaders by managing their secretaries through his chief secretary and their guards through his chief of guards. Although he surrounded his rivals with his men, he was never sure they were not spying on him through his women.

Mao's wife, Jiang Qing, suffered from hypochondria; aversion to noise, light, cold, and heat; and compulsive quarreling. Having driven her mad with boredom, dependency, and enforced idleness, Mao at first tried to spare her the knowledge of his love affairs. But when he needed her as a political proxy, he brought her into the inner circle. Like her equally sick colleague Lin Biao, Jiang once in power flowered into robust health, making friends with Mao's favorite female companion to get better access to the source of power.

Dr. Li shows us Lin Biao in the arms of his wife, crying with pain from a kidney stone; Hua Guofeng sitting in Mao's anteroom for hours unable to see the great leader because his companion and gatekeeper, Zhang Yufeng, is napping; Zhou Enlai kneeling on the floor before Mao to trace the route of a proposed motorcade; Jiang Qing in fury as a sick Mao hands control over the whole country to Zhou, only to recover and outlive him.

Of all Mao's followers, only Zhou kept relatively aloof from the byzantine networks that laced the court. Because he did so, Dr. Li and the other courtiers ironically viewed him as disloyal and dangerous. For Zhou to report information to appropriate colleagues in the formal chain of command struck the others as a sign of weakness and treachery.

At the end, the most loved man in China was friendless. During his long decline, his servants' chief obsession was to avoid blame for his demise. Only his favorite, Zhang Yufeng, had the decency to treat him like a human being by quarreling with him, fearless of being accused of angering him to death. But as he weakened, she found other interests, having become indispensable because only she could decode his slurred speech.

Dr. Zhisui Li's frank, round, slightly smiling face stands out from the rows of stony-faced retainers in the group photographs of Mao's household. His open expression, soft cheeks, and neat clothes betray him as the one who came back from the West. His foreign tincture made him doubly valuable, denoting both competence and dependency. For Mao was secure to the extent that Dr. Li was vulnerable. Surviving under Mao's protection, he stuck to his business, maintaining the health of the man whose acts cost the lives of millions.

Only a certain willingness to look away from evil can make a man the ideal guardian of a dictator's life. Dr. Li's limits as an observer of history were one of his qualifications for his job. But politics sometimes forced itself on him. Mao sometimes insisted on talking about events or on sending Dr. Li away from the court to observe and report. At court, Dr. Li had to learn who protected and who opposed him. Aside from Mao, his patron was Wang Dongxing, chief of bodyguards. Their alliance provides the book's bias, but also much of its insight into court politics.

Since he left China, Dr. Li has been all but erased from official history. Of the countless books on Mao's personal life published by

Chinese presses, only one or two mention him. Apparently, there has been a central directive to treat him as a non-person. But his image survives in unretouched film footage and photos, and reliable sources confirm his identity. Official and semi-official works corroborate many details in his account but differ from his in leaving out aspects of the story that would embarrass the regime, which still rules by the soft light of Mao's official image. No authorized account offers a portrait of Mao that rings as true as Dr. Li's. It is the most revealing book ever published on Mao, perhaps on any dictator in history.

In 1981, five years after Mao's death, the Chinese Communist party Central Committee adopted an official verdict on his life, "Resolution on Certain Questions in the History of Our Party Since the Founding of the People's Republic of China." It called Mao a great revolutionary whose contributions outweighed the costs of his mistakes. This book tells a different story. It shows how excessive power drives its possessor into a shadow world, where great visions become father to great crimes.

PREFACE

BY DR. ZHISUI LI

In 1960, *China Youth* magazine contacted me through Tian Jiaying, one of Mao Zedong's secretaries. Tian asked if I would write articles for the magazine.

Tian was a neighbor of mine in Zhongnanhai, and was aware of my habit of keeping a journal of my daily activities. In fact, he had read some of my writing; this is why he suggested that I select a few of my journal entries for publication.

I had started writing a journal in 1954, when I was appointed Mao's personal physician, and soon writing became a hobby. It helped while away the time, and served as a record of my experience. Initially I took notes only on major episodes, but after a while I wrote down many other things I happened to observe. Still, I had never intended to publish my writings, and I turned down the magazine's request.

By 1966, I had compiled more than forty volumes of notes. In the latter half of that year, the Red Guards began to search the houses of their political enemies. At that time I lived in a residence complex in Gongxian Lane in Beijing, where three vice-ministers of the Ministry of Public Health also lived. As victims of the Cultural Revolution, they were under constant attack by the Red Guards, and their living quarters were frequently raided by the young rebels. Sometimes the Red Guards knocked at the wrong door and entered my residence by mistake. My wife, Lillian, was alarmed, for she was afraid that they might accidentally get hold of my notes, which contained many candid observations on Mao's public and private activities.

Unable to find a safe place for these notes, we made the painful decision to burn them. But we could not do this at home because we were afraid that our neighbors might observe us and suspect that we were destroying criminal materials. Ultimately, I thought of the incinerator at Zhongnanhai that was used to burn the unneeded documents and letters of Mao Zedong and his wife, Jiang Qing.

I took my notes there and fed them into the incinerator. As I reached the last dozen or so volumes, Wang Dongxing, director of the Central Bureau of Guards, phoned and asked to see me immediately. He said that Jiang Qing's chef had reported to him that I was destroying documents in the incinerator. I promptly assured him that I was burning only my personal notes, not official documents. He asked me what was wrong with the notes. I said that they touched on Mao's activities and that it would be risky to keep them. He said that if I burned them I would be inviting trouble, and that if the chef reported the matter to Jiang Qing, it would be disastrous.

Still, I figured that since I had already burned a major portion of the notes, I might as well finish the lot. So I went back to the incinerator and burned what was left.

The next day, Wang Dongxing yelled at me, "I told you not to burn the notes, but you did it anyway. This time, the Chairman's chef has made a report to me of your activity. If this gets out of my hands, it will be a catastrophe. So stop it. If you do it again, I will have you arrested."

I told him there was nothing left to burn. The job was finished. So much for the diaries I had kept for a dozen years.

During the Cultural Revolution, I was in constant fear for my safety and dared not make any more notes.

In 1976, after the death of Mao and the arrest of the Gang of Four, Lillian said to me with a sense of regret, "What a pity! If we had kept the notes, nothing would likely have happened. We burned them for nothing." She urged me to write down again my experiences of those earlier years.

One day in the summer of 1977, Marshal Ye Jianying came to the 305 Hospital, of which I was the director, for a checkup. Chatting with me, he said, "You worked for the Chairman for twenty-two years. That is a long, long time. You should write your life story. It's part of history." He told me that if I published a book, he would help promote it.

Subsequently, many newspapers and magazines requested that I contribute articles. I turned down these requests, as I had done before, for I knew what happened to writers who wrote truthfully of their experiences: They were condemned as rightists or reactionary intellectuals. And I certainly did not want to write anything to praise the powerful or to whitewash the terrible events I had witnessed.

And yet I did not want my memory of those twenty-two years to fade away without a trace. I decided to rewrite my life story. Beginning in 1977 I wrote intermittently for some time, eventually producing more than twenty volumes of notes. Because Mao's language was so colorful and vivid and deeply etched in my brain, I was able to recall verbatim much of what he had said. My survival and that of my family had always depended on Mao's words; I could not forget them. Still, I had no intention of having my recollections published; I knew that no publisher in China would print this type of work, and I did not want to get into trouble by publishing it myself. I kept the notes simply as a remembrance of the life that Lillian and I had shared in those bygone days.

In February 1988, Lillian was found to be suffering from chronic renal failure. She was hospitalized that May; by July her condition had deteriorated. My two sons, John and Erchong, and their wives, Linda and Mae, who had gone to the United States in the early 1980s, urged me to bring Lillian to this country for treatment.

In August, Lillian and I and our granddaughter, Lili, arrived in Chicago. While Lillian was undergoing treatment, I helped take care of her diet and medical needs. It was at this time that she suggested I produce a manuscript for publication based on my notes. But I hardly had the desire or the time to do so.

In December, Lillian caught a severe cold, and her condition worsened sharply. Though we had her admitted to a hospital and did everything possible to save her, she was to die on January 12, 1989.

Before she went into a coma, she urged me again and again to write down the events of the previous forty years. She said, "You must do it, for yourself, for me, for our posterity, for our grandson who will soon be born. I am sorry I cannot help you anymore."

In March 1989, I unpacked the volumes of notes from my luggage and began work on the present book. I consider this publication a permanent tribute to Lillian.

I hope that reading these pages will give people a deeper understanding of the tumultuous life of Mao Zedong. If, by reading this book, people can value more their own ideals and cherish more their freedom, that will be a fulfillment of the fondest hope that Lillian and I shared.

． ． ．

In 1949, after twenty-two years of bloody war, the Communist party finally defeated the Guomindang and established the People's Republic of China.

In 1948 I had gone to work as a surgeon for the Australian Oriental Company in Sydney, where I stayed until the summer of 1949. That summer I received a letter from the vice-minister of public health of the Chinese Communist party's Military Affairs Commission, who, at the suggestion of my eldest brother, invited me to work in China. I accepted the invitation and went to Hong Kong to meet my wife, Lillian; together we went back to Beijing, my native city. I was twenty-nine years old then.

The vice-minister put me to work at Fragrant Hills Clinic, in a western suburb of Beijing, a medical facility under the jurisdiction of the General Office of the Communist party's Central Committee. Later I worked at the Zhongnanhai Clinic at Communist party headquarters.

I worked diligently at my job, winning the respect of many high-level cadres as well as others. In 1952, the General Office unanimously elected me a Grade-A model worker, and in the same year I was admitted to the Communist party of China. I was successively appointed director of the Zhongnanhai Clinic, director of the Administrative Office of the Bureau of Health, deputy secretary-general of the Medical Science Committee of the Ministry of Public Health, and president of the 305 Hospital of the People's Liberation Army.

In 1954, at the recommendation of Wang Dongxing, director of the Central Bureau of Guards, with the consent of Yang Shangkun, director of the General Office, and Luo Ruiqing, of the Ministry of Public Security, and with the approval of Prime Minister Zhou Enlai, I was appointed personal physician to Mao Zedong and later director of the medical team for Mao. From then until Mao's death in 1976, for a period of twenty-two years, I was in charge of Mao's health, at his side almost constantly, whether in Beijing or elsewhere.

When I started working for Mao, I was greatly surprised by his life-style, which was much different from that of the average person. He followed no schedule at all in eating or sleeping. To him, the division of a day into twenty-four hours or the difference between day and night had little meaning. His public and private activities, including his meetings with foreign heads of state, were arranged strictly according to his preferences.

Mao liked to conduct his activities on the spur of the moment, without giving adequate advance notice. Even the people who worked closely with him could not tell what his next demand would be. In addition, the Chinese Communist party was a very tightly controlled organization, and very secretive. As Mao instructed us, "Don't talk about the things that go on around here." As a result, his real life was shrouded in a thick mist, and he appeared all the more mysterious and powerful.

Until 1959, I revered him. Though I was physically near him at all times, a mystical, impregnable wall seemed to separate us. I could not see through this wall to know what his real life was. After 1959, I gradually penetrated this invisible barrier and was able to see Mao's real face. Like an actor, Mao appeared onstage with elaborate makeup but showed a different face backstage.

In the early 1950s, as Mao concluded the Sino-Soviet Treaty of Friendship, Alliance, and Mutual Assistance and advocated a "leaning-to-one-side" foreign policy, many people believed that he was very close to the Soviet Union. But they did not know that even as far back as the 1930s he had been considered a dissident by Stalin and the Soviet Communist party, a "turnip—white on the inside and red on the outside." In his first official visit to the Soviet Union in the winter of 1949–50, he was received very coldly; he stayed there for two months, achieving nothing. It was only after he threatened to return to China that Stalin agreed to sign the friendship treaty. Mao regarded Russia as a great threat to China, determined eventually to gobble it up. But it was not until the early 1960s that the break in Sino-Soviet relations became widely known.

In the 1930s, following their visit to the Communist-base area in northern Shaanxi, Edgar Snow and other American journalists told the world about the near-miraculous existence of the Chinese Communist party. From then on Mao looked favorably upon the United States, and especially the American people. In the 1950s, when he advocated the "learning-from-the-Soviet-Union" policy, many Chinese studied Russian, considering it the most important foreign language. But Mao did not. Instead, he studied English. He said of himself, "My words and my deeds are inconsistent."

Among his staff, a number of people were classified, to use the communist jargon, as intellectuals, all of whom, myself included, had received British and American educations. He never allowed a Soviet-educated individual to work for him.

The Korean and the Vietnam wars brought China and the United States into conflict. One of the many causes of these wars was that Americans misunderstood Mao's personal preference for the United States and allowed American political leaders hostile to Chinese communism to take charge of America's China policy, with tragic results. Beginning in the late 1960s, Mao devoted himself to the improvement of Sino-American relations and accomplished this objective before he died.

Mao regarded Chiang Kai-shek as his lifelong enemy but gave him credit for a strong sense of nationalism, not subservient to the United States. He said, "Chiang Kai-shek and I both claim there is only one China. On this point we are in complete agreement."

The power struggles at the highest level of the Chinese Communist leadership were complicated and tangled. From the "anti-rightists" movement of 1957 to the so-called "criticizing Peng Dehuai anti-party group" campaign of 1959 to the Cultural Revolution of 1966—all these and other political upheavals seemed to arise for a variety of reasons. In reality, there was only one fundamental cause: Mao wanted to retain total power.

For example, Mao considered the anti-Stalin, anti-personality-cult campaign launched by Khrushchev and the Soviet Communist party at its Twentieth Congress in 1956 a threat to his own position as the supreme leader of the Chinese Communist party, and he responded accordingly, with a series of measures to assure his leadership. As Wang Dongxing said, "Mao considers no one in the whole Communist party indispensable to the party except himself."

Mao led an appalling private life. Publicly, he appeared composed and dignified as well as friendly and personable, creating an image of a respected elder gentleman. But in reality he was a dedicated philanderer. As he grew older, his sexual adventures became all the more scandalous and wide-ranging. He had no other recreational activity except for these adventures, which involved an uncountable number of young women. As Wang Dongxing observed, "Is it because he feels he is going to die soon that he has to grab as many girls as he can? Otherwise, why is he this interested in [sex] and why is he this energetic?" And Mao's wife, Jiang Qing, said of him, "In the matter of political struggle, none of the Chinese and Soviet leaders can beat him. In the matter of his personal conduct, nobody can keep him in check either."

I am not writing a biography of Mao. I am instead recording what I saw and heard during the twenty-two years when I was Mao's personal physician. This book is dedicated to the memory of my wife, Lillian, who endured with me the hardship of life with Mao. Without her unfailing support and constant encouragement when she was alive, I could not have finished this work.

ACKNOWLEDGMENTS

BY DR. ZHISUI LI

I would like to thank the people who helped make this book possible.

The late Dr. Tian Beichen brought some of my diaries from Beijing to the United States. Professor Tai Hung-chao of the University of Detroit translated my Chinese manuscript into English, a difficult task given its specialized terminology. Anne Thurston's contribution was invaluable in making the book accessible to non-Chinese readers. I would also like to thank Jason Epstein of Random House and his able assistants, Maryam Mohit, Mallay Charters, and Joy de Menil. Professor Andrew Nathan of Columbia University has been involved in the publication of this book from its beginning. Yamin Xu has worked closely with both the original Chinese text and the English manuscript, and under Anne Thurston's supervision has compared my recollections with those of others who have written about Mao; he has also contributed to the biographical sketches and the chart of the General Office and has made many helpful suggestions. I am grateful to Dr. Yuan Yu Hsia, who has allowed me to use his map of Zhongnanhai. I am grateful to Mr. Robert Barnett, my literary agent, for his strong support and good advice through difficult times. I would also like to thank Lesley Oelsner, Benjamin Dreyer, Sybil Pincus, Shelley Garren, and Sandra Lambert of Random House.

I want very much to thank the following scholars who were kind enough to read and comment on the English draft in its various stages: Arthur Kleinman, a psychiatrist and anthropologist at Harvard University; Kenneth Lieberthal, of the Department of Political Science at the University of Michigan; Michel Oksenberg, the president of the East-West Center in Honolulu; Roderick MacFarquhar, of the Government Department at Harvard University; Lucian Pye, professor emeritus of the Political Science Department at M.I.T.; Michael Schoenhals, of the Center for Pacific Asia Studies at the University of Stockholm; and Ross Terrill. Their advice and encouragement have been extremely valuable. I would also like to thank Veronica Windholz for her excellent copyediting.

Nancy Hearst, the librarian at Harvard's Fairbank Center for East Asian Research, provided invaluable help early in the project by making her extensive collection of Mao memoirs available to Yamin Xu. Later, she read and commented on the manuscript, helped with difficult fact-checking, assisted in proofreading the galleys, and expanded Yamin's original bibliography to include the most recent memoirs of Mao.

Most of all, I want to thank my wife, Lillian, without whose constant love and encouragement this book would never have been written.

CONTENTS

CHINA

miles 0 200
km 0 600

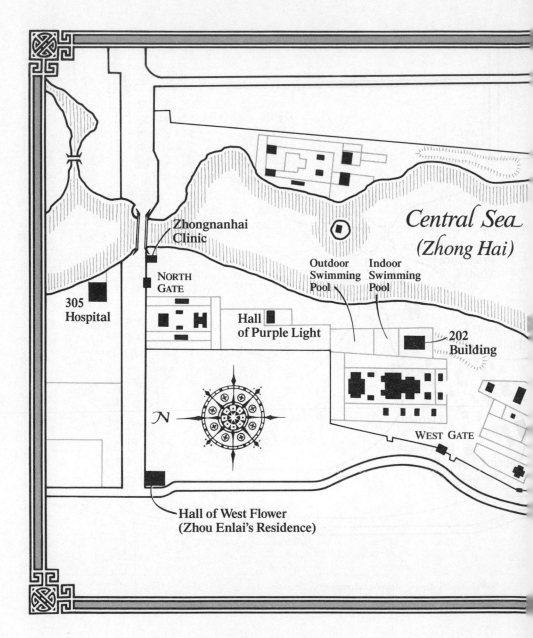

Central Sea
(Zhong Hai)

Zhongnanhai
Clinic

NORTH
GATE

305
Hospital

Outdoor
Swimming
Pool

Indoor
Swimming
Pool

Hall
of Purple Light

202
Building

N

WEST GATE

Hall of West Flower
(Zhou Enlai's Residence)

Map of Zhongnanhai as I Knew It in the Early 1970s

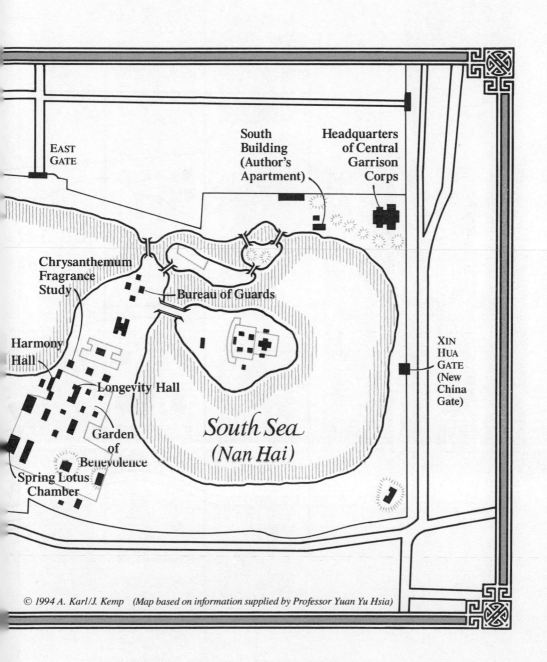

EAST
GATE

South
Building
(Author's
Apartment)

Headquarters
of Central
Garrison
Corps

Chrysanthemum
Fragrance
Study

Bureau of Guards

Harmony
Hall

Longevity Hall

Garden
of
Benevolence

Spring Lotus
Chamber

XIN
HUA
GATE
(New
China
Gate)

South Sea
(Nan Hai)

© 1994 A. Karl/J. Kemp   *(Map based on information supplied by Professor Yuan Yu Hsia)*

THE ORGANIZATION OF THE CHINESE COMMUNIST PARTY IN THE MID-1950s

CHAIRMAN
Mao Zedong

Politburo Standing Committee (after 1956)
Mao Zedong, Liu Shaoqi, Zhou Enlai, Zhu De, Chen Yun, Lin Biao

Politburo

Secretariat
(Shuji Chu)
responsible for implementing politburo decisions
(general secretary after 1956: Deng Xiaoping)

Investigation Department
(Diaocha Bu)
Li Kenong

Rural Work Department
(Nongcun Gongzuo Bu)
(abolished in 1956)
Deng Zihui

General Office
(Bangongting)
Yang Shangkun

Propaganda Department
(Xuanyan Bu)
Lu Dingyi

Organization Department
(Zuzhi Bu)
An Ziwen

Youth League
(Qingnian Tuan)
Jiang Nanxiang &
Feng Wenbing

All China Labor Union
(Chuanguo Zonggonghui)
Liu Changsheng

United Front Department
(Tongzhan Bu)
Li Weihan

All China Women's Federation
(Chuanguo Funu Lianhehui)
Cai Chang

Department of Foreign Liaison
(Duiwai Lianluo Bu)
Wang Jiaxiang

Guangming Daily
(Guangming Ribao)

Red Flag Magazine
(Hongqi Zazhi She)
Chen Boda

People's Daily
(Renmin Ribao)
Deng Tuo, Wu Lengxi

New China News Agency
(Xinhua She)
Zhu Muzhi

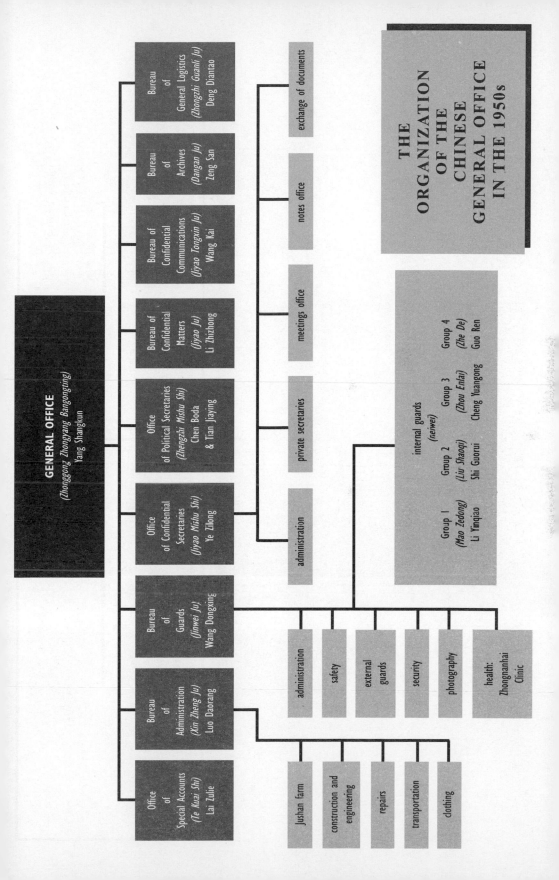

THE ORGANIZATION OF THE CHINESE GENERAL OFFICE IN THE 1950s

GENERAL OFFICE
(Zhonggong Zhongyang Bangongting)
Yang Shangkun

Office of Special Accounts (Te Kuai Shi) Lai Zulie

Bureau of Administration (Xin Zheng Ju) Luo Daorang

Bureau of Guards (Jinwei Ju) Wang Dongxing

Office of Confidential Secretaries (Jiyao Mishu Shi) Ye Zilong

Office of Political Secretaries (Zhengzhi Mishu Shi) Chen Boda & Tian Jiaying

Bureau of Confidential Matters (Jiyao Ju) Li Zhizhong

Bureau of Confidential Communications (Jiyao Tongxin Ju) Wang Kai

Bureau of Archives (Dangan Ju) Zeng San

Bureau of General Logistics (Zhongzhi Guanli Ju) Deng Diantao

administration
private secretaries
meetings office
notes office
exchange of documents

Jushan farm
construction and engineering
repairs
transportation
clothing

administration
safety
external guards
security
photography
health: Zhongnanhai Clinic

internal guards (neiwei)

Group 1 (Mao Zedong) Li Yinqiao

Group 2 (Liu Shaoqi) Shi Guorui

Group 3 (Zhou Enlai) Cheng Yuangong

Group 4 (Zhe De) Guo Ren

I

The Death
of Mao

1

"Chairman, you called for me?"

Mao struggled to open his eyes and move his lips. The oxygen mask had slipped from his face and he was struggling for breath. I leaned over. "Ah . . . ah . . . ah . . ." was all I could hear. His mind was clear, but his speech was hopeless.

I was Mao's personal physician, in charge of the medical team—sixteen of China's best doctors and twenty-four excellent nurses—trying to save his life. For more than two months—since June 26, 1976, when Mao suffered his second myocardial infarction—we had been on duty around the clock. Eight nurses and three doctors were constantly by Mao's side while another two doctors monitored his electrocardiogram. The shifts changed every eight hours. I was always on call, sleeping fitfully some three or four hours a night. My office was a cubbyhole just outside Mao's sickroom.

The citizens of China had not been told their leader was ill. They had traced Mao's physical decline only through occasional photographs of his rare visits with foreign dignitaries. The last of them was the photograph of Mao meeting with Laotian leader Kaysone Phoumivan in May 1976. The press continued to say he was healthy, but the photograph with Kaysone Phoumivan proved that their leader had grown shockingly old. Still, hundreds of millions had begun that morning, September 8, 1976, chanting in rhythm, "Ten Thousand Years to Chairman Mao."

But those of us on duty in Mao's sickroom that night knew the end was hours, even minutes, away. He had been failing since June. Two members of the Communist party politburo, paired by rank and political proclivity—moderate party vice-chairman Hua Guofeng with radical party vice-chairman Wang Hongwen, radical politburo member Zhang Chunqiao with moderate politburo member Wang Dongxing—also kept vigil twenty-four hours a day, rotating every twelve hours.

Hua Guofeng, in charge of the efforts to save the Chairman's life, was genuinely loyal to Mao, deeply concerned about his health and comfort, conscientiously trying to understand the doctors' explanations, trusting that we were doing all we could to save Mao. When we recommended new, and sometimes uncomfortable, medical procedures, like running a tube through Mao's nose and into his stomach for feeding, Hua Guofeng alone among the leaders had been willing to try the new procedures first on himself. I liked Hua Guofeng. His integrity and sincerity were rare amid the corruption and decay among the party elite.

I had first met Hua Guofeng in 1959, during the Great Leap Forward, when I accompanied Mao on a visit to his native village of Shaoshan, in Hunan province. Hua was the first party secretary of Xiangtan, the prefecture where Mao's village was located, and Mao had liked him enormously. Two years later, when local officials continued to pretend that food production was increasing even as the Great Leap Forward had plunged the country into economic depression, Hua Guofeng had the courage to say that "the people are losing weight, the cattle are losing weight, even the land is losing weight. How can we talk about increases in food?"

"No one else tells the truth like Hua Guofeng," Mao said to me then.

Hua had come to his present position in April 1976, an early victor in the power struggle that was unfolding as Mao's death approached. In January 1976, Mao had appointed Hua acting premier to succeed the deceased Zhou Enlai as head of the State Council, in charge of the daily affairs of government. In early April, hundreds of thousands of people gathered in Tiananmen Square to mourn Zhou's death and protest the policies of such radical leaders as Mao's wife, Jiang Qing, and her Shanghai cronies Zhang Chunqiao, Yao Wenyuan, and Wang Hongwen. The demonstrations were publicly declared "counterrevolutionary," and Mao placated the radicals by purging the moderate Deng Xiaoping, charging him with having fomented the disturbance. Always the balancer, Mao then disappointed the radicals by appointing Hua first vice-chairman of the party. Hua

Guofeng was thus confirmed both as head of government and as Mao's chosen successor to head the party. This made me very happy. I thought Mao had chosen the right person to lead the party and the government. Even Jiang Qing's chef was delighted, commenting that at last the Chairman had made a sharp decision. But the radicals had begun accusing him of leaning to the right.

As a result, Hua decided he could no longer continue. I was at the swimming pool on April 30, 1976, when he told Mao that the attacks against him made it impossible for him to serve. After the meeting, Hua had told me of their conversation and showed me the notes Mao had written. There were three of them: "With you in charge," Mao had scrawled, "my mind is at ease"; "Act according to the decisions laid down"; "Don't be nervous; take it easy." By then, Mao's speech was incomprehensible, and he had to communicate by pen.

Mao's scribbled blessing became the document that legitimized Hua's succession.

Shortly before midnight on September 8, 1976, the doctors had administered an intravenous injection of *shengmai san,* a traditional Chinese herbal concoction consisting primarily of ginseng, in an effort to stimulate Mao's heart. His blood pressure had risen from 86 over 66 to 104 over 72 and his pulse had firmed up a bit, but the improvement, I knew, would be fleeting.

Hua Guofeng pulled me aside just after we administered the injection. "Dr. Li," he whispered as politburo members Zhang Chunqiao and Wang Dongxing strained to hear. "Is there anything else you can do?"

I said nothing. Hua knew there was no hope, and I did not know what to say. I could not yet bring myself to use the word *death.*

Silently, I looked at Hua Guofeng. The air was frozen. The whirring of Mao's respirator was the only sound in the room. Then I shook my head. "We have done all we can," I whispered hoarsely.

Hua turned to Wang Dongxing, director of the Central Committee's General Office in charge of party affairs and longtime head of Mao's bodyguards. Wang had first met Mao in Yanan, and for decades he had been in charge of the Chairman's safety. Few men had a longer or closer association with Mao.

"Ask Comrade Jiang Qing and the politburo members in Beijing to come here immediately," Hua instructed Wang, "and notify the politburo members in other parts of the country to report to Beijing." Wang turned to go.

As Wang was leaving, a nurse rushed up to me. "Dr. Li, Zhang Yufeng says that Chairman wants to see you." I rushed to his side.

Once a stewardess on the special train that Mao used in his travels through China and now his confidential secretary, Zhang Yufeng had long been Mao's close companion. I first saw Zhang Yufeng and Mao together one evening in Changsha. She was an innocent-looking eighteen-year-old girl with big round eyes and lovely white skin, and she asked the Chairman to dance. I watched them later as they left the dance floor together.

The relationship had sometimes been tumultuous, and Mao had had many other women in his life as well. Even now two young dancers were serving unofficially as nurses, sponging his body and feeding him. But Zhang Yufeng had been with Mao the longest, and though I thought she had grown coarse—and fond of alcohol—she had managed to retain his trust. In 1974, after Xu Yefu, Mao's confidential secretary, was hospitalized with lung cancer, Zhang took over the task of sending and receiving the voluminous documents that Mao read and commented upon each day, and when Mao's eyesight failed, she read the materials to him as well. In late 1974, she had been officially appointed Mao's confidential secretary by Wang Dongxing.

As Mao's doctor, I was allowed unimpeded access, but everyone else had to go through Zhang to get to Mao. After 1974, even Mao's wife, Jiang Qing, and ranking members of the politburo had to go through Zhang Yufeng, and she treated even the highest leaders with disdain. One day in June 1976, when Hua Guofeng had come to see Mao, Zhang Yufeng had been napping and the attendants on duty were afraid to rouse her. Two hours later, when Zhang had still not gotten up, Hua, second in command only to Mao, finally left without seeing his superior. Earlier in the same year, Deng Xiaoping had been ill and under political attack, separated from his family. His youngest daughter, Deng Rong, had written to Mao for permission to stay with her father. Zhang Yufeng did not deliver the letter to Mao, and Deng Rong was never permitted to be with her father.

Much of Zhang Yufeng's power came from the fact that only she could understand his speech. She had to interpret even for me.

"Dr. Li," she said as I went to Mao's side, "Chairman wants to know if there is any hope." With some effort, Mao nodded and slowly extended his right arm, taking my hand. His hand felt limp as I took his pulse, and the pulse itself was weak and difficult to find. The roundness of his cheeks, so familiar to the Chinese people, was gone and his skin was ashen. His eyes stared vacantly, without their usual luster. The line on the electrocardiograph fluttered.

We had moved Mao into this room in Building 202 of Zhongnanhai six weeks previously, in the early morning hours of July 28, 1976, when Beijing, and much of that part of China, had been hit by an earthquake that completely destroyed the city of Tangshan, some one hundred miles east of Beijing. More than 250,000 people had died instantaneously. In Beijing few people had died, but there was much damage, and fears of another earthquake led millions of residents to spend the next several weeks living in makeshift tents in the streets. Mao's sickbed in his study beside the indoor swimming pool, where he had moved early in the Cultural Revolution, had been violently shaken by the quake. We had to move him to safer ground.

Building 202 was the only choice. Connected to the swimming pool by a corridor, Building 202 had been constructed especially for Mao in 1974 and was meant to withstand a major earthquake. That evening, after we had moved him, another major aftershock hit in the midst of a heavy rain, but we barely felt it in Building 202. The whole sky could have fallen in at that point and I would not have noticed, so completely was I focused on saving the Chairman's life.

Now Hua Guofeng, Zhang Chunqiao, Wang Hongwen, and Wang Dongxing walked quietly up to Mao's bed. From behind the screen I could hear others come quietly in. The room was filling in preparation for the midnight change of shift.

As I stood there holding Mao's hand and taking his pulse, with the four politburo members standing behind me, Jiang Qing suddenly stormed in, shouting, "Will someone tell me what is happening?"

Jiang Qing was Mao's fourth wife, if you count the marriage his parents arranged for him as a teenager, which Mao refused to accept. Mao had married Jiang Qing in Yanan in 1938. I am told that she had gotten along well with others in Yanan. But after 1949, bored by her life of inactivity, the wife of the country's highest leader became increasingly irascible and demanding. Not until the Cultural Revolution did she finally come into her own, seizing the opportunity to settle her personal vendettas when she was finally appointed a member of the politburo. Mao and Jiang Qing had been leading separate lives for years, but Mao had never seen fit to divorce her, for he would then have been free to marry one of his other women. This he preferred to avoid. During the Cultural Revolution, Jiang Qing had moved to one of the huge villas in the complex of the Diaoyutai state guesthouse, but she had returned to Zhongnanhai, to the Spring Lotus Chamber, after her husband's June heart attack.

It had not been easy for Jiang Qing to accept the hold Zhang Yufeng had over Mao, but when she finally bowed to the inevitable, she began courting Zhang herself as a way of communicating with Mao. Jiang also had difficulty accepting the fact of Mao's illness and his impending death. She was torn between the fear that her own power rested finally on Mao and the hope that with his death she would be selected to rule in his place. His sickness and incontinence disgusted her.

Hua Guofeng tried to quiet her. "Comrade Jiang Qing," he said politely, "Chairman is talking with Dr. Li right now."

I tried to reassure Mao, even though I knew there was no hope. His health had been deteriorating for years. The turning point began shortly after September 1971, when Lin Biao, then vice-chairman of the party, vice-chairman of the Military Affairs Commission, and the man Mao had chosen as his successor, the leader all of China referred to as Mao's closest comrade in arms, had turned against Mao and conspired to unseat him. Believing that his plots had been discovered, Lin Biao had commandeered a plane and fled, heading for the Soviet Union, together with his wife and son. The plane had run out of gas and crashed near Undur Khan, in Outer Mongolia, and everyone on board was killed. The episode left Mao depressed, listless, and unable to sleep. Finally, he became ill.

He was still sick, rebelling against his doctors and refusing all medical treatment, several weeks before President Nixon's historic first visit to China, in February 1972. Only three weeks before Nixon was scheduled to arrive, Mao finally told me to begin treatment. His condition was so serious that a full recovery was out of the question. When Nixon arrived, Mao was still so weak he could hardly talk. His lung infection was not fully cured, and he was troubled by congestive heart failure. He was so bloated that he had to be fitted with a larger suit. I greeted President Nixon as his car pulled up to Mao's residence and directed him to Mao's study, retiring then to the corridor just outside the reception room, where I was able to hear their conversation clearly and was ready with mobile rescue equipment should Mao need it.

Now, at eighty-three, Mao's body was ravaged by a multitude of diseases. His lifelong addiction to cigarettes had destroyed his lungs, and for years he had faced frequent bouts of bronchitis, pneumonia, and emphysema. As the bronchial lining of his lungs lost its elasticity, convulsive coughing had torn away the walls of his left lung, leaving three large air bubbles, making it hard for Mao to breathe. He could draw air in but could not easily exhale and was comfortable only lying on his left side, the weight of his body compressing the air bubbles and allowing his healthier right lung to breathe. Often he could breathe only with the aid of an oxygen mask, and during episodic emergencies we relied on the American-made respirator that Henry Kissinger had sent in 1971 after his secret mission to China.

In 1974, Mao had been diagnosed as suffering not from Parkinson's disease, as so many in the West supposed, but from a rare, incurable, and ultimately fatal motor neuron disease—amyotrophic lateral sclerosis, or Lou Gehrig's disease as it is popularly known in the West. In the ordinary progression of the illness, the motor nerve cells in the medulla and spinal column, which control the muscles of the throat, the pharynx, the tongue, and the right hand and leg, degenerate and die, leading to muscular atrophy and then paralysis of the affected parts. As the disease progresses, patients lose the ability to speak and to swallow and must be fed by a nasal tube running to the stomach. The affected muscles become useless, and breathing becomes increasingly laborious. The patient fights a continuing battle with lung infections. There is no cure and no effective treatment, and most patients die within two years of the initial diagnosis.

Mao's disease had progressed just as the specialists predicted. But it was not only the amyotrophic lateral sclerosis that was killing him now. It was his heart, weakened by age and chronic lung disease. Mao had suffered his first myocardial infarction in mid-May 1976 in the midst of an argument with Zhang Yufeng, and a second one on June 26. His third heart attack was on September 2. The doctors all knew, though none dared say it, that death was imminent.

The party chairman, however, was fighting on.

"It's all right, Chairman," I said to him, his hand still in mine. "We will be able to help you." For an instant Mao's eyes seemed content. Slowly, pinkish patches began to appear on his cheeks. He exhaled deeply. His eyes closed. His right hand dropped lifeless from mine. The line on the electrocardiograph turned flat. I looked at my watch. It was 12:10 A.M., September 9, 1976.

I felt no sorrow at his passing. For twenty-two years I had been at Mao's side, with him every day, accompanying him to every meeting, traveling wherever he went. More than his physician, I had served for many of those years as his personal and political confidant, closer to him longer than anyone but—possibly—Wang Dongxing.

In the beginning I had adulated Mao. He was China's savior, the country's messiah. But by 1976 this had long since passed. My dream of a new China, where all men would be equal and exploitation ended, had been shattered years before. I had no faith in the Communist party, of which I was still a member. "An era has ended" was the best thought I could summon as I stared at the flat line on the electrocardiograph. "Mao's time has passed."

The thought was fleeting. Immediately, I was filled with dread. What would happen to me? As Mao's doctor, I had lived for years in constant fear.

Looking up from Mao's inert body and into the faces of the people gathered round, I realized that everyone else in the room must also have been calculating his fate. Life within the walls of Zhongnanhai had always been precarious. I found myself staring at Jiang Qing.

"What were you people doing?" she snapped at me. "You will be held responsible."

Her accusation was no surprise. Jiang Qing found plots and conspiracies in the most innocent acts. The difficulties in our relationship had begun twenty years before, and four years earlier, in 1972, she had accused me of being a spy.

Hua Guofeng intervened, walking slowly toward her. "We've been here all along," he said gently. "The comrades on the medical team—all of them—have done their best."

Wang Hongwen confirmed Hua's statement. "Yes, the four of us have been here all this time," he began, his face turning red. Wang Hongwen was the youngest member of the politburo and was often referred to sardonically as the "rocket"—a reference to his meteoric rise to power from a minor security cadre in a Shanghai factory to the highest reaches of political power. No one could understand why Mao had taken such a liking to the young man or pushed for his rapid promotions. Wang was tall and handsome and looked intelligent, but his looks were misleading. He was poorly educated—a middle-school graduate only—ignorant and not very smart. He had nothing to contribute to the leadership of China. In May, when Mao suffered a major health setback, Wang had come to me with a cure: He wanted Mao to eat ground pearls. They had already been delivered to Beijing. Wang expected me to administer them to Mao. I waffled. Mao was never given ground pearls.

As Mao lay dying and Wang was supposed to be on duty, he would often go rabbit shooting in the fields near the secret military airport at Xiyuan. He spent much of his time watching movies imported from Hong Kong. Wang, I am convinced, had never been a particularly good man, but power had corrupted him even more. "The medical team has been reporting to us on every detail," he defended himself to Jiang Qing. "We knew clearly—"

"Then why didn't you let me know the situation earlier?" Jiang Qing interrupted.

But Jiang Qing had been repeatedly informed of Mao's condition. Her response had usually been to accuse the doctors of exaggerating his illness. She would say that we were bourgeois and that only a third of our advice should be heeded. On August 28, after she was formally told how serious Mao's condition was, she defied us all by leaving Beijing for an "inspection trip" to Dazhai, the nationwide model agricultural brigade of which she was a particular supporter. Hua Guofeng called her back on September 5. She had not even troubled to ask about Mao's condition when she returned. She was tired, she said.

On September 7, when Mao's condition turned critical and we thought his death was imminent, Jiang Qing had come to meet with the medical team. She went around the room shaking hands with each of the doctors and nurses in turn, repeating to each of them, "You should be very happy now; you should be very happy now." She seemed to have convinced herself that she would take control when Mao died and believed we would be pleased with her leadership.

The other doctors, meeting her for the first time, were stunned by her callousness. "There's nothing strange about it," Wang Dongxing told me. "Jiang Qing believes that the Chairman is the only thing keeping her from ultimate power." She was waiting for him to die. The power struggle gained momentum even as Mao lay dying and intensified before his body turned cold.

Jiang Qing was the leader of the radical faction, supported by Zhang Chunqiao, Wang Hongwen, Yao Wenyuan, and Mao's nephew Mao Yuanxin. Zhang Chunqiao was a Shanghai-based leftist theoretician and a leading exponent of the Cultural Revolution. "Socialist weeds are better than capitalist wheat," he used to say. Now, with Jiang Qing's outburst, he began pacing the floor, his hands clasped behind his back, eyes on the ground.

Mao's nephew began wandering glumly around the room as though looking for something. Mao Yuanxin was the son of Mao's younger brother, Mao Zemin, who had been executed by the governor of Xinjiang province, in China's far northwest, during the Second World War. The governor—Sheng Shicai—had first welcomed Mao Zemin to his fold but switched his political allegiance from the Soviet Union and the Chinese Communist party to Chiang Kai-shek and the Guomindang after Germany's invasion of the Soviet Union. Mao

Zemin's wife was arrested then, too, and Yuanxin was born in jail. When Yuanxin's mother remarried, Mao took responsibility for rearing his nephew, bringing him to Zhongnanhai after 1949, though he rarely saw him.

I had watched Yuanxin grow up. As a child he had not gotten along well with Jiang Qing, but Yuanxin was in his mid-twenties when the Cultural Revolution began in 1966 and joined the rebel side. He wrote to Mao apologizing for his earlier relations with Jiang and announcing that he was joining her. Now only in his mid-thirties, Mao Yuanxin had been appointed political commissar of the Shenyang Military Region, in China's northeast, and late in 1975, after Mao became too ill to attend politburo meetings, Yuanxin had started attending for him, serving as the liaison between Mao and the highest leadership of the party. He had considerable power. Jiang Qing trusted him.

As the physicians and nurses stood with heads bowed in terror at Jiang Qing's outburst, Wang Dongxing was engrossed in a conversation with his subordinate, Zhang Yaoci, the commander of the Central Garrison Corps. The enmity between Wang Dongxing and Jiang Qing was also longstanding. Wang had nothing to fear from Jiang Qing and ignored her outburst. He had amassed remarkable power and held many positions. He was not only the head of the Communist party's General Office but had served for years as director of the Central Bureau of Guards, and was party secretary of the Central Garrison Corps charged with protecting the party leadership and providing security at their residences and offices. Until the Cultural Revolution, he had been vice-minister of China's Ministry of Public Security, too.

Zhang Yaoci, like Wang Dongxing, was a veteran party member and participant in the Long March, and they both came from Jiangxi province. The two security officials had much to plan. Mao's body would lie in state at the Great Hall of the People. With tens of thousands of people filing past to pay their respects, security would have to be tight.

Suddenly, Jiang Qing's expression relaxed. She turned pleasant. Perhaps she had just concluded that her greatest obstacle to power was gone, that she would soon assume leadership over China. "All right," she said. "You all have really had a hard time. Thank you very much." Turning to her nurse, she ordered her to have the black silk dress already made for the occasion of her husband's death ironed. She was ready to mourn.

Hua Guofeng turned to Wang Dongxing. The two had become

close only recently. "Call a meeting of the politburo right away," he instructed.

Most of us were turning to leave the room when Zhang Yufeng suddenly wailed. "The Chairman is gone," she cried. "What will happen to me?" Jiang Qing walked over to her, put her arm around Zhang's shoulder solicitously, and smiled, urging her not to cry. "You can work for me now," she said. Zhang's tears stopped immediately, and she burst into a smile. "Comrade Jiang Qing, thank you so much."

"From now on, don't allow anyone else into Chairman's bedroom or living room," I heard Jiang Qing whisper to her. "Collect all the Chairman's documents, keep them in order, and deliver them to me." She headed toward the conference room, two doors down from Mao's sickroom, where the politburo meeting would soon begin. Zhang Yufeng trailed behind, promising to follow Jiang Qing's orders.

Zhang Yaoci, the commander of the Central Garrison Corps, came to me from Mao's bedroom, obviously worried. He wanted to know if any of the medical staff had seen Mao's watch.

"What watch?" I inquired.

"The one Guo Moruo gave the Chairman during the Chongqing negotiations." Mao had never been in the habit of wearing a watch—he ran on his own time—but the Swiss Omega given to him in August 1945 by Guo Moruo—writer, calligrapher, multifaceted scholar, head of the Chinese Academy of Sciences until his death in 1978, good friend and, finally, sycophant of Mao—had great historic value. The Americans had used the Chongqing negotiations to encourage the Guomindang and the communists to work out their differences and form a coalition government. The collapse of the negotiations had marked the inevitability of civil war and the end of the cooperation between the Communist party and the United States.

"We were all busy trying to save Chairman's life," I answered. "Nobody was paying attention to a watch. Why don't you ask Zhang Yufeng?"

"I saw Mao Yuanxin scurrying around, touching this and that," Zhang Yaoci replied. "He must have taken it."

"No one on the medical team would have dared to take it," I repeated. Zhang Yaoci rushed back into Mao's sickroom.

A moment later, Wang Dongxing walked out of the room where the politburo had begun to gather and called me privately into an adjoining room. The politburo had just decided that Mao's body would have to be preserved for two weeks in order for people to pay their respects. Beijing is still hot in September, and they wanted us to begin immediately, to prevent Mao's body from deteriorating. Wang told me to hurry.

None of us had dared raise the question of Mao's funeral arrangements while the Chairman was alive, but the request to preserve Mao's body for a few weeks came as no surprise and would cause us no problems.

As I went on my way to begin the arrangements, a captain in Zhang Yaoci's Central Garrison Corps stopped me. "Dr. Li, you'd better prepare yourself," he said ominously. "The politburo is meeting now, and I suspect the news for you won't be good. If anything goes wrong, you won't be able to run away." A moment before, I had been filled with a sense of my impending doom. I was surprised at the utter calm that descended upon me with the officer's remark.

I fully expected to be charged with Mao's murder.

I come from a long line, at least five generations, of doctors. Late in the Qing dynasty, during the reign of the Empress Dowager Cixi (1835–1908), my great-grandfather had been so respected that he was summoned from Anhui province to serve as physician to the imperial court. One of my ancestors took care of the Tongzhi emperor (1856–74) and continued later to serve as physician to him and the imperial household.

Folklore has it that the Tongzhi emperor was fond of slipping out of the imperial palace, disguised as a commoner, to visit the brothels that dotted the narrow alleys crisscrossing Beijing just south of the Forbidden City. According to my family history, my great-grandfather diagnosed the Tongzhi emperor as suffering from syphilis. The Empress Dowager Cixi was furious with the judgment. She snatched a jade pin from her hair and threw it on the ground in displeasure, refusing to permit the treatment my great-grandfather prescribed, and insisted that the Tongzhi emperor be treated for smallpox instead. The emperor died, and my great-grandfather was "de-hatted," losing his noble rank, though he continued to serve in the imperial hospital. He died without being exonerated, so the hat that designated his noble status was placed in his coffin by his side rather than on his head. One part of my family tradition survived: My ancestors continued to serve as doctors. But my great-grandfather's admonition against serving in the imperial court was also faithfully handed down from generation to generation and just as faithfully observed. No ancestor since had served in the imperial court.

But one does not refuse a summons from the highest reaches of power. I had protested my appointment as Mao's physician, but the honor could not be turned down. I tried to leave several times, but Mao always called me back.

My work was secret from all but my family and closest friends. The organizations charged with Mao's security were afraid that conspirators would use his doctor to do the Chairman in. People who did know of my work had always expected my service to end badly, and they often warned me of the potentially dire consequences of serving as Mao's physician. "You have a grave responsibility," one of my cousins admonished me in 1963. "Chairman Mao's health is a matter of great concern to the whole party and the whole nation. If any member of the Central Committee is ever dissatisfied and decides to criticize your work, you will be in serious trouble."

Other friends refused to visit my home, even after my family moved out of Zhongnanhai and visits were permitted. One friend from Kunming, in Yunnan province, had been a close friend of Tan Furen, the onetime commissar of the Kunming Military Region who had been assassinated by one of his own bodyguards during the Cultural Revolution. "After his assassination, everybody who had ever set foot in Tan's house was intensely interrogated—in isolation," she told me. "Fortunately, I had never been to his home." She would not visit me, either.

The allegations that Stalin's doctors had conspired to murder the Soviet leader had always weighed heavily on my mind. I fully expected similar allegations against me and my medical team. As Mao's death grew near, I had begun to prepare for my arrest. At the beginning of September, just after his third heart attack, I returned home briefly, for the first time in months, to pack a small bundle of clothes—my quilted cotton jacket and trousers and an overcoat. I expected to be held in an unheated jail. I visited each room in our apartment, silently saying goodbye, fearing I would never return. My wife was at work and my children were at school. My wife told me later that our housemaid told her that I came back home in a great hurry and seemed worried. The maid added that she thought something bad might have happened.

So when I heard the captain's warning only minutes after Mao's death, I prepared for whatever might come. Mao liked to say that "a dead pig is not afraid of boiling water." I felt like a dead pig, numb.

It was still dark when I phoned the minister of public health, Liu Xiangping, at her home and asked to see her immediately. I refused to explain why and told her only that we must meet in person. Liu Xiangping was the widow of the late minister of public security Xie Fuzhi. They had both been leftists and devoted to Jiang Qing. I assumed that her appointment as minister of public health in the midst of the Cultural Revolution had been recommended by Jiang Qing, since Liu Xiangping had no qualifications for the position.

She still lived on the grounds of the Ministry of Public Security just off Changan Avenue, north of the old legation area, in an elegant old Western-style house that had once been a foreign embassy. She was waiting for me in an anteroom and not yet fully awake.

"Chairman Mao passed away at ten minutes past midnight," I began. She screamed even before I finished my sentence. "We have lots to do right now and cannot waste any time," I continued impatiently. "The central authority wants us to preserve the Chairman's body for two weeks. We must rush. They are waiting for us."

She wiped her eyes. "What shall we do?" She was weeping.

"We have to talk with people at the Academy of Medical Sciences," I said. "The anatomy and histology departments have specialists."

"All right. But first we should ask Huang Shuze and Yang Chun to come here for a talk." Liu Xiangping relied on Huang Shuze, one of the vice-ministers of public health and a doctor himself, when she needed medical advice. Yang Chun was party secretary at the Academy of Medical Sciences.

"We'll waste a lot of time if we ask them to come here," I said. "Let's call the specialists first and then we'll all meet in Yang Chun's office at the academy." Liu agreed and began calling them while I drove to the academy.

Yang Chun and Huang Shuze were already waiting when I arrived. Two experts in the preservation of human bodies were there, too—Zhang Bingchang, a research associate in the department of anatomy, and Xu Jing, a fortyish-looking female assistant researcher in the department of histology. The minister of public health had not told them why they had been summoned so mysteriously in the middle of the night, and Zhang Bingchang, obviously worried, was staring out the window. I learned later that this was not the first time he had been called to the academy like this. During the Cultural Revolution, he had often been awakened to sign the death certificates of people who had been murdered or committed suicide. Since the militant young Red Guards responsible for the deaths did not want such unpleasant facts to be recorded, Zhang Bingchang was often "struggled against" and beaten. "I didn't mind being beaten," he told me. "What I feared most was being labeled a counterrevolutionary." Not long before, he had been called during the middle of the night to perform an autopsy on the body of former minister of public security Li Zhen, who had died from an overdose of sleeping pills. Because of his report, he had been jailed by the Ministry of Public Security for more than two months.

He relaxed visibly when I told the group of Mao's death.

The specialists agreed that Mao's body could easily be preserved for two weeks. It was only a matter of injecting two liters of formaldehyde into a leg artery. Huang Shuze and Yang Chun had no objection to the method, so Zhang and Xu fetched their syringes and medical supplies and accompanied me to Zhongnanhai. The streets were deserted. It was four o'clock in the morning and still dark. The Chinese people would not learn of their leader's death for hours.

The politburo was still meeting in the conference room. "Director Wang Dongxing has asked for you several times, and Marshal Ye Jianying was looking for you, too," said the officer in charge of the armed guards standing watch as soon as he saw me. "The politburo has approved an announcement of the Chairman's death—'A Message to the Whole Party, the Whole Army, and the People of All Nationalities of the Country.' It will be broadcast at four o'clock this afternoon."

This was the announcement I had been waiting for. It would give the official verdict on the cause of Mao's death—and say whether I and the team of doctors would be blamed. "What did it say about the illness and death of the Chairman?" I asked anxiously.

He handed me a copy. "Take a look," he said.

I grabbed the sheet of paper and quickly scanned the first paragraph. ". . . received excellent medical care during his illness," I read, "nevertheless in the end his condition was beyond help. He died at ten past midnight on the morning of September 9, 1976, in Beijing." There was no need for me to read further. I had been exonerated. Several days later, on September 13, my name would appear in the *People's Daily* as the director of Mao's medical team. I was safe.

Wang Dongxing came up to me as soon as I entered the room where the Beijing-based politburo members—seventeen people in all—were gathered. "Let's go somewhere else," he said. "We need to talk."

As we stepped into an adjoining room, he asked, "Did you see the announcement?"

"Yes, I just saw it. I only read the first paragraph," I responded.

He grinned, then continued. "The politburo has just made a decision. The Chairman's body is to be permanently preserved. You'll have to find out how it can be done."

I was astonished. "But you told me the body only had to be preserved for two weeks," I objected. "Why do you want to preserve it forever? In 1956, Chairman Mao was the first person to sign the pledge to be cremated. I remember that clearly."

"It's a decision of the politburo. We decided just a moment ago," Wang Dongxing said.

"But it's impossible," I protested. "How do you feel about it?"

"Premier Hua and I both support the decision," Wang answered.

"It just can't be done," I argued. "Even iron and steel corrode, to say nothing of the human body. How can it not deteriorate?" I was remembering my trip to Moscow with Mao in 1957 and our visit to the remains of Lenin and Stalin. The bodies had seemed shrunken and dry, and I had been told that Lenin's nose and ears had rotted away and been replaced by wax and that Stalin's mustache had fallen off. Soviet embalming techniques were far more advanced than China's. I could not imagine how we could preserve Mao's body.

"You must have some regard for our feelings," Wang responded, blinking.

"Yes, of course," I agreed. "But Chinese science simply isn't advanced enough for this."

"That's why you're going to have to find people to help you. Whatever you need—equipment, facilities, anything—just let me know," Wang assured me. "The central authority will make sure you have everything."

The elderly Marshal Ye Jianying joined us. One of the earliest members of the Communist party, a founder of the People's Liberation Army, and one of my favorite politburo members, Marshal Ye asked what I thought about the permanent preservation of Mao's body. I reiterated my objections. After a short silence, he said, "Under the circumstances we have no choice but to accept the decision of the politburo, Dr. Li. But why don't you consult with some people you trust, some instructors at the Institute of Arts and Crafts, to see if they can make a wax dummy of Mao? Tell them to try to make it look real. Later maybe we can use the model as a substitute, if that becomes necessary."

I was relieved. At least Ye Jianying, a vice-chairman of the Military Affairs Commission and a key member of the politburo, would not insist on the impossible.

Wang Dongxing concurred, but told me not to say a word.

To this day, I do not know how many members of the politburo were involved in that decision. It is possible that Jiang Qing herself never knew.

I returned to Mao's sickroom. His body was still there, the room still full of medical equipment. We moved him to a more spacious room adjacent to the conference room where the politburo was meeting. The temperature was 78 degrees Fahrenheit, much too high for the body. I ordered the attendants to lower the temperature to 50 degrees. "We can't do that," they told me. "The top leaders are all here, and Comrade Jiang Qing has set stringent requirements about room temperature. You have to get their permission." Zhongnanhai was directly connected to two of Beijing's power plants, and backup generators guaranteed heat in the winter and air-conditioning in the summer, even if power everywhere else in the city was out. But even in Building 202, built especially for Mao, there was no way to control the temperature in individual rooms. I went to the conference room and got politburo permission. The meeting adjourned shortly thereafter.

When I returned to Mao's makeshift morgue, Zhang Bingchang and Xu Jing were just finishing the injection of formaldehyde. I told them about the politburo's decision to have the body permanently preserved. They were astonished. "It's impossible," they agreed. "We have no idea how to do it."

I sympathized but insisted, "We just have to figure out some way to do it. Somebody has to go to the library at the Academy of Medical Sciences. Find out if there are books on the subject."

Xu Jing went immediately to the medical library and phoned us a little more than an hour later. "There is a procedure for preserving the body for a relatively long time," she explained. "Another large dose of formaldehyde—as much as twelve to sixteen liters, depending on the size of the body—has to be injected within four to eight hours of death. When the tips of the fingers and toes are filled with liquid, enough has been injected." But Xu Jing was still uncertain. She had found the formula in a Western journal but had no idea whether it would work. She suggested we consult with the politburo.

I spoke with Wang Dongxing. "You people are just going to have to talk it over and decide among yourselves," he said. "But you'd still better ask Premier Hua's opinion first."

I found Hua Guofeng and told him about Xu Jing's proposal. He thought for a while and said, "We can't call another meeting now. Even if we were to meet, it wouldn't do any good. We politburo members know nothing about these things. Why don't you just go ahead and do it? I can't think of any other way."

At the makeshift morgue, Zhang Bingchang and Xu Jing had been joined by two newcomers. A man named Chen, an intern with the department of anatomy at the Academy of Medical Sciences, was there to help administer the formaldehyde. A Comrade Ma from the department of pathology of the Beijing Hospital came as an expert in making up the dead. I told them to begin the injection. Altogether we injected a total of twenty-two liters, some six more than the formula called for, hoping that the extra would provide some additional guarantee. The process took hours. We did not finish until ten o'clock in the morning.

The results were shocking. Mao's face was bloated, as round as a ball, and his neck was now the width of his head. His skin was shiny, and the formaldehyde oozed from his pores like perspiration. His ears were swollen, too, sticking out from his head at right angles. The corpse was grotesque. The guards and other attendants were aghast. "What have you done to make Chairman look so terrible?" Zhang Yufeng complained. "Do you think the central authority will approve of what you have done?"

Xu Jing remained calm throughout the ordeal, but I was worried about Zhang Bingchang. He was pale and clearly anxious. "Don't worry," I tried to reassure him. "We'll think of something."

Somehow we had to restore Mao to his original appearance, but there was no way to remove the formaldehyde. "It's all right if his body stays bloated," I said. "His clothes will cover it. But we had better try to fix his face and neck."

"Maybe if we massage them we can squeeze some of the liquid back into the body," Zhang suggested. The team started working on Mao's face with a towel and cotton balls, trying to force the liquid down into the body. When Chen pressed a little too hard, a piece of skin on Mao's right cheek broke off. Chen trembled in fright. "Don't worry," Ma consoled him. "We can apply some makeup." He used a cotton swab to dab some Vaseline and a flesh-colored liquid onto the spot. The makeup worked. The damage was invisible.

The four of them continued working until three o'clock in the afternoon. Finally, Mao's face looked normal. His ears no longer stuck out. The neck remained swollen, but the guards and attendants agreed that Mao looked much better—given the circumstances. When they tried to put the suit on Mao's body, though, his chest was so swollen the jacket would not button. They cut a slit in the underside of the jacket and trousers to accommodate Mao's new bulk.

Xu Shiyou, the commander of the Guangzhou Military Region, had just arrived in Beijing and came to pay his respects while we were dressing the body. Xu Shiyou was one of China's most famous generals, a party member since his youth and a survivor of the Long March. When still a child, Xu had been forced by poverty to become a Buddhist monk in Henan's Shaolin Temple, famous the world over for its martial arts. Xu's family were peasants, and he was never educated. The Red Army taught him to read. He was a coarse and ignorant man, but Wang Dongxing used to say that Xu Shiyou could take on twenty men singlehanded and beat them all. Xu had never liked Jiang Qing but was fiercely loyal to Mao.

When he saw Mao's body, Xu Shiyou bowed to it three times in the traditional Chinese manner. Then he leaned forward to look at the skin on Mao's chest. Suddenly, he turned to me and asked, "How many *ga ma* did the Chairman have before he died?" I had no idea what he was talking about.

"Everybody has twenty-four *ga ma*," Xu insisted. "How many did Chairman have?"

I remained speechless.

"You are a smart physician," Xu began baiting me. "Don't you know about *ga ma*?"

To this day I do not know what a *ga ma* is. Friends who know more about Buddhism than I say that Buddhists believe that every living body has twenty-four *ga ma*, but I knew nothing about such things.

Xu Shiyou circled the body twice, muttering to himself. "What the devil," he said. "Why are there bluish bruises on his body?" He bowed deeply again three times, saluted Mao, and left.

Ma redid the makeup. Satisfied that we had done our best and that the body really did look like Mao, we finally finished dressing him, draping the body with the Communist party flag—the crossed hammer and sickle against a bright red background. At around midnight on September 9–10, some twenty-four hours after his death, we placed Mao's body in a crystal vacuum-sealed casket. Several members of the politburo had their pictures taken facing the coffin. Mao's body was then loaded into the back of an ambulance. I sat with it as we left the gates of Zhongnanhai and headed south, traveling through the darkened, deserted streets of Beijing to the Great Hall of the People, where Mao would lie in state for a week.

The intense power struggle that had begun during his illness was now centered on the custody of Mao's documents. Jiang Qing and Mao Yuanxin visited Mao's living quarters, where Zhang Yufeng was still staying, and asked her to give them Mao's papers, especially transcripts of Mao's conversations during an inspection tour in south China from August 14 to September 12, 1971, just before Lin Biao's disastrous abortive flight to the Soviet Union. Mao's talks during that trip had never been made public but were known to contain not only criticisms of Lin and several of his closest colleagues but assessments of several other top Communist party leaders, including Jiang Qing and her colleagues Zhang Chunqiao, Wang Hongwen, and Yao Wen-yuan, soon to be labeled the Gang of Four.

Wang Dongxing, responsible for safeguarding Mao's documents, was staying in the Great Hall of the People while Mao's body lay in state, for he was also in charge of the security arrangements within the Great Hall. Tens of thousands of carefully selected citizens were coming daily to pay their respects, and the country's top leadership was standing vigil. Wang knew nothing of Jiang Qing's efforts to remove Mao's documents until Zhang Yaoci, the commander of the Central Garrison Corps, informed him. Wang went immediately to Zhang Yufeng. "Your responsibility is to take care of the documents, not to give them to others," he yelled at her. "They belong to the central authority of the party. No one has permission to take them away."

Zhang sobbed and mumbled, "Comrade Jiang Qing is a politburo member and Chairman Mao's wife. Mao Yuanxin is his liaison to the politburo and the Chairman's nephew. What can I do to stop them?"

"All right," Wang responded. "I'll send someone here to inspect all the documents. In the meantime, you have to ask Jiang Qing to return the papers."

Jiang Qing refused to return the documents until Hua Guofeng insisted. "Chairman Mao's body has hardly turned cold," she complained, "and already you people are trying to drive me out." Wang Dongxing later told me that parts of the documents seemed to have been falsified, and implied that Jiang Qing had attempted to expunge Mao's criticisms of her.

In the meantime, I had begun to organize a special team for the permanent preservation of Mao's body, recruiting more than twenty leading specialists in anatomy, pathology, and organic chemistry from medical schools around the country.

We investigated China's ancient means of preservation. Recent archaeological finds had unearthed bodies hundreds of years old that had been astonishingly well preserved. We quickly concluded that the ancient techniques were of no use to Mao. Buried deep in the ground, the bodies had never been exposed to oxygen. They had been covered with a sort of balsam and immersed in a liquid that scientists thought was mercury. The bodies had disintegrated immediately upon being exposed to the air.

We wanted to know how Lenin's body had been preserved, but China's relations with the Soviet Union had so deteriorated that sending a research team there was out of the question. Instead, we sent two investigators to Hanoi to find out how Ho Chi Minh (1890–1969) had been preserved. The trip was a failure. No one in Vietnam was willing to explain the process, and the two researchers never saw Ho Chi Minh's body. They were told confidentially that Ho's nose had already rotted away and that his beard had fallen off.

Another two researchers in England visited Madame Tussaud's Wax Museum to learn how to make wax figures. The team concluded that in this technique, at least, China was already far more advanced than England. The waxen figure of Mao made by the Institute of Arts and Crafts looked remarkably lifelike. The replicas in Madame Tussaud's were obviously wax.

Finally, from our reading of scientific journals, we concluded that the only way to preserve Mao's body was through a modification of the method we had already used. We would leave Mao's brain intact—we did not want to open his skull—but remove the viscera—the heart, lungs, stomach, kidneys, intestines, liver, pancreas, bladder, gallbladder, and spleen. These we would preserve in separate jars of formaldehyde should there ever be any question about the cause of Mao's death. The visceral cavity would then be filled with formaldehyde-saturated cotton. A tube inserted into Mao's neck would allow the team to replenish the formaldehyde at periodic intervals. The crystal coffin would be filled with helium. Work on Mao's body was scheduled to begin just after the official period of mourning and would be done in the utmost secrecy. The "May 19 underground project" was our worksite.

The May 19 underground project dated back to the border clashes between China and the Soviet Union over Zhenbao (Treasure) Island, in northernmost Heilongjiang. Sometime after the hostilities began on March 2, 1969, Mao became convinced that the Soviet Union, not the United States, was the main threat to China's security. His conviction led to the later détente with the United States, but in the meantime Chinese everywhere were called upon to "dig tunnels deep, store grain everywhere, and never seek hegemony"—implying that China loved peace even as the country prepared for war. In urban areas throughout the country, citizens were mobilized to dig underground air-raid shelters as protection against Soviet attack. Beijing is still crisscrossed with these underground tunnels, and keepers of the underground maze boasted that the entire population of the city could be underground in three minutes.

While the citizens of Beijing were constructing these underground tunnels, the Chinese army's corps of engineers was secretly building the huge May 19 underground complex, named for the day in 1969 that the decision to construct it was made. Inaccessible from the citizens' air-raid shelters, the huge complex was to house the military high command in time of war. It contains a highway large enough for four trucks abreast and links Zhongnanhai, Tiananmen, the Great Hall of the People, Lin Biao's former residence of Maojiawan, and the People's Liberation Army 305 Hospital, in the heart of the city, with the military headquarters in the western hills outside, where many military officials reside. In addition to the military command center, there are offices, telephone and telegraph communications facilities, living quarters, and a modern, well-equipped hospital, for use only in case of war. This special hospital was just underneath 305 Hospital, where I served as director, and became our secret workplace.

Sometime after midnight on September 17, 1976, at the conclusion of the weeklong mourning period and as all of Beijing slept, Mao's body was removed from the Great Hall of the People and placed in the back of a mini-bus. Hua Guofeng and Wang Dongxing, riding in separate cars, joined the heavily guarded motorcade and so did the minister and one of the vice-ministers of public health and leading members of the medical team responsible for preserving the body. I rode in the van with Mao's body as we raced through the darkened streets of Beijing to Maojiawan, deserted since Lin Biao's death, where a pair of soldiers stood guard over the entrance to the underground complex. The soldiers waved us through, and the mini-bus descended into the bowels of the underground highway, heading for the special hospital beneath 305 Hospital, some ten to fifteen minutes away. There, Mao's body was removed and placed in one of the clinic's operating rooms, where work on its preservation would soon begin. Days later, the waxen dummy arrived and was placed nearby in another locked room, where I saw it for the first time. The skill of the artists at the Institute of Arts and Crafts was indeed impressive. The waxen figure looked uncannily like Mao Zedong.

Known only to a small handful of people, the two Maos, one preserved by formaldehyde and one a waxen effigy, remained in the underground hospital for a full year, where I continued to inspect them once a week. Even the soldiers who stood guard over the hospital had no inkling of what they were protecting. In 1977, with the completion within Tiananmen Square of the Memorial Hall, where Mao's body was to be put on public display, both Maos—and the several formaldehyde-filled jars containing his vital organs—were transferred to the huge vault beneath the public hall. An elevator raises and lowers the remains to and from the viewing area, the exposed casket resting on the elevator floor. Xu Jing, the female assistant researcher from the department of histology at the Chinese Academy of Medical Sciences, who had participated in the efforts at preservation, was put in charge both of Mao's remains and of the mausoleum where tens of thousands of ordinary Chinese and visiting foreign tourists would come each day to pay their respects to the man who had been the chairman of the Chinese Communist party for some forty years.

The memorial service for Chairman Mao was held on September 18, the day after I delivered his body to the secret underground vault. The weather was scorchingly hot, and I arrived at Tiananmen—the Gate of Heavenly Peace, once the southern entrance to the Forbidden City, where the emperors of the Ming and Qing dynasties had lived—at two o'clock in the afternoon, an hour before the proceedings began. Mao's portrait was still atop Tiananmen, as it had been since the communist victory, and it was flanked on both sides by revolutionary slogans proclaiming the worldwide unity of the proletariat and wishing the People's Republic of China a life of ten thousand years.

In the nearly thirty years since my return to China, I had come often to Tiananmen. I had been there on October 1, 1949, when the People's Republic of China was established, and later with Mao to review the twice-yearly parades—on the October 1 anniversaries of the founding of the People's Republic, and again for Labor Day, on May 1. Early in the tumultuous Cultural Revolution (1966–76), I had gone with him to review the millions of cheering Red Guards from the country's middle schools and universities. Today, the vast square that stretches south of the Gate of Heavenly Peace, flanked on the west by the massive Great Hall of the People, where Mao had lain in state, and on the east by the huge Museum of Revolutionary History, was filled with half a million somber mourners, specially chosen for the occasion and drawn from all walks of life.

At three o'clock in the afternoon, all of China came to a halt. For three minutes, the whistles of every factory and train in the country blasted their final tribute. An equal period of silence followed. Then, as all Chinese work units throughout the country conducted their own tributes, Wang Hongwen opened the national service. Looking out over the crowd, I was dripping with perspiration. The exhaustion I had managed to stave off for months suddenly overcame me. As Hua Guofeng began the eulogy, I tottered, and had to struggle not to fall. Since Mao's first heart attack in May, I had been on duty night and day. I had not slept more than four hours a night. My weight, normally 175 pounds, had dropped to 120. My mind was in a cloud during the service. I knew only that when it was over, at last I would get some sleep. Maybe I could return to my family.

At five-thirty in the afternoon, I went back to my office in Zhongnanhai, curled up on the cot, and fell asleep.

Minutes later, the phone awakened me. It was Wang Dongxing. The politburo had scheduled a meeting for the morning of September 22, four days from then, in the Great Hall of the People. We would be expected to present a report on Mao Zedong's illness and treatment and explain how he had died. The whole medical team was ordered to attend, and I was to read the report. "This is a very important meeting," Wang emphasized. "You must be fully prepared." The next day, my name appeared again in the *People's Daily* heading the list of Mao's doctors.

But I had not been exonerated. The relief I had felt at reading the announcement of Mao's death had been premature. That statement, praising Mao's medical care, had been a public presentation for the Chinese masses. Now, the entire politburo would meet to make its official determination of how and why Mao died. If my report was approved, the official verdict would be that Mao died of natural causes. The medical team would be cleared. If the politburo did not approve my report, the consequences would be disastrous. It was a matter of life and death for me and the entire medical staff.

I called the medical team together, and we agreed that I would draft the report and that we would reconvene to discuss it. I began immediately, spending the entire night of September 18 and all the following morning writing. The report was comprehensive, some fifty pages long. It began with our successful attempt to save Mao's life after his first congestive heart failure in January 1972 and described the progressive degeneration from his amyotrophic lateral sclerosis and his three myocardial infarctions. I explained how Mao's illnesses had been diagnosed and treated and outlined the cause of his death. The medical team offered several revisions. We finally finished the report on the morning of September 20.

Wang Dongxing did not want to read the report and suggested that Hua Guofeng review it instead. After reading the report carefully, Hua was worried that many of the medical terms might not be clear to the politburo members. He also said the report did not clearly state the cause of death. He asked for revisions.

My colleagues were reluctant to change the medical terminology and thought that many of the terms would be extremely difficult to convey in lay language. They suggested that I explain these terms orally. They were also reluctant to ascribe Mao's death to a single cause. He was an old man, after all, and had suffered the cumulative effect of old age and several serious diseases. They thought I should emphasize his difficulty in breathing—the result of his series of heart attacks, his advanced emphysema, and his motor neuron disease—as the immediate cause.

I submitted the revised report to Hua Guofeng on September 21 and told him of my colleagues' opinions. "Some politburo members might raise questions at the meeting," he warned me. "Try your best to give them a thorough explanation—one that they will understand."

The meeting was already in session when my colleagues and I arrived at the Great Hall of the People on the morning of September 22. The politburo members were sitting on comfortable chairs placed in a casual circle around the room, with small wooden tables in front of them holding cups of tea. Several notetakers from the Bureau of Secretaries [*mishu ju*] were there, too, and a number of younger interns were scurrying about. I sat in an easy chair directly behind Premier Hua Guofeng and Marshal Ye Jianying, the man who had suggested making a waxen image of Mao. Chen Xilian, the commander of the Beijing Military Region, was talking. "I cannot do my job anymore," he was saying. "I want to be relieved of my duties."

"Relax, Comrade Xilian," Hua Guofeng replied. "We'll discuss your problem later. Let's listen to the report from Chairman Mao's medical team now. They have worked day and night for four months trying to save the Chairman's life. Dr. Li will present the report." I never learned why Chen Xilian wanted to resign.

Ye Jianying told me to speak loudly. Several members of the politburo were old and hard-of-hearing. I was interrupted a number of times as various members asked about some of the medical terms.

When I began to describe how Chairman Mao had turned critically ill in June 1976, General Xu Shiyou suddenly rose and walked menacingly toward me. "Why were there black-and-blue marks on the Chairman's body?" he demanded, standing directly in front of me. "What was the cause?" It is a popular folk belief in China that the body of someone who has been poisoned to death will be covered with bruises.

I tried to explain. "In the last days of his life, the Chairman could hardly breathe. He was seriously short of oxygen. That is the reason for the bruises."

"I have fought field battles all my life and have seen lots of dead people," Xu challenged me. "But I never saw anyone in that condition. When I saw the bruises on the Chairman's body on September 9, I asked you how many *ga ma* he had, but you couldn't answer the question. I believe the Chairman was poisoned. Only poison could produce bruises like that. We must interrogate the physicians and nurses to find out who poisoned the Chairman."

An elaborate system to prevent Mao from being poisoned had been in effect since the first days of the People's Republic. I tried to explain the system to Xu. "Each medicine we used was first agreed to by the medical team," I explained. "A prescription was then written, and each prescription was certified by two nurses and further verified by the doctors on duty. The prescription was taken to the special pharmacy that serves only our top party leaders. It was then delivered in sealed containers that could only be opened by the doctors at Mao's side."

"This could be a plot cooked up by everyone involved," Xu insisted. "We have to have a thorough investigation." Xu Shiyou really did believe that Mao had been poisoned as part of an elaborate plot. He suspected Jiang Qing and her close associates were the masterminds. Unaware of how strained my relations with Jiang had been, he thought that I and the other doctors had been persuaded to go along.

When Xu Shiyou finished, the entire room was quiet. Xu was standing in front of me, his hands on his hips. He glanced in mute accusation at Zhang Chunqiao, who stared at the ground, his left hand propping up his chin. Jiang Qing, still in her black silk dress, was sitting on the sofa staring at Xu. Hua Guofeng stiffened. Wang Dongxing was pretending to read documents. Wang Hongwen, looking flushed, glanced nervously around the room.

Then Marshal Ye Jianying and General Li Desheng, commander of the Shenyang Military Region, turned to me and whispered, "Why were there bruises on Chairman Mao's body?"

"There were three large air bubbles in the Chairman's left lung," I said, "and he had pneumonia in both lungs. He was having great difficulty breathing and was therefore seriously short of oxygen. Bruises like this—death patches, we call them—normally appear about four hours after death. When Comrade Xu Shiyou saw the body at four that afternoon, Chairman had already been dead for sixteen hours."

At this moment, Mao's widow, Jiang Qing, rose and said, "Comrade Xu Shiyou, the medical team has been working very hard for four months. Why don't you just let them finish their report?" Wang Hongwen, as though on cue, rose too, and said, "Since Chairman turned critically ill, Guofeng, Chunqiao, Dongxing, and I were taking turns—"

Xu pushed up his sleeves and walked toward Jiang Qing. He

pounded the table in front of her so hard the teacups fell to the carpet. "You aren't allowing the members of the politburo to speak at a politburo meeting," he bellowed at her. "What kind of tricks are you people playing?"

Hua Guofeng intervened. "Comrade Shiyou, let's calm down," he urged. He turned to me. "Dr. Li, why don't you and your people leave now. We'll take up this matter later." The medical team, silent and despondent, returned to Zhongnanhai. I had delivered only the first ten pages of my report.

"Director Wang Dongxing says not to say a word about what happened at the politburo meeting," Zhang Yaoci warned me. "You are just to wait for the politburo's decision."

I expected to be summoned back at any moment.

At lunch, I repeated Zhang's warning to the medical staff. They continued to be apprehensive. None of us could eat.

I had expected to be accused of helping to kill Mao. The surprise was that the accusation came from Xu Shiyou and that Jiang Qing, who had done nothing but criticize the doctors during Mao's illness, had come to our defense. I speculated that since Jiang Qing's close colleagues Wang Hongwen and Zhang Chunqiao had helped supervise the medical team, they would also have to be held responsible for any medical errors. If the politburo concluded that there had been a plot to poison Mao, then Wang Hongwen and Zhang Chunqiao would be implicated. This is why Jiang Qing had to insist on the innocence of the medical team.

Days went by and there was no word from the politburo. I was consumed with anxiety. The members of the medical team were told to return to their medical institutions. Some of them thought the crisis was over.

But I was not so sure. I knew, better than they, that the power struggle in Zhongnanhai had just begun. In July, two months before Mao's death, Wang Dongxing had told me he was considering arresting Jiang Qing immediately, while Mao was still alive. Even as Wang Dongxing feigned indifference to her and Hua Guofeng remained unfailingly polite, I knew that the two were going to arrest her and her radical supporters. Thus, while Jiang Qing was behaving as though Mao's power would soon be hers, she must have known that she was not safe. With the power struggle still unsettled, the medical team's position would remain precarious, too. Accusations and counteraccusations about Mao's death would be part of the debate.

And even if the power struggle were temporarily settled and Jiang

Qing and her colleagues removed, how long would it be before another struggle, another round of recriminations, began? After twenty-seven years in Zhongnanhai, I had learned how uncertain life there could be. Having presided for twenty-two years over Mao's health—his illnesses and, finally, his death—I knew I would never be safe again.

II

1949–1957

2

I was in Sydney, Australia, a twenty-nine-year-old ship's doctor, when I read that the city of my birth had been conquered by the communists without a shot. On January 31, 1949, the citizens of Beiping, as the city was then called, had lined the streets to welcome their "liberation." Now the entire leadership of the Communist party was moving there to establish the People's Republic of China. The new capital would be there, too, and the city would thus return to its rightful name and function. Beiping, meaning "northern peace," was the name given Beijing when Chiang Kai-shek moved his government to the "southern capital" of Nanjing. Now the city would become Beijing, the "northern capital," again. The civil war with Chiang Kai-shek's Guomindang forces continued, but everyone knew that the communists would emerge victorious.

Beijing was my home. I had spent my first thirteen years there, living in the elegant traditional style, in a "four-cornered courtyard" complex my grandfather had had built. Ours was a wealthy, upper-class home, the walled compound comprising numerous one-story tile-roofed buildings facing a series of three separate flower-filled courtyards containing over thirty rooms. The complex was situated south of the Forbidden City in the area called Liulichang—"Glazed Tile Factory"—for the factory that had made the golden-colored tiles for the roofs of the Imperial City during the Ming dynasty (1368–1644).

My grandfather died before I was born, but the family tradition he exemplified permeated our home. His portrait hung in a special room, where we gathered to pay homage to his memory several times each year. Just inside the family compound, my grandfather's medical offices were maintained unchanged, and the Pei Zhi Tang apothecary he had established continued to thrive nearby, still owned by my family but managed by a trusted herbal pharmacist.

My grandfather had been wealthy, but he was honored for the special kindness he had shown to the poor. He had opened the Pei Zhi Tang apothecary in order to provide free medicine and had offered his medical services free to those who could not afford to pay. My ancestors were famous in Liulichang, and much of Beijing, for their generosity. I grew up believing that the poor suffered unduly and should be treated with charity.

But my wealth and destiny separated me from the poor. Though poverty was pervasive in Beijing, my mother never permitted me to play with children of the poor. From my earliest childhood, I was expected to carry on the family tradition by becoming a doctor, and I believed that my family was special. I was proud of my ancestors and wanted to excel at whatever I did.

My uncle—my father's younger brother—had also become a doctor and devoted his energies to the disadvantaged. When Henan province was struck by a typhus epidemic, he volunteered to go there, contracted typhus, and died before the age of thirty. His widow and two children, whom I called my elder brothers, continued to live in our family compound. So did my elder brother from my father's first marriage. My father had married my mother after his first wife died.

Only my father had eschewed the family tradition. In 1920, he went to France on a work-study program, leaving my mother and me, then only an infant, behind. He stayed more than seven years. Zhou Enlai was among the students in his group, and the two remained friends until my father's death. But while Zhou became a communist leader, my father joined the nationalists, the Guomindang, and became a high official under Chiang Kai-shek.

My father's sojourn in France brought scandal to the family, for he returned with a new French wife, who moved into our compound. My mother was a traditional Chinese woman—simple and illiterate, with bound feet and a generous and compassionate nature. Her highest ideal was to be a good wife and mother. It was legal then in China for a man to have more than one wife and many of the wealthy did, but multiple wives had not been part of my family tradition, and my father's second wife was regarded as a disgrace.

Nevertheless, my father's French wife was a good and decent

woman and highly educated. She taught French at Peking University and was always especially kind to me, plying me with sweets, but I sensed my mother's unhappiness in her frequent outbursts of anger and the beatings I often suffered at her hands. I was well into adulthood before I saw that they were the result of her unhappiness over my father.

Even in childhood, I greatly resented my father. I rarely saw him, but his influence on me was profound and largely negative. Others in my family had taught service and sacrifice for the good of mankind. But my father craved power. My ancestors had placed great emphasis on the moral path, but my father strayed. Not long after their return to China, he and his new wife moved to Nanjing to join Chiang Kai-shek's government. A few years later, after his French wife died, my father became a womanizer. He never married again. I was ashamed of his private behavior and resolved to become a self-sacrificing doctor in the service of humanity. My father's position in the Guomindang government contributed to my distaste for the nationalists and my early and ready acceptance of the Communist party. Perhaps my distaste for my father's moral failings also contributed to my later dismay at Mao's private life.

Like most Chinese of my generation, I grew up patriotic, proud of our Chinese culture, our literature, poetry, and art, and the richness and glory of our four thousand years of history. But I was profoundly troubled by the decline of my country that had begun a century before. As a student in primary school, I learned of China's defeat by Great Britain during the Opium War of 1839 and studied the series of invasions by France, Japan, and Russia that had undermined China's sovereignty and left the country divided and weak. I learned about the foreign concessions that had grown up in so many cities, oases of foreign law immune from Chinese rule. From my boyhood, I knew of the famous sign at the entrance to the riverside park along the Shanghai Bund—"Chinese and dogs not allowed"—and had been deeply offended. Like many, I attributed China's decline to the foreign powers that had established themselves in our country—what we later called imperialism.

In 1931, when I was eleven years old, the Japanese took over the northeastern provinces of Manchuria and established the puppet state of Manchukuo. My mother and I fled Beijing and went south to Suzhou, where I attended Suzhou University Middle School, established by American Methodist missionaries. My education there was entirely in English, decidedly American, and filled with religion. I studied the coming of the *Mayflower* and the Boston Tea Party and learned how George Washington chopped down the cherry tree. In 1935, at the age of fifteen, I was baptized a Christian.

I turned toward communism at about the same time. My elder brother from my father's first marriage was studying medicine at Aurora University in Shanghai, where he became a member of the Communist party in 1935. This was unusual for a man of his background and wealth, but it was motivated by patriotism and his lifelong concern with the plight of the poor. Every weekend, visiting us in Suzhou, he enthralled me with tales of the evils of capitalism and its oppression of workers and talked about the communist belief in equality and a world without exploitation. He accused the Guomindang of corruption and a lack of will in the struggle against the Japanese invaders of Manchuria. The communists, he assured me, were fighting the Japanese. I looked up to my elder brother and was enraptured by his utopian dreams—China rich, prosperous, and fully sovereign once more, with equality and justice for all. I devoured the books he gave me—*The Story of the First Five-Year Plan,* Nicolai Ostroevsky's *How the Steel Was Forged,* and a book by French journalist Henri Barbusse lauding Stalin's contributions to the revolution. My brother taught me that only communism could save China and that two men—Zhu De and Mao Zedong—were leading the country toward that goal. China's salvation rested with them. Zhu Mao we called the duo, as though they were a single man, and from that time on, I regarded Zhu Mao as our country's messiah, a belief that was only strengthened when I learned that Lu Xun, my favorite writer, was also an admirer of communism.

It was about this time, in 1936, that my cousin introduced me to a classmate from her middle school. Wu Shenxian—Lillian Wu—was her name, and it was love at first sight—or nearly so. Lillian was a Christian, too, and wealthy. It would be a decade before we married, but even as the widening war forced our families to flee further and further inland, we always managed to end up in the same place.

The Japanese armies continued their advance, and my mother and I fled to Wuhan, in 1937, and then to Chongqing, in Sichuan province, where Chiang Kai-shek moved the Guomindang capital, in 1938. In the fall of 1935, the Communist party, forced out of its base in Jiangxi by Chiang Kai-shek's encircling armies, had completed its epic Long March and established a new base area in northwest China's Shaanxi province. My elder brother and one of my cousins both made their way there.

In 1939, I began medical school at West China Union University Medical School, established almost a century earlier by Canadian missionaries, in Chengdu, Sichuan province. After the Japanese took over Beijing, many faculty and students from Peking Union Medical College (PUMC) fled to Chengdu, and after 1941 West China Union University Medical School and Peking Union Medical College were amalgamated for the duration of the occupation. Since Peking Union Medical College was American-run and Rockefeller-funded, so too was the West China Union University Medical School. Most of my professors were American. Our courses and books were all in English and my training was modern and Western. I received two diplomas— one from West China Union University Medical School and the other from the State University of New York.

Lillian studied sociology briefly at Fudan University in Chongqing and then transferred to Jinling Women's College, an American-run Christian school, in Chengdu.

I completed my internship in surgery in 1945, the year the Japanese surrendered, and took a job at the modern and well-equipped Central Hospital in Nanjing, where the staff was all Western-trained. I intended to specialize eventually in neurosurgery. In November 1946 I finally married Lillian, who was then working as a librarian at the British Council.

The Guomindang and the communists were facing civil war. Inflation was creating tremendous financial insecurity. Lillian's salary from the British was relatively high, the equivalent of $150 a month, and she was paid in British pounds. But my pay was paltry—the equivalent of $25 a month—paid in Chinese currency. I took my pay to the black market as soon as I got it, exchanging the Chinese currency for U.S. or Mexican silver dollars. Inflation was so severe that the pile of money that would purchase three eggs in the morning would buy only one egg by the afternoon. People carried their money in carts, and the price of rice was so high that citizens who in ordinary times would never have dreamed of stealing were beginning to break into grain shops and make off with what they could.

In the midst of this upheaval, my classmate and friend Danny Huang, then practicing medicine in Hong Kong, suggested I join him there, where life was more stable and doctors could earn a good living.

It was a difficult decision. In Hong Kong we would surely prosper, but medicine was not nearly so advanced in what was then only a backwater of China. My skills as a surgeon would not progress. But as the civil war expanded, Lillian urged me to go, and in December 1948, I left Nanjing for Hong Kong.

I did not stay. I took a job with the Australian Oriental Company, practicing medicine in Sydney and sailing the seas between Australia and New Zealand as a ship's surgeon. My income was substantial. Lillian moved to Hong Kong, rented a house, and got a job with the British. I did not want her to join me in Australia, which had a "whites-only" policy. As a Chinese, I could live there temporarily, practice medicine, and make good money, but I could never become a citizen. My pride and self-respect cried out against this racist policy. Still, I stayed in Sydney, in a small boardinghouse, surrounded by Australians who thought China was hopeless. I became increasingly depressed. My main reason for staying was the money I made. But I did not want to live in Hong Kong, a British colony, either. I was too proud to become the disenfranchised subject of a foreign king.

My spirits lifted, though, when the communists took over Beijing. And I was literally thrilled in February 1949, when the communists triumphed over a British warship attempting to prevent them from crossing the Yangtze River. I was sure that a communist victory would mean the end of the foreign concessions and imperialist incursions. China could finally assume her rightful place in the world.

Then, in April 1949, I received a letter from my mother, now back in Beijing. She enclosed a letter from my elder brother, who had returned home as one of the communist liberators and was now serving in an administrative position with the department of public health (*weisheng bu*) under the Communist party's Military Affairs Commission (*zhonggong zhongyang junshi weiyuan hui*). He was happy to be home again and wanted me to go back, too.

"China is short of qualified physicians," he wrote. "The new government could offer you a good job. Our whole family could be united once more."

I was in a quandary. Life in Sydney was comfortable and secure. Lillian could join me eventually, and my mother could join us, too, if she wanted, or I could send her enough money to live comfortably in Beijing.

But I knew I would never be able to become a neurosurgeon in Australia, where such opportunities were not available to Chinese. And no matter how much money I made, I could never be comfortable there. Outside China, I would always be drifting, in exile, and I was too patriotic for that.

Easter was approaching. I was planning to spend the holiday with my closest friend in Sydney, Alex Yang. Alex had been born in Australia but had maintained many of his Chinese customs. He and his wife were hardworking people, owners of a small grocery store on Elizabeth Street.

When we met, my friend sensed immediately that something was troubling me. I told him of my indecision about returning to Beijing.

"It's a big decision," Alex said.

"What do you think?" I asked.

"We're different people," Yang replied. "My whole family is in Australia. Even if I were offered a very good salary, I would have no reason to go to Beijing. Even with the whites-only policy here, the population of this country is small. You could make a good living. Why don't you write your brother to find out more about what kind of job they are offering and what kind of salary. Then you can compare."

His talk only rekindled my patriotism. I was not so interested in whether I would make more money. If China under the Communist party could become rich again, I was willing to suffer hardship for my country.

But I agreed with Alex that I needed to know more. I wrote my brother that night.

The reply came in early May. My brother again urged my return. He enclosed a letter from his boss, Fu Lianzhang, the deputy director of public health under the Military Affairs Commission. Fu Lianzhang—Nelson Fu, as he was known to Westerners—was famous in Chinese medical circles. He was probably the only Western-trained Christian doctor to have participated in the Long March. He treated Mao for malaria in 1934, just before the Long March, and in the party's wartime headquarters in Yanan had served as the physician to leaders of the Communist party.

Fu's letter was brief, but it seemed warm and sincere. He welcomed my return and urged me to encourage other physicians to go back, too. He made no mention of salary and gave no hint of what my assignment in Beijing might be, but he assured me that it would be suitable.

I was elated. That such a high-ranking official should urge me to return suggested that the Communist party really did want well-trained people. There would be a place for me in new China. I decided to return immediately.

Alex Yang held a small farewell party. Two other Chinese doctors were also there. "You must write after you return," they insisted, "and if you aren't happy, by all means come back. You can always find good work here."

I never did write my friends in Sydney. Thirty-six years later, in 1985, I visited again as a guest of the Australian Medical Association and returned to Elizabeth Street to look for my old friend Alex Yang. But everything had changed. His little shop was gone. I never found my friend.

Lillian and I were reunited in Hong Kong. It was mid-May 1949, and the British colony was in chaos, crowded both with refugees leaving the mainland in flight from the communists and with people converging in preparation to return. It was a strange and perplexing phenomenon. When I visited Danny Huang, he shook his head in regret over my decision to return. "Wouldn't it be nice if we could work together here?" he asked. I told him about Fu Lianzhang's letter. Danny said, "Well, try it for a while. If things work out, write me. Maybe I'll return, too." I never wrote him, either.

Lillian and I visited one of her former professors from Fudan University, Zhang Jinduo, who was also returning to Beijing. He had been invited to serve as a delegate to the Chinese People's Political Consultative Conference (CPPCC). The Communist party was calling for a united front with non-party intellectuals, and the CPPCC had been established, we believed, to give leading intellectuals and scientists, artists and actors, and members of the non-communist "democratic parties" a political voice and power. The new communist-led government would use our energy and education and talent to transform the country, we thought. "China is so full of hope now," Professor Zhang said when we met. "The whole country is going to revive."

The CPPCC held its first meeting at the end of September 1949. It voted to establish the People's Republic of China and elected the leaders of the new central government. Mao Zedong would serve as the chairman of the new republic. Mao's colleague Liu Shaoqi and Song Qingling, the widow of Sun Yat-sen—the man credited with overthrowing the Qing dynasty and establishing the Republic of China in 1912—were among the several vice-chairmen. But the Chinese People's Political Consultative Conference turned out to be a tragic joke, for the Communist party ran everything, including the central government. The CPPCC came to be referred to as a vase of flowers—pretty to look at but of no use at all. Members who had the temerity to express opinions and offer advice at odds with what the communists wanted to hear would find themselves declared rightists and subjected to horrible abuse. Professor Zhang Jinduo was one such innocent. In 1957, he was labeled a rightist and sent to a hard-labor camp for reform. When he was exonerated more than twenty years later, in 1979, he was a feeble old man, blind and unable to care for himself.

In the beginning, though, before the persecutions began, it seemed perfectly natural to me that China should be governed by the Communist party. I worshiped the party. It was the hope of new China. I had been like a blind man in Australia, with no idea where I was going. The united-front policy had shown me the light. My talents would be used in new China. We intellectuals would have power and prestige. When I saw glimmerings that the party was not all I believed it to be, I dismissed them as trivial exceptions to the rule.

The friend with whom we were staying in Hong Kong introduced us to a man named Yan, reputed to be a high-ranking member of the Communist party and charged with recruiting intellectuals to return. Our friend encouraged us to give Yan a gift to pave our smooth return. "With Yan's help, you might land a good-paying job in a medical college in Beijing. Maybe you could give him a Rolex watch. He pays the seafare for the people he sends to Beijing, so you would still save some money."

I doubted that Yan was paying the fares out of his own pocket and detested the bribery that had plagued Chinese officialdom for so many thousands of years. I believed that the Communist party was aloof from the corruption that had turned so many millions of people against the Guomindang. I refused to give Yan a gift. "The Communist party is honest," I told my friend. "I can depend on my own abilities to earn my living."

I never got in touch with Yan again. But he resurfaced in China as the alleged leader of a "democratic party." In reality, he was a member of the Communist party's central Department of Investigation, disguised—like many others in the CPPCC—as a member of a "democratic party."

In 1956, when I told Mao the story of my friend's encouragement to offer Yan a bribe, Mao laughed uproariously. "You bookworm," he chided me. "Why are you so stingy? You don't understand human relations. Pure water can't support fish. What's so strange about giving someone a present? Didn't Guo Moruo give me a watch during the Chongqing negotiations?"

The turbulence of Hong Kong that spring of 1949 was disquieting, but I was young and naive and full of dreams. I would return to my homeland and get a job with one of the leading hospitals in Beijing. I would live according to my family tradition and the Hippocratic oath, curing illness and treating rich and poor alike. I would be a great neurosurgeon. Medicine would be my contribution to building a new China, wealthy and strong, where all men were equal and corruption was ended.

We left Hong Kong for Beijing in the middle of June 1949. I had not been home for seventeen years.

3

The city was shabby and drab. After eight years of Japanese occupation and four years of civil war, the streets were unkempt and the thick walls surrounding the city had crumbled. The painted wooden signboards that had once hung outside the multitude of small shops, lending Beijing so much color and life, had disappeared. My favorite bookstores in Liulichang had closed.

The people seemed as poor and drab as the city, men and women alike dressed in communist blue or gray cotton washed so often as to be almost completely faded. Everyone wore the same black cotton cloth shoes, and hairstyles were identical, too—short-cropped crewcuts for men, straight, short bobs on the women. With my Western-style suit and tie, leather shoes, and hair that suddenly seemed long, I felt like a foreigner. Lillian, colorfully dressed and wearing high-heeled shoes, her hair stylishly cut and freshly permed, was a bright red poppy in a field of yellow wheat. I quickly borrowed a properly communist suit, and Lillian visited a tailor for a set of subdued new clothes.

The change in my mother was dramatic. She had become old and frail, reduced to a tiny eighty pounds, and her hair had turned a silver gray. But she was delighted to see me, pleading with me as soon as we met never to leave again. I promised to stay.

The mood of Beijing was a startling contrast to its physical decline. The whole city seemed happy. Beijing had been liberated, and the population genuinely welcomed the new communist government. The city was filled with a spirit of anticipation and hope. The few friends and relatives who thought we were foolish to return were the exceptions.

My brother arranged for me to meet Fu Lianzhang, who would arrange for my work. I visited Fu at his home in the compound of what would soon become the Ministry of Public Health. Located in Bowstring (Gongxian) Lane, just north of the busy Wangfujing shopping area, the compound, once the home of a Manchu prince, had been occupied by a high-ranking Guomindang general until the communist takeover. The estate in Bowstring Lane was built in the same traditional style as my own family home but was far grander and more elegant, with six courtyards and seven or eight grape arbors, a traditional garden with a false mountain of rock, and ceramic-tile floors.

Fu Lianzhang was lying on a chaise longue made of bamboo and wicker. He was tall, gaunt, and sickly-looking, with a broad forehead and sharp, piercing eyes. He was fifty-five years old then, twenty-six years older than I, and from the perspective of my youth he seemed elderly indeed.

Fu did not bother to get up when I entered, extending me a limp handshake from his position in recline. His soft hands were those of an intellectual. I felt honored to be granted an audience with such a high official.

"I have had tuberculosis for years and cannot talk to you for long," he explained after welcoming me back and asking about my educational background and work experience. "But your job has been arranged. Just report tomorrow morning to the Health Section." Until the new people's government was formally established, the functions of governance were being administered by the Military Affairs Commission, and the Health Section was under its aegis.

My greeting at the Health Section was warm. "Welcome, welcome," said the official who showed me around. "We are short of physicians here. I know your brother. He was my boss for many years.

"Vice-Minister Fu has instructed that you be treated like one of us," the official explained. "We operate here on a free-supply system. The government will give you everything you need—your room and board, clothes, even your shoes. Since you are a senior physician, you are entitled to grade-two kitchen privileges. Your food allowance will be slightly more than the average staff member's."

The free-supply system meant that I would be receiving no salary. The Communist party had two systems for paying its employees. People new to the revolutionary cause, working for the party for the first time, were ordinarily given a salary. Veteran revolutionaries were on the free-supply system. Since I was considered to have "voluntarily joined the revolution," I was given the honor of being put on the free-supply system even though I was a newcomer to the cause.

This did not make me happy. My family burdens were large, for in addition to my wife, I would be supporting my mother, two aunts, and my wife's parents. I had considerable savings in gold and U.S. dollars, but without a salary and with so many people depending on me, my savings would soon be used up.

Only when I was introduced to Comrade Lei was I given any hint about what my work with the Health Section might be. "Comrade Lei will accompany you to your job at the outpatient clinic at Labor University in the Fragrant Hills," I was told. "Go home now and get your belongings together. Report back here a week from today. A truck will take you then to the Fragrant Hills. Comrade Lei will go with you."

The meeting was unsettling. No one had ever asked me whether I actually wanted the job. I was confused. I had never heard of Labor University, and while I was happy to be given work at a university, I did not know whether it would have a hospital affiliated with a medical school, which is what I wanted. The reference to an outpatient clinic did not sound promising.

Moreover, I learned that the Health Section could not find appropriate work for Lillian. She was given a temporary job in a kindergarten at a training institute for public-health workers in Tong county, a suburb some twenty kilometers east of Beijing. Her talents and training would be sorely underused. It was a far cry from the high-paying, challenging job she had been offered by the British Council in Hong Kong. Our homecoming seemed less than auspicious, and for a few fleeting moments I thought maybe I should have given that Rolex watch to Mr. Yan.

"You are new here and don't understand what's going on," my brother encouraged me. "Here, people don't choose jobs; jobs choose people. This is called 'being obedient to the organization.' As for the problem of pay, you can manage on your savings now. The rest will be worked out later." Party discipline prevented him from saying more.

The place called Labor University was located in Xiangshan—the Fragrant Hills—several miles to the northwest of Beijing and a few miles beyond the old imperial Summer Palace. Once the emperor's hunting grounds, the hills were dotted with buildings from the reign of the Qianlong emperor. The area was also famous for two ancient Buddhist temples—the Temple of the Sleeping Buddha and the Temple of the Azure Clouds. In autumn, the white-barked evergreen pines and the red-leaved smoke trees transform the hillside into a brilliant patchwork of color. Labor University sprawled across much of the Fragrant Hills and had a bustling, well-populated feel to it.

The place was peculiar, though. Armed sentries were posted everywhere. I was shown around by two high-ranking veterans of the Communist party—Wu Yunfu and Luo Daorang, who were the director and deputy director of the Bureau of Administration under the General Office of the Chinese Communist party's Central Committee. The whole place was filled with Communist party officials. When Wu Yunfu issued me my free supplies and the badge that identified me as an official with the Labor University, he warned me to be very careful not to lose the badge. "And don't talk to anyone else about what is happening here," he cautioned. "Your work is secret." I had no idea why.

My quarters sat among the trees along one of the wooded slopes, but my room was a far cry from the imperial edifices that could be seen throughout the hills. It was a rude and tiny peasant hut, the likes of which I, as a wealthy child of the city, had never even imagined. The floor was made of clay, the roof leaked, and the only electricity was a bare light bulb overhead. The lone piece of furniture was the bed—a wooden board placed atop two wooden stools, one at either end of the plank, with no mattress or bedding at all. There was no running water, of course, and an outdoor public latrine served as the toilet. I used a thin cotton pad for a mattress and filled an enamel basin with boiled water drawn from a nearby well to wash. The measure of my status as a doctor was the fact that I did not have to share my quarters with others. The conditions were so primitive that my wife could not join me there, so we met only on weekends, when I returned to my mother's house to visit—and take my weekly bath.

My meals were another sign of my status. We ate only twice a day, as is the custom among Chinese peasants—once at ten in the morning, then again at four in the afternoon. Unlike peasants, who rarely eat meat, however, my grade-two kitchen privileges entitled me to meat almost every day, and while the cafeteria was hardly less primitive than my living quarters, the food was tasty and well prepared, and the simple kitchen was reasonably clean.

The clinic, though, was even more astonishing. It was also a peasant hut, with packed clay floors and no medical equipment at all—just a few thermometers and some devices for measuring blood pressure. The only medicines available were aspirin, cough syrup, and a few drugs to combat bacterial infections. My stethoscope and medical experience were the only tools I would have to aid in making diagnoses. I could only hope that none of my patients were seriously ill.

Here too, though, the upbeat mood of the staff was a stark contrast to the physical condition of the clinic. The staff—about thirty people in all—had been anticipating my arrival long before I was even aware of my assignment, and they greeted me with obvious delight. They were all young—most of them younger even than my own twenty-nine years. Even the two section chiefs were still in their mid-twenties. They were all rural people, recruited by the party, and the most educated among them had only finished primary school. They could do minor first aid—bandage a small wound—and knew how to give aspirin for colds, but they had no scientific knowledge of disease and would not have known how to make a diagnosis. "We really hope you can teach us modern medicine," they told me. "We know so little about it." They wanted me to give lectures. I was aghast. How was I going to manage in circumstances like this?

That first weekend, an old friend I had not seen for eleven years visited me at home. We chatted about old times and what had happened since. My friend had joined the Communist party many years before and was now working with the New Democratic Youth League.* I told him I had just started work at the medical clinic at Labor University in the Fragrant Hills. "It's a huge university with armed sentries everywhere," I said. "It's unlike any university I've ever seen."

My friend turned serious. "Actually, I have permission from the leading cadre of our organization to talk with you," he said. "He asked me to warn you about several things. You are new to revolutionary work, and it is easy to make mistakes out of ignorance."

I was willing to concede my ignorance, but I still had no idea what he was talking about. "I am a doctor," I said. "When I see patients, I do my best. What mistakes could I make?"

"Let's start again," he said. "Now, tell me again where you work."

I repeated that I worked at Labor University. "I know very little about the place. I just see patients every day. But there are very few patients and none of them has any serious illness. It's really a waste of time."

He laughed. "Why do you think you've never seen another university like it? Why are there armed sentries everywhere? Why is your work so secret? You're not at a university, my friend. All the leading organizations of the Communist party are located on the site of Labor

*The name of the New Democratic Youth League later changed to Communist Youth League.

University. Your clinic serves the members of these organizations. They are temporarily located there, out of the city, for the sake of safety and secrecy because Beijing was so recently liberated. That's why your work is such a secret.

"You will learn more in time," he continued, becoming serious again. "But don't look down on the clinic. It may be poorly equipped and you may see few patients, but it is a very important place. You will be meeting many extremely important people. This is why our leading cadre allowed me to talk with you."

I dared not ask the name of the leading cadre to whom he referred, but Jiang Nanxiang, later to become minister of education (1965–66), was the deputy secretary of the New Democratic Youth League then. I assumed the information was coming from him.

I had returned to China with dreams of becoming a surgeon and serving my country through medicine, only to be plunked unsuspecting into the very center of the Chinese Communist party. Though the communists had taken over Beijing, the civil war still continued. The People's Republic of China had yet to be established. Until the new government could take over, the leaders of the Communist party would remain outside the city, in the Fragrant Hills. The central secretariat of the Chinese Communist party and all its subordinate agencies were located there. Of the five top secretaries of the Communist party, three—Mao Zedong, Liu Shaoqi, and Zhu De—lived in the Fragrant Hills, in the old imperial buildings that dotted the grounds. Only Zhou Enlai and Ren Bishi lived elsewhere. The clinic where I worked was not part of a university at all but an agency under the jurisdiction of what became, after the establishment of the People's Republic of China, the Communist party Central Committee's General Office, headed by Yang Shangkun, who, forty years later, in 1988, would become president of the Chinese People's Republic. The General Office was responsible for the safety, well-being, and organizational efficiency of its ranking members—Mao and the other top four secretaries. It was, and remains, among the most secret of all party organizations, and even members of the staff are not told its organizational structure and functions. Only high-level cadres or people who have worked within the organization for years could begin to describe the organization.

In the early 1950s, the General Office had eight major divisions, equal in status.*

---

*The General Office was reorganized several times during Mao's reign. This is a description of its organization in the early 1950s.

The Bureau of Administration, headed by Wu Yunfu and Luo Daorang, who had escorted me around "Labor University" on my first day there, was responsible for the basic physical needs of the party leadership—for providing them with food and supplies, for the construction and repair of the buildings where they lived and worked, for their transportation and communications, and for administering finances.

The Central Bureau of Guards, headed by Wang Dongxing, who later was simultaneously a vice-minister of public security under Luo Ruiqing, was responsible for the security and health of the highest-ranking leaders of the party. While charged with protecting all of the party's ranking leaders, Wang also served as the chief of Mao's bodyguards, and his primary loyalty was unquestionably to Mao. Even then, security arrangements for the highest leaders were elaborate. Wang's responsibility for the health of the highest leaders overlapped—and occasionally collided—with Fu Lianzhang's separate Ministry of Public Health. The official photography office, for reasons I never understood, also fell within the purview of Wang Dongxing's bureau.

The Office of Confidential Secretaries, headed by Ye Zilong, was responsible for arranging all the meetings called by ranking members of the party, for recording notes of those meetings, and for sending and receiving party documents. Ye Zilong was also Mao's chief confidential secretary. As such, he served as the chairman's chief steward, responsible for arranging Mao's private life, food, and personal finances, and for storing and taking care of the many gifts he received. The functions of the confidential secretaries were primarily logistical.

The substantive work was done by the Office of Political Secretaries, which was responsible for keeping the top leadership informed of issues and for writing reports and documents. In 1949, the Office of Political Secretaries was headed by Chen Boda, who was also Mao's chief political secretary. Mao had several other political secretaries as well—his wife, Jiang Qing, Hu Qiaomu, and Tian Jiaying. Other top leaders also had their own political secretaries, among whom, invariably, were their wives.

The Bureau of Confidential Matters, headed by Li Zhizhong, and the Bureau of Confidential Communications, headed by Wang Kai, were the most secret of the organizations under the General Office. The Bureau of Confidential Matters was staffed by young people capable of remarkable feats of memory, for it was their job to memorize a secret telegraph code. This code, different from the ordinary Chinese telegraph code, changed frequently, and it permitted secret communications by telegraph both within the central leadership and to leaders in the provinces and the army. Each of the Chinese ideographs was assigned a number, and the young staff, trained at a special school in Zhangjiakou, Hebei, memorized the entire code and used it without reference to a codebook or other material. Beyond a certain age, when memorization is no longer easy, the staff would be assigned other jobs.

The Bureau of Confidential Communications was responsible for transmitting secret documents to party and army leaders throughout the country. Most of the staff members were simple and uneducated, often illiterate. They served as couriers, carrying documents among various ministries of the State Council, to the provinces, and to the far-flung corners of the country. Absolute political reliability rather than intelligence was required for the job.

The Bureau of Archives, headed by Zeng San, was responsible for maintaining the historical records of the Communist party. The Bureau of General Logistics, headed by Deng Diantuo, was responsible for providing supplies to all the bureaus and ministries of the party.

The Fragrant Hills Clinic, under the combined jurisdiction of Luo Daorang and Fu Lianzhang, was responsible for the health of everyone who worked in these organizations. The entire staff of the General Office, from the highest-ranking leaders to ordinary members and their families, were my patients. The group as a whole was young and healthy. Their medical complaints by and large were minor, of no great interest to me, since I had aspired to be a surgeon. I was disappointed not to be pursuing my dream of a medical career, but as the only Western-educated physician at the Fragrant Hills Clinic, I came to know many cadres, high and low. Still young and idealistic, and so recently returned to Beijing, I felt honored to be working so close to the levers of Communist party power. I had tremendous respect for the men and women who became my patients. These people had made the Chinese revolution and were working to bring it to fruition. They had left their homes and their families as mere youths, sacrificing everything to build a better, more just, and stronger China. They were the Long Marchers, who had undergone unthinkable danger and hardship to establish the guerrilla base areas from which to challenge Chiang Kai-shek and his corrupt and wasteful government. These Communist party cadres devoted every ounce of energy to their work, selflessly indifferent to their personal gain or interest. I had never known such people, and I was overcome with admiration. They were the embodiment of China's hope.

· · ·

As a new member of the heart of the Chinese revolution, I was privileged not only to witness the ceremony formally establishing the People's Republic of China but to have a front-row seat.

On October 1, 1949, the whole population of the Fragrant Hills was awakened at five o'clock in the morning to the type of crisp, clear, and chilly day that makes autumn in Beijing the most magnificent season. We rode by truck from the Fragrant Hills and arrived in Tiananmen Square a little before seven, taking our places near the marble bridge just at the foot of the Gate of Heavenly Peace, which serves as the entrance to the Forbidden City. Tiananmen Square was smaller then than it is today, surrounded by the dilapidated buildings that once served as rest houses for officials awaiting an audience with the emperor. The Great Hall of the People and the Museum of Revolutionary History would be constructed in 1959, in celebration of the tenth anniversary of the founding of new China.

When we arrived, the square was already swarming with people, carefully chosen from all walks of life. I had a perfect view of the podium from which the leaders would proclaim the establishment of the People's Republic. Above the sea of people thousands of banners were unfurled, waving in the autumn breeze, their colors transforming the shabby city. The crowd was shouting slogans—"Long Live the People's Republic of China," "Long Live the Chinese Communist Party"—and singing revolutionary songs. The enthusiasm was contagious, and everyone grew more excited with every new slogan and song.

At ten o'clock sharp, Mao Zedong and the other top leaders appeared on the podium overlooking the square. The effect was electric. Mao had been my hero since my brother first told me he was China's messiah, and this was my first glimpse of my savior. Even working in the Fragrant Hills, so close to Mao's residence, I had never seen him before. He was fifty-six years old then, tall and healthy and solid. His face was ruddy, his black hair thick, his forehead high and broad. His voice was powerful and clear, his gestures decisive. He no longer wore the military uniform so familiar to us from his photographs. The founding of the new government was a state occasion and Mao officiated in his position as the chairman of the People's Republic of China, representing the central government rather than the party. He wore a dark brown Sun Yat-sen suit (only later would the style be referred to as the Mao suit) and a worker's cap for this civil occasion and stood among a number of non-communist political personalities as testimony to the reality of the united front. The beautiful Song

Qingling, widow of Dr. Sun Yat-sen, who had toppled the imperial system and brought China to political modernity, was among them.

Mao Zedong was the center of attention, but his manner was dignified, and there was an air of modesty about him, with no trace of arrogance. I had seen Chiang Kai-shek many times during the height of his power, and he had always been aloof, demanding subservience from everyone around him. The effect was invariably alienating.

Mao, though, was a truly magnetic force. Mao did not speak standard Mandarin. But the Hunan dialect he spoke is easy for Mandarin speakers to understand, and its rhythm and tones are pleasant to the ear. Mao's voice was soft, almost lilting, and the effect of his speech was riveting. "The Chinese people have stood up," he proclaimed, and the crowd went wild, thundering in applause, shouting over and over, "Long Live the People's Republic of China!" "Long Live the Chinese Communist Party!" I was so full of joy my heart nearly burst out of my throat, and tears welled up in my eyes. I was so proud of China, so full of hope, so happy that the exploitation and suffering, the aggression from foreigners, would be gone forever. I had no doubt that Mao was the great leader of the revolution, the maker of a new Chinese history. Though I was standing so near him, he still seemed very far away. I was only an ordinary doctor and he was the great revolutionary leader of the People's Republic of China. Never in my wildest imagination, standing in Tiananmen that day, could I have suspected that soon I would become his personal physician, the director of his medical team, that I would be with him for twenty-two years and present at his death.

In December 1949, not long after the celebrations, Mao Zedong left for Moscow, where he spent several months negotiating a treaty of friendship with Stalin and the Soviet Union. Upon his return in February 1950, Mao moved from his hideaway in the Fragrant Hills into the city of Beijing, to Zhongnanhai, the former royal garden within the grounds of the old Forbidden City. Other ranking party leaders followed him, living and working in regal splendor. So, too, did most of the central administrative offices and staff. Only a few of the original offices—the Bureau of Administration and the Bureau of Confidential Matters, for instance—remained in the Fragrant Hills. The Fragrant Hills Clinic was split in two, with one section going to Zhongnanhai to take care of the top leaders there, the other remaining in the Fragrant Hills. I stayed in the Fragrant Hills. If not for an accident, the story of my life would have been entirely different.

4

A case of fatal encephalitis led to my move to Zhongnanhai. Outbreaks of encephalitis, transmitted through the bite of a mosquito, are common during summer and autumn in Beijing, and knowledgeable doctors have learned during the encephalitis season to be particularly attuned to the symptoms of this potentially fatal inflammation of the brain. Encephalitis can be treated and cured with Chinese herbal medicine if it is caught in the early stages, when it often appears as nothing more serious than a flu. If undetected, the patient becomes disoriented and often dies.

In the damp, rainy Beijing summer of 1950 the mosquitoes were especially numerous. When a staff member in Zhongnanhai contracted encephalitis, the young and inexperienced clinic "doctor" diagnosed the illness as a simple flu. The staff member died. Yang Shangkun and Zhou Enlai, concerned about Mao's health, were alarmed. The staff member's apartment compound was very near Mao's. If a mosquito could kill someone so close, the disease could also be carried to Mao.

The young director of the Zhongnanhai medical clinic was fired, the clinic was reorganized, and a campaign against disease-carrying pests was launched. The Fragrant Hills Clinic was moved to Zhongnanhai as part of the reorganization. The move changed my life.

Backward and poorly equipped, the Zhongnanhai Clinic was being refurbished for the country's new leaders, along with the rest of Zhongnanhai.

Zhongnanhai, dominated by the Middle and South lakes, from

which its name derives, is magnificently landscaped, surrounded by the same vermilion wall that once enclosed the Forbidden City. The place is so secret and so well constructed that it is impossible to see in or over the walls from anywhere in the city, and never since the communists came to power have I seen a book that accurately describes the layout. Armed soldiers from the Central Garrison Corps, under the command of the army's general staff, kept guard at the gates, and entry into the grounds was limited to people who lived and worked there and to specially invited official visitors. The offices of the State Council, headed by Zhou Enlai, occupied the buildings in its north—in the area of the Middle Lake. In addition to Mao, several other of the country's top leaders—Zhu De, Liu Shaoqi, Zhou Enlai, Peng Dehuai, Deng Xiaoping, Li Xiannian, Dong Biwu, Li Fuchun, and Chen Yi—lived within Zhongnanhai, in elegant traditional courtyard-style walled compounds. Ranking staff members lived there, too. I was given a small apartment on the grounds. Later, when I was assigned a larger apartment, Lillian and our infant son, John, moved in with me.

Even within the grounds, security at Zhongnanhai was tight. Access from place to place was restricted, and sentries checked everyone's passes. Working in the clinic, near Mao's residential compound, I carried a B pass and was restricted to the clinic and the area around the apartment building where I lived. Lillian also had a B pass, but her freedom of movement was more restricted.

As director of the Zhongnanhai Clinic, I cared for many of the top leaders, those living both in Zhongnanhai and elsewhere in Beijing. I treated their family members, too. Having spent eight years fighting Japan and another four years in civil war against the nationalists, many of the leaders had only recently married, and a minor baby boom was erupting. I treated the children, too. My workload was heavy, and I had little time for leisure or rest.

I applied to join the party, but my background was problematic. Obviously, I was not the stuff of which good communists were made. My father had been a high-ranking official in the Guomindang government, and while Zhou Enlai had invited him to return to Beijing and provided him protection, many still viewed him as "reactionary." My father-in-law had been a wealthy landlord in Anhui province, and with nationwide land reform still in progress, he had been declared an "enemy of the people," denied all rights of citizenship, and deprived of all means of livelihood. He was utterly dependent on me.

My wife was suspect, too. Before liberation she had worked for both the United States Air Force and the British Council, and there were rumors that she had been a secret agent for these two "imperialist" countries.

My activities as a youth also made me suspect. In the detailed autobiography I wrote when applying for party membership, I said that while I was in middle school in Suzhou, all the tenth graders were required by the Guomindang government to undergo three months of military training. After training, I had been expected to join the Guomindang's National Renaissance Society. At the end of military training, nothing more was said about the society, nor was I ever involved in any of its activities. As it turned out, the National Renaissance Society was the predecessor of the Three Principles of the People Youth League, a political organization connected with the Blue Shirt Society, one of the Guomindang's secret spy agencies. The party members investigating my application could not believe I had never been actively involved in the Renaissance Society. How could anyone have joined such a notorious organization without participating in its activities?

They were also suspicious because part of my internship after medical school had been spent working as a military doctor under the Guomindang.

The party sent agents to investigate my background, certain, no doubt, that I had been an active member of the Renaissance Society, perhaps even a spy myself. A decision on my party membership was indefinitely delayed.

Nonetheless, I wanted to contribute to the unfolding revolution. I volunteered to join a land-reform team going into the villages to direct the redistribution of land and property from the big landlords to the poor, landless peasants. Though my own parents-in-law had already lost all their property, I still supported the movement. Land reform was a means to end the centuries of oppression in the countryside and to improve the lot of the rural poor. Only years later did friends who had participated dare tell me how violent the movement had often been, and how frequently unfair. But I was not allowed to participate in the land reform. My medical services, I was told, were needed in Zhongnanhai.

When the Korean War broke out in the summer of 1950, I volunteered. I had not participated in the war of resistance against Japan or in the civil war against the nationalists, but I wanted a chance to serve my country, even though I was certain that China would be defeated. The United States was so much more advanced than China, and American equipment was much better.

I followed the war closely, surprised and thrilled that China was not only holding its own but was actually defeating the United States forces in battle after battle. It was the first time in more than a century that China had engaged in war with a foreign power without losing face. I was appalled, too, over reports that the United States was using bacteriological warfare in Korea. Even as the Korean War dragged on inconclusively, I was proud to be Chinese. But my superiors refused to allow me to participate, arguing again that my services were more valuable in Zhongnanhai.

I became depressed, frustrated at not being allowed to contribute to the revolution, disappointed at not being able to continue my career as a surgeon. I felt remote from the revolutionaries who were my patients and was unhappy that my application for membership in the party was so long delayed.

In the midst of my malaise, in the spring of 1952, I had my first encounter with Mao's family. It happened when Mao's son Anqing, then about thirty years old, was brought to the clinic in the midst of a psychotic episode—unable to sleep, constantly pacing the floor and talking to himself. Mao had had two sons—Mao Anqing and Mao Anying—by Yang Kaihui, the first of his freely chosen wives. Yang Kaihui was executed by the Guomindang in 1930 for refusing to betray her husband even as Mao, hundreds of miles away in the Jiangxi soviet base area, had already married He Zizhen. After Yang Kaihui's execution, the two boys went to Shanghai, where they had to fend for themselves like vagabonds, barely eking out enough to live. Some who knew Mao Anqing attributed his mental illness to the brutal beatings he had suffered at the hands of the Shanghai police. The two children were discovered only years later, after the party had established its base area in Yanan. Mao sent them to the Soviet Union to study.

With the outbreak of the Korean War, the elder son, Anying, went to the front, where he died early in the hostilities during an American bomb attack. Meanwhile, Anqing worked as a translator in the Propaganda Department of the Communist party's Central Committee.

During the "three-anti" campaign that began in 1952 to counter the corruption, waste, and bureaucratism of Communist party cadres, Anqing discovered that one of his colleagues had stolen the royalties from some of his writings by forging his signature on various forms. In a fit of anger, Anqing struck the man. Mao was furious when he learned of the incident and reprimanded his son severely. Mao's anger seemed to have triggered the onset of the episode I was treating in the clinic. But I was not trained in psychiatry and the clinic could only offer short-term emergency treatment. I kept him sedated, waiting for the right moment to tell the family that he needed psychiatric care in a hospital.

One evening while I was in my office reviewing patient records, a nurse ran in, out of breath. Jiang Qing had come to see Mao Anqing and wanted me to tell her about his condition. She urged me to hurry.

Jiang Qing was waiting in the reception area adjoining Anqing's room accompanied by a smart-looking nurse. I had seen Mao's wife several times, but always at a distance. She had been an actress before joining the communists in Yanan, and I had expected her clothes to be different from the drab Mao suits that were the fashion of the day. But I was not prepared for her to be so elegantly dressed—in a neat wool Western-style suit, its open collar revealing a beige silk blouse underneath. She was wearing stockings, too, a real luxury in those days, and low-heeled black leather shoes. Her hair was thick and black, permed, and neatly combed into a bun. Her eyes were big and round, clear and dark, and her delicate skin was the color of ivory. She was about five feet three or four inches tall, rather thin, and her upper body seemed longer than the lower. She was then thirty-eight years old. I was thirty-two.

"You must be Dr. Li," Jiang Qing greeted me in a cultured Beijing dialect after I had taken a seat opposite her. Not waiting for my response, she asked, "How is Anqing?" Despite her elegance, she struck me as cold. Some say that in her youth Jiang Qing was very pretty. I found her nice-looking but certainly not pretty. She was too aloof and haughty.

I described Anqing's case in detail and suggested that he be transferred to a psychiatric hospital or a sanatorium since the clinic at Zhongnanhai was not equipped to treat psychiatric cases.

She thought for a while before responding. "I will take your suggestion to the Chairman. Let him make the decision," she finally said. We shook hands as she left, and I noticed that her fingers were long and soft, her nails tapered at the tips. She thanked me as she walked into the courtyard, where three security guards were waiting. She had seemed mistrustful, her eyes constantly probing, as if she was trying to uncover something beneath my words and behavior.

Shortly thereafter, Mao Anqing was diagnosed by other doctors as schizophrenic and sent to the seaside town of Dalian, in China's northeast. He lived in a private home, where he was cared for by a full-time nurse. Anqing and the nurse fell in love, but the family had arranged a marriage for him—to the younger sister of his brother Anying's widow—and the disappointed, heartsick nurse was forced to return to Beijing.

In the autumn of 1953, more than a year after the incident in the clinic, I met Jiang Qing again at the home of Hu Qiaomu, one of Mao's political secretaries and the leading party secretary of the Propaganda Department. Hu respected my medical work and we had become friends.

I had gone to Hu Qiaomu's residence in Zhongnanhai to treat him for an allergy and an ulcer. While I was examining him, his wife, Gu Yu, who worked in the Chinese Academy of Sciences, came running in. Jiang Qing had just arrived. "Quick. Put on your clothes," she told her husband. Hu apologized that we had to stop the examination.

I met Jiang Qing on my way out. "Isn't this Dr. Li?" she asked, shaking my hand as Hu explained why I was there. My impression of her did not change with this brief second encounter. If anything, she seemed even colder.

As director of the Zhongnanhai Clinic, I was responsible for treating ordinary staff members, too, and because I treated everyone equally, without regard to rank, my reputation grew. Many people praised my work. They trusted me and often came to share their personal and family troubles as well, knowing they could rely on me to keep their secrets.

In the fall of 1952, I was unanimously voted a Grade A model worker by the General Office. It was a tremendous honor.

After that, I was finally admitted as a candidate for membership in the Communist party. The party investigators had found no evidence against me. They had located a man named Xu Bin who had served as company commander during my military training in 1936 and who was now undergoing hard labor at a camp in Guizhou province as part of his "educational reform." Xu could not remember me at all. They spoke with a number of my schoolmates, all of whom confirmed that I had never participated in politics. Everyone they met attested to the truth of my autobiographical statements and my basically apolitical nature. The searching and checking had delayed my party membership for a full two years.

My "class background" and alleged political activities would come back to haunt me later, as China was swept by one political campaign after another, but in November 1952, I took the party oath, promising to devote my life to the Chinese Communist party and to sacrifice for the cause. My education in the fundamentals of Marxism did not extend beyond a reading of the *Communist Manifesto* and two articles by Mao, the enthusiastic education my brother had provided during my youth, and a few Marxist slogans—like the socialist principle "From each according to his abilities, to each according to his needs."

In fact, I never really became one of "them." The vast majority of party members working within Zhongnanhai were a very special group, longtime veterans of the cause. They had joined the party when they were very young, often as teenagers, and they had endured the Long March. Most came from humble backgrounds and were woefully uneducated and still steeped in peasant ways. Many of them respected and admired me, and I, in turn, respected their revolutionary zeal and the sacrifices they had made for the revolution. But the gulf between us was unbreachably wide. I would always be an intellectual, a doctor, from an "exploiting class," and therefore problematic, a target to "absorb, utilize, and reform." My value to the party rested solely on my medical skills.

Just how valuable those medical skills were I learned on the evening of October 2, 1954, when Wang Dongxing phoned and invited me to his home. Wang, as director of the Central Bureau of Guards, was responsible for the overall safety of the country's leaders and was also the chief of Mao's bodyguards. I had met him while working in the Zhongnanhai Clinic, where he, his wife, and children always requested me when they were sick. We had become friends. He, too, was a veteran party member and a survivor of the Long March. He had turned toward communism as a ten-year-old peasant child, when, unschooled in the ways of urban life, he was threatened with arrest by a policeman who caught him urinating on a city street. Only a healthy bribe from Wang's father saved the young boy from jail. Disgusted with the corruption of the ruling Guomindang, Wang joined the Communist party. He met Mao and began to work with him in Yanan. After 1949, he was suddenly catapulted to a position of tremendous political responsibility, but he retained a deep respect for intellectuals and seemed to regard me, a Western-educated doctor, with particular esteem.

On the phone, he refused to tell me why he wanted to see me, insisting that we had to talk in person. I was puzzled. Wang was normally straightforward.

We met in the spacious room he shared with his wife within the grounds of Zhongnanhai. It served as his office, living room, dining room, and bedroom. His children and baby-sitter lived in another building, just across the courtyard. Wang poured a cup of tea and handed it to me. "It's this year's Longjing," he said. "Give it a try." Grown in Hangzhou, Longjing is the finest, most delicate tea in China. Unlike wine, which is best when it is aged, tea is at its best and most expensive when consumed the year it is picked. Wang was a connoisseur.

I savored the tea. "Is there something I can do for you?" I finally asked, curious about why he had called me there.

Wang turned serious. "Do you know why I have kept you in the clinic for so long, refusing to allow you to be transferred elsewhere?" he asked.

"No, I don't," I responded, still puzzled.

"I have watched you for several years," he said. "You are very well liked by the people in Zhongnanhai. You give everyone the same good care no matter who they are. You are never snobbish. Your medical skills, your easy manner, and your great dedication to your job have made a deep impression on all the comrades here, including the top leaders. Even Chairman Mao has heard good things about you.

"We have been looking for a personal physician for the Chairman for some time now, but it has been very difficult to find one," he continued. "I have spoken to both Luo Ruiqing [the minister of public security] and Yang Shangkun [head of the General Office] and suggested that you become Chairman Mao's physician. I have made the same recommendation to Premier Zhou Enlai. They all agree. So yesterday I spoke to the Chairman about it. He has tentatively agreed, but naturally he wants to talk with you before making his final decision. You must prepare yourself. He will want to meet with you soon."

I was shocked. I knew that following Ren Bishi's sudden death in 1950 all of the ranking leaders had been assigned personal physicians, but I could not imagine myself with such an assignment. From the clinic, I had often gazed out at Mao's compound. It seemed to me the heart of the entire nation. Its pulse affected everyone in China. But I had never imagined setting foot in the place. Mao himself remained distant and remote. My mind was suddenly a jumble of thoughts. "This isn't the job for me. I'm completely inappropriate. What about my background? The suspicions that I had been associated with the Guomindang? My father's real association with the Guomindang? My wife? All those rumors that she was a spy? She is not a member of the party, could never become a member of the party. No, this is a job for the son of a worker or peasant. I cannot change my past." Besides, Chairman Mao already had his own personal physician.

My great-grandfather's disgrace came to mind as well—his honest insistence that the Tongzhi emperor was suffering from syphilis, the

Empress Dowager Cixi's ire, my great-grandfather's demotion and his admonition, passed on through the generations, that his descendants were never to serve as physicians in the imperial court.

I refused the offer, sharing my misgivings with Wang Dongxing. He laughed aloud. "Why are you so worried? Your family background was thoroughly investigated before you joined the party. It is no longer a problem. Luo Ruiqing, Yang Shangkun, and Premier Zhou have all cleared you for this assignment. They know about your family background. Only after they were all convinced did I recommend you to the Chairman. As for the story of your great-grandfather—those were feudal times. His experience has nothing to do with now. You need not hesitate." He laughed again.

"Does Fu Lianzhang know?" I asked. It was Fu Lianzhang's encouragement, after all, that had brought me back to China. He had found me my original job. Fu had become a vice-minister of the newly created Ministry of Public Health under the government's State Council. As chief of its Bureau of Health he was in charge of the health of the country's top leaders. He saw himself as Mao's close friend and loyal follower and was particularly interested in the Chairman's health. He would want to be consulted about my appointment.

"The decision was made by the central authority," Wang responded. "Fu is your supervisor now, but he need not be involved." Fu Lianzhang would be unhappy about being left out.

"I need to think about this," I told Wang. His assurances had not convinced me. I was an outsider in Zhongnanhai, a member of the party without really being a part of it. My family background would never change. If I were to become Mao's physician, I would be under constant surveillance. My smallest mistake would be noted, recorded, and blamed on my bad family background. Any little error and I could be charged with plotting against the party. How easily I could be declared a "class enemy." And what a terrifying crime!

"No, there is no room for reconsideration," he responded. "We have already decided."

Only then did I realize that I had no choice. "If I must accept this job, of course I will do my best," I told him. "But no one is perfect. If I make a mistake, I hope it will not reflect badly on you." Wang Dongxing was taking a great risk in sponsoring me for the position. If I got into political trouble, he would be held responsible and could lose his job, too. The tie would bind us until Mao's death.

"Don't worry," Wang assured me. "Of course you must be very careful. You will often have to get advice from your superiors. But you also have to do what you think is right. You have your own opinions.

You will have to take responsibility for what you do. That's all. I think you will do a good job. I don't think I have chosen the wrong person.

"Now, get yourself prepared for a meeting with the Chairman. After all, the final decision will be his. Just wait for my word. When he is ready to see you, I will let you know."

Wang gave me Mao's medical records and asked me to look them over. He said that Mao would soon be leaving Beijing for a rest in the south. I was to continue working in the clinic until called.

Even as I waited, I had intimations of the danger ahead. Chen Zongying, the widow of Ren Bishi, one of the top five Communist party secretaries, warned me the job would be tough. After Ren Bishi's sudden death in the fall of 1950, Chen Zongying had become deeply unhappy. Nothing could bring her husband back. I could only try to comfort and console her. Chen Zongying was a marvelous woman, a good wife and loving mother. We had become friends.

I was accompanying her, on party instructions, on a trip to Shanghai and Hangzhou when she called Mao an old codger (*Mao laotou*) and warned me to be extremely careful. "He has a terrible temper and can turn mercilessly against you at the slightest provocation," she said. "His wife, Jiang Qing, is notorious, cruel to everyone around her. She's a seductress, too. Don't allow yourself to be deceived by her. If you get in trouble there, no one would dare hire you. You could land in jail if anything were to go wrong."

Chen Zongying's warning was shocking. I worshiped Mao. He could do no wrong. He had yet to be elevated to the equivalent of emperor, but his prestige was already unassailable. No one dared criticize him. Moreover, at that very moment a campaign against counterrevolutionaries was unfolding. If anyone had known of Chen Zongying's warning, she could have been accused of being a counterrevolutionary, anti-party element herself.

I never forgot her warning, and in later years her words often returned to haunt me. Even today I remain deeply grateful to her for having spoken so frankly.

The unfolding campaign against counterrevolutionaries in Zhongnanhai frightened me. Wang Dongxing, the director of the Central Bureau of Guards and the man sponsoring my appointment as Mao's doctor, was in charge, and the personal physicians of the country's highest leaders were a major target, accused of being members of an anti-party group.

I sat in the audience, stunned, as day after day for weeks on end the "struggle sessions" against the doctors continued. Every day, the staff at Zhongnanhai would gather to criticize the doctors, and everyone in the audience was expected to participate. The meetings lasted four or five hours, from late in the afternoon until well in the evening. Each day, I listened as the accusations against my fellow doctors became more and more exaggerated. The doctors had not been happy with their work. Each physician was responsible for the health of one party leader, but despite Ren Bishi's sudden death, the other leaders were all in good health. The doctors had little to do, but their appointments prohibited them from practicing medicine elsewhere. They were even younger than I, in the prime of their lives, and they felt their talents and training were being wasted. They had complained about not being able to do other work. Their "crime" was one of frustration at being asked to sacrifice their careers on behalf of a single healthy party leader. For this they were accused of being members of an anti-party group.

As the attacks against them continued, their "crimes" became twisted, blown out of all proportion. Jiang Qing's physician, Xu Tao, who had also served briefly as Mao's doctor, was a particularly hapless victim. His alleged anti-party crimes included torturing the Chairman's wife. The accusations would have been absurd if the potential consequences for Xu Tao had not been so great. The security guards, under Jiang Qing's direction, accused the doctor of pulling down the window shades too slowly when she ordered them drawn. The sun, she said, had permanently damaged her eyes. Xu Tao had deliberately given the Chairman's wife a chill by lowering the temperature below the eighty degrees upon which she insisted. When he showed her the thermometer reading precisely eighty degrees, she accused him of inflicting mental anguish. For this, Xu Tao was declared a member of the anti-party group.

In the end, all but one of the doctors were dismissed. The ones who were expelled were lucky. They went to Beijing Hospital, where they continued their medical careers, which was what they had wanted. Xu Tao, who had suffered the most grievous attacks, was the only doctor to remain behind, continuing, ironically, as Jiang Qing's personal doctor.

My heart went out to the doctors. They were my colleagues. I knew they had done no wrong. Certainly they were not members of any anti-party group. But I could not speak out on their behalf. To have defended them in public would have meant risking being declared an anti-party element myself.

My mental anguish was indescribable. It continues to this day. It had begun shortly after my return to China, when Lillian could not find work and I knew that had I given that Rolex watch to Yan, she would have found a suitable job. The anguish returned in 1952, during the "three-anti" campaign, against corruption, bureaucratism, and waste, when my brother and cousin were attacked. They were my relatives, the men who had introduced me to the Communist party, and I knew that they were innocent. But I was afraid to speak out. Had I defended them, I, too, would have been attacked.

Even before I began my work for Mao, I had violated my conscience. I could not say what was really in my heart. Ordinarily, when faced with a situation that ran contrary to my own beliefs, I tried to remain silent. But during the campaign against the physicians, I was forced to join in the attacks—for my own survival and for the survival of my family. I had to lie. It was the only way to save my job and be promoted. I wanted, above all, to survive.

But I did not accuse the doctors of opposing the party. I could not do that. Instead, I said they had been wrong to complain, that they had not done their jobs well, that they should learn to work better in the future.

Looking back over that period almost forty years later, from the perspective of safety in the United States, I know I would behave that way again. I felt I had no other choice. Too many family members were depending on me. There was no escape. If I were to return today and be asked to support the atrocities committed by the Chinese army on June 4, 1989, I would have to do so. Even today, the Communist party continues to demand that people attack the innocent. It requires people to pledge public support for policies with which they do not agree. Survival in China, then and now, depends on constantly betraying one's conscience.

What I did not know in the midst of my anguish during the purge of the doctors in 1954 was that the physicians were mere pawns in a power struggle between Wang Dongxing and Fu Lianzhang.

The roles of the two men put them inevitably in conflict. As a vice-minister of public health, Fu Lianzhang was responsible for the health of the party elite, and the leaders' private physicians had all been appointed upon his recommendation. Not having easy access to Mao or the other leaders, he used those appointments to his own advantage, ordering the men to report to him not only on the health of the leaders but on what they were saying and thinking. It was his way of reading the prevailing political winds, sniffing out potential political trouble. Mao, as the supreme leader, was his ultimate and most important concern.

But Wang Dongxing, as a high public-security official and head of the security guards, was responsible for the overall safety of the leaders, and thus their health was also his concern. Wang had considerably more power than Fu, was more ambitious politically, and had more direct access to Mao. Wang not only relied on the security guards to report to him on the leaders' activities but also tried to gather information from the doctors and nurses appointed by Fu, attempting thereby to create his own monopoly on information. Fu saw Wang's use of the doctors as interference; Wang thought Fu was trying to exert too much influence on the medical personnel.

The conflict was reaching a climax when Wang called upon me to serve as Mao's physician, which further exacerbated their enmity. Fu Lianzhang urged Mao to reject me, citing my problematic family background. Wang countered by taking advantage of the campaign against counterrevolutionaries to attack the physicians appointed by Fu. Wang won. The doctors were his unwitting victims. The rift between Wang Dongxing and Fu Lianzhang widened.

The campaign against the doctors was a painful education. The individual in China had no independent will. One had to obey one's "superiors" absolutely. There was no room for even the slightest disagreement. A single careless remark could be interpreted as defiance of one's superior and bring the wrath of the whole organization against you. "Struggle sessions" could be convened to criticize you; the "masses" could be organized to humiliate you.

The individual was merely a tiny cog in a large and complex machine. If the cog performed its functions well, it could be of use to the machine. At the slightest complaint, the smallest deviation from the norm, the cog could be thrown aside.

Much as I adulated Mao, my new assignment troubled me. "You will be granted no mistakes," Lillian warned me, "not even minor ones." Lillian knew better than anyone else how difficult my new position would be. We had been back in China for five years by then, and she had already grown disillusioned. The attacks against her—as the daughter of a landlord, as a suspected spy—had been unrelenting. But she also knew that I could not refuse the assignment. She was constantly worried.

Months went by after my meeting with Wang. I waited in anticipation, but the summons from Mao still did not come.

5

On April 25, 1955, at about three o'clock in the afternoon, the head nurse at the Zhongnanhai Clinic came to me with a message. She seemed tense and puzzled. "Group One just telephoned," she whispered. "You're wanted at the swimming pool." Group One was the code name designating Mao and his staff.* The "swimming pool" was Mao's.

There were two swimming pools then in Zhongnanhai. The outdoor pool, open in the summertime, was used by the entire staff. The indoor pool had been constructed for the top-level leadership, but over time the other leaders had stopped using it and Mao took it over as his. Later he would spend so much time there that additions were built—a reception room and study and a bedroom. In 1967, during the Cultural Revolution, Mao finally moved his residence to the building that housed the swimming pool, living there until only weeks before his death. It was there that he received President Richard Nixon, Premier Tanaka, and many other foreign leaders. Even in 1955, the "swimming pool" always referred to Mao.

My order to meet the Chairman had come.

My clinic was busy that day—it always was—and several patients had been waiting for several hours. I attended to them before riding my

---

*Group Two referred to Liu Shaoqi, Group Three to Premier Zhou, Group Four to Zhu De, and Group Five first to Ren Bishi and then, after his death, to Chen Yun.

bicycle to the indoor pool. Li Yinqiao, the deputy chief of Mao's bodyguards, who was constantly at his side, was waiting. "Why are you so late?" he asked anxiously, rushing up to me. "You kept Chairman waiting."

"I couldn't leave my patients," I explained. "It took some time to finish with them. Is Chairman ill? Does he need medical care?"

"No, no. He just wants to talk to you."

Li Yinqiao escorted me into the indoor pool area.

Mao was lying on a wooden bed, naked beneath an open terrycloth robe, his lower body loosely covered with a towel. He was reading. His body was as strong and large as I remembered from my first sight of him atop Tiananmen. His shoulders were broad, and his belly was big. His face had the same healthy glow, and his hair was still thick and black, his forehead broad, his skin like butter, delicate and hairless. His legs were rather thin for such a robust man. He wore coffee-colored socks. His feet were large.

Li Yinqiao announced my arrival, and I apologized immediately for being so late, explaining that I could not leave the patients who had already waited hours to see me. Mao was not irritated at all. He put aside his book and asked Li to pull up a chair so I could sit next to him. Mao's bodyguards doubled as his personal attendants, and a group of four were on duty, organized by teams, day and night, twenty-four hours a day.

"Zhang Zhidong did not follow a regular schedule for eating and sleeping," Mao said, referring to a high-ranking official of the Qing dynasty. "I am just like Zhang. I came over here right after I woke up. What time is it now?"

"It's four-thirty in the afternoon," I replied.

"This is my morning. What time do you get up?"

I was confused. Most Chinese take a short nap after lunch, and since I did not yet understand Mao's habits or how he went about eliciting information, I was not sure whether he was asking what time I woke up from my afternoon nap or what time I got up in the morning. "Usually I get up a little after six in the morning," I replied, "and then I take a short nap in the afternoon."

"You are a doctor," Mao said with a smile. "You take good care of your health and follow a regular schedule." Mao's eyes seemed full of wisdom, and he exuded good feeling—less by his words than by the expression on his face. I was overcome. I felt that I was in the presence of a great man.

He was smoking a British-made "555" cigarette, puffing through a cigarette holder. "Song Qingling suggested the cigarette holder," he said, referring to the widow of Sun Yat-sen. "It has a filter inside that is supposed to eliminate nicotine. I have smoked for many years, but I still wonder how nicotine affects me. Do you smoke?"

"Yes, I do," I responded, "but not much." I usually smoked three or four cigarettes a day after work.

"You are the first smoking doctor I have met, then." He smiled, taking several deep puffs and looking at me with a mischievous grin. "Smoking is also a deep breathing exercise, don't you think?" I could not tell whether he was joking or serious, so I did not know how to respond. I just smiled at him in silence.

He looked at my hair. "You are just a little over thirty. Why do you have so much more gray hair than I?"

I tried to explain that my prematurely gray hair was probably inherited, part of my genetic makeup. "To look at our hair," I said, "I seem much older than the Chairman."

"You are flattering me," Mao laughed.

His conversation had put me at ease.

He asked about my educational background and my professional experience, listening attentively as I responded. "Since you started high school, your education has been completely American," he said, "and during the war of liberation against Chiang Kai-shek and the Guomindang, the Americans helped Chiang. The Americans also fought against us in Korea. Still, I like having American- or British-trained people working for me. I am interested in foreign languages. Some people think I should learn Russian, but I don't want to. I'd rather learn English. You can teach me."

I agreed.

Mao paused for a while, becoming more serious. "You were only fifteen years old in 1935, when you joined the National Renaissance Society—just a kid. You didn't know anything then. Besides, you have already told the story to your superiors. I can't see that this is a problem." He told me how the founding emperor of the Tang dynasty (A.D. 618–907), Li Shimin, had refused to listen to the advice of his ministers and had placed such trust in a general with a questionable background that he allowed the general to sleep by his side. The general was extremely talented and became quite useful to the emperor. The two learned to work well together. "What it takes," Mao said, looking at me, "is sincerity. We have to treat each other with sincerity. Both the relationship and our sincerity have to be tested over a long period of time.

"Take Xu Shiyou, for instance," he continued, referring to the onetime Buddhist monk who was then the commander of the Nanjing

Military Region. Xu Shiyou had originally been a follower of Zhang Guotao, one of the founders of the Chinese Communist party, who in a disagreement with Mao had defected to the Guomindang. Xu Shiyou refused to follow Zhang Guotao, declaring his loyalty to Mao instead. "During the rectification campaign in 1942 in Yanan, many people questioned Xu's loyalty because he had once worked for Zhang Guotao," Mao explained. "They criticized him severely. Xu was desperate and was thinking about pulling his army out of Yanan. Kang Sheng wanted to arrest him and have him shot. I said that we had to wait. I needed to talk to him. Many comrades did not like this. They were afraid he might harm me. I disagreed.

"When Xu saw me, he burst into tears. I told him not to cry. I just wanted him to answer two simple questions. 'Do you believe in Zhang Guotao or me?' I asked. 'Of course I believe in you,' Xu answered. 'Do you want to go or stay?' I asked. 'Of course I want to stay,' he answered. So I told him, 'Okay, stay. Continue to command your troops. That's it.' Hasn't Xu Shiyou done a fine job since?"

Suddenly, after years of anxiety and depression, I felt safe. Mao had solved the problem of my family background and political past. Others had used my past to attack me, to deprive me of party membership, to make me insecure. "You were just a kid," Mao had said. "What matters is sincerity." His logic was so simple, but it relieved all the weight of my past. Mao was the supreme leader. No one could challenge him. I was grateful. Mao had saved me.

A bodyguard entered and began serving Mao his meal. He invited me to share it. There were four dishes—fish, pork mixed with hot peppers, a favorite of Mao's, lamb with leeks, and a platter of vegetables. They were swimming in oil but had no soy sauce and little salt. For most people, life was still difficult in the mid-1950s. Food was scarce, and oil was a precious commodity. I was not accustomed to eating oil and only picked at the meal we were sharing.

"You don't want to eat," Mao chided me. "This fish is very good—and the pork, too."

"I'm not very hungry," I apologized. Only much later would I become accustomed to his tastes.

"This is both my breakfast and lunch," he said. "I only have two meals a day. Maybe this isn't your mealtime."

We continued to chat. He asked whether I had ever studied philosophy.

"When I was a student, I could not even finish my medical texts," I answered. "I had little time for other reading. Since then I have spent all my time treating patients. So I have had little opportunity to read philosophy. But I have read two of Chairman's essays—'On Practice' and 'On Contradiction.' "

I had really liked both essays. Mao wrote well—simply and to the point. "On Practice" had taught me that real knowledge comes from doing rather than from reading about how to do—a useful lesson for an aspiring surgeon. "On Contradiction" had helped me understand that the solution to any problem requires locating the major contradiction—going to the root and treating the cause rather than concentrating on the symptoms.

Mao smiled. "During the War of Resistance against Japan [1937–1945], I was asked to give a lecture on philosophy at the 'Resist Japan University' in Yanan. I thought then that I needed to summarize the experiences of our revolution by integrating the theory of Marxism with the concrete reality of China. So I wrote those two articles. 'On Practice,' I think, was more important than 'On Contradiction.' I spent two weeks writing 'On Contradiction,' but it only took me two hours to deliver it as a lecture."

Years later, when I sometimes looked back and wondered why I had made such a good impression on Mao during that first meeting, I returned often to this part of our conversation. Only after being in Mao's inner circle for some time did I realize how important Mao himself thought those two articles were. He believed they were a major contribution to the philosophical development of Marxism-Leninism —an explication of "socialism with Chinese characteristics." The Soviets, however, accorded them no such honor and branded them revisionist instead. I heard rumors that Stalin had designated P. F. Yudin, a renowned Soviet philosopher of Marxism-Leninism, as the Soviet ambassador to China in order to study Mao's thoughts and report on their orthodoxy. Mao often visited Yudin, and the two would argue late into the night. But Yudin persistently rebuffed Mao's views. Mao was vexed. "Did philosophy really reach its limits with Marx and Lenin?" he would sometimes wonder out loud. "Can't the inclusion of China's revolutionary experience produce new philosophical thought?"

That first afternoon, however, I knew none of this, and Mao himself was circumspect. "I think you should read some philosophy," he said. "It might do you a lot of good as a physician. I have just finished Engels's *Dialectics of Nature*. Take it with you. I have heard that in American universities the highest degree in the humanities, science, and engineering is called the doctor of philosophy. It seems that they also consider philosophy important for all the academic disciplines. I also think it's important to study history. Without studying history, we can't know how the present has come about. You should also study literature. As a doctor, in touch with so many different people, if you only know medical science, you'll be boring. You won't share a common language with others."

He paused.

"Well, we can stop here for today. We will have many chances to talk in the future." He extended his hand and shook mine firmly.

It was shortly past seven in the evening when I left the swimming pool area, and my mind was racing. The meeting had been full of surprises, from finding Mao in bed to the discovery of his unusual sleeping habits, his wry sense of humor, and his ability to get me to relax and speak my mind. He was formidable and approachable, wise and iconoclastic. My tension had evaporated, and I suddenly felt more secure than I had in years. There was still a vast gulf between Mao and me, and I knew little about him, but I was certain I had been in the presence of a great man. I was proud to be called upon to work for him in such an intimate capacity. It was an opportunity I had never imagined. But could I do a good job? How should I prepare myself? What really would be required of me? I went to see Wang Dongxing immediately.

"You spent quite a long time with the Chairman," he said in greeting, obviously pleased. If the meeting had not gone well, Mao would have dismissed me much earlier. "What did you talk about?"

I reported our conversation.

Wang was delighted. "See? I told you. You can do the job. It's a good beginning. Keep it up."

The phone rang. It was Mao's bodyguard, Li Yinqiao. I had made a very good impression on Mao. I had passed the test. Mao wanted me to serve as his personal physician.

"I'll report to minister of public security Luo Ruiqing," Wang said. "Go home now and get a good rest. Keep all this confidential. Don't tell anyone about your job unless they really have to know."

Lillian was the only person I told. She also thought that I had made a good first impression. Otherwise Mao would not have talked with me so long or invited me to dinner.

I was happy that Mao had seemed to like me, but I was still worried about the job. "We'll just see whether my work goes this well, too," I said.

"You know the job will be very demanding," Lillian said.

Fu Lianzhang phoned the next day and invited me to visit him in Bowstring Lane. I bicycled to his home.

"You saw Chairman yesterday," he greeted me enthusiastically.

This time he came to the door to welcome me, taking my hand tightly in his. "Tell me how everything went."

I never learned how the news had traveled so fast. Fu listened attentively, growing increasingly excited as I described my meeting with Mao. He poured a cup of tea for me, then circled twice around an end table, talking as though to himself. "It was a matter of luck," he mumbled.

He turned to me, smiled, and said, "You really are lucky. The first time you met the Chairman, and you talked with him for so long. What a precious occasion!" Fu, I sensed, was jealous and puzzled that the meeting had gone so well.

"In 1934, when the Chairman was suffering from malaria and about to go into battle, he asked me to treat him," Fu said. "I gave him quinine.

"Then, when he was about to go to war again, he asked me to take care of his pregnant wife, Comrade He Zizhen. I delivered her baby." Fu Lianzhang was not clear about exactly how many children He Zizhen had borne, and I never learned for certain either, but I had heard that she had two boys before the Long March began in the fall of 1934 and that both were left behind with a peasant family when the communists evacuated their southern base area and that later efforts to find them had proved fruitless. Fu Lianzhang became excited as he remembered those times, his cheeks turning red and perspiration breaking out on his forehead. He took a few sips of boiled water. "I don't drink tea or take anything stimulating," he said.

"Later, Chairman Mao saved my life," Fu continued, turning the conversation in another direction. "I had been accused of being a member of the Guomindang's Anti-Bolshevik Corps, and Chairman Mao protected me. When I was still a young man, I contracted tuberculosis, and Chairman Mao treated me with great kindness. During the Long March, when everyone else was on foot, he let me ride a horse. He made sure because of my poor health that I had a whole chicken to eat every day." Chicken was expensive and difficult to come by in those days, and to eat a whole chicken every day was an unimaginable luxury.

Fu offered me some more tea and continued. "I'm telling you these stories because I want you to understand the Chairman."

I knew little about the early history of the Communist party or of Mao's past. I asked Fu to continue. "What you're telling me is very helpful."

Fu smiled and went on. "The Chairman has a serious case of insomnia. During the Jiangxi soviet period, in the early 1930s, I had to

go to Shanghai disguised as a businessman to buy sedatives—Veronal
—and glucose to treat him. I suggested that the Chairman take both
the Veronal and the glucose before going to bed. The sleeping medication worked, so the Chairman was very happy. You can see I am very
loyal to the Chairman. He and I are the same age, but my health is not
as good."

Fu looked at me intently. "Your new assignment means that the
party trusts you," he said. "This is a very noble assignment. But it is
also very difficult."

The meal was served. "Yesterday Chairman treated you to dinner.
Today I will do the same," Fu said. The dishes were light and included
a bowl of steamed chicken. "I still eat one chicken a day," he explained. He ordered wine and raised his glass to me. "Ordinarily I
don't drink wine at all," he said, "but I want to share some with you
today.

"You must be very careful in your work as Chairman Mao's
physician. Whenever you have any difficulties, no matter what they
are, just tell me. I will help you." I had no idea what help Fu could be.
He obviously wanted to know as much about Mao and his activities
as he could.

Fu stopped eating after he had finished his chicken. "I eat five
meals a day, just a little each time," he explained. "You must eat more.

"Chairman wants you to help him study English," he continued.
"This is a good opportunity to befriend him. It seems he likes you. Try
to be accommodating. In addition to treating him medically, you
should do whatever else he wants, too."

I bridled at Fu's suggestion. I was a physician. To allow myself to
become involved in nonmedical matters was to diminish my role as a
doctor. "If I were to do as you suggest," I responded without thinking,
"I would have little time for medical practice."

Fu became solemn. "You shouldn't see things that way. Chairman's knowledge is as deep and as wide as the seas. You have much
to learn from him. You are a doctor. You should try to broaden your
knowledge. This way, you will have more opportunities to talk with
him. You will be able to understand him better."

Mao, too, had encouraged me to broaden my knowledge, and I
realized that Fu had a point. Mao was still young and healthy, and for
many years I would not be treating his illnesses but would have to find
ways of maintaining and improving his health. I would have to understand his temperament, his character, and his habits, and to do this I
would need his trust. Fu was right. I would have to expand my knowledge so I could talk more often with Mao. I thanked Fu for his advice.

He responded warmly, taking my hand in his, gripping it firmly. "Please come visit every week," he urged me, "with or without business."

The streets were crowded with people, and the atmosphere around me was festive as I bicycled home from Fu Lianzhang's. Beijing was preparing for May Day, and the buildings were festooned with colorful posters and banners. I felt good.

I had become disillusioned after my return to China. My dream had slipped away. Other members of my generation, my brother, cousins, and friends, were finding their places in this new revolutionary society. They were veteran revolutionaries, men who had made their way to Yanan in the 1930s to make revolution. With the establishment of the new government in 1949, they had been rewarded with important positions. Some had been criticized during the "three-anti" campaign, but they had retained their jobs, and now they were respected by everyone, successful. My schoolmates, too, were making something of their lives. Their medical careers were blossoming. They were becoming highly respected specialists in major hospitals throughout the country.

I had been adrift, assigned a job I never wanted, forced to abandon surgery and become a general practitioner instead, devoting my time to petty illnesses. My career was stymied. Premier Zhou Enlai had recently announced that my clinic at Zhongnanhai would soon be combined with the clinic set up to serve the State Council, and he had appointed me director of the new facility. But all these reorganizations were unsettling. I had no idea what the future would bring. My appointment as Mao's doctor would free me from the clinic and the petty pressures that work entailed.

As Mao's physician, I would enjoy a new respect. Mao was the paramount leader of China, worshiped by millions. But he lived in secret, shut off from even his closest political colleagues. He was tightly guarded. To ordinary people, he was a mysterious and faraway presence whom they could never dream of knowing. Even the highest party officials saw him only at meetings. As his doctor, I would be constantly at his side, with him every day, tutoring him in English, talking with him about philosophy, privy to the workings of his inner court.

My whole world had changed. The sky had opened up and the earth had embraced me. I was no longer a nobody. When I met Fu Lianzhang in 1949, just after my return, he had not even stood up from his chaise longue to greet me and still I had felt honored that such a high official had received me. Now he was meeting me at the door, almost obsequious. Indeed, I soon noticed that many top leaders became suddenly courteous and outgoing, eager to talk to me. I was no longer an ordinary physician. I was proud of myself, exhilarated. I was Chairman Mao's doctor. I was ecstatic!

6

Just before midnight on the eve of the May Day celebrations, only days after my first meeting with Mao, I was summoned by one of his bodyguards to go to the Chairman immediately.

I rushed to Mao's residence, assuming that he had taken ill. Why else would I be called so late?

I had never been to Mao's home, and I approached it with reverence. Walking through the gate and into the outer courtyard, I felt I was completing my own long march from ordinary doctor to the center of the revolution. From this day on, I thought, my life will be rooted in this sacred, forbidden land. I was thrilled.

Mao is always described as having led an ascetically simple life, setting an example of frugality. When his residence was opened following his death, his worn-out clothes, robes, and slippers were exhibited to the public as evidence that he had sacrificed luxury in order to stay in contact with the masses. Mao was a peasant and he had simple tastes. He dressed only when he absolutely had to and spent most of his day in bed, wearing a robe and nothing on his feet. When he did get dressed, he wore old clothes and worn-out cloth shoes, donning the "Mao suit" and leather shoes only for formal, public occasions. He had someone else—one of his bodyguards, usually—break in his new cloth shoes. The photographs showing him neatly dressed, working in his office, were staged. He conducted virtually all his business from his bedroom or from the side of his indoor pool.

But he still lived an imperial life. His compound was located in the heart of Zhongnanhai, in the center of the old imperial grounds, just between the Middle and South lakes and facing south, in the manner of emperors. It must have been the best-protected place on earth. Foreigners visiting Mao would notice the absence of armed guards, but in fact they were everywhere in Zhongnanhai, discreetly placed, fanning out in a series of concentric circles with Mao at the center. Mao's bodyguards (*neiwei,*) who doubled as attendants, carried pistols, but security at the outer edges of the concentric circles, at the walls of the compound, was so strict that the effect was of a sealed-off cocoon. Beyond Mao's immediate bodyguards, both within his compound and posted at intervals around it, were the so-called "external guards" (*waiwei*), members of Wang Dongxing's Central Bureau of Guards. They, too, were armed.

Armed combat soldiers from the Central Garrison Corps, formally administered by the army chief of staff but in fact under the direct supervision of Wang Dongxing as vice-minister of the Ministry of Public Security, stood guard at the perimeters of Zhongnanhai. This series of protective layers was duplicated wherever Mao went.

Mao's whereabouts were kept secret from all but the highest party leaders. When he was visiting outside Zhongnanhai on ceremonial occasions, his car would be parked somewhere else lest his license number be seen and remembered. Even so, the number was frequently changed. Much of the security system had been copied from the Soviet Union shortly after the communist takeover, but it was also reminiscent of the elaborate precautions taken to protect Chinese emperors during the imperial age.

Mao's compound had once been the emperor's library and retreat, built during the reign of the Qianlong emperor (r. 1736–1795). The complex had not been properly maintained for decades and had begun to decay. The buildings had yet to be fully restored to their former splendor, and renovations were still in progress. Entering for the first time, I was struck more by the functional simplicity of the interior than by its elegance. But the presence of the Qianlong emperor was everywhere.

The south-facing main gate to Mao's walled compound was traditional, old-fashioned and colorfully painted. The wooden placard above bore the legend FENGZEYUAN, Garden of Abundant Beneficence, and had been inscribed by the Qianlong emperor himself. Indeed, all the wooden placards at the buildings' entrances had been inscribed by the emperor. The roof tiles were gray rather than the golden yellow of those in the adjacent Forbidden City, but the style of the buildings was like that of the imperial abode.

Just inside the main gate, on either side of the entrance, were two small rooms where bodyguards stood duty around the clock. The walled compound could be entered only by those holding the special A pass. There was a large courtyard just inside, and straight ahead was a spacious building designated Yinian Tang, or Longevity Hall, where Mao held meetings, received foreign dignitaries, and hosted banquets before the construction of the Great Hall of the People in 1959. Just behind Longevity Hall was another building, Hanhe Tang, Containing Harmony Hall, which housed Mao's large collection of books. It was almost always locked.

Mao's private quarters, known as the Chrysanthemum Fragrance Study (Juxiang Shuwu), were in the second courtyard, connected to the first by a covered corridor. The courtyard was lovely, with magnificent ancient pines and cypresses towering over the wicker tables and chairs where Mao, in the summertime, often held outdoor meetings. Mao's living quarters consisted of two main buildings and several smaller ones. The huge room that served as Mao's study and bedroom was in one building, separated from Jiang Qing's bedroom by a large dining room. The second main building, connected by a corridor to Jiang Qing's bedroom, served as a sitting room for Mao's wife. Adjacent to Jiang Qing's bedroom, and sharing the same interior wall, was the home of Ye Zilong, the head of the Office of Confidential Secretaries, who served also as Mao's chief steward and looked after his personal needs.

To the west of Ye Zilong's quarters and in another building connected to Containing Harmony Hall was the huge kitchen. Ye was in charge of Mao's food. The system of procuring Mao's food was complex—also copied from the Soviets, but similar to the imperial system, too—falling under the larger aegis of Wang Dongxing's Central Bureau of Guards.

Shortly after Mao's return from Moscow in early 1950, two Soviet food specialists had been assigned to the Central Bureau of Guards to help set up a system for inspecting and supplying food to the leaders in Zhongnanhai. At the heart of the system was the Giant Mountain (Jushan) farm, which grew high-quality vegetables, meat, chicken, and eggs for Mao and other top leaders. Mao's chef would send his shopping list to the Central Bureau of Guards' Department of Supply, located near Beihai Park, just north of Zhongnanhai, and the Department of Supply in turn would send the requests to Jushan farm. The food would be delivered to the supply station at Beihai Park, where it would pass through two laboratories—one to analyze the food for freshness and nutritional value and the other to test for poison. After passing the tests, the food was sent to a food-tasting service, where tasters sampled the food before it was given to Mao. The same expensive system existed for all the ranking leaders and was widely duplicated for leaders in the provinces. This cost the public a great deal of money.

Mao's bedroom was connected by a corridor to another building that ostensibly served as his office. The office was locked year-round, opened only for formal picture-taking sessions. Mao never used it.

Adjacent to the compound occupied by Mao and Jiang Qing was another family courtyard, where Li Min, Mao's daughter by He Zizhen, and Li Na, his daughter by Jiang Qing, lived with Jiang Qing's sister, Li Yunlu. Li Yunlu was much older than Jiang Qing—her feet were bound—and she had reared Jiang Qing after their mother died. Later she became a concubine to a businessman. After the party leadership moved to Zhongnanhai, Jiang Qing invited Li Yunlu and her son to live there and help rear Li Na and Li Min. Neither Mao nor Jiang Qing took much interest in their children, and they rarely saw them. They studied in boarding schools, and even when they came home for vacation they only occasionally joined Mao or Jiang Qing for dinner—never more than a few times a year.

A fourth compound consisted of the offices of Mao's medical staff and secretaries and the living quarters of Mao's nephew, Yuanxin, then a young boy of middle-school age. There was a room for playing Ping-Pong here, too, and a large room where Mao's gifts, his clothes, and many of Jiang Qing's belongings were stored. Some of the country's most famous painters, such as Qi Baishi and Xu Beihong, had sent Mao gifts of their art, and these were kept in storage here, but most of the gifts were from foreigners. Later I saw huge, elaborately carved wooden boxes full of Cuban cigars sent by Fidel Castro and cases of aged brandy from Romania's Ceauşescu and a beautiful gold-and-silver cigarette case from the shah of Iran. Ye Zilong, in addition to being responsible for Mao's kitchen, was also in charge of this storeroom.

The courtyard in this area was the largest, with a lovely water fountain and many evergreens and bamboo trees and a grape trellis. In summertime, it was particularly comfortable, several degrees cooler than anywhere else. A large vegetable garden was attached, and in the late 1960s, an air-raid shelter was built under it.

The fifth compound, entered by a separate gate, much simpler than the southern entrance, was dominated by Diligent Administration Hall (Qinzheng Dian). Until the construction of the Great Hall of the People, ambassadors from foreign countries came here to present their credentials. The dormitories of Mao's bodyguards and Jiang Qing's nurses, on duty around the clock, were also in this compound. Mao's food, stored in three 1940s-style General Electric refrigerators, the daily supplies for his household, and medical supplies were kept in these offices, too.

The offices of Mao's bodyguards, where Mao's calendar and the log of his activities were kept, were located just inside the back door of the fourth compound. Anyone wishing to see Mao, including the staff who worked directly for him, had to report first to the bodyguards stationed here. It was to this courtyard that I rushed around midnight, April 30, 1955, certain that Mao had taken ill. A bodyguard greeted me as I came in.

"What's wrong?" I asked.

"The Chairman has taken sleeping pills twice but still cannot sleep," the guard explained. "He wants to talk to you."

I was escorted to Mao's bedroom. It was huge, almost the size of a ballroom. The furniture was more Western than Chinese, contemporary and functional, and the four windows were covered in heavy velvet drapes, which were, I realized later, always kept closed. Inside Mao's room it was impossible to tell whether it was night or day.

Mao was lying on a huge wooden bed, half again the size of an ordinary double bed, constructed especially for him by one of the carpenters in Zhongnanhai. Two thirds of the bed was stacked with books, and I noticed that on the side where Mao was now reclining, the edge was raised about four inches higher than the rest of the bed. Li Yinqiao told me later that this was a safety measure to prevent Mao from falling out. It would be years before I realized that the incline had more to do with his sex life than his safety.

Just next to the bed was a large square table, which doubled as his office desk and dining table. Mao took most of his meals alone, in his bedroom. He and Jiang Qing, even then, lived very separate lives and seldom ate together.

"I haven't had my supper yet," Mao said in greeting, fully alert. "I want to have a chat with you." He was wearing a robe, open to expose his chest. He was holding an ancient Chinese book bound together by linen string.

Mao put down his book and I pulled up a chair to sit next to him, sipping the tea his bodyguard had served.

"Is there any news?" he began. I was puzzled. All my news came from the *People's Daily,* which I assumed Mao also read. Surely I had no information that he did not. "For example," Mao continued, noting my confusion, "whom did you see in the last couple of days? What did you talk about?"

"Is there any news?" was to become Mao's daily greeting, and he asked the same question of every staff member. It was his way of gathering information and keeping continual check on us. It was his way of controlling us, too. He expected us to repeat all our conversations and activities and encouraged us to criticize each other. He liked to play one member of the staff off against another. He permitted no secrets.

I told him of my conversation with Fu Lianzhang.

Mao listened attentively. Then he began talking about how Fu Lianzhang had come to accompany the communists on the Long March from the soviet-base area in Jiangxi province to the headquarters of the new base area in Shaanxi. "During our internal struggle against the Guomindang's Anti-Bolshevik Corps in the early 1930s, the Communist party executed five members of Fu Lianzhang's family, including his daughter and son-in-law. They were members of the party themselves but had been accused of being secret members of the Guomindang's Anti-Bolshevik Corps." It was during this time, I knew from Fu Lianzhang's own story, that Fu had also been treating Mao for malaria.

"Fu was not then a member of the Communist party, but I asked if he wanted to join us on the Long March anyway," Mao continued. "He did. We gave him a horse, but he did not know how to ride, so he fell into a river and almost drowned. But he stayed with us all the way to Shaanxi. He's a good man, Fu Lianzhang. But you don't have to listen to everything he says. You really don't have to consult with him about my health problems. When I don't feel well, talk to me about the treatment, not him. If I agree to the treatment, I won't blame you if anything goes wrong. If you don't discuss the treatment with me, then you can't claim credit for healing me, even if I do get better."

I was happy not to have to discuss Mao's health with Fu Lianzhang but was disconcerted that Mao expected to be so closely consulted. Did Mao really want me to describe the physiological and pathological changes the body undergoes during illness? Would I really have to explain every treatment? Would he actually have to be persuaded to accept my treatment? Where would I find layman's language to explain everything to him?

Mao would not be an easy patient.

Dinner was served. Again, the food was swimming in oil. Mao was sixty-two years old and weighed just over 190 pounds—a bit heavy even for his five-foot-ten-inch frame. Later, I would often criticize his diet and caution him against eating so much fat, but he never listened. He had been in the habit of eating fatty pork since boyhood, and he would do so until the end of his life.

He offered me a dish of bitter melon cooked with hot peppers. "How does it taste?" he wondered.

I had never eaten such a dish. "It's hot and bitter," I replied.

Mao roared with laughter. "Everyone should taste some bitterness in his life," he said, "especially a person like you. You studied medicine and became a doctor. You have probably never eaten bitterness."

Chi ku, "to eat bitterness," can mean, literally, to eat something bitter or to suffer hardship, and I was not certain whether Mao was referring to the food we were eating or playing on words to let me know he regarded me as soft, a product of an easy upper-class life. "I have never eaten this kind of bitter melon before," I replied, sticking to the question of food, "but it's tasty."

"Well, good," he replied. "You must be prepared to taste some bitterness."

Mao's answer made clear that he was sure I had never faced hardship or difficulty, and he wanted me to taste my share. Mao, I would discover, thought everyone—from his daughters Li Na and Li Min to the country's highest leaders—should *chi ku.* Most of the leaders, coming as they did from peasant pasts and having struggled for decades to bring the revolution to victory, had already had their share of bitterness. But Mao thought they had become soft after gaining power and settling into luxurious lives in the city. Without periodic exposure to suffering, he thought, those at the top would forget the real China. In years to come, he would make certain that everyone around him, myself and the highest leaders included, ate more than a little bitterness.

He turned to other topics. China has made three great contributions to the world, he said—Chinese medicine, Cao Xueqin's novel *The Dream of the Red Chamber,* and mah-jongg. He wanted to know if I played mah-jongg.

Mah-jongg is a gambling game that four people play with a set of 136 small tiles, and for many Chinese the game becomes addictive. My family had always disapproved of gambling, and since middle school I had regarded mah-jongg and opium addiction as two cancers eating away at Chinese society. I had never learned to play.

"Well, don't look down on mah-jongg," Mao chastised me.

"With a total of 136 tiles, every player has to watch not only over his own pieces but all the other pieces on the table. You have to observe how the others are playing and put all this complicated information together to calculate the possibility of winning and losing. If you knew how to play the game, you would also understand the relationship between the principle of probability and the principle of certainty."

Mah-jongg is indeed a game of strategy, and Mao was both China's great strategist and a superb mah-jongg player. But I think his strategic brilliance came from other sources—from Sun Zi's ancient *Art of War,* from his reading of Chinese history, from the *Romance of the Three Kingdoms.* But sharpening his strategic wit was not the only reason he played mah-jongg. His partners, I learned later, were usually pretty young girls. While his hands were busy with the tiles, he was also flirting with his partners, using his feet to touch this one's feet or that one's legs under the table.

"*The Dream of the Red Chamber,*" Mao continued, "is about the rise and fall of feudal society—a condensed history of China over the last two thousand years. I don't ordinarily read novels, but I like *The Dream of the Red Chamber.*"

I had only skimmed *The Dream of the Red Chamber,* unable to read it from cover to cover. It is indeed the greatest of all Chinese novels, but the story is complicated, and the characters numerous. Every time I picked the book up, I laid it aside in boredom after only two or three pages. One of its themes is the decline of the very wealthy Jia family and the corrupt society in which the family is embedded. Mao saw it as a classic study of corruption and the decline of "feudalism" in China. But Chinese for centuries had read it as the tragic love story of Jia Baoyu, who falls in love with a young woman whom his family refuses to allow him to marry. Alienated from society and his family, Jia eventually becomes a monk, but his early rebellion takes the form of pleasure seeking and the pursuit of beautiful women. Later, when I knew Mao better, I understood that he saw much of himself in Jia Baoyu. Even his compound, the Garden of Abundant Beneficence, seemed almost a replica of the opulent Jia family home. Mao, too, was a rebel who liked to seduce young women, and he surrounded himself with female companions. But Mao, unlike Jia Baoyu, never became a monk. "Don't think I'm a saint," Mao warned me early in our relationship. "I'm not at all a saint, and I'm not a monk. I don't want to be."

Mao attributed China's large population to the efficacy of Chinese medicine. For thousands of years, he told me, China had gone through continual war and natural disaster. But our population now was more than 500 million. Was it because of Western medicine that we had this many people? Western medicine had been practiced in China for only about one hundred years. For thousands of years before, our people had depended on Chinese medicine. Why were there still people who dismissed Chinese medicine? The only Chinese books he had not yet read, he said, were those on Chinese medicine and Buddhism. He wondered if I had read books on Chinese medicine.

My ancestors had been devoted to Chinese medicine, but my training had been Western and I had never given much thought to the contributions of traditional medicine. But I did not believe that China's large population was the result of Chinese medicine. I told Mao that I had read some ancient Chinese medical books but could not really understand them, especially those relating to the theory of the five elements—metal, wood, water, fire, and earth. I did not understand the theory.

Mao laughed. "The theory of *yin* and *yang* and the five elements really is very difficult," he said. "The theory is used by doctors of Chinese medicine to explain the physiological and pathological conditions of the human body. What I believe is that Chinese and Western medicine should be integrated. Well-trained doctors of Western medicine should learn Chinese medicine; senior doctors of Chinese medicine should study anatomy, physiology, bacteriology, pathology, and so on. They should learn how to use modern science to explain the principles of Chinese medicine. They should translate some classical Chinese medicine books into modern language, with proper annotations and explanations. Then a new medical science, based on the integration of Chinese and Western medicine, can emerge. That would be a great contribution to the world."

He paused to reflect. "Even though I believe we should promote Chinese medicine, I personally do not believe in it. I don't take Chinese medicine. Don't you think that is strange?"

I agreed that it was strange. Publicly, the Chairman was the leading advocate of traditional medicine, but he refused to use it himself.

"Tomorrow is May Day," Mao said as our nocturnal visit drew to a close. "Come with me to the top of Tiananmen to watch the celebration. It will be a good education for you." He asked how old my child was.

"Five," I replied.

"Take him, too, and let him see the scene," Mao suggested.

"That might not be such a good idea," I replied. "All the top leaders will be there. I will go because of my work, but he really has no reason to go. No one else takes his children. Besides, if he makes trouble, I would be criticized."

Mao smiled. "All right. You don't have to take him. Now go home and get some sleep."

It was three-thirty in the morning when I reached home, long past my ordinary ten o'clock bedtime. Lillian was still waiting up for me. I told her of my talk with Mao. "He is still in good health," I said a bit irritably. "He doesn't need daily medical care. I feel as though he is using me to make idle chatter rather than as a doctor."

Lillian urged me to be patient and accommodate the Chairman for now. "You are just starting your job," she pointed out. "He seems to have a very good impression of you. Don't rush things."

That was the first of countless nocturnal chats I had with Mao. He led an isolated life, seldom saw Jiang Qing, and had no friends. The "Yanan spirit"—the comradeship of the survivors of the Long March—was a myth. Occasionally, Liu Shaoqi or Zhou Enlai would come to meet with Mao on business, but most of their communications took place either through notes on the documents that were constantly being exchanged among them or at the meetings of the politburo standing committee that Mao convened irregularly in the living room of Longevity Hall—or in whatever city he happened to be staying. There was no coming and going, no visiting back and forth between Mao and other ranking party leaders. His bodyguards were his closest everyday company, and they were young, uneducated peasants with whom the possibility of conversation was limited. He talked to them about their girlfriends, offered them romantic advice, and sometimes even helped compose their love letters. But it was impossible to talk to them about the subjects that interested him most—Chinese history and philosophy.

So Mao made me his conversation partner, encouraging me to read his favorite historical and philosophical texts, and spent hours every week talking to me. When insomnia struck, he would sometimes read a book or call a meeting—no matter how late and inconvenient for others—but often he would simply call someone in to chat, and I was frequently that person. It was not unusual to receive a summons from Mao at three o'clock in the morning. His insomnia was always particularly acute just before National Day and May Day, when he was to review the parade and receive the crowds at Tiananmen.

Lillian was right to urge patience but wrong that the need to accommodate Mao would be temporary. Mao was a dictator. There were no other preferences but his. Those of us around him had to grant his every wish. To assert one's individuality in Mao's imperial court would have been an invitation to disaster.

7

The morning after our first nocturnal chat was May Day, and I reported to the duty office at Mao's residence at a little after nine, emergency medical bag in hand. Wang Dongxing was already there, and Mao soon emerged from his bedroom, dressed in a woolen Sun Yat-sen suit and a pair of brown leather shoes. He was excited about the upcoming event and greeted us with obvious delight.

Luo Ruiqing, minister of public security, arrived, and gave Mao a military salute. At Mao's signal, we all piled into the waiting limousines to be whisked off to Tiananmen.

I had attended every National Day and May Day celebration since my return to China in 1949, and the holidays had always thrilled me. I loved the excitement of the huge crowds gathered in the square, the parade, the music, and the flags. I loved watching the leaders atop the Gate of Heavenly Peace, reviewing the parade and waving to the throngs. The celebrations had always made me proud to be Chinese. But today, I was no longer one of the crowd. I, too, would be standing atop Tiananmen, with the country's highest leaders, watching the celebration below.

I sat in the lead car with Luo Ruiqing. As we pulled up to the staging area behind the Gate of Heavenly Peace, Luo jumped out and rushed to Mao's car, opened the door, and offered his hand. Mao glared at the public-security minister, got out of the car himself, and said angrily, "Don't be so thoughtless. There's no need to help me. Help Vice-Chairman Song Qingling." May Day was a state occasion, and the communist government still maintained the facade of a united front with the non-communist, "democratic" parties. Sun Yat-sen's widow, Song Qingling, was the most prominent spokesperson for the united-front policy. Luo rushed to Song's car, but she was already out.

Song Qingling must have been about sixty then, but she was still as beautiful and graceful as the first time I saw her atop Tiananmen. She was warm and outgoing and came forward to greet us, graciously shaking hands with everyone.

The other so-called democratic personages, by contrast, seemed senile and cold, taking their time about greeting us, moving with the deliberate, painful slowness of the very old. Mao greeted them pleasantly, though, then turned to Song Qingling and gallantly asked her to lead the way to the reception room atop the Gate of Heavenly Peace, helping her climb the rough-hewn outdoor stone stairs.

We reached the top of Tiananmen to applause from the already-assembled guests, and I was surprised to discover a spacious indoor reception area furnished with numerous comfortable overstuffed chairs, arranged in a large semicircle. Snacks, fruits, and drinks were laid out in abundance. So this was how the top leaders were able to spend five or six hours reviewing parades with never a hint of discomfort!

Mao shook hands with many of the guests, then turned toward the balcony that overlooked the square. Decorated with colorful red lanterns and banners, it was separated from the reception area by a huge screen and could not be seen from inside. I followed Mao to the podium and watched in wonderment as he waved to the crowd, slowly and deliberately walking back and forth across the length of the balcony, extending his blessing to every corner of the square. His expression was impassive, but I knew he was thrilled. I was overcome with excitement. The square was a sea of color, filled with thousands of young students dressed head to toe in white, the bright red Young Pioneers' scarves a splash of color around their necks. Thousands of carefully selected cadres and workers were carrying huge banners of every imaginable hue. The crowd went wild the moment Mao appeared, waving their banners and leaping into the air, shouting slogans supporting the Communist party, new China, and Mao.

Peng Zhen, the mayor of Beijing, opened the celebration. Just at the foot of Tiananmen, near where I had been standing on October 1, 1949, a military band played the Chinese national anthem. Cannons fired a twenty-one-gun salute. The band kept playing—"The East Is Red" ("The east is red; the sun shines; China has brought forth a Mao

Zedong"), "The Internationale," "The March of the People's Liberation Army."

The festivities began.

The military paraded by first, the army, navy, and air force troops in full military dress, displaying their weapons—tanks and cannons and so on. The band continued its martial music as Mao and all the other government leaders stood in review. Then waves upon waves of cadres, workers, and students marched by—with national flags, factory flags, school flags, colorful banners, waving their greetings to Mao and the other leaders. The parade continued for hours. Only rarely did the exhilarated Mao return to the reception room to rest.

The final contingent, thousands of children dressed in white and sporting red scarves, did not arrive at the foot of the podium until mid-afternoon. Raising their huge bouquets of flowers in another colorful salute, the children began shouting slogans of praise for China and the Communist party. That the crowds loved and respected Mao there was no doubt. Everyone participating in the parade had been specially selected. They were meant to love Mao.

Participate in these celebrations and you will receive an education in patriotism, Mao had told me. "Participate and you will love your country even more." He was right. On May 1, 1955, accompanying him for the first time, standing near him as he reviewed the crowds, thrilling to the martial music and the sea of color and the displays of China's military might, I was indeed overcome with patriotism.

The parade ended at about four-thirty in the afternoon, and we returned to Zhongnanhai. As Mao returned to his residence in the Chrysanthemum Fragrance Study, Luo Ruiqing reminded him that we would be returning to Tiananmen at seven o'clock for the evening fireworks display.

"It's been a long, hard day," Luo Ruiqing said, turning to us. "Be back here at six-thirty. Don't be late."

I returned to my apartment in Zhongnanhai's South Building, where my wife and son, John, were waiting, playing chess. I had promised to take them to the park that afternoon, and we had planned to go to my mother's house for a holiday dinner. Our plans were ruined.

"What should I tell Mother?" Lillian wondered. I sent them off, promising to join them as soon as I could, and told them to return home if I had not showed up by nine. I returned to my office in Group One and quickly ate a bowl of noodles.

As the other staff members gathered, the secretaries and guards began complaining that they had not had enough time for supper. "Don't worry," Wang Dongxing assured them. "There will be plenty of snacks at Tiananmen. Just don't all get together and eat at the same time or people will say that the staff of Group One gets special treatment—eating food intended for the leaders."

Seven o'clock came and Mao did not emerge from his quarters. "Big Beard Wang is cutting the Chairman's hair," Wang Dongxing explained. At seven-thirty, Luo Ruiqing turned to Wang Dongxing. "You'd better let the Chairman know it's time to leave," he said. Wang disappeared into the Chrysanthemum Fragrance Study. I followed to take a look.

Mao was sitting on a wicker chair in his dining room, a white sheet wrapped around his neck, holding an old-fashioned linen string-bound book, reading, shifting first this way and then that with no regard for the difficulties he was causing old Big Beard Wang. The back of the chair was too high, which gave Wang problems, and Mao's constant shifting from one position to another kept Wang in constant motion. He was perspiring heavily.

Big Beard Wang, whose real name was Wang Hui, was then in his sixties. He had been cutting Mao's hair since the late 1930s. When the party launched a rectification campaign in 1942, Mao told me later, Big Beard Wang had been accused of some sort of perfidy against the party. As the campaign against hidden traitors continued and the accused were pressured to confess, Big Beard Wang was among those who did, saying he was a secret assassin and had intended to kill Mao with his razor.

"I had my doubts when I heard about Big Beard Wang's confession," Mao told me. "Big Beard Wang had been cutting my hair and shaving me for years and had never so much as nicked my face. If he had wanted to kill me, he could have done it long before. I asked Big Beard Wang to come see me. He cried when he saw me, kneeling down and confessing that he had planned to kill me. 'So why haven't you killed me already?' I asked. Wang said he was waiting for the Guomindang to come, then he would kill me. 'If the Guomindang comes, they'll kill me. You won't have to,' I told him. I urged Wang to tell me the truth, and he explained that his interrogators had been keeping him awake day after day, not allowing him to sleep, trying to get him to confess. Only when he confessed was he finally allowed to sleep.

"So I halted the campaign," Mao continued. "I stressed that people had to tell the truth, not be forced to lie."

Big Beard Wang had remained impeccably loyal. Indeed, many

members of Mao's inner court, those closest and most loyal to him, had once been similarly saved by Mao.

Luo Ruiqing came in. "Can't you hurry it up?" Luo whispered to Wang.

"Minister Luo, you can't hurry him," Wang Dongxing whispered in reply. "If he hurries, he might accidentally hurt the Chairman. Then what a mess!"

After the haircut was finished, Big Beard Wang began shaving Mao, an even more difficult task. Big Beard had to crouch on his knees to get at Mao's chin while the Chairman continued to read, chin down, face thrust into his book. It was getting later and later.

Finally, Wang was finished, and the motorcade set out. Riding with Wang Dongxing and Luo Ruiqing, we talked about the problem of Mao's haircuts. Luo wanted to bring in a barber's chair from the Beijing Hotel and set it up in a special room.

But Wang had already made the same suggestion to Mao. He did not want the barber's chair. "The Chairman prefers it this way," Wang said.

"But Big Beard Wang is so old. His hands are trembling," Luo continued. "If he accidentally cuts the Chairman's face, it would be terrible."

"But it's even more difficult to find someone else," Wang said. "The Chairman won't allow him to be replaced. He doesn't trust a new barber moving around with a sharp razor."

Luo was silent. I thought he should have known better. He should have understood the difficulties Mao faced in finding people to trust. He should have known how important trust is. Luo Ruiqing, loyal though he was, never did understand the Chairman. I realized that someday I might have to use syringes and needles, maybe even a scalpel, on Mao. His permission for me to treat him would also depend on trust, and I would have to win that trust before I could do my work as his doctor. To do that, I would have to get closer to him, let him know me better. We would have to become friends.

The fireworks began as soon as Mao reached the top of Tiananmen. All the major buildings in the city had been strung with white lights, and we could see the white outlines of the buildings traced against the night sky. It was a spectacular sight—the colors of the shooting fireworks against the white lights and thousands upon thousands of colorfully dressed people performing folk dances in the square below.

As the fireworks were still splashing across the sky, Premier Zhou Enlai came to ask Mao to have his picture taken with some of the foreign dignitaries attending the occasion. Vietnamese leader Ho Chi Minh, then sixty-five years old, was among the guests, lean and energetic, with a long, wispy white goatee. Ho was dressed like a peasant, his bare feet in rough straw sandals. Ho had spent much of his adult life in China, and his Chinese bodyguard told me that the Vietnamese leader was fond of practically everything Chinese—food, clothing, transportation, houses. He spoke fluent Chinese. Ho was still spending most of his time in China then, in the two southern provinces of Guangxi and Yunnan, which border on Vietnam. I was introduced to him and liked him enormously. Mao commanded great respect, but Ho was more personable, less awesome.

The fireworks were over around ten. No one involved in the preparations for the evening would tell me how much the lavish food and refreshments had cost, but I learned that about half a million *renminbi* had been spent on the fireworks alone. The average monthly wage of workers then was thirty *renminbi*. Later, I would come to regard these festivities as almost criminally wasteful, particularly when they continued uninterrupted through the "three bad years," when millions starved. They lost their meaning for me then.

They would lose their meaning for Mao as well. National Day and May Day were the only two days of the year that he had to rise early and was expected to appear on time. He was always excited before the celebrations, and his insomnia would grow worse. Often he would get no sleep at all the night before the festivities. He was exhilarated by the crowds and their adulation and his energy always carried him through the event, but he often caught cold afterward. Sometimes the cold would become bronchitis, and he would be miserable for weeks. As he got older, the bronchitis would sometimes turn into pneumonia.

He hated having to dress for those occasions. One of the reasons he later resigned from his position as chairman of the republic was his disaffection with the National Day and May Day celebrations. He wanted to be relieved of the burdens of ceremony and official formality. The decision in the mid-1960s to celebrate National Day only once every five years was not motivated, as he claimed, by a concern for wasteful expenditures. During the Cultural Revolution, at the height of the internal struggle for power, Mao went eight times to Tiananmen to review millions of Red Guards from all over the country at a far greater cost than any National or May Day celebration. In his struggles against his political opposition, cost was of no concern to Mao. After Lin Biao's disastrous abortive flight to the Soviet Union in September 1971, Mao never participated in the celebrations again.

On May Day 1955, however, Mao still reveled in the excitement, and the twinge I felt over the cost of the extravaganza quickly evaporated in my elation at being there.

Nonetheless, I was looking forward after the day's excitement to returning home to my family. But that was not to be. Mao, I was astonished to learn, was hosting a dance. Ballroom dancing had been prohibited after the revolution as decadent and bourgeois, and the dance halls had been closed. But behind the walls of Zhongnanhai, in the huge Spring Lotus Chamber (Chunou Zhai), just to the northwest of his walled compound, Mao held dancing parties once a week. When he returned from the evening of fireworks, Mao planned to spend the night dancing and I was expected to join.

I walked into the huge chamber with Mao. Immediately, he was surrounded by a dozen or so attentive, attractive young women from the Cultural Work Troupe of the Central Garrison Corps, flirting with him and begging him to dance. A band from the Cultural Work Troupe was performing Western music—fox-trots, waltzes, and tangos—and Mao danced with each of the young girls in turn, his ballroom style a slow, ponderous walk. After each dance, his young female partner would sit with him and chat, only to be replaced by a new one a few minutes later. Jiang Qing was not there that evening, having left not long before for Hangzhou, but Zhu De and Liu Shaoqi were. Only Mao and the other two party leaders sat at tables. The hundred or so others, most of them cadres from the General Office and young people from the Cultural Work Troupe, sat in chairs lining the walls of the huge ballroom. Since I was young, Mao's doctor, and one of the few men in the room, the young women invited me to dance, too.

Periodically, the Western dance music would stop and the room would fill with the sounds of Beijing opera. Beijing opera is a folk tradition rather than high art, and the stories it tells are often earthy, filled with intrigue, romance, and deceit. Some are pornographic. The music itself can be distressing to Western ears—loud and cacophonous, the antithesis of Western dance music. I was surprised that night to hear tunes from *Shushan Qijie,* an opera about a prostitute who falls in love with a student, and even more astonished when Mao took to the floor as it was playing to indulge in his form of Western ballroom dance.

As the evening wore on, my presence seemed superfluous. I assumed that my responsibilities for the day were over. When I went to Li Yinqiao to tell him I was leaving, the bodyguard warned me to stay. "Please don't go," he said. "Chairman may be dancing, but he is still paying attention to his staff. He knows who is around and who is not. If you leave now, he will think that you and I don't get along well, and I will be blamed."

"But how could that be?" I wondered. "There are no problems between us."

"Yes, but you don't understand Chairman yet. You will understand after you have worked here for a while."

Li Yinqiao was right. Even when he was relaxing, Mao knew where everyone was and insisted that they be nearby. A year later, in Hangzhou, I was tired and went to my room to rest rather than attend the dance the party committee had organized on Mao's behalf. Just as I was settling in, there was a knock on my door. One of Mao's bodyguards was standing there. "Chairman wondered if the other guard failed to tell you about the party," he said. "You'd better come." Still later, in 1958, in Hunan, when I decided to forgo the evening entertainment because of a heavy downpour, the director of Hunan's public security came personally, at Mao's direction, to escort me to the performance. Thus I learned never to miss one of Mao's parties.

It would be several years before I understood the purpose of these dancing parties. The Cultural Work Troupe of the Central Garrison Corps had been organized to provide entertainment not only for the Central Garrison Corps but also for Mao. The troupe contained a pool of young women, selected for their looks, their artistic talent, and their political reliability. Over time, the role of these dancing parties, and of some of the young women who participated in them, became too obvious for me to ignore.

In 1961, one of Mao's specially made beds was moved to the room adjacent to the ballroom where Mao would retire to "rest" during the course of an evening of dance. I often watched him take a young woman by the hand, escort her to the room, and close the door behind them.

Peng Dehuai, a vice-chairman of the Military Affairs Commission, had criticized Mao's use of the Cultural Work Troupe twice, once in 1953 and again at a politburo meeting in 1957. Peng was the frankest, most honest man on the politburo, the only top leader who consistently dared to confront Mao. He accused him of behaving like an emperor, with a harem of three thousand concubines, and criticized Luo Ruiqing and others as well. The Cultural Work Troupe was disbanded, but Mao continued to have plenty of female partners. Dancing girls from other cultural troupes—from the Beijing Military Region, the air force, the special railway division, the Second Artillery Corps, and from the provinces of Zhejiang, Jiangxi, and Hubei—came to serve him. So did many young, attractive, and politically reliable women from the Bureau of Confidential Matters.

I knew none of this at that first dancing party on May Day 1955. I knew only that I wanted to go home to my family. But the dance did not end until two o'clock in the morning. I declined Wang Dongxing's offer to join him for a snack and hurried home to Lillian, who had waited up.

As we shared a bowl of fried rice, she told me how disappointed she was that the family holiday had passed without me. My mother had prepared a huge feast, and they had waited until ten o'clock before finally eating. My son, John, had been so tired that he fell asleep at my mother's and was spending the night there.

Less than a week had passed since my first meeting with Mao and already my whole life had changed. My regular schedule had been turned upside down. "You've already picked up Chairman Mao's habits," Lillian said. From that point on, for more than two decades, my life with Lillian and my family would never be the same. I loved Lillian very much, but I was rarely at home. We had once looked forward to our holidays—National Day, May Day, Chinese New Year—and the whole family usually spent them with my mother, but in all the time I worked for Mao, we were never again able to celebrate together, and in twenty-two years I had only one weeklong vacation.

Mao's schedule often required me to be with him through the early hours of the morning, so I could return home only just before dawn. Lillian would often wait up for me, and she was always worried.

Mao traveled constantly, and I accompanied him wherever he went, sometimes staying away for months at a time, occasionally not returning for an entire year. Lillian was particularly anxious during these extended trips, unable to eat or sleep well. My second son, Erchong, was born while I was away in 1956.

Not only were we often separated, but Lillian was excluded from my life in the inner circle even when I was in Beijing. She never became a party member. Because of her family background and prior work with the British and Americans, she was considered irredeemably unreliable politically. Only my own position as Mao's doctor protected her in the series of devastating political campaigns that were to destroy so many lives.

During those years, she sacrificed herself to make my own work easier, carrying the entire burden of our household, caring for both our children and my aged mother. Lillian had returned to China a vivacious and outgoing young woman, full of energy and zest for life. But she changed over time, and the changes were painful to watch. Gradually, with her constant worry over my job, her pain at being excluded from so much in new China, and her own difficulty finding work, she became quiet and withdrawn. "We live like drifters," she would say. "Our family is really no family." Her spark seemed to die.

8

In mid-July 1955, some six weeks after standing with Mao atop Tian-anmen, I was summoned unexpectedly to Beidaihe, the resort town on the Bohai Gulf where the top party leadership retreated each summer to escape the Beijing heat. Mao and his entourage had left only a few days earlier, accompanied by Zhou Zezhao, the doctor I had been appointed to replace. I was still working as director of the Zhongnan-hai Clinic and was not yet traveling with the Chairman. That I should be summoned so urgently meant something was wrong.

I took the special train that went back and forth daily carrying official documents and ferrying officials and staff and arrived in Bei-daihe the same day I had been called.

Mao, I learned, had had difficulty sleeping the night before and rose early for a morning swim. His bodyguards had tried to dissuade him. Beidaihe had been struck during the night by a spectacular thun-derstorm. The wind was still high, and the sea was choppy. The guards were afraid Mao could drown in such turbulent waters. Mao insisted, however, and headed for the beach with his guards trailing behind.

The guards had alerted Wang Dongxing, who rushed to the shore and tried to talk Mao out of his adventure. Mao ignored them all, plunging into the stormy waters and swimming determinedly out to sea with a flock of strong young bodyguards paddling quickly behind.

Wang Dongxing was desperate. If anything should happen to the Chairman, he would be responsible. He called Luo Ruiqing and Zhou Enlai, hoping to pass responsibility for the Chairman's safety up the ladder to them. Mao was already far out to sea by the time the two leaders arrived. Zhou, in exasperation, immediately reported the incident to still higher levels—to Liu Shaoqi, second only to Mao—hoping that Liu could persuade the Chairman not to risk his life. Liu refused to intervene. He was either too smart or too reticent to attempt to thwart Mao's will.

Jiang Qing was also at the beach and so was Dr. Zhou. Jiang Qing was furious with the physician, a diffident man, then in his fifties, some twenty years my senior. "The Chairman just swam into the storm," she yelled. "If he gets in trouble, what are you going to do? Just stand there?" But Dr. Zhou did not know how to swim.

Two soldiers helped the doctor into a small lifeboat and tried to row to Mao. But the waves were so strong the soldiers could not maneuver, and the doctor became hopelessly seasick. Mao had already returned from his swim while the doctor's boat continued to battle the waves. When the shaken doctor finally returned to shore, he climbed unsteadily out of the boat, collapsed on the sand, and vomited. Jiang Qing was furious. It was then that she sent for me.

Mao was furious with Wang Dongxing. "You bastard!" he cursed him. "You should know that I can swim under these conditions. But you not only tried to stop me yourself, you tried to intimidate me by getting the other party leaders involved."

Wang Dongxing and Luo Ruiqing were not only Mao's protectors. They were his loyal and devoted followers. But they were faced with an insoluble dilemma. They were responsible for the Chairman's safety. If anything went wrong, their loyalty would not matter, nor would the fact that Mao himself had ignored their pleas not to risk his life. They could lose not only their jobs but their lives.

But Mao saw their efforts as an infringement on his freedom, and he resented the idea that other members of the politburo were trying to rein him in. His will would not be thwarted, and he was quick to lash out at anyone who tried. The Beidaihe episode was a turning point in Mao's relations with Wang Dongxing and Luo Ruiqing. His anger would fester for years, until he finally turned against them both.

The episode was a turning point for me as well. At the end of the summer, Dr. Zhou was quietly relieved of his duties, leaving Zhongnanhai to become head of Beijing Hospital, and I became Mao's exclusive personal physician. My job was not merely to treat Mao's illnesses but to keep him as healthy as possible. If he ever got a disease that could have been prevented or suffered needless pain or discomfort, the blame would be mine. Thus my job and my life were constantly on the line, and I had to be alert to any changes in the Chairman's health.

To do this, I had to know him intimately, to be with him constantly. When Mao returned from Beidaihe, I began seeing him every day. The excuse we often used was his study of English. I accompanied him wherever he went, in Beijing and out.

I needed to conduct a medical exam both as a benchmark against future changes and because I had noticed in Mao's medical records that his white blood cell count had been higher than normal for the past two years—a little over 10,000cmm. rather than the normal 6,000–8,000. The Chairman was suffering from a chronic mild infection and I had to find out why.

I was reluctant to raise the topic with Mao. He prided himself on his physical prowess and hated to be sick, and I knew he had an aversion to doctors. In 1951, a team of Soviet physicians had examined him, poking and prodding for so long that Mao had lost his temper.

I took the opportunity of our English lesson—we were reading Engels's *Socialism: Utopian and Scientific*—to broach the subject, explaining to Mao that his high white blood cell count indicated a minor infection.

"Why?" Mao wanted to know. He was almost completely ignorant of modern medicine.

"It's nothing serious," I said. "I just need to find out where the infection is." I told him I would examine his sinuses, teeth, throat, and prostate and assured him the exam would be brief—no longer than half an hour. He agreed.

Nothing was wrong with his nose and sinuses. I looked into his mouth. Mao never brushed his teeth. Like many peasants from southern China, he simply used tea to rinse out his mouth when he woke, eating the leaves after drinking the water. He had resisted all attempts to get him to see a dentist. Peng Dehuai, the straight-talking military leader who so openly spoke his mind to Mao, had already suggested that I encourage the Chairman to improve his oral hygiene. "The Chairman's teeth look like they are coated with green paint," he had told me, and as I looked into Mao's mouth, I saw that his teeth were covered with a heavy greenish film. A few of them seemed loose. I touched the gums lightly and some pus oozed out. He had never complained of discomfort, even though an infection of that sort ordinarily causes considerable pain. I suspect that Mao had a high tolerance of discomfort and so hated doctors and illness that he often endured his pain in silence.

"Can you do something about it?" Mao wanted to know when I explained the problem. I said that my medical training did not include dentistry, and I advised him to see a dentist.

Mao smiled. "Confucius said, 'To know what you know and what you don't know, that is true knowledge.' It seems you don't pretend to know things you don't."

I examined his prostate. His foreskin was exceptionally tight and difficult to pull back, and I was concerned about the possibility of infection. Mao had stopped bathing after he moved to Zhongnanhai. He considered it a waste of time. Instead, his attendants rubbed him down with a hot, wet towel every night as he reviewed documents, read, or talked.

I noted, too, that the left testicle was smaller than normal and that his right testicle was not in the scrotum or groin. An undescended testicle, a congenital defect where the testicle remains in the abdomen, does not affect sexual function but does increase the likelihood of testicular cancer. I would have to watch this abnormality.

I needed a sample of Mao's semen to test for further infection. His prostate was small and soft. I massaged it to extract the secretion for laboratory tests.

A few days later, Mao let me arrange for a dentist from Beijing Medical College, Dr. Zhang Guangyan, to treat him. Zhang had been a schoolmate of mine, two years my senior, at West China Union University Medical School's department of dentistry.

The dental procedure, like Mao's haircut, was to be performed in the dining room of the Chrysanthemum Fragrance Study, the high-backed wicker chair transformed for the occasion into a dentist's chair. Zhang was nervous as he laid out his equipment, asking what my own examination had revealed and wondering about the Chairman's habits and temperament. Having assumed my post only a few months earlier, I had no great insight to share. "I do know that he likes things done quickly and without too much talk," I said, and assured him that since Mao had agreed to see him, he would make every effort to cooperate.

The Chairman was reading a history book when we went to meet him. He often held a book when greeting guests. Mao, for all his power, was sometimes ill at ease when he met people for the first time, and he knew that guests, viewing him as a demigod, were also nervous in his presence. The book was a way for him to relax and open the conversation. He liked to help people relax by telling jokes and making small talk, and he was good at this. At first meetings, he was usually attentive and humorous. By putting people at ease, he could coax them to speak frankly. It was a way of gathering information.

"Ah, so you've arrived," Mao said when he saw us. He put the book aside. "Reading can really carry you away." He stood up and shook hands with Dr. Zhang, then motioned for us to sit.

We were served tea. A bodyguard handed Mao a hot towel, which he used to wipe his face and, meticulously, to clean his hands.

Mao asked Zhang's given name. The dentist explained that it was *guang yan*—*guang* meaning "to glorify" and *yan* meaning "the Han people." China is a multi-ethnic nation, but the dominant race, some 93 percent of the population, is the Han—the group most people associate with "Chinese."

"So you intend to glorify the Han people," Mao responded. "Your name would have been very popular during the campaign against the Manchus in the last days of the Qing dynasty." The Qing dynasty that collapsed in 1911 had been non-Han, run by the Manchus from north of the Great Wall. Much of the anti-Qing sentiment had been racial, directed at the fact that the dynasty was ethnically "foreign."

When Mao asked where Zhang was from, he explained that he was originally from the province of Hebei, meaning "north of the river," but that he had lived in the province of Sichuan, meaning "four rivers," for many years.

"Ah, Hebei province. Do you know what river 'north of the river' refers to?" Mao asked.

"Yes, the Yellow River," the dentist replied. The Yellow River has changed its course many times in Chinese history and was just south of Hebei when the province received its name. Today, the river at the same longitude is much further south, flowing through Shandong.

Mao lit a cigarette. "And in Sichuan," he continued, "what are the four rivers?"

Zhang responded without thinking. "The Min, the Tuo, the Jialing, and the Jinsha," he said.

Mao corrected Zhang with a smile. "The last one is not the Jinsha River, I believe. It's the Wu River, which is much larger than the Jinsha."

Zhang smiled too. "I was thinking of one of your poems about Sichuan, which has a line, 'The waters of the Jinsha River hit the cloud-covered banks.' So I thought the Jinsha must be one of the four rivers."

Mao laughed. "It's only a poem."

Mao began talking about West China Union University Medical School, which had been funded by the United States, and the fact that Zhang had actually studied in America. Mao was delighted by this. "During the war against Japan, the United States sent a military mission to Yanan," Mao said, "and we all got along very well. An

American physician named Dr. George Hatem came and stayed with us for good and has made great contributions to our campaign to eliminate venereal disease. He is in the same profession as you." Dr. Hatem (1910–1988) had gone to the party's northern base in Baoan, Shaanxi, with Edgar Snow in 1936, staying in China and serving as a physician.

"The United States has also trained many skilled technicians for China," Mao continued, a remark that would have been unthinkable for ordinary Chinese. The United States was still publicly reviled as China's Enemy Number One and to praise it was counterrevolutionary. "So all of you belong to the British-American school," Mao said. "I like people trained in England and the United States." He told Dr. Zhang that he was studying English with me. "We're reading Engels's *Socialism: Utopian and Scientific. Shehuizhuyi* is pronounced 'socialism' in English, isn't it?"

"Yes, that's right," Zhang replied.

Seeing that Mao's banter seemed to have calmed Zhang's nerves, I suggested we begin the checkup. Mao agreed.

Zhang cleaned Mao's teeth, removing the heavy layer of plaque and accumulated food residue. "Chairman, you need to brush your teeth every day," Zhang suggested. "There was too much plaque."

"No," Mao protested. "I clean my teeth with tea. I never brush them. A tiger never brushes his teeth. Why are a tiger's teeth so sharp?"

Mao's logic was often unorthodox. Zhang and I were speechless.

Mao winked at his small victory. "See, there are a lot of things you doctors can't explain."

"Quite a lot," Zhang agreed politely. He told Mao that one of his upper left teeth needed to be extracted. "The gum surrounding the tooth is full of pus, and it is very loose. If the tooth isn't taken out, the teeth next to it could be affected, too."

"Is it really that serious?" Mao wanted to know.

"Yes, I wouldn't dare fool you," Zhang replied.

"Okay. But I'm afraid of pain. Use a lot of anesthetic."

Zhang turned to me and whispered, "Is the Chairman allergic to Novocain?"

"No," I responded. Mao had already had quite a few shots of both penicillin and Novocain. He had never been allergic.

"Do we really need an anesthetic?" Zhang continued in a whisper. "I can easily pull out the tooth."

"I think we'd better use it," I replied. "He'll be less nervous."

Dr. Zhang used the Novocain, and the tooth came out with a gentle yank.

Mao was delighted. "The British-American school has scored a great victory!" he shouted.

A few days later, Mao's white blood cell count had returned to normal.

Again, Mao was pleased. "You solved a problem that had been with me for several years," he said. "You have scored a great victory! Long live the British-American school!" he repeated. He asked me to get him a toothbrush and toothpaste and began brushing his teeth. But after a few days, he stopped. Rinsing his mouth with tea was deeply ingrained, one of many peasant habits that he would never change. Besides, Mao did not like routine, even in such basic matters as washing his face and brushing his teeth.

As the years went by, the problems with his teeth continued and so did his aversion to dentists. His teeth became blackened and began falling out. By the early 1970s, all his upper back teeth were gone. Fortunately, his lips usually covered the remaining few teeth even when he talked and smiled, so the absence of so many and the color of the few that remained were not often noticed.

The laboratory tests from the prostate examination came back, revealing that he was infertile. The sperm were dead. Mao had fathered several children by his three wives, and the last of them, his daughter with Jiang Qing, Li Na, was then some fifteen years old. The infertility apparently had begun sometime in mid-life, for reasons I was never able to discern. But the problem could not be corrected.

"So I've become a eunuch, haven't I?" was Mao's response when I told him about his infertility. He was genuinely concerned.

"No, not at all," I replied. Most eunuchs serving in the imperial courts had been deprived of their entire genitalia, though some had lost only their testicles.

I soon saw that Mao lacked even rudimentary knowledge of the workings of the human reproductive system. Our discussion was the first he knew of his undescended right testicle, but neither that abnormality nor his infertility made him in any sense a eunuch.

I tried to explain. "Your sperm are abnormal, and this makes you infertile. But you still have normal sexual desires and normal sexual potency. This will not be affected by your abnormal sperm."

Then I realized that Mao was not worried about his infertility but was afraid of becoming impotent. He had long believed that sexual activity is confined to the period between twelve and sixty. His own sexual experiences, I would learn later, had begun when he was still a teenager in his hometown of Shaoshan, and he was fond of recalling a youthful sexual encounter with a pretty twelve-year-old village girl.

Mao had turned sixty in December 1953, and when I came to work for him in 1955, he feared the end of his sexual activity was approaching. He had begun to experience bouts of impotency and linked sexual desire to health. So long as he wanted sex, he was healthy. My predecessors had given him frequent injections of an extract of ground deer antlers, an aphrodisiac according to traditional Chinese medicine, but his impotency persisted and he worried greatly. He was determined to stay alive, healthy, and sexually active until eighty, and one of my jobs was to help him do that.

Thus he was exasperated when I cautioned him against using deer antlers. I had no idea what effect they had and wanted to be sure they were harmless. "You doctors!" Mao responded. "One of you says this; another says that. I am only going to listen to doctors seventy percent of the time."

Mao did not insist on the shots of ground deer antlers, but he did demand that I find some other treatment for his impotency and his longevity. In this, as in so many other matters, he followed the tradition of Chinese emperors. The legendary first emperor of China, the Yellow Emperor, father of the Han race and the man from whom all other Chinese are said to have descended, is reputed to have become immortal by making love with a thousand young virgins. Emperors ever after have believed that the more sex partners they have, the longer they will live—hence their thousands of concubines. Qin Shi-huangdi, the founding emperor of the Qin dynasty, with whom Mao often identified, is said to have sent a Daoist priest and five hundred virgin children across the sea in search of the elixir of immortality. Legend says that the Japanese are their descendants.

Shortly after I began working for him, Mao heard that a Romanian physician, a woman named Lepshinskaya, had a new formula that would lengthen life, enhance sexual potency, and renew overall strength and endurance when taken daily by injection in small doses. Mao was interested, but he wanted me to test the drug first. If it worked for me, he said, he would take it himself.

I pointed to the difference in our ages—I was only thirty-five and he was sixty-two—assuring him that I was still young and vigorous, untroubled by the symptoms that bothered him. Dr. Lepshinskaya called her formula vitamin H3, but the substance was merely Novocain. While I did not believe in such allegedly magic potions, I knew Mao was not allergic to Novocain, and therefore had no strong medical objections to letting him test it. He took vitamin H3, injected in the buttocks, for about three months and then stopped for lack of results.

In all the years I worked for him, I was never able to educate Mao in medicine. His thinking remained pre-scientific. As a Western-trained doctor, however, I suspected that the bouts of impotency that so concerned him were more psychological than physiological. After consulting a number of urologists and neurologists and assuring myself he had no physical problem, I began treating him with a placebo. I prescribed some capsules of glucose and ginseng and gave them to him under the guise of a "body-building tonic."

In time I could see that Mao's problem with impotence was most pronounced when he was embroiled in a political struggle whose outcome was uncertain. By the early 1960s, as his power rose to new heights, he rarely complained about impotence. At the height of the Cultural Revolution, in the late 1960s, he and Jiang Qing were sexually estranged, but Mao had no problems with the young women he brought to his bed—their numbers increasing and their average ages declining as Mao attempted to add years to his life according to the imperial formula.

Even as Mao searched for an elixir of long life, he never really doubted that his life would be extraordinarily long. He believed the couplet he had written as a youth proclaiming that he would live two hundred years and swim against the current three thousand *li*.* Mao's remarks to foreigners in the mid-1960s that he was preparing to meet God—or Marx—were mere strategic tricks. Mao had never been healthier than at the beginning of the Cultural Revolution, and his health remained good for several years thereafter. Mao often took to his bed when he was the object of political attack, but he also used ill health as a political ploy. Mao's health and the country's politics were often intertwined.

Mao was not above feigning ill health, either, and in 1963, at a low point in Sino-Soviet relations, he put on a great dramatic performance before the Soviet ambassador to China as a way of testing Soviet reaction to his possible death. He first rehearsed his act several times in front of me and other members of the staff, covering himself with a terry-cloth blanket, feigning lethargy and pain, pretending to have great difficulty talking. "Do I look like I'm sick?" he wanted to know. Then he called the Soviet envoy to his bedside and staged an excellent dramatic performance.

Similarly, in 1965, when Mao told his old friend the journalist Edgar Snow that he was going soon to meet God, he was testing the

*A *li* is a third of a mile.

U.S. government's response to his death and trying to foster a change in U.S. policy toward China. Mao was convinced that Snow, whose *Red Star over China* had become a classic in both Chinese and English, was a CIA agent and a conduit of information to the highest levels of the American government. And in 1965, when Mao told French culture minister André Malraux that he did not have long to live, he really wanted to watch European reaction to the news.

Mao frequently accused others of fomenting conspiracies, but he was the greatest manipulator of all.

9

Most of Mao's medical problems during the first years of my service were minor—common colds and occasional bronchitis, itchy skin, corns on his feet, or lack of appetite. He was so frequently constipated that one of his bodyguards administered an enema every two or three days, and his bowel movements were a daily topic of discussion. A normal bowel movement became cause for celebration among his staff.

For me, however, the most nerve-racking problem was Mao's persistent insomnia.

He was a man of tremendous energy. In his iconoclasm and refusal to accept routine, Mao rebeled against time as well. Sleep, like bathing, was a waste of time. His body refused to be set to the twenty-four-hour day. He stayed awake longer than others, and much of his activity took place at night. If he went to bed one day at midnight, the next night he might not sleep until three in the morning, and the day after that he would not sleep until six. His waking hours grew longer and longer until he would stay awake for twenty-four, or even thirty-six or forty-eight, hours at a stretch. Then he could sleep ten or twelve hours continuously, and no amount of noise or commotion would wake him. I am not sure when the pattern began. Possibly, his biological clock had always been askew. Fu Lianzhang talked about treating him for insomnia in the early 1930s. Certainly, the two decades of revolutionary struggle before the establishment of the People's Republic and the many years of guerrilla war would have upset anyone's normal sleep patterns.

When he wanted to sleep but could not, Mao would turn to physical activity to wear himself out—swimming, dancing, walking. But he was also addicted to sleeping pills and had been for more than twenty years before I became his doctor. Fu Lianzhang had given him Veronal in the 1930s, and after 1949 prescribed sodium amytal, a powerful barbiturate, in 0.1 gram gelatin capsules. When one pill was not effective, Mao would take two, three, or four. Often nothing worked. As he grew more tired, he would become more hyperactive and would start to wobble on his feet. His staff worried that he might fall or suffer a stroke.

Even before I took up my post, Fu worried that Mao might accidentally overdose on barbiturates. Secretly, without telling Mao, he had reduced the sodium amytal in the capsules from the original 0.1 gram to between 0.05 and 0.075 grams, but Mao's response was simply to take more tablets.

I was extremely distressed to learn that Mao was taking barbiturates. I had never prescribed such powerful drugs for a patient, and I, too, was worried about the possibility of an overdose. When I first learned of his habit, I warned Mao not to take the drugs. "Then you don't want me to sleep," he said, and insisted on continuing the medication. I had no way to stop him. He was my boss and refused to listen to me.

Then one day he called me into his room. "How many days do you think there are in a year?" he asked.

It was another of his unorthodox questions. "Three hundred and sixty-five, of course."

"Well, for me there are only two hundred days, because I get so little sleep," he said.

I was puzzled until I realized that he was talking about the number of cycles of waking and sleeping he went through in any given year. "If you count your days by your waking hours, Chairman, you have more than four hundred days in your year. If you look at it this way, your life is like the immortal described in the poem—'there are no sun and moon in the hills, a thousand years slip by unnoticed.' "

Mao roared with laughter. "If you are right, then insomnia would be a means to longevity!" He was joking, but I knew that he wanted me to do something to relieve his insomnia.

I recommended a change in strategy. While the sodium amytal prescribed by Fu Lianzhang was effective in inducing prolonged sleep, it was slow to take effect. I suggested that Mao take two 0.1 gram capsules of sodium seconal twenty minutes before his last meal of the day, which would put him to sleep quickly. After the meal, he would take one capsule of the sodium amytal to prolong his sleep. Moreover, I disagreed with Fu Lianzhang's method of secretly reducing the dosage without telling Mao. I thought Mao should be told frankly what type and amount of medicine he was taking. The medicine was being dispensed by his bodyguards, simple and uneducated young peasants with no knowledge of medicine, and with Mao's health now my responsibility, I wanted to make certain they did not give him too much.

Since Fu Lianzhang was still my boss, I first presented my suggestions to him. He agreed. But when I assured Mao that the new method would work better, he was skeptical. "A boasting doctor has no effective medicine," he said, quoting a popular folk saying. But he agreed to try.

The new prescription did improve Mao's sleep and soon I was able to reduce the amount of sodium seconal, filling the capsule with more glucose, still to good effect. When I told Mao, he said, "Your medicine bag is full of skimpy capsules, but they still work."

But sometimes Mao became so agitated that even my method became useless.

In fact, Mao suffered from two different types of insomnia. His biological time clock really was different, but he also suffered from what we called neurasthenia.

Though neurasthenia is no longer a recognized disease in the United States, its symptoms, by whatever name, were very common in China, and both Mao and Jiang Qing frequently suffered from them. Neurasthenia is usually induced by some sort of psychological malaise, but because admitting to psychological distress is simply too shameful for most Chinese, its manifestations are usually physical. Insomnia is the most frequent symptom of neurasthenia. Headaches, chronic pain, dizziness, anxiety attacks, high blood pressure, depression, impotence, skin problems, intestinal upsets, anorexia, and bad temper are others.

In time, I came to regard neurasthenia as a peculiarly communist disease, the result of being trapped in a system with no escape. I first became aware of the syndrome in 1952, when my elder brother suffered from severe neurasthenia, with high blood pressure as its major symptom, after being attacked during the "three-anti" campaign. After the campaign against the rightists in 1957, when so many innocent people were falsely accused, the incidence of neurasthenia increased dramatically. I had not been aware of such a high incidence of neurasthenia under the Guomindang government. Under the Guomindang, no matter how bad things got, it was always possible to run away. Under the communists, there was nowhere to go. Major psychoses, such as schizophrenia or manic depression, were more or less acceptable under the communist system, but minor psychological troubles fell under the category of "ideological problems." For a Chinese to see a psychiatrist because of personal problems would be such an unbearable loss of face that treatment for such things did not even exist while Mao was alive. Every doctor knew that behind his patient's neurasthenia was some great personal difficulty. But the doctor's response was to treat the patient medically rather than inquire into the roots of the illness.

I never used the term *neurasthenia* when confronted with Mao's anxieties. Mao would have resented this and I would have been summarily dismissed. Nor did he himself use the word. When Mao took to his bed with depression, he would simply say that he was unhappy and ask me to help, which I would do by prescribing ginseng and vitamins B and C. Mao's neurasthenia manifested itself in a variety of symptoms—insomnia, dizziness, itchiness, impotence. At its very worst, he suffered from anxiety attacks. Once, in an open field, he suddenly became disoriented and would have fallen except for the help of his bodyguards. Such attacks occurred occasionally at public functions. Once Mao was meeting with an African delegation when several members of the group surrounded him, talking with great animation, gesturing and pointing at the Chairman. I could see him begin to totter, and an aide came immediately to his rescue. Wherever he went, whenever he walked or received guests, an aide was always next to him in case he lost his balance. When he was relaxed, his symptoms disappeared, and none of the many examinations I ordered of his heart, brain, or inner ear indicated any physical problem.

The underlying cause of Mao's neurasthenia was different from that of ordinary people. As the most powerful leader in the country, he was the cause of others' personal problems. Mao's neurasthenia was rooted in his continuing fear that other ranking leaders were not loyal to him and that there were few within the party whom he could genuinely trust. The symptoms became much more severe at the beginning of a major political struggle. While Mao was plotting his strategy and until he finally got his way, his sleep would be interrupted for weeks and months at a time. What I did not know when I took over as Mao's doctor was that he was then locked in a struggle over the question of agricultural collectivization and that the sleeplessness I was dealing with was a result of this political battle.

Mao's goal was to transform China—the sooner, the more thoroughly, the better. He was not satisfied with the rural reforms that had been carried out in the early 1950s, just after the establishment of the People's Republic, when land and farm tools were seized from the rich and distributed to the poor. Private ownership still prevailed. Mao wanted socialism, and that meant agricultural collectives. He did not want to wait for agricultural mechanization, for China was too poor and mechanization would take too long.

Cooperatives had been introduced into China's rural areas as early as 1953, but the rapid pace of the movement and the tendency to establish unmanageably large collectives and to deprive peasants of their tools and animals had been opposed both by the peasants and by many of Mao's lieutenants. In some parts of the country, the collectives were being abolished almost as quickly as they were formed, and Deng Zihui, the director of the Rural Work Department, was giving the orders for dissolution. Mao was furious with both Deng Zihui and other party officials he saw as thwarting his plan. Mao forced Deng Zihui to step aside and later abolished his Rural Work Department and demoted Deng to a meaningless position. "Deng Zihui supported us during the democratic revolution," Mao told me later, referring to the period during the civil war when the party followed moderate policies of land reform, "but after liberation he went another way." The disagreements had been particularly intense during the summer of 1955, when the party leaders were gathered at Beidaihe and Mao took his defiant swim, and they continued through the fall.

I scrupulously avoided politics when I first worked for Mao and did not realize as I was worrying about his white blood cell count, his impotence, and his insomnia that he was spending most of his time plotting a counterattack against the more conservative members of the party. Throughout the fall and winter of 1955–56, he held a series of meetings to promote his notion of socialist transformation, and in late fall and early winter he began working on a book, *Socialist Upsurge in China's Countryside,* gathering reports on collectivization from all over the country, editing and writing introductions to the articles himself, calling for a rapid socialist transformation of the rural areas. It was his attack on the central party leadership, a way of pushing the party toward rapid socialization, and during this time he became agitated and unable to sleep.

One day in the late fall of 1955, while still working on the book, Mao went for three days with only fitful sleep and then stayed awake for more than thirty hours straight. The sleeping pills I had given him no longer worked. He tried to exhaust himself by swimming. Then he sent for me.

He was lying on a chaise longue when I arrived at the indoor swimming pool and looked flushed, excited, and worn out. I politely refused his offer to take a swim myself, explaining that I didn't even have time for lunch—I was still working in the Zhongnanhai Clinic—

let alone for a swim. "I haven't eaten either," he said smiling, "and I haven't slept. I swam for an hour. I have taken sleeping pills three times and I still can't sleep. Are you giving me those skimpy capsules again?"

"No, the capsules are full-strength," I assured him.

"Well, what can you do to get me some sleep?"

I suggested liquid chloral hydrate, even though Fu Lianzhang had told me that Mao did not like liquid medicine. I explained that the medicine would taste bitter—a bit hot and biting.

"That's okay," he said. "I like hot things."

I went to the pharmacy in Gongxian Lane, where Fu Lianzhang continued to control the drugs for Mao and the other ranking leaders, relying on a company in Hong Kong to supply medicines and medical supplies from the United States, England, and Japan. As an additional measure of safety, Mao's drugs were always prescribed under the pseudonym Li Desheng. He had taken the name, meaning "Li of superior morality," when the party was forced to evacuate Yanan in 1947 in the face of Guomindang attack. As the pharmacist was filling Mao's prescription, Fu Lianzhang rushed in to warn me that the Chairman did not like liquid medicine and that chloral hydrate does not taste good. "If Chairman gets angry about this, what are we supposed to do?" he wanted to know.

"I have explained everything to Chairman, Vice-Minister Fu," I responded. "He wants to try it. He's waiting for me. I have to hurry. I'll let you know later how it goes." I turned to leave.

"How can you be so rash—not even consulting me first?" he called after me. Fu Lianzhang took his position as my boss seriously and wanted to be involved in every decision involving Mao's health. He took great pride in his longstanding relationship with Mao and was convinced both that he understood the party chairman and that Mao would always welcome and follow his advice. But Fu was no longer in regular contact with Mao. Mao and I were developing our own relationship.

The Chairman was waiting at the swimming pool, expecting me to join him for dinner. "It would be best to take the medicine first, before dinner," I told him.

I poured fifteen milliliters of 10 percent chloral hydrate into a cup and he drank it down in one gulp. He said it did not taste so bad, that he did not usually drink wine, but that this stuff tasted like wine. "Let's see if it works," he said.

As we ate and the medicine began taking effect, Mao began drifting into euphoria. By the end of the meal, he was ready to sleep, so tired that he did not even return to his residence at the Chrysanthe-mum Fragrance Study. He lay down on the bed by the side of the swimming pool, fell asleep at around two in the afternoon, and slept for ten hours straight.

His guard summoned me in the middle of the night and told me that my cannon had hit the bull's-eye.

Mao was still resting, his eyes closed, when I arrived. Opening his eyes, he lit a cigarette. "What is this miracle drug?" he wanted to know. "It's wonderful!"

"It was one of the first medicines used to induce sleep," I told him. "Chloral hydrate first became popular in the nineteenth century and its effects are well known. Clinical studies show it to be very safe."

"Then why didn't you give it to me earlier?"

"I knew Chairman does not like liquid medicines," I explained. "Besides, it doesn't taste good. So I didn't suggest it until I felt it absolutely necessary." In fact, there is no great difference in the efficacy of sodium amytal and chloral hydrate. He was near exhaustion when he summoned me, and my description of the drug's potency had had a decided psychological effect.

I think Mao knew that the causes of his neurasthenia were as much psychological as physiological, and he understood the power of placebos. Once, when he had been very ill as a child, his mother took him to a Buddhist temple to pray and burn incense for her ailing son. Mao had recovered. "I am opposed to destroying Buddhist temples," he would tell me, even as Buddhist temples all over China were being demolished by party leaders. "Poor people need to rely on their idols when they are sick. When they beseech Buddha for a cure, all they get are the ashes from the incense they burn. But incense ashes ease their mind and help them back to health. Don't sleeping pills work the same way? Don't they just ease the mind?

"So you've kept a lot of tricks in that medicine bag of. yours, huh?" Mao teased. "Okay, go home now and get some sleep. I'll start to work."

From then on, Mao relied on chloral hydrate to sleep, often taking it with sodium seconal. In time, he became addicted to the medication not only because it put him to sleep but because it stimu-lated his appetite and made him euphoric as well. Then he became addicted to the euphoria, taking the pills when receiving guests and attending meetings. He also took them for his dance parties.

10

I remained disengaged from politics, ignorant of the growing tension between Mao and the central leadership. But by early 1956, I was beginning to sense that the Chairman was in the grips of a gnawing, still inchoate political malaise. Looking back, I know that 1956 was a turning point, the year that the seeds of the Cultural Revolution, the massive political upheaval that would convulse the country a decade later, were sown. Khrushchev's secret speech against Stalin at the Soviet Union's Twentieth Party Congress in February 1956 was the watershed.

Mao did not attend the Moscow meeting. Zhu De, the grandfatherly founder, together with Mao, of the Red Army and the wartime commander in chief of the guerrilla forces, headed the delegation instead. Zhu De was about seventy then, a kindly old man with thick black hair and a ready smile. He had no political ambition. He had gone into semi-retirement after liberation, serving largely in honorary roles—as a vice-chairman of the Central People's Government Council (1949–54), as vice-president of the republic (1954–59), and as a vice-chairman of the National Defense Council. He devoted his time to official inspection trips and to raising orchids in his Zhongnanhai greenhouse—he had over a thousand flowers in all. His position as vice-president of the People's Republic was a sinecure, but we still called him commander in chief and he continued to be greatly respected by all Chinese for his role in bringing the Communist party to power. Zhu De had not been prepared for Khrushchev's attack, and when he cabled Mao with the news and asked for instructions on how to respond, the former military commander suggested that China support Khrushchev's critique. Mao was furious. "Zhu De is an ignorant man," he fumed. "Khrushchev and Zhu De are both unreliable."

Mao had an almost mystical faith in the role of the leader. He never doubted that his leadership, and only his leadership, would save and transform China. He was China's Stalin, and everyone knew it. He shared the popular perception that he was the country's messiah. Khrushchev's attack against Stalin forced Mao to the defensive, threatened to undermine his rule, and called his own leadership into question. For Mao to agree to the attack against Stalin was to admit that attacks against himself were permissible as well. This he could never allow. In 1953, after Stalin's death, Mao had welcomed Khrushchev's assumption of Soviet leadership. Following his attack on Stalin, though, Mao turned bitterly hostile, convinced that the new Soviet leader had violated a fundamental tenet of revolutionary morality— that of unswerving loyalty. Khrushchev owed his own position to Stalin. He had turned against the very man who had made him what he was.

And he saw Khrushchev's attack as playing into the hands of the Americans—the imperialist camp. "He's just handing the sword to others, helping the tigers harm us," Mao complained. "If they don't want the sword, we do. We can make the best use of it. The Soviet Union may attack Stalin, but we will not. Not only that, we will continue to support him."

I had always admired Stalin. He was to the Soviet Union what Mao was to China—the great leader and savior. But Mao's refusal to accept de-Stalinization had nothing to do with his respect for the man. In fact, Mao despised Stalin. I was shocked, listening to Mao describe the history of his relations with the late Soviet leader, to hear that he and Stalin had in fact never gotten along. No doubt the history that Mao imparted to me in early 1956 was colored by his anger. Only now do I realize that Mao often lied to suit his political ends.

Mao had a deep-seated personal antagonism toward Stalin that traced back to the days of the Jiangxi soviet, in the early 1930s.

In 1924, when the Chinese Communist party was barely three years old, the Comintern had directed the new party to form a political alliance with the Guomindang. China was in chaos, with no real central government, and the Comintern wanted the Chinese communists to cooperate with the nationalists to overthrow the regional warlords and unite the country under a single rule. A united front was established, but in 1927, Chiang Kai-shek turned ferociously against the urban-based communists, decimating the party in the cities. Mao returned to the countryside of his native Hunan, where he witnessed peasants in revolt. Traditional Chinese rebellions had often emanated from the countryside, and Mao was convinced from this experience that the twentieth-century Chinese revolution would also be rural, relying on the peasantry as the leading force. He proposed a daring strategy, unorthodox in Marxist-Leninist terms but well suited to China's historical conditions: He wanted the Communist party to lead the peasant revolts. Mao established a rural base in the remote and backward mountains of Jiangxi province, where he set about mustering peasant support, working to reform the rural landholding system while launching guerrilla attacks on Chiang Kai-shek's forces, hoping eventually to so weaken the nationalists that the peasants could take over the cities. Gradually, under Mao's leadership, the Jiangxi soviet expanded.

In 1930, Stalin appointed Wang Ming, then only twenty-five years old and fresh from several years of study in the Soviet Union, as his Comintern representative in China. Wang Ming himself never took over leadership of the Chinese Communist party, but his faction, according to Mao, did and then insisted on returning the locus of revolutionary activity from the countryside to the city, leading the still weakened communists into battles they could ill afford to fight. Mao was labeled a conservative by the international communist camp and pushed aside. "A turnip, that's what Stalin called me—red on the outside but white on the inside," Mao said.

The Jiangxi soviet began to flounder. Chiang Kai-shek encircled the mountain base area and launched a series of deadly military assaults—"extermination campaigns," Chiang called them. The campaigns nearly succeeded. With Chiang's fifth attack on the Jiangxi soviet, the annihilation of the Communist party was imminent. It was then that the party made the decision to break out of the encirclement and begin the epic retreat that came to be known as the Long March. Only en route was Mao's leadership restored.

Mao blamed Stalin and the Comintern for the party's early disasters. He thought the Comintern had taken a good situation and turned it into a mess. "In the Guomindang-controlled areas of China then," he said, "our losses were one hundred percent. In the soviet base areas, our losses were ninety percent. But we didn't blame Stalin or the Soviet Union for the disaster. We blamed our own comrades for their errors of ideological dogmatism." Wang Ming, the faithful follower of Stalin's line, rather than Stalin himself, was blamed for the disasters, charged by Mao with being a "left adventurist."

Mao also accused Stalin of bowing before American might after the Second World War, trying to convince the Chinese Communist party to follow the example of the French, Italian, and Greek Communist parties by surrendering its guns to the government—the Guomindang. Mao refused. During the civil war between the nationalists and the communists, Stalin offered no help, refusing to give the communist forces a single gun or bullet, "not even a fart," Mao said. Stalin had urged them to stop their campaign north of the Yangtze River and allow the Guomindang control over the south. "We didn't pay attention to him," Mao said.

I had always heard that much of the weaponry the Chinese communist forces used during the civil war was from the Soviet Union, left behind when the Soviets evacuated Manchuria at the end of the Second World War. Mao, though, could not admit that the Soviets had helped at all, and I was in no position to argue.

He said that when the communists took over the Guomindang capital in Nanjing and Chiang Kai-shek was forced to flee to Guangzhou (Canton), the embassies of England and the United States remained in Nanjing, prepared to do business with the new government. The Soviets, however, supported the Guomindang, moving their embassy with Chiang to Guangzhou, refusing to have anything to do with the communists. Stalin, Mao said, did not want the communists to win.

"Then in the winter of 1949, only months after liberation, I went to the Soviet Union for negotiations," Mao continued. "But Stalin didn't trust me. He let me stay there for two months without negotiating. So finally I got mad and said, 'If you don't want to negotiate, then let's not negotiate. I'll go home.' That was how the Sino-Soviet Treaty of Friendship, Alliance and Mutual Assistance was finally concluded."

The Korean War was yet another source of tension between Mao and Stalin. I had always thought that China and the Soviet Union had cooperated during the war, but Mao insisted they had not. "During the Korean War, when the American army reached the border between China and Korea at the Yalu River, I told Stalin we had to send our forces down there to fight," Mao said. But Stalin had said no. He thought it would be the beginning of the Third World War. Mao had told Stalin that if he did not want to fight and if the Americans conquered all of Korea, both China and the Soviet Union would be threatened—like teeth getting chilled through broken lips. Mao would fight anyway, but he wanted Soviet weapons. If the Soviet Union was afraid of being accused by the United States and England of assisting China, then China would buy the weapons from the Soviet Union.

China would do its own fighting and not involve the Soviet Union in any other way. Mao also accused Stalin of trying to further divide China by supporting Gao Gang, trying to make Gao the emperor of Manchuria, hoping to create a separate communist party there.

Mao's assertions astonished me. By all public accounts, the Soviet Union was China's big brother, the model for our own socialist development. China and the Soviet Union were the closest of allies. But the relationship in reality, Mao said, was more like that of emperor and subject. "They're trying to eat us up," he said. Mao refused to be subject to anyone. History had taught him to befriend distant states and be wary of those that are near, and he continued to distrust Soviet expansionism.

But Mao never allowed his complaints to become public. The legitimacy of his own revolutionary leadership was still too closely linked to Stalin.

Khrushchev's speech was a watershed in China's domestic politics, too. Zhu De's suggestion that China support the attack on Stalin was a terrible affront to Mao. I never believed that Zhu De was a threat to Mao and always felt Mao's anger against him was misplaced. But Mao and Zhu had clashed once before, in Jiangxi, and Mao insisted that Zhu De's initial stance on Khrushchev's speech was "a reflection of his personal character." He remained suspicious of Zhu De's loyalty.

On May Day 1956, two months after Khrushchev's speech and Mao's outburst against the commander in chief, Zhu De was taken ill. His health should have prevented him from attending the festivities atop Tiananmen. But the May Day photograph of China's ranking leaders was an important political scorecard, and Zhu De was worried about the public message his absence would send. "If I don't go," he told Ren Bishi's widow, my friend Chen Zongying, "people will say I have committed some terrible political mistake and was not allowed to attend." Zhu De, pale and drawn, was present when the photograph was taken, assuming his official place in the political lineup not far from Chairman Mao.

Mao never forgave Khrushchev for attacking Stalin. But as 1956 progressed, I saw how dissatisfied he was with the leadership of his own Communist party. At first he focused on what he saw as their obsequious, uncreative imitation of the Soviets.

By 1956, much in China had already been borrowed from the Soviet Union. A massive state bureaucracy, extending down to the rural townships, had been established under the direct control of the Communist party. Agricultural collectivization was complete, and major factories and shops in the cities were under state control. Smaller, less developed handicraft factories and shops had also been collectivized or taken over by local governments. Economically and bureaucratically, the socialist transformation seemed complete.

But the transformation of the spirit, the dynamic rebirth of China that Mao sought, was more elusive. With the massive bureaucracy in place, onetime revolutionaries had become bureaucrats themselves, more devoted to their own comfort and the social status quo than to Mao's revolutionary ideal. Mao was impatient. He wanted to move quickly, continuing the revolution. But the party bureaucrats, including ranking leaders, preached caution, clinging to the notion of gradual development, in accordance with the Soviet model. Their emulation of the Soviet Union, Mao thought, lacked creativity. Institutions and organizational arrangements were being copied without regard to the special circumstances of China. Mao was irritated with his own lieutenants.

Mao's revolution demanded daring, verve, and struggle and Mao felt that China's other party leaders lacked these qualities. That some of them had even agreed with Khrushchev's attack on Stalin was a challenge to his leadership. Mao's guard was up. He did not want any of his underlings becoming Chinese Khrushchevs after his death, writing "black reports" attacking him. He was constantly alert to attempts to undermine his rule.

It was this disaffection with his own party that would fester for years and grow, leading finally to the catastrophe of the Cultural Revolution.

11

Mao described himself best. I am *heshang dasan,* he told Edgar Snow in 1970, literally meaning "a monk holding an umbrella." But *heshang dasan* is only the first half of a couplet. The second, more important and meaningful, half, *wufa wutian*—is always left unsaid. The sound *wufa wutian,* meaning "without hair, without sky," is the same as an expression that means "without law, without god"—a man subject to the laws of neither man nor god. Mao's interpreter that day was a young woman without a classical education, and she translated the Chairman's self-description as "a lonely monk walking the world with a leaky umbrella." Edgar Snow and numerous scholars after him concluded that Mao had a tragic, lonely view of himself. Nothing could have been further from the truth. Mao was trying to tell Edgar Snow that he was a god and law unto himself, *wufa wutian.*

"I graduated from the University of Outlaws," Mao used to tell me. He was a consummate rebel. He rebelled against all authority and had to be in control of every situation—from decisions at the highest reaches of political power to the most mundane details of his everyday life. Nothing that occurred within Zhongnanhai happened without his consent, not even the clothing chosen for his wife to wear, and he expected to be consulted on every major decision in China.

It is true, though, that Mao had no friends and was isolated from normal human contact. He spent little time with his wife and even less with his children. So far as I could tell, despite his initial friendliness at first meetings, Mao was devoid of human feeling, incapable of love, friendship, or warmth. Once, in Shanghai, I was sitting next to the Chairman during a performance when a young acrobat—a child—suddenly slipped and was seriously injured. The crowd was aghast, transfixed by the tragedy, and the child's mother was inconsolable. But Mao continued talking and laughing without concern, as though nothing had happened. Nor, to my knowledge, did he ever inquire about the fate of the young performer.

I never understood his apparent callousness. Perhaps he had seen so many people die that he had become inured to human suffering. His first wife, Yang Kaihui, had been executed by the Guomindang, and so had his two brothers. His elder son had been killed during the Korean War. Several other children had been lost during the Long March in the mid-1930s and never found. But I never saw him express any emotion over those losses. The fact that he had lived while so many others died seemed only to confirm his belief that his life would be long. As for those who had died, he would simply say that "lives have to be sacrificed for the cause of revolution."

Mao was never isolated from information, however. While he spent much of his time in bed and often went days without dressing, he read constantly and was always soliciting reports, both written and oral, from everyone around him, seeking to know all that he could about what was going on everywhere in China and the world, from the petty machinations within his inner court to the remote areas of the country to the far-flung reaches of the globe.

He hated protocol and ritual. Shortly after becoming head of state in 1949, when his chief of protocol, Yu Xinqing, suggested that Mao follow international convention by wearing a dark-colored suit and black leather shoes when receiving foreign ambassadors, Mao rebelled. "We Chinese have our own customs," he insisted. "Why should we follow others?" He began wearing what we then called the Sun Yat-sen suit and a pair of brown leather shoes. When other leaders imitated their Chairman, the name of the outfit changed. The gray "Mao suit" became the uniform of the day. The protocol chief who had had the temerity to suggest that Mao act in accordance with international protocol was fired. He committed suicide during the Cultural Revolution.

Mao saw schedule and routine, protocol and ritual, as a means to control him, and he refused to be subordinate to them. He reveled in his own unpredictability. When he went for a walk, he would always return by a different route. He never retraced his steps, never took the same path twice. He was always in search of the new, the untested, the untried, both in his private life and in the affairs of the nation.

What fascinated him most and absorbed much of his time was Chinese history. "We have to learn from the past to serve the present," he often said. He had read the twenty-four dynastic histories—the series of official chronicles compiled by each new dynasty for the one it had just defeated and covering the years from 221 B.C. to A.D. 1644—numerous times.

But Mao's view of history was radically different from that of most Chinese. Morality had no place in Mao's politics. I was shocked to learn not only that Mao identified with China's emperors but that his greatest admiration was reserved for the most ruthless and cruel of our country's tyrants. He was willing to use the most brutal and tyrannical means to reach his goals.

One of the emperors Mao admired most was the Shang dynasty tyrant Emperor Zhou, who had reigned during the eleventh century B.C. The Chinese people have always regarded Emperor Zhou with revulsion, horrified by his cruelty. The lives of his subjects had meant nothing to Emperor Zhou, and he was in the habit of displaying the mutilated bodies of his victims as a warning to potential rebels. His swimming pool was filled with wine.

But Zhou's excesses were nothing compared to his contributions, Mao argued. Emperor Zhou, Mao pointed out, had greatly expanded China's territory, bringing the southeastern coastal area under his control and unifying many divergent tribes under a single rule. He had killed some loyal and able ministers, to be sure—the famous Bigan was the most notable example—but Bigan was killed because he had counseled against further expansion. Yes, Emperor Zhou had lived luxuriously. Of course he had had thousands of concubines, but what emperor had not?

Qin Shihuangdi (221–206 B.C.), the founding emperor of the Qin dynasty and of the imperial China that was to last for nearly two thousand years, the man credited with building the Great Wall, was another of Mao's favorites and the emperor with whom he was most often compared. Qin Shihuangdi, like Emperor Zhou, had expanded China's territory and consolidated a multitude of small countries into a single state. He had introduced unified measures and weights. He had constructed roads. But the Chinese people hated him because he had executed the Confucian scholars and burned the classic books. But Qin Shihuangdi killed the scholars, Mao argued, only because they got in the way of his efforts to unify China and build the Chinese empire. And he only killed 260 Confucian scholars. Where was the great tragedy in that? One ought not, in looking at Qin Shihuangdi, exaggerate the trivial and ignore the great.

Empress Wu Zetian (A.D. 627–705), one of the few women ever to attain supreme power in China, a rank to which Jiang Qing would later aspire, was also a favorite. When Mao asked my opinion of her, I responded honestly. "She was too suspicious, had too many informers, and killed too many people," I told him.

"Well, Wu Zetian was a social reformer," Mao said. "She promoted the interests of the medium and small landlords at the expense of the nobility and the big families. If she had not been suspicious, if she had not relied on informers, how could she have discovered the plots the nobles and the big families were hatching to overthrow her? And why shouldn't she execute the people who were plotting to kill her?"

Similarly with Emperor Sui Yangdi (A.D. 604–618). In the eyes of the Chinese people, Sui Yangdi was one of the worst. He liked women and drink and lived in decadent opulence, using beautiful young girls attached to silken cords to pull his pleasure boat upstream. Countless people died when Sui Yangdi ordered the building of the Grand Canal. But Mao ranked Sui Yangdi with the best. China's rivers all flow west to east. The Grand Canal linked the country north to south, serving as a belt to bind the country. Sui Yangdi was also a great unifier.

While Mao was most interested in Chinese history, he had also read something about the great leaders of the West. Napoleon was his favorite. Napoleon's concentrated use of cannon fire, in Mao's view, was a revolution in military strategy. The French general, moreover, combined military expansion with academic study, taking with him to Egypt not only soldiers but also scholars and scientists, who studied the origins of Western civilization. Mao wanted to organize similar studies in China and in 1964 planned a scholarly expedition to the source of the Yellow River, in remote Qinghai province. The Yellow River had long been considered the seat of Chinese civilization, and Mao wanted to trace that civilization back to its roots.

Wang Dongxing was put in charge of logistics and assembled a team of historians, geographers, geologists, water specialists, and engineers. He obtained horses from Inner Mongolia and supplies and equipment from the army, and Mao and I began practicing horseback riding together. Our trip, scheduled to begin on August 10, 1964, was canceled five days before that. Informed that the United States was sending more troops to Vietnam, Mao wanted to stay and monitor the situation, finally deciding to send Chinese soldiers—secretly, and wearing Vietnamese uniforms—to fight the United States.

·   ·   ·

Not only were Mao's views of history astonishing, they revealed a great deal about him. He used the stories of China's past both to understand and to manipulate the present and saw himself in terms of his own contributions to the country's ongoing history. I am convinced that the intrigues in China's ancient imperial courts were a far more powerful influence on his thought than Marxism-Leninism. True, Mao was a revolutionary. His aim was to transform China, to make it rich and powerful again. But he turned to the past for instruction on how to rule, for guidance on how to manipulate the conspiracies that plagued those in the highest reaches of power.

But Chinese history was little help in the type of transformation Mao sought. Chinese culture, Mao believed, was moribund and stagnant. His goal was to reinvigorate it, and this necessitated learning from abroad, adapting foreign ideas to the Chinese situation. He often said that the result would be "neither Chinese nor foreign, neither a donkey nor a horse, but a mule."

Socialism was Mao's means to unleash the creative energies of the Chinese people and thus to recapture China's ancient glory. He had to turn to the Soviet Union for inspiration because the Soviet Union was the preeminent socialist state, and from the very establishment of the People's Republic, Mao insisted that China "lean to one side." The Soviet Union was the model for China's new government to follow. But his vision of socialism was always socialism with Chinese characteristics, socialism for the wealth and glory of China, for the reawakening of Chinese culture, socialism creatively adapted to the Chinese case. Wholesale importation of foreign things without digestion and re-creation is no good, he often said. He never intended the Soviet model to be adapted uncritically, without modification.

Moreover he retained, from the first day I met him, an admiration for the technology, dynamism, and science of the United States and the West. His propensity to "lean to one side" was always tempered by a recognition that the Soviet Union was not the only potential source of lessons in revitalization.

Mao had grandiose ideas of his own place in history. He never had any doubt about his own role. He was the greatest leader, the greatest emperor, of them all—the man who had unified the country and would then transform it, the man who was restoring China to its original greatness. Mao never used the word *modernization* with me. He was not a modern man. Instead, he talked about making the country rich and returning it to its original glory. A rebel and iconoclast, he would dare to transform China and make it great. He would build his own Great Walls. His own greatness and China's were intertwined. All of

China was Mao's to experiment with as he wished. Mao *was* China, and he was suspicious of anyone who might challenge his place or whose vision differed from his. He was ruthless in disposing of his enemies. The life of his subjects was cheap.

I did not immediately understand, because it was so hard to accept, how willing Mao was to sacrifice his own citizens in order to achieve his goals. I had known as early as October 1954, from a meeting with India's prime minister Jawaharlal Nehru, that Mao considered the atom bomb a "paper tiger" and that he was willing that China lose millions of people in order to emerge victorious against the so-called imperialists. "The atom bomb is nothing to be afraid of," Mao told Nehru. "China has many people. They cannot be bombed out of existence. If someone else can drop an atomic bomb, I can too. The deaths of ten or twenty million people is nothing to be afraid of." Nehru was shocked.

In 1957, in a speech in Moscow, Mao said he was willing to lose 300 million people—half of China's population. Even if China lost half its population, Mao said, the country would suffer no great loss. We could produce more people.

It was not until the Great Leap Forward, when millions of Chinese began dying during the famine, that I became fully aware of how much Mao resembled the ruthless emperors he so admired. Mao knew that people were dying by the millions. He did not care.

During our early, shocking conversations about Chinese history, the lessons I drew were more immediate and personal. Mao's view of history held lessons for me as well. Mao was the center around which everyone else revolved. His will reigned supreme.

Loyalty, rather than principle, was the paramount virtue. From his subordinates his wife and female companions, his household staff, the political leaders with whom he ostensibly shared power—he demanded total and indivisible loyalty.

That loyalty was based less on trust than on dependence. Incapable himself of affection for others, Mao expected no such feelings toward him. Repeatedly in my years with Mao I watched him win loyalty from others in the same way he had won it from me.

He would begin by charming people, winning their trust, getting them to open up, to confess their faults—just as Big Beard Wang confessed that he had plotted to murder Mao and Xu Shiyou admitted that he had once been loyal to Zhang Guotao and I had told him about my problematic bourgeois past. Mao would then forgive them, save them, and make them feel safe. Thus redeemed, they became loyal.

His loyalists, in turn, would become dependent on him, and the longer they depended on him, the more they had to depend on him, the more impossible life outside his circle became. From the outside looking in, it was inconceivable that anyone serving the Chairman would want to leave, so greatly was Mao worshiped, so glorious was working for him considered to be. Only those who were not absolutely loyal to Mao could want to leave his circle; only those who were not loyal would be expelled. No one anywhere in China would dare shelter anyone suspected of being less than loyal to the party chairman.

Some were genuinely loyal, both because Mao had personally saved them and made them feel secure and because they saw him as the savior of all of China. But others were mere sycophants. Mao basked in the flattery, even when he suspected it was not sincere, knowing that over time he would be able to distinguish the genuine political loyalists from the sycophants. Those could be discarded when their usefulness was gone.

The slogan "Serve the People" was Mao's, and the message called out from billboards everywhere in China—white characters, written in Mao's own hand, set against a bright red background. Behind the elaborate Xinhua (New China) Gate, which served as the southern entrance to Zhongnanhai, the characters were inscribed in gold, and the billboard blocked any glimpse ordinary Chinese might get into the modern-day Forbidden City, where China's highest leaders lived and worked. Within Zhongnanhai, at our periodic "political study" sessions, we too were reminded to serve the people and the party rather than ourselves. The message had always inspired me. It was one of the reasons I had wanted so fervently to join the Communist party.

But I had not worked long for Mao before realizing that he was the center around which everything revolved, a precious treasure that had to be protected and coddled and wooed. Everything was done for Mao. He never had to raise a hand, never put on his own socks or shoes or trousers, never combed his own hair. When I pointed out to Wang Dongxing that the energies of Group One were focused not on serving the people but exclusively on serving Mao, he pointed out that "Serve the People" is an abstract expression. "We must have a concrete person to serve," he said. "To serve Mao, then, is to serve the people, isn't it? The party assigned you your work here. You are working for the party, aren't you?"

Young and naive as I was, I thought Wang Dongxing was right.

Later I would see that just as Mao condoned emperors who had been ruthless in dispensing with ministers who had not fully agreed with their views, so Mao could be ruthless in dispensing with those who did not fully agree with him. It is true that in the early years, top officials sometimes disagreed with Mao without being purged. But Mao harbored grudges, and when he convinced himself that an underling's loyalty had waned, when the political time was ripe, he could cast an old revolutionary aside without a second thought. Men like Zhou Enlai seemed to know this and were completely loyal to Mao. Others, like Liu Shaoqi and Lin Biao, did not and thus were cast aside. Whenever a leader became too independent of Mao, he was purged.

When Mao suspected that members of his staff were becoming too close to other leaders—whether Zhou Enlai, Lin Biao, or Liu Shaoqi—he would dismiss them immediately. "Disaster," Mao warned me, "comes by way of the mouth." Thus I knew that my survival depended on my silence. In the political campaigns that would sweep China over the next two decades, I took Mao's lessons to heart, confining myself to looking after the Chairman's health. I was his doctor. Even as I became aware of his ruthlessness, I protected myself by watching in silence. There was no independent will but his. I still worshiped Mao. He was China's guiding star, our country's savior, our tallest mountain, the leader of us all. I thought of China as one huge family and believed we needed a head. Chairman Mao was the chief. I would serve him and, through him, serve the Chinese people.

12

It was only when I began traveling with Mao that I began to understand the lavish and wasteful arrangements that were always made on
his behalf. No measure to protect his safety and health was too great.
His comfort and happiness were paramount. I knew that the arrangements for Mao's safety were elaborate, but in Zhongnanhai the security measures were so routine I barely noticed them. When we traveled,
the extravagances became obvious.

Mao traveled constantly. He was rarely in Beijing. He never felt
at home in the "northern capital." He was a southerner by both
inclination and birth, and Guangzhou (Canton), Hangzhou, Shanghai,
and Wuhan were his favorite cities. He would travel for months at a
time, returning to Beijing only for mandatory appearances on May
Day and National Day and for visits with foreign guests. He traveled
whimsically, too. If in the morning he decided to visit Hangzhou, we
could be on our way by afternoon. Even those of us traveling with him
were not told his ultimate destination, and though Mao might know
about the trip well in advance, we were ordinarily informed only the
night before. The security staff was afraid that word of his impending
departure might leak. Rarely did we have more than a day or two to
prepare.

He traveled ordinarily in his own private, elegantly appointed
train, eleven cars in all. It was housed in a special shed far away from
the central Beijing train station, another way of assuring that his
arrivals and departures took place in the utmost secrecy. Mao and

Jiang Qing each had a separate car, though Jiang Qing traveled with us only once. A third coach served as the dining room and kitchen. Mao's quarters were luxurious, outfitted with one of his huge wooden beds and a large supply of books, which took up much of the space.

Four dormitory cars crammed with bunk beds housed Mao's bodyguards, the armed guards from the Central Garrison Corps, the railroad staff responsible for maintenance, and his personal staff—photographers, confidential aides, and the chef who always accompanied him. Another car served as their dining room. One car was filled with emergency medical equipment, and another was a spare.

My only complaint about the train was the absence of air-conditioning, which made for sweltering summertime travel. But in the early 1960s Mao got a new train, built in East Germany and extremely luxurious, with recessed lighting, every conceivable modern appliance and, of course, air-conditioning. On the new train, Wang Dongxing, Mao's confidential secretary Lin Ke, and I had our private car, sharing a common living room. We had our own individual living compartments, which were large and comfortably furnished, each with a washbasin, table, bed, and hot running water.

Similarly astounding were the security precautions along the route. All train traffic along the entire rail line was stopped for the duration of Mao's journeys, and traffic throughout the country would often become so snarled that schedules did not return to normal for an entire week. Train stations, ordinarily teeming with frenzied travelers and vendors hawking their delicacies, were cleared of all but security personnel. Coming into empty train stations, seeing only sentries along the platforms, was always an eerie experience. When I and other members of the staff commented to Wang Dongxing on the unnatural absence of vendors, he arranged to add reality to the scene by having security personnel pose as vendors.

The leadership of each province through which Mao's train passed was responsible for the Chairman's safety while he was there, and each province provided a special driver and engine for that leg of the trip. When the train passed through a province, the local director of provincial public security had to be on the train until the next province was reached. Then the director of public security of that province would replace the previous one. In addition to guards from Beijing, who traveled on the train and stood watch nearby when it stopped, the provincial public security bureaus also provided troops to protect the route, and hundreds of sentries were posted at regular intervals, one every fifty meters, along the entire way. I once spoke to the director of a local security office on the rail line between Beijing and

Manzhouli—the town on the Manchurian border with the Soviet Union—who had stood watch during Mao's return from Moscow in January 1950. For two weeks in the dead of winter several hundred miles of the rail line had been guarded around the clock by soldiers and militiamen stationed every fifty meters. The guard himself had crouched for two weeks in a ditch along the route. Everyone knew that some top-ranking leaders would be passing through, but only much later did they learn that the train had been carrying Mao.

Mao had no schedule when he traveled, because the train moved only when he was awake and stopped while he was asleep. Since his sleep patterns were erratic, so was the progress of his train. When he slept, the train would pull into sidings within the walled compounds of military airports, railway yards, or factories. Protecting him was easier that way, and the factories were always emptied before his arrival.

Occasionally, Mao would fly. The first plane trip I took with him was in the summer of 1956. After he spent the winter working on *Socialist Upsurge in the Chinese Countryside,* visiting Hangzhou and Shanghai, and trying to push his plans for rapid agricultural collectivization, he wanted to fly—just for the experience of flying, he said. Mao had flown only once before, in August 1945, when U.S. ambassador Patrick Hurley brought him by American plane from Yanan to Chongqing to participate in the ill-fated negotiations between the communists and the nationalists aimed at preventing the outbreak of civil war.

Everyone responsible for his security was nervous about the flight, and the safety precautions were especially elaborate. Minister of public security Luo Ruiqing worked directly with the head of the Chinese air force, General Liu Yalou, to select, test-fly, and equip the plane—a Soviet-made LI-2, reputed to be the safest of the Soviet models.

On the morning of our departure, General Liu came personally to escort Mao and his entourage to the West Garden (Xiyuan) military airport in the western suburbs, not far from the Summer Palace. All air traffic everywhere in China was grounded for the duration of our flight, and several fighter planes patrolled our route. There were four planes in the entourage. Luo Ruiqing, Yang Shangkun, Wang Dongxing, and a coterie of secretaries, security guards, and aides took off first in another Soviet-made plane, an IL-14. Mao's two drivers, his chef, a photographer, two "food technicians," and more security guards were divided between two other planes. Other members of his staff, a retinue of some two hundred people, had been sent ahead on Mao's special train, together with his car—a bulletproof, armored Soviet-built luxury "ZIS" limousine built specially for him. His car was thus there to whisk him from the airport to his villa in Guangzhou, and the train sat in a shed at the White Cloud airport in case Mao should decide to continue his travels by rail.

Mao's plane, the LI-2, was small, with a single propeller. The original twenty-four seats had been removed and the entire interior remodeled. In the front were a bed, a small table, and two easy chairs for the Chairman. At the back were four other comfortable chairs for those of us accompanying him—two bodyguards, a confidential secretary, and me.

Air force colonel Hu Ping was our pilot.

"So I must trouble you with this flight," Mao greeted Colonel Hu when we boarded the plane, summoning his usual charm to put the pilot at ease.

"It is my great honor and good fortune to fly for Chairman," Hu Ping responded. I would soon discover a strong correlation between the flattery Mao received and the speed with which the flatterers were promoted. During the Cultural Revolution, Hu Ping rose to become chief of the headquarters of the air force general staff. In 1971, however, he would be implicated in Lin Biao's plot against Mao and jailed, and all record of his service to the Chairman expunged.

We made the journey in two legs, passing time in the air by studying English. Around noon, we stopped in Wuhan for lunch. We were greeted by an impressive array of local leaders, including provincial first party secretary Wang Renzhong and Wuhan municipal party leader Liu Kenong, who hosted an elaborate banquet in a magnificent guesthouse that had been a villa of Chiang Kai-shek's. Located on the city's scenic East Lake, the villa was just across from the famous Wuhan University, and the waiters, trained by the British and French in the foreign hotels that had been a feature of Wuhan before 1949, were gracious and attentive. The Wuchang silver carp, a favorite of Mao's, was delicious.

The trip gave me an opportunity to witness the elaborate flattery Mao received wherever he went, and Wang Renzhong's was particularly extravagant. "Stalin and the Chairman cannot be compared," he said to Mao. "Stalin killed so many people. But our party not only tolerated your rival Wang Ming but tried to maintain unity with him."

Mao responded warmly. "Of course we have to differentiate between contradictions within the ranks of the people and contradictions between us and the enemy," he said. "When dealing with contradictions within the ranks of the people, we must never arrest and kill people at random."

"This is possible only under the Chairman's leadership," Wang responded in what seemed to me to be calculated praise. Wang's political star continued to rise until the Cultural Revolution. He became one of its deputy directors when the movement began, plunging from grace only after insulting Jiang Qing by making a public speech without her explicit approval.

We arrived at Guangzhou's White Cloud airport at about six that evening, where our greeting was no less impressive. Guangdong's first party secretary, Tao Zhu, was there, together with provincial leader Chen Yu. Peering through the windows of the limousine to catch my first glimpse of Guangzhou as our cavalcade sped through, I was struck by the dirt and the clamor. Trash was strewn everywhere, and sewage flowed through the streets. The noise was a combination of the singsong chattering of Cantonese and wooden thongs clacking against the pavement.

Mao's presence in Guangzhou was a closely guarded secret, and the staff of Group One was sequestered, prohibited from leaving our enclave, making phone calls, or receiving visitors or mail. Our occasional letters home were sent through special couriers outside the regular mails. Only days before we left did Wang Dongxing finally send us sightseeing, with members of the Guangdong provincial security bureau as our guides.

Mao's comfort was second only to his safety.

The practice of confiscating elegant old villas and building new ones for the exclusive use of the party elite had begun shortly after the liberation of Beijing, when Yang Shangkun's General Office had five villas constructed for the top five leaders—Mao, Liu Shaoqi, Zhou Enlai, Zhu De, and Ren Bishi—in the Jade Spring Hills (Yuquanshan), near the Fragrant Hills. A swimming pool was added for Mao, built under the specifications of his non-swimmer guardians Luo Ruiqing and Wang Dongxing. With Mao's safety their paramount goal, the two security officers specified that the pool be only the length of two bathtubs and barely knee deep.

Mao was furious at being presented with such a useless toy, and his fury was only further fueled when the irrepressible Peng Dehuai spoke out at a politburo meeting against using state funds to indulge Mao's private pleasures. Mao used his private funds to reimburse the state for the pool's construction, but he never went near the villa.

The confiscation and construction of villas and pools continued in Beidaihe. In 1950, Yang Shangkun's General Office began expropriating old mansions there, assigning one villa to each of the ranking leaders. A brand-new one—designated Building 8—was constructed especially for Mao.

Then new villas started cropping up in other provinces, with provincial leaders competing to build the structure most closely in tune with Mao's tastes.

There were miscalculations. Assuming that modern was best, many provincial leaders provided Mao with soft Western-style mattresses and sit-down toilets. Mao countered by traveling with his own hard wooden bed and insisting on a squat-style privy. Even when he went to Moscow in 1949–50, Mao took along his own wooden bed, and during his visit in 1957 he squatted over a bedpan because the toilets in the Kremlin were all of the sitting variety.

Tao Zhu had been one of the first of the provincial leaders to construct a luxurious new villa for Mao and Jiang Qing, and he had been guilty of fewer miscalculations than other provincial leaders. Mao liked to visit Guangzhou.

The Islet (Xiao Dao) guesthouse where we stayed was a complex of villas situated on a small island flanked by two branches of the Pearl River. The grounds were luxuriant with sweetly scented flowers, banana trees, and tropical plants.

Three buildings at Xiao Dao were reserved especially for Mao. One was Dr. Sun Yat-sen's old villa, but because Tao Zhu considered it too small he had another, Building 1, constructed. It had separate bedrooms for Mao and Jiang Qing, with a spacious meeting room, large enough for showing movies, in between. A third building was for recreation, reading, and dining, and an Olympic-size swimming pool was built later. Villas 4, 5, and 6, located nearby, were ordinarily reserved for Liu Shaoqi, Zhou Enlai, and Zhu De. In June 1956, Luo Ruiqing, Yang Shangkun, Wang Dongxing, Mao's secretary Lin Ke, and I were housed there.

Security was always tighter in Guangzhou than elsewhere. Tao Zhu, Luo Ruiqing, and others in the public-security apparatus feared some sort of hostile intrusion from Hong Kong. The British colony, some ninety miles away, was teeming, they believed, with Guomindang spies and other subversive agents intent on doing the Chairman in. Armed soldiers from the Central Garrison Corps were posted all over the island. All river traffic was stopped, and patrol boats constantly circled, alert to possible intruders. With all this protection, the place was eerily silent. Only the tropical birds continued to sing.

Wang Dongxing's Central Garrison Corps had sent an entire company to Guangzhou, so Mao's retinue from Beijing alone totaled some two hundred people. Most were housed eight to ten to a room in a Guangdong public security bureau building located just at the end of the bridge that joined the islet with the mainland.

With such a large entourage, the capabilities of the Guangdong public security bureau and the staff at the Islet guesthouse were taxed to the limits. There was not enough space, equipment, or kitchen staff to accommodate us all. Mao's separate kitchen was well equipped and sanitary, posing no great difficulties in either health or management. The Chairman's food was flown in daily from Giant Mountain Farm in Beijing and prepared by Mao's chef. Mao often sampled the fine fruits and vegetables and the fish of Guangdong, but he still preferred his oily, spicy Hunan food to the more subtle Guangdong fare.

But the kitchen serving the security guards posed a real problem. There were no refrigerators, and with food for two hundred people sitting around in the heat, the risk of food poisoning was great. The trash was also difficult to manage, and garbage was an invitation to rats and disease.

Wang Dongxing assigned some of the personnel from Beijing to assist the Guangzhou kitchen staff, and a system for sanitation and purchasing and handling food was set up. I was put in charge of all medical work.

Wang Dongxing and Luo Ruiqing endeavored to shield Mao from the troubles his elaborate security staff were causing, but the Chairman could not help but notice. "You've got guards all over us, as if you're getting ready to confront a major enemy," he complained to Wang Dongxing. "You want to do everything yourself, as if you don't trust the local leaders, much less the masses." Mao never felt the same sense of threat as his security personnel. The masses, he knew, loved him. Who would want to do him harm?

Shortly after we arrived, Liu Shaoqi, Zhou Enlai, Zhu De, and Chen Yun also began arriving, followed by provincial and local-level leaders. Mao had called a meeting. The top leaders took up residence in the Islet guesthouse, and I moved to the public-security building across the bridge. The provincial and local-level leaders were scattered in several different guesthouses managed by the Guangzhou Military Region and the Guangdong provincial government.

Tao Zhu hosted a banquet to welcome the new arrivals, inviting Mao as guest of honor. Cantonese cuisine was one of the country's national treasures, he said, and he hoped that Mao would give it a try. But Mao could not be bothered by such social niceties and declined the invitation, deputizing Wang Dongxing, Ye Zilong, and me to represent him. He wanted me to report on the banquet.

An hour and a half before the banquet was to begin, I received a visit from Tian Chou, the chief of the office staff for the Central Bureau of Guards. He was alarmed. The food analysts had found cyanide in the food. The kitchen had been quarantined and the staff forbidden to leave. Wang Dongxing told me to go to the kitchen immediately.

When I arrived, the seven banquet tables were already elegantly set with white tablecloths, awaiting the arrival of the distinguished guests. I went to the laboratory in the room adjoining the kitchen where the two food analysts from Beijing were testing the various delicacies, the rice, and the drinks that were supposed to be served at the banquet. They were tense and perspiring heavily, but relieved to see me and anxious for my advice.

The deputy director of the Guangdong public security bureau, a man named Su, explained that the backgrounds of the people working in the kitchen had been checked many times and no one seemed to have any political problem. But he was worried. Hong Kong, with its thousands of spies, was too close. Maybe some "bad element" from there had managed to sneak in and slip poison in the food.

Only the bamboo shoots contained cyanide. The other dishes were fine. Bamboo shoots are a delicacy in China, and these had been grown right in one of the guesthouse gardens. I had fresh bamboo shoots dug out for further testing. Again the test showed a trace of cyanide. I ordered a car and went immediately to the library at Sun Yat-sen Medical College, a short drive from the guesthouse. Bamboo shoots, I discovered, naturally contain a trace of cyanide, but well within safe limits.

Tao Zhu was delighted with my discovery. Grinning, he took my hand and thanked me profusely, promising to honor me with a toast at the banquet.

The deputy director of the Guangdong public security bureau also thanked me profusely. "You have done us a great favor," he said. "A moment ago Secretary Tao was so upset he was going to discipline me and my staff. Now the whole thing has been cleared up, and the banquet can be held on time. Without you, we would have had a terrible problem on our hands."

When I stood up at the banquet to thank Tao Zhu for his toast, he turned to Wang Dongxing and repeated the old Chinese adage "a powerful general commands no weak soldiers." Wang was delighted with the compliment, proud that his choice of me to serve as Mao's doctor had been so publicly vindicated.

I went to see Mao as soon as the banquet was over. He was lying in bed reading a history of the Ming dynasty. I told him the story of the cyanide. He blamed the Soviet Union.

"I don't think it's such a great idea to copy everything indiscriminately from foreign countries," he said, referring to the food-tasting system, which, like the elaborate security arrangements, had been copied from China's big brother. "Now they're doing this food tasting not only in Beijing but in other parts of the country, too. It upsets everyone for no reason. Tell Wang Dongxing to stop it."

Wang was irritated that I had talked to Mao.

If I hadn't told him, someone else would have, I said. I knew that every time I greeted Mao he would begin by asking, "Any news?" and wanted to hear what was happening within his staff. If he had heard about the cyanide from someone else, the story could have been distorted, and he would have blamed me for not telling him sooner.

Wang knew I was right. And he knew he would be forced to institute changes in Mao's food-supply system.

Shortly thereafter, the two food laboratories and the tasting service in Beijing were abolished, and the Central Bureau of Guards turned management of the Jushan farm over to the city of Beijing. But the changes were largely cosmetic. Most of Mao's food continued to come from Jushan farm, even though the supply station was authorized to purchase Mao's food not only from there but from several other markets as well.

When I told Mao about the changes, he smiled. "When I say 'Learn from the Soviet Union,' we don't have to learn how to shit and piss from the Soviet Union too, do we? I'd rather not learn from the Soviet Union. I want to learn from the United States."

13

Jiang Qing was in Guangzhou, too, and we were in frequent contact.

"You'd better brief Jiang Qing on the Chairman's health," Mao's bodyguard Li Yinqiao had said to me only two days after we had arrived.

"Why?" I wanted to know. "Didn't we all see her the first day we got here?"

"If you don't, she'll say you look down on her," Li insisted.

I followed his advice. At nine that morning, I was ushered into her study in Sun Yat-sen's old villa, Building 2. She was seated, dressed in a pastel blue suit and white low-heeled leather shoes, her hair done up in a bun, reading *Reference Materials,** the highly confidential newsletter, circulated daily to the country's highest leaders, that contained important foreign and domestic news, completely uncensored, much of it from the foreign press. Jiang Qing had copied Mao's habit of greeting visitors with book in hand, but to considerably less effect. She only pretended to read, often waiting until the visitor's arrival had been announced before picking up her book.

She motioned for me to sit as I greeted her politely, remembering

*China at that time had three "internal" sources of news. *Reference News* (*cankao xiaoxi*) contained news from foreign newspapers and wire services as well as domestic reports from the New China News Agency that were not openly published. This was read by ordinary cadres. *Reference Materials* (*cankao ziliao*) was reserved for top leaders and contained news reports from foreign sources. *Internal Reference News* (*neibu cankao*) contained domestic Chinese news reports and was also reserved for top leaders.

the repeated admonitions of Li Yinqiao and the nurses that the Chairman's wife must be treated with special courtesy. "The Chairman's health is good," I told her. "His irregular schedule is unfortunate, but he has been living like this for a long time. If we forced him to change now, it could do more harm than good."

"You mean you think there is no need to persuade the Chairman to follow a regular schedule?" she inquired curtly.

"That's right," I responded. "Otherwise his insomnia might become worse."

"Isn't that something of a physician's opinion?" Her voice was full of sarcasm. Already the meeting was not going well.

"It is my opinion," I replied. I was, after all, a physician.

She raised her eyebrows and stared at me. "Have you reported your opinion to the Chairman?"

"I have."

Jiang Qing was taken aback. She began tapping her finger on the end table next to her. "And what did the Chairman say?" she demanded.

"The Chairman agreed with me. He said he is getting old and is no longer able to change his habits so easily," I explained.

She lowered her head for a moment, then lifted it, lightly patting her hair with her hand. I knew that Mao's habits greatly distressed his wife and that she would like to see them changed. But she could not afford to disagree with her husband. Jiang Qing was the most pathetically dependent, the most slavishly loyal, and the most unabashed flatterer of anyone in the inner circle. Without Mao she was nothing. "I agree with this opinion," she responded disingenuously. "In the past, a number of leaders have encouraged the Chairman to change his habits. I have not agreed." She smiled. Then she asked. "And what about his sleeping pills?"

"The Chairman has had insomnia for many years. The pills help him sleep, and he needs the rest."

"It looks as though you are not suggesting any changes," she responded.

"That's right—as long as he does not increase the dosage."

"No doctor, it seems to me, thinks it's such a good idea to take sleeping pills," she said, baiting me again. "Do you take them yourself?"

"No, I don't."

"You do not. You do know, don't you, that sleeping pills are harmful to one's health?" she asked superciliously.

"Of course it is best not to take any medicine if you can help it,"
I agreed. "But for years the Chairman has had this habit—"

"Did you tell the Chairman he can continue taking sleeping pills?"
she interrupted icily.

"Yes, I did. I have been calculating the Chairman's sleep pattern.
Every day he goes to sleep two or three hours later than the day before.
Sometimes he doesn't sleep for twenty-four or thirty-six hours. But
after going so long without sleep, he then sleeps for ten or twelve hours.
The cycle averages about five or six hours of sleep a day. The pattern
looks irregular at first, but actually it has a regularity of its own."

"Then why haven't you told me all this before?" she demanded.

My patience was wearing thin. "I have not had a chance," I
responded. "The Chairman has only recently told me this."

"All right. Let's stop here," Jiang Qing concluded coldly. "In the
future, when you have other ideas, let me know first before telling the
Chairman."

I had no intention of consulting with Jiang Qing first. She had no
way of controlling her husband and was trying to control me as a way
of exerting some small measure of power over Mao. If I consulted with
her before discussing the issues with Mao himself, I would have to do
things her way. I would not fall into her trap. I bade her a polite
goodbye while ignoring her command.

A heavy rain was falling when I left her study, so I waited in the
anteroom for it to stop. She walked out to find me still there. "You are
too reserved, Doctor," she said, her voice turning kind when I explained why I was waiting. "Come in and let's have a chat."

She asked about my schooling and then told me a story about
visiting a doctor in Shanghai when she was seriously ill. The doctor
had looked at her perfunctorily and prescribed some medication without even asking her to describe what ailed her. Jiang Qing had complained, but the doctor ignored her and encouraged her to leave. Jiang
Qing became angry. "You are just a running dog of Western capitalists," she had shouted at him. "The way you treat patients is shameful." She left without the medicine.

She paused for a moment after telling me the story. Then she
continued. "You Western-trained physicians are all alike. None of you
care about patients."

"Not all physicians are that way," I protested, still trying to be
polite. I tried to explain that many physicians make tremendous sacrifices on behalf of their patients.

"That's nothing but petit bourgeois humanitarianism," she shot back.

"But there are many moving stories . . ." I tried to explain. My protest was to no avail. Service to mankind without regard to class did not exist for Jiang Qing. She believed only in "revolutionary humanism," which could be practiced only by workers and peasants and meant confining aid to members of one's own class. Class enemies, the bourgeoisie, were not worthy of being cured.

But I believed in treating everyone regardless of class, whether friend or enemy. Jiang Qing could not believe this and certainly she did not consider it revolutionary humanitarianism but capitalistic and bad.

"You are a doctor and I am a patient," she answered me. "I don't like people debating me." Having stumbled unwittingly into a struggle with Mao's wife, I was summarily dismissed.

Later, Jiang Qing told one of her nurses that I was very arrogant. "He thumbed his nose at me today," Jiang Qing said. "I have never seen such a person. He is opinionated and stubborn and refuses to change his mind about anything. We're going to have to do something to get him."

I reported my conversation with Jiang Qing to Mao. "We don't object to humanitarianism in its entirety." Mao smiled. "We are simply opposed to practicing humanitarianism on the enemy." Jiang Qing, though more strident, had been reflecting Mao.

But he tried to make peace between us. "It looks as though Jiang Qing has something against you," he continued. "Why don't you say something to flatter her? That way she'll be happy."

Wang Dongxing concurred with Mao. He wanted me to show her more respect and seemed worried about the consequences if I did not. I suspected that he, too, had had problems with Jiang Qing.

Their advice surprised me. I had been taught to be sincere, to avoid courting favor through flattery.

I would not flatter her and to sympathize with her was difficult, but I was forced to try to understand her. She lived a life of luxury. Everything she wanted, she was given. But she had nothing to do. Her life had no meaning. Jiang Qing was adrift. Mao was both busy and indifferent to her, and she no longer shared his life. There was a twenty-year age gap between them, and their tastes and preferences were completely different. Jiang Qing insisted on schedule and routine; Mao rebelled against all regularity. Mao read voraciously. Jiang Qing was too impatient to read. Mao prided himself on his health and physical prowess; Jiang Qing wallowed in her illnesses. They would not even eat the same food. Mao relished his hot and spicy Hunan dishes while Jiang Qing insisted on either blandly cooked fish and vegetables or fancied herself a connoisseur of the "Western" food she had eaten in the Soviet Union—pot roast and caviar.

Efforts had been made to give her meaningful work. In 1949, she had been appointed deputy director of the Film Guidance Committee of the Ministry of Culture, but she had behaved so arrogantly, claiming to speak for Chairman Mao, that no one could get along with her. She was transferred to Yang Shangkun's General Office in Zhongnanhai as deputy director of the Office of Political Secretaries. Again she was so intimidating to everyone that Mao had ordered her to resign.

He appointed her one of his secretaries instead, putting her in charge of reading and compiling reports from *Reference Materials*. Not having time to read it himself, Mao relied on secretaries to scour the news and cull what was most important. It was a task most other leaders had also delegated to their wives.

Jiang Qing could often be seen with a copy of *Reference Materials,* but she rarely bothered to read it. When she did, she had no way to distinguish what was important, so her efforts were useless to Mao. Lin Ke actually compiled the reports.

Jiang Qing was what the Chinese call *xiao congming*—"penny wise"—clever at small details but muddled when it came to large matters, and devoid of analytic ability. She knew little of China's history and even less of the world beyond. She had heard of the major countries and a few of the most important world leaders, but her knowledge was limited. She knew nothing, for instance, about Spain— where it was, its political past, its current leadership. She frequently missed the point of what she read. She once told me that England was not as feudalistic as China because it had often been ruled by queens. Since Chinese paternalism was regarded as feudalistic, rule by a woman constituted modernity, she thought. Despite her ear for the Beijing accent, her knowledge of the Chinese language was limited, although she hid her ignorance of words she did not know by pretending to ask how they were pronounced in the Beijing dialect. Looking up words in a dictionary was too burdensome for her.

Despite her own intellectual shortcomings, she was fond of mocking the deficiencies of others. Mao had once teased me by claiming that I had learned all my history from Beijing opera—an insult that impelled me to a more systematic and determined reading of China's past. But Jiang Qing continued to delight in Mao's comment long after the joke had worn thin, often repeating it to me sarcastically.

Mao was perturbed by his wife's indifference to history and current events and often sent her books, documents, and compilations of the news, demanding that she study the same official documents he did. Always, she demurred.

She watched imported movies from Hong Kong instead. She watched movies incessantly—morning, afternoon, and evening. She was sick, she said. Jiang Qing was always sick. She watched movies as a treatment for her neurasthenia.

In 1953, the Ministry of Public Health and the Central Bureau of Guards had responded to her malingering by assigning her a personal physician, Dr. Xu Tao. Xu Tao was originally Mao's physician, but since Mao was so vigorous and Jiang Qing was so ill, Xu Tao's services, Mao said, were better devoted to his wife.

Jiang Qing had made life miserable for Xu Tao, instigating the attacks against him during the 1954 campaign against counterrevolutionaries in Zhongnanhai and continuing her abuse after the campaign was over. In Guangzhou, he came under vicious slander again, accused of making improper sexual advances toward one of Jiang Qing's nurses.

The nurse was anemic and often felt dizzy and weak, so she asked Dr. Xu for a checkup shortly after Jiang Qing and her entourage arrived in Guangzhou. Dr. Xu conducted the examination in an anteroom of the guesthouse where they were staying. One of the bodyguards—an ignorant peasant youth of dubious morality, with no knowledge of medical etiquette and a peasant's suspicion of sex—somehow walked in during the course of the examination. The youth accused Dr. Xu of sexual impropriety.

Wang Dongxing, in charge of the bodyguards, was responsible for investigating the matter. He did not believe the accusation. He knew Xu Tao too well and thought that the young bodyguard was not only ignorant but deficient in character.

I, too, was shocked at the allegation. That Dr. Xu could have done such a thing was inconceivable. He was a cautious man, a bit stubborn perhaps, but he had a strong sense of morality. Besides, he had already been implicated as a member of the anti-party group and would surely do nothing so foolish as to destroy his entire future. I defended him at the meeting Wang Dongxing was forced to call, pointing out that Dr. Xu's personal integrity and professional career were at stake. We had no right to saddle him with a completely unsubstantiated charge.

In the end, even Mao defended the doctor's integrity. Dr. Xu was exonerated and his accuser was fired—probably the first time ever that a member of Mao's medical staff was fairly treated in a clash with the security personnel.

But Jiang Qing's harassment of her doctor was unrelenting. She assigned him the task of screening all her movies, demanding that he select only those that would relax her and allow her to sleep. When she did not like one of his selections—and often she did not—she accused him of mental torture. Xu pleaded to be relieved of the responsibility. A doctor ought not to be required to screen films, he said, but Jiang Qing insisted. Watching movies was a treatment for her neurasthenia, she argued, and screening the films was therefore a doctor's responsibility.

Jiang Qing's neurasthenia was the result of a life without meaning and her incessant fear that she would be abandoned by Mao. Her illness took the form of a general malaise and restiveness, an excessive sensitivity to noise and light, and an impossibly bad temper. She was an inveterate pill-taker, but she also tried to take solace through psychological escape. Movies were her main form of escape.

But Jiang Qing did not like most of the movies she saw and her critiques were often scathing. She had a way of taking a perfectly good movie and making it impossible for others to enjoy. She often watched *Gone With the Wind,* all the while deriding it as propaganda for the Southern slave system and accusing those of us who openly enjoyed the movie of being "stinking counterrevolutionaries." In the mid-1950s her words had little bite. Years later, during the Cultural Revolution, her vicious indictments would destroy careers and lives.

Even when she approved of Dr. Xu's movie selections, she still could not be satisfied. Sometimes the lighting on the screen was too bright, and she claimed it hurt her eyes. When the lighting was turned down, she could not see the picture. If the lighting was right, then something would be wrong with the temperature in the room.

The staff set up two rooms for her—one for watching movies and the other for sitting and resting. Just when the temperature and light in one room had been painstakingly adjusted to meet her demands, she would move back to the other. Never could all her demands be met at once. Whether the room was too bright or too dark, too cold or too hot, too stuffy or too drafty, the fault was always with her staff, whom she accused endlessly of torturing her.

When Guangzhou was struck by a brief cold wave, the staff assigned to stoke the coal furnace had to crawl past her sitting-room window on hands and knees lest the outside activity disturb her uneasy tranquility. When a guard argued with her about whether the tango has four steps or five, she ordered him to stand outside for two hours without moving. While en route back to Beijing, she ordered her plane to land in Jinan so she could put off her doctor and a guard with whom she had disagreed. Her continual demands kept five or six people constantly scurrying in response to her every whim. It was considered an honor to work for the Chairman's wife, but the level of distress and anxiety among those who served her was high indeed.

Later I would come to understand that it was her husband's incessant womanizing that was most distressing to Jiang Qing. Since I was in charge of her nurses, who were often attractive young women and easy prey for Mao, she occasionally urged me to warn them against becoming involved with her husband. Once in Zhongnanhai, I happened upon her crying on a park bench just outside Mao's compound. She urged me not to tell anyone about her tears, saying that just as no one, Stalin included, could win in a political battle with her husband, so no woman could ever win the battle for his love. Her greatest fear, which intensified over the years as his womanizing became more flagrant, was that her husband would leave her.

Mao made some effort to save Jiang's face where his many female companions were concerned, but as time went on, he became less careful. Several times Jiang Qing came upon her husband with other women, including one of her own nurses. She had always taken great pride in her beauty and her competence. Her husband's behavior hurt her deeply, but she could never openly display anger to Mao. She was too afraid that he would leave her. She was powerless to stop his philandering.

Mao knew this. "Jiang Qing is always worried that I may not want her anymore," he told me before I was fully aware of his philandering. "I've told her that this isn't true, but she just can't stop worrying. Don't you think that's odd?" Mao could not understand that Jiang Qing was actually hurt by his behavior, that no wife wants her husband to be involved with other women. Nor could he understand her continuing insecurity.

Isolated, lonely, and frustrated, she took out her frustrations on everyone around her. Whether it pained her I do not know, but Jiang Qing had to agree with Mao in every detail of all matters, and she would do nothing without his permission. Powerless before Mao, she used her position as his wife to lord it over her staff, and her insecurity made her mean and vicious. She often became upset with the security guards, because she knew that some of them were instrumental in procuring women for Mao. But because they worked directly for Mao and were under the supervision of Wang Dongxing, there was little she could do to harass them. Her personal staff usually suffered the brunt of her hostilities, and her medical staff was particularly hard hit.

Much as she accused others of torturing her, the fact is that she inflicted incessant mental torture on those around her. She seemed to believe that if she was unhappy, everyone around ought to suffer as well. Few of her staff stayed for long, asking to be transferred when they could stand her demands no more.

In the fall of 1956, Xu Tao asked to leave. After the campaign against counterrevolutionaries and the slander over his alleged sexual indiscretions, he had found escape by devoting himself to study, and he wanted to return to a hospital, where he could use and improve his medical skills. He went to Peking Union Medical Hospital, financed by the United States with money from the Rockefeller Foundation. It was one of the country's best hospitals. By that time, I envied him his release.

14

If Jiang Qing was the most dependent member of Mao's inner circle, Ye Zilong was the most useful. Everyone around Mao had a use.

Formally, Ye was the director of the Office of Confidential Secretaries and the head of Mao's small group of confidential secretaries—in charge of arranging and recording meetings and serving as Mao's chief steward, responsible for the personal details of Mao's life—his food, his clothing, his financial affairs.

Later I learned from Wang Dongxing, and from Ye Zilong himself, that he also helped with Mao's women friends. They came from several places, especially the Bureau of Confidential Matters and the Cultural Work Troupe of the Central Garrison Corps. The girls were young, innocent, uneducated, politically correct, and completely loyal to Mao.

Ye's home was right in Mao's compound—to facilitate his job as Mao's steward and confidential secretary. Many of Mao's women friends stayed in Ye's house awaiting their audience with the Chairman. Ye Zilong would arrange for the young women to enter Zhongnanhai. The women would then hide in Ye's house until Jiang Qing was safely asleep and Mao was ready to receive them. The young women were then led through the dining room and into Mao's bedchamber. In the early hours of the morning, they would be escorted out.

Ye was also in charge of the generously endowed special bank account Mao kept in the office of special accounts under the General

Office. By 1966, on the eve of the Cultural Revolution and before the little red book of Mao's quotations had sold hundreds of millions of copies, Mao had already earned 3 million *renminbi* from his *Selected Works* alone. Even in the 1950s, he was one of the richest men in China. He could afford to be generous with his money. He supported several of his former teachers, friends, and associates, assuring that they continued to live comfortably even after the new communist government had robbed them of their possessions and right to earn a livelihood. He used his money to show appreciation to the various women brought before him, too. Mao never touched money himself, so Ye Zilong was in charge of paying all these people—anywhere from a few hundred *renminbi* to a couple of thousand at a time.

I found Ye to be an unsavory man, ignorant and nearly illiterate. He was a peasant who had joined the party as a youth. He had started working for Mao in the late thirties, just after participating in the Long March. Before arriving in Beijing in 1949, he had never visited a city or used electricity or seen a neon light. The party's takeover of Beijing was a genuine liberation for him, and he was quick to credit Mao with having transported him in one gigantic leap from rural deprivation to a paradise of riches. He was not one of those simple peasants who unwittingly was tempted by the bright lights of the city. His character, I believe, was wanting long before he arrived in Beijing. What had been lacking in the past was the opportunity.

I had first come across Ye Zilong in the Zhongnanhai Clinic before I started to work for Mao, and I had never liked him. My first memory of him is from 1951, when Ye asked me for five vials of penicillin. He told me that one of his peasant relatives in Hunan had syphilis. The rural health clinic there had no modern drugs. But in those days China did not manufacture penicillin, and the two imported vials we had stored in the clinic were precious. To Ye's great consternation, I refused his request.

The head nurse in the clinic had been astonished. Ye was known even then to be very close to the Chairman and thus to have considerable clout. Most people would have tried to court Ye's favor by granting his request, and the nurse was certain I had offended him. It never occurred to me that my path would cross Ye's again or that we would be thrown into constant, almost daily, contact.

Like all of us in the early 1950s, Ye Zilong was on the free-supply system. He had no money for the luxuries he craved. But he was able to get what he wanted for free, since people were eager to ingratiate themselves with Mao's confidential secretary as a way to curry favor with the Chairman himself. When the party was teaching the virtues of simplicity and frugality, Ye could enjoy every pleasure, every luxury. When the elegant club for high-ranking cadres was established, Ye Zilong got to know the new managers, who regularly treated him, free of charge, to the best banquets the club could offer.

Guards charged with prohibiting ordinary Chinese from entering his favorite pleasure haunts—the exclusive high-cadres' club and the Beijing Hotel—never asked Ye for his pass. Anyone could tell that he was an important man, a high-ranking party official. Only his rough, uncultured speech revealed his peasant past. Otherwise, he cut a handsome figure. His skin was white and smooth, and when all of Beijing was wearing faded, patched, and baggy cotton, Ye was dressed in woolen Mao suits, well cut and perfectly tailored. Ye officiated when Mao was fitted for clothes, and the Chairman's grateful tailor supplied Ye's impressive wardrobe for free.

As chief steward, Ye was in charge of Mao's private storeroom, where the Chairman's many gifts were kept, in much the same manner that trusted eunuchs had managed such treasures during imperial days. Mao was generous in disbursing his gifts—everyone within the inner circle had been a recipient—and Wang Dongxing told me that Ye's East German cameras, Swiss watches, and Japanese-made transistor radio came from Mao's storeroom. He became an expert on the leading brands of a whole range of foreign-made electrical products, though he would not have been able to locate their countries of origin on a map.

Ye also followed the old adage that the manager of the kitchen gets to eat there, too. Tuanhe reform farm, whose prisoners raised a wide range of foods—meat, fish, vegetables, and rice—was one source of Ye's food, which he paid for with token sums. When the Communist party seized power, the new government set up "reform farms" all over the country, filling them quickly with both genuine criminals and political prisoners. Conditions on the reform farms were harsh. Most of the early political prisoners were lowly sorts—former foot soldiers or low-level local officials under the Guomindang. The ranking officials had either fled or been welcomed into the communist fold. My father was one who had been welcomed. When the communist armies were approaching Nanjing, Zhou Enlai had sent an intermediary urging him not to flee. Later, with Zhou's help, my father moved to Beijing and was given a sinecure, with a comfortable salary and housing.

Tuanhe, run by the Beijing municipal bureau of public security, was the leading reform farm in the capital. Ye Zilong, like many other high-ranking cadres, was certainly able to keep himself well supplied with all the food he needed. Even during the famine of 1960–1962, when millions of people were starving. Ye continued to receive plenty of high-quality food.

Ye was married and never divorced his wife, but he developed a close friendship with a staff member from the Bureau of Confidential Matters whom he met at one of Mao's dances in the Spring Lotus Chamber. When the young woman's boss heard of this, Ye's friend was shipped secretly out of Beijing. No one would tell Ye where she had gone.

Ye met her again by chance at another dance in 1958, when he was with Mao in Wuhan. The two renewed their friendship. Ye helped her to get a divorce, a difficult thing to arrange in those days, and to move to the industrial city of Tianjin, some 100 kilometers east of Beijing. There was no highway then and the roads were always clogged, so the drive was six hours from Beijing. Ye arranged a job and a house for the woman, and he visited her often, sometimes using Jiang Qing's car when the Chairman's wife was out of Beijing. Ye's friend, too, was well fed when many in China were hungry. Their friendship was interrupted again during the Cultural Revolution, when Ye came under scrutiny. But in 1980, when Ye Zilong was rehabilitated and appointed vice-mayor of Beijing, the two became reacquainted—Ye a bald old man and the woman a gray-haired old lady.

My entry into Group One did not sit well with Ye Zilong. He had not forgotten my refusal to supply him the penicillin. As a veteran cadre, a peasant, and a Long Marcher, he saw me as a bourgeois intellectual tainted by the values of the old society. That I had been appointed by his enemy Wang Dongxing only added to his antagonism toward me. Knowing that I was uncomfortable with my new position, he and Fu Lianzhang had tried to have me dismissed. Jiang Qing told me they took their concerns directly to Mao, arguing that my bourgeois past made me politically unreliable. Mao did not agree.

Working closely and frequently with Ye Zilong in Group One only made me dislike him more.

Mao's security personnel were also offensive. Their offices were right next to those of the medical staff, so it was impossible not to notice the differences between the two groups. The nurses concentrated on their work, talking only about business. Xu Tao was particularly silent. Labeled a member of the anti-party group and recently accused of antisocial behavior, he knew that the slightest slip of the tongue could get him even further into trouble.

But the security personnel were always chattering with each other, often very loudly, freely, and about subjects the medical staff would not have dared discuss. Sex was a favorite topic.

I had already been surprised by how casually Mao discussed sex. Mao did not understand the human reproductive system, but I quickly learned that he was remarkably preoccupied with sex. He was extremely curious, for instance, about the sex life of Gao Gang, the onetime head of Manchuria, who had taken his own life after having been accused in 1954 of an "anti-party alliance." Gao Gang was said to have amassed so much power that his good friend Stalin had called him the king of Manchuria. Wang Dongxing had told me that Gao and his alleged co-conspirator, Rao Shushi, were purged because they had pretensions of usurping the leadership of Liu Shaoqi.

In his conversations with me, Mao spoke little of Gao Gang's political mistakes. Instead, he marveled at the allegations that Gao had engaged in sex with more than one hundred different women, and was fascinated with the means Gao had used to snare so many partners, including the dance parties Gao hosted. "He had had sex twice on the very night he committed suicide," Mao told me. "Can you imagine such lust?

"Gao's sexual adventures were really a trivial matter," Mao continued. "If he hadn't made serious political mistakes, they wouldn't be worth our concern. Even with his political mistakes, we could still have made use of him if he had thoroughly confessed his faults."

Jiang Qing also spoke freely about sex. I was surprised, not long after beginning my service, to hear her announce proudly on several occasions that she and Mao had made love the night before. She praised the Chairman's sexual prowess.

Given the atmosphere, perhaps I should not have been so shocked that sex was a frequent topic of discussion among Mao's guards.

Jiang Qing was another favorite subject of theirs. When she was out of earshot, the discussion always turned eventually to her, and the guards mocked her mercilessly. One young guard in particular, Xiao Zhang, used to do scathing imitations of the Chairman's wife. Xiao Zhang was clever, effeminate, almost pretty, and a very good actor. Jiang Qing's clothes were kept in the guardroom—the washing and ironing (even Jiang Qing's silk underwear was ironed) were done by the bodyguards there—and Xiao Zhang used to dress up in one of Jiang Qing's raincoats and wear one of her straw hats, prancing around, twisting his body this way and that, in uncanny imitation. The other guards would laugh uproariously, and once even Mao walked by to catch sight of the act, grinning without saying a word.

But the ambience in the guardroom made me very uncomfortable, and I tried to distance myself from the security personnel. I was quiet around them, and my disapproval of their behavior was no doubt obvious. Ye Zilong noticed this and accused me of putting on airs and looking down on him.

Unknown to me, he went directly to Mao, saying that I put on airs because I was a doctor and charging me with looking down on cadres from worker and peasant backgrounds—another sign of my political unreliability.

It was the type of accusation Mao loved. Mao never wanted his underlings to band together against him, so he was constantly gathering information to play us off against each other. He made sure that relations within Group One were always strained. Jiang Qing, for instance, was constantly bickering with Ye Zilong and Li Yinqiao. She and Ye had once been close, but their relationship cooled as Mao depended more on Ye. She did not like Li Yinqiao, either, because he had once accused her of running away to Hangzhou to avoid the scrutiny of an unfolding political campaign. Wang Dongxing and Ye Zilong had disliked each other for years. Ye Zilong and Li Yinqiao did not get along because they were competing for Mao's favor. Mao cultivated the discord, and when the divisions threatened to go too far, he would step in to mediate the dispute, serving as the peacemaker, bringing us back to what was always an unstable, short-lived equilibrium.

"Doctors always put on airs," Mao complained to me one day in Guangzhou. "I just don't like it."

"Doctors may put on airs to others," I responded, "but not to you."

"Not necessarily," Mao shot back. "Haven't you put on airs?" It was then that I learned of Ye Zilong's accusations against me.

In fact, if measured by the standards of Mao's entourage, I had put on airs. Both my family's social standing and my training as a doctor had taught me that my profession was prestigious and that physicians deserved respect. Mao's revolutionary values were supposed to have changed those notions. Pride of place now rested with the peasants and workers. But my own thinking was not so easily changed. I still took pride in my work and could not help but be offended by the coarseness of Mao's staff.

Ye thought I should be dismissed, but Mao played the peacemaker. He told Ye to stop complaining about me. But he also gave instructions, through Jiang Qing, to me. She urged me to show some respect to Ye Zilong, suggesting that I try to say something nice to him. Ye Zilong came to the Chairman even earlier than she had, Jiang Qing explained. Even she had to accommodate him.

But I had no intention of sweet-talking Ye Zilong, just as I refused to sweet-talk Jiang Qing. I told Mao frankly what I thought of both Ye Zilong and Li Yinqiao, adding that others found them offensive, too. Mao said, "They are useful to me. Try to maintain good relations with them." It would be several years before I learned why the two men were so useful to Mao.

Already, though, I found my situation oppressive—not because of Mao, whom I still revered, or even Jiang Qing, who was so difficult, but because of the staff of Group One. I was disgusted by Mao's syco-phants and the advice that I sweet-talk this person and toady up to another. I was a member of Mao's imperial inner court. We seemed a privileged, exalted group. But the staff of Group One treated me like a nobody. Ye Zilong and Li Yinqiao, the confidential secretaries and bodyguards in general, were like the eunuchs in the imperial court, at the emperor's side from morning till night, transmitting his imperial edicts, using their power to intimidate and humiliate others. I was expected to swallow my pride and become a sycophantic courtier myself. I was Chairman Mao's personal physician, but I was at the mercy of louts like Ye Zilong and Li Yinqiao.

I was proud, and the humiliation was excruciating. I took stock of my situation. Mao's health was still good. He had no need for a full-time physician. I could never develop into a first-class physician if I stayed, and my dream of excelling as a doctor was still strong.

I decided to resign.

I told Wang Dongxing first. He was incredulous. "You have done a great job for the Chairman," he encouraged me. "You solved his white blood cell count problem. You gave him new sleeping pills. You have to look at this from a broader perspective. You have to take the needs of the party into consideration. It's not easy to be appointed to the position you have. Besides, if you don't think this whole thing through, if you leave here without very clear reasons, you may find yourself without another job."

Wang's final point was chastening. Other people who had left Group One without good reason, including one of Mao's previous doctors, had had difficulty finding work. Everyone assumed they had left under some sort of political cloud. Why else would anyone leave the privileged circle of Zhongnanhai? No one was willing to risk hiring a politically suspect person. With my family history, my departure would surely be suspect. I was trapped. I felt terribly unsafe in Group One, but if I tried to get out, I could end up nowhere.

But as I continued to think about my situation, the answer was still the same. I wanted to leave the job, the sooner the better, no matter what the consequences.

I went to Jiang Qing. "I have been thinking about my situation here," I explained to her. "I am an intellectual from the old society. I don't meet the political requirements for the Chairman's personal physician. I think we need to find a replacement for me—someone who comes from the right class and who has no political problems in his past."

Jiang Qing asked if I had talked with Mao. I explained that I had told him clearly about my personal background when we first met but that I had not talked to him about my intention to leave.

Jiang Qing thought for a moment. She told me not to talk to the Chairman. She would talk to him herself.

Jiang Qing called me to her quarters the next day. She had spoken to Mao. They had made a decision. She explained that while I and my family had political problems, these were a thing of the past. It is unfair to blame you for your family's past, she said. Besides, Wang Dongxing, Luo Ruiqing, and Yang Shangkun had all investigated my background and concluded it was not a problem. Zhou Enlai had also been informed of my case. "So you can feel at ease and go back to your work," she said. "Forget about your political problems."

Wang Dongxing was delighted. "At last we know what the Chairman thinks of you," he said proudly. "Isn't he nice to you? Didn't I say that when I size up a person, he is bound to be good? Now all you have to do is work hard. You'll have no more problems at all."

I was trapped.

Jiang Qing became much friendlier to me after that, making certain that I was served tea when we met and often inviting me to join her to chat. She was learning to imitate Mao's conversational style, feigning his relaxed and easygoing manner, encouraging me to speak without restraint, trying to probe my mind without revealing hers, circumspect about jumping in too quickly with her own views. She did quite a good imitation of her husband—Jiang Qing had once been an actress, after all—but it was not a style that came naturally to her or one that she could maintain for long. Her opinions continued to come straight from her husband, and I often disagreed with her, though I had to be cautious about expressing myself. I had no way of knowing then that a decade later Jiang Qing would be unleashed and that even the most innocent comment one made about a novel or poetry could ruin a person's life. But from the beginning I had an uneasy feeling about her and was often tense and on guard during our visits.

• • •

In the early summer of 1956, while we were still in Guangzhou, Jiang Qing's nurse came to tell me that Jiang Qing wanted to see me. "There is good news for you," she said.

Jiang Qing, who was quite a good amateur photographer, was studying some of her photographs when I went in. She put them aside. "Doctor, I hear you have been perspiring a lot," she said.

I was embarrassed. I had no clothes for Guangzhou's tropical climate. I took off my jacket during work, but there was no air-conditioning and my heavy trousers were uncomfortably warm. I perspired all day.

"I didn't bring my summer clothes," I explained to Jiang Qing.

Jiang Qing pointed to several bolts of fabric on a table nearby. "Take one of these and have a tailor make a new suit for you," she said. "Your clothes are too heavy."

I hesitated. "I can get by—just wearing my shirt without the jacket." Her nurse tugged me by the sleeve, silently encouraging me to accept Jiang Qing's gift, but I continued. "I appreciate your concern, but no thank you." Jiang Qing's offer was both her way of apologizing for our many disagreements and an attempt to ingratiate herself with me. But I did not want to be accused of accepting special favors from the wife of the party chairman.

"Please take it," Jiang Qing insisted. She instructed one of the attendants to accompany me to the tailor.

Jiang Qing's offer put me in an extremely uncomfortable position. She had a reputation for being impossibly stingy, but now she had suddenly become generous, singling me out as the object of her new magnanimity. With so much backbiting and petty jealousies within Group One, there was likely to be gossip if I accepted the gift. But by refusing I would risk insulting Jiang Qing and possibly even Mao.

I took my dilemma to Wang Dongxing. "If you don't take it, she will accuse you of looking down on her," he said. "If you do, others will be jealous. Let me talk to her and see if I can explain the problem and get her to change her mind."

But Jiang Qing would not change her mind. "She wondered why one comrade should not show concern for another," Wang Dongxing told me. "She says she's not trying to buy you over. If others make a fuss behind your back, I'll explain the situation to them."

I was forced to take the gift. But the gossip was even worse than I had feared. "Jiang Qing has always been such a stingy person," Li Yinqiao sniped. "Her goodwill gesture to Dr. Li is certainly a first." Then Ye Zilong and Li Yinqiao began circulating a rumor that Jiang

Qing and I were *hao,* which literally means "good," but implied that we were sexually involved. The rumor went all the way to Mao. I think he half believed it.

As soon as I learned of this rumor, I went immediately to Mao.

I asked the Chairman if he knew about Jiang Qing's gift. "Yes, I knew about it ahead of time," he said. "Go ahead and take it." I told him there had been rumors about Jiang Qing and me. He had already heard.

Jiang Qing would never dare to have an affair. An affair would have provided Mao an excuse to get rid of her, and her fear of abandonment was too strong. But she would go to great lengths to ingratiate herself with people who were close to Mao, and she was happy to allow herself to be amused by other men.

By mentioning the rumor to Mao, I was also denying its truth. I needed to say no more. Mao believed me. " 'A gentleman acts according to his conscience,' " he said. The rumor ended there.

15

The weather in Guangzhou was unbearably hot. It was already June. Mao moved to Building 3, setting himself up in the spacious reception hall, where attendants brought five big barrels of fresh ice every day in an effort to keep him cool. The rest of us used electric fans, which only circulated the heat.

The mosquitoes had arrived. If we slept without mosquito nets, we were bitten. If we used nets, we suffocated. Mao, too, was bothered by the pests and accused his guards of not doing enough to get rid of them. But the guards passed the responsibility over to me. Mosquitoes might carry malaria, they said, and hence were a doctor's concern.

The problem seemed intractable. We were on an island, and the mosquitoes were breeding in the surrounding waters. The ceilings in the buildings were nearly fifteen feet high, and the windows were covered with heavy drapes. The mosquitoes hid in the curtains, emerging after sundown for their nocturnal attacks. Our efforts to eliminate them were hopeless. The problem wasn't solved until we ordered DDT from Hong Kong.

But the heat was still oppressive, and the staff was becoming restive. They wanted me to persuade Mao that the time had come to leave. "I don't mind the heat," Mao said. "And there are still a few things I have to do here. Let's wait for a while." I assumed that important political business was brewing. During Mao's absence from Beijing, the central leadership had begun publishing criticisms of "adventurism" in the editorials of the *People's Daily,* saying that industrial and agricultural production should advance with steady steps. The Chinese public surely did not understand at the time—nor, in fact, did I—but the "adventurism" the party leadership was attacking was Mao's own, for it was Mao who insisted on rapid collectivization and intensified industrial production.

Shortly after I had tried to persuade Mao to leave, Luo Ruiqing and Wang Dongxing came to see me, wondering whether the Pearl River was clean. I was taken aback. The Chairman had just announced that he intended to swim in three rivers—the Pearl in Guangzhou, the Xiang in Changsha, Hunan, and the Yangtze in Wuhan, Hubei. Luo Ruiqing and Wang Dongxing were convinced that Mao's plan was too dangerous, and so was the provincial leadership in the places where he wanted to swim. Tao Zhu said that the Pearl in Guangzhou was too polluted. Wang Renzhong was saying that the Yangtze in Wuhan was too wide and that its whirlpools were too dangerous. Mao was not listening. Now Luo and Wang wanted my official judgment on whether the Pearl River was too polluted.

I was certain the water could not be particularly clean. We were downstream from Guangzhou's industry. But without testing, I could not say how polluted the water was.

They wanted me to test the water for bacteria and pollutants and to report to them as soon as the results were in.

The next morning, before my tests were complete, one of Mao's bodyguards rushed in to fetch me. The Chairman was furious. "It's about the swimming," the guard told me. Luo Ruiqing and Wang Dongxing were meeting with Mao. They wanted me there, too.

I went immediately, running into the two security officials, both flushed and perspiring heavily, just as I entered Mao's quarters. Wang smiled at me awkwardly. The test results no longer mattered. The Chairman was about to go swimming.

Just then, Mao emerged from his bedroom wearing a white robe, white swimming trunks, and a pair of leather sandals. He walked quickly toward the dock, arms swinging, and boarded a waiting yacht. Tao Zhu, Wang Renzhong, and Yang Shangkun were following close behind, and I ran to join them. Mao was showing that his determination was not to be challenged.

He had begun swimming as a child, using the pond on his father's property to learn, and was a good swimmer. Now, however, everyone responsible for his safety had tried to persuade him not to swim, but the more his security staff tried to protect him, the more he insisted on swimming. He was defying us all, telling us symbolically that it was useless to attempt to restrain him.

The yacht sailed upstream a short distance and stopped as four sampans immediately surrounded it. Mao descended a ladder over the side and plunged into the water, trailed by a squadron of twenty to thirty guards, followed by the other leaders. I plunged into the water after them, joining the protective circle around Mao. Mao's decision had come so unexpectedly that he was the only one wearing a bathing suit. The rest of us were in our underwear.

The river was more than a hundred yards wide, and the current was slow. The water, just as I had feared, was filthy. I saw occasional globs of human waste float by. The pollution did not bother Mao. He floated on his back, his big belly sticking up like a round balloon, legs relaxed, as though he were resting on a sofa. The water carried him downstream, and only rarely did he use his arms or legs to propel himself forward.

I was no swimmer and had to use all my energy just to stay afloat. Mao noticed my efforts and called me over to him. "You have to relax your body," he instructed. "Don't move your arms and legs so much. When you want to change position, just move lightly against the water. This way you can stay in the water for a long time without so much effort. Give it a try."

I tried, but to no avail. I had to move my arms and legs or drown.

"Maybe you're afraid of sinking," he said. "Don't think about it. If you don't think about it, you won't sink. If you do, you will."

Yang Shangkun and Wang Renzhong were faster learners. They, too, got swimming lessons from Mao and soon were floating along with him. Several years and many more tries in the ocean, in swimming pools, and in rivers would be necessary before I could master his style.

We floated down the Pearl River for nearly two hours, covering some six or seven miles. Then we took showers and had lunch on board the well-equipped yacht, joined by Jiang Qing, who had been observing our swim from the deck.

Mao was as elated as if he had just won a war. "You people told me that Dr. Li said this water was too dirty," he said to Luo Ruiqing.

"Yes," I interjected. "I saw human waste floating by."

Mao laughed heartily. "If we tried to follow the standards of you physicians, we wouldn't be able to live. Don't all living things need air and water and soil? Tell me which of these things is pure? I don't believe there is any pure air, pure water, pure soil. Everything has some impurities, some dirt. If you put a fish into distilled water, how long do you think it would live?"

I was silent. Mao was clearly not going to accept my views on sanitation.

When I met with Mao again that evening it was clear that another spat was brewing between him and his protectors. "I want to swim in all three rivers," he told me. "Luo Ruiqing and Wang Dongxing didn't want me to swim in any of them. After we swam in the Pearl River today, they still said that it's not a good idea to swim in the Yangtze— too many strong waves and whirlpools. If I'm trapped there, they say, no one will be able to rescue me. Tao Zhu didn't want me to swim in the Pearl, but he doesn't care if I swim in the Xiang. Wang Renzhong doesn't want me to swim in the Yangtze, but when I asked him if I could swim in the Pearl and the Xiang, he said that I could."

The problem was one of jurisdictional responsibility. Luo Ruiqing and Wang Dongxing, responsible for Mao's safety wherever he went, did not want him to swim in any of the rivers. Tao Zhu, as first party secretary of Guangdong, did not want him to risk the Pearl. Mao's safety in the Yangtze was Wang Renzhong's concern.

"I don't need their protection," Mao argued. "They don't even know what's going on in the water. So I've sent Han Qingyu and Sun Yong to do a test swim in the Yangtze and to report their findings to me." Security officers Han Qingyu and Sun Yong were very good swimmers, among the coterie who always accompanied Mao into the water.

That Mao should swim in the Yangtze was truly unthinkable. It is the mightiest of China's rivers, the swiftest and most dangerous, with strong currents and whirlpools. Even boats have difficulty maneuvering. No one had ever swum in the Yangtze River before—not even the people who lived along its banks. But Mao wanted to swim the Yangtze anyway.

When Han Qingyu and Sun Yong returned from their test swim, both agreed that the Yangtze was much more dangerous than the Pearl. Anyone trapped in one of the whirlpools could not be saved. Moreover, the water was infested with snails carrying schistosomiasis, a debilitating disease.

Luo Ruiqing suggested to Wang Renzhong that he report the findings to Mao. But Wang wanted the two swimmers to tell him. Wang knew that Mao would not listen to him.

Luo Ruiqing instructed the two guards to tell Mao the truth. "Don't just tell him what we know he wants to hear," Luo insisted. The two men agreed.

We all went together to see Mao. Han Qingyu, never very articulate, was so nervous to be brought before his great leader that he began squirming and stammering and couldn't talk at all. After a few false starts, Mao finally interrupted him.

"All right, don't say anything," Mao ordered. "I'm going to ask you one question at a time. You answer each one as it comes." Han became even more tense.

Mao began. "Is the river very wide?" he asked.

"It is very wide." Han nodded.

"Are there many whirlpools?" Mao wanted to know.

"Many whirlpools," Han responded.

"If trapped inside, is it possible to get out?" Mao continued.

"No, impossible to get out." Han shook his head emphatically.

"It's not good for swimming?" Mao demanded.

"Not good for swimming," Han agreed.

Suddenly, Mao pounded his fist on the table and exploded, "I bet you didn't even go into the water. How could you know? How can you serve as captain of our guards?

"*Gun dan!*" he yelled, using the vulgar phrase that roughly translates as "Get your balls out of here!" It is not language the Chinese people expect from their highest leaders.

Han's face turned ashen. He stood frozen in terror.

Again Mao exploded. "*Gun dan!*" he repeated.

Han backed out of the room. No one else moved.

Mao turned next to Sun Yong. "Now, you tell me what the Yangtze is like."

Sun knew exactly what to say. "Chairman," he responded immediately. "You can swim there."

Mao smiled. Sun started trying to say something else, but Mao stopped him. "That's enough. Don't say anything more. Just get ready to go swimming."

Wang Dongxing was furious with Sun Yong. "Why did you say that to the Chairman?" he demanded. "Didn't you agree to tell him the truth?"

Sun's face turned red. "Vice-Minister Wang," he said. "Didn't you see what happened to Han? If I had said the same thing, he would have ordered me to get my balls out of there too. I can't help it."

Han, too, confronted Sun, accusing his fellow officer of selling him out.

Wang Dongxing tried to reassure Han, promising to protect him from Mao's fury. But he could not. After we returned to Beijing, Han was transferred out of Group One. Sun Yong, who had both lied and betrayed his colleague, continued as one of Mao's guards and was promoted up the ranks.

•　•　•

Summer of 1954, in Zhongnanhai.
Dr. Zhisui Li standing outside Mao Zedong's walled compound,
in a photograph taken by Wang Dongxing.

Summer of 1961, at the new Lushan guesthouse, where
Mao Zedong encountered his third wife, He Zizhen.
From left to right: provincial security officer Lu, Wang Dongxing,
confidential secretary Xu Yefu, confidential clerk Li Yuanhui,
Dr. Li, head nurse Wu Xujun, Mao Zedong, nurse Zhou,
and two bodyguards.

December 26, 1963, Mao Zedong's seventieth birthday. Dr. Li and
Mao pose in front of Room 118, in the Great Hall of the People.

(*at left*) December 26, 1964, Mao Zedong's seventy-first birthday.
In front of Room 118, in the Great Hall of the People, from left
to right: bodyguard Xiao Zhang, security guard Wang Yuqing,
Central Garrison Corps commander Zhang Yaoci, Mao, head nurse
Wu Xujun, Dr. Li, political secretary Lin Ke, and bodyguard
Zhou Fuming.

It was late June 1956 and Mao was finally ready to leave. He wanted to go next to Changsha, the capital of his native province of Hunan, to test the Xiang River, where he had often gone swimming in his youth. We traveled on his special train.

The weather in Changsha was miserably hot, hovering around 104 degrees. Mao took his first swim the day after we arrived.

The Xiang River was reaching the flood stage and in some places was two hundred yards across. Mao's party, scores of people altogether, began approaching the river in a wide line from a road that ran parallel to the water. Suddenly there was a commotion ahead and to Mao's left. "Get him to a hospital," people were yelling. Li Xiang, the director of Hunan's bureau of public security and the man in charge of local security arrangements for Mao, had been bitten by a water snake.

Mao was coolly unconcerned, but the protective circle of some thirty security guards tightened around him. Luo Ruiqing, visibly shaken, moved over to me. "Do you have medicine for snake bites?" he asked. I assured him that I did. He was not worried about Li Xiang, and I was not expected to offer medical assistance to the stricken official. My responsibilities were exclusively to Mao.

Luo Ruiqing wondered how there could be a snake on Mao's route and why the security people had not done a thorough check of the area.

But Mao had changed his plan at the last minute. The security staff had readied another site for his swim. They had no chance to clear the path he finally chose.

Mao's unpredictability only added to the burden of his security staff. Wang Dongxing decided that in the future, the security check for Mao's swims would have to extend ten *li* in either direction from the spot where Mao said he would enter the water.

The current of the Xiang River was much faster than that of the Pearl, but Mao swam the same way he had in Guangzhou, slowly moving to the center and floating downstream in the current. He floated to a small island in the middle of the river—Orange Island, it was called—a place he had visited in his youth.

As soon as he set foot on the island, one of the accompanying patrol boats landed, too. Mao's attendants brought him a robe and his sandals and a pack of cigarettes. The rest of us followed barefoot, wearing nothing but our swimming trunks. The orange trees for which the island had been named were nowhere in sight. Suddenly, some peasant children, who had recognized the Chairman, appeared and began to chant "Long Live Chairman Mao!" The security people tried to chase them away, but Mao insisted that they stay. He loved contact with the "masses."

Only a few families lived on the island, and their houses were dilapidated.

Cigarette in hand, Mao walked up to an old woman in threadbare clothes and started a conversation. The old lady was concentrating on mending other garments that seemed equally worn out.

"How is your life here?" Mao asked. If the old lady knew she was being questioned by the chairman of China's Communist party, she gave no indication. She continued her work without bothering to respond. Mao repeated the question.

"Mama huhu," the woman finally answered, not even bothering to look up. "So-so."

A small crowd of island folk had gathered. Mao began talking about how he used to swim to the island when he was young. The place had been deserted then.

It was deserted when we went back several years later, in June 1959. Mao's unscheduled stop had so terrified the security personnel that immediately after he left, the provincial public security bureau and the soldiers of a nearby military unit had searched the island for "bad elements" and moved everyone away. They transformed the place into a magnificent park filled with orange trees—beautiful when they bloomed in autumn. I asked Li Xiang, the head of Hunan's public-security apparatus, what happened to the old woman, but Li said he did not know. He did know, of course. He was just not willing to say.

On the third day of our visit to Hunan, Mao went swimming again. All of us were trying to float like him, catching the river's current, when suddenly the hapless Han Qingyu, who had cautioned Mao against swimming in the Yangtze, got caught in a manure pit. Manure pits are usually right on the riverbank, but this one had been submerged when the river started to flood. Han was covered with human feces. Awful as it was, I had to join the others in laughing.

As Mao's doctor, though, I was concerned about the Chairman's health. I mentioned it to him that evening.

Mao laughed, pointing out again that the food we eat takes its flavor from the manure with which it is fertilized. "The problem is that the Xiang River is too small," he continued. "I want to swim in the Yangtze. On to the Yangtze River!"

Within hours, we were on the train to Wuhan.

Wang Renzhong had made elaborate preparations for Mao's swim. We stayed again at the East Lake guesthouse. Wang had found an elegant steamer, the *East Is Red Number One,* which could accommodate two or three hundred people and had a large outer deck, many berths, a full bath, and plenty of toilets. Mao, the leaders accompanying him, and a swelling staff that included both his own and local security personnel, boarded the boat at a factory that had been emptied of workers and filled with security guards instead. As Mao boarded the *East Is Red,* eight boats filled with security people encircled it, moving together with the steamer out to the middle of the river. Four motorboats were patrolling a still wider radius, on the lookout for anything untoward.

As the steamer reached the middle of the Yangtze, just downstream from the huge bridge that was then under construction, Mao descended the ladder and got into the water, the other leaders following. Immediately, some forty security guards formed a protective circle around the Chairman.

As I stepped from the ladder into the water, the rapid current immediately carried me some fifty yards downstream. I managed to keep my balance, floating with the water, moving my arms and legs as little as possible, trying to imitate Mao's style. The feared whirlpools were nowhere in sight, and after the initial shock I felt at the strength of the current, I was calm, floating effortlessly downstream, basking in the midday sun, as though melting into the warm brown water. The Yangtze was in flood, and from the middle of the river the banks were barely visible. It was a wonderful way to relax.

Suddenly I heard people on the *East Is Red* shouting and saw several small boats racing toward it. A number of sailors jumped into the water near the steamer. I moved closer to Mao to find out what was going on. But neither he nor anyone else knew.

Only when we got back on board did we learn that three-star general Chen Zaidao, the commander of the Wuhan Military Region, had decided to enter the water alone shortly after we left. But the rapid current frightened him and he tried to swim upstream back to the boat. The powerful current overwhelmed him, and he swallowed great quantities of water. By the time the sailors reached him to haul him out, he was nearly drowned.

After about an hour of floating, Luo Ruiqing and Wang Dongxing urged me to try to convince Mao to stop.

But Mao wanted to continue. "Swimming in the Yangtze River isn't so frightening after all, is it?" he asked.

"No, not this way," I responded.

"It seems to me," he continued thoughtfully, "that even the most difficult thing, the most dangerous thing, is not to be feared so long as one prepares for it well. Without good preparation, even an easy thing can create complications."

I had to agree. But he was not just talking about swimming in rivers, I suspected. His words had other implications, too.

We floated for another hour. Again, Luo and Wang urged me to get Mao back on the *East Is Red.* We were about to reach the part of the river that was heavily infested with the schistosomiasis-carrying snails.

I told Mao. "What infested area?" he demanded. "They just want to get me back on the ship."

"But two hours is enough," I said. "A lot of people didn't have a chance to eat before we started. They must be very hungry by now."

"All right," he agreed. "Let's go back and eat."

One of the sailors swimming with us estimated we had gone about fifteen miles, but I thought we had gone much further. The current was very swift. We both agreed that the swim had been effortless. We had not been exercising at all.

Yang Shangkun agreed. "This isn't swimming," he said. "It's just floating with a little effort."

Once Mao was finally on board, the leaders in charge of his safety breathed a collective sigh of relief. Wang Dongxing had been particularly worried. He wondered out loud what would have happened if it had been Mao rather than Chen Zaidao who nearly drowned. "I would have been accused of committing an unpardonable crime," he said.

Sun Yong, who had assured Mao that the Yangtze was swimmable, was equally relieved. He knew that if anything had gone wrong, he would have lost his life.

Mao invited us to join him for lunch on the ship. He was exhilarated with his success, and soon the flattery began. Wang Renzhong poured a glass of wine for Mao. "Chairman, please have a drink," he said. "It can keep you from catching cold."

Mao laughed. "In this hot weather how could anyone catch cold?" he asked. "But let's have a drink anyway. Everybody can have a drink." Taking a sip from his own glass, Mao turned to General Chen, who was still recovering from his ordeal. "Comrade Chen Zaidao, I think you need a drink. People normally swim with the current. Why did you try to swim against it?"

Chen was speechless.

Wang Renzhong began his fatuous flattery. "Chairman, we have been following you for many years but did not know you were such a great swimmer, a man of such strong determination. When you were young you said, 'Struggle against heaven, struggle against earth, struggle against people—the happiness is endless.' This is really true. After swimming with you today, our happiness is endless. We have learned a great deal from the Chairman. I hope you continue to teach us more and criticize us more in the future."

Luo Ruiqing, who had so strenuously opposed the swim, joined in. "We have been followers of the Chairman for a long time," he said. "But we have not digested what we have learned from him. I am not one of those people Chairman has often talked about whose brains are as hard as granite. I can change myself."

Yang Shangkun had not opposed Mao's swim but he had remained silent. Yet he had called our swim "floating with a little effort," and I knew that he had been unimpressed with Mao's physical feat. Now he, too, joined the chorus. "Speaking of the strength of the Chairman," he began with a smile, "no one can match it. No other world leader looks down with such disdain on great mountains and powerful rivers. But Chairman can. No one in history can match him."

Even Wang Dongxing, who had done everything he could to prevent Mao from swimming, put his earlier objections behind him. "Chairman, we need to draw some lessons from this experience," he said. "We should not just think about the problem of safety. We have to think about the great consequences of Chairman's actions for the whole nation. The people of our nation can draw lessons from Chairman's example: Think what used to be considered unthinkable, and do what used to be considered undoable."

Mao basked in the praise. "Don't flatter me," he protested, loving every word. "There is nothing you cannot do if you are serious about it. Remember, when you face something unfamiliar, don't oppose it right away. And if your opposition fails, don't be indecisive. Instead, make serious preparation for it. Comrade Wang Renzhong opposed my swimming before, but then he switched his position and made serious preparation for the swimming. That is the right attitude."

Jiang Qing reserved her praise until everyone else had spoken. She had not wanted Mao to swim in the Yangtze. But when she saw how determined he was, and how angry toward those who opposed him, she shifted gears. "What's so dangerous about swimming?" she had asked in her cold, disdainful voice.

Looking at the guests with smug satisfaction, she now said, "In Guangzhou you people opposed the Chairman's swimming. You were scared to death. I disagreed with you. I am a supporter of swimming."

"Only Jiang Qing completely supports me," Mao often said. He was right. Jiang Qing always supported Mao in all that he did. She had to.

I looked around the table at the assembled guests, ranking leaders of the Communist party. I recalled Mao's remarks about his staff. "They are always competing with each other, courting my favor," he had said. "They are good to me. I can make use of them." But these leaders of the Communist party were also mere sycophants and courtiers. What use would Mao make of them?

The whole lunchtime conversation and the fawning of the assembled leaders would have been ludicrous if the comments had only referred to Mao's three-river swim. But the praise he was receiving had political implications, too. Mao's plans for China were grandiose, dangerous, and daring, and in insisting on the rapid transformation of China into a socialist state, he was defying the more deliberate and cautious central leadership. Mao's criticism of those who opposed the unfamiliar without thinking was a criticism of the conservatives in Beijing, too. The problems encountered in the course of rural collectivization and urban economic restructuring were the result of incomplete preparation, not the policy of socialist transformation itself, Mao believed. If Mao himself could defy received wisdom by swimming in dangerous rivers and emerge healthy and triumphant, so China could risk transforming the entire economic and social structure to reclaim China's glory and international prestige. And if China's central leadership would not support him in his grandiose plans, provincial leaders like Tao Zhu and Wang Renzhong would. Essential to his schemes was the cooperation of provincial and local-level leaders, hence his frequent departures from Beijing to muster the support he was not getting in Beijing. His trip in the summer of 1956 was thus a major success.

Mao governed China the way he swam, insisting on policies that no one else had ever imagined, dangerous, risky policies like the Great Leap Forward, the people's communes, and the Cultural Revolution, all of which were designed to transform China. In June 1956, the most grandiose and daring of his political schemes—the Great Leap Forward and the Cultural Revolution—were still years away. The ten grand monuments to his rule, constructed to celebrate the first ten years of the Communist party's "liberation"—including the Great Hall of the People and the Museum of Revolutionary History—had yet to reach the drawing board. But it was in Wuhan, after Mao's first swim in the Yangtze, that I began to have an inkling of how extravagant Mao's ideas were.

I joined Mao for a meeting with the director of the Yangtze Valley Planning Office, a man named Lin Yishan, while we were in Wuhan, where I learned of his plan to build a huge dam along the middle reaches of the Yangtze. Listening to Lin's description and looking at the design for the dam, I was aghast, doubly so because Lin Yishan was a veteran revolutionary, not a scientist or an engineer. The project was a huge engineering feat designed to transform the whole Yangtze River valley. The undertaking would require extraordinary scientific know-how, and the results, it seemed to me, were unpredictable. But Mao was enthusiastic. "The Three Gorges will be gone in the future," he said to me, referring to the most famous section of the Yangtze, with its high peaks and swiftly flowing currents, its breathtaking scenery that has been honored in painting and poetry for centuries, "and only a great reservoir will be left."

That evening, after our visit with Lin, Mao composed a poem to celebrate his swims, the rivers, and the daring of men determined to change the world.

> After swallowing some water at Changsha
> I taste a Wuchang fish in the surf
> and swim across the Yangtze River that winds
>   ten thousand *li.*
> I see the entire Chu sky.
> Wind batters me, waves hit me—I don't care.
> Better than walking lazily in the patio.
> Today I have a lot of time.
> Here on the river the Master said:
> "Dying—going into the past—is like a river flowing."
>
> Winds flap the sail,
> tortoise and snake are silent,
> a great plan looms.
> A bridge will fly over this moat dug by heaven
> and be a road from north to south.
> We will make a stone wall against the upper river to the west
> and hold back steamy clouds and rain of Wu peaks.
> Over tall chasms will be a calm lake,
> and if the goddess of these mountains is not dead
> she will marvel at the changed world.

Nothing could stop Mao, not even the storm and waves from the central leadership in Beijing. Like Qin Shihuangdi, the founding father of imperial China, who had built the Great Wall, Mao too wanted a massive monument that would live for centuries after him. The dam to tame the mightiest and most famous of China's rivers was only one such project.

Scientists and engineers were later brought into the Yangtze River project. Knowing Mao's dream of a dam surely must have colored their recommendations. They ingratiated themselves with Mao by agreeing that the project was feasible. Truly conscientious scientists, I think, would not have acceded so easily. Later, honest scientists and engineers under the State Council and the Chinese People's Political Consultative Conference expressed their reservations, but the project was nonetheless approved, more than fifteen years after Mao's death, in April 1992.

Mao swam in the Yangtze for the next two days, emerging each time triumphant. After his third swim, he suddenly announced that we would return by train to Beijing immediately. It was already well into July. Because I was focused on the day-to-day safety of the Chairman and the internecine squabbling of his inner court, I had completely ignored the political battles that Mao was fighting even while he was away. I never asked what was happening, and I did not want to know. My responsibility was Mao health. My survival depended on keeping out of politics. I learned of the vast changes sweeping the country only through what Mao himself chose to tell me, from the party documents that passed my way, and from the reports that my friend Tian Jiaying, Mao's political secretary, provided me. With our return to the capital, my detachment would not be so simple.

16

Back in Beijing, Mao began pulling me more tightly into his circle. His confidence in me was growing, and he wanted me to become more politically involved, serving not only as his doctor but as one of his secretaries, too. "My health is okay," he said, "and your work is not so heavy. I think you are a good person." He wanted me to play a role similar to that of Lin Ke. In addition to reading *Reference Materials,* the daily top-secret compilation of reports from international news agencies, Mao wanted me to make my own political investigations, write reports, and offer him advice.

I did not want the job. If I were to serve as Mao's secretary, I would be sucked into an unpredictable and dangerous political maelstrom. I still did not understand politics and I did not want to become involved. Wang Dongxing encouraged me to accept Mao's offer. With me as one of Mao's secretaries, Wang's own links to the Chairman would be tighter. But I knew that the other staff members in Group One would become even more jealous of me, and their sniping and bickering would intensify. The envious would lie in wait, ready to pounce on my slightest mistake. The prospect was frightening. My life was precarious enough with my work confined to medical matters. As Mao's secretary, I would be in perpetual danger. I had to refuse his offer.

I explained that I had no competence in administration and that I could never be as good a secretary as Lin Ke. I wanted to continue as his doctor.

Mao did not give up. He began showering me with personal favors, sucking my family in, too. As the summer of 1956 progressed and the time for our yearly sojourn in Beidaihe approached, he suggested that my two little boys come with us to the seaside resort.

I objected. My younger son was just an infant, and John, the older one, was not well behaved. All the high-ranking leaders would be in Beidaihe. It wouldn't look right for me to take my children.

"You're too cautious," Mao admonished. "No wonder Jiang Qing says you are too reserved. If children like Li Na, Li Min, and Yuanxin can come, why can't yours come, too?"

Mao's favoritism put me in a difficult position within Group One. Ye Zilong and Li Yinqiao were clearly displeased. "Then take them along," Ye had said without enthusiasm, a bite to his voice, when I told him Mao's suggestion. The situation made me uneasy.

Wang Dongxing thought I had to do as the Chairman said, but he was worried about the morale of the security personnel if I took my children along when others could not. He suggested that I get the Central Bureau of Health to make the arrangements. That way the security guards would make less of a fuss.

I still had two masters—Wang Dongxing and his Central Bureau of Guards and the Central Bureau of Health. Since most of China's ranking leaders summered in Beidaihe, medical staff from the Central Bureau of Health went with them to run a clinic for the leaders and their staff. The Central Bureau of Health staff agreed to take my children on the train with them to Beidaihe. In the end, though, I only allowed my elder son, John, then six years old, to go. Erchong stayed in Beijing with Lillian and my mother.

Before we left, Jiang Qing suggested to Wang Dongxing that I tutor Li Min, Mao's nineteen-year-old daughter by his second wife, He Zizhen, while we were in Beidaihe. Li Min was honest, simple, well mannered, and polite, but not very bright. She had spent World War Two in the Soviet Union, and her education had suffered there. In 1956, she was a high-school student and needed help with mathematics, physics, and chemistry. Wang Dongxing, without consulting me, agreed that I would become her tutor.

I had no objection to tutoring Li Min. But Jiang Qing's requests did not stop there.

Jiang Qing had heard that my wife's English was very good, Wang Dongxing told me. She wanted Lillian to tutor Li Na in English. Wang had agreed to that request, too.

I was shocked. For me to teach Li Min was one thing, but for Lillian to tutor Li Na was quite another. Li Na was Jiang Qing's daughter, sixteen years old, but I found her caustic and mean, not merely lacking in basic good manners but downright rude. Lillian was a kind and gentle woman. How could she manage Li Na?

Wang Dongxing insisted. "I already promised Comrade Jiang Qing. Please don't let me down."

I was firm. "No," I reiterated. "Lillian is extremely busy with her work." One of my wife's former professors had arranged for her to work with the Foreign Affairs Association, and she was often away escorting foreign delegations around the country. "She is not a member of the party. It would be inappropriate for her to come and go at the Chairman's residence. Besides, her parents were landlords and her brothers and sisters are in Taiwan. She has serious political problems."

Wang insisted. Luo Ruiqing and the security apparatus had already cleared her for the work.

I became adamant. "I have enough problems as it is," I said. "I can't let Lillian work here, too. That would make things even more difficult for us."

Wang was growing increasingly irritated. "Don't you trust our party leadership?" he shot back. "Minister Luo and I both agreed, but you refuse. Don't you know you are making things difficult for us, too?"

"It is not my intention to make things difficult for you," I responded. "But you know as well as I that Jiang Qing is an extremely difficult woman. Li Na is mean and brash. Then there are people like Ye Zilong and Li Yinqiao who spread rumors and create trouble for nothing. My wife is a simple, gentle person. She would have no idea how to cope here in Group One."

Wang was still annoyed. "Okay," he said. "Don't you bother about this. I'll talk to your wife myself. Tell her to come see me."

I rushed home as soon as I could, imploring Lillian not to agree. I urged her to explain to Wang Dongxing how busy she was. "You get home late every day," I reminded her. "You have no time. Be firm."

She agreed and went immediately to see Wang. I waited anxiously for her return.

She was calm when she came back an hour later. Just seeing her allayed my fears. "We had a good talk," she began. "I told Vice-Minister Wang about my work—about all the foreign visitors I am responsible for hosting, about how I often accompany them on tours to different parts of the country. I explained that it would be impossible for me to commit myself to any specific time for Li Na."

I was relieved. "You spoke very well," I complimented her. "What did he say?"

"He listened to me carefully. He agreed that the assignment would be difficult. He said we could discuss the matter later. That's all."

"Your wife is a very busy person," Jiang Qing commented when I saw her the next day.

"She certainly is," I agreed. "She has to host so many foreign guests. She comes home late every day."

Jiang Qing nodded. "Let's talk about tutoring Li Na later. Can you start tutoring Li Min?"

"Yes," I agreed. "For two hours a day."

I left with Mao for Beidaihe, traveling on his special train, in late July 1956. Mao and Jiang Qing again set up residence in Building 8; Jiang Qing's sister, Mao's two daughters, and his nephew, Yuanxin, lived in a villa once owned by Zhang Xueliang, the man who had held Chiang Kai-shek hostage in 1936 and who was then under house arrest in Taiwan. Lin Ke and I stayed in Building 10.

Beidaihe was charming. Lillian and I had been there in 1954, in what turned out to be our last vacation together for more than two decades, and we had fallen in love with the place. Beidaihe had originally been a tiny fishing village on the coast of the Bohai Gulf, in northern Hebei. Sometime after the Opium War, the British had developed it into a beautiful summer resort, connecting the town to Beijing by train. The village had continued to prosper even after the British left, as Chinese officials and wealthy businessmen came to build their own villas, and the town now bustled with restaurants and shops. The red-brick British-built villas, set in the midst of evergreens, were outlined against the blue and white of the sky. The ocean was a kaleidoscope, too, its color changing, so the local fishermen told us, with the color of the various schools of fish swimming through. We were all particularly fond of the fish that turned the waters a shimmering silver.

When Lillian and I had been there, we would wake at two or three in the morning, when the tide was at its furthest ebb, and wade out in the sand to collect mussels and seashells. At around four in the morning, the fishermen would begin selling their morning catch, and we would buy our food for the day. The crabs were especially good, but Lillian and I liked the kind of flounder the Chinese call *bimuyu*. The eyes of the *bimuyu* are both on the same side, and we remembered the Chinese love poem about the two *bimuyu* swimming out to sea together.

The weather during this visit with Mao in 1956 was a marvelous respite from the heat of Beijing. A gentle, misty, salty sea breeze blew in every morning and evening, and those times of day were particularly pleasant and cool. Just in front of our villa was a smooth, sandy beach stretching east and west some seven miles, and we could see colorful, old-fashioned fishing junks bobbing in the distant horizon. Four lush plum trees, dripping with fruit, stood in front of our building, and the egg-sized purple plums were cool and sweet and free for the picking. Mushrooms were another delicacy of Beidaihe, and after a rain, we would organize small delegations to scour the forest for the big, sweet mushrooms, redolent of pine, that would spring up in the damp. We would present our chef with a bagful to be mixed with dried shrimp, and he would make a rich, delicious soup. Mao never liked our fresh mushroom soup, but Jiang Qing loved it.

The whole place was enchanting, and our routine was relaxed. There were movies every night, including the latest foreign films, and Mao hosted dancing parties on Wednesday and Saturday evenings in a big hall with an outdoor deck just at the edge of the beach. Liu Shaoqi and Zhu De would occasionally join the dances, too. I would tutor Li Min for two hours in the morning, then go swimming with Mao in the afternoons, accompanied by a whole squadron of security guards and assorted staff from the General Office—thirty or forty people in all. The security staff had set up a raft some two thousand meters offshore, where Mao would rest for a while, sunning himself, before swimming back to the beach.

Beidaihe was often hit by violent summer thunderstorms, and the surf would stay rough long afterward, completely submerging the raft. Mao insisted on swimming nevertheless, and Wang Dongxing and Luo Ruiqing seemed to have given up trying to prevent him. I had to swim with him in the rough and choppy waters—an exciting, often frightening experience. The waves would lift us up and toss us into the air, then slam us down to the bottom of the sea, and I would fight my way back to the surface, gasping for breath. Often, I would exhaust my strength swimming in the direction of Mao's raft only to be thrown back to the beach in one quick flip of a wave.

"Don't you think it's fun to do battle with the wind and the waves?" Mao would ask after such adventures.

"I've never had this experience before," I would answer, not sure that I wanted such excitement again.

"It's like 'riding the great wind and breaking the powerful waves for ten thousand miles,' " Mao would insist.

The ocean was infested with sharks, and Mao's security staff had erected a net just beyond the raft to keep them out. Occasionally the security personnel would actually catch a shark, and they would put it beside the path to the beach to make certain Mao saw it, a silent warning against swimming out too far. Wang Dongxing knew that if

Mao were actually cautioned against swimming beyond the nets, he would insist on taking the risk. Silently displaying the captured shark was much more effective.

Mao would stay at the beach, reading documents or talking with other party leaders, until late in the afternoon, protected from the sun by a canvas awning that served as his lounge.

My son John adjusted quickly to life in Beidaihe and was soon having the vacation of his life, becoming strong and tan. The security guards befriended him, taking him swimming in the afternoons and to the movies at night. Li Min liked him, too, and often played with him and kept him company. He stayed with me, making my bed neatly each morning and seeing that our clothes were clean. He was not so naughty after all, and I was proud that he behaved so well.

The other top leaders were also in Beidaihe, but Liu Shaoqi and Zhu De were the only two I saw regularly. Mao's presence was inhibiting to the other leaders, and they kept separate lives, swimming at their own beach and holding their own dances in the East Hill facilities set up by the State Council. Rarely did they venture into Mao's section of town. I never went to visit them, either, for Mao expected our undivided devotion and worried that if we were in contact with others, his secrets might be revealed.

Zhu De, though, seemed unaware that Mao was still angry with him and would often come to the beach when the Chairman was there, sometimes joining Mao under the awning for a chat. The former commander in chief did not know how to swim but would often go into the water with a life preserver. He was a fan of Chinese *xiang* chess, and when other players were scarce would invite my son to play. He was unfailingly polite and friendly to me, always solicitous of the Chairman, invariably asking after Mao's health, wondering whether the Chairman was busy and if he had been sleeping well.

Liu Shaoqi—tall, lean, silver-haired, and slightly stooped—was the only other party leader who often came to the beach while Mao was there. He usually arrived at about three or four in the afternoon. Reserved, dignified, and very alert, Liu Shaoqi was then Mao's chosen successor, the number-two man in the party, in charge of day-to-day domestic affairs. Mao and Liu worked closely together, but they were comrades rather than friends and rarely met in Beijing, communicating instead through party documents. When the party center composed a document for Mao's approval, it would first be sent to Liu, who would write his own comments and recommendations in the margins before sending the document, via the Bureau of Confidential Communications, on to Mao. Mao would then write his comments and return the document to Liu for implementation.

Wang Guangmei, the latest of Liu's several wives, usually accompanied him to Beidaihe. Like many of the leaders' wives, Wang was much younger than her husband. She was then about thirty and had thick black hair, an oblong face, and slightly buck teeth. She was not pretty but was attractive and very outgoing and enjoyed the limelight. Wang Guangmei would greet Mao warmly whenever she saw him and sometimes swam with him out to the platform. Jiang Qing made little effort to hide her displeasure with Liu's wife and I sensed a certain jealousy toward her. Wang was much younger than Jiang Qing, and far more relaxed and sociable. Jiang Qing always seemed ill at ease at the beach. She had never learned to swim and was embarrassed that her right foot had six toes. She kept her feet covered with rubber shoes even when she waded into the ocean.

Liu had numerous offspring from his several marriages, and a number of them were also at Beidaihe that summer. Liu Tao, a sixteen- or seventeen-year-old daughter of Liu's former wife, Wang Qian, was also very active and outgoing and friendly to Mao. She, too, would occasionally swim with him out to the raft and at the twice-weekly dancing parties often asked Mao to dance. She asked in innocence, and Mao never took the same liberties with Liu Tao that he did with so many other young women. Jiang Qing nonetheless was angered by the young woman's open and friendly personality.

But Jiang Qing was often angry, and I was trying then to inure myself to her nastiness. Never could I have imagined in bucolic, enchanting Beidaihe that a decade later her petty jealousies and insecurity would lead to such viciousness and vindictiveness that she would set out to destroy every member of Liu Shaoqi's family.

Nor could anyone have predicted in the summer of 1956 that Mao himself would later turn with such vehemence against the man we all then believed to be closest to him.

But the seeds of that split were already sown, for Mao and Liu had different ideas of what Liu's role should be. Mao considered his own rule supreme. He viewed Liu Shaoqi as his assistant in the daily affairs of the party, responsible for doing Mao's bidding. But Liu Shaoqi came to view himself as Mao's equal, or nearly so, and indispensable to the running of the state. The more equal Liu believed himself to be, the more dissatisfied with him Mao became.

The summer of 1956 was a turning point in Mao's relations with Liu. I discovered this circuitously, only after my own relationship with Mao had suffered a wounding blow.

17

The thunderstorms and gusty winds of summer were the greatest upset I had expected in bucolic Beidaihe. Instead, Mao turned against me in a sudden fit of anger. Fu Lianzhang was to blame.

Shortly after we returned to Beijing in July 1956, Fu Lianzhang had asked me to brief him on the Chairman's health. Fu's intrusive interest in Mao's well-being continued, and he had written Mao a letter that he wanted me to deliver. He wanted Mao to try a new barbiturate from West Germany called Phanodorm, and he wanted a team of physicians to give Mao a thorough physical examination.

I bridled at Fu's suggestions. Mao's insomnia had improved since I had changed his medication, and so long as he continued averaging six to eight hours of sleep a day, I saw no reason to experiment with new drugs. And Fu should have known better than anyone else that Mao would not take kindly to a physical exam. Fu himself had told me how angry Mao had been with the Soviet doctors who had examined him in 1951 and had cautioned me about how much he disliked physical exams.

I explained my objections to Fu.

Fu agreed not to raise the question of new sleeping pills, but he insisted I encourage Mao to have the exam. He had followed the Chairman since the 1930s, Fu said, and Mao had always trusted him. "Just tell him that I made the suggestion," Fu said. He named two specialists in internal medicine at Peking Union Medical College who could administer the exam. I was about to reiterate my objections when he stopped me with an icy look. "Come on," he said. "Cut the excuses. It's settled."

Fu Lianzhang put me in a difficult position. Technically, he was still my superior, and I could not easily refuse his request. But I knew that Mao would resent Fu's suggestions and that I, as his messenger, would take the brunt of Mao's ire. I was reluctant to raise the issue.

Two days went by. Fu called to complain about my delay and urged me again to give the letter to Mao.

I could not refuse. I went to see Mao immediately.

The Chairman had just finished swimming and was sunbathing by the pool. "Why haven't you been swimming lately?" he wanted to know. "Doctors should watch out for their health."

I changed into swimming trunks and went into the pool.

"Try for endurance. Don't worry about speed," Mao coached me from the side.

"I still haven't mastered the Chairman's style of swimming," I responded. "I need more practice."

He motioned me closer so he could demonstrate his style. "You look very healthy," he encouraged me.

This was my cue. "When we were in Wuhan," I said, "the Chairman went swimming in the Yangtze River, two hours each time. The Chairman's heart and circulation are much better than average."

"You are flattering me again," he smiled.

"No, I'm telling the truth. Many people much younger than you cannot swim that long. One sailor swimming with us went into shock."

"Why didn't I know about it then?"

"There were so many people around, and Comrade Wang Renzhong was afraid they would be upset if they found out."

"It's nothing to get upset about," Mao responded. "Everyone has a different constitution."

"It would be a good idea for the Chairman to have a physical exam while he is still in excellent health," I suggested. "This would give us a baseline for comparison later." I did not mention Fu Lianzhang yet, not wanting Mao to accuse me of listening to Fu without taking responsibility myself.

Mao looked at me and shook his head. "That's just doctor talk," he said. "When rural folk get sick, they do nothing. Even when they are seriously ill they often don't see a doctor. Medicine is good for curable diseases, not for incurable ones. Is your medicine really good for everything? Take cancer, for instance. Can a doctor cure cancer? I don't think so."

I explained that cancer could be cured in its early stages if it had not metastasized. I argued for the benefits of surgery. "But without a checkup, cancer in its early stages cannot be detected," I continued.

"Give me some examples," Mao challenged.

Most of the top communist leaders were relatively young and healthy then. None of them could serve as an example. I mentioned a few cases where breast cancer had been successfully cured.

Mao smiled. I had just proved his point. "Breast cancer is just on the surface of the body," he said. "It's relatively easy to detect and cure. What you should say is that some types of cancer can be cured with early detection. It isn't true for every type of cancer." He paused. "Are you telling me you want me to have a physical checkup?"

"Vice-Minister Fu has written Chairman a letter," I responded. "Please take a look."

Mao read the letter. "That Fu Lianzhang," he said, exasperated. "He just doesn't have anything else to do. I don't have time for a checkup now. Let's wait till we go to Beidaihe."

We agreed that the doctors Fu had suggested would go to Beidaihe to administer the exam there.

Fu Lianzhang was delighted with the news. "Didn't I tell you?" he said. "I knew if you said the suggestion had come from me the Chairman would certainly agree." Fu was out of touch with Mao. He had completely misunderstood.

Both Mao and Jiang Qing were scheduled for physical exams at Beidaihe. Doctors Zhang Xiaoqian and Deng Jiadong from Peking Union Medical College would examine Mao, and doctors Lin Qiaozhi and Yu Aifeng would examine Jiang Qing. Jiang Qing's examination was completed without delay, but the doctors scheduled to examine Mao waited for two weeks and still Mao's summons did not come. Mao was busy, and I hesitated to press him. Finally, Fu Lianzhang called me to complain. The doctors were needed in Beijing, he insisted. He wanted me to see that the exam was carried out.

It was a simple matter, I thought. Mao had already agreed to have the physical exam, and we needed only to set a convenient time. Trying to be casual, I raised the question with him during our English lesson the next day, explaining that the doctors had been waiting for a couple of weeks and inquiring about when he would have the checkup.

"Let them stay here and relax for a while," Mao responded.

"What should I tell them?" I wanted to know.

"About what?" Mao asked.

"Aren't we talking about your checkup?" I inquired.

Mao turned sullen. "Who said I will have a checkup?"

"Didn't Chairman say before we left Beijing that he would have a checkup in Beidaihe?" I reminded him.

Suddenly, Mao lost his temper. "Can't I change my mind?" he yelled. "Even the decisions of the politburo—I can change those, too. That bastard Wang Dongxing must be behind all this. I will not have a checkup. Tell him to get out of here."

I had no idea what had sent Mao into such a rage, nor did I know to whom he was referring when he said to get "him" out of here.

"It was Vice-Minister Fu Lianzhang who suggested the checkup, not Wang Dongxing," I responded awkwardly.

"Then get the bastard Fu Lianzhang out of here, too," Mao yelled.

"But he's not even here," I muttered weakly. I assured Mao nonetheless that I would cancel the plans for his physical.

I was shaken. Mao had no reason to be angry with me. A physical exam was a perfectly natural thing for a doctor to suggest, and certainly I had meant no harm. If Mao had not wanted the physical, he could have declined it—politely.

"Chairman is not really upset with you," Li Yinqiao tried to explain when I emerged from Mao's room. No conversation with Mao was private. Li Yinqiao and bodyguard Xiao Zhang had been listening at the door. "The politburo has met several times in the past couple of days, and there have been meetings with ministers in the State Council and with party secretaries from the provinces. Lots of issues are being discussed, and the Chairman has said some nasty things about his security arrangements. He thinks there are too many guards on his special train. He's complaining about some of the arrangements for his swim in the Yangtze. I'm not sure what's going on."

So perhaps Mao was not really angry with me. Maybe he was angry with people in the party leadership and was taking it out on me.

"If the Chairman doesn't explain to you tomorrow, Jiang Qing will," Li encouraged me. "Don't let this upset you. Don't even think about it."

But all I could think about was Mao's outburst. I had seen him lose his temper and had watched his rudeness toward others, but this was the first time he had been furious with me or had used such crude language toward me. I was extremely upset. How could I work for such a difficult, unpredictable, and hot-tempered man? Suddenly the job seemed too difficult, too dangerous. I wanted to leave. I wanted to work in a hospital.

I returned to my room to reflect and began to blame myself. I knew Mao did not want a physical exam. He had not wanted one when I raised the subject in Beijing. I had had to persuade him. He agreed only to placate me, shut me up. Since I was still trying to stay away from politics, I knew little of his activities in Beidaihe. I had proposed the physical exam without knowing what else might be bothering him. How simpleminded I was!

Mao summoned me the next evening. He smiled as soon as I walked into his room. "It's not so easy to work for me, is it?" he said. I smiled too. "Getting upset is just one of my weapons," he told me. "When they force me to do something I don't want to do, I get upset. Then I don't have to do it. I got upset so I wouldn't have to have the physical. Don't worry about my temper tantrum. I've always thought we should criticize both each other and ourselves. If I do anything wrong in the future, tell me. Just don't talk behind my back. What I don't like is people talking behind my back."

"Chairman," I responded. "I was impetuous to suggest a check-up."

"I have lots to do in Beidaihe," Mao explained. He said that the Eighth Congress of the Chinese Communist party would be convened in a few weeks, and he was busy preparing. He did not have time for a checkup. "Tell the doctors I'm too busy," he said. "We'll have the checkup later." He paused. Then he continued soothingly. "Take good care of the doctors. If they like, they can stay here a while longer. Dr. Zhang Xiaoqian is a fellow Hunanese. Maybe I'll have a chat with him."

I still knew little about the political situation, but I knew then that the Chairman was angry with someone besides me.

Mao became conciliatory after that. His confidence in me seemed to return. We met every day to study English, and often when he was unable to sleep he called me in for late-night chats. He talked mostly about his disaffection with the Soviet Union and the need for China to learn from the West. He worried about China's cultural stagnation and thought Western ideas would reinvigorate China. He wanted to borrow from the West without becoming subordinate to it, to create something new that was neither Chinese nor Western but a hybrid. When I pointed out the vast differences between the two cultures, he accused me of being unimaginative, lacking the spirit of adventure. It was the same accusation he was making against the party leaders.

It was around this time, in the late summer of 1956, that Mao first told me he was planning to resign as chairman of the republic. I did not believe him. I had yet to understand that Mao never engaged in idle talk. Sometimes it was months or years before I fully understood the importance of our conversations, and he often used them to help think things through. His intention to resign was still a secret when he first told me, though it was under discussion among the top party leadership. Only three years later, in 1959, did the resignation become public and take effect. Mao's health and his desire to retreat to the "second line," where he could focus on important matters and be free from petty detail, were offered as reasons. The truth was somewhat more complex.

Mao's health was one factor. He never slept well before the Tiananmen celebrations and sometimes did not sleep at all, so often after the ceremony he would catch colds, which would sometimes linger and become bronchitis. Mao did not like wasting time being sick.

Mao's dislike of formality was another factor in his resignation. The position of chief of state was ceremonial, and he hated to dress up. Accepting credentials from foreign ambassadors and meeting with them on state occasions was a waste of time. By 1956, even the luster of the Tiananmen celebrations had worn thin.

But I later understood that Mao's resignation was also a political tactic to test the loyalty of other ranking party leaders—especially men like Liu Shaoqi and Deng Xiaoping—of whom he was already suspicious. Khrushchev's speech attacking Stalin had put Mao on the defensive, and the response of Chinese party leaders—their initial support of Khrushchev, their affirmation of the need for collective leadership, and their criticisms of Mao's adventurism—had called their loyalty into question. By letting his intention to resign circulate secretly within the party, Mao was offering the party leadership a chance to prove its loyalty by begging him to stay on. When they did not, he devised other means to retain his power. By withdrawing from the battle, leaving Beijing for his long trip south early in the summer, Mao could observe the political maneuverings from afar. He had no intention of relinquishing power. In fact, he wanted more power rather than less. If he wanted to rid himself of petty detail it was only to ensure the supremacy of his rule and to devote himself to the more important matter of transforming China.

In his test of the party leadership, Mao did not have long to wait. The Eighth Party Congress, convened in September 1956, confirmed Mao's worst suspicions of both Liu Shaoqi and Deng Xiaoping.

18

The congress was scheduled to open on September 15, 1956. The other party leaders returned to Beijing sometime before the meetings, but Mao stayed behind in Beidaihe. The weather was beginning to turn cool, but Mao liked chilly weather, and we continued our afternoon swims until the water became too cold even for him. We left just before the congress opened.

The Eighth Party Congress was the first to convene since 1945, when the party was still in Yanan before the establishment of the People's Republic, and it would both elect a new Central Committee and lay down the guiding principles for the newly established socialist system. Mao wanted the congress to lay down his policies of radical reform and to confirm his position as the country's unparalleled leader. But he left the details of the meetings to Liu Shaoqi and Deng Xiaoping, and I think the two men let their own self-importance overwhelm their political good sense. They had misunderstood Mao's plan to resign as chairman of the republic, and their management of the congress was a slap in the face to the Chairman. He accused them of taking control and pushing him to the second line, not only on nonsubstantive and formal matters but on issues of vital interest as well.

Liu Shaoqi was charged with delivering the party's political report, the most important speech of the congress. Ordinarily, Mao would have been actively involved, commenting on Liu Shaoqi's various drafts. But Mao told me—and repeated the claim on numerous occasions during the Cultural Revolution—that Liu Shaoqi did not let him see it.

"I am going to resign the chairmanship of the republic," Mao complained to me, "but I am still the chairman of the party. Why didn't they consult me about the party congress? They did not give me a chance to participate in drafting the political report. They did not even let me see the text in advance. They said they were short of time. Well, I was not out of the country. Why did they say they were short of time?"

I did not know whether Mao had read the draft of Liu's speech, but he clearly did not like what he had learned of it, and I think his statement to me must have been an example of the exaggeration he often engaged in when he was angry. The general line laid out at the Eighth Party Congress never had Mao's support, and all of his political initiatives thereafter—the party rectification, the Great Leap Forward, the socialist education campaign, and the Cultural Revolution—were efforts to undermine the general line laid down by the congress. Not until the Twelfth Plenum of the Eighth Party Congress of 1969, which formally purged Liu Shaoqi and Deng Xiaoping, ousted the majority of representatives of the Eighth Party Congress, and enshrined Mao's thought as the country's leading force, was Mao's revenge complete.

Deng and Liu worked closely together, and their views of how China should be governed were, I think, fundamentally different from Mao's. They saw the party as a decision-making organ, and Khrushchev's attack on Stalin only confirmed their belief that decisions ought to be made collectively. They viewed Mao as the first among equals. Mao's view, however, was more imperial. He saw himself and his will as supreme and resented any indication to the contrary.

Mao gave the opening address to the congress, and I accompanied him for both the opening and closing sessions and listened offstage to Liu Shaoqi's political report. I knew immediately, listening to both Liu and Deng Xiaoping, that Mao would be furious. I, too, was very surprised. Mao had good cause to feel slighted. The reports lauded the principle of collective leadership and decried the cult of personality, and Deng Xiaoping assured the party delegates that China would never have a cult of personality. The new constitution described by Deng deleted the phrase that took Mao's thought as the country's ideological guide and created a new position for Mao, that of honorary chairman, which he would assume upon resigning the chairmanship of the party—suggesting that even his party chairmanship would not be permanent and that others expected him to step down from that post, too.

The praise of collective leadership, following Khrushchev's example, was particularly disturbing. If the party adhered to the principle of collective leadership, everyone would be equal and important issues would have to be jointly determined. Mao's role would be diminished. But Mao wanted to stay at the top. He wanted a cult of personality.

I agreed. Mao was supposed to be the leader, not Liu Shaoqi or some collective body.

Similarly, while Mao said that he wanted to retreat to the second line, he still expected to be consulted on all important matters. The problem, Mao said, was that what Liu and Deng regarded as important and sent to Mao for consideration, Mao regarded as unimportant; what Mao regarded as unimportant, Liu and Deng sent to Mao's attention.

The Eighth Party Congress was the first time I was aware that there were differences between Mao and Liu Shaoqi, his chosen successor, and the meeting was a turning point in Mao's relations with both Liu and Deng. Mao was convinced the top leaders were trying to diminish his power.

But Mao had a way of deflecting his anger, lashing out first not at the real targets of his rage but at their underlings. Just as Mao's earlier anger at Stalin had been directed instead toward his representative, Wang Ming, so Mao's fury against Liu Shaoqi and Deng Xiaoping was initially directed against their subordinates, Luo Ruiqing and Wang Dongxing. His anger brought quick and dramatic changes to my life.

The explosion occurred one evening shortly after the Eighth Party Congress and just after the October first National Day celebrations in 1956. Most of the Zhongnanhai staff were in Huairen Hall watching a performance of Chinese opera. Mao was in his bedroom, and I was reviewing some medical records in the duty office nearby. Suddenly, Li Yinqiao walked into my office and phoned Huairen Hall, instructing Luo Ruiqing and Wang Dongxing, both attending the opera, to report to Mao immediately.

The two men arrived within minutes, puzzled at Mao's unceremonious summons and wondering what could be so urgent.

"The Chairman wants to see you," was all Li Yinqiao would say.

Mao began yelling the moment the two officials walked into his room, cursing them in the crudest of language. The meeting lasted an hour, and Li Yinqiao and another bodyguard took it all in by eavesdropping at the door. Mao had already criticized Luo and Wang in

Beidaihe. Their security arrangements, he had said, were excessive, wasteful, and obsequiously modeled on those of the Soviet Union. He was still angry with Wang Dongxing for opposing his swim in the Yangtze. But what really infuriated him was something that he could not admit—that they were too subservient to the party bureaucracy. Both were in the habit of reporting directly to the party center, under the supervision of Liu Shaoqi and Deng Xiaoping.

But Mao was the chief, the head of the party secretariat, and there was no institutional necessity for Luo and Wang to report to someone else. They did so not out of loyalty to Liu Shaoqi and Deng Xiaoping and certainly not to antagonize Mao. So far as both men knew, the relationship between Mao and the other top leaders was solid as a rock. They reported to the party center because they were terrified that Mao's defiance of their security arrangements could lead to some sort of accident. They wanted to make certain that the other top leaders just under Mao would share responsibility if anything went wrong.

That the two officials reported so often to the party center had always vexed Mao, and after Liu's behavior at the Eighth Party Congress, Mao was more infuriated still. His fury was further fueled by Li Yinqiao. Li told Mao that Luo and Wang were determined, despite Mao's criticisms at Beidaihe, to provide the Chairman with "maximum protection."

Li knew that Mao did not want "maximum protection." He wanted to be free to swim where he wanted, to mix with the masses, and to indulge undetected in his private life, too. Maximum protection meant maximum exposure to guards who were strangers to Mao and loyal to Luo and Wang. The more bureaucratically appointed guards he had, the more people were privy to his private affairs, and the greater the possibility that his activities would be reported to the central party leadership. Mao needed more freedom to maneuver. He did not want the party leadership to know everything he did. He needed guards who were loyal only to him and willing to skirt the bureaucratic hierarchy. He could not say this, though, because he could not yet admit his disaffection with the men who were supposed to be his comrades.

"I don't believe that old Hunanese saying that when the butcher dies you have to eat unskinned pork," Mao shouted at Luo Ruiqing and Wang Dongxing, which meant that he could do very well without their services. "You two are fired."

Mao told Luo Ruiqing that he was being demoted, removed as minister of public security and appointed to the much less distinguished position of governor of Hunan province. Wang Dongxing was to be relieved as head of Mao's security guards and vice-minister of the Ministry of Public Security. He would go first to be "educated" at the Communist party's Central Cadre School in Beijing and then be sent back to his home province of Jiangxi for further reform.

The two men were pale and shaken when they left Mao's room. Luo Ruiqing was particularly upset. He could not understand why Mao resented his well-intentioned protection.

"What happened?" Luo asked, his lips trembling, as the two came into the duty office. He wanted to report immediately to the party center and to call a meeting at the Ministry of Public Security. He still could not understand that his penchant for reporting everything to the party center was why Mao had dismissed him.

Wang Dongxing, who was closer to Mao, understood him better. He knew that if Luo called a meeting or went to the party center, the chance for compromise would be lost and Luo's break with the Chairman would be complete.

He urged Luo Ruiqing not to act rashly, suggesting that the meeting could wait until they found out what had gone wrong. Luo was persuaded.

Later, Luo Ruiqing wrote a letter apologizing to Mao, confessing his mistake. When he called a meeting at the Ministry of Public Security it was to make a public self-criticism.

Mao relented. Luo continued as minister of public security. He never went to Hunan.

Wang Dongxing also wrote a letter apologizing to Mao and made a self-confession. But Wang was not exonerated. He was fired.

Wang Dongxing's dismissal left me bereft. He had been my friend and protector—my only support within Group One. He had given me advice and kept me informed and helped me when things went wrong. Wang Dongxing had brought me into Group One, over the persistent objections of people who remained behind and who would benefit from his departure. Both Ye Zilong and Li Yinqiao were delighted that Wang was gone, and their enmity toward me persisted. Without Wang I felt naked, helpless against the constant skirmishes within the palace walls. I had no way to survive. I would be eaten alive. I, too, would have to leave Group One. I began planning my escape.

19

Jiang Qing's health intervened. This time she really was sick.

The doctors had taken a routine Pap smear during Jiang Qing's physical examination in Beidaihe, and initial results showed a malignancy. Wanting further confirmation, her two doctors, Lin Qiaozhi and Yu Aifeng, sent slides to two of the country's leading pathologists—Liang Boqiang, at Sun Yat-sen Medical School in Guangzhou, and Hu Zhengxiang, at Peking Union Medical College. Both doctors concurred. The sample was malignant. The diagnosis was cervical cancer in situ. The cancer had not yet spread. It was in its very early stages, and they believed the disease could be cured.

But Jiang Qing was Mao's wife and the doctors had to be certain. Dr. Yu Aifeng flew to the Soviet Union with another slide. Again the diagnosis was confirmed. Fu Lianzhang, who had been coordinating the efforts of the doctors, wrote a report to Mao explaining what was wrong.

Mao called a meeting with the doctors. Dr. Lin Qiaozhi, the female gynecologist who had taken the Pap smear, suggested sending Jiang Qing to the Soviet Union for cobalt 60 treatment. Chinese hospitals were providing radium therapy then but were not equipped for cobalt 60 treatment. The Russian doctors insisted that cobalt 60 was better. Dr. Lin's suggestion was as much an effort to protect herself and her Chinese colleagues as it was good medical opinion. None of the Chinese doctors wanted to be responsible if their optimistic prognosis proved wrong.

"I'll let you decide," Mao said after listening to their recommendations. "When you are ill, you have to listen to doctors." Dr. Lin's advice was taken. Jiang Qing would be sent to the Soviet Union, accompanied by Dr. Yu Aifeng.

Jiang Qing had had intimations that something was wrong, but she had not been told. Mao wanted the physicians to tell her. He first treated us all to dinner.

Jiang Qing was inconsolable when the doctors broke the news. Only when they assured her repeatedly and unequivocally that the treatment would cure her completely was she finally mollified. Within days she left by plane for the Soviet Union.

It was early November. I had to make my move.

I had explored two possibilities—one was an opportunity to study tropical medicine in Great Britain, the other was a course in neurology at Beijing Hospital under the direction of a famous Soviet neurologist, a man named Rushinski, who was then working in China. The heads of leading neurology departments from all over the country would be participating, and at the end of the course Beijing Hospital planned to establish a new institute for advanced neurological studies.

I told Mao about both training programs. "You mean you want to go?" he asked.

"If you agree, I hope to go," I responded.

"Tropical medicine?" he mused. "That has nothing to do with me."

I knew immediately that for Mao, my "going" would be temporary. He would want me to come back.

"If you want to go," he said, "join the training program here in Beijing. That way, you will be able to help me more." Mao's most persistent complaints, after all, were symptoms of neurasthenia. A training program in neurology would better prepare me for my future work with him.

"If it meets with Chairman's approval," I responded, "I will take the matter up with the Ministry of Public Health." I still intended to leave Group One permanently, but I would have to take one step at a time. The Ministry of Public Health was responsible for placing physicians in jobs.

"Who will take over while you are gone?" Mao asked.

I had already thought of that. I wanted Dr. Bian, an internist at Beijing Hospital about five years my junior and a graduate of a very fine medical school in Nanjing, to replace me.

"I don't know him," Mao responded. "If he comes, do you intend to leave here permanently?"

I assured Mao that I would return later if he wished.

"Tell Fu Lianzhang that I can get by without a substitute for now," Mao responded. "Let's decide on this later."

Fu Lianzhang was happy to see me go—he had never wanted me to serve as Mao's doctor—and insisted, despite Mao's objections, on appointing Bian to replace me. Bian moved immediately to Zhongnanhai, and I began the training program. It was mid-November.

I rejoiced in my newfound freedom! I loved the program. My schedule was tight, and I quickly became absorbed in my new studies. I was thrilled to be working with medical colleagues. Conversation was easy, and we got along well. I often worked until two or three in the morning, but still I felt more energetic and relaxed than I had in Zhongnanhai, when my "colleagues" were Ye Zilong and Li Yinqiao. Dr. Ji Suhua, the vice-president of Beijing Hospital, invited me to stay after completing my training and promised to find me a place in the new neurology institute.

Lillian was elated with my new assignment, too, happier than she had been in years. My long hours still left little time for leisure, but her life was returning at last to normal. Her parents came from Nanjing, living with my mother, Lillian, and our two sons in the old family compound. They were delighted to be there. Their political rights had recently been restored, after the local Nanjing authorities discovered that I was the doctor of some high-ranking official in Beijing. They had been reclassified, respectably, as poor urban residents. They, too, were much more relaxed, and took pleasure in doting on their two grandsons.

But I kept my apartment in Zhongnanhai, even though we were rarely there. Luo Daorang, the man who had taken over temporarily as acting director of the Central Bureau of Guards after Wang Dongxing's dismissal, allowed me to move my official work unit to Beijing Hospital but would not allow me a complete break with Mao. He wanted to make it easy for me to return. Mao had already fired three doctors before me. Luo was afraid there would be trouble if he let me leave and the Chairman wanted me back.

Immersed in my studies, I was oblivious to the changing political situation in China, only vaguely aware that Mao had introduced a new policy of "letting one hundred flowers bloom, one hundred schools of thought contend." I knew that on February 27, 1957, he had given a talk and called on intellectuals and members of the so-called democratic parties to offer criticisms of the party's performance, and afterward, we in the training program were offered the opportunity to raise our own criticisms of the party as well. Meetings were called at Beijing Hospital. But I was too engrossed in my studies to participate in the meetings. The political movement seemed far away, like war in a distant land, and no one insisted that we take part.

By spring 1957, I was still absorbed in my studies and grateful to be back in my own milieu.

Then on May 4, 1957, Li Yinqiao came to see me at the hospital. The Chairman had caught a cold and wanted to see me. I was being summoned back.

I did not want to go.

I asked Li about Dr. Bian, who was supposed to be taking care of the Chairman.

Dr. Bian had seen Mao a couple of times after I left, Mao's bodyguard explained, but Mao could not get used to him. Mao had arranged to be introduced to the young doctor at one of his dancing parties, hoping that the festive atmosphere would put the physician at ease. But Bian had still been extremely nervous, literally trembling in Mao's presence. Mao did not like him. He was without a doctor. Mao had just returned from Guangzhou, and Jiang Qing was back from the Soviet Union. Li Yinqiao told me they both wanted me back. "When the Chairman wants you, how can you turn him down?"

But I was on duty at the hospital. Regulations required me to request permission to go, but only the party secretary at the hospital knew that I was the Chairman's doctor. Mao's security personnel had insisted that my position remain secret. They were afraid that would-be assassins could somehow use me to poison Mao. If I left the hospital without permission, I could be criticized for abusing my privileges, coming and going as I pleased. It would create a bad impression.

"Your superiors are already aware of this matter," Li informed me. A man named Wang Jingxian had by then taken charge of Mao's security after Wang Dongxing's demotion. Wang had given the directive for my return, instructing Li Yinqiao to fetch me. A car was waiting.

I insisted on reporting to my superiors.

"You don't have time," Li Yinqiao insisted. "The Chairman asked me to send for you right after he woke up. It's not good to keep him waiting. You can go see him first and report to the others later."

I had never really escaped from Group One. I was only on loan to the Ministry of Public Health. The Central Bureau of Guards still had real control over my life. I had no choice. I returned to Zhongnanhai with Li Yinqiao, my medical bag in hand.

Mao was lying in bed when I arrived, looking tired and pale. He asked me to sit next to him on the bed. A guard served tea. I asked him how he felt. "Not good," he said. "Caught a cold."

He had had a cold and a cough for more than two months, he said, since just after his February 27 speech, and he had lost his appetite.

He let me examine him. Nothing was seriously wrong. He just had a bad cold. I suggested that he take some cough syrup and some medicine to improve his digestion.

"Okay, I'll take them," he agreed. "You can write the prescriptions and give the guards the directions. You don't have to come here each time I take the medicine."

I agreed and got ready to leave.

"Please sit for a while," Mao insisted. I sat back down. "It's not so easy working for me, is it?" he asked with a smile, recalling the time he had lost his temper in Beidaihe. I smiled too. "You're thinking of leaving here permanently, aren't you?" he wanted to know. "But I don't have a new doctor yet. Let's work out a gentlemen's agreement. You come back to your job. I know you don't have much to do here. You can't give me a checkup every day. We'll find some other things for you to do. I remember something about the minister of public health under the Guomindang—Zhou Yichun or something like that, I can't remember his name exactly—but he earned a doctorate from Germany by studying the ovaries of rabbits. See, he earned an advanced degree by studying a seemingly insignificant thing. You can use your spare time here to do some research. Maybe you can get together some animals, buy some equipment, and set up a research laboratory. I will finance the whole thing with my own funds, not the government's. What do you think?"

But I did not think setting up an animal laboratory in Zhongnanhai was a good idea. I would be severely criticized. No animals were permitted within Zhongnanhai—not even cats or dogs. The health and security people were afraid that animals could pass infectious diseases to Mao and the other leaders. Later, Jiang Qing would cause quite a stir when she got a pet monkey. It simply would not do for me to have a laboratory with animals.

"Maybe when I have nothing to do here I can just read more books," I suggested to Mao.

He thought for a moment. "That's all right," he said. "But it's not enough. Knowledge cannot be acquired without practice. Well, let's settle it this way. You take care of my health and then decide later how best to use your time."

This was not a gentlemen's agreement. It was a command, politely phrased, from the party chairman. No one could disobey Mao. His word was law. If I refused, I would never find another job. My wife would be fired, too, and she would never find work again. I could even be arrested, tortured perhaps, if I ignored his command.

"I asked you to be my secretary," Mao reminded me after a pause. "But you didn't want to. There are quite a few famous personalities in modern China who began their careers in medicine and ended up in politics, you know. Sun Yat-sen, Lu Xun, and Guo Moruo all started out in medicine. Practicing medicine is fine, but there is no reason to limit yourself to it. It's also a good idea to know something about the social sciences."

Mao could force me to serve as his doctor, but he could still not persuade me to become his secretary. I was not a politician, and I would never debase myself by becoming part of the scramble for power.

"You still don't want to be my secretary?" Mao continued. "All right. Just be my physician. But let's try to develop some common language between us, try to broaden our mutual knowledge. You can read more of the *Reference Materials* even if you aren't my secretary. This way we can talk together and have a peaceful coexistence."

I was miserably disappointed. I had finally found peace in my work at Beijing Hospital and wanted very much to stay. Working with Mao, I would not even be able to visit my medical colleagues again. Loyalty to Mao meant giving up one's friends. I hated the thought of having to work with Ye Zilong and the others in Group One again, in that hateful atmosphere. But my fate still rested with Mao. I was forced to return to his side.

"I really am resigning as chairman of the republic," Mao continued. The news of Mao's resignation was still secret, but the decision was now definite. "The central authority has issued a statement to the high-level leaders of the party and government for discussion. Ye Zilong, Li Yinqiao, and some others in Group One don't like the idea. I told them my resignation is good for my health. But they don't see the point. They think when I'm no longer chairman of the republic, they won't be able to profit from my position. They think working for the chairman of the republic is more glorious."

•   •   •   •

Mao's cold, I sensed, was not his only problem. Enormous political changes had taken place during my six-month absence. I had ignored the rumblings while I was at the hospital, but now I was back in the political world.

I never returned to Beijing Hospital, not even to collect my belongings or to explain why I had to withdraw from my studies. I called the party secretary to explain that Mao had called me back, and a guard went to get my things. That very night I was back in Zhongnanhai, trapped in Group One once more. This time there was to be no escape.

III

1957–1965

20

Lin Ke tried to fill me in on what had happened during my absence.

Mao was furious over the slights he had received at the Eighth Party Congress—the call for collective leadership, the assertions that China would never have a cult of personality, the removal of Mao's thought as the guiding principle for the nation, and the criticisms of adventurism. He still saw many of the ranking party leaders as too conservative and slow at instituting revolutionary change. He was still angry at the Second Plenum of the Eighth Central Committee that had met in mid-November, just as I was beginning my studies. In his speech to the meeting, Mao announced his intention to launch a "rectification" of the party, to wipe out what he called "subjectivism, sectarianism, and bureaucratism."

It was just after the November meeting, Lin Ke said, that Mao took to his bed, staying there for months, as he often did in the midst of an unresolved political struggle, rising only to use the bathroom and make an occasional speech. Mao used these apparently debilitating depressions to plot his next political moves.

Mao's February 27, 1957, speech was part of his strategy. Mao had risen from his bed to talk to the Supreme State Conference, convened under his authority as chairman of the republic. The meeting was attended not only by the party politburo, ranking leaders of the Military Affairs Commission, and high-level government officials, but by the leaders of the "democratic parties" as well. Mao harshly criticized the party bureaucracy, and he urged members of the "democratic parties" to voice their own criticisms of the party's mistakes and to suggest means of reform. He declared the revolution a victory and socialism a success, arguing that the time for class struggle was over. Counterrevolutionaries continued to exist, but their numbers were so small—a few weeds in the midst of a field of grain—that they could do no harm. Henceforth, social contradictions were "non-antagonistic," easily manageable differences among the people. In the upcoming rectification of the party Mao would call on intellectuals from outside the party to criticize the party's faults.

Rectification movements were not new to the Communist party. Mao had directed the first one in Yanan, in 1942. The difference between this and earlier party rectifications was that this one would not be an exclusively internal affair. Mao no longer trusted the party to rectify itself. He intended to call upon the public at large, and especially intellectuals within the "democratic parties," to speak out in criticism of the party. It was a highly unusual move. The Chinese Communist party was a tightly knit, powerful, and secretive organization, and non-party people had never been allowed to criticize it. Those who did risked being labeled counterrevolutionary, as hundreds of thousands of often innocent people already knew.

Moreover, Mao was deeply suspicious of China's intellectuals. Publicly, he advocated uniting with and using them, but he continued to doubt their loyalty. Politically, intellectuals had to be reformed. "Thought reform" of educated Chinese had begun immediately after liberation, which meant teaching them to toe the party line. When they did not, the most recalcitrant and vociferous were singled out for vitriolic attack.

The writer Hu Feng had been the most recent object of attack. An outspoken critic of Mao's insistence that literature should serve his political ends, Hu Feng had not feared to offer constructive criticisms directly to the Ministry of Culture. But his most outspoken attacks had been private, voiced only in conversations and letters with friends. Some of these friends were party loyalists who had handed their letters over to the authorities. In 1955, Hu was imprisoned as head of a "secret anti-party clique" for criticism he had naively believed to be private. Hu Feng's arrest did not incline other intellectuals to speak frankly, even among friends.

Mao's policy of encouraging intellectual debate, of letting "one hundred flowers bloom and one hundred schools of thought contend," was a gamble, based on a calculation that genuine counterrevolutionaries were few, that rebels like Hu Feng had been permanently intimidated into silence, and that other intellectuals would follow Mao's lead, speaking out only against the people and practices Mao himself most wanted to subject to reform.

Mao had reason to believe that his gamble would work. Every time he met with representatives of the "democratic parties," he was showered with the same obsequious flattery I had first witnessed from the provincial party leaders during our trip south in the summer of 1956. With the Hu Fengs silenced, the remaining intellectuals, loyalists, could be expected to follow Mao's lead.

At the Supreme State Conference in February 1957, after Mao blamed his own failure in leadership for the country's decline in economic production, Zhang Zhizhong, onetime Guomindang general and leading negotiator in the talks between the communists and the nationalists in 1945, rose to defend the Chairman. Zhang had defected to the communists in 1949, at the urging of Zhou Enlai. He had become an ardent, outspoken supporter of his erstwhile adversaries.

"I often compare the Chairman with Chiang Kai-shek," Zhang said at the Supreme State Conference. Chiang Kai-shek, Zhang said, always blamed others when anything went wrong. He never took responsibility himself. Mao, though, blamed no one. "He takes responsibility himself. What a difference! How admirable!"

The criticisms Mao called for were slow in coming. Most intellectuals were afraid to speak out. Mao was such an overwhelming presence, surrounded by the aura of righteousness and power, that even the brave and the honest were overcome by awe, suddenly obsequious before him. The truth Mao so often extracted in private, face-to-face meetings was in the form of confessional, abject apologies for having doubted or wandered in the past. The confessions would be followed by promises of loyalty. Nothing about Mao's presence, in public or in private, encouraged dissidents to speak the truth and so he believed that his popular support was nearly universal.

When the intellectuals remained quiet, Mao rose from his bed and took to the podium again. At a National Propaganda Work Conference, held from March 6 to 13, 1957, attended by ranking party leaders and non-party "democratic elements," Mao repeated the message of his February speech and again invoked the policy of "letting one hundred flowers bloom, one hundred schools of thought contend," urging leaders of the "democratic parties" to overcome their hesitations and speak out. Newspaper articles repeated his theme and party leaders in local work units throughout the country took up the gauntlet. The more one loved the party, the saying went, the more one would speak out in criticism of it.

The rebukes, when they began, were mild and often petty.

Finally, the "democratic elements" began to oblige and criticism increased.

It was at this point, in early May, just as the criticisms were becoming strident, that I returned to Mao's side.

As days went on, the "mistakes" of the party were subjected to increasingly ruthless criticism. Finally, the very right of the party to rule was questioned. Not only were individual members of the party called to account, but the party as an institution was rebuked. People were suddenly arguing that the Communist party had no intrinsic right to rule, that power should be shared. Some people called for a multi-party system or a policy of political rotation, in which each party had a turn. A few misguided souls even argued that the "democratic parties" should have their own armies.

In the end, Mao's own leadership was criticized. The Communist party was likened to a Buddhist monastery where the abbot (Mao) dictated the "scriptures" that were then echoed by the monks—the leaders under Mao. Some people complained that they were allowed to criticize only the minor monks and not the abbot himself.

Mao of course was shocked. He had never intended that any of the criticisms be directed against him. He had never meant the party as an institution to come under attack. Accustomed as he was to the flattery of everyone he met, certain that his real enemies had been eliminated or put in jail, he had not realized the depth of the intellectuals' dissatisfaction.

By mid-May, the criticisms were reaching a zenith. The tide of Chinese public opinion seemed to be turning against the party. Even members of the State Council's Office of Counselors, high-level intellectuals from the "democratic parties" to whom the government frequently turned for advice, were joining the attacks. When one counselor stood up to make a speech defending the party, no one paid attention. The *People's Daily,* the Communist party's own newspaper, headed then by Deng Tuo and under the supervision of the deputy director of the party's Propaganda Department, my friend Hu Qiaomu, also ignored the counselor's speech.

Mao had grossly miscalculated. He stayed in bed, depressed and apparently immobilized, sick with the cold that called me back, as the attacks grew ever more intense. He was rethinking his strategy, plotting his revenge. He was furious.

On May 15, only days after my return, Mao wrote an article entitled "Things Are Changing," which was secretly circulated to high-level leaders. The nature of the rectification campaign was soon to be transformed. Mao was planning a counterattack against those who had spoken out so vociferously in criticism. In the next few days, as local leaders and newspaper editors learned of the coming counterattack, newspapers were encouraged to continue publishing criticisms of the party while allowing defenses of the party and attacks against the "rightists" to be published, too.

"We want to coax the snakes out of their holes," Mao told me around this time. "Then we will strike. My strategy is to let the poisonous weeds grow first and then destroy them one by one. Let them become fertilizer." The intellectuals were still being encouraged to speak out, but party leaders now knew that a counterattack against them was about to begin.

"I wanted to use the democratic parties to rectify the Communist party," Mao told me. "I never realized they were so unreliable." He thought members of the Democratic League, formed in the 1940s by a group of intellectuals hoping to find a moderate solution somewhere between the communists and the nationalists, were the worst. "They are nothing but a bunch of bandits and whores," he said. Khrushchev's attack on Stalin in February 1956 and the Hungarian revolt in the fall of that year had set off a tide of worldwide anti-communism, he thought, and in China both party officials and ordinary people had succumbed. Mao accused them of being muddle-headed.

He turned his wrath on Hu Qiaomu for having done nothing to stop the *People's Daily*'s attacks on the party. "If you can't manage the newspaper," he told Hu, whose job was to keep the editor of the party newspaper in check, "then resign and let others do it." He told Hu to prepare for an attack on the rightists.

On June 8, 1957, the *People's Daily* published the first open hint that the policy of encouraging intellectuals to speak out was about to change. An article written by Mao, "What Is This For?," accused a small number of people of attempting to overthrow the socialist government and called upon the masses to begin a counterattack.

On June 19, 1957, the speech Mao had given on February 27, in which he first encouraged intellectuals to speak out, was finally published in the *People's Daily*. Titled "On the Correct Handling of Contradictions Among the People" and presented as an almost verbatim transcript of the original speech, it was in fact very different from Mao's original talk. Its tone completely reversed the liberal, conciliatory Mao. People who had heard the original speech said that in it, Mao had set no conditions on acceptable criticism. Critics were strongly encouraged to speak out, to let one hundred flowers bloom. There was no mention of "poisonous weeds" or of snakes coming out of their holes. But in the June 19 version of the speech, Mao set forth six constraints: Criticisms must serve to unite rather than divide; must serve to build socialism and to consolidate the people's democratic dictatorship; must help the socialist system, the leadership of the Communist party, and the unification of the international communist movement.

Just as Mao felt betrayed by the intellectuals who had spoken out, now it was the intellectuals' turn to feel grievously betrayed by Mao. His message to speak out had been echoed in newspapers and work units everywhere in China. Reluctantly, they had voiced their criticisms. And when they did, Mao turned against them.

Mao knew the intellectuals felt betrayed. "Now some of the rightists are saying that I plotted against them," he said after the June 19 version of the speech was published. "They say that I urged them to participate in the blooming-and-contending campaign and then retaliated when they did as I said. But I haven't hatched any 'secret plot.' I did it openly. I told the rightists to criticize us in order to help the party. I never asked them to oppose the party or to try to seize power from the party. I told them from the very beginning not to make trouble. 'It won't be good for you to make trouble,' I warned them. 'Just try to be helpful to the Communist party.' Some of them listened. But most of them didn't." Mao, I know now, was being disingenuous. His strategy of using the intellectuals to criticize his foes within the party had backfired.

It was around this time, toward the end of June, about six weeks after my return, that the new security chief, Wang Jingxian, came to see me. "Get ready to take a trip," he told me. Mao was leaving Beijing. Where he was going was still a secret, but Wang knew we would be gone for a while. The period of blooming and contending was over. Mao's campaign against the rightists had begun.

21

We traveled as usual on Mao's luxurious train, the schedule still tied to the Chairman's unorthodox sleeping habits. But the security arrangements were completely changed. Mao's personal entourage had been reduced to less than a tenth of the force that used to accompany us when Wang Dongxing was in charge. Wang Jingxian, a timid man who had taken over as head of Mao's security forces, had been reluctant to take on his awesome assignment. He was following Mao's wishes to the letter, reducing the Zhongnanhai security staff to a minimum and relying primarily on local security forces for protection.

Once Mao decided on a counterattack, his health quickly revived; his cold was gone and his old vigor and spirit were back. He had plenty of time to talk en route, and so did Lin Ke, and my conversations with both helped me catch up on news of the events in my absence. Often I would hear my late-night conversations with Mao delivered a day or two later in the form of a speech.

"I handle opponents by letting them attack first," Mao told me. "Only later do I strike back. I have three rules: First, I follow the ancient philosopher Laozi. I, the father, do not initiate action.* When under attack, I retreat, doing nothing, remaining silent. We let the enemy feel he has scored a few points." If we were to answer enemies immediately, Mao said, they would not dare to show their true face.

---

*Laozi, in Chinese, means both Laozi the philosopher and "father." Mao intended both meanings.

So he wanted to wait until they exposed themselves. Only then do we retaliate, doing to them what they have been doing to us, Mao said. "This is the Confucian way."

It was not really the Confucian way but a tactic Mao used with both the rightists and his foes within the party.

"In the beginning, people didn't know who the rightists were or what they looked like, and it was hard for us to explain," Mao continued. "But now we can identify them clearly. They are counterrevolutionaries. No—don't call them counterrevolutionaries. That doesn't sound good. Just call them rightists."

Mao's second rule was that he did not imprison his opponents unless they had committed some egregious deed, something, he said, that really antagonized the people. "They can work," he said. "Why should we waste their productive power by imprisoning them? If they aren't qualified to be leaders, their labor can still produce something of value. This method has a long tradition in Chinese history."

Mao's third rule was that opponents would be reformed within their own work units. The work unit would be responsible for observing the rightists' behavior and listening to what they said. Rightists teach by negative example, he said, letting us know what is wrong and bad. If rightists can be properly reformed, Mao said, that was fine. They'll feel good after they have been rectified. Those who cannot be rectified, whose minds are as hard as granite, will just die with their granite brains intact. "There is nothing else we can do," he said. But he doubted that many people were that hardheaded.

Mao thought that just about everyone could be reformed. Everyone can become a good person, he said. "A cow is not born tilling the land or giving us milk. An untrained horse can't be ridden. Cows and horses have to be domesticated in order to benefit man. A counterrevolutionary—or, for that matter, a spy—must have some sort of special talent. If not, how could he become a counterrevolutionary or a spy or a rightist? So why can't we reform them and make use of their talent?"

Mao's greatest anger was reserved for the Democratic League. "There's not a single good person in it," he said. "We thought about disbanding the League, but we wanted to try to unite with them. But now the Communist party is going to rectify the Democratic League and all the other democratic parties. We're going to single out hundreds of thousands of rightists. We won't kill anyone, though, because if we were to kill anyone we would have to kill them all. This is a rule we laid down during the rectification campaign in Yanan in the early 1940s, when Wang Shiwei launched an attack on the party and published *Wild Lilies*. When we investigated, we discovered that Wang was a Trotskyite and a secret agent, but I insisted that he not be killed. It was when we were retreating from Yanan under Guomindang attack that our security forces executed him. They were afraid he might try to run away. I criticized them for killing him."

The writer Wang Shiwei had published scathing criticisms of the party in Yanan, accusing the leaders of living the good life even as they preached asceticism and egalitarianism. While the leaders danced, ordinary Chinese were suffering desperately in the struggle against the Japanese invasion. Critical though he was, Wang was no Trotskyite, and when I read *Wild Lilies* years after my conversation with Mao, I knew that Wang's accusations had been correct. He had been criticizing the same corruption I saw later in Zhongnanhai. The degeneration of the party had begun as early as Yanan, I realized.

We stopped first in Jinan, Shandong, and then traveled on to Shanghai, where we were hosted by one of Mao's most ardent supporters, mayor Ke Qingshi. Ke Qingshi was the only party leader who had actually seen Lenin. He had been studying at the University of the Orient in the Soviet Union and was working in a factory when Lenin gave an address. Mao said that Ke had never forgotten the scene, as though the influence of seeing Lenin had led Ke Qingshi to become a great revolutionary. "See how powerful the influence of a great leader can be on the people?" Mao said when he told me the story.

Ke had arranged for the Chairman to stay in the opulent bronze-roofed marble mansion once owned by Silas Hardoon, a Jewish businessman who had made his fortune in Shanghai in the 1910s. Located in the heart of the city and enclosed by high brick walls, the grounds of the estate were still magnificent, the rolling green lawns dotted with frog-filled lily ponds and ancient trees. But Mao was uncomfortable with this Western-style opulence and insisted, over Ke's objections, on moving back to his train.

Unlike Mao's earlier trips, this visit to Shanghai was a public event. Everyone knew he was there. He wanted the country to know that he was in charge and that a campaign against rightists had begun.

The anti-rightist campaign in Shanghai was already unfolding. We visited a factory where workers had already put up "big character posters"—huge sheets of paper covered with large characters whose messages attacked the rightists. Mao declared the big character posters a great creation. He delivered a speech to local party, army, and government cadres. He met with the city's leading leftist artists—the writer Ba Jin, the actor Zhao Dan, his wife, Huang Zongying, and the actress Qing Yi.

Mao in attack was Mao on the move. We soon left the bustle of Shanghai for the peace of Hangzhou, the most beautiful of China's cities, its West Lake the most enchanting spot in the world. I have never seen anything so exquisite as the place where we stayed. Liuzhuang, it was called. Now remodeled and modernized for Mao, it had once been the home of a fabulously wealthy tea merchant. Located on a flower-filled, secluded peninsula that jutted into West Lake, Liuzhuang was smaller and more tasteful than the Summer Palace in Beijing, its gardens bigger and more opulent than those of Suzhou. Built in the traditional style, the numerous tile-roofed buildings were set in the middle of ponds and streams and connected to each other by graceful arched white-marble bridges. The fish were as plentiful as the flowers, and our chef was deft in transforming the daily catch into delicious dishes.

Soviet leader Anastas Mikoyan came to meet Mao in Hangzhou. He was on a secret mission to soothe Mao's feelings over the recent Malenkov-Molotov purge—and for some difficult talks on China's proposed development of nuclear weapons. Mao asked me to see him.

A short, stooped man of about sixty, the Soviet leader was suffering from arthritis in his back and legs and wondered whether acupuncture would help. I arranged for him to see a famous acupuncturist in Beijing, but as we chatted about his health, he offered me a glass of vodka and switched the topic to the perils of nuclear war. His discussions with Mao had clearly shaken him, and he needed to talk. He was greatly distressed by Mao's nonchalance about the massive loss of human life.

Mao had been expounding his "paper tiger" theory again, arguing that China could afford to lose tens of millions of people in a nuclear war. Mikoyan wanted to impress on me the horrible destructiveness of the atom bomb. He hoped that China would learn from the experience of the Soviet Union and cease trying to build the bomb. The cost—millions and millions of rubles—was only one consideration. He also described the debilitating illness—aplastic anemia, in which the bone marrow loses the ability to produce blood cells—that had killed a senior Soviet official in charge of testing the bomb.

"I am a physician," I had replied to his warnings. "I know very little about the atom bomb. But from the point of view of medical ethics, I oppose it. It is just like other weapons. It kills people."

I had no right to discuss such sensitive issues with leaders of foreign countries and felt compelled to report the conversation to Mao. But for Mao the issue of the atom bomb was one of control, not human lives. "Mikoyan told me, too, that the Soviet bombs were enough for both our countries," he said. " 'The Soviet nuclear umbrella can cover us all.' But the Soviet Union wants to control us," he insisted. "That's why they don't want us to have the bomb. The fact is they can never control us. The Soviet Union is worried that we don't listen to them. They're afraid we might provoke the United States. But we're not afraid of getting into trouble with other countries. I will definitely develop the atom bomb. You can count on it. Nobody should try to restrict us. Nobody should try to intimidate us. No one can lord it over us."

If Mao was willing to lose so many ordinary Chinese people to nuclear war, why should he not be willing to allow the deaths of tens of thousands of rightists? He might not order their executions, just as he had not ordered the death of Wang Shiwei, but he would do nothing to intervene.

Mao gave another talk in Hangzhou and then rested a few days, but we soon moved on to Nanjing, staying at a villa once owned by a Guomindang official. It was already July and Nanjing was sweltering, the temperature often climbing to over one hundred degrees. Mao was always less bothered by the heat than I. His aides would bring fresh barrels of ice to his room each day; as Mao discoursed on the anti-rightist campaign, the ice melted and I sweated.

The campaign was swirling like a tempest outside. Mao was reading the domestic *Internal Reference* with relish, savoring the criticisms of the rightists that filled its pages. Our nocturnal chats became more frequent, often extending into the early-morning hours. That he was sleeping less seemed only to exhilarate him, as did the unfolding political drama.

Lin Ke, who had been in close contact with Mao while I was at Beijing Hospital, told me his political analysis of Mao's new mood. He thought that Mao was being forced to make temporary peace with his opponents within the party in order to launch a united counterattack against the intellectuals outside the party who had been so vociferous in their rebukes. Deng Xiaoping was put in charge of the anti-rightist campaign. Deng had sometimes irritated Mao, but he was not one of those Mao had accused of foot-dragging. Only much later would I learn with what vengeance Deng conducted the anti-rightist campaign and how viciously he attacked those who would undermine the party's rule.

From the vantage of hindsight, I see Mao's attempts to rectify the party in 1957 as an abortive Cultural Revolution. What we remember most about 1957 today are the terrors committed against the rightists outside the party. But in the beginning Mao's antagonists were actually leading members within the party, men who had slighted him, belittled his power, and urged caution when Mao insisted on plunging ahead with his utopian socialist dreams. Mao wanted these opponents attacked, perhaps even ousted. But he did not want the socialist system or the right of the Communist party to rule called into question. Above all, he did not want his own rule to be undermined. Faced with attacks from outside the party, Mao was forced back into temporary alliance with his opponents within the party. They, in turn, now joined him enthusiastically because their right to rule, even more than Mao's, had also been called into question.

But Mao had put the party leadership on notice that he could call upon outsiders to attack them, and the implicit threat stood as a sword over the heads of those who might challenge his rule. Most leaders, for the time being, fell in line with Mao's demands. Fear that Mao would again unleash his own anger, and the wrath of the intellectuals, against them was as much a reason for their support of his later Great Leap Forward as their shared belief in his utopian dreams. Mao was still testing the party leadership. The Chairman was struggling to regain control, regrouping his forces, mustering his strength, prepared to strike back at a later time.

In the meantime, he wanted to call a party meeting to take stock of the situation. Nanjing was too hot. Jiang Weiqing, the crippled first party secretary of Jiangsu province, where Nanjing is located, assembled several provincial leaders to come up with a more hospitable venue.

They decided on Qingdao, the coastal resort in Shandong province once controlled by the Germans, where the weather was cool and the swimming excellent. The weather was too hot for the Chairman to travel by train, so we flew in two Soviet-built IL-14 airplanes, stopping briefly in Jinan, where Mao gave a rousing speech against the rightists—an abbreviated version of the meandering discourses of our late-night chats—to a group of party and military cadres from the Shandong region.

Qingdao, cooled by a refreshing sea breeze, was a welcome respite from the furnace of Nanjing. The town was hilly like San Francisco and German in flavor, with rows of neat red-brick, red-roofed houses set among lush shrubbery and trees, surrounded by red-brick walls. Mao and his personal entourage stayed in the magnificent hilltop castle that had once housed the region's German governor. The view was spectacular—a panoramic vista of the city and the sea.

Mao visited the town's most famous attractions—the aquarium, which was considered the best in China; Shandong University, where Jiang Qing claimed to have audited the lectures of the noted Shakespearian scholar Liang Shiqiu; and a locomotive factory, where Mao and the workers both seemed delighted to meet, even though Mao only waved and did not speak. Security measures in Qingdao were heavy. Mao's presence in the resort was supposed to be secret, but between his sight-seeing excursions and the extensive security precautions, the residents surely had cause to wonder. Many of Qingdao's streets remained closed to both vehicles and pedestrians.

The meeting of provincial and municipal-level party secretaries began on July 17, 1957, shortly after our arrival, and went on for several days, with the discussions focusing on the unfolding antirightist campaign and how to further the socialist transformation. The *People's Daily* published Mao's report from the conference in an article entitled "The Political Conditions in the Summer of 1957." It was yet another attack on the rightists and a restatement of his vision of socialism—modern industry and agriculture built by a huge army of socialist-minded technocrats. Mao spoke in paradoxes—of the centralization of power and of democracy, of discipline and freedom, of unity through ideology and of individual will. The task, he said, was to surpass the United States economically within forty or fifty years, beginning from 1953, and to move from socialism to communism. Something was germinating in Mao's mind. It was not yet clear what it was.

From the protective cocoon of Mao's personal entourage, living in unimaginable luxury, shielded from the mundane world, I had no way of conceiving what the anti-rightist campaign was really about— how widespread the attacks might be, what it meant to those who were singled out, what types of punishment were being handed down. Even Mao's conversations had an air of unreality. The implications of what he said were almost impossible for me to grasp.

And I was very busy in Qingdao, preoccupied with problems that had nothing to do with politics.

22

My problem was Jiang Qing. She had returned from the Soviet Union in April, just before Mao called me back, and was with us in Qingdao. The cobalt 60 treatment had been successful, but her bout with cancer had left her more demanding and hypochondriacal, and more difficult to deal with than ever. After only two days in the castle, she had kicked out Mao's entourage, complaining about the noise we made. The flushing of our toilet disturbed her. "Whose rest did we come here for, anyway?" she demanded. "Yours or mine?"

She was still under the care of her two gynecologists, but since Xu Tao's departure in the fall of 1956, she had had no internist. She asked me to serve as her doctor. I demurred, pointing out that my obligations were to Mao, that I always traveled with him, and she was not often along on the trips. She understood, she assured me, but wanted me to take care of her when she and the Chairman were together. "I won't need much help," she said, "and if you are not around, my nurse can call you for instructions and prescriptions." I could not refuse.

The arrangement soon ran into difficulty. Several days after our expulsion from the castle, in the midst of a torrential downpour, Jiang Qing's nurse called me. It was about eleven o'clock at night, but Jiang Qing wanted to see me immediately. She had a stuffy nose. After determining that her pulse was normal and she was running no fever, I suggested to the nurse that Jiang Qing take some allergy medicine, and I promised to go and see her first thing in the morning. I had no car and saw no use getting soaked in the downpour over Jiang Qing's stuffy nose.

Minutes later, my phone rang again. Jiang Qing was furious and had asked her nurse to tell me that it was irresponsible for a doctor to prescribe medicine without seeing the patient first.

I was furious, too. It was very late, and Jiang Qing knew it was raining heavily. Her "illness" was a mere stuffy nose. She was utterly inconsiderate demanding me to see her in those circumstances. "She does not have to take the medicine if she doesn't want to," I assured the nurse. "I will see her tomorrow."

Jiang Qing snubbed me the next day. Her two gynecologists were about to return to Beijing, and she had scheduled a farewell banquet in their honor. Protocol required that I be there, too, but she pointedly refused to invite me, spreading word through her staff that I was being punished for my misbehavior. In fact, I was happy not to go. Eating with Jiang Qing was an ordeal. She took her medication at meals and had a pill for each of her many disorders. Her guests were forced to sit through her disquisitions on each pill and its functions—this one for her poor digestion, another to build her blood, tranquilizers for her nerves, a host of vitamins for a range of ills. Those who came expecting good food and lively conversation soon found their appetites disappearing as Jiang Qing monopolized the conversation with her maladies.

Then Mao caught a cold, too. Qingdao had stayed cool and wet even in July, but the Chairman still went swimming every day at the private beach the Shandong public-security officials had cleared for him. His cold started shortly after the meeting was over, and he developed a cough, lost his appetite, and turned listless. My Western medicine did no good, and after a few days I suggested he stop taking it. Shu Tong, the first party secretary of Shandong, persuaded Mao to see a famous doctor of Chinese medicine from Jinan. It was the first time Mao had agreed to be treated by traditional methods. He still did not believe in Chinese medicine, even though he continued to promote it, and he did not like the hot, bitter herbal liquid that was the trademark of the traditional cure. But he was frustrated that he could not shake the cold and he decided to give it a try. "You don't want me to take more of your Western medicine," he said to me, "so what am I supposed to do?"

I never understood the theory behind Chinese medicine, but many of the herbal cures seemed to work. My father had once been cured by a famous doctor of Chinese medicine when Western medicine failed. I thought Mao should give it a try.

"So let the doctor come and treat me—under your supervision," Mao said.

The doctor, Liu Huimin, was a tall, thin sixty-year-old man, unsophisticated and honest. Mao treated him in the same disarming manner he always used when meeting people for the first time. "*Huimin* means 'beneficial to the people,' " Mao said, commenting on the doctor's given name. "Please give me the benefit of your treatment."

Dr. Liu felt Mao's pulse and looked at the Chairman's tongue. "The Chairman has a cold deep inside his body," the doctor announced seriously. "We need to administer medicine to get the cold out."

Mao already knew he had a cold and was not interested in further confirmation. He only wanted to be cured. "I don't understand Chinese medicine. You just talk to Dr. Li about how to treat me," he said, motioning us both away. Dr. Liu bowed deeply to Mao, in the traditional manner of respect, and I accompanied him and Shu Tong to discuss the treatment.

Dr. Liu wanted to administer two doses of herbs, stewed in broth, just before his bedtime. Mao was then to sleep under heavy blankets, to induce sweat. I knew the Chairman would not like the prescription. He did not like bitter liquids, and he kept his room cool, covering himself with a terry-cloth towel rather than a blanket.

I had to explain the proposed treatment to Mao. He frowned. "Chairman does not like this treatment, does he?" I asked. "But Chairman can try it this once. If it doesn't work, you don't have to try it again."

Mao was still reluctant. "If I cover myself with a heavy blanket, I'll perspire without his medicine. Why do I need to take the medicine, too?"

"Perspiring with his medicine and without it are two different things," I explained. "If you try it, you'll be able to tell the difference."

Mao agreed. "I'll try it just this once. If it's no good, I won't do it again."

Shu Tong's wife prepared the medicine. I checked all the ingredients to satisfy myself that the herbs were harmless, but since the medicine would not go through the elaborate poison control of Fu Lianzhang's pharmacy, I had to confer with the Central Bureau of Health in Beijing about how to guarantee that the herbs were safe. Mao always had special telephones installed when he traveled, with six or eight secure lines going directly to his confidential secretaries in

Zhongnanhai. I used one of them to call. The bureau concluded that since Shu Tong was a member of the party Central Committee and first party secretary of Shandong province, the doctor he had proposed must be reliable. But they were puzzled over the question of how to protect against the possibility of poison. In the end, four identical portions of the medicine, a dark brown bitter-tasting brew, were prepared. One bowl was sealed and put in custody with the Central Bureau of Health. Then Shu Tong and I served as guinea pigs, drinking the medicine first. When we suffered no immediate adverse effects, Mao drank his.

Mao spent an uncomfortable night sweating under his heavy blanket. He felt no better the next day. Dr. Liu encouraged him to repeat the procedure.

On the morning of the third day, Mao still did not feel well. Dr. Liu felt the Chairman's pulse and looked at his tongue again. The Chairman, he concluded, had been cured.

Mao thought otherwise. He was still sick. He had a cold and a cough. His symptoms had not gone away. After another three days of the medicine, Mao had still not improved.

Dr. Liu was puzzled. He examined Mao again, taking his pulse and looking at his tongue. This time he concluded that the real source of the Chairman's discomfort was not the cold but exhaustion. The cure was a concoction of ginseng and herbs designed to replenish lost nutrients. The herbs were the stock-in-trade of traditional Chinese medicine, and while dubious about the need to "replenish" Mao's nutrients, I saw no great harm in the prescription. The Central Bureau of Health again approved. Four batches were prepared, and Shu Tong and I again served as guinea pigs.

Still Mao did not improve. The doctor was puzzled. I thought warmer weather might help, and while Shu Tong assured us every day that the cool, damp weather was highly unusual and would surely change, it did not. Finally, I suggested to Mao that we return to Beijing. He agreed. We arrived back in Zhongnanhai in early August. His cold immediately improved.

23

Mao wanted me to experience the anti-rightist campaign firsthand.

"You're like a hermit, hiding in the mountain and seeing no one," he said shortly after our return to Beijing. He suggested I visit Peking Union Medical Hospital and tell him what was happening there.

The old Peking Union Medical Hospital, financed with Rockefeller funds, had been one of the finest and most comprehensive in the country, with the best doctors and the most up-to-date equipment. But the hospital had been completely reorganized, following the Soviet model, since 1949. Some of the hospital's most distinguished doctors had been assigned elsewhere, and management had been put under party control. Power was now in the hands of the first party secretary, Zhang Zhiqiang. While the party leadership regarded Zhang Zhiqiang as a doctor because he had been trained during the war by communist medics, the Western-trained doctors on the staff did not. Zhang was a coarse and uneducated man, but he was an old revolutionary, and in those days being revolutionary was considered qualification enough.

The real doctors on the staff, my friends and former teachers among them, had been distressed by the organizational changes, believing that the overall quality of the hospital had suffered. They thought the Ministry of Public Health, in overall charge of hospital management, was interfering in their affairs. When urged to speak out during the blooming of the hundred flowers, several of them had. I carried their concerns back to Mao.

He did not like my interpretation of the hospital's problems, accused me of having stopped eating after only a taste, and sent me back for further investigation.

I attended one of the meetings to criticize the hospital's "rightists." Li Zongen, the director of the medical school, and Li Kehong, the medical director of the hospital, were the primary objects of attack, and their main accusers were the hospital's young lab technicians and nurses, uneducated people with little understanding of how to run a modern hospital. The younger doctors, who did know something about how the hospital should have worked, had too much respect for their senior colleagues to participate in the attacks. The two Dr. Lis were accused of attempting to undermine party leadership over the hospital and of overstepping their authority by trying to control personnel, finance, and administration. The meeting was lively, and the crowd was excited and angry.

I sympathized with the two doctors, but I also thought they had been foolish to criticize the party openly. No one criticized the party. I had already worked for Mao for three years, and I still revered him. I had no independent will or opinions. What Mao thought, I thought. It was not that I had contrary opinions that I had to suppress or keep to myself. Mao's opinions were mine. The possibility of differing with the Chairman never crossed my mind.

After the meeting, I went to see Dr. Zhang Xiaoqian, one of the senior physicians originally scheduled to administer the physical exam to Mao in Beidaihe and, like Mao, a native of Hunan province. Zhang had been the director of his alma mater, the Yale-in-China Medical School in Hunan, before liberation and was one of the country's best doctors. During the spring, Dr. Zhang had spoken out, too, criticizing the party secretary for failing to consult him about the transfer of doctors from his department to other hospitals. Now, as the anti-rightist campaign unfolded, Dr. Zhang was greatly distressed. "I made a terrible mistake talking so much," he told me. "I shouldn't have said what I did. But I never meant to grab power in personnel matters. I only said that the head of a department should have the right to say something about his physicians, especially about their performance." Dr. Zhang asked me to "reflect his views to the proper authorities," meaning Mao.

When I reported on my second visit, Mao smiled, convinced that I finally understood the situation in the hospital. He explained that power over personnel, finance, and administration was the concrete manifestation of party authority. If those powers were given away, party leadership would be impossible. "We won these powers only after years of civil war and after countless casualties. And now the rightists want to take them away." But he forgave Zhang Xiaoqian. Dr. Zhang is different,

Mao said, just a simpleminded person who has been manipulated by others. Zhang Xiaoqian was never persecuted for having spoken out.

Doctors Li Zongen and Li Kehong were not so lucky. Only weeks after my visit, they were officially labeled rightists and exiled to the countryside for "reform." Li Kehong, one of the best doctors in China, was reduced to serving as a librarian in a small medical college in Yunnan, in China's far southwest. Dr. Li Zongen, also an outstanding physician, was exiled to remote Guizhou. Neither doctor ever returned to Beijing. Both died prematurely, soon after having been sent away.

Even as the anti-rightist campaign broadened and Mao's net spread wider and wider, I barely knew what the campaign really meant. I did not know how many people were being sent to labor reform or what torture this "rectification" really was. In fact, listening to Mao talk, I actually thought the Chairman was generous to his enemies, giving them a chance to reform. When Mao told me that he did not believe in killing his opponents, I believed him. So I supported Mao and supported the anti-rightist campaign. Mao was good and the Communist party was good. They had saved China.

Only three years later, in 1960, when China's foreign minister, Chen Yi, told me that half a million people had been labeled rightists, did I know that the numbers were just too large and that most of those people had been falsely accused. What was most disturbing was that the various work units charged with finding rightists had been assigned a quota. Every place had to declare 5 percent of its members guilty of being rightists, whether they really were rightists or not. Hundreds of thousands of people had been falsely accused.

It was only later, too, that I began to understand what it meant to be labeled a rightist, how many people lost their jobs, were sent to labor reform camps, and died miserable deaths. It is true that Mao did not kill his opponents right away. But the physical and mental hardship of his "reforms" often meant a torturously slow and painful death. Only when I was sent myself to participate in hard labor for a mere two weeks did I begin to have an inkling of what life in the labor reform camps was like. They could take a man who could carry only twenty *jin* of stones and force him to carry forty, and when his body broke and he could go no further, they would say it was because he was a rightist. And as he lay there shattered and broken, helpless, they would force him to confess to his crimes and then to betray other people. People died in those labor reform camps, where death seemed better than Mao's reform.

I should have known. I had opportunities to know. Mao himself had given me plenty of hints. "If we were to add up all the landlords, rich peasants, counterrevolutionaries, bad elements, and rightists, their number would reach thirty million," he said to me one day. "If we put them all together in one area, they would constitute a good-size nation. They could make all sorts of trouble. But dispersed among the various party and government organs, they're just a tiny minority. Of our total population of six hundred million people, these thirty million are only one out of twenty. So what is there to be afraid of? Some of our party members cannot see this point. I've told them to just stand firm when they're under attack. Stick it out. But some of them thought it was disastrous to be attacked. They couldn't stand it anymore, and some of them even wanted to leave the party and join the rightists to attack us. Now we have identified all these people, and we are going to attack them."

This was the first I had heard that there were some 30 million "enemies of the people." The figure seemed enormous. But by then I knew that Mao rarely spoke without good reason, and his figure must have come from a reliable source. Later I would come to believe the figure was even higher.

I had had intimations, too, of how little the lives of his countrymen meant to Mao.

"We have so many people," he would say. "We can afford to lose a few. What difference does it make?"

I am grateful that I did not understand Mao at the time, did not know how widespread his purges were, how horribly my fellow intellectuals were suffering, how many people were dying. I had tried to escape from Mao's circle so many times, and always Mao had pulled me back. Now I was trapped, with no hope of leaving. There was much that I could have seen then but did not. What if I really had known clearly what was happening outside my protective cocoon? What if I really had understood the depth and extent of the purges? I could never have accepted it, but I would have been powerless to do anything, either. I would not have been able to leave the circle and I would not have been able to live within it.

The Chinese have an expression, *nande hutu,* which means that it is difficult to be muddle-headed—but lucky. It is an expression reserved for situations like mine. Looking back, I know that I was muddle-headed during those years. I had to be. It was the only way to survive.

24

The Soviet Union was celebrating the fortieth anniversary of its founding in November 1957, and Khrushchev had invited leaders of communist parties from all over the world to join the festivities. The Chairman
was sixty-three then and had left China only once before—in late 1949,
just after the founding of the People's Republic, when he had gone to
Moscow to negotiate the treaty with Stalin.

Mao wanted to go to Moscow. In China, the anti-rightist campaign was still in full swing, and he was ebullient. The country was
united and optimistic as never before. Socialism had been introduced
to both city and countryside and the revolution was pushing rapidly
forward. Mao could return to Moscow triumphant, the most senior
foreign leader of the communist camp, head of a huge delegation, rival
and challenger of Khrushchev.

We planned to leave on November 2.

I was in charge of medical preparations. Huang Shuze, the deputy
director of the Central Bureau of Health, was to serve as doctor to the
delegation, and I would go as Mao's personal physician.

Jiang Qing suggested that Liu Huimin, the doctor of traditional
Chinese medicine who had treated Mao in Qingdao, come, too. It
would be a way of honoring the doctor and repaying him for his
treatment, and the doctor's presence on the delegation would send a
message to Moscow that the Chairman really was an advocate of
traditional Chinese medicine. Dr. Liu was thrilled with the invitation
and deeply honored, but his enthusiasm quickly turned to anxiety. He

was afraid of the Moscow cold, and nothing I said could convince him that the buildings would be so well heated that he would never feel the weather. Dr. Liu was several years younger than Mao, but his health and temperament were those of a considerably older man. He was afraid of losing face if he were to catch cold. What if the Chairman became ill and the doctor was too sick to treat him? The humiliation would be unbearable. Dr. Liu was worried that the standard heavy wool coat being provided each member of the delegation would not be enough. He wanted a fur coat and hat and relaxed considerably when Ye Zilong, in charge of logistical arrangements, agreed.

Dr. Liu's worries turned then to Mao's health. He had to prepare for every eventuality. The Soviet Union had none of the medicinal herbs Dr. Liu would need if Mao were to become ill. He would have to bring them with him. He had to have enough herbs to treat Mao for a whole range of possible maladies. Gathered together, Dr. Liu's herbs filled more than three huge trunks, and their pungent odor wafted through the sealed containers and lingered in the air. Dr. Liu wanted the trunks to accompany him on the plane.

We negotiated. A trainload of gifts would be going to Moscow ahead of the delegation. The doctor could take a week's supply of herbs on the plane, but the three trunks and the huge clay pot he would use to boil his concoctions would be packed in a specially made wooden crate and shipped ahead on the train.

Mao would also need a nurse to assist in case of medical emergency. I nominated the most capable and experienced nurse I knew— Xu Tao's wife, Wu Xujun, the head nurse at the Office of Health in Zhongnanhai. Ye Zilong, though, wanted one of the attendants who had accompanied Jiang Qing to the Soviet Union the year before. It would be a way of saving money. The party was paying for the winter wardrobes for the delegation, and Jiang Qing's attendant already had the right clothes. But the attendant had no medical training. For once, Jiang Qing supported me, intervening on my behalf to argue that having a good nurse to serve the Chairman was far more important than saving a little money. Wu Xujun was chosen to go.

The Soviets also assigned a doctor to Mao. His sole responsibility was to escort the Chairman to Moscow and to look out for the Chairman's health en route. I was responsible for entertaining the doctor during his short stay in Beijing. The head nurse and I, together with Lai Zhulie, the director of Zhongnanhai's Office of Special Accounts, introduced him to Beijing duck at the renowned Quanjude Restaurant, where the city's most famous delicacy was still considered the best. The doctor was ecstatic over the meal, as effusive in his praise of the powerful *maotai* liquor he imbibed without restraint as he was of the duck. He was happily intoxicated when I dropped him off at the Soviet embassy and even happier when I presented him another bottle of *maotai.*

The Soviets sent two of their own planes, TU-104s, to fly us to Moscow. Mao, Song Qingling, the Soviet doctor, and I traveled together on one plane, and the rest of the large Chinese delegation went on the other. The stewardesses kept us well supplied with caviar, fish and chips, and sandwiches, and we were given buffets of cold cuts at each of the several refueling stops we made en route. Mao did nothing to disguise his feeling about Russian food. "It's not to our liking," he declared with disdain. The Russian doctor drank liberal quantities of vodka during the early stage of the journey, prattling on about the harmful effects of smoking and the benefits of drink. Intoxicated with the benefits of vodka, he spent the second leg of the journey sleeping it off.

Nikita Khrushchev greeted us at the airport, together with a group that included the bearded, somber, and dignified Nikolai Bulganin and my old friend Anastas Mikoyan. Mikoyan greeted me warmly in Russian, but I understood nothing he said, and we had no interpreter. I presumed he was saying something about the acupuncture treatments I had recommended. The only female among our official hosts was the minister of culture, Yekaterina Furtseva, an attractive woman in her fifties who kept herself busy scurrying here and there, over what I never could tell.

The Chinese delegation was the most senior of the sixty-four attending the conference, and Khrushchev was friendly and respectful to Mao, personally escorting him to the Kremlin palace where he was to stay and encouraging him to take a rest when the conference was over—either at a dacha in the suburbs or at the Black Sea coastal resort of Sochi. Mao demurred. From the beginning, he was reserved and even a bit cool with Khrushchev. He was still angry about the attack on Stalin. His private barbs against the Russian leader began almost immediately after we arrived. Driving in from the airport, Mao had noticed, as I had too, that the people in the streets seemed lackadaisical and unenthusiastic, even sullen. The contrast with China, still in the throes of post-revolutionary enthusiasm, was striking. "Khrushchev lost the support of the people when he started the campaign against Stalin," Mao said. "No wonder they have lost their enthusiasm."

The arrangements for Mao and his entourage had been made with the greatest of care. The palace where he stayed, a former residence of the empress Yekaterina, was an opulent maze of corridors and huge, spacious rooms filled with elegant antiques. The floors were covered with thick, lush carpets, and the high ceilings were hung with glittering chandeliers. Portraits still lined the walls. Yekaterina's bedchamber, Mao's private quarters, was huge and magnificently furnished, the most opulent room of all. Mao had not brought his own bed this time, but he insisted on using his own chamber pot in lieu of the flush-style sit toilet in the adjoining bathroom.

Ye Zilong, Wang Jingxian, Lin Ke, Li Yinqiao, bodyguard Zhang, two chefs, ten members of Mao's staff, including several interpreters, and I stayed in the palace near Mao. The delegation's ranking leaders from both the party and government—Song Qingling, Deng Xiaoping, Peng Zhen, Peng Dehuai, Lu Dingyi, Yang Shangkun, Chen Boda, and Hu Qiaomu—stayed in the palace, too. The rest of the staff stayed in various hotels or in the Chinese embassy, and I rarely saw them.

Lin Ke and I shared a room in the palace. Our surroundings were not as sumptuous as Mao's, but the accommodations were elegant indeed, and we were provided with a continual supply of apples, oranges, chocolates, orange juice, mineral water, and cigarettes. Liquor was plentiful, and the food was excellent.

Mao stayed in high spirits, feisty and combative. He never commented upon, or even seemed to notice, the luxury of his surroundings, but he did take note of the treatment he and the Chinese delegation were receiving, comparing it sarcastically to his reception in 1949 during the negotiations with Stalin. "Look how differently they're treating us now," he snapped, his voice sharp, his lip curled in a smile of disdain. "Even in this communist land, they know who is powerful and who is weak. What snobs!" It was a biting, bitter remark, and I could hardly believe Mao was serious.

We visited the Lenin mausoleum to lay wreaths before the glass-covered caskets of Lenin and Stalin—a disquieting experience for me. The bodies of the two Soviet leaders were shrunken and dry, and I learned that their extremities had already rotted and been patched with wax. I had no idea that twenty years later I would head the team charged with preserving the body of Mao.

Mao evinced little curiosity about Russian culture. He ate alone, apart even from other members of the Chinese delegation. Each of his meals included a huge spread of both Russian and Chinese food—the Soviets had assigned him two Russian chefs, and one of his own cooks was a specialist in Western-style cuisine—but Mao ate only the Hunanese fare concocted by his favorite chef. I could appreciate his love of

Chinese food. The heavy Russian fare, though excellent, was not to my taste either, and when Mao asked me to join him for dinner one evening, I devoured the meal with delight, even though I had just eaten my Russian-style meal. "It doesn't look to me as if you've just eaten," Mao quipped.

Mao's one foray into Russian culture was an embarrassing failure. He agreed to accompany Khrushchev to a performance of *Swan Lake*. I went, too, sitting with them in Khrushchev's special box. We arrived late, after the second act had begun, and Mao was bored immediately. He had never seen Western ballet, and no one had prepared him for it. "I could never dance that way in my life," he said to Khrushchev. "How about you?" The Soviet leader agreed that he, too, could not possibly dance on his toes. At the end of the second act, Mao announced that he was leaving. "Why did they dance that way, prancing around on their toes?" he asked me. "It made me uncomfortable. Why don't they just dance normally?" I suspected, though, that he was deliberately refusing to appreciate Russian culture. He enjoyed carping about Khrushchev and the shortcomings of the Soviet Union.

Only when we visited the Chinese students studying at Moscow University did Mao finally evince a flash of admiration. The food in the Soviet dining hall was much better than the meager rice and vegetables Chinese students were accustomed to eating, and the student dormitories at Moscow University were far better than those in China. At Moscow University, only two students shared a room. In China, the same size room was shared by eight. "We just cannot compare," Mao said.

Mao ordinarily attended meetings during the day and spent the evenings alone in his room, leaving me and the other staff members with plenty of free time. Lin Ke and I spent one evening at an elaborately staged, extravagant song-and-dance performance, put on especially for the visiting delegations, enjoying ourselves thoroughly. Most evenings, however, we spent in the palace movie theater watching American films of World War Two vintage, of which the palace had an abundant supply. *The Great Waltz* was our favorite, and we were content to confine ourselves exclusively to American films. But Han Xu, from the Ministry of Foreign Affairs, later to become China's ambassador to the United States, was afraid that our hosts might be insulted if we watched only American movies, so we occasionally tried to please them by requesting Soviet films as well. I started to watch the newly released *And Quiet Flows the Don,* based on Sholokhov's novel about the coming of World War One and the October Revolution, but there were no subtitles in either Chinese or English, and since I understood no Russian, my interest quickly flagged.

Our delegation was particularly popular with the Russian staff. We had brought huge quantities of gifts—a magnificent carved ivory boat, cloisonné vases, and a gold-leaf Comintern flag for our more distinguished Soviet hosts, and a large supply of Chinese cigarettes and *maotai* as more modest gifts for the staff. We began distributing our booty shortly after arriving. Soon we began getting late-night knocks on our doors from people requesting more. I suspect that it was the abundance of our gifts, coupled with a mistaken belief that Chinese doctors enjoyed both high status and pay, that motivated one of the room attendants to profess her devotion to me. Lin Ke had noticed the young woman expending special effort making my bed, and later she passed the word through our interpreter, Yan Mingfu, that not only was she interested in becoming my friend but was even willing to return with me to China. Yan Mingfu turned her down on my behalf, and our delegation had a good laugh.

Other cultural misunderstandings were less amusing, brought on by the venality and insensitivity of some of the Long Marchers Mao kept on his staff. In addition to the food and drink the attendants always placed in our rooms, they also put a full bottle of toilet water in our bathrooms each morning. But every day the bottles would disappear. Ye Zilong thought someone in our delegation was stealing the cologne and insisted on searching everyone's luggage. His attitude was terribly insulting, but I had little choice. My luggage was searched along with everyone else's. The investigation revealed nothing, though, and the toilet water continued to appear each morning and to disappear soon thereafter. Only after the routine had continued for several more days did we realize that the attendants themselves were taking the toilet water away. Mao was annoyed when he heard about Ye Zilong's pettiness and insisted that the matter be dropped. "What are you going to do when you prove that the attendants took it?" he asked. "If they're taking it behind your back, doesn't that mean they don't want you to know?"

Toward the end of our visit, Lai Zhulie, the director of special accounts in Zhongnanhai, suggested that he, I, and an interpreter from the Chinese embassy pay a visit to thank the doctor who had accompanied Mao to Moscow. We went to his apartment—a nice-sized, well-furnished place with carpets on the floor, a real rarity in China. The doctor was delighted to see us and a gracious host, but when we presented him our gifts—two bottles of *maotai* and a few trinkets—he became befuddled, pacing the floor in obvious confusion. Finally he took three 100-ruble notes from his pocket and gave us each a 100-ruble bill. I was embarrassed, declining the money, which Lai grabbed from my hand and pocketed. On the way back he told me that all gifts to the delegation became property of the Chinese government.

The parade celebrating the fortieth anniversary of the October Revolution was held on November 7, and we all went to Red Square to participate. Mao watched with Khrushchev from atop the Lenin mausoleum, and I stood next to the mausoleum with the head of the Estonian Communist party, a man who had lived in Great Britain for several years and spoke excellent English. He hoped to visit China someday, he said. It was such a faraway, mysterious place.

The May Day and October first parades in China had been modeled on the Soviet archetype, but by then I had already tired of the military displays and the extravagant waste. Even Red Square, with its cathedrals and palaces and its cobblestone walks, held no great allure. Two years later, when Tiananmen Square was enlarged in commemoration of the tenth anniversary of the Chinese revolution, I suspected that China was competing with the Soviet Union to build the biggest square on earth.

Despite his differences with Khrushchev, Mao was genuinely delighted with the outcome of the Moscow conference and with the joint declaration issued at its conclusion. "In 1848, Marx and Engels issued the *Communist Manifesto* and launched a worldwide communist movement," he said. "Now, more than one hundred years later, the Moscow Declaration has summarized the experiences of that movement and charted our future." Mao was optimistic about the future, exhilarated by the prediction he had made in his own speech. Within fifteen years, Mao said to the assembled delegates, the Soviet Union will overtake the United States in the production of steel and other major industrial products and China will overtake Great Britain. Within fifteen years, he asserted, the material conditions in the communist world will be transformed, their economies surpassing those of the capitalist West. With the transformation of the material base, the whole world would be ripe for the communist revolution.

Mao saw steel as the fundamental indicator of economic development and talked about the need to increase its production in China. "Our country produces too little steel," he said. "We have to do everything we can to increase our material strength. Otherwise, people will look down on us." He spoke positively of the Cold War and of Dulles's brinkmanship and of international tension. "Let there be tension in the world," he said. "Tension is good for us. It keeps our country united. So long as others are sharpening their sabers, no one will find me asleep."

Later, from his memoirs, I knew that Khrushchev had been appalled by the irresponsibility of Mao's speech in Moscow in November 1957. Mao was like a frog looking at the sky from the bottom of a well, thinking he was seeing the world. He had no basis for asserting that the communist world would overtake the capitalist one within fifteen years, no knowledge of what the capitalist world was like. To favor brinkmanship and the perpetuation of international tension in the nuclear age was foolhardy in the extreme. But Mao's speech, like his late-night conversations with me, was no idle chatter. A new strategy was germinating in his mind. The seeds of his Great Leap Forward— the most utopian and misguided of all his policies—had been sown.

25

Mao had been energized by the Moscow meetings, and when we left on November 20, 1957, he was gearing up to launch an all-out drive to increase production. The Communist party was the major impediment, and his first task was to whip up its support.

Shortly after our return from Moscow, we joined Jiang Qing for a couple of weeks in Hangzhou. Then we flew south to Nanning, in Guangxi Autonomous Region, for a party conference. Mao's pushing and goading began en route.

Hunan's first party secretary, Zhou Xiaozhou, came to pay his respects to Mao during a refueling stop in Changsha, and Mao began baiting the leader of his native province. "Why can't Hunan increase its agricultural production?" Mao wanted to know. "Why do the Hunan peasants still plant only one crop of rice a year?"

Zhou replied that the weather in Hunan permitted only a single crop of rice. Mao disagreed, pointing out that Zhejiang province, where Hangzhou is located, had essentially the same natural conditions and the peasants there still planted two crops of rice. Why not in Hunan? Mao insisted. The exchange was embarrassing to Zhou, and he did not know how to reply.

"You're not even studying other experiences. That's the trouble," Mao argued.

"We will study the matter, then," Zhou replied obediently.

"What do you mean study?" Mao demanded. "You won't get anywhere with your study. You can go now." He picked up a book and began reading. Zhou was humiliated. He said goodbye to the others in the cabin and then turned back to Mao. "We'll try to start two plantings right away," he promised.

When Zhou left, Mao tossed his book aside in exasperation. "He'll try to start two plantings!" he said sarcastically. "He doesn't even want to study others' experiences. What's the use?"

Over the next few months, this type of interchange between Mao and the more cautious provincial party leaders was repeated in both private meetings and party conferences as the Chairman gradually herded the less adventurous onto his own utopian path.

The Nanning meeting was his first big effort to get the party in line.

Nanning is a quaint, old-fashioned town, colorful and clean. The roadways are narrow, and the second-story balconies of the small shops overhang the street, protecting pedestrians from the frequent rains. The area is warm, wet, and lushly green year-round, and even in early January the temperature was a mild 78 degrees. The orange and grapefruit trees were covered with white blossoms, and the air was filled with their fragrance. The people were colorful, too. The area is populated by the Zhuang national minority, whose women dress in short swirling skirts and gaudy headpieces.

The people of Nanning are unsophisticated and honest, and the place is neither rich nor economically developed. Local officials took great pride hosting Mao and did the best they could. Official propaganda described Mao and his wife as simple and frugal themselves, and having taken that propaganda to heart, officials in Nanning were confident that their best would be welcomed by Mao. When we arrived in early January, several days before the conference began, Mao and his wife were housed in two separate buildings in the complex of the province's official guesthouse, located on a quiet, tree-covered hill. The spot was magnificent, the view superb. Mao had no complaints. Jiang Qing, though, found her accommodations impossible.

She sent for me a few days after our arrival. Her nurses were torturing her, she said, and she demanded that I call a meeting to criticize them. My responsibilities included supervising Jiang Qing's nursing staff, and when Jiang Qing was unhappy with them, I was expected to intervene.

The nurses, she said, were deliberately trying to make her catch cold. The guesthouse had no central heating, and when the temperature dropped in the evenings, Jiang Qing's attendants would hook up an electric space heater. But the heater had no thermostat. When it was on, Jiang Qing was too hot. When it was off, she was too cold. Local officials, frantically trying to find a solution, sent a team to Hong Kong to purchase a more modern space heater—a portable radiator, with heated water circulating through its internal tubing. The radiator provided steady heat, and Jiang Qing's temperature problem was solved.

But there were no showers in the Nanning guesthouse, and Jiang Qing was in the habit of bathing before she retired at night. Her nurses tried to manage by filling several containers with warm water and pouring the water over her, container by container. But the water from the last of the containers was always somewhat cooler, and Jiang Qing accused the nurses of deliberately trying to make her catch cold. When local officials learned of this problem, they dispatched another team to buy shower equipment in Hong Kong. But Jiang Qing would have to move out of the guesthouse temporarily in order to have the shower installed. She refused, preferring to blame her nurses instead. When I tried to mediate, she turned on me, accusing me of trying to force her to move to a hotel.

In exasperation, unable to reason with her, I raised the problem with Mao.

"Jiang Qing is a paper tiger," he told me. "Some things you can just ignore. Try to stick it out. Tell the nurses not to be afraid of her, and let them know that I appreciate their work."

Jiang Qing, equally exasperated, also took her problem to Mao. "You know the expression 'A parent sick for one hundred days will have no filial sons,' " one of the guards heard Mao say to his wife. "These people just work for pay. They have no spirit of service." Mao criticized Jiang Qing and praised the nurses in front of me, but he criticized the nurses in conversations with her. Apparently, though, he encouraged his wife to seek a reconciliation with me.

"Do you know that I often try to accommodate you?" Jiang Qing asked me one day in the midst of the squabbles.

I assured her that I did not.

"Both your strengths and your shortcomings are striking," she continued. "You are good at finding solutions, and you often act decisively. The Chairman also thinks you are imaginative. He thinks you have good judgment. But you are conceited, too. You put on airs. Once you've taken a position, nobody can change your mind. But since you have done such good work for the Chairman, I cannot criticize you. Do you know that?"

"No, I don't know what you mean," I responded.

"Sometimes I just can't take you anymore," she said in exasperation. "But the Chairman wants you. He is used to you now. You know, you and I are colleagues, both working for the Chairman. I have told you my opinion of you. What is your opinion of me?"

"I don't have any opinion," I said. "But I feel that both my competence and my personal background make me unsuitable to work here. I still hope someone can replace me."

Jiang Qing was becoming increasingly impatient and annoyed. "Whether you are suitable to work here is a question for the Chairman to decide," she responded.

One of the guards had been eavesdropping on our conversation. "Dr. Li, from her perspective Jiang Qing really is trying to be nice to you," he pointed out to me as I left her quarters. "The Chairman is also quite frustrated with her. Not long ago, just after she left his room, I heard him say to himself, 'Even when we are so busy, you still make such a fuss. It's just not reasonable!' "

But Jiang Qing continued to make a fuss. Her shower problem had not been solved. She continued haranguing the nurses, and the nurses kept running to me in tears. I could find no one to help. Mao's new security chief, Wang Jingxian, was a good man but said his job was confined to security. Ye Zilong also insisted that Jiang Qing's bathing problem was not his responsibility. I could only continue trying to persuade the Chairman's wife to move to a hotel for a day. Finally, she relented, and the shower was quickly installed.

Still, Jiang Qing was not satisfied. Now she said there was too much noise around her building. All the local officials and security people charged with catering to Mao and his wife were forced to move down the hill, and all traffic everywhere on the mountain was stopped—just to satisfy her whim.

The Nanning conference was attended by both national- and provincial-level party leaders. From the day it began, January 11, 1958, the atmosphere was tense. The majority of party planners did not share Mao's goal of catching up with England in fifteen years, and Mao spent much of the eleven days attacking the cautious leaders in charge of planning, development, and finance. Few escaped his whip. Even Zhou Enlai and Chen Yun were criticized.

Four days after the conference began, alternate politburo member Chen Boda called me to his hotel room. He had caught cold and wanted me to treat it. In fact, he wanted to return to Beijing, but Chen Boda had also been criticized by Mao and was afraid the Chairman would accuse him of running away if he left. Chen was having trouble sleeping. The person in the room just above his head had stayed awake the whole night before, pacing the floor. He wanted me to find out who it was and ask him not to pace. But whoever was pacing the floor had to be a high-ranking party leader. All the hotel guests were. I had no right to order party leaders not to pace the floor. I did find out, though, that the room just above Chen's was occupied by Bo Yibo, the chairman of the State Economic Commission. Bo was a leading economic planner, known for his caution. Also under Mao's gun, he too was under great psychological strain.

Huang Jing, the chairman of the State Technology Commission, responsible for encouraging technological development and Jiang Qing's former husband, cracked under the strain. Mao had attacked him severely, and as the meeting was drawing to a close, Shanghai mayor Ke Qingshi asked me to take a look at him. Huang was behaving strangely.

Huang Jing was lying in bed, staring at the ceiling, muttering incomprehensibly, when I entered. He was totally bewildered to see me. "*Rao ming a; rao ming a*—Save me, save me," he kept begging me.

Yang Shangkun arranged for him to go to nearby Guangzhou for medical treatment, accompanied by Li Fuchun, a vice-premier and chairman of the State Planning Commission, and Xi Zhongxun, the secretary-general of the State Council. Huang's bizarre behavior continued on the plane. He knelt down before Li Fuchun and kowtowed, head to the floor, begging Li to free him and spare his life. He was put in a military hospital in Guangzhou, where he tried to escape by jumping from a window, and broke a leg in the process. I lost track of him after that. Later I learned that he died in November 1958.

Mao's mood contrasted sharply with the palpable tension his anger was engendering. Once he had lost his temper a few times, the Chairman began to relax. By the end of the conference, he broke his ordinary prohibition and joined the concluding banquet festivities, taking particular delight in the delicacy known as Dragon Battling Tiger—a dish consisting of poisonous snake (the dragon) and wildcat (the tiger). The "delicacy" was very fatty and difficult for me and many other participants to eat, but Mao consumed it with relish.

The next day he went swimming in the Yong River, just outside Nanning. The water temperature was now less than 70 degrees, and it seemed too cold to swim. But Mao insisted, and I had to join him. He floated on the river in his usual style for an hour. The next day he came down with a cold and a cough.

He refused my medicine until he was thoroughly miserable. Only then did he follow his doctor's advice. His cold quickly improved.

·   ·   ·

The Nanning conference was only the first of a series of meetings Mao called over the next several months. At each one he goaded, cajoled, and badgered the party into shape, accusing first this provincial leader and then that party planner of dragging his feet, being too slow, holding the country back. And at the end of each meeting, the targets for agricultural and industrial output had increased, and when the second session of the Eighth National Congress met in May 1958, the stage had been set for his Great Leap Forward.

26

It was in early 1958 that I first sensed a change in Mao, a new and often irrational suspicion that grew stronger over the years, until the Cultural Revolution. We had left Nanning and flown to Guangzhou and then back to Beijing, staying only a couple of weeks. Mao was keeping the pressure on. After suspending the rectification campaign to attack the rightists, he had begun it again in the fall. This time it was to be an internal affair, party member against party member.

In early March, we flew to Chengdu, the capital of Sichuan province, the rice bowl of China. Mao was calling another meeting.

We stayed at a place called Golden Ox Dam, about seven miles west of the city. The grounds were as lush and vast as a botanical garden, covered with bamboo trees, blue pines, and cypresses, and the paths were lined with palm, banana, and grapefruit trees. The camellias and azaleas were in bright red bloom. It rained often during our stay, and after the rains the tropical forest would be shrouded in a mysterious mist, like in a Chinese landscape painting. Some of Mao's poetry—about misty gardens and flowers splashing the mountainside—had come from scenes like this, he said.

I was happy to be there. It was my first visit to Chengdu since graduating from medical school some fourteen years before, and the city was my second home. I visited my old university as soon as I could.

The campus of West China Union University Medical School had also been a lush botanical garden, the biggest and prettiest in China, and when I was a student, it had been my paradise on earth. But everything had changed. A large road had been built through the old campus, and many buildings had been destroyed. Those left were in disrepair. The gardens had been neglected. The name of the university had changed to Sichuan Medical College; and the old liberal arts college had been amalgamated with Sichuan University. My visit with Sun Yuhua, the president of the medical college and my old friend, filled me with nostalgia, but I dared not meet with other friends. My work with Mao was too sensitive, and the upcoming party conference was secret. Seeing old friends would be too awkward.

Mao sympathized, pointing out that people always feel sentimental when they visit a place after a long absence. He recited an ancient poem from the fifth or sixth century:

> The willows planted in years gone by
> Are lovely hugging the Han River on the south.
> Now leaves fall to the ground
> And even the river is sad.
> If nature can be so sentimental
> How do I feel?

He thought I should meet my old friends.
But I stayed with Mao.

Not long after we arrived, Li Jingquan, the first party secretary of Sichuan, invited Mao to a Sichuan opera being held in an auditorium on the grounds of Mao's guesthouse. Mao had been skeptical about attending—he preferred Beijing opera—but was so carried away by the performance that at one point he put the lighted end of a cigarette into his mouth as he watched. After that, we attended Sichuan opera every night, and word of Mao's love of opera spread quickly to other provincial leaders. They were always curious about Mao's tastes because they all hoped to host Mao themselves someday and wanted to do it right. After 1958, all the new provincial villas included an auditorium for watching opera.

It was in Mao's attitude toward the indoor swimming pool at Golden Ox Dam that I sensed a new, irrational fear. The pool, constructed on orders from Li Jingquan, was supposed to be a replica of the indoor pool at Zhongnanhai and it was meant especially for Mao. Mao encouraged me and other members of his staff to swim there, but he was uneasy about it himself. He refused to swim there and asked me several times whether I thought the pool was different from the one in Beijing. He said he was afraid it was poisoned. None of us who swam in it suffered any ill effects, and Mao's attitude left me more curious than concerned. Only in retrospect, as the condition worsened, did I see in his suspicion the seeds of a deeper paranoia.

Mao was restless. He was still dissatisfied with the party leadership. He had tried whipping them into shape, coaxing them out of their lethargy, but had met with only partial success. He had called the conference to prod the party leadership some more.

The meetings, held from March 8 to 26, 1958, were a continuation of the Nanning conference, with Mao criticizing and goading the party leaders responsible for economic development. He was still trying to get them to come up with plans to catch up with Great Britain in fifteen years and thought that the output targets were too low and the party planners too cautious. Mao had brought the public criticisms of the party to a sudden halt with the anti-rightist campaign in the summer of 1957, but his confidence in the party had not been restored. During our talks in Chengdu, he complained about the country's lack of leadership and described the party elite as "a bunch of zombies with a slave mentality." He wanted them to have more courage and determination.

It was their unoriginal copying of the Soviet Union and their mindless, superstitious recitation of Marx that bothered him most. "Marxism didn't just drop from heaven," Mao would say. "We shouldn't do everything according to the books, slavishly copying every word." He traced the party's slave mentality to China's Confucian past. So awed were Chinese by Confucius that they could not even call him by name, addressing him instead as Sage. Now the party was similarly awed by Marxism, taking it as dogma, refusing to deviate an inch from the texts. The effect was the same: Confucianism had stifled creativity in the past, and Marxist dogma was stifling it today. Marx was a new Confucius, crippling China, preventing the country from moving forward. Much as Mao disliked Stalin, he thought the Soviet leader had been right to criticize Marx. Stalin knew that Marx was not always right and had pushed ahead courageously to develop the theory and practice of socialism.

The party leaders, Mao thought, were similarly cowed by intellectuals, bowing humbly before them, convinced of their own inferiority. Thus he doubted that the Chinese Communist party could lead the transformation of China. "Our cadres' perspective is too narrow," he said. They led the good life, eating their fill from morning to night, their energy diverted from their brains to their stomachs.

But he still had faith in the young and the unschooled. "The young and the uneducated have always been the ones to develop new ideas, create new schools, introduce new religions," he said. "The young are capable of grasping new situations and of initiating change, brave enough to challenge the old fogies. Confucius started his new school of thought and began recruiting students when he was twenty-three. What learning did Jesus have? But hasn't the religion he created lasted to this day? Sakyamuni developed Buddhism when he was nineteen years old. Sun Yat-sen was not a man of learning. He had only a high school education when he began his revolution. Marx was also very young when he began developing his theory of dialectical materialism. His learning came later. When he was twenty-nine years old, he was writing books challenging the theories of well-established bourgeois scholars like Ricardo, Adam Smith, and Hegel. He was only thirty when he wrote the *Communist Manifesto,* and by then he had already created a new school.

"The great scholars have always been overthrown by the young and uneducated," he said. "It didn't matter that they were young and not so knowledgeable. What is important is to seize the truth and move courageously forward."

There was no irony in Mao's words. He never acknowledged that just as Confucius was never called by name, addressed only as Sage, so no one called Mao by name, referring to him only as Chairman. Soon his words, too, would become dogma. And Mao often distorted history for his own purposes. Sun Yat-sen had been a medical doctor, a member of a wealthy intellectual elite, when he launched the revolution of 1911.

Years later, in 1966, when Mao launched the Cultural Revolution—calling upon the country's youth to rise up in criticism against their professors and the Communist party—I would remember conversations like this. He had been mulling over the strategy for years.

In Chengdu, though, Mao still depended on the party to work his will. He was on the attack again, criticizing anyone who had preached caution, arguing, in terms they could accept, that to be against his insistence on "rapid advance" was to be against Marxism—and therefore to be a rightist. He whipped the economic planners like horses, trying to get them to go faster. It was in Chengdu that I first remember hearing the slogan "Go all-out, aim high, and build socialism with greater, faster, better, and more economical results."

In Chengdu, I also became aware of a change in Mao's understanding of socialism. Even with the establishment of a socialist economic system, he argued, classes continue to exist. Workers and peasants belonged to the laboring class and thus were "good." But the remnants of imperialism, of feudalism, and of bureaucratic capitalism still existed, and so did the rightist bourgeoisie. The national bourgeoisie, who had supported the communists in the struggle against the Guomindang, still existed, too, and could be expected to oppose the socialist transformation. And Mao put the intellectuals in the bourgeois camp. "Intellectuals are unstable," he told me, "swinging with the wind. They read a lot of books, but they are ignorant of real life." He was beginning to talk about class struggle.

From Mao's perspective, the Chengdu conference was a success. Production-output targets were going up. The conference produced thirty-seven new documents, each one revising upward the earlier—conservative, more realistic—targets for economic output.

But a change was coming over the party, and it was soon to have disastrous results for China. Mao's voice was so powerful, his point of view so strong, that it was becoming difficult for the cautious to disagree. To express skepticism about the unrealistically high output targets was to risk being labeled a rightist. The force of Mao's will gradually silenced those who disagreed, and those who pandered to him began to lie, agreeing to higher targets even when they knew those targets were impossible to obtain, claiming to have reached those targets even when they had fallen short. The party was beginning to lie, and Mao seemed to like best the most outrageous liars. Fear was setting in.

27

While we were in Chengdu, the party rectification campaign was intensifying in Beijing. My friend Lin Ke, the secretary responsible for briefing Mao on the contents of the daily *Reference Materials* and another of his English tutors, was one of the first to come under attack. Lin Ke left Chengdu for Beijing as soon as he learned he had been implicated. He had to be present to defend himself.

Known later as the Black Flag Incident, the episode was the most bizarre and complicated among the political struggles I had yet to witness within the inner circle. It would destroy lives and ruin careers. Meanwhile, I learned an unforgettable lesson.

The nature of the political-appointment system within the Communist party explains much about how the Black Flag Incident evolved. Much of the problem centered on the concept of responsibility. When a Chinese official suggests someone for appointment and the candidate is appointed, the official also assumes responsibility for the actions of the person he appoints. For the system to work, the subordinate must become absolutely subservient to his superior and carry out his orders even when they violate his better judgment. The fundamental tenet of party membership is discipline, and party discipline means absolute obedience to one's superiors, the subordination of one's own will to the dictates of the party, compliance with higher-level commands. The party, and one's superiors within the party, are always right. Thus, criticism of one's superiors is a violation of everything a party member has been taught. An attack on one's leader is an attack on the party itself. Loyalty is the paramount virtue.

The benefit of subservience is protection. Since the subordinate is always following orders from his superior and the superior is responsible for his actions, the superior must therefore protect his subordinate from attack. Similarly, any higher-level purge begins with attacks on the target's underlings. If a lower-level person is guilty of political misdemeanor, so is his superior. Thus, the endless series of political struggles that I witnessed over the years always began not at the top but somewhere in the middle. The goal may have been higher-ranking leaders, but the route was through their subordinates.

Mao fervently opposed this system, which he thought caused the party to lack daring and courage. Everyone was always trying to pass responsibility further up the ladder, and because the price for mistakes was so high, initiative, independence, and boldness were stifled. If one person fell, so did many others—not only the actor himself, but his boss and everyone under him. It was assumed that if the party boss had allowed one person under him to go astray, others under his command must similarly have committed mistakes.

Mao revived the party rectification campaign in the fall of 1957 as a way of shaking up this stultifying system, hoping to liven up the leaders by giving their subordinates more say. He called upon lower-ranking party cadres to expose the misconduct of their superiors—especially any conduct that might be construed as conservative and therefore "rightist."

But for those asked to participate it was an unusual and frightening request. What if the criticisms were not upheld? What if the party leader remained in his post? The leader could take revenge, use his higher-level position to make life miserable for the people who had dared to criticize, and condemn them as anti-party, rightist, or worse. These were the lessons of the anti-rightist campaign.

Thus, when Mao launched the rectification campaign again, most party members remained silent. I certainly did. I had grievances against people like Ye Zilong and Li Yinqiao, but I would never have spoken out.

Some people within Zhongnanhai did speak out, however. Eight political secretaries—staff members of the Office of Political Secretaries under the Zhongnanhai General Office headed by Yang Shangkun—got together to criticize their boss, He Zai, the deputy director of their office. He Zai's primary crime was his arrogance. The dissidents accused him of taking credit for everything that went right and blaming his subordinates for everything that went wrong. They accused him of toadying to his superiors and intimidating his subordinates.

Lin Ke was one of the eight who participated in the attack.

But He Zai passed the responsibility upstairs, saying that real decision making rested not with him but with his boss, the much higher-ranking Yang Shangkun. By this logic, to accuse He Zai of being a rightist was tantamount to accusing Yang Shangkun and hence politically more dangerous. He Zai further argued that to attack him was to attack the party and that the eight accusers were the real rightists. He mobilized other staff members within the Office of Political Secretaries to attack the eight and spread the word that my friend Tian Jiaying—another of Mao's political secretaries and, like He Zai, one of the deputy directors of the Office of Political Secretaries—had instigated the attack against He Zai. By March, when we were in Chengdu, He Zai had marshaled sufficient support within the General Office that the eight staff members, Lin Ke included, were about to be officially declared an anti-party, anti-socialist, rightist clique.

It was only after the Chengdu meetings were over and Lin Ke had returned to Beijing that I realized how serious the accusations were. I had left Chengdu with Mao, going first to Chongqing and then for a boat ride through the Yangtze River gorges, stopping in Wuhan for another discussion of the Yangtze River dam project, and then traveling on to Guangzhou, arriving in late April. Ye Zilong and Tian Jiaying joined us there, and I learned that Yang Shangkun had suspended the eight secretaries, including Lin Ke, and ordered them to write "self-evaluations." The investigation of their anti-party activities was continuing.

Tian Jiaying was distressed. The accusations were unfair. But he was in a quandary. As a deputy director, he was of the same rank as He Zai. The eight staff members were also his subordinates. Rumors were circulating that he had instigated the eight to make their accusations, and he was on the verge of being investigated himself. He wanted to discuss the issue with Mao but was afraid of getting into further trouble if he did. Tian Jiaying, like everyone else in Group One, served two masters. He worked directly for Mao, but he still served under the overall command of the General Office of the party. If Tian Jiaying took his concerns directly to Mao, he could be accused of going over the head of Yang Shangkun and the General Office. But with the decision already made by the General Office, Mao himself was the only one who could override it.

I, too, was distressed by the news about Lin Ke. I was vaguely acquainted with all of the accused, but Lin Ke and I had worked closely together over the past several years, often sharing a room when we traveled. Lin's job as Mao's secretary was the same one Mao had offered me, and I could easily have been in his position. Lin Ke spoke bluntly and his frankness was sometimes offensive, but I had never heard him utter a word against the party. To accuse him of being an anti-party element was preposterous. Besides, he was Mao Zedong's secretary. How could Mao's secretary be anti-party?

In Guangzhou, Group One was abuzz with talk about the case. But when I came to Lin Ke's defense, saying I could not imagine him doing anything against the party and wondering whether his attackers had some kind of grudge, Ye Zilong challenged me. "You're not in Beijing. How do you know?"

"If Lin Ke is really opposed to the party, it would be awfully difficult for him not to give the slightest hint," I responded. "In my presence, he has always been loyal. How could he suddenly become anti-party?" My resolve to keep quiet was slipping.

Wang Jingxian signaled me, and I joined him in an adjacent room. He cautioned me against speaking so rashly. The decision has already been made, he said, and my voice had no political weight. "If you keep talking like this, people will say you are covering up for Lin Ke. Then you'll be charged with opposing the decision of the party. You could be implicated, too." Ye Zilong, delighted to see Lin gone, had already reported the decision to Mao. If I continued defending Lin Ke, Ye Zilong could take out after me, too.

Wang was right. There was nothing I could do.

But I was still uneasy. The attack was unfair. It was not right that no one dared to speak out in Lin Ke's defense.

I believed that if Mao knew the full story, he would support Lin Ke. When Ye Zilong reported on his case, Mao had said nothing, a sign that he disagreed. Ye had misinterpreted, taking Mao's silence as agreement. I thought otherwise. But if I came to Lin's defense, Ye Zilong would accuse me of interfering in a decision of the party. My only hope was for Mao to raise the question himself.

Mao called for me later that afternoon. Wearing a bathing suit and covered with a robe, he was sprawled on a lounge chair on the deck of the yacht near his guesthouse. He wanted an English lesson. But shortly after we began, Ye Zilong interrupted to report further on the "anti-party group" in Zhongnanhai. I rose to leave. The matter was no official business of mine. Mao encouraged me to stay. "This is no secret," he said. "We'll study English in a bit."

Mao wondered why a report on the anti-party group was coming from Ye. Yang Shangkun and his deputies were responsible for the investigation. The information should be coming from them. But Yang Shangkun's deputy had asked Ye to report.

Mao was silent. Ye Zilong left.

I knew that Mao was unhappy, but I still did not dare to speak. I was under the jurisdiction of the Public Health Ministry's Central Bureau of Health and the controversy was taking place within the Office of Political Secretaries under the General Office. The matter was none of my business, and party discipline required me to stay out. My meeting with Mao was not private. No meeting with Mao ever was. His guards, continually coming and going, pouring us tea, wiping Mao's face with a hot washcloth, eavesdropped on everything, hanging on to every word, and when they were not in the room, they listened at the door. If I brought up the question of Lin Ke, they would tell Ye Zilong and Lin Ke's enemies within Group One would turn on me, too. I could not take the initiative. I had to wait for Mao.

I picked up our lesson for the day. We were reading the English version of Liu Shaoqi's political report to the second session of the Eighth National Congress, scheduled for May. Liu Shaoqi was giving Mao plenty of time to comment, and its thrust was pure Mao—"go all-out, aim high, and build socialism with greater, faster, better, and more economical results."

Mao stopped me. He was quiet, thinking. "Do you know about this problem at the Office of Political Secretaries?" he asked.

"I know about it, but not in detail," I responded. "I was surprised to learn from Director Ye that Lin Ke is in such serious trouble."

"Do you know the eight people involved?"

"I am acquainted with them all, but Lin Ke is the only one I know well."

"What do you think of Lin Ke?"

My opportunity had come. I had to be careful. Others were listening. I had to present Lin Ke's faults as well as his strengths. "In the past three or four years, we have spent a great deal of time together," I began. "We have talked a lot. I don't think Lin Ke is in any way against the party. He's a little egotistical, that's all."

"Who isn't egotistical? But we're not talking about that. I'm asking whether you think Lin Ke is against the party."

I explained that so far as I knew, Lin Ke had never said anything against the party. Maybe he had been critical of particular individuals or leaders, but I never heard him utter a complaint against the party itself or against the Chairman. In fact, I assured the Chairman, he seemed very loyal.

"Right. During the anti-rightist campaign last year, Lin Ke and the other seven were all very active. How is it that when the rectification campaign starts they suddenly become opposed to the party?"

"I don't know the details of the case," I responded. "But Comrade Tian Jiaying is here now. He knows."

Mao wanted to talk to Tian Jiaying.

Tian Jiaying and Wang Jingxian were incredulous when I told them about my conversation. Wang thought me brave. But Tian Jiaying was still concerned. Yang Shangkun was also his boss, and Tian did not want to give the impression of opposing Yang or going over his head. But Mao had asked to discuss the matter with him. He decided to tell the whole story. The two talked that evening.

At four o'clock that morning, I was awakened from a sound sleep by one of Mao's bodyguards. The Chairman wanted another English lesson. I splashed my face with cold water and hurried to Mao's bedroom.

"I wanted to wake you two hours ago," Mao said, "but I knew it was still too early." One of the guards served me a cup of strong tea.

I knew Mao wanted to talk about Lin Ke, but first we read some English. Then Mao stopped. He had talked to Tian Jiaying, he said. "I think I understand the situation now. The eight staff members criticized the leading cadres of the Office of Political Secretaries for having rightist leanings. Then He Zai and Yang Shangkun tried to help each other out by attacking the eight. But they completely distorted the case. I think the eight staff members are right. Some of the leaders do have rightist tendencies. The way they've gone about striking down the eight staffers shows they have rightist leanings, doesn't it? Those eight were enthusiastic supporters of the anti-rightist campaign last year. How could they suddenly become rightists themselves? The leaders making the charges against them are the ones who are rightists. They're using this notion of party discipline to scare their subordinates. They're ruthless. The eight have no way to survive."

Mao compared the case to a similar episode during the Tang dynasty when eight young and courageous reformist officials had offended the landlords and bureaucrats with their proposals for change. The landlords and bureaucrats had struck back at the reformists by sending them all into exile.

"I have ordered Tian Jiaying back to Beijing," Mao continued. "We'll go back soon."

We returned to Beijing at the end of April, three days before the May Day activities. Mao spent three hours talking with Lin Ke, listening to his view of the case. The mood in Zhongnanhai changed dramatically with Mao's return. Yang Shangkun had arranged a big "struggle session" against the eight. Then Tian Jiaying returned to report that the case would not be settled until Mao himself investigated. The party chairman did not agree with the decision of the General Office. Now He Zai and Yang Shangkun were in a quandary.

Just after May Day, Mao called Tian Jiaying, Lin Ke, He Zai, and two staff members from the party organization at the General Office—Liu Huafeng and Xiao Lan—to a meeting in his room. He asked me to sit and listen.

Mao was in bed, wearing only his robe, and he was calm, conciliatory, trying to find a way to compromise. He said that the rectification movement within the Office of Political Secretaries had not been properly conducted and reiterated what he had already told me—that the eight staff members had supported the anti-rightist campaign. They were leftists, not rightists. The case had to be handled on the basis of fact. Proletarian problems could not be solved with bourgeois means— you attack me and I overthrow you.

Had everyone present agreed with the Chairman, the case against the eight could easily have been dropped. But Xiao Lan, one of the staff members from the General Office, a woman in her forties, disagreed. She pointed out that the eight had criticized the leaders of the General Office, and the General Office had already determined that the eight were opposed to the party. They had been suspended from their work and ordered to make self-evaluations.

Xiao Lan was challenging Mao, and while I disagreed with her point of view, I had to admire her courage. But she was also stupid and naive. Committed to the supremacy of the party and its leadership, educated to subordinate herself to party discipline, she did not understand why Mao had launched the rectification movement. Mao was dissatisfied with the conservatism of the party leaders. He wanted them criticized. He thought the eight staff members had been right.

Xiao Lan was also stupid to think that the party itself was supreme or that decisions of the party were final. She did not understand that above the party was the emperor. She had just challenged the emperor.

The change in Mao's attitude was instantaneous. He sat upright, pushed the terry-cloth towel from his body, looked around the room. He was ready for battle. "All right," he said coldly. "Both sides continue to insist on their own points of view. I cannot change your minds. We'll organize a meeting to handle the case. Everyone has to go. Let's have a thorough debate, clear the whole thing up once and for all. The meeting will begin tomorrow. Order the staff members of all the offices in Zhongnanhai to be there. Now you can all leave."

Mao had dropped a bombshell, and nothing could prevent its explosion. He was supporting the cadres who had criticized their boss and hoped that other staff members would, too.

Yang Shangkun, who was both director and party secretary of the General Office and party secretary of the Central Committee's General Headquarters (*zhongzhi jiquan*), was clever. He Zai was his subordinate, and He Zai's defense had been that he had merely been carrying out the orders of Yang Shangkun. Knowing that Mao did not support He Zai, Yang Shangkun made a "self-criticism," distancing himself from He Zai by apologizing for not paying sufficient attention to He Zai's work or to the rectification movement within the Office of Political Secretaries. "I am asking all of you to speak up and identify those who tried to strike down our leftist comrades," he said at the first meeting. "If anyone thinks I did something wrong, then speak up against me, too." It was a clever maneuver.

Xiao Lan persisted in her attacks against the eight even after knowing Mao's stand, and her attack gave the incident its name. The Lin Ke group, she insisted in meeting after meeting, had not been raising a red flag in support of the Communist party but a black flag of opposition.

The meetings continued for a month. I did not have the stomach to attend. The eight were finally exonerated, as they had to be once Mao intervened. But it was not until the Cultural Revolution that I fully understood Mao's strategy during the Black Flag Incident. Yang Shangkun, as the highest-ranking party member involved, was the real object of Mao's suspicion even then, and above Yang Shangkun, behind the scenes, was his boss, Deng Xiaoping. The Black Flag Incident was but one episode in Mao's lengthy test of Yang's behavior, a test that Yang Shangkun would ultimately fail. In 1958, Yang Shangkun was allowed to continue as director of the General Office, but the General Headquarters of the Central Committee, of which he was party secretary, was abolished—a major diminution of his authority but still a way of saving his face. During the Cultural Revolution the Black Flag Incident would be resuscitated to destroy him and presented as one of his two major crimes.

The middle-ranking cadres, the staff members just under Yang, were the ones punished in this round of trials. Two staff members, Li Dongye and Liu Huafeng, good men who had acted under orders from Yang Shangkun and Zeng San, were made scapegoats, sent down to lower-level organizations for reform, where their life was very hard. Only in 1980, after Mao's death and the return to power of both Deng Xiaoping and Yang Shangkun, were they finally exonerated.

He Zai, the original target of the staff members' criticisms, fared even worse. He was expelled from the party and also sent down to lower levels for reform, to be exonerated only in 1980.

Xiao Lan, the woman who had led the challenge against Mao, insisting that the eight had been waving a black flag of opposition, was destroyed. She lost her job and was expelled from the party and sent to be reformed. She was never exonerated and died in hard labor.

But nothing was ever as it seemed. The rumors about Tian Jiaying had been true. He was behind the eight staff members in their struggle against He Zai, and both He Zai and Yang Shangkun were his targets. As the case evolved, however, Tian Jiaying saved Yang Shangkun from being fired by claiming that Yang Shangkun was telling the truth when he said he did not know what He Zai was doing. When He Zai was demoted, Yang Shangkun rewarded Tian with a promotion.

We in Zhongnanhai were a privileged group, often shielded from the harsh realities outside, but the Black Flag Incident taught me how dangerous the intricate political struggles within Zhongnanhai itself could be. Mao had called upon subordinates to criticize their superiors as a way of shaking up the conservative elite. But the elite had power and the means to counterattack, and the risk of being declared a rightist or counterrevolutionary was great for an underling. Only Mao's personal intervention could save a subordinate from doom. And Mao was not yet willing to go straight to the top and overthrow the leaders with whom he disagreed. The outcome of any political struggle was always uncertain, and some people always lost. Those people were the middle-ranking cadres, men like me and Lin Ke, and the signals we received were conflicting. Party loyalty required subservience to one's superior and obedience to his command. Following Mao meant criticizing one's superior and risking being declared a rightist. I was grateful once more that I did not have Lin Ke's job and resolved anew to remain silent and out of the political fray.

28

In the summer of 1958, all of China was mobilized in the construction of massive water conservancy projects, and much of the country was participating in the backbreaking labor required to build them. Mao led the way. The projects were not merely economic, though the reservoirs were meant to improve China's irrigation system and thus to boost agricultural production, too. Mao also wanted to use the construction projects to honor manual labor and make it a respected form of work. It was part of his lifelong disdain for the arrogance of parasitic intellectuals and his glorification of the hardworking peasants and workers.

In Beijing, hundreds of thousands of people had volunteered—so party propaganda said—to build a new reservoir adjacent to the magnificent Ming tombs—the site, some thirty miles outside of town, where thirteen of the sixteen Ming emperors are buried, the ruins of their tombs tucked away in the rolling foothills. Army soldiers, party and government staff, workers from schools, factories, and shops—even the staff from foreign embassies—were all putting in their time. Every resident of Beijing must have been called in for a stint on the project.

Then China's leaders began participating, too, taking turns shoveling dirt as cameras clicked, recording the event for history.

In the afternoon of May 25, 1958, six buses filled with China's top party and government officials set out from Zhongnanhai, with Mao's bus in the lead. The Chairman was ebullient, sitting in the next to last row, chatting with everyone around. I was just behind him. "Normally, we big shots are waited on by others," he said. "Now it's our turn to do some manual labor ourselves. Everyone says it's good to do some manual labor, but once they actually start working, they change their minds. People are working on the reservoir here for different reasons. Some really want to work. Some feel they have to. Still others consider manual labor some kind of golden trademark. Whatever the reason, doing some manual labor is better than not doing any at all."

The site was swarming with people. Soldiers made up the main workforce, but there were paid construction workers, peasants from the surrounding area, and "volunteers" from the city, too. Mao's arrival was electrifying, and the huge crowd roared in approval, chanting slogans of welcome, as General Yang Chengwu, commander of the Beijing Military Region and director of the reservoir project, greeted the Chairman when he stepped off the bus. An entire company of soldiers was needed to clear the path so Mao and his entourage could work their way through the crowd to the tent that served as General Yang's command post. Yang briefed Mao on the work as we looked out over the site.

In the distance, the dam was under construction. In the foreground, in a vast bed of sand and rock, was a sea of humanity. Thousands of people were digging out huge rocks and great quantities of sand with nothing more than shovels, dumping the rocks and sand into huge baskets that were then transported by shoulder pole to waiting railroad carts that shuttled them to the dam. In front of the dam the process was reversed, as thousands took turns using their shovels to remove the rocks and sand from the carts and dump the dirt into huge baskets, which were then carried by shoulder pole to an agitator cart that ground the stones into gravel. There the gravel was gathered up again and transported by shoulder pole to the dam itself. It was backbreaking work.

Mao walked, followed by General Yang, the party leadership, and me, to the foot of the dam, where he took a shovel and began digging the gravel. The rest of us followed. We picked up our own shovels and began to dig. Mao was dressed casually, in a white shirt, light gray trousers, and black cloth shoes. It was very warm that day, and the sun was strong. Mao's face soon turned bright red, and he was quickly covered with a fine yellow dust. As he began to perspire, the furrows of water traced a cobweb pattern on his face. After little more than half an hour, General Yang urged the Chairman to stop working. "It's been a long time since I've done such work," Mao said. "So little effort and already I'm dripping with sweat." Mao retired to the command tent for a rest and some tea.

"Why don't you people from Group One come here for a month?" Mao said to me as he relaxed. "You need to experience some hardship. So many others from Beijing have come. The staff in Group One can't just leave."

Mao's rectification of the party was continuing, directed not just at those who had "made mistakes" but at ordinary people like me. We were guilty, in the jargon of the day, of being "divorced from the masses." The staff in Group One was living the good life—too good a life, Mao thought. We ate and dressed too well and were waited on by others. He wanted us to experience the life of the workers and peasants, to be tempered and reformed by living and suffering like them. Mao believed in the benefits of hard labor. He wanted us all—particularly me, a child of privilege whose life had always been soft—to eat a little bitterness. I was about to get my own taste of labor reform.

Mao's suggestion was not a matter of choice. I was hardly enthusiastic about the backbreaking labor, but I had to agree. "All right," I responded. "But we need to go back to the city first to gather our things."

Mao agreed.

The next morning a picture of Mao, shovel in hand, surrounded by smiling officials and ordinary people, appeared on the front page of every newspaper in the country. This classic photograph—testimony to the Chairman's devotion to the masses, to the respect he accorded physical labor, and to his willingness, despite his exalted position, to remain one with the people by participating in labor—has been reprinted in newspapers and magazines countless times and is included in every volume that sings the praises of Mao. It was the only time in the twenty-two years I worked for him that Mao engaged in hard labor, and he had wielded the shovel for less than an hour. Never in humankind has such a simple symbolic gesture galvanized a nation to such a frenzy of enthusiastic, backbreaking work.

Late in the evening of Mao's symbolic act, we met at the indoor swimming pool to plan Group One's participation in the water-conservancy project. Mao had just taken a swim, and he and Jiang Qing were resting by the pool, drinking tea. "This Ming tombs reservoir project is a major undertaking," Mao said. "Hundreds of thousands of people have volunteered their time and their labor. Even foreigners are involved. We can't let them down. Starting tomorrow, the staff in Group One—you, the secretaries, the bodyguards—will go there to work for ten or twenty days. The job is simple. You just dig gravel, deliver it, walk around in the sunshine or rain. Just work until you are exhausted. If you really can't stand it, let me know. I'll bring you back."

Mao would not go back to the site. He was too busy, he said. He wanted one secretary and one guard to stay behind. Everyone else in Group One was to go. "Do it for me," he said. "Represent me."

"Your health is not good," he said, turning to Jiang Qing. "You don't have to go. But don't drag others' feet. Let your staff go."

"I just need two nurses," Mao's wife replied. "The others can go." The reduction in her staff would be a hardship for Jiang Qing.

We left the next day, led by Ye Zilong and Wang Jingxian, the new head of Mao's security. Cadres from all the central organizations of the party and government and from the Beijing municipality had committed themselves to working at the site for twenty days. Group One was a bit laggard. Most other organizations had already been at work for five days.

Even at hard labor, Group One remained a privileged elite. Others were living outdoors, in makeshift lean-tos of woven reed mats, open to the elements. General Yang Chengwu found us quarters in a class-room in one of the middle schools of neighboring Fangshan county. The room was bare and only about twelve square meters. We slept on the floor, using our quilts as bedding. The nine of us were packed like sardines, able to fit only by sleeping on our sides. If one person moved, everyone else was forced to shift his body, too. With the noise and the heat and bodies perpetually in motion, sleep was almost impossible. Under the circumstances, however, we were grateful for our high-class accommodations.

General Yang also assigned us the best shift, from midnight to eight in the morning, another mark of our privilege. By late May, the days were already scorching, and working at night spared us the worst of the heat. We ate our breakfast after returning from work—a coarse cornbread called *wowo tou,* rice porridge, and pickled, salty vegeta-bles—then spent each morning in study sessions devoted to convincing us that all advances in human civilization were the result of hard labor. Lunch was a bit better than breakfast—some cooked vegetables, some rice, and a bowl of soup—but the ingredients were coarse and poorly cooked, and my appetite was gone. We would sleep after lunch, waking at nine or so in the evening to begin preparing for work.

The site was an hour's walk from the school. We would set out a little before eleven. Mao said that the work was simple, and he was right. I used a shovel to dig stones and earth from the riverbed, emptying them shovelful by shovelful into big baskets. When two baskets were full, I attached them to a carrying pole, hoisted the pole onto my shoulders, and carried them to one of the open railway carts that were transporting the gravel to the dam site. I was still young—only thirty-eight years old—and very healthy. I had been athletic in my youth—a gymnast and a basketball player. But this was the most arduous work I had ever done in my life, and the muscles I was using were completely different from the ones I had used in sports.

The nights were cool, but after an hour or two, I was soaked with perspiration and my body ached all over. For others, digging with a shovel seemed as natural and easy as lifting a fork was for me, and many people at the site were able to suspend six baskets from their carrying pole without apparent effort. There was a certain rhythm to their gait, as beautiful as a dance. They would trip along with the carrying pole bouncing up and down, their bodies bobbing, so that when the carrying pole was up, their shoulders were down, and they never seemed to carry the full weight of the load. In front of the railway cart, they used another motion, first swinging the baskets back and then directing them forward, so the heavy load seemed to fly out without effort, dumping the rocks and sand right into the proper spot. Most members of Group One had grown up in the countryside and were used to work like this. But to me, every hoist of the shovel was like lifting a thousand pounds, and I staggered under the weight when I slung the carrying pole over my shoulder, and it cut into my flesh.

Much as I tried to imitate my peasant comrades, I continued to stagger awkwardly under the load and my body never stopped aching. One night, exhausted, I lost my balance completely, dumping my baskets and landing in the cart myself—to the great amusement of everyone around. "It's a little different from using a stethoscope and scalpel, isn't it?" they joked. For the first time in my life, I had a fleeting sense of inferiority. I was able to console myself in the knowledge that these peasants and workers would look equally awkward with a stethoscope or a scalpel in their hands. For the first time, too, I began to get a concrete sense of how horrible life must have been for the rightists who had been sentenced to reform through hard labor. At most, I would be forced to suffer for twenty days. Rightists were forced to do such nearly unbearable labor day after day, month after month, year after year. How many of them could survive?

Some people suggested that I switch jobs and serve as the doctor treating work injuries instead. The proposition was tempting and I would have liked to accept it, but Mao had sent me to taste a little bitterness. If I had served as the site doctor, he would accuse me of shirking my assignment.

People tried to make my job easier, explaining how best to conserve my strength, demonstrating how to carry the pole without taking the weight. But it was hopeless. One night, when a rainstorm hit and I was soaking wet and trembling with cold, Wang Jingxian suggested that I quit and go back to the middle school. But everyone else was still working, and I could not leave. So I worked even harder and was soon covered with sweat despite the rain and the cold.

By the fifteenth day, I was totally exhausted. I had hardly slept or eaten, and I had used up every reserve of energy my body could muster. The aches persisted in every muscle, and at every step I was filled with agony. The original twenty-day working period for party and government cadres was over, but since Group One had arrived five days late, we had to decide whether to continue. No one—not even the physically strong Long Marchers—wanted to continue. But no one wanted to risk being labeled a backward element by suggesting we quit and go home. We decided to continue for another five days.

General Yang Chengwu saved the day. He came to congratulate us on our work. "Your labor here shows your enthusiastic support for this project," he said. "Whether you work fifteen days or twenty doesn't matter. The Chairman needs you. One hour of work for the Chairman is more valuable than five days of work here. As the director of this project, I order you to leave." He laughed. We burst out laughing, too, delighted with his command. We had been ordered back to Zhongnanhai!

The meeting continued, though. We had to select a model worker from our team.

I was nominated. "Dr. Li made heavy demands on himself," one member of our group said. "He is so educated, but still he never put on airs. He worked right beside us, never lagging behind, persevering to the end. That's not easy." The majority agreed.

I could not accept the honor. It would be ridiculous to be designated a model worker for a job I despised. I had come because Mao had ordered me to, not because I wanted to work. And for me the honor was of little value. I was a doctor. My pride came from my medical skills. Besides, I knew Group One. If I, the doctor and intellectual, should be singled out as a model in manual labor, staff members like Ye Zilong would surely resent me. They would have one more excuse to continue their sniping.

I rejected the honor. "As an intellectual, I have to be reformed through labor," I insisted. "I cannot be named a model worker. Otherwise my reform would have no meaning." Some members of the group continued to insist. But I was adamant.

Ye Zilong decided the matter. He did not want me to be selected. "The doctor has already insisted several times that he does not want the honor," he pointed out. "I think we should respect his wish."

But the team could not agree on another model worker. Again, General Yang Chengwu found the solution. "All of you work for the Chairman," he said. "All of you are dedicated to your work. All of you have set a fine example. Every one of you is a model worker. So we will name your team a model team." The matter was settled. Everyone was delighted. We could return to Beijing with honor.

I did not return home when the van dropped us off in Zhongnanhai. I had not bathed for more than two weeks, and I was filthy. I could not face my family like that. I went instead to Xinghua Yuan, one of the few old-style luxury bathhouses still operating then. For five *yuan,* the equivalent of the price of ten pounds of pork, I was ushered into my own private room with a comfortable cot and a bath. An attendant drew a tubful of hot water, and I immersed myself in the bath, allowing myself to relax for the first time in weeks. After I had soaked for a while, the attendant rubbed my dirty body with a hot towel, let the water out of the tub, and drew another full, hot bath. After I had soaked some more and washed myself with soap, the attendant lathered and scrubbed my back, let out the water again, and filled the tub a third time with hot water. Again, I immersed myself, succumbing to the pleasures of the bath. My bath complete, my body clean at last, I lay on the cot while the attendant massaged my aching muscles. In the meantime, my filthy clothes, which had been taken away to be scrubbed, reappeared clean, dry, and neatly folded. After two hours of luxuriating at the bathhouse I was finally ready to present myself to my family. I went to my mother's in Liulichang.

My appearance was still a jolt to my mother and my wife. "You have lost so much weight!" they both exclaimed. My wife could sympathize. She had spent only one day working in the reservoir and had returned sunburned and exhausted. They encouraged me to stay at home and rest.

I dared not rest. Mao was waiting, and I wanted to be the one to tell him of my misadventures. I gobbled down my mother's delicious dumplings and went immediately to the Chairman.

He was resting with Jiang Qing by the side of the pool. "Look at you," he teased. "You're not strong enough to catch a chicken! So you fell into the cart, huh? Lucky you got out fast. You could have been delivered to the dam along with the gravel!" I had come too late. The story of my two weeks at hard labor had already been reported.

"How was it?" Jiang Qing wanted to know. "Was it fun in the cart?" I knew from her nurse that Jiang Qing had been gloating. "They all eat so well and stay in nice places and get the best treatment everywhere just because they're on the Chairman's staff," she had said. "Now it's their turn to suffer a little."

"You almost didn't make it," Mao commented.

"I'm exhausted," I had to confess. "It wasn't exactly pleasant."

"You intellectuals only know how to talk and write. You have no idea what it is to do manual labor. It's not idle talk when I say intellectuals ought to do manual labor every now and then. It's a way to get close to the masses and to appreciate the collective power of the people. You should try to participate in labor more often. It'll be good for you." Mao's words were frightening. I did not look forward to going back.

The story of my two-week bout with hard work made the rounds of Zhongnanhai. For a long time thereafter my ignominious tumble into the railroad cart was the standing joke.

29

After Jiang Qing's return from the Soviet Union, she had become obsessively hypochondriacal, convinced she was seriously, alarmingly ill. She was certain that her cervical cancer had recurred, that she had a tumor in her liver, her stomach, her brain, that her body was riddled with disease. She was troubled by a ringing in her ears and said it felt as though insects were trying to crawl in. She could not bear light or noise. She complained about drafts. She had no appetite. She could not sleep. She took first this kind of sleeping pill and then another, one kind of medicine and then, convinced she was allergic, another. She was addicted to pills, to medicine, to her own illnesses.

But her radiation treatment had been successful. Her cancer was completely cured.

Her health, when she and Mao were together, was my responsibility. I was forced to take her complaints seriously.

In several of the blood tests I had drawn since her return from the Soviet Union I had noticed a slight irregularity in Jiang Qing's blood count. I was certain it was nothing serious, just part of the body's gradual readjustment after radiation, but Jiang Qing was nearly hysterical with worry, and I wanted to assuage her fears by having her examined by a team of the country's leading physicians. Shortly after my stint at hard labor, the Central Bureau of Health—the division under the Ministry of Public Health responsible for high-level leaders—gathered together a number of specialists, working under my direction, to administer a thorough physical, checking for every conceivable malady. The process took a full two weeks, with Jiang Qing behaving more imperiously than ever, changing the schedule at whim, treating the doctors with disdain, ordering them around like servants.

After all the exams had been completed and the test results were in, I called a meeting of the physicians. We all reached the same conclusion. Jiang Qing was not sick. Her cancer was cured. Her blood count was a minor problem. There was no evidence of any illness. Indeed, from the time she returned from the Soviet Union in the spring of 1957 until her arrest twenty years later, she remained in perfectly good physical health.

The problem, we all agreed, was psychological. I could understand how it had evolved. Jiang Qing was genuinely frightened about her health, and she had little understanding of the workings of the human body. She was naturally suspicious and nervous and could not trust anyone, not even her doctors. Nothing we said could allay her fears. Caustic and selfish, she was preoccupied with herself. She drove potential friends away, and her relationship with Mao was not normal for husband and wife. Her isolation and loneliness only exacerbated her anxiety. We described her overall psychological problem as neurasthenia. There was no other label we could use. But we were physicians, specialists in illnesses of the body. We had no way to cure Jiang Qing's psychiatric problems.

We wrote a report and submitted it separately to both Mao and Jiang Qing, explaining that we had performed a complete, detailed examination on every aspect of Comrade Jiang Qing's health, that the radiation therapy had been successful and she was recovering well. We agreed that she should take vitamins to strengthen her resistance to disease and suggested she involve herself in cultural, literary, and athletic activities. We recommended that she increase her social activities while taking a temporary leave from work. We were being polite. Jiang Qing had no work to leave. Inactivity was one source of her problems.

Jiang Qing rejected the report and insisted that she was seriously ill. The doctors were incompetent, she said. Or we were lying. She ordered us to rewrite the report.

We met again, but not to discuss her physical health. We needed to decide how to write a report that would convey our ideas to Jiang Qing and still be acceptable to her. We decided to say that her process of recovery would be long and gradual and that her neurasthenia would naturally intensify. The physical discomforts she was experiencing were a result of this natural intensification.

But she was no more satisfied with the second report than the first.

"Can you guarantee that I won't get sick in the future?" she demanded. Her question was absurd. Of course no one could make such a guarantee. She also thought the report was too abstract. She wanted us to work out a weekly schedule for her, filled with specific cultural, literary, and athletic activities.

We suggested that she spend her time watching movies, listening to music, perfecting her photography, and attending dancing parties and concerts. We also suggested that she begin practicing *tai ji chuan,* the traditional martial art of shadowboxing. *Tai ji chuan* requires intense concentration, both to control the breath and to move the body, and the practice, properly performed, has a soothing effect. We thought it would help keep Jiang Qing calm.

Mao was skeptical about Jiang Qing practicing *tai ji.* But he agreed that she could try it for a while to see how she liked it. The Central Bureau of Health found a teacher named Gu, recommended by the Shanghai Athletic Commission, and Gu began daily instruction in the basic techniques. Mao and his wife were spending a couple of weeks in a new villa in the western outskirts of Beijing—a complex for the top leaders called Six New Buildings. I accompanied Gu there for the daily lessons.

Though Jiang Qing was intensely serious about learning *tai ji,* she was a dismal student. Gu was a cautious and reticent man, but he was devoted to his art, strict in his demands even on the Chairman's wife. Jiang Qing would become irritated when he corrected her posture or breathing, and I had to caution him to tread gently and not be too concerned about her slow progress.

Summer was upon us again, and in July, I left with Mao and Jiang Qing for Beidaihe. Gu, after a little more than a month of instruction, came too, to continue the program.

In Beidaihe, Jiang Qing's psychological problems returned with a vengeance. She complained incessantly. She was afraid of bright lights and ordered her nurses to pull down the shades to keep out the sun. But she wanted fresh air, so she ordered the windows open. When the windows were open she hated the draft. When they were closed it was too stuffy. The slightest noise, even the rustle of her attendants' clothes, drove her to distraction, and she was constantly yelling at them about the noise they made when they moved. She was bothered by color. Pinks and browns were especially troublesome. They hurt her eyes. She had everything in her residence—walls and furniture alike—painted a pale light green.

Her nurses were under constant attack and continually ran to me in tears complaining about the Chairman's wife. There was nothing they could do to satisfy her. Within a month, her nurses had been changed five or six times. "With six hundred million Chinese, we have enough people around," Jiang Qing would say after dismissing yet another nurse. "If they don't want to work for me, they're welcome to leave. We have plenty of other people."

I was responsible for Jiang Qing's nursing staff and at a loss about what to do. I talked to Shi Shuhan and Huang Shuze, the director and deputy director of the Central Bureau of Health, hoping that their experience overseeing the health of the country's highest leaders might help. They, too, were at a loss. Huang Shuze and I went to explain the problem to Yang Shangkun. "Jiang Qing doesn't think much of me," Yang said. "What good can I do?"

Finally, Shi Shuhan, Huang Shuze, and I decided to take the problem to Zhou Enlai. We all respected the premier tremendously, and Shi Shuhan had already faced a similar problem with Lin Biao, one of China's marshals and a vice-chairman of the National Defense Council, who was then in semi-retirement. Lin Biao also suffered from neurasthenia and had refused to listen to his doctors. Zhou Enlai had talked to Lin, telling him that Chairman Mao and the party really hoped he would follow the doctors' advice. For a while at least, Lin Biao had complied. We thought that if Zhou understood the problems Jiang Qing was causing, he would work out a similar solution.

We were wrong.

We requested a meeting with Premier Zhou, outlining our reasons. Zhou pleaded busy. He suggested we meet with his wife, Deng Yingchao, the premier's closest adviser and confidante and herself a highly respected member of the Central Committee. My contact with Zhou's wife had been minimal, but I had long admired her from afar. Big Sister Deng, we called her. It would be an honor to meet her.

I was charged with making the presentation. I described Jiang Qing's situation to Deng Yingchao in detail, explaining that Jiang's problems were not physical and hence were beyond any medical solution. I explained that I thought Jiang Qing's psychological problems derived from her isolation and from her lack of interest in work. I thought, though, that if the proper person were to speak to her, she might be persuaded to change her behavior and perhaps her problems would diminish. I told Deng Yingchao that we were asking for her help because we did not know where else to turn or what else to do.

Deng Yingchao listened attentively throughout my presentation. Only when I was finished did she respond. "The Chairman has devoted his whole life to the revolution," she said. "Eight members of his family have sacrificed their lives for the cause. The Chairman's contributions have been extraordinary, and the respect we owe him is tremendous. We must realize that the Chairman now has only his wife, Comrade Jiang Qing. His first wife, Yang Kaihui, died for the revolution. The Chairman's second wife, He Zizhen, is herself suffering from a mental disorder. Now Jiang Qing is ill. We must do everything we can to help her, as a way of showing our gratitude to the Chairman. We must take proper care of Comrade Jiang Qing no matter how difficult the job.

"You say Comrade Jiang Qing has mental problems. This makes us very, very sad. You should not have said that. It isn't fair to the Chairman. The party has assigned you the responsibility of providing Comrade Jiang Qing with the best medical care possible. You have no right to do anything but that."

I was astounded. Deng Yingchao was not being honest. Clearly, she had consulted with Zhou Enlai. She would not be saying this without his agreement. This was their joint response. Suddenly, I realized that Zhou Enlai was Mao's slave, absolutely, obsequiously obedient. Everything he did was designed to court favor with Mao. Everything he did, he did to be loyal to Mao. Neither he nor his wife had a shred of independent thought. Deng Yingchao was a tough and clever woman. I had come to her with a genuine problem, and she knew the problem was real. But she had to be holier than thou, accusing us of failing in our duties to the Chairman, of lacking her devotion to Mao, of lacking her husband's devotion to Mao. If Mao were ever to learn what she said at this meeting, her standing and the standing of her husband would rise a few notches—and mine would most certainly fall.

I felt betrayed. She had managed to twist my intentions and put me on the defensive, making my inability to solve Jiang Qing's problems a test of my loyalty to Mao. Deng Yingchao was treacherous, and I never trusted her again. I left in disgust, shaken.

I was left with no other choice but to talk to Mao directly, without Jiang Qing. The opportunity came when Khrushchev made his secret visit to China.

Khrushchev arrived in Beijing on July 31, 1958. Mao returned to Beijing by train from Beidaihe to meet him. En route, I raised the question of Jiang Qing's health.

Mao was surprised. "Didn't you people already give me a report? Is there some new problem?"

I explained that there was no new problem but that the report had not contained all that the doctors wanted to say. Mao put out his cigarette and asked me to give him the full report.

"The physicians believe that Comrade Jiang Qing really has no serious physical problems," I began. "Her problem is psychological." I handed him a statement to this effect, signed by the doctors who had examined her. Mao read it.

"The physicians think that Comrade Jiang Qing often substitutes her own opinion for reality," I continued. "She changes her mind a lot. They think it would be best for her to have more social activities, more contact with other people. Maybe that would help."

Mao was silent.

I continued. "I understand that when Marshal Lin Biao was ill, his doctors had a hard time getting him to listen. But when Premier Zhou asked him to follow doctors' orders, he listened. That helped with his treatment. The problem is that Comrade Jiang Qing does not listen to any of us. We just don't know what to do."

Mao closed his eyes and lit another cigarette. He took a deep puff. "Jiang Qing does listen to the orders of the party," he said slowly. I knew that when he spoke of the party, he was referring to himself. Mao said that his wife's thinking was often bourgeois but that we were seeing only one of her problems without seeing the other. "What really bothers her is that she is afraid that one day I might not want her anymore," Mao said. "I've told her many times that it's not true and that she should stop worrying about it. Now, you tell the nurses that I do appreciate their service to Jiang Qing. I know she is not nice to them. Tell them they don't have to listen to her all the time. Sometimes they will just have to turn down her demands."

"They wouldn't dare," I said. "How can they reject her demands? If they refuse to do what she wants, they could be accused of being counterrevolutionary. They can't satisfy her even when they are doing their very best. She accuses them of working only for pay."

Mao smiled. "I tell her often that a parent sick for a hundred days will have no filial sons. She's been in poor health for a long time. She ought to be a little more accommodating."

"The nurses don't expect her to be accommodating. They just hope she won't criticize them all the time and that she'll stop making such impossible demands."

"I think the worst of her disease is over," Mao said. "Please thank both the nurses and the physicians for me."

I told Mao the physicians hoped that he would not tell Jiang Qing what they had said.

Mao agreed. "No, I won't tell. I think Jiang Qing will listen to the words of the party. If you have any more problems with her, tell her directly, though—and tell me, too. Don't avoid talking to her, and don't talk to others about her behind our backs. That would be bad."

"I've never said things behind your back," I replied. "I'm telling you all this because I'm having such a hard time." Talking to Deng Yingchao had been going behind Mao's back. But I could not admit that to him, and I had already come to regret my meeting with the premier's wife. I would never do it again.

Mao smiled. "Let's all just do what we have to do," he said. Our conversation was finished.

I met with Shi Shuhan, Huang Shuze, and Cui Yitian—a vice-minister of public health—to report my conversation with Mao. They were worried, afraid of the repercussions on the doctors and the Central Bureau of Health if Jiang Qing should ever find out. They advised me not to talk with Mao about Jiang Qing again.

Afterward, I could tell that Mao had talked to Jiang Qing about her behavior toward the nurses. She made an effort to treat them better. Even so, several of them were dismissed that summer in Beidaihe. I began to suspect that Jiang Qing's problems with her nurses were not confined to her dissatisfaction with their service to her. I now realize she was also worried about Mao's attraction to the young women. Jiang Qing was in the habit of interviewing prospective nurses during the dancing parties, where she said the atmosphere was more relaxed. Mao was always there, too, and the young, innocent girls were always awed by the spectacle and overcome with admiration when they saw their great leader Chairman Mao. Once, Jiang Qing became upset when one of the young nurses stopped to shake Chairman Mao's hand, greeting him warmly, before delivering the medicine she had brought for Jiang Qing. I explained that it was only natural for a young nurse to behave so enthusiastically when meeting a man she so greatly admired.

Jiang Qing thought otherwise. "Doctor, you don't understand the Chairman," she replied. "He is very loose with his love life. His physical pleasure and his mental activity are separate, and there are always women willing to be his prey. Don't you understand? You have to teach these young nurses something about morality. They should be courteous to their leader, but they should also be careful in their contact with him."

Jiang Qing's comment puzzled me at the time. I was still ignorant then of Mao's sexual excesses and remembered the conversation in which he had mentioned both his wife's worries that he would leave her and his own assurances that he would not. I did not yet know that in some matters Jiang Qing saw reality more clearly than I. Mao's appetite for sex was enormous, and sex and love were separate.

30

Khrushchev arrived for a secret visit to Beijing on July 31, 1958. Mao returned the extravagant hospitality given him in the Soviet Union with a slap in Khrushchev's face. He received the Soviet leader by the side of his swimming pool, clad only in his swimming trunks. When Mao suggested that Khrushchev join him and don swimming trunks himself, the Soviet leader surprised us all by accepting the offer, changing into one of the bathing suits that were kept in ample supply in the dressing rooms alongside the pool, and plunging into the water with Mao. Khrushchev did not know how to swim and wore a life preserver in the water, surrounded by me and a couple of bodyguards, with the interpreters trying to manage their work from the side.

Superficially, the two men were cordial, and Khrushchev did not then acknowledge the insult, but the talks between the two men did not go well, and Khrushchev's memoirs record the disdain he felt for Mao's unorthodox ways. He had originally planned to stay a week, but he left after only three days. The Chairman was deliberately playing the role of emperor, treating Khrushchev like the barbarian come to pay tribute. It was a way, Mao told me on the way back to Beidaihe, of "sticking a needle up his ass."

Mao's catalog of complaints against the Soviets had grown, but could be reduced to a single, overriding concern. "Their real purpose," Mao said, "is to control us. They're trying to tie our hands and feet. But they're full of wishful thinking, like idiots talking about their dreams." The Soviets, he said, had proposed the creation of a joint fleet and wanted to build a long-range radio station in China.

Mao accused Khrushchev of trying to use China as a pawn in the Soviet effort to improve relations with the United States. Khrushchev, he said, wanted a promise from China not to attack Taiwan. He was also criticizing China for beginning a program to amalgamate the agricultural collectives into huge people's communes.

"I told him we could build a joint long-range radio station," Mao said, "but he has to give us the equipment and technology. We could also create a joint fleet—with his ships and our captains. I told him that whether or not we attack Taiwan is our own domestic affair. He shouldn't try to interfere. As for the people's communes, what is so wrong about trying them out? So I summarized everything for him. We could create a joint radio station and a joint fleet—in accordance with my conditions. We will do something on the Taiwan front. We will definitely give the people's communes a try."

Hidden from the world, unbeknownst to the West, the Sino-Soviet dispute had begun.

On the way back to Beidaihe, Mao continued to fume. "Khrushchev just doesn't know what he's talking about," he complained to me. "He wants to improve relations with the United States? Good, we'll congratulate him with our guns. Our cannon shells have been in storage for so long they're becoming useless. So why don't we just use them for a celebration? Let's get the United States involved, too. Maybe we can get the United States to drop an atom bomb on Fujian. Maybe ten or twenty million people will be killed. Chiang Kai-shek wants the United States to use the bomb against us. Let them use it. Let's see what Khrushchev says then.

"Some of our comrades don't understand the situation. They want us to cross the sea and take over Taiwan. I don't agree. Let's leave Taiwan alone. Taiwan keeps the pressure on us. It helps maintain our internal unity. Once the pressure is off, internal disputes might break out."

Mao's talk was baffling. I had no knowledge of radio stations or joint fleets and knew little about Taiwan. I even dared to hope when he raised the question of Taiwan that peace talks between the two sides might soon begin. I had not heard about the movement to establish people's communes. We had just finished the transition to higher-level agricultural cooperatives.

It would be several weeks before the real meaning of Mao's talk about Taiwan became clear. But I was about to get a firsthand look at the new people's communes.

On August 2, 1958, at three o'clock in the morning, after our return to Beidaihe from the meeting with Khrushchev, I was awakened from a sound sleep by one of Mao's bodyguards. The Chairman wanted an English lesson. I rushed to his room, where we began reading Engels's *Socialism: Scientific and Utopian.* That and the *Communist Manifesto* were his two favorite English books, and we read them over and over. Mao never really learned English. He used the lessons as a way to relax, and our lessons were an occasion to chat. We stopped around six in the morning. Mao asked me to join him for dinner.

While we were eating, he handed me the current issue of *Internal Reference,* the compilation of secret reports written by journalists all over China and edited by the New China News Agency. Distributed daily to leaders at the ministerial level and above, *Internal Reference* kept the highest-level leaders informed about events the party did not want the rest of the people to know. The reporting was often critical, focusing on problems that had yet to be solved or on disparities between party ideals and the reality of everyday life. During the period of "blooming and contending" in 1957, when everyone was being encouraged to speak out, the *Internal Reference* was filled with the most scathing criticisms of the party. Sometimes the reporting was sensational—stories of rapes and murders that were never reported to the public.

With the beginning of the anti-rightist campaign in the summer of 1957, however, the character of *Internal Reference* had changed. Some journalists who had reported honestly on the dark side of Chinese society, men like Li Shenzhi, were labeled rightists and removed from their positions, and some were sent into exile in remote areas of the country. By early 1958, with the new drive for internal party rectification and Mao's efforts to whip up party support for his go-all-out fast approach, *Internal Reference* had turned 180 degrees, glorifying the great advances that were taking place throughout the country—particularly in the rural areas. The copy Mao showed me that morning had a report about the creation of a people's commune, an amalgamation of many smaller agricultural cooperatives into one gigantic organization, in Chaya Hill, Henan province.

"This is an extraordinary event," Mao said. "This term *people's commune* is great. Lots of rural cooperatives have been united to form one big people's commune. The commune will be the bridge linking socialism to communism. But there are lots of things we don't know. How is this people's commune organized? How does it work? How does it allocate income and verify how much people have worked? How do they implement the idea of uniting agricultural labor with military training?"

Sometime in the spring and summer of 1958, when the massive water conservancy campaign had led to shortages of rural labor, some places had begun amalgamating the agricultural producers' cooperatives into huge organizations. At first, the new organizations had a variety of names. Mao had not yet visited the new rural units and the politburo had yet to approve them, but Mao liked the idea of huge rural organizations, and the name people's commune appealed to him, too.

Mao wanted me to investigate some of these new people's communes. "Have a look," he said. "Stay a month. Get a clear picture of the situation, and then come back to tell me about it. Do you have any pressing business here?"

In the midst of a long, quiet summer in Beidaihe, I had, at Mao's suggestion, been translating a book on aging from English into Chinese, sharing the translation with Mao. He had loved the first few chapters but became bored with the section on the effect of aging on the body's cells. I had continued the translation, though. It was a way to pass the time and kept me in contact with medical literature. But I assured him I could stop my work for the trip he proposed.

"The book is of no great interest," he said. "You can translate it later. The people's commune is a great event. It affects the political system of our nation. Back in 1949, when our army crossed the Yangtze River, an American wrote a book called *China Shakes the World*—or something like that. Now, ten years later, with the creation of people's communes, China is going to shake the world again. So you go and take a look. Don't go by yourself, though. Ask Ye Zilong and Huang Shuze to go, too."

My knowledge of life in China's rural areas was limited to the walks I had taken to villages when Mao's train stopped for him to rest, and I had been appalled by what I saw: abject poverty and peasants subsisting on a staple diet of steamed buns made from coarsely ground corn. They were simple and honest people, and once when I tried to buy some buns, they insisted on presenting them as gifts. I had eaten one myself and taken another to Mao. He was less surprised by the poverty, but he encouraged me and the rest of his staff to continue such "social investigations" whenever we could.

Even as he spoke about sending me to inspect the people's communes, Mao was falling asleep and his speech was slurred, his voice nearly inaudible. He had taken his sleeping pills just before we started eating and he had brought up the idea of the investigation in the midst of that half-awake, half-asleep euphoria he entered as the drug began to take effect. I was not sure whether his suggestion was real or part of a drug-induced dream. "I'll talk to the others. We can be ready to go in two or three days," I responded.

"There's nothing to talk about," he snapped, momentarily alert. "Tell them to get ready today and get going tomorrow."

The Chairman fell asleep. It was eight o'clock in the morning. I went immediately to tell Ye Zilong about Mao's new assignment.

A month in the countryside—traveling without Mao and thus by ordinary train, sleeping in humble guesthouses, eating the coarse food of the peasants—was not Ye Zilong's idea of a desirable assignment. He seemed to have no interest in national policy, and, not surprisingly, he did not want his comfortable routine to be interrupted.

"The Chairman just eats till he's full and has nothing else to do," Ye complained. "What the fart good can this trip of ours do?"

I insisted we had to go. The Chairman wanted us to investigate.

"You go tell Huang Shuze about it," he said. "Then we'll get together and talk about it. But we can't leave tomorrow. I need a few days."

His talk was making me nervous. We could not delay. "Chairman asked us to leave tomorrow," I insisted. "We can't refuse his orders." I suggested that Ye Zilong talk with Mao himself, and I went to inform Huang Shuze, the deputy director of the Central Bureau of Health.

Huang was an idealistic follower of Mao. The Chairman's word was gospel, and his instructions had to be followed. He was honored with Mao's assignment and could easily be ready to go the next day.

Still, I was troubled by Mao's orders. The suggestion had come while he was under the influence of the barbiturates. Maybe the suggestion was whimsy. I decided to raise the matter with Jiang Qing.

She was still in bed, eating a breakfast of almond yogurt and toast, when I was ushered into her room around noon. I explained my dilemma. "I don't think the Chairman would treat such a matter casually," she replied. "But I'll talk to him when he wakes up."

I ran into Mao's political secretary Tian Jiaying. Tian was my good friend and was always exceptionally well informed—not just from the reports that came in through *Internal Reference* but because he was continually receiving confidential background material from the provinces and from his friends and lower-level political secretaries all over China. He knew all about the new people's communes. He was skeptical.

Tian pointed out that when advanced cooperatives were introduced in 1956, the peasants complained that we were going too fast. The administration of the lower-level cooperatives had not been straightened out before the higher-level cooperatives were introduced. Now we were trying to adopt a still higher form of organization—people's communes. They were, he thought, economically unsound, a way for the provincial leaders to escape Mao's whip, a new method of courting favor with the Chairman.

After Mao's goading and prodding at the meetings in Chengdu and Nanning, he said, the provincial leaders wanted to show that they were doing their best to carry out the decisions. They used all sorts of tricks to get the central authority's attention and went into a frenzy competing with each other to increase production targets. They all wanted to be in the vanguard. But Tian encouraged me to go have a look for myself.

After lunch, I packed my luggage, prepared to leave the next day. Then I lay down for a nap. I had been up since three in the morning.

At seven in the evening Mao's bodyguard Xiao Li woke me. Chairman Mao was waiting to see me.

Ye Zilong and Jiang Qing had both talked to him. "I've decided to go take a look myself," he said. "Such a big event, how can I not go see? We'll leave in a couple of days. I want to visit quite a few places. So get yourself prepared again. And take along an assistant if you need someone to help you out." Huang Shuze, Mao said, was "liberated." He did not have to go. Mao needed a nurse instead. He was still taking the ginseng that I had prescribed for his impotence, and we were preparing it the traditional way—boiling the root in water. The nurse would be responsible for making and administering the concoction. I suggested Wu Xujun, who had accompanied us to Moscow.

Mao cautioned me that the journey was absolutely secret and made clear that my role on the trip was not merely to serve as his personal physician. "It's no good for medical personnel to confine themselves to treating illness," he said. He did not want me "isolated from society," especially when society was undergoing such a fundamental change. He wanted me to see how the changes were affecting the people. He saw our trip as an exploration in the relationship between the particular and the universal—a chance to see how the particularity of individual people's communes fit their socialist principles.

Two days later, we set out from Beidaihe, ensconced in the luxury of Mao's private train. Thus began—partly in defiance of Khrushchev, partly the whimsy of a drug-induced stupor, and partly Mao's genuine need to know—what was to become the most sensational "nationwide inspection tour" the Chairman had ever made.

Our train headed south. This social investigation, it was clear from the beginning, would be different. The Great Leap Forward had begun.

31

The weather that summer was spectacular, the best in years. It rained every night, and the days were sunny and mild, so there was no doubt that the fall harvest would be the best in China's history. All of China was in a frenzy, bubbling with optimism and excitement.

We traveled first through Hebei province, visiting several newly formed communes. The optimism of the peasants was captured in the names of the new organizations, all of which promised a glorious and revolutionary future—the Communist Commune, Dawning, Morning Sunshine, Red Flag.

Then we went to Henan, where first party secretary Wu Zhifu—small, fat, and honest—escorted us by car through the dusty, unpaved back roads of his province. We traveled in a cavalcade of cars, tens of people in all—a contingent of armed guards from Zhongnanhai under the supervision of Wang Jingxian, a group of Wu Zhifu's provincial security officers, reporters from the New China News Agency, and some journalists from the Henan party newspaper. Mao had cautioned me that the trip was secret, but the journalists made it public.

The August weather was scorchingly hot. We relied on big broad-brimmed straw hats to protect us from the sun and were greeted with wet washcloths each time we stopped. The two truckloads of sweet, juicy watermelons that followed us from place to place were our best relief from the heat. Mao, as usual, was little bothered by the weather and seemed indifferent to the watermelons, but many of us in the entourage gorged ourselves on the succulent fruit.

Mao enjoyed himself. He liked being among rural folk again. When he stepped on a patch of dung, dirtying his shoes, he was delighted and refused to let anyone wipe it off. "It's fertilizer—a useful thing," he said. "Why wipe it off?" Only when he took off his shoes that night could one of his guards wipe them clean. The fields were lush with crops, crowded with peasants at work. In China north of the Yellow River women rarely work in the fields, but everywhere we looked women and girls, dressed in bright red and green, were laboring alongside the men.

In Lankao county, Mao wanted to swim in the legendary Yellow River and sent the faithful Sun Yong, who had encouraged him to take his first swim in the Yangtze, to test the waters. But the Yellow River suffers from oversilting and the water was a thick brown brew, only chest-deep. Sun and the other security officers sank in mud up to their knees at every spot they tested. Mao gave up his plan to swim.

On August 6, accompanied by the usual large entourage, Wu Zhifu took us to visit Seven Li village, in Xinxiang county. The fields en route were filled with chest-high cotton, and the white round bulbs were the size of a fist. The harvest for Seven Li village was going to be abundant.

As our cars pulled into the village square, a big red banner strung across the front door of the village headquarters cried out in greeting: SEVEN LI VILLAGE PEOPLE'S COMMUNE. Mao grinned as he stepped from his car. The huge new collectives had a variety of names. This was the first time we had actually seen the word *people's commune* associated with a place. "This name, 'people's commune,' is great!" Mao said. "French workers created the Paris commune when they seized power. Our farmers have created the people's commune as a political and economic organization in the march toward communism. The people's commune is great!"

Three days later, in Shandong, Mao repeated his comment: "The people's commune is great!" An attentive New China News Agency journalist had been standing nearby and immediately the words appeared on the front page of newspapers all over the country, instantaneously becoming a new slogan. It was treated by party secretaries at every level as a new imperial edict to transform China's cooperatives into gigantic people's communes, organizations that would combine government and agricultural production and become the foundation of Communist party power in the countryside.

People's communes had already been established in most of the places we visited, and traveling from one to the other was an exciting experience. Something big was happening in the Chinese countryside, something new and never before seen. History was being made. China had finally found the way from poverty to abundance. The salvation of the Chinese peasantry was at hand. I, too, supported the movement to establish people's communes. Chairman Mao was right. People's communes were great.

Returning by train to Beidaihe, Mao was still excited. I had never seen him so happy. He was convinced that the problem of food production in China had been solved, that the country was now producing more food than the people could possibly eat.

We arrived in Beidaihe on August 13, and four days later Mao convened an enlarged meeting of the politburo, which lasted until August 30, 1958. In the midst of the meetings, on August 23, Mao's answer to Khrushchev became public. China began using those artillery shells Mao had said were wearing out and started a massive bombardment of Quemoy, an island just off the coast of Fujian province still held by the Guomindang. It was Mao's challenge to Khrushchev's bid to reduce tensions between the Soviet Union and the United States, his demonstration of China's importance in the triangular relationship among China, the Soviet Union, and the United States. Seeing Khrushchev's efforts at world peace as an attempt to control him and China, Mao deliberately tried to trip up the game. Mao was convinced that Chiang Kai-shek wanted the United States to drop an atom bomb on Fujian province, and Mao would not have minded if it had. His shelling of Quemoy was a dare to see how far the United States would go. He shelled the island for weeks. Then on October 6, at Mao's instruction, the Communist party announced a one-week cease-fire. On October 13, the cease-fire was extended for two more weeks. When the American fleet moved in to protect the Straits of Taiwan, Mao ordered the bombardment resumed. On October 25, a new policy was proclaimed. If American ships stayed away, the communists would give the cannons a rest on even-numbered days and bomb Quemoy, and the island of Matsu, on odd-numbered ones.

Mao knew that "comrades" like Khrushchev—and some within China, too—thought he wanted to retake Taiwan. But that was never Mao's intention. He did not even want to take over Quemoy and Matsu. "Quemoy and Matsu are our link to Taiwan," he said. "If we take them over, we lose our link. Doesn't everyone have two hands? If we lose our two hands, then Taiwan is no longer in our grip. We let it slip away. The islands are two batons that keep Khrushchev and Eisenhower dancing, scurrying this way and that. Don't you see how wonderful they are?"

For Mao, the shelling of Quemoy and Matsu was pure show, a game to demonstrate to both Khrushchev and Eisenhower that he could not be controlled and to undermine Khrushchev in his new quest for peace. The game was a terrible gamble, threatening the world with atomic war and risking the lives of tens of millions of ordinary Chinese.

Two momentous decisions were made during the enlarged politburo meetings that August. People's communes—huge amalgamations of agricultural cooperatives—were to become the new form of economic and political organization throughout rural China. The movement to establish people's communes was official. And China's steel production was set to double within a single year. Most of the increase would come through backyard steel furnaces.

The country was in a frenzy. Mao had said that people's communes were great, and suddenly the whole country had established people's communes. The enlarged politburo had decided to double steel production by relying on small backyard steel furnaces, and immediately the whole country was building backyard steel furnaces. Mao wanted to see them.

32

On September 10, 1958, Mao set out again, traveling by plane, train, and boat, to see for himself the vast changes taking place in the country. His popular adulation grew at every stop we made.

We flew first to Wuhan. Two of Mao's most enthusiastic admirers—"democratic personage" and Guomindang defector Zhang Zhizhong and Anhui's first party secretary Zeng Xisheng—visited him there. Mao thrilled Zhang Zhizhong by inviting him to come along on his inspection tour, and Zhang obliged by showering Mao with flattery. "The condition of the country is excellent indeed," he said to Mao. "The weather is favorable, the nation is at peace, and the people feel secure."

Zeng Xisheng, too, was courting Mao's favor. He wanted the Chairman to visit Anhui province. Zhang Zhizhong, a native of Anhui himself, joined Zeng in encouraging the visit. Mao agreed. We took a boat down the Yangtze to the city of Anqing, just on the border of Anhui, where first party secretary Zeng Xisheng escorted our party by car to Anhui's capital, Hefei. There, we witnessed new miracles. "Backyard steel furnaces" were the local specialty.

I saw the first such furnace—a makeshift brick and mortar affair, four or five meters high—in the courtyard of the offices of the Anhui provincial party committee. The fire was going full-blast, and inside were all sorts of household implements made of steel—pots, pans, doorknobs, and shovels—being melted down to produce what Zeng assured Mao was also steel. Zeng Xisheng picked up a hot nugget from the ground, plucked from the furnace only moments before, to show Mao the fruit of the mill, and nearby were samples of finished steel, indisputable evidence of the success of the backyard steel furnace. Mao had called upon the country to overtake Great Britain in steel production within fifteen years, by using methods that were quick and economical. Even now, I do not know where the idea of the backyard steel furnaces originated. But the logic was always clear: Why spend millions of dollars building modern steel plants when steel could be produced for almost nothing in courtyards and fields? The "indigenous," or "backyard," steel furnace was the result.

I was astounded. The furnace was taking basic household implements and transforming them into nuggets called steel, melting down knives into ingots that could be used to make other knives. I had no idea whether the ingots were of good-quality steel, but it did seem ridiculous to melt steel to produce steel, to destroy knives to make knives. The backyard steel furnaces were everywhere in Anhui, all producing the same rough-looking ingots.

Toward the end of the visit, Zhang Zhizhong proposed that Mao ride through the streets in an open car so the citizens of Hefei could see their great leader. In the summer of 1949, Mao had entered Beijing in an open jeep and the citizens lined the streets to welcome their liberation. In September 1956, during a visit by Indonesian president Sukarno, Mao had ridden in an open cavalcade. But he rarely appeared so openly before the masses. The Chairman's provincial visits were almost always secret, and security was tight. When he visited factories, his exchanges with workers were carefully controlled. Mao's face-to-face meetings were ordinarily confined to high-ranking party elite or leaders of the "democratic" parties. His twice-yearly appearances on the top of Tiananmen were not really exceptions. The crowds in the square were carefully chosen. The risk of appearing publicly before the masses was not only to Mao's security. The Chairman did not want to be accused of fostering his own cult of personality.

Mao believed that the masses needed a great leader and that the chance to see him could have an inspirational, potentially transformative, effect. But he needed the illusion that the demand for his leadership came spontaneously from the masses themselves. He would not be guilty of having actively promoted his own cult of personality. "Democratic personage" Zhang Zhizhong, sensitive to Mao's dilemma, was well suited to push Mao into the limelight. "You seem very concerned about the development of a personality cult," Zhang said to Mao.

Zhang argued, though, that Mao was the Lenin, not the Stalin, of China. Mao, like Lenin, had led the Communist party and the Chinese people to revolutionary victory, living on to lead in the construction of socialism, too. Unlike Lenin, who had died only eight years after the success of revolution, Mao would bless the people of China with his leadership for another thirty or forty years, they hoped. The difference between Mao and Stalin was that Stalin had promoted his own cult of personality. Mao had not. Mao, said Zhang, had a democratic style of leadership that stressed the "mass line" and avoided arbitrariness and dictatorship. "How can our country have a personality cult?" he wondered. "Progress is so fast, and the improvement in the life of the people so great that the masses spontaneously pour out their sincere, passionate feelings for you. Our people truly love their great leader. This is not a personality cult." Mao loved Zhang's flattery. The two were a perfect pair. The Chairman agreed to show himself to the citizens of Hefei.

On September 19, 1958, over 300,000 people lined the streets of Hefei hoping for a glimpse of Mao. He rode slowly through the city in an open car, waving impassively to the throngs, basking in their show of affection. I suspect that the crowds in Hefei were no more spontaneous than those in Tiananmen. The gaily colored clothes, the garlands of flowers around their necks, the bouquets they held aloft as the motorcade passed by, the singing, the dancing, the slogans they shouted—"Long Live Chairman Mao," "Long Live the People's Communes," "Long Live the Great Leap Forward"—suggested that Zeng Xisheng had left little to chance. These crowds had also been carefully chosen, directed by the Anhui bureau of public security. But the crowds were no less enthusiastic, no less sincere in their adulation, for having been carefully chosen. At the sight of their Chairman, they went wild with delight.

Mao was beginning to talk about establishing a free-food-supply system in the rural people's communes, so people could eat all they wanted without having to pay. He talked about taking cadres off salaries and returning them to a free-supply system similar to the one that had existed until 1954—the same system that had depleted my foreign savings. Salaries would cease. Basic necessities would be provided by the state along with a small allowance to cover incidental expenditures. His idea was to revive the system first in Zhongnanhai's General Office, starting with us in Group One.

On September 15, Zhang Chunqiao, the director of propaganda in the Shanghai party committee, had written an article promoting a free-food-supply system. Mao was so enthusiastic about it that when we stopped in Shanghai a few days later, he invited the city's propaganda chief to meet with him on the train. It was the first time I met the man who would rise to such prominence during the Cultural Revolution and later become one of the Gang of Four. Zhang was a silent, unfriendly, and brooding type, and conversation with him was difficult. I disliked him at once, and his proposal to reintroduce the free-supply system sent a chill down my spine. I opposed it. My entire savings had been dissipated two years after my return to China because of the free-supply system. The free supplies and petty allowance would not be enough to keep my family alive. In addition to my wife, mother, two small children, and my wife's parents, I had been subsidizing several other relatives, too—two aunts and a cousin. Without my salary, we would all have to rely on my wife's much smaller income. There was no way we could survive.

No one in Group One wanted a revival of the free-supply system. Ye Zilong, with us on the trip, was equally concerned. His salary was high, and he loved his life of luxury. Privilege gave him access to all sorts of free supplies, but he wanted his salary, too. When he discovered how I felt about the supply system, he encouraged me to raise my concerns with Mao. It was a clever suggestion. I might be successful in persuading the Chairman not to introduce the plan, in which case Ye's generous salary would continue. If Mao was not convinced and introduced the system anyway, I would be the one to be labeled a backward element. Ye's salary would be gone, but politically he would still be safe.

Mao's mind was still not made up, and he really did want to hear the opinions of his staff before reaching a decision. But no one was willing to risk being seen as a backward element. The issue was a matter of my family's survival. I had to tell Mao my doubts.

Mao was lying in his bed reading when I went into his compartment.

"Any news?"

"We've been talking about the free-supply system."

"Any brilliant ideas?"

I explained the difficulties I would face with no salary and so many family members to support.

Mao thought the problem could be solved by establishing communes in the cities, too. City residents, even the young and the old who had no work, could get their supplies from the commune. Children would be sent to public nurseries. This was the route to communism. "Wouldn't that solve all your problems?" he asked.

I explained that my elderly relatives were not in good health and would be unable to work in a commune. But they also had great pride and would not want to live off the labor of others. Moreover, if the commune had to support them as well as my children, the cost to the government would surely be higher than my salary.

Mao agreed that this was a problem. "Before we decide, we will have to calculate carefully the amount of labor available to the urban commune and the commune's capacity to support non-working people. If there are too many old or young, we really would have a problem." He was prepared to wait if the time did not seem ripe.

Xiao Zhang, one of the bodyguards, had been eavesdropping on our conversation and gave me thumbs-up as I left Mao's compartment. He was no more willing than I to see the free-supply system introduced. I, too, was pleased with my conversation with Mao. He was exhilarated about the vast changes taking place but was still thinking reasonably then, willing to listen to voices of caution, weighing the consequences of the many changes being proposed. He even had doubts about the backyard steel furnaces and whether such small-scale mills were the way to catch up with Great Britain in fifteen years. "If these small backyard furnaces can really produce so much steel," he wanted to know, "why do foreigners build such gigantic steel mills? Are foreigners really so stupid?"

Tian Jiaying was a voice of caution. He was distressed about Zhang Chunqiao's call for a free-supply system and accused Zhang of writing irresponsibly in order to ingratiate himself with the Chairman. "We ought not to adopt these slogans lightly," Tian argued. "We cannot ignore our low level of agricultural production or disregard the need to feed and clothe our hundreds of millions of people. It is absurd to think we can march into a communist society by dragging a naked and starving population along with us. In the past, our party has always sought truth from facts, but this isn't what we are doing now. People are telling lies, boasting. They have lost their sense of shame. This is a violation of our party's great tradition." Some of the reports coming in from the provinces, Tian said, were claiming average grain yields per *mu** of ten thousand pounds. "This is ridiculous," he said. "It is shameful."

He blamed the deceit on the atmosphere created by Mao. "When the king of Chu was looking for a consort with a pretty figure, all his concubines starved to death trying to lose weight," Tian remarked. "When the master lets his preference be known, the servants pursue it with a vengeance." Mao's plan for the Great Leap Forward was grandiose, utopian—to catch up with Great Britain in fifteen years, to

*One *mu* equals .16 acre.

transform agricultural production, using people's communes to walk the road from socialism to communism, from poverty to abundance. Mao was accustomed to sycophancy and flattery. He had been pushing the top-level party and government leaders to embrace his grandiose schemes. Wanting to please Mao, fearing for their own political futures if they did not, the top-level officials put pressure on the lower ones, and lower-level cadres complied both by working the peasants relentlessly and by reporting what their superiors wanted to hear. Impossible, fantastical claims were being made. Claims of per-*mu* grain production went from 10,000 to 20,000 to 30,000 pounds.

Psychologists of mass behavior might have an explanation for what went wrong in China in the late summer of 1958. China was struck with a mass hysteria fed by Mao, who then fell victim himself. We returned to Beijing in time for the October first celebrations. Mao began believing the slogans, casting caution to the winds. Mini–steel mills were being set up even in Zhongnanhai, and at night the whole compound was a sea of red light. The idea had originated with the Central Bureau of Guards, but Mao did not oppose them, and soon everyone was stoking the fires—cadres, clerks, secretaries, doctors, nurses, and me. The rare voices of caution were being stilled. Everyone was hurrying to jump on the utopian bandwagon. Liu Shaoqi, Deng Xiaoping, Zhou Enlai, and Chen Yi, men who might once have reined the Chairman in, were speaking with a single voice, and that voice was Mao's. What those men really thought, we never will know. Everyone was caught in the grip of this utopian hysteria.

Immediately after the October first celebrations, we set out again by train, heading south. The scene along the railroad tracks was incredible. Harvest time was approaching, and the crops were thriving. The fields were crowded with peasants at work, and they were all women and young girls dressed in reds and greens, gray-haired old men, or teenagers. All the able-bodied males, the real farmers of China, had been taken out of agricultural production to tend the backyard steel furnaces.

The backyard furnaces had transformed the rural landscape. They were everywhere, and we could see peasant men in a constant frenzy of activity, transporting fuel and raw materials, keeping the fires stoked. At night, the furnaces dotted the landscape as far as the eye could see, their fires lighting the skies.

Every commune we visited provided testimony to the abundance of the upcoming harvest. The statistics, for both grain and steel production, were astounding. "Good-news reporting stations" were being set up in communal dining halls, each station competing with nearby brigades and communes to report—red flags waving, gongs and drums sounding—the highest, most extravagant figures.

Mao's earlier skepticism had vanished. Common sense escaped him. He acted as though he believed the outrageous figures for agricultural production. The excitement was contagious. I was infected, too. Naturally, I could not help but wonder how rural China could be so quickly transformed. But I was seeing that transformation with my own eyes. I allowed myself only occasional, fleeting doubts.

One evening on the train, Lin Ke tried to set me straight. Chatting with Lin Ke and Wang Jingxian, looking out at the fires from the backyard furnaces that stretched all the way to the horizon, I shared the puzzlement I had been feeling, wondering out loud how the furnaces had appeared so suddenly and how the production figures could be so high.

What we were seeing from our windows, Lin Ke said, was staged, a huge multi-act nationwide Chinese opera performed especially for Mao. The party secretaries had ordered furnaces constructed everywhere along the rail route, stretching out for ten *li* on either side, and the women were dressed so colorfully, in reds and greens, because they had been ordered to dress that way. In Hubei, party secretary Wang Renzhong had ordered the peasants to remove rice plants from faraway fields and transplant them along Mao's route, to give the impression of a wildly abundant crop. The rice was planted so closely together that electric fans had to be set up around the fields to circulate air in order to prevent the plants from rotting. All of China was a stage, all the people performers in an extravaganza for Mao.

The production figures were false, Lin Ke said. No soil could produce twenty or thirty thousand pounds per *mu*. And what was coming out of the backyard steel furnaces was useless. The finished steel I had seen in Anhui that Zeng Xisheng claimed had been produced by the backyard steel furnace was fake, delivered there from a huge, modern factory.

"This isn't what the newspapers are saying," I protested.

The newspapers, too, were filled with falsehoods, Lin Ke insisted, printing only what they had been told. "They would not dare tell the public what was really happening," Lin said.

I was astonished. The *People's Daily* was our source of truth, the most authoritative of all the country's newspapers. If the *People's Daily* was printing falsehoods, which one would tell the truth?

Our talk was dangerous, and my agitation was worrying Wang Jingxian. "Let's not talk anymore," he interrupted. "It's time to go to bed." He pulled me aside privately, as he had when I had come to Lin Ke's defense before, and cautioned me against speaking so freely. "You could get into trouble," he warned.

I did not really believe Lin Ke. I was swept away by the drama of the Great Leap Forward, caught up in its delusions. I still trusted the party, Mao, the *People's Daily*. But Lin's revelations were distressing. The situation was troubling.

If Lin Ke was right, why was no one telling Chairman Mao? What about the Chairman's advisers—men like Tian Jiaying, Hu Qiaomu, Chen Boda, Wang Jingxian, Lin Ke, and leaders like Zhou Enlai? If they knew the reality, why did they not inform the Chairman? But no one, not even those closest to him, dared to speak out.

I wondered whether Mao, despite his outward enthusiasm, had his own private doubts.

From my conversations with Mao, I doubted that he really knew. In October 1958, Mao's doubts were not about the production figures or the miraculous increases in grain and steel production. There were exaggerations, perhaps, but he was worried most about the claims that communism was at hand. With the establishment of people's communes, the introduction of public dining halls, and the abundant harvest soon to come, word was spreading that communism was just around the corner. The creative enthusiasm of the Chinese peasantry had finally been unleashed. Mao's problem was how to maintain that mass enthusiasm while checking the belief that communism was upon us. "No one can deny the high spirits and strong determination of the masses," he said to me one night. "Of course, the people's commune is a new thing. It will take lots of hard work to turn it into a healthy institution. Certain leaders, with good intentions, want to rush things. They want to jump into communism immediately. We have to deal with this kind of problem. But other people are still suspicious about the general line, the Great Leap Forward, and the people's communes. Some hopelessly stubborn people even secretly oppose them. When they go to see God, they'll probably take their marble heads with them."

When Mao called central and local-level leaders to a conference in Zhengzhou, Henan, from November 2 to 10, 1958, the mood was still optimistic. Spirits were high. Mao stressed to the participants what he had already told me—that the general line, the Great Leap Forward, and the people's communes had to be reaffirmed. For the transformation to communism, though, patience was required. China could not rush prematurely into the future. And the peasants were being worked too hard. Cadres at all levels had to pay attention to the well-being of the masses. Months earlier, Mao had been whipping and goading the cadres into action. Now he was trying to slow them down. He was putting a brake on the most fantastical claims. But about the production figures and the backyard furnaces, he had no complaints.

It was at Zhengzhou in November 1958 that the curtain that had prevented me from seeing Mao clearly began to lift. In the ebullience of the Great Leap Forward, Mao was less secretive about his private activities. I could see for myself. Mao was staying on his train but going each night to the dances held in his honor at the Zhengzhou guesthouse. A young nurse who was also on the train accompanied Mao openly to the dances, and I knew that she was staying with him at night.

The last contingent of Chinese volunteers had just returned from Korea, and the Cultural Work Troupe from the Twentieth Army was in Zhengzhou to be welcomed back personally by Mao. The young girls from the troupe swarmed around Mao at the parties, lavishing attention on him, competing with each other for the honor of a dance—and then putting on quite a performance when Mao agreed. I still remember one young girl dancing in perfect step with Mao, becoming bolder and bolder, leaning her body this way and that, twisting and turning in rhythm to the music, loving every twist and turn. Mao was delighted, too, and he often stayed at the parties from nine in the evening until two in the morning.

After the Zhengzhou meetings, we went by train to Wuhan. The Twentieth Army Cultural Work Troupe came, too, and so did the young nurse. Mao's spirits were still high. Wang Renzhong had made sure that Mao's view from the train was of extravagantly abundant crops, thriving backyard steel furnaces, and gaily dressed women. Everyone, it seemed, was singing. As a doctor, I could not help but notice that many of the women were standing in paddy fields with water up to their waists. Paddy fields are not ordinarily that deep, but deep planting was another innovation of the Great Leap Forward. For the women, though, the low-lying fields were an invitation to gynecological infections.

In Wuhan, Mao called the Sixth Plenum of the Eighth Party Central Committee into session. Wang Renzhong put the most capable of Hubei's security staff in charge of security and logistics, and as usual the accommodations were excellent. The best local chefs were on hand to prepare sumptuous meals of the choicest delicacies, and our rooms were continually supplied with liquid refreshment and fruit. Mao was warning against believing that communism was at hand, but living as we were in a communist paradise, for us it had already arrived. Even as Hubei public security wrapped a tight cloak of secrecy around the Chairman's activities on the train, Mao became more brazen about his female companions. The dances and lavish nightly entertainment continued, and Mao brought the young nurse openly to the nightly festivities.

Mao gave me and all his personal staff a few days' leave to visit our families in Beijing, my only vacation in twenty-two years, so I was not in Wuhan for all the meetings. The Sixth Plenum was in session from November 28 to December 10 and continued the effort to bring more reality to the Great Leap Forward. Cadres and citizens were encouraged to be more realistic. China was not yet on the verge of entering communism, and people were still to be paid on the basis of how much they worked. The enthusiasm that had swept the country was a good thing, but analyses had to be based on concrete facts. Mao had recognized that the claims for economic output were too high, so projections were scaled down and so were targets for future increases. Mao's resignation as chairman of the republic finally became official. The Central Committee agreed that he would not serve as chairman when the next session of the National People's Congress began.

But Mao resigned as chairman only to become emperor. He was still the supreme leader and coming to be seen as infallible and nearly omnipotent. The mood in Wuhan was still ebullient, and the problems, such as they were, were the type Mao liked—over-optimism, too much enthusiasm, daring, and verve. Mao's enthusiasm for the people's communes continued unabated. He was critical of the Soviet Union for insisting that mechanization had to precede collectivization. The people's commune was the route to rural prosperity. The masses, at last, had become creators of history. If mistakes were to be made, better that they be leftist than rightist. Rightists lost their jobs, were imprisoned, sent to hard labor, suffered to the point of death. Leftists got only a gentle slap on the wrist.

I returned to Wuhan shortly before the meetings closed and was there for the celebration banquet Mao hosted for the other top leaders. Liu Shaoqi, Zhou Enlai, and Deng Xiaoping attended, as did all the provincial party secretaries. The toasts were all tributes to Mao. Wang Renzhong, sycophantic as usual, effusively led the way. "The proclamations from this meeting are the *Communist Manifesto* of today," he exclaimed. "Only under the brilliant leadership of the Chairman can such a red sun rise in the East."

Zhou Enlai rose to add to the flattery. "Comrade Chen Boda has said that one day under a truly communist society equals twenty years in a non-communist one. Today, we have that kind of productive power."

Ke Qingshi followed suit. "It is not correct to say that no one can outdo Marx," he said. "Haven't we already outdone Marx in both theory and practice?"

There were toasts in criticism of the Soviet Union. "For decades, the Soviet Union has tried to establish an advanced form of social development, but always they have failed. We have succeeded in less than ten years."

Liu Shaoqi and Deng Xiaoping joined in the toasting and drinking, but neither proposed a toast himself.

Mao ordinarily drank very little, but as China's leaders lifted their glasses in toast after toast, he joined them and his face turned a bright red. Then he turned the flattery to Zhou Enlai, his faithful servant, the most loyal of his lieutenants. "Premier Zhou can drink a lot," he said. "Let's toast the premier."

I took the lead in toasting Zhou Enlai, standing in front of him to clink glasses. "Bottoms up," I said.

"Oh, we must celebrate," Zhou replied loudly as others joined in toasting him. Zhou's capacity for liquor was enormous, and his face never turned red. But that night Zhou got drunk, and he woke up in the middle of the night with a nosebleed. Luo Ruiqing blamed me, berating me the next morning for having started the round of toasts, arguing that a doctor should know better than to urge others to drink. I thought I had only been following Mao's lead.

Agricultural production in the fall of 1958 was the highest in China's history. But by mid-December, the nation was seriously short of food. Even as China's leaders drank to the brilliant leadership of Chairman Mao, the disaster that had been brewing unseen for months was finally bubbling to the surface.

In Wuhan, feted by Wang Renzhong, the party leadership remained sheltered from the unfolding crisis. But during my visit home in the middle of the meetings, I had discovered there was no meat or oil in Zhongnanhai. Rice and basic staples were hard to come by. Vegetables were few. Something had gone awry.

Much, in fact, had gone wrong. A large portion of the huge harvest lay uncollected in the fields. Massive numbers of able-bodied male peasants had been transferred from the fields to work in the backyard steel furnaces. The women and children could not bring in the harvest. The labor was backbreaking, more than they could endure, and crops rotted in the fields.

In fact, I did not know it then, but China was tottering on the brink of disaster. The leading cadres of the party and first party secretaries in the provinces were ingratiating themselves with Mao, disregarding the welfare of hundreds of millions of peasants. The preposterous claims of vastly increased production were taken seriously by the upper-level leaders, to whom they were made. But how could one *mu* of land produce fifty, one hundred, or two hundred thousand pounds of rice? Rural areas were taxed on a percentage of what they produced, and areas that falsely claimed gigantically high yields were taxed according to their faked reports. Some places were delivering all they had produced to the state. Other places were giving so much there was little left for their inhabitants to eat. Peasants were beginning to go hungry. Soon they would starve. The greater the falsehoods, the more people died of starvation.

Ironically, much of the grain that was sent to the state as taxes was exported. China was still repaying its debts to the Soviet Union and much of the grain went there. It was a question of face. Mao could not admit that the communes Khrushchev had so vigorously opposed were anything less than a success.

To minimize their losses and keep enough food to eat, communes were saying that they had been struck by natural disasters. Their harvest had been abundant, but the weather had destroyed it. Such communes were thus able to keep the grain they would otherwise have owed in taxes. Or they were granted relief grain from the state.

The backyard steel furnaces were equally disastrous. As the drive to produce steel continued at an ever more frenetic pace, people were forced to contribute their pots and pans, their doorknobs, the steel from their wrought-iron gates, shovels, and spades. There was not enough coal to fire the furnaces, so the fires were fed with the peasants' wooden furniture—their tables, chairs, and beds. But what came out of the furnaces was useless—nothing more than melted-down knives and pots and pans. Mao said that China was not on the verge of communism, but in fact some absurd form of communism was already in place. Private property *was* being abolished, because private property was all being given away to feed the voracious steel furnaces.

Still, Mao's euphoria continued. I think at this point he was still being shielded from the impending crisis. I had misgivings. I could see disaster brewing. But I did not dare to speak. I worried that Mao was being deceived and no one was willing to tell him the truth. Of the men closest to Mao, Tian Jiaying was the best informed, the most skeptical, and the most honest. I thought he should be the one to inform Mao. But Tian Jiaying was in Henan, investigating the situation there. Realistic reports would have to await his return. Mao trusted him. Mao would believe what he said.

33

The criticisms of Mao had now begun. But they were too oblique to be understood.

Zhou Xiaozhou, first party secretary of Hunan province and still under fire from Mao for his caution about pushing agricultural production, was the first to criticize Mao. We left Wuhan in mid-December, stopping briefly in Changsha, where Zhou Xiaozhou invited Mao to a Hunan opera—*Sheng Si Pai* ("The Board of Life or Death"). It was a complicated tale about a young woman falsely accused of murder. Hai Rui (1513–1587), an upright Ming dynasty (1368–1644) official in the court of the Jiajing emperor, was the hero, arriving just in time to prevent the young woman's execution. Peng Dehuai, China's honest, outspoken minister of defense, who had so often dared to criticize Mao, had seen the opera during his November visit to Changsha and had enjoyed it immensely. Hai Rui, renowned for his fairness, integrity, and commitment to reform, was the hero of several local folk operas, all extolling the courage and honesty of the official who had risked his life for the good of the country and the people and who dared to challenge the vainglorious and misdirected emperor. Zhou Xiaozhou's choice of opera could not have been accidental. Surely he regarded himself as an upright official with the good of the country at heart, under siege from a foolhardy emperor.

If Mao caught the implicit criticism of him, he gave no indication. He loved the opera and was fascinated with the character of Hai Rui. That same night, in Changsha, he asked Lin Ke to get him some Ming dynasty histories with more examples of Hai Rui's courage and integrity. Within months, he was encouraging party leaders to study Hai Rui's example.

We did not stay in Changsha. Jiang Qing was waiting in Guangzhou. Mao continued to talk excitedly about the latest production statistics. He had become curious about the works of the Soviet economist Leontief, wanting to compare economic organization in the Soviet Union with the new economic structures in China, and asked Chen Boda, Tian Jiaying, and Deng Liqun to join him in Guangzhou to study Leontief's book on political economy.

In Guangzhou, Tian Jiaying reported on the situation he had seen in Henan. I did not have a chance to talk to him then and knew only that Henan had problems and that people there were hungry. In my nighttime meetings with the Chairman, I noted a new measure of concern. He wondered occasionally whether land really could produce ten thousand pounds per *mu* and was also suspicious about the quality of steel being produced in the backyard steel furnaces. "Is that steel really useful?" he would wonder out loud. I could not answer him because I knew no better than he. But feeding knives and shovels and pots and pans into small steel furnaces in order to make new knives and shovels and pots and pans did not make sense. In the frenzy of production, nothing was being done with the so-called steel that was being produced.

Whatever Mao's doubts, they were overridden by the rationale of his Great Leap Forward, which had stirred the creative enthusiasm of the Chinese masses. He did not want to throw cold water on it. Mao stood on the side of the masses, and he represented their interests. His leadership lay in his capacity to motivate people to action, to unleash their great creative force, and his policy of the Great Leap Forward, he believed, did precisely that. His faith in his own leadership, in the Great Leap, and in the Chinese masses continued undiminished.

We were in Guangzhou on December 26, 1958, for Mao's sixty-fifth birthday. When Tao Zhu, the first party secretary of Guangdong province, threw an elaborate banquet in Mao's honor, the Chairman refused to attend. "When I was young, I was happy to celebrate my birthday," he said, "but now every birthday means I have aged a year, matured a year, and have one less year to live." It was polite talk. Mao was in his prime. He did not believe that he was headed toward death. His aversion to banquets had recurred, I think, because he was beginning to lose face. The Great Leap Forward was not going as he wanted, and he was reconnoitering, trying to understand why.

Mao spent the night of his sixty-fifth birthday in bed, sending me and others from Group One to the banquet Tao Zhu had arranged. He asked me to report to him as usual when it was over. The banquet was sumptuous, and the toasts to the Chairman's health were as extravagant as the food. I was so drained by the wine that I went to bed immediately after the banquet without making my usual report to Mao.

Li Yinqiao woke me in the middle of the night. We were leaving immediately for Beijing.

Jiang Qing had wakened earlier in the night wanting a glass of water and another sleeping pill. When her nurse failed to respond to her call, Jiang Qing looked for her in the duty room, and when the nurse was not there, the Chairman's already suspicious wife stormed into Mao's bedroom and discovered her nurse with Mao.

Li Yinqiao told me what had happened. For the first time since I had met her, Jiang Qing lost her temper with Mao. As her fury spilled forth, other suspicions came pouring out, too. There was a recent visit from the daughter of a former servant of Mao. Mao had stayed in contact with the servant and had encouraged her daughter's education, sending her three hundred *yuan* to enroll in school. The young woman visited Mao in his bedchamber during her winter break in 1958. She had paid a similar visit to the Chairman during his November-December stay in Wuhan. Jiang Qing had found out and suspected her husband of having affairs not only with her nurse and the young girl but with the young girl's mother, the former servant, as well. All this came out during the couple's late-night quarrel.

Mao's response to his wife's fury was to leave. He returned to Beijing immediately, leaving the fuming Jiang Qing behind.

We left in the middle of the night, so quickly I had only minutes to dress, grab my things, and rush to the train.

Jiang Qing quickly regretted her outburst. Her apology arrived shortly after our return, in the form of a simple note quoting a line from *Journey to the West,* the most beloved of China's folk stories. When Xuan Zang, the Chinese monk who goes to India in search of Buddhist scriptures, and hence in a quest for truth, leaves Monkey behind at the Water Curtain Cave in a pique of anger, Monkey is bitterly disappointed and lonely. "My body is in Water Curtain Cave," Monkey says to Xuan Zang, "but my heart is following you." Mao was delighted to read the same words from Jiang Qing. Mao was the modern-day Xuan Zang, on a dangerous mission in a quest for truth in the form of communism. His women were trivial when compared to the perils on the journey to communism. Mao now had Jiang Qing's implicit permission to carry on his affairs.

34

With the approach of the new year, 1959, Beijing was in panic. Rumors that urban communes were soon to be established had swept the city, and people thought their private property was about to be confiscated by the state. The city was a gigantic garage sale as people sold their precious private possessions in the hope of holding on to the cash when their property was handed over to the communes.

My family's situation had deteriorated markedly since the Great Leap Forward began, and because I had spent most of 1958 traveling with Mao, I had been of little help. I was happy to be back.

My mother was terrified that she would be forced to work in the new urban commune. But she was too old and too tired and was busy during the week looking after my two sons while my wife was away at work. Who would look after the children once the commune was formed? Mao wanted them sent to state-run nurseries.

As rumors persisted, Lillian and I were offered extra space in Zhongnanhai for my mother and sons. But I did not want to involve my family any more than necessary in life in the inner court. And I wanted a place to escape to whenever I could. My old family home was still a haven—the only place where we could really be a family, forget the cares of the world, laugh and enjoy ourselves without restraint. It was the only place we all felt safe. I wanted to preserve that haven.

Mao heard the hue and cry of the urban residents and soon abandoned his plan for urban communes. But most of my family's property was confiscated anyway. Watchful neighborhood officials had noticed that my mother and our two sons occupied only five of the rooms in our huge thirty-room complex. My mother had been allowing relatives to live in some of the other rooms and rented out the rest for token sums. In the winter of 1958–59, when the leftist political atmosphere was at its height, our local neighborhood association, the Beijing Housing Administration, and the local public security bureau decided to confiscate all but the rooms my mother and sons were using. They did not call such expropriation "confiscation," of course. My mother was to be "compensated" for the "voluntary" sale of her house, and she was to share in management of the property when the new tenants moved in.

Still, she was distraught, and so was my wife. The house was our inheritance, passed down through the generations. My wife urged me to talk with my superiors in the Central Bureau of Guards and the Central Bureau of Health. Maybe some sort of compromise could be reached.

I, too, was upset. But I could not ask for special treatment. My family had been privileged, and most of the people I worked with came from humble peasant pasts. My superiors had no reason to help save my family home—certainly not in the prevailing leftist atmosphere. Compared to others, we still lived a life of luxury. The likely result of my efforts to save our house would be another offer for the whole family to move into Zhongnanhai, and that I wanted to avoid. So we gave up our family home—all but the rooms occupied by my mother and sons. The sum from the sale was so paltry that it was an outright gift to the state, and my mother had no control over the tenants.

I consoled my mother as best I could, pointing out that she was lucky to own five rooms in a city where housing was crowded and most people owned no property at all.

In the same winter of 1958–59, the food shortage hit, causing further hardship for my mother. Lillian still ate in the dining hall at Zhongnanhai, and I joined her when I was there. There was no meat and the quality of the food had gone down, but the quantity was sufficient. Zhongnanhai would be the last place affected by a food crisis. But for my mother, even the basic necessities were in short supply. There was no meat at all, and oil and rice were difficult to buy. People waited in long lines to buy even basic foodstuffs.

My mother was over seventy then, and her health began to decline. She developed hypertension. We arranged for neighbors to help her, to wait in line and do her shopping. But the economic situation was becoming worse every month, and Tian Jiaying warned that this was only the beginning. The whole nation faced a serious shortage of food, and no end was in sight.

With the crisis continuing to deepen, I expected Mao to stay for a while in Beijing. I was wrong.

One afternoon in late January 1959, I was visiting Hu Qiaomu in Beijing Hospital, where he was convalescing after a recurrence of his ulcer, when I received an emergency call to return to Group One immediately. Mao must have taken suddenly ill. I rushed out, not even bothering to grab my sweater, hopped on my bicycle, and was pedaling out the front gate of the hospital when bodyguard Xiao Li arrived by car. The Chairman had decided to visit Manchuria. He was leaving immediately.

Mao had already left for the airport by the time I arrived in Zhongnanhai. My medical supplies had gone with him, and a car was ready to take me to the airport immediately. I had no time to pack a toothbrush, let alone any clothes. We arrived at the airport just after Mao's plane had taken off. Another plane was waiting, engines running and ready to go. Xiao Li and I were the only passengers, and the plane took off as soon as we were on board.

A few hours later, I stepped out of the plane in Shenyang, Liaoning, the coldest region of China during the coldest month of the year, with no overcoat or even a sweater. The buildings were, blessedly, well heated, but I was miserably cold outdoors. "Did you sell off your clothes because of the Great Leap Forward?" Mao joked when he saw my discomfort. "Or did you give them to the people's commune?" Fortunately, the trip lasted only five days.

The Chairman had come north because it was the largest coal- and steel-producing region of China, and he wanted to know how steel was produced and whether the quality of the backyard steel furnaces was good. He had wanted to decentralize steel production both as a way of allowing the creative energies of the peasants full flower and to deprive the central-level economic bureaucrats of their stultifying power. But Mao had still not settled the question he kept raising with me. Why, if good steel can be produced in tiny backyard furnaces, does the technologically advanced West rely on gigantic factories for production? He was also interested in the question of how the furnaces were fueled. In rural China, where the demand for cooking fuel had long since denuded the forests, peasants were resorting to burning their doors and furniture to keep the mini-furnaces stoked. The steel factories in the northeast were huge and modern, and coal supplies were plentiful. Mao wanted to see both steel factories and coal mines.

What he learned during his visit was conclusive. High-quality steel can be produced only in huge modern factories using reliable fuel, like coal. But he gave no order to halt the backyard steel furnaces. The horrible waste of manpower and materials, the useless output from the homemade furnaces, was not his main concern. Mao still did not want to do anything to dampen the enthusiasm of the masses.

We returned briefly to Beijing, but Mao was quickly off again to Tianjin, Jinan, Nanjing, Shanghai, and Hangzhou. He invited Luo Ruiqing and Yang Shangkun to join him. He wanted to use the tour to "educate" them, he said. Both men had fallen out of favor with the Chairman and were honored by the invitation. Luo Ruiqing, ever loyal to Mao, was still trying to win the Chairman's favor—removing himself from active involvement in security arrangements and even taking up swimming as a way to show his support. But Mao's trust had not fully returned, and Luo had been depressed.

Yang Shangkun, still smarting from Mao's dissolution of his General Headquarters post after the Black Flag Incident months before, was also trying to ingratiate himself with Mao. He was lying low, concentrating on administration rather than politics, presenting himself as a faithful servant without political ambition. Isolated and insecure, he had hooked himself to Deng Xiaoping as the rising leader most likely to protect him from the vagaries of political change and to grant him his political due. Yang's opportunities to see Mao were rare, and he was elated to join him on the trip.

The trip was another "inspection tour," and we visited factories, universities, people's communes, and schools. The provincial party and military leaders showered the Chairman with praise, enthusiastically professing their loyalty. Even as the economic situation worsened, the cult of Mao was growing. If food was scarce, people reasoned, the fault lay not with Mao but with their local leaders. The Chairman, everyone supposed, had come to put things right. The popular attitude toward Mao was rooted in Chinese tradition. The emperor was never wrong, only misguided by his advisers and court officials. Huge, enthusiastic crowds turned out to welcome him, greeting him with thunderous applause and shouts of "Long Live Chairman Mao."

Mao wanted Luo and Yang to see for themselves how greatly he was loved by the masses. Indeed, Luo Ruiqing and Yang Shangkun were properly impressed. Mao had given them great face by inviting them along. They basked in his reflected glory. It was a heady experience.

Yang Shangkun had only one regret. Mao had spoken often during the trip—about how to organize the relationship between industry and agriculture, how the people's communes ought to be structured, how to arrange for equitable distribution and pay for labor performed. But no notes had been taken on the Chairman's remarks. One night, chatting with Luo Ruiqing and others on the staff, Yang Shangkun said he wanted to find a way to record Mao's remarks. Mao often discussed matters of policy when he toured the provinces, but the central secretariat, with no record of what the Chairman had said, had no way to transform them into written policy instructions. Local officials were at a similar loss. They could pass Mao's informal comments up to higher levels—to Liu Shaoqi and Deng Xiaoping—but with no official record, no one was willing to take responsibility for taking local-level reports as the basis for policy.

"We have to think of a way to record the Chairman's words and send the minutes to the central secretariat for future reference," Yang Shangkun said. It was a thoughtful suggestion by a grateful subordinate.

Ye Zilong told me Yang Shangkun had suggested that he request Mao's permission to bring a stenographer along on future trips, so the center could have a complete record of everything the Chairman said. But Mao did not want a stenographer, Ye Zilong said. He saw his remarks as casual talk, and he knew the power of his words. All of rural China had rushed to establish people's communes when they knew Mao had said "people's communes are great." He did not want further casual remarks to be translated so hurriedly into policy. The responsibility was too great.

Not long afterward, an elite team of technicians from the Public Security Ministry came aboard Mao's train to put bugging equipment in Mao's sleeping compartment and in the reception area where he often held meetings. The tiny imported devices were so cleverly hidden—in lampshades, wall lamps, and flower vases—that Mao would never find out. The microphones were linked to recording equipment in another compartment, and a technician from the General Office, a young man came to record Mao's conversations and maintain the equipment. Mao was never told the nature of his work, but the young man began accompanying us on all of Mao's travels. Later, I was told that similar high-tech bugging devices had also been installed in the provincial guesthouses Mao frequented.

Along with everyone in Group One I was sworn to absolute

secrecy. The decision to bug the Chairman had been made at the highest levels, it was whispered. If the secret were ever to be revealed, the consequences would be dire. We all stayed quiet. The party had spoken, and we obeyed. None of us could have known then how disastrous the decision would be....

35

When the Seventh Plenum of the Eighth Party Central Committee met in Shanghai from April 2 to 5, 1959, Mao was still optimistic. His faith in the Great Leap Forward and the people's communes was apparently undiminished. Minor problems had developed, but they were manageable. The organization of the communes had to be perfected, and guidelines had to be laid down about how to allocate labor between the backyard steel furnaces and agricultural work. Too many strong laborers had been pulled from the fields. Payment procedures within the communes needed to be revised. Projections for economic output needed to be scaled back again, too. Output for 1958 had been grossly exaggerated, and the targets for 1959 had to be more realistic.

Mao's greatest fear was not that food was short or that targets were too high or that backyard steel furnaces were wasting labor and producing worthless iron. He was afraid that the creative energies of the masses, unleashed by the Leap, would somehow be dampened. If he knew the country was careening toward disaster, he gave no hint. I did not really know, either. Food was short in Beijing, and Tian Jiaying was warning that the crisis had only begun, but I still thought the problems were temporary, a result of misreporting at the lower levels. Inside Mao's circle, I remained oblivious to the world outside.

Mao stayed on his train during the Shanghai meetings, both because he was uncomfortable with the opulence of Hardoon's former residence and because he was still involved with the young railroad nurse on his special train. His boldness continued, and the young woman accompanied him every evening to the exclusive Jinjiang Club, formerly owned by the French and now an exclusive retreat for top-level leaders. Aware of Mao's penchant for female companions, the Shanghai public security authorities had arranged for the Chairman to meet Shanghai's most famous actresses and singers. But their choices did not interest Mao. The women were too old, too sophisticated, too worldly-wise for him. Mao preferred younger, less experienced women. They were easier to control. The Shanghai authorities then arranged for nightly performances by cultural troupes of younger, more inno-cent girls, who were capable of greater devotion.

There were movies, too, and local operas every evening. Ke Qing-shi arranged the performance of another opera about Hai Rui, whose story had first captivated Mao in Changsha the year before. In the Shanghai performance, Hai Rui was imprisoned for remarking ironi-cally that the emperor's name (Jiajing) had the same sound as the saying that meant the emperor had bankrupted the nation. At first, the Jiajing emperor threatens to kill Hai Rui. But after reading the offi-cial's memorial a second and third time, the emperor finally realizes that Hai Rui is a good and upright man, willing to sacrifice his own life for the good of the nation. Hai Rui remains in prison, but the emperor stays his execution. One day, when the prison guard presents Hai Rui with a lavish meal, the official assumes it is his last and that his execution is at hand. Only when he finishes eating does the guard congratulate Hai Rui and tell him that the emperor is dead. Hai Rui, genuinely loyal to the emperor, is so saddened and shocked to learn that the emperor's death and not his own is the occasion for the sumptuous repast that he vomits up the meal.

Again, Mao was enthusiastic about Hai Rui. Hai Rui was both courageous in chastising the emperor and genuinely loyal to him. Mao began to promote the Hai Rui spirit. Hai Rui's biography was re-printed and distributed to the meeting participants, and Mao urged them to follow Hai Rui's example. Later, Mao encouraged historians to do research on Hai Rui, and their articles were published in newspa-pers throughout the country. In Shanghai and Beijing, modern dramas about Hai Rui began to be staged. The Ming dynasty official was becoming a national folk hero.

At the same time, Mao's dissatisfaction with the party was return-ing. He was blaming the party leadership for the dislocations of the Great Leap Forward. False reports and inflated statistics were ram-pant. "There are so many lies," he said to me. "When there is pressure from the top, there will be lies from the bottom."

There was irony in Mao's promotion of Hai Rui. Because that Ming dynasty official later became such an important symbol of the party's dissatisfaction over the purge of Peng Dehuai and in how the Cultural Revolution started, I have often reflected on the meaning of Hai Rui for Mao. Mao was a complex and often contradictory man. As the emperor, he believed in his own infallibility. If wrong decisions were made, wrong policies introduced, the fault lay not with him but with the information provided him. The emperor could not be wrong, but he could be deceived.

Hai Rui's appeal to Mao was threefold. Hai Rui told the truth and was genuinely loyal to the emperor, so loyal that he was willing to die, even unjustly, without a word of blame—for the glory of the emperor and the good of the nation. And when things went wrong, Hai Rui blamed not the emperor but the emperor's deceitful and misguided ministers.

Mao did want to be told the truth. Even in my disillusionment, I still believe that had he fully understood the truth early in the Great Leap Forward, he would have brought a halt to the disaster long before he did. But the truth had to come to him on his own terms, from a modern-day Hai Rui. He could not accept it when it included criticisms of him or when it came from conspiring ministers who might be contenders for his power. The truth had to come from political innocents.

But few political innocents made it to the highest reaches of political power in China. There were few thoroughly selfless, disinterested top-level officials who put the welfare of the nation above all else. Immersed as he was in Chinese history, and thus in the power struggles and political intrigues that were part of every court, Mao expected political intrigue within his own imperial court, and he played the same games himself. Even if aspirants to power told Mao the objective truth, he could not accept it because he saw conspiracies everywhere.

Thus Mao's encouragement to study Hai Rui, like his call for the intellectuals to criticize the party, became part of his own conspiratorial strategy. While Mao did want to hear the truth from loyalists without political intent, his promotion of Hai Rui was also a ruse to bring his enemies out in the open, just as in 1957 he had spoken of coaxing snakes out of their holes. As the emperor, only Mao had the power to decide who were the genuine loyalists and who were the ones merely criticizing the emperor as a way of enhancing their power.

But there were flaws in Mao's logic. Just as the emperors the Chinese people most reviled—Qin Shihuangdi, Emperor Zhou, and Sui Yangdi—were the ones Mao most admired, so most people reading the story of Hai Rui saw the Jiajing emperor as vainglorious and unfair. Many of Mao's closest colleagues believed that they were as loyal to Mao as Hai Rui had been to the Jiajing emperor. Mao argued that under "pressure from the top," those at the lower levels had lied, and he blamed his own high-level lieutenants for the pressure. But the real pressure had come from Mao. In 1957, he had declared his critics rightists and punished them without mercy, then goaded the party into action, whipping the leaders to set ever higher production targets. He himself had created the atmosphere that made it so difficult for party leaders to tell the truth, and the party leaders had followed his lead out of loyalty to—or fear of—Mao. Mao saw the fault not in himself but in other leaders, the evil ministers in the court of Jiajing. His promotion of Hai Rui was another attempt to deflect criticism from himself and blame others. But others, like Zhou Xiaozhou, read the story differently. They were Hai Rui, loyalists unjustly accused and punished, and Mao was the emperor who was no longer benign.

We returned to Beijing in mid-April 1959 for the first plenary session of the Second National People's Congress—the nominal Chinese legislature. Under instructions from the party Central Committee, which had just met, the National People's Congress finally accepted Mao's resignation as chairman of the republic and elected Liu Shaoqi in Mao's stead. Zhu De was made chairman of the standing committee of the National People's Congress, and Song Qingling and Dong Biwu were elected vice-chairmen of the republic.

Mao's resignation and the designation of Liu Shaoqi as the new chairman of the republic had been long in coming, and the official announcement was anticlimactic and passed without fanfare or great public note. Until then, the two posts that carried the title chairman (*zhuxi*)—chairman of the Chinese Communist party and chairman of the republic—were both held by Mao, and thus there was only one chairman. The English rendering of *president* to denote chairman of the republic misses what was a major problem for Mao. When Liu Shaoqi took over as chairman of the republic, there were two men with the title of chairman in China, where titles are important. This Mao would never accept.

That two men now held the title of chairman, when Mao wanted to reign supreme, had political implications that I, and most of China, could not have known at the time.

A subtle change began to come over Liu Shaoqi after 1959. Before he took over as chairman of the republic following Mao's resignation, we had all called him Comrade Shaoqi. Then suddenly he was being addressed only as Chairman Liu. The title carried with it great power, and Liu took his new title and power seriously, gradually expanding his control over the country's day-to-day affairs and often acting without consulting Mao. But Mao's struggle to reassert himself as China's only chairman had already begun, and would end with the purge of Liu Shaoqi, when the title of chairman of the republic would be struck down, together with the man.

We stayed in Beijing only a month, then set out by train, heading south, at the end of May.

36

Everything had changed. The fires from the backyard furnaces were out, the brightly dressed peasant women gone. The fields were empty. No crops. No people. Wuhan, still under the direction of Mao's friend Wang Renzhong, was in terrible shape. We stayed, as usual, in the Meiyuan guesthouse along East Lake, but there was little to eat. In the past, our rooms had been copiously stocked with tea and cigarettes, and every meal had been a banquet. Now there was no meat, because the cows and chickens had starved and the pigs were too skinny to eat. Occasionally, we were served fish. Vegetables were scarce. There were no cigarettes or matches anywhere in the province. The warehouses had been depleted. Everything had been consumed. Only months earlier, Wang Renzhong, Mao's great sycophant, had been bragging that Hubei was producing ten or twenty thousand pounds of rice per *mu*. Now there was famine.

Wang Renzhong claimed that the famine was the result of natural disasters. But there had been no natural disaster in Hubei. The weather in 1958 and 1959 had been splendid. Much of the abundant crop had simply not been collected.

Changsha, in Mao's home province of Hunan, was different. Food was less plentiful than before, but no one was starving, and the small open-air restaurants were serving customers. We stayed in the magnificent Lotus Garden guesthouse, with beautiful modern buildings and lotus trees set among rolling lawns. The tea and cigarettes supplied to our rooms were stale. They had been taken out of storage in honor of our visit. But the warehouses had not been depleted and the tea and cigarettes were China's best. We ate meat in Hunan, too—the tasty ham for which the province is famous.

The irony of the contrast between Hunan and Hubei was not lost on Zhou Xiaozhou, the first party secretary of Hunan, who had been so severely criticized by Mao in 1957 for his failure to implement double cropping and who had introduced Mao to Hai Rui. Wang Renzhong was accompanying Mao's entourage to Changsha, and one day as Luo Ruiqing, Wang Renzhong, Zhou Xiaozhou, and I were chatting, Zhou could not resist needling Wang about the contrast. "Wasn't Zhejiang praised for its high output last year?" he asked bitterly. "And Hunan was criticized for not having worked as hard. Now look at Hubei. You don't even have stale cigarettes or tea. You used up all your reserves last year. Today, we may be poor, but at least we have supplies in storage." Wang Renzhong stalked out without saying a word as the rest of us stood in embarrassed silence. But Zhou Xiaozhou was right. Even on the streets, the contrast was obvious. The province of Hunan still had food.

Mao decided to return to Shaoshan, the Hunan village of his birth. He had not been back since 1927, thirty-two years before.

Mao's trip to Shaoshan was his way of seeking to learn the truth. He did not believe the leading cadres. There could be no carefully staged performances for Mao in Shaoshan. He knew the place too well. He could see through any attempt to deceive him. Besides, the village folk would speak frankly to him. They were honest and simple, and Mao was one of them. He trusted them.

37

The day was sunny and hot when we set out by car from Changsha on June 25, and the country roads were unpaved and dusty. Our car had no air-conditioning, and the dust came floating in through our open windows. We were perspiring so heavily that by the time we arrived in the Xiangtan prefectural seat some two hours later, we must have looked as if we were made of mud.

The party secretary of Xiangtan prefecture, Hua Guofeng, welcomed us. It was the first time I had met the man who would become Mao's successor some sixteen years later. We rested for a while in Xiangtan, chatting with Hua, but the prefecture chief did not accompany us on the final lap of our trip. Mao was afraid that the peasants of Shaoshan might speak less frankly with the head of their prefecture around.

Shaoshan village was a forty-minute drive from Xiangtan. Mao stayed on a hilltop in an old guesthouse once owned by Christian missionaries (even in as remote a village as Shaoshan, the missionaries had set up a church), and I stayed in a school at the bottom of the hill. The weather was hot and humid even at night, and the mosquito net covering my bed was stifling. I could not sleep.

Li Yinqiao phoned me at a little after five the next morning. Mao had not slept either. He wanted me to join him now for a walk. I met Mao at his guesthouse, and we began walking down the back of the hill, with Luo Ruiqing, Wang Renzhong, Zhou Xiaozhou, and a host of bodyguards following. Partway down, in the middle of a small pine grove, Mao stopped before a burial mound. It was only when he bowed from the waist in the traditional manner of respect that I realized we were standing before his parents' grave. Shen Tong, one of the security officers accompanying us, quickly gathered a bunch of wildflowers. Mao placed the flowers on the grave and bowed three times again. The rest of his entourage, standing behind him, bowed too. "There used to be a tombstone around here," Mao said. "It has disappeared after all these years." When Luo Ruiqing suggested that the site be repaired and restored, Mao demurred. "It's good just to have found the place," he said.

We continued walking down the hill, in the direction of the Mao clan ancestral hall. Again Mao stopped, puzzled, looking for something. We were standing on the spot where the Buddhist shrine Mao had referred to so often in our conversations once stood—the shrine his mother used to visit when he was sick, where she burned incense and fed the ashes to her son, certain of their curative powers. The tiny shrine, like the tombstone, had disappeared, torn down only months before with the establishment of the commune. The bricks were needed to build the backyard steel furnaces, and the wood had been used as fuel.

Mao had fallen silent on our walk. The destruction of the shrine had saddened him. "It's such a pity," he said. "It should have been left alone. Without money to see doctors, poor farmers could still come and pray to the gods and eat the incense ashes. The shrine could lift their spirits, give them hope. People need this kind of help and encouragement." I smiled when he said this, but Mao was serious. "Don't look down on incense ashes," he said, repeating his admonition that medicine is good only for curable disease. "Incense ashes give people the courage to fight disease, don't you think? You are a doctor. You should know how much psychology affects medical treatment." People could not live without spiritual support, Mao believed.

My smile was not meant as disagreement. I have always believed that one's state of mind has a profound effect on health.

We went then to visit Mao's old family house. No one lived in it then. The personality cult surrounding Mao was still in its early stage, so the family house was still in its original state, old farming equipment neatly displayed on the porch. Only a wooden board above the entrance designated the place as Mao's childhood home. The style of the house was typical of that area—simple mud walls and a thatched roof. There was nothing modern about it. But with eight rooms built around a courtyard, the home was obviously that of a wealthy peasant.

The land Mao's father had once farmed, with help from temporary laborers, was now part of the people's commune. Just beyond the house was a pond lined with trees. "That's where I used to go swimming and where the cattle drank water," he said.

He began reminiscing about his childhood. "My father was tough," he said. "He always beat us. Once when he tried to beat me, I ran away, and he chased me around this pond, cursing me for being an unfilial son. But I told him that an unkind father will have an unfilial son."

Mao described his mother as kindhearted and always willing to help others. She, Mao's younger brother, and Mao often formed a "united front" against Mao's father. "My father died a long time ago, but had he lived to this day, he would have been classified a rich peasant and been struggled against," Mao said.

Mao began contacting his relatives to learn firsthand how the Great Leap Forward had affected them. Only the women and children were at home. The men were away working on the backyard steel furnaces or water conservancy projects. Mao did not have to delve far to learn that life was hard for the families in Shaoshan. With the construction of the backyard steel furnaces, everyone's pots and pans had been confiscated and thrown into the furnace to make steel—and nothing had been returned. Everyone was eating in the public mess halls. The families had no cooking equipment. Even if they still had had pots and pans, their earthen hearths had been destroyed so the mud could be used as fertilizer.

When Mao took a swim in the newly constructed Shaoshan reservoir that afternoon, he talked to the local folk about the project. Everyone criticized it. The reservoir had been poorly built, one old peasant pointed out. The commune secretary was in such a rush to finish that it leaked. The reservoir's capacity was too small, and when it rained, water had to be released to prevent flooding.

The commune directors called the menfolk back to meet with Mao in the evening, and Mao hosted a dinner party for them at his guesthouse—some fifty people in all. Everyone complained about the mess halls. The older people did not like them because the younger people always cut in and grabbed the food first. The younger people did not like the mess halls because there never was enough food. Fistfights often broke out, and much of the food was wasted when it ended up on the floor.

Mao asked about the backyard steel furnaces. Again he heard nothing but complaints. Indigenous raw materials were scarce. They used locally mined low-quality coal to fuel the furnaces, but there was not enough coal and no iron ore at all. The only way to comply with the directive to build the furnaces was to confiscate the peasants' pots, pans, and shovels for iron ore and their doors and furniture for fuel. But the furnaces were producing iron nuggets that no one knew what to do with. Now, with no pots or pans, people couldn't even boil drinking water at home, let alone cook. The commune kitchens were no help with the water problem, because the cooks had to devote all their energies to preparing food.

When Mao's questions stopped, the room fell silent. An air of gloom descended. The Great Leap Forward was not going well in Shaoshan. "If you can't fill your bellies at the public dining hall, then it's better just to disband it," Mao said. "It's a waste of food. As for the water conservancy project, I don't think every rural community has to build a reservoir. If the reservoirs are not built well, there will be big problems. And if you cannot produce good steel, you might as well quit."

With these words, Shaoshan probably became the first village in the country to abolish the public dining halls, halt its water conservancy project, and begin dismantling the backyard steel furnaces. Mao's comments were never publicly released, but they spread quickly through word of mouth. Soon many areas were dismantling their projects.

Thus it was that I, and certainly Mao, began to be aware that the economic situation in the country had deteriorated. Mao's return to Shaoshan awakened him to reality, shaking him into a growing awareness that trouble was brewing. When he returned to Wuhan, his previous ebullience had evaporated. But there was still no doubt in his mind that the programs themselves were basically sound, that they simply needed further adjustment. Mao still did not want to do anything to dampen the enthusiasm of the masses. The problem was how to bring the cadres back to reality without crushing their spirit or spreading gloom to the people. It was a question of propaganda—how to mobilize cadres and peasants alike to the right level of realistic enthusiasm. Mao decided to call a propaganda meeting to discuss the issues. It would be held in Wuhan.

We arrived in Wuhan on June 28. The weather was scorchingly hot and would only become hotter as the summer progressed. Wang Renzhong thought the meeting would be best held in a more hospitable climate. He suggested Qingdao, the site of the meetings in the summer of 1957, but Mao remembered the month-long cold he had contracted during his stay and refused to return to Qingdao.

Shanghai mayor Ke Qingshi suggested Lushan, the famous mountain resort along the Yangtze River in Jiangxi province where

Chiang Kai-shek used to convene meetings of the Guomindang. At nearly fifteen hundred meters' elevation, the weather would be cool, and the facilities, built for Chiang and the Nationalist party elite, were excellent. There was even an auditorium for meetings. Besides, Lushan was not too far from Wuhan—just down the Yangtze by boat. Many of the party leaders had already begun gathering in Wuhan. Transporting them to Lushan would be easy.

Mao agreed. The party would convene in Lushan.

38

The situation in Mao's native Shaoshan was good compared with the rest of China. A horrible famine was sweeping the country. The province of Anhui, where party secretary Zeng Xisheng had first shown Mao the backyard steel furnaces, had been badly hit, and so had Henan, where we had gone in August 1958 to see the new people's communes. People in some of the more remote and sparsely populated places, like Gansu, were starving. Peasants were starving in Sichuan, too—the nation's most populous province, larger than most countries and known as China's rice bowl. During the meetings in Chengdu, Sichuan, in March 1958, Mao had pushed his plan to overtake Great Britain in fifteen years. In many provinces, tens of thousands were fleeing, just as Chinese peasants always had done in face of famine.

I never witnessed the terrible famine myself. Group One was protected from the awful realities. I learned about the famine on the way to Lushan, sailing down the magnificent Yangtze River with Mao, his staff, and several provincial leaders. Tian Jiaying was on board, and the memories of his six-month inspection tour of Henan and Sichuan were still fresh. I was standing on deck with him, Lin Ke, and Wang Jingxian, who had been put in charge of Mao's security after Wang Dongxing was sent away. Tian Jiaying described the famine in Sichuan. The government's efforts to alleviate the crisis had been inadequate. The overly optimistic target for steel production in 1959 had been cut from 20 million tons to 13 million. But 60 million able-bodied peasants, strong and healthy men who ought to have been at work in the fields, were still working on the backyard steel furnaces. The dislocation of labor was disastrous. The fields were not being farmed. The problem was getting worse.

Tian Jiaying was distressed not only because so many people were starving but because so many in authority were lying. Falsehoods are flying and getting more absurd with every passing day, he said. But the people speaking falsehoods are being praised; the ones who tell the truth are being criticized.

The conversation turned first obliquely and then more directly to Mao. Mao was a great philosopher, a great soldier, and a great politician, but he was a terrible economist. He had a penchant for grandiose schemes. He had lost touch with the people, forgotten the work style that he himself had promoted—seeking truth from facts, humility, attention to details. This was the source of the country's economic problems.

Wang Jingxian began telling us about Mao's many girlfriends. The Chairman's private life, Wang said, was shockingly indecent.

I was incredulous. I had known the economic situation was bad, but not that famine had swept the country and that millions were starving. I was surprised at the criticisms against Mao. My friend Tian Jiaying was ordinarily cautious, but the forthrightness with which he was speaking was dangerous, even among so close and sympathetic a group. Wang Jingxian's revelations were startling, too. Wang was charged with safeguarding the Chairman, and even among friends he should have been more careful. I remained silent and so did Lin Ke. Still grateful to Mao for having saved him during the Black Flag Incident, Lin Ke knew better than to criticize the Chairman.

Ke Qingshi, Wang Renzhong, and Li Jingquan, the first party secretary of Sichuan province, joined our conversation, wondering what we could be discussing with such intensity.

"We are talking about the famine," Tian Jiaying replied. "People are dying of starvation."

"China is a big country," Li Jingquan responded. "Which dynasty has not witnessed death by starvation?" He was right. Episodic famine is part of China's history. But in 1959, China was supposed to be in the middle of a Great Leap Forward. Even as people starved, official propaganda was making fantastic claims.

"The people are showing greater enthusiasm for work than ever before in our history," Wang Renzhong said, mimicking the Chairman's words. Both provincial secretaries were well tuned to Mao's political line.

Ke Qingshi, too, followed Mao's political lead. "Some people pay attention only to the minor things and not the major ones," he said. "They always see the negative side of things, complaining about everything. The Chairman says this kind of person could stand right in front of Mount Tai [Taishan] and still not see it."

Even before we reached Lushan, the battle lines were being drawn. Wang Renzhong, Li Jingquan, and Ke Qingshi, under pressure from Mao to increase production or lose their jobs, sacrificed truth on the altar of Mao. They extolled the Great Leap and minimized their economic problems, feeding the central authority unrealistic economic statistics because they knew what the center wanted to hear. They were supported by central officials like Luo Ruiqing and Yang Shangkun, whose official responsibilities were unrelated to economic questions but who were attuned to Mao's policy preferences, had been criticized by Mao in the past, and wanted to do nothing to anger him again. They supported Mao not out of conviction but for self-preservation, remaining, whether deliberately or naively, ignorant of the real extent of the country's economic problems. They offered nothing but support for Mao.

Mao's critics were generally of two types. One consisted of economic planners like Bo Yibo, the head of the State Economic Commission, and Li Fuchun, in charge of the State Planning Commission. Their offices were responsible for setting production targets and for working out the plans that would ensure that those targets could be fulfilled. Early during the Great Leap Forward, Bo Yibo had resisted setting such unrealistic production targets, but later, under pressure from Mao, he had caved in and done everything he could to push his subordinates to meet them. When Bo realized how serious the economic crisis was, he instructed his staff to prepare an honest and comprehensive report detailing the problems. But sensing that Mao would not welcome criticism, he balked at submitting the report. In a telephone conference with his subordinates around the country, he instructed them to continue doing their utmost to fulfill the production plan and to press ahead to achieve the stated, still bloated, goals. He was uncomfortable with Mao's economic audaciousness, certain that his plan would fail. But he dared not challenge Mao. He refused to speak out. Bo Yibo never publicly criticized the Great Leap. Nor did Li Fuchun.

The second type of critic consisted of those who had been on inspection trips to local areas and knew firsthand how bad the disaster was. They were neither economic planners nor responsible for implementing Mao's grandiose schemes, but they had witnessed the deteriorating, chaotic conditions in the countryside. Mao's political secretaries—Tian Jiaying, Hu Qiaomu, and Chen Boda—were among them. Their job was to report the truth.

But while the critics talked among themselves, as we did on the boat down the Yangtze, conversation with the people making the preposterous claims was almost impossible. Those who insisted on the truth, and were thus willing to offend Mao, were rare indeed. Most trimmed their sails to the wind. Even people like Tian Jiaying, who had been on inspection tours and knew the truth, or provincial leaders like Zhou Xiaozhou, who knew the extent of the crisis and was privately critical of both the Great Leap and of Mao himself, were reluctant to challenge Mao directly. On the boat, Tian Jiaying was willing to talk with Lin Ke about the country's problems. But when Mao's close supporters—Ke Qingshi and Li Jingquan—joined us, he fell silent.

We docked at Jiujiang, Jiangxi province, on July 1, 1959. Wang Dongxing, still in Jiangxi for his "reform," had become a vice-governor of the province and came on board to welcome Mao. He had been in close contact with the masses, truly educated by his experience, Wang assured Mao.

The Chairman was delighted. "People cannot always stay at the top," he said. "Let's make a new rule. Everyone who works at the central level should take turns working at lower-level organizations."

The highway from Jiujiang to Lushan was well paved, and we reached the sprawling mountain resort in little more than an hour. Logistical arrangements for the party leaders were under the direction of first party secretary Yang Shangkui, chairman of the Jiangxi provincial people's congress Fang Zhichun, who was married to Mao Yuanxin's mother, and vice-governor Wang Dongxing. Wang was directing the security arrangements for Mao, thus putting himself into immediate conflict with Wang Jingxian. Wang Jingxian ignored Wang Dongxing's arrangements, claiming that Wang Dongxing had been out of touch with Mao for so long that he no longer understood the Chairman. It was an insult Wang Dongxing would never forget, and Wang Jingxian would pay for it later.

Mao stayed in Chiang Kai-shek's two-story villa, and I was housed in a building nearby. The weather on the mountaintop was cool and damp, and we were so high up that when I left my windows open, clouds would float in through one window and out another.

When Mao opened the enlarged politburo meeting on July 2, the day after our arrival, he dubbed the gathering a "fairy [*shenxian*] meeting." Fairies live in the heavens among the clouds, just as we were living then, and they have no cares and no limits on their behavior. Fairies can do whatever they please. Mao wanted no fixed agenda for the meeting. Party leaders could talk about whatever they wanted. Mao proposed nineteen possible topics for discussion, and the participants were encouraged to talk about them freely. When the meeting began, Mao knew there were problems with the Great Leap, and he believed measures were being taken to correct those problems. He had no reason to believe there would be trouble. In his short opening address, Mao praised the achievements of the Great Leap Forward, alluded to the problems, and said he hoped that the participants would appreciate the energy and creativity of the Chinese people.

Mao's confidence in the Great Leap Forward remained unshaken, and I do not know how much of the real situation Mao knew when he spoke then. His visit to Shaoshan had given him a clear sense that there were problems. He certainly knew that something had gone awry and that there were major shortages of food. He knew that in many places there was no rice to eat, and he was willing to discuss those problems and work to solve them. But I do not think that when he spoke on July 2, 1959, he knew how bad the disaster had become, and he believed the party was doing everything it could to manage the situation. The purpose of the "fairy meeting" was to discuss both how to solve the problems and how to retain the enthusiasm of the masses. But his solution was simply for people to work harder still.

My notes record him as saying that "some people have asked, 'If our production is so high, why is our food supply so tight? Why can't female comrades buy hairpins? Why can't people get soap or matches?' Well, if we cannot clearly explain the situation, let's not explain it. Let's just stick it out and carry on our work with even greater determination and energy. We will have more supplies next year. Then we will explain everything. In short, the situation in general is excellent. There are many problems, but our future is bright."

Following his speech, the party leaders broke into small groups, divided geographically—north, northeast, northwest, east, central-south, and southwest—to discuss problems in their own regional areas.

When I met with Mao that night, he said the meetings would continue for about two weeks, and he was relaxed and in good spirits. He wanted to go sightseeing. Lushan was a vast mountain range, famous for its scenic spots—caves and temples and magnificent lookout points. Mao wanted to see them all.

Dr. Wang Shousong, the director of Jiangxi Hospital and a graduate of a Japanese medical school, had set up a clinic for the meeting participants and their entourages, staffing it with four young and energetic nurses from the nearby Lushan sanatorium. The Jiangxi provincial leadership arranged for evening entertainment, and performances by the Jiangxi provincial music and dance troupe were followed by the dances Mao so enjoyed. The young nurses joined the dancing parties, and within days, Mao was rotating between a young nurse and a member of the cultural troupe. The Chairman was becoming bolder about his dalliances. Security surrounding Mao's building was tight and the Chairman's privacy was still closely protected, but Mao himself did little to hide the fact that he was entertaining young women in his room.

The meetings were going so smoothly and Mao was having such a good time that he phoned Jiang Qing in Beidaihe and told her not to come to Lushan. He would join his wife when the meeting was over.

Five days after we arrived in Lushan, a great quarrel broke out in Group One. Li Yinqiao was angry with me and Lin Ke, complaining that he had to wait on the two "intellectuals." The building where Lin Ke and I were staying had no telephone, and if the Chairman wanted either of us, Li Yinqiao had to dispatch one of the guards to get us. The guards resented the walk and suggested we set up a duty office on the first floor of Mao's residence. We objected, both because space was tight and because it was awkward to witness the frequent comings and goings of the Chairman's female guests, and we did not want to see or know. We were afraid Mao would think we were spying on his private affairs. Without explicit orders from him, Lin Ke and I thought it best to stay in our own residence.

But our disagreements over the logistical arrangements quickly spilled over into other longstanding grievances within Group One: the peasants against the intellectuals—Li Yinqiao and the guards on one side, Lin Ke and me on the other. Mao had lost his appetite since coming to Lushan and was complaining that he did not like the dishes his chef, Li Xiwu, had been preparing. Li Yinqiao wanted me to solve the problem, and when I protested that Mao's food was not my responsibility, he accused me of putting on airs and shirking my responsibilities. We met and squabbled for several days, oblivious to the party meetings around us.

Tian Jiaying brought me out of my own problems and into the reality of what was happening in the Lushan meetings. "You know, the big Lushan meeting is getting just as tense as your little Lushan meeting," he said to me one day. I did not take him seriously at first. Mao had been relaxed and was obviously having a good time when the meetings started. I was so deeply embroiled in the mini-Lushan meetings of Group One that I had had no idea anything had gone wrong. But Mao's mood had changed. He had become less talkative and seemed lost in thought, pondering something, which is why he lost his appetite.

The regional small group meetings had been going on without an agenda for several days. Mao was not participating but found out what was going on by reading the daily reports. In the small group settings, people were beginning to speak their minds, complaining about the lies that were being transmitted as production statistics and reporting on the widespread starvation in many rural areas. The more time passed, the more boldly people were speaking out.

Watching in silence from the sidelines, Mao was learning where party leaders stood on the question of the Great Leap Forward. His critics had miscalculated, forgetting the tone Mao had set when he opened the conference, ignoring the Chairman's insistence that the situation was good and the problems were minor. They were misinterpreting his silence now, reading it as approval when in fact Mao was becoming more and more disgruntled. Mao often said that he did things openly (*gao yangmou*) and never engaged in conspiracies (*gao yinmou*). He believed he had openly set the parameters of discussion at the first meeting.

But something was going seriously wrong. Mao's "fairy meeting" was falling apart. The worst was yet to come.

39

On July 10, eight days into the Lushan meetings, Mao convened a meeting of the regional leaders. Again he spoke. He emphasized that only through unity and shared ideology could the party resolve its problems. The general line, he argued, referring to the policy of the Great Leap Forward and catching up with Great Britain in fifteen years, was completely correct. The achievements of the past year were great. There had been failures, to be sure, but those failures were relatively minor. "Doesn't each person have ten fingers?" he asked. "We can count nine of those fingers as achievements, only one as a failure."

He warned against the idealism of those who thought China was on the verge of entering communism. At the present stage of development, he said, the people's communes must be considered merely rural cooperatives—advanced cooperatives, to be sure, but not communist organizations. If people look at communes this way then there should be no serious problems at all. People—cadres and ordinary folk alike—have had unrealistically high expectations of the people's communes. Now expectations had to be lowered. In waging revolution, we have to pay a certain "tuition" for the experience. The nation had lost some 2 billion *renminbi* in the endeavor to build steel furnaces, but people everywhere in the country had learned a new skill—how to make steel. The money lost is really just tuition for learning a new skill.

Mao did not wait to hear the comments after his speech, and I left with him as soon as it was over. But Tian Jiaying told me later that everyone fell silent after the Chairman left. His speech had served as a warning to criticize no more.

Peng Dehuai, though, continued the debate. He did so discreetly, in a private, handwritten letter that he delivered to Mao on July 14. It was a long letter, and while I did not know at first what it said, I knew that Mao was unhappy. He did not sleep the night after receiving it.

In the first part of his letter, which I read later, Peng praised the accomplishments of the Great Leap Forward in 1958, citing the great increases in agricultural and industrial production. He discussed the people's communes, pointing out that their shortcomings had been largely corrected through revised organizational guidelines proposed at a series of meetings in November 1958. The backyard steel furnaces also had produced both losses and gains. The furnaces had prompted a nationwide geological survey in search of natural resources to run the furnaces. Many people had learned new technical skills in running the furnaces, and cadres had improved their organizational skills. These were gains. In the process, however, considerable amounts of both natural resources and manpower were wasted. These were losses. He thought the losses were greater than the gains.

In the second part of his letter, Peng Dehuai emphasized the need to learn from the Great Leap Forward. He argued that the Leap had fostered leftist tendencies—that production claims had been greatly inflated and that many people had been infected with a petit bourgeois fanaticism. He concluded with a plea that the party differentiate clearly between right and wrong and that it elevate ideological thinking to a high level. He did not want to blame specific individuals. To do so would not be good for the unity of the party or for the work still ahead. It was a mild and honest letter, thoughtful and well balanced. Peng Dehuai was not a politician. He was a simple and honest man, a soldier incapable of political intrigue. But he was exceptionally courageous. He was telling the truth when many others were lying, and unlike most other party leaders, he had no fear of Mao.

On July 16, clad only in a white robe and slippers without socks, Mao called the politburo standing committee to a meeting at his villa. Liu Shaoqi, Zhou Enlai, Zhu De, and Chen Yun were the only members then at Lushan. Deng Xiaoping was in Beijing Hospital. On May 2, he had slipped and broken his leg while playing billiards at the high-level cadres' club north of Zhongnanhai. I had sent him to Beijing Hospital for surgery, following which his leg was put in a cast. He stayed there for weeks, receiving round-the-clock treatment from a young nurse originally sent from Shanghai to Beijing to serve Mao. (The director of the Central Bureau of Health, Shi Shuhan, told me that the young woman became pregnant during this time and was transferred back to Shanghai and forced to have an abortion.)

Lin Biao was not there, either. He continued to suffer from neurasthenia and was often ill. I learned later that he had phobias about water, wind, and cold, and the clouds of Lushan, the daily rain, and winds would have been torture for him.

Mao's staff listened as the standing committee talked.

Mao told the party leaders that rightists outside the party had already criticized the Great Leap Forward and that now some people within the Communist party were criticizing it, too, saying that the Great Leap Forward had done more harm than good. Peng Dehuai was one such person, as evidenced in his letter to Mao.

Mao said he was going to have Peng's letter distributed to the participants in the Lushan meetings so they could evaluate its contents themselves. He said, ominously, that if the party were to split in two, he would organize a new one—among the peasants. If the army were to split apart, he would organize another army.

The standing committee then began discussing the contents of Peng's letter. Mao had already impressed upon them how serious the issue was. His colleagues' remarks were guarded.

Following the standing committee meeting, Peng's letter was distributed to the small group meetings for discussion. Few people dared to agree with Peng. But some did. On July 19, Huang Kecheng, chief of the general staff and a close friend of Peng's, expressed his support for the letter, and so did Zhou Xiaozhou, the first party secretary of Hunan province, who was already so upset with the way the economic crisis was being handled. Both men praised the intent of Peng's letter while arguing that some of its phrasing was a bit too harsh. Li Rui, who had recently begun serving as one of Mao's political secretaries, also agreed with Peng, saying that his letter had put the problems of the Great Leap into sharp focus and had shattered the stifling atmosphere that prevented honest criticisms even among the party elite.

On July 21, in another small group meeting, vice–foreign minister Zhang Wentian, who had been educated in the Soviet Union, made a stunning, lengthy attack on Mao's leadership and the Great Leap. In the early 1930s, after his return from the Soviet Union, Zhang had been a member of the Wang Ming faction, opposed to Mao's leadership. But later he had supported Mao and was known as a man who could be counted upon to follow the Chairman. He had served as ambassador to the Soviet Union for a period but had no position of great responsibility after 1949.

Zhang Wentian pointed out that when the free-supply system and public dining halls were introduced in the people's communes, some people thought that communism had arrived. Zhang disagreed. He argued in favor of using the mass line to seek truth from facts. But this, he said, is more easily said than done, as Chairman Mao himself often pointed out. Zhang was arguing, obliquely, that Mao's words and deeds had been inconsistent—that he had said the party ought to listen to the masses, had argued that the party ought to seek truth from facts, but then had ignored his own dicta in practice. Chairman Mao often tells us we should be courageous enough to propose ideas that differ from his, Zhang Wentian pointed out, that we should pull the emperor off his horse even if that means losing our heads. These words are correct. But who is not frightened by the prospect of losing his head?

Zhang ended by arguing in favor of the spirit of democracy and free speech. "We need to create a lively, fresh atmosphere in which people can freely speak their minds," he said. "Only then can we develop a fighting spirit. Our leadership must adopt a work style and create an environment in which the rank and file can freely present their ideas. Peng Dehuai's letter is intended to evaluate and to summarize our experiences. Its intentions are good."

Other participants in Zhang Wentian's small group, especially people like Shanghai mayor Ke Qingshi, Anhui first party secretary Zeng Xisheng, and Shandong first party secretary Shu Tong, took exception, frequently interrupting Zhang's talk, refuting his arguments, rebuking him for speaking so directly against Mao. Zhang Wentian responded by saying that he would rather die telling the truth than live in misery.

On July 23, Mao called another plenary session of the enlarged politburo. Again he spoke. Now people both inside and outside the party have joined in attacking us, he said. Some people outside the party are rightists. Now some people inside our party are rightists. Let me offer a word of advice to those comrades inside our party, he said. When you speak, you must know in which direction you are going. You should not waver in a moment of crisis. Some of our comrades lose their composure in the midst of great storms. They don't stand firm. They swing like farmers doing the rice-planting dance. They display the same kind of unreliability and pessimism as the bourgeoisie. They are not rightists, but they are moving closer and closer to the rightists—maybe just thirty kilometers away. Dangerously close.

Mao refuted the Peng letter point by point, focusing especially on Peng's references to petit bourgeois fanaticism and accusing him for saying that we had gained less than we lost.

The meeting became tense.

While Mao spoke, Peng Dehuai was sitting quietly in the last row of the auditorium. He was already angry. Even before Mao spoke, Peng had confronted the Chairman privately, demanding to know why Mao had taken a private letter addressed to him and distributed it to the conference participants without his permission. Mao had responded disingenuously that Peng had not instructed him not to distribute the letter. Peng was so angry he could not continue the conversation.

After Mao finished his speech, Peng quickly slipped out the door. I left with Mao, and we bumped into Peng Dehuai outside. "Minister Peng, let's have another talk," Mao said as soon as he saw the military leader.

But Peng Dehuai was livid. "There's nothing more to talk about. No more talk," he said, his face turning red as he raised his right arm over his head and brought it down hard against thin air.

"We have our differences, but we can still exchange opinions," Mao responded.

"Talk is useless," Peng said, and walked away.

The chorus of criticisms of Peng Dehuai began, echoing Mao's charge that Peng and his sympathizers were rightists. Then Mao decided to call the Central Committee of the Eighth Party Congress into its eighth plenary session. The Central Committee was the highest organ of power in China. Any formal action against Peng Dehuai would require its approval.

Jiang Qing arrived in Lushan the next day. She had called Mao to say she wanted to be there. Mao had changed his mind. He wanted her there, too.

Ye Zilong, Wang Dongxing, and I met her at the Jiujiang airport on the morning of July 24, where she greeted me curtly. "How is Chairman's health?" she asked coldly. I explained that Mao had lost his appetite and complained about his food for a few days but that the problem had been solved when Wang Dongxing brought in an excellent chef from Nanchang. The Chairman's appetite had returned, and he was enjoying especially the turtle soup that was one of the chef's specialties.

Jiang Qing had come to Lushan with a political mission, and her demeanor had suddenly changed. Her illnesses and lethargy had disappeared. She was ordinarily exhausted at the end of a trip and would take a long nap when she arrived. But the tension at Lushan had fired her energy. Mao was still asleep when she arrived, so she went immediately to see Lin Biao, who had also just arrived. He was staying at the bottom of the mountain, away from the damp and the cold. They talked for two hours. Then she went up the mountain to pay separate and lengthy calls on Zhou Enlai and his wife, Deng Yingchao, on Vice-Premier Li Fuchun and his wife, Cai Chang, and on Shanghai mayor Ke Qingshi. Jiang Qing had never been active in politics before. When she married Mao in Yanan, the politburo had set one firm condition. Mao's wife was to stay out of politics. Jiang Qing did nothing without Mao's permission. That she should come to Lushan to meet with the other high-ranking leaders meant that Mao had a very big problem. She was there to defend her husband. It was evening by the time she finished her rounds. By then Mao was awake.

I went to see her the next morning. "I rushed here because I was worried about the Chairman," she said. "But he seems to be in high spirits and good health. You must take good care of him. Last night, Li Yinqiao told me that the Chairman had not been eating well. You must bear in mind that you are the person responsible for the Chairman's diet. Make sure the kitchen staff continue to improve their work."

I knew that Li Yinqiao had been criticizing me to Jiang Qing again. I was a doctor, not a dietician, and continued to resent being called upon to find new chefs and deal with his changes in appetite. My insistence on retaining my integrity as a physician was one of the reasons Li Yinqiao had criticized me during Group One's mini-conference. I could respond to Jiang Qing only by reminding her that the problem with Mao's food had been solved. She nodded, then added a word of caution. "Doctor, you are an intelligent and knowledgeable person. You're different from people like Li Yinqiao. You have to be sensitive about political matters. Don't let other people fool you. While you are here, try not to make contact with others." Jiang Qing's warning was a gesture of goodwill, an effort to protect me from the effects of the political fallout that would surely result from the controversy at Lushan. She wanted me to avoid contact with people known to disagree with Mao—people like my friend Tian Jiaying.

When the Eighth Plenum of the Eighth Central Committee opened on August 2, Mao was again on the attack. "We took it easy when we first arrived in Lushan," he said. "We held a sort of 'fairy meeting,' chatting with each other without an agenda. There was no tension. Later, I became aware that some people felt they had not had a chance to speak their minds freely. The kind of loose talk we had had was not to their liking. They could not grasp the essence of our discussions. They want a tense situation. They want to attack the general line, to destroy the general line. Now, the signs of a division have gradually appeared. In the last nine months, we have opposed leftist tendencies. Today, the problem is different. At the Lushan conference we are not opposing leftist tendencies but rightist ones. Right opportunists are launching a furious attack on the party, on the leadership of the party, the work of the people, and the great and dynamic socialist reconstruction."

Mao's opening speech to the Central Committee set the tone for the meetings that followed. By calling upon the participants to criticize the divisive activities of the "anti-party group," Mao had turned Peng into an enemy, and no amount of talk or exchange of opinions could save him. For the next week, from August 3 to 10, the Central Committee broke up into small working groups, charged with criticizing both Peng's letter and those who supported him. The meaning of the incident was being transformed, blown out of proportion. There was in fact nothing anti-party or anti-Mao about Peng's letter. But under Mao's direction, the letter was coming to be seen as part of a conspiracy. Peng and the men who had shared his views were being called upon to explain to the Central Committee how they had "plotted together both before and during the meeting." I began to understand better some of Mao's exaggerations and distortions in his conversations with me. "History" as Mao told it often diverged from the truth.

Suddenly, the conversation I had participated in on board ship to Lushan, when Tian Jiaying had reported so many deaths from starvation in Sichuan and Wang Jingxian had spoken so freely about Mao's sex life, took on an ominous importance. Three of Mao's political secretaries—Tian Jiaying, Chen Boda, and Hu Qiaomu—had been sent to the provinces to investigate the results of the Great Leap Forward. All had witnessed economic disaster and widespread death by starvation—Tian in Sichuan, Chen in Fujian, and Hu in Anhui. All had reported honestly. Now the first party secretaries of those three provinces—Li Jingquan, Ye Fei, and Zeng Xisheng—came forward to defend themselves against the secretaries' reports and to attack the men who had made them.

Shanghai mayor Ke Qingshi, Hubei's Wang Renzhong, Guangdong's Tao Zhu, and security chief Luo Ruiqing all came forward too, viciously attacking Peng and his supporters, and singling out my friend Tian Jiaying in particular. "What does a young man like you know about Marxism?" Luo Ruiqing demanded of Tian Jiaying, shaking a finger in his face. "You are speaking nonsense. What right do you have to speak before the plenary session of the Central Committee?" The trip Luo had taken with Mao in 1958 had only strengthened his loyalty to the Chairman.

Li Rui, the newest of Mao's political secretaries, was also attacked. When he tried to defend his position, Zhou Enlai stopped him. "This is a plenary session of the party Central Committee," he said. "You are neither a member nor an alternate. You have no right to speak."

As the meetings progressed and the criticisms continued, Chen Boda, Hu Qiaomu, and Tian Jiaying were all in danger of being condemned as members of this new "anti-party group."

The final determination was Mao's. He spoke at another session on August 11. "Peng Dehuai and his supporters do not have the ideological preparation necessary for the proletarian socialist revolution," he said. "They are bourgeois democrats who made their way into our party by pretending to be followers of Marxism. Chen Boda, Hu Qiaomu, and Tian Jiaying are our party's scholars. We still need them. As for Li Rui, he is not in the same category. He is not a party scholar." With these words, Tian Jiaying, Chen Boda, and Hu Qiaomu were saved. Li Rui was condemned to the anti-party group.

Mao's staff also came under criticism. Luo Ruiqing called us together on August 12 to give us a good tongue-lashing. "You are blind to your own good fortune," he said. "The party has shown great confidence in you by letting you work for the Chairman. But you have no self-esteem. I have heard some of you do not get along with each other and do not cooperate with each other as you should. Instead, you try to push your own responsibilities off on others. And you, Wang Jingxian, have spoken carelessly, letting the anti-party elements make use of your bad-mouthing. We will look into this matter when we return to Beijing." Luo laid down one rule: We were not to tell anyone, no matter who, anything about what happened in Group One or about Mao. We were not even to chat among ourselves about the Chairman or the situation in Group One. I sensed that the issue was not yet settled, that there were dismissals and purges to come.

In a party document that circulated at the final meeting on August 16, Mao wrote that a great struggle had occurred at the Lushan conference. "It is a class struggle," Mao said, "a continuation of the life-and-death struggle between the two great classes—the bourgeoisie and the proletariat—and has been going on for the last ten years of socialist revolution." With these words, Peng Dehuai and his supporters were condemned to the ranks of the bourgeoisie.

The Lushan conference approved the document condemning Peng as an anti-party element and defending the general line of the Great Leap Forward. The party would launch yet another nationwide campaign against rightists, this time against party members and cadres who shared Peng Dehuai's critical views of the Great Leap Forward and were deemed, by virtue of their realism, to be suffering from a new malady the party dubbed "right opportunism."

The latest party decision left me befuddled and anxious. To place the problem with Peng Dehuai in the category of "class struggle," to see him as an "anti-party element" and a "right opportunist," was to put him in a category almost as bad as the Guomindang. I knew Peng was not an enemy of the party. I knew him to be a good and honest man.

I was not in any political danger myself, though my good friend Tian Jiaying was being put through the political wringer and even though, on the boat ride down the Yangtze, I had been privy to conversations critical of Mao. I had Mao's trust, and I had never said a word against him. I was both too cautious for that and too naive.

But what happened at Lushan had been excruciatingly painful to watch, and my tension was compounded by the backbiting within Group One. The tension began to take a personal toll. My ulcer, previously only a mild annoyance, flared up with a vengeance. I was in constant pain, unable to eat, and had to force myself to swallow liquids. I was bleeding internally, and my stools turned black. The medicine I had prescribed for myself was doing no good. I was weak and losing weight rapidly. Dr. Wang Shousong, in charge of the Lushan clinic, urged me to leave the conference to get treatment in nearby Nanchang. But if I suddenly left in the midst of the political conflict, people might suspect that I had political problems, too, and was using illness as an excuse to escape them. Mao was keeping a close eye on his staff, attempting to gauge our loyalty, calculating where we stood on the continuing political debate. He wanted our full support. If I told him my problem, he might not believe me, and if I left to get treatment, he might doubt my loyalty and suspect me of supporting Peng Dehuai. So I stayed, never mentioning my problem to Mao, trying to nurse myself with a liquid diet and medication.

But the bleeding persisted. By the time the Central Committee meetings had concluded, I was thin and weak. When Hu Qiaomu came to see me with a cold, he saw immediately that I was thin and ill. He urged me to get treatment immediately, arguing from his own experience with a recurring ulcer that further delay could only prolong my recovery. He promised to speak with the Chairman himself and get permission for me to leave.

Hu went directly to Mao. The Chairman agreed that I should return immediately to Beijing and get the best possible treatment. Huang Shuze, the deputy head of the Central Bureau of Health, was instructed to arrange for my hospitalization, and Ye Zilong would get me on one of the planes that were ferrying documents and personnel between Jiujiang and Beijing.

I went to say goodbye to Jiang Qing. The beauty of Lushan had presented her with many opportunities to practice her photography, and she was looking at some of her pictures when I went in. She, too, was shocked by my appearance. Both she and the Chairman had been terribly busy in the past several weeks, she said, and they had not known how sick I was. Still, she was hesitant about letting me return to Beijing. She wanted me to stay a bit longer and accompany her and Mao when they left. It was a gesture of goodwill on her part, a way of saying that I still enjoyed Mao's trust and that they would both protect me. But I was too sick to accept.

"It wouldn't be convenient to have a sick man like me along," I explained. "I'd better go back to Beijing."

Jiang Qing agreed. I told her Huang Shuze could take over my responsibilities in my absence.

I asked Jiang Qing to wish Mao goodbye for me, but she urged me to see him in person.

He was lying in bed, reading a Ming dynasty history. Perhaps he was rereading the story of Hai Rui, who had had the courage to tell the emperor the truth.

I explained that Huang Shuze would be substituting for me. Mao urged me go to Beijing Hospital. It was no ordinary hospital. It was the most exclusive country club in China. Its patients were all government and party officials of the rank of vice-minister and above or leading "democratic personages" like Guo Moruo. Established by Germans around the turn of the century, its medical facilities and staff were the finest in all of China.

Mao hoped that I would soon be well and warned me not to tell anyone in Beijing about what had happened at the Lushan conference. "Observe the decisions of the party," he said.

Huang Shuze was reluctant to serve as my substitute, but he had little choice. I gave him Mao's medical records and briefed him on the Chairman's health. He was efficient and gracious in making the arrangements for my return to Beijing, phoning Shi Shuhan, the director of the Central Bureau of Health, and Ji Suhua, who had become the president of Beijing Hospital, arranging for them to meet me at the airport the following day.

I said goodbye to Luo Ruiqing and Yang Shangkun. Luo, like Mao, urged me to take care of myself and get the best treatment, and he cautioned me about the political situation. "Keep everything you have learned here secret," he warned. "You must be sensitive about political matters."

Yang Shangkun attributed my illness to the tensions of our mini-Lushan conference. "Group One is like a big barrel of dye," he said. "Nobody can stay in it without being painted some sort of color. You have heard a lot in Lushan. When you are in Beijing, maybe you can visit Comrade Deng Xiaoping. He has checked out of the hospital now."

While Mao and Luo Ruiqing had impressed upon me the secrecy of everything that had happened at Lushan, Yang Shangkun wanted me to report to his superior. But I knew that the only way to stay out of trouble was to remain silent. Beijing Hospital would be my shield against the political storm. China's leaders often use Beijing Hospital to nurse their political wounds, too, withdrawing from worldly involvement to ride out the latest storm. I vowed to stay there as long as I could and to use the opportunity to find a way out of Group One. I wanted to find another job.

Wang Dongxing and head of the Jiangxi people's congress Fang Zhichun saw me off at the airport, laden with gifts—a big basket of fruit, tins of Lushan tea, and ten bottles of Jiangxi wine. I could not drink wine with an ulcer, but Wang insisted I take it to share with my friends.

Even as the car made its way down the winding mountain road, my tension began to ease. I was leaving behind a party rent by internal divisions. My dreams for China and the party had been destroyed. My image of Mao had been shattered. My only hope was to save myself. The further we traveled from Lushan, the less the pain in my stomach. I was relieved to be leaving. I had found it impossible to sleep in Lushan, but as soon as the airplane took off, I fell fast asleep. I was still asleep when we landed in Beijing. I had been the only passenger on board.

40

Lillian met me at the airport, together with Shi Shuhan and Ji Suhua. Lillian and I visited my mother briefly before I checked into the hospital.

As the economic crisis deepened, my family's situation had continued to deteriorate. My mother's health was declining. Her hypertension had not improved, and she developed a heart condition, too. She often ate only one meal a day—not just because food was so scarce but because she had no appetite. And with me so often out of Beijing and my wife working from early morning to late at night, she still had primary responsibility for our two sons.

She was distressed to see me. I was her only son. She loved me very much and worried about me constantly. Seeing me sick and thin only worried her further. Not wanting to upset her already precarious health, I left for Beijing Hospital after only a few minutes.

My ulcer was not serious, and Wu Jie, the head of internal medicine and my former professor, now in charge of my case, assured me that if I followed his regimen of medicine and diet I would recover quickly without surgery. Indeed, after three days, I began to improve. The bleeding stopped, and I felt much better. My major irritation was the woman in the room next door, the wife of one of the vice-ministers of health. She knew I worked for Mao and was mustering all her persuasive powers to learn what she could about the relationship between Mao and Jiang Qing. So irritating and incessant were her overtures that Ji Suhua, the hospital's president, helped me change rooms.

Just as I was beginning to recover, my mother was rushed to the emergency room of nearby Tongren Hospital with a heart attack. The attack was not severe, and she was soon out of danger. But she needed weeks of convalescence in the hospital. An aunt began caring for our two sons as Lillian plied back and forth between Tongren and Beijing hospitals. I was well enough to leave the hospital for occasional visits and sometimes joined her to see my mother.

The hospital became my sanctuary. The new campaign against "right opportunism" was heating up, and I wanted to stay out of the fray. Beijing mayor Peng Zhen, an enthusiastic supporter of the new campaign, had the streets festooned with huge red banners calling out the new political slogans. "Long Live Chairman Mao!" "Long Live the General Line!" "Long Live the People's Communes!" "Long Live the Great Leap Forward!"

My elder brother, by my father's first marriage, still working with the Ministry of Public Health, was implicated in the movement. He had been demoted after the "three-anti" campaign in the early 1950s, but he was still director of the institute testing drug safety and efficacy. He was a loyal party member but still came under suspicion in every campaign. I was not in contact with him then, and Lillian wanted me to make inquiries within the ministry, but there was nothing I could do to help. My intervention would only bring attention to myself. I wanted to stay away from politics altogether.

And I wanted to leave Group One. It was not so much Mao who made working there impossible but Ye Zilong and Li Yinqiao. They were crass and lowly, and the longer they stayed in Group One, the more offensive they became. Ye Zilong had renewed his acquaintance with his female friend in Wuhan in 1958, and then Li Yinqiao started a friendship with a woman. I disapproved of their behavior, looked down on their pettiness, despised them as human beings. But they lorded it over me, demeaning me, forcing me to deal with Mao's appetite as well as his health, and I was engaged in hopeless, endless mediations between Jiang Qing and her nurses. I was nearly forty, and my career was stifled. I wanted to work as a surgeon.

Ji Suhua offered me a position in Beijing Hospital directing the hospital's Office of Health. I would be responsible for overseeing the health of the high-level leaders admitted to the hospital. But leaving the politics of Zhongnanhai for the politics of Beijing Hospital made no sense to me. I bided my time recuperating, looking into jobs in Shanghai and Nanjing.

Mao returned to Beijing in early September, and not long after his return, Li Yinqiao and one of Mao's confidential secretaries, Luo

Guanglu, visited me, encouraging me to check out of the hospital. The tenth anniversary of the founding of new China was not far away. The celebration would be huge. For the past ten months, millions had worked to complete Mao's ten great construction projects in time for the tenth anniversary. Every citizen of Beijing had participated in the work—a new form of corvée labor at the behest of China's twentieth-century emperor. Just as Qin Shihuangdi had built the Great Wall and every emperor thereafter had had his own massive construction project, so Mao had decreed ten great buildings to commemorate the tenth year of his reign. Tiananmen was expanded to the huge square it is today, capable of holding half a million people, with the massive Great Hall of the People and the Museum of Revolutionary History flanking either side of the square. The parade of military might and the fireworks display would be the most extravagant in the history of new China. Li Yinqiao and Luo Guanglu did not want me to miss the great event. But I did not want to go.

I did not join Mao at Tiananmen. The tenth anniversary of the founding of new China came and went. I stayed in the hospital.

My mother continued to recuperate in Tongren Hospital. Then one day in late November, in the midst of her daily hot bath, she suddenly fainted and went into shock. By the time I reached the emergency room, she was sinking fast, her blood pressure dangerously low. The doctors held out no hope. She died only hours later, disappointed at not being able to see her two grandsons again.

We held no funeral service. Three days after her death, with the help of the Central Bureau of Health, my mother was cremated, and her ashes were given to me. I put the box on my desk at home, reluctant to send them to Babaoshan cemetery. Maybe one of the hospital positions in Nanjing or Shanghai would come through, and I could take my mother's ashes there.

With my mother gone, holding on to the five rooms in our family home became even more difficult. I wanted to move out of Zhongnanhai and back to my mother's house, but Luo Daorang, the acting director of the Central Bureau of Guards, would not agree. He suspected I was trying to leave Group One but knew I was wanted back. As Mao's personal physician, I had to live in Zhongnanhai. He wanted my whole family to move there and offered to allocate an extra room for our two sons. "Think it over, Dr. Li," he said. "When you come back to Group One, you will be taking lots of trips. If your wife and kids were at your mother's house, with you traveling all the time, you would no longer have much of a family life."

Luo was right. I did not want to return to Group One, but if I did, holding on to my mother's rooms made no sense. Lillian and I decided we had no choice but to move the whole family to Zhongnanhai. Our older son could ride his bicycle to his nearby school, and we would board our younger son, then only three years old, in the Beihai nursery during the week and bring him home on weekends. My wife and I and our elder son would take our meals in the Zhongnanhai dining hall.

I left the hospital briefly to help arrange the family move, and then, upon Lillian's urging, checked back in. Lillian visited me often and brought our two sons on weekends. My call to rejoin Group One would be coming soon, and she wanted me to be fully recovered before returning to the stress of the job.

The Beijing Housing Administration soon discovered that my mother's rooms were vacant and asked me to turn full title of the property over to them. I had no choice. Finally, ten years after the founding of "People's China," more than a decade after I had returned as a young idealist to serve my country, I had become a genuine proletarian, a member of the propertyless class. All my family's private property had now been confiscated by the state.

I was depressed. It is not easy, even for an idealist, to hand over a beloved home that has been in his family for generations. After the Japanese invasion, when I fled with my mother to Suzhou, I had left for seventeen years. But I had spent my childhood in that home, and the best memories of my adulthood after returning to China were from there. Our last bastion of warmth, contentment, and peace was lost to us forever.

41

My summons from Group One came toward the end of December. Xu
Yunbei, a vice-minister of public health, came to visit. He had already
discussed my case with my doctor, Wu Jie. When Li Yinqiao tried to
extract me, Wu Jie had protected me, claiming I needed more time to
recuperate. It took a vice-minister of public health to override him. Wu
Jie finally agreed that I could check out.

But I wanted to stay. I wanted more time to recuperate. Xu
insisted. My substitute, Huang Shuze, had left. His mother had died,
and Huang had returned to Tianjin for her funeral. I was needed in
Group One.

Still I resisted.

But my convalescence had become a political matter. "The campaign against right opportunism is spreading like wildfire," Xu Yunbei
warned. "It would not look good for you to stay in the hospital with
no serious medical problem."

It was political blackmail. Much had changed during the four
months I had spent in the hospital. Peng Dehuai had been removed
from his military posts, and so had his deputy, the chief of the general
staff, Huang Kecheng. Luo Ruiqing had been promoted, taking over
Huang's position as chief of the general staff. And Lin Biao, a vice-
chairman of the Military Affairs Commission and a vice-chairman of
the National Defense Council, had succeeded to Peng Dehuai's position as minister of defense. Many wondered why Mao had appointed
a man in failing health to take over such an important position.

Lin Biao's first act in his new role as defense minister was to attack his predecessor at an enlarged meeting of the Military Affairs Commission, accusing Peng Dehuai of being both "anti-party" and a rightist. Then he turned against Marshal Zhu De. "What kind of commander in chief is Zhu?" Lin asked sarcastically of the man who had joined Mao to found the Red Army. "He never fought any major battles, never won any great victories. He was nothing but a black commander in chief." Lin's speech had been cleared in advance by Mao. The Chairman had turned against his old colleague Zhu De.

If I stayed in the hospital, Xu Yunbei could accuse me of siding with Peng Dehuai. I could be implicated in the campaign against right opportunism.

I promised the vice-minister that I would leave as soon as I received my official checkout papers. Xu assured me that would not be necessary. Xu's word as a vice-minister of health was all the notarization the hospital would need.

I was back in Group One the next day.

Mao was in Hangzhou. Wang Jingxian had called two days before I left the hospital, insisting that I go there as soon as possible.

I left with Li Yinqiao by plane on December 22, 1959. We encountered heavy snow en route, and the plane began to shake so violently that we had to land in Nanjing. A massive snowstorm was sweeping the region, extending south to Hangzhou. To continue by plane was dangerous. The director of the Jiangsu provincial bureau of public security arranged for a car to take us to Mao. We spent the night in Nanjing and left the next morning in heavy snow, working our way slowly by car to Hangzhou, arriving finally at about three in the afternoon. Mao was asleep. I did not meet with him until that evening.

He was bleary-eyed and tired, coughing constantly, with another of his colds. "I've been miserable for several days," he said. "How have you been?"

"I have recovered. But Chairman seems to have a cold."

"I don't know. Just don't feel well."

"Let's have a checkup."

Mao had a slight fever, but his heart, blood pressure, and pulse were normal. He had a severe cold and acute bronchitis.

Mao wanted a quick recovery. A new round of party meetings was coming up. He wanted to be well for them.

I suggested that he take antibiotics for his bronchitis and other medicine for his cold. He agreed.

By the next evening, Mao was much better and his temperature was normal. The coughing had subsided. He was cheerful. "The bragging doctor has some good medicine," he joked.

The Chairman's sixty-sixth birthday was approaching. I delivered a message from Zhejiang's first party secretary, Jiang Hua, inviting Mao to a banquet in his honor. Mao declined, saying that he did not like birthday parties anymore and claiming he needed more time to recuperate. He asked Group One to join in the dinner and report to him on the food. But he warned us against having too extravagant a feast and asked that we view the gathering not as his birthday party but as an opportunity to chat and have fun. Mao was still losing face because of the food crisis and did not want to indulge in extravagance when so many ordinary folk were suffering.

The other leaders had no such empathy with the masses.

Ye Zilong, ever ready for fine food and drink, planned to have a good time. He told me he intended to get Wang Fang, the director of Zhejiang public security, drunk. "Doctor, you have done us all a great favor," he said to me gratefully when I told him about the invitation.

The next day, December 26, was Mao's birthday. His entire staff went to pay their respects. Mao had recovered completely, and his spirits were high. He thanked me for the treatment I had given, and we had a photograph taken together.

Eight tables of ten people each were set for the banquet that night, and the entire provincial leadership of Zhejiang participated. First party secretary Jiang Hua and head of provincial public security Wang Fang represented all the guests and went to wish Mao a happy birthday.

Mao's warning against overindulgence was ignored. The feast that night was as extravagant as any I have ever had, consisting of the finest, most expensive delicacies Chinese cuisine can offer. We had real bird's-nest soup with baby doves, one of the rarest of Chinese dishes, and shark's-fin soup cooked in a special clay pot, also rare and expensive. Nothing could top those two delicacies, but the other food was only slightly less delectable. The wine was superb as well, and Ye Zilong succeeded without great effort in getting Wang Fang drunk.

Midway through our extravagant meal, Wang Jingxian turned to me. "It's shameful for us to be consuming such a feast," he whispered. "So many people are starving to death."

I agreed. Outside, beyond the protective walls of Group One, beyond the special privileges of the country's leaders, the peasants of China were starving. The harvest of 1959 had been worse than the one the year before. The deaths were now in the millions, and before the famine was over tens of millions would die. As so many of my countrymen starved, I sat with Lin Ke and Wang Jingxian, with Ye Zilong and Li Yinqiao, and with the leadership of Zhejiang province celebrating the sixty-sixth birthday of the absent emperor Mao, the tables laden with expensive, extravagant delicacies. The head of the provincial public security bureau was falling-down drunk. I was miserable.

But I felt that I had no choice. Had I refused to participate, I would have risked bringing political trouble to myself. "Those who brave the battle alone are always shot down," Lin Ke often said, quoting from Lu Xun. "Survival in Group One requires us to violate our consciences." The only way to be at peace with my conscience was to leave Group One. But I had just tried once more and failed.

I lived in a world apart. We in Group One had no rules. There was no law. It was a paradise, free from all restraint, subject only to the whim of Mao and the guilt that gnawed those of us whose consciences remained intact.

42

Corruption within the party grew worse even as the food crisis deepened and more people died. In early January 1960, several days after Mao's sixty-sixth birthday, we left Hangzhou for Shanghai, where an enlarged meeting of the politburo was scheduled for January 7. Mao spent the nights on his train, but the meeting participants and members of his entourage were housed in the elegant, formerly French-owned Jinjiang Hotel. Inside the hotel, shielded from reality, the meetings produced one fantastical document after another as the politburo veered further and further to the left. Production targets went up. Steel production was to increase to 18 million tons. Small-scale business enterprises were to be set up at the level of the county and the people's communes. Irrigation projects would be expanded. Large pig farms would be established.

During the day, China's leaders deluded themselves by formulating unworkable economic plans. At night they played and were entertained by acrobats and music and dance troupes from all over the country, serenaded by leading stars of Beijing and local operas.

And they shopped. Now it was Shanghai mayor Ke Qingshi's turn to stage an elaborate charade for Mao and the party elite. Even as the nation lay crippled from an awesome shortage of foodstuffs and consumer goods, the stores within the compound of the Jinjiang Hotel were brimming with high-quality, reasonably priced merchandise of every description—bicycles, leather shoes, fine woolens, all of which were unavailable in local shops. China's leaders, the staff of Zhongnanhai, and we in Group One went on a shopping spree. I did too, and bumped into Yang Shangkun and Ye Zilong one afternoon as they emerged from a shop laden with purchases.

As the country's economic situation worsened, Ye Zilong's work for Mao had begun to suffer. This made Li Yinqiao happy, and Li began maneuvering to wrest away some of Ye's power. Finally, prodded by Jiang Qing, Mao acted, transferring some of Ye Zilong's control of his funds to Li Yinqiao.

Ye Zilong was furious.

"Fart! I have done his dirty business all these years, and look how I'm treated," he complained to me one day.

"It seems to me that the Chairman has been quite good to you," I said, trying to humor him.

Ye cursed. "He's taking away my power and telling people I'm bad. He's trying all sorts of things to squeeze me out. It's worse than being dismissed. This isn't the place for me. What a sad result."

Talking to Ye Zilong, something inside me snapped, too. Among other things, I could no longer pretend that I didn't know about Mao's infidelities. For years, I had stayed away when I thought Mao might be entertaining his female guests, feigning ignorance. But now I could no longer hide the truth from myself.

After my release from the hospital, Mao no longer attempted to hide his affairs. While I was in the hospital, Mao had met a new clerk in the Bureau of Confidential Matters, a young, white-skinned woman with clear, dark eyes and delicately arched eyebrows. She had attracted Mao at once when she told the Chairman how she had defended him against his detractors when she was in primary school. Many of her schoolmates had vilified Mao as a "bandit" and spread rumors that the party was intent on communizing both marriage and property. The young woman had defended Mao and the communist party and once was hurt in a fight when her schoolmates beat her for her devotion to Mao.

After that, the young woman was often with Mao, and their relationship became increasingly public. She was with Mao in Shanghai, accompanying him day and night, often dancing with him until one or two in the morning. Mao was inexhaustible and often consented to return to the train only when his new companion was too tired to continue.

She was the first of Mao's women who made no effort to hide that relationship from Jiang Qing. She was proud of her relationship with Mao and was warm and outgoing to Jiang Qing, treating the Chairman's wife as a friend. Jiang Qing seemed to return the friendship, and

I presumed her apology to Mao after discovering him having an affair with her nurse had forced her finally to accept the inevitability of Mao's other women.

His complaints about impotence subsided after I left the hospital. My faith in the Chairman had been shattered by the purge of Peng Dehuai, and once I could no longer avoid the truth of his private life, I felt only revulsion for the man I had once revered.

But having Li Yinqiao in charge of Mao's personal affairs did not clean up Group One.

In 1958, we in Group One became aware that Li Yinqiao had befriended a woman on Mao's staff. Li's work began to slip, and Mao began to notice. One day he complained to me that the two were sticking together like glue, working for each other rather than him.

While Mao was asleep on the train, Li Yinqiao and his friend began slipping off the train to the Jinjiang Hotel. One day when Ke Qingshi came to pick Mao up to escort him to the party meeting, Mao's personal bodyguard was nowhere to be seen. Mao was furious when Li finally returned. "Li Yinqiao, you're with that woman night and day. Who do you think you are?"

Ke Qingshi was worried. Li Yinqiao was charged with the Chairman's safety. Mao's well-being in Shanghai was Ke Qingshi's responsibility. Ke spoke with his counterpart from the capital, Beijing mayor Peng Zhen. Other ranking leaders were contacted. Everyone agreed that something had to be done. Mao's safety was at stake.

The problem worsened when we left Shanghai for Guangzhou. Three days after our arrival there, Li Yinqiao's friend came to me, distraught. She was pregnant. She wanted me to help her get an abortion in Guangzhou.

I was reluctant. As a matter of policy, we tried not to use local medical facilities except in emergency. The woman said she had become pregnant in Beijing. Why could she not return and get the abortion there, I asked. Why did she have to get it in Guangzhou?

Two days later, Li Yinqiao came to plead his friend's case, begging me to help. It would be "inconvenient" for her to have the abortion in Beijing, he explained. Too many people knew her there. She would have no way to keep the problem secret. Ye Zilong had given his okay for the abortion to take place in Guangzhou.

Ye Zilong's permission, I knew, was an exchange for Li Yinqiao's silence on another matter. Just after we arrived in Guangzhou, Ye had asked me for a prescription to treat his baldness. The Japanese-made lotion would have to be imported from Hong Kong, which could only be done if I wrote the prescription and charged it to a government account. This time I wrote the prescription. Ye Zilong still remembered that I had not given him penicillin to treat his relative's syphilis, and I knew Ye would make my life miserable if I refused him again. It was the type of petty blackmail that went on daily in Group One. Ye Zilong agreed to the abortion with the understanding that Li Yinqiao would not tell Mao about the imported tonic.

As I delayed, Li's friend came again to plead her case. She was already two months pregnant. She did not want to wait any longer.

Still uncomfortable to be using my position as Mao's doctor, I nevertheless arranged for the abortion through the president of the People's Hospital in Guangzhou. Li's friend checked into the hospital that afternoon.

Jiang Qing found out immediately. Confronting me that same evening, she wondered—disingenuously, I was sure—why the woman had been hospitalized. When I told her that she was having an abortion, Jiang Qing did not ask whose baby it was. "This is intolerable!" she said, hitting the table with the palm of her hand.

Still the friendship continued, and its reverberations affected all of us in Group One. Back in Beijing, Li Yinqiao began spending time with his friend while his wife was away. It was about this time that the woman's husband tried to commit suicide. The woman came running to my apartment one afternoon frantically yelling for help. Her husband was dying, she said, crying, and urged me to hurry to see what I could do.

He was lying on the floor of their apartment, his breathing labored. "I cannot live anymore," he said to me. "I have lost too much face." He had swallowed the mercury from a thermometer. But his most serious injury was his loss of face. His vital signs were normal, and he did not even have to be taken to the hospital.

Li Yinqiao still did not break the friendship.

Ye Zilong was still unhappy. "Mao does not say outright he wants me to leave, but doesn't let me do anything for him either," he complained. Mao began criticizing Ye before other members of the staff. Ye Zilong began looking for a way out and talked to Beijing mayor Peng Zhen about finding a job with him. Ye continued to gossip about Mao, and the circle of people who knew about his indiscretions widened to include some of the country's ranking leaders—Peng Zhen and Yang Shangkun among them. Mao's private escapades were an open secret among the party elite, but Ye Zilong's talk was dangerous.

Ye Zilong's talk was his undoing. Mao never knew what Ye was saying, and I am not certain what he would have done had he known.

Wang Dongxing told me that Liu Shaoqi did find out. Liu Shaoqi acted to protect the Chairman and moved quickly and ruthlessly against Ye. Ye has slandered the party, Liu declared when he heard what Mao's confidential secretary had been saying. He wanted to arrest him and have him shot. Only when Zhou Enlai and Peng Zhen intervened on Ye's behalf did Liu Shaoqi agree to spare Ye Zilong's life.

It was no surprise, given Mao's private life, that others in Group One followed the Chairman's example. Mao's staff was young and the men were handsome, and at the dancing parties in which we all participated, opportunities to meet pretty young women were plenty. But the standards for Mao and other top leaders were different from those imposed on the lesser ranks. Mao was subject to discipline from no one and could do whatever he wanted, but the demands the party made on his staff were strict. Now something had to be done. The solution began when Mao ordered the return of Wang Dongxing.

43

Wang Dongxing returned to Zhongnanhai in October 1960. Sobered by the severity of exile, his political instincts razor-sharp, he had a new law of political survival—absolute subservience to Mao. Never say no to Mao was his rule. "If Mao says one, it's one. If Mao says two, it's two." Henceforth, Wang believed, his reading of the Chairman would have to be unfailingly accurate. He never wanted to be exiled again. He would make no more mistakes.

Obeying Jiang Qing was the first mistake to avoid. Before he went to Jiangxi, Wang treated an order from her as an order from Mao. But there was no way to satisfy Jiang Qing, and despite Wang's attempts, she turned against him. Mao had criticized his efforts. "If you follow Jiang Qing's orders, then you're working for her, not me," he said. So Wang listened only to Mao. Jiang Qing could no longer intimidate him. "I was sent down for four years," he said, "and I didn't die. The worst that could happen now would be to be exiled again. So if she thinks she can push me around, she's dreaming."

Wang's first task was to consolidate his power within Group One by clearing out his enemies and drafting men guaranteed to be loyal to him. The corruption within Group One had grown so blatant that even Mao could no longer ignore it, and this served as Wang's excuse to launch an internal rectification campaign.

Wang Dongxing had long been sensitive to issues of corruption within Group One. In the early 1950s, Wang himself had been accused of corruption, of leading the good life when the party was preaching austerity. Wang had taken the criticisms to heart, and his personal behavior was exemplary.

Still, in 1952, when minister of public security Luo Ruiqing began the "three-anti" campaign against corruption within the Ministry of Public Security, Wang had a problem. One day Luo Ruiqing called a meeting of ranking members of the party's security apparatus and invited the participants, Wang Dongxing among them, to confess to the assembled group any misdemeanors they might have committed. The audience remained silent as Luo prodded them to speak. No one had anything to confess. As minutes went by and no one spoke, Luo Ruiqing began. "Wang," he yelled. "Why don't you speak up? Don't you have some kind of problem you want to tell us? You can't get away with it."

Wang is a common surname in China, and Wang Dongxing was not the only Wang at the meeting. The two Wangs exchanged glances. Neither spoke.

"Wang Dongxing, why are you looking at somebody else?" Luo yelled from the podium. "You'd better confess. Otherwise you'll be in serious trouble." Wang Dongxing, who told me the story, was dumbfounded.

"You stole something from the Chairman and sold it, didn't you?" Luo demanded.

Wang Dongxing could not imagine what Luo meant.

"You're still not talking after all these hints?" Luo demanded. "Look, what do you think this is?" Luo was holding a piece of paper.

It was a letter from a local shopkeeper alleging that Wang Dongxing had stolen a camera from Mao and consigned it to his shop for sale. An attached receipt was signed by Wang Dongxing.

But Wang had not taken a camera from Mao and knew nothing of the incident. The name was his but the signature was not. Eventually, Wang was able to prove that his name had been forged, and he did his best thereafter to uncover corruption wherever he found it.

Mao was ordinarily less concerned with corruption than Wang. The honesty of his staff was not a major concern. If an underling was useful, no matter what his other failings, Mao would protect and keep him safe. Once an aide had lost his usefulness, Mao was ruthless, kicking him out without a twinge of regret. His closest aide, his closest political ally, could become an enemy overnight.

Wang's goal upon his return to Group One was the purge of his enemies, Ye Zilong and Li Yinqiao.

Mao was also dissatisfied with Ye and Li, but he could not easily act against them. The two men had been too deeply involved in the

Chairman's personal life for him to censure them openly and risk provoking them into revealing secrets he preferred to keep hidden. Mao did, however, work against them from behind the scenes.

Revenge and a quest for power were prime motives in Wang Dongxing's attempt to purge Ye Zilong and Li Yinqiao. The two men had maneuvered to turn Mao against him, and Wang blamed them for his four years in exile. Back in Zhongnanhai, his time for retribution had arrived.

But he was motivated also, I believe, by a genuine sense of fair play. In the rural areas of Jiangxi he had seen suffering and hardship, and having eaten so much bitterness himself, the special privileges he saw in Group One were galling. What is more, the famine had finally hit Zhongnanhai. The vermilion walls that ordinarily shielded the privileged residents from reality could no longer stave off hunger. Our rations had been reduced to sixteen pounds of grain a month. Meat, eggs, and cooking oil were nowhere to be had. We were allowed to buy vegetables on the open market, but there were hardly any for sale. Some people organized expeditions to hunt wild goats, but soon goats became extinct too.

Malnourishment was rampant in Zhongnanhai, and edema and hepatitis were endemic. My own family was suffering greatly. Lillian was among those hit with malnutrition, and she developed edema, but she worried more about our sons than about herself. When I managed occasionally to bring some soybeans home, she would give them to our children. My trips out of town with Mao, instead of distressing her, became cause for the family to celebrate. They ate better when I was away, because they still received my monthly sixteen pounds of rice.

Mao of course was immune to the tribulations of famine, and everyone tried to shield him from its effects, but he knew the severity of the crisis. The documents he received every day now allowed him no escape from the truth. Reports were coming in from all over the country, and by the summer of 1960, he had become so depressed that he took again to his bed. He seemed psychologically incapable of confronting the effects of the famine. When I told him that edema and hepatitis were everywhere, he accused me of inventing trouble. "You physicians have nothing better to do than scare people," he snapped. "You're just out looking for disease. If no one were sick, you'd all be unemployed."

When I insisted that doctors were not out looking but rather confronting the effects of malnutrition in their clinics every day, he said, "What's the difference? We're in the middle of a food shortage. You doctors are just upsetting people by talking about disease. You're making it difficult for everybody. I just don't believe you." He gave me a copy of *Internal Reference* that contained an article suggesting that people increase their intake of protein and carbohydrates as a way to strengthen resistance. Yang Shangkun began fostering what he called the "Long March spirit" among General Office staff, urging us to accept hardship, become self-reliant, and grow our own vegetables and melons. Soon everyone was tending tiny vegetable plots, and many took time off from work to nurture their precious gardens. Still, our stomachs were always half empty. Gardening had no immediate effect on the widespread malnutrition and consequent disease.

I thought Mao was ruthless to close his eyes to the illness that was everywhere around him. But I allowed him his illusions and never mentioned the subject again, behaving in his presence as though hunger and disease had miraculously disappeared. He continued to resent party leaders who dwelled on what he called the "dark side" of things. "The more they talk about the dark side of things," Mao often said, "the darker our future looks." He saw leaders who dwelt excessively on the country's difficulties as trying to bring pressure on him.

Mao did make one concession to the famine. He stopped eating meat. "Everyone is starving. I can't eat meat," he said.

Liu Shaoqi and Zhou Enlai were afraid that Mao's sacrifice would affect his health and encouraged me to change his mind. When the northeastern provinces sent some tiger and deer meat as a present to the country's ranking leaders, I encouraged Mao to try it. He refused. "Send it to the public dining hall, where everyone can have some," he said.

"Can't we save some for you?" I asked.

"I'm not eating meat now," Mao replied. "Let's wait for a while."

His sacrifice had no effect on the famine. A few people in Zhongnanhai may have eaten better because Mao shared the tiger and deer, but none of the crops revived. Still, the Chairman's gesture won him the admiration of everyone who knew.

It was against the backdrop of the famine that Wang Dongxing conducted his internal rectification campaign. The special privileges of Group One had never endeared us to the less pampered cadres who worked in Zhongnanhai. Everyone knew of our frequent travels, that our accommodations were always the best, that we dined free and never had to pay for our drinks. They could see the Rolex watches and the Leica cameras—booty confiscated from Taiwan spies arrested on the mainland that public security officials sold to members of Mao's inner circle for a pittance. They knew we had access to scarce luxury goods—wool suits, silks, and leather shoes—that no ordinary citizen could buy. That we continued to flourish even in the midst of famine only furthered our comrades' antagonism.

As part of his bid to increase his power within Group One, Wang Dongxing attacked these luxurious practices. He focused on body-guard Li Yinqiao. "Ye Zilong and I are equal in rank, and he has worked for the Chairman longer than I," Wang Dongxing explained. "If I were to take action against him, he could make trouble for me." If Wang were to attack both Ye and Li simultaneously, the two might unite against him. His tactic was to isolate Ye and concentrate his fire on Li.

Mao agreed. Ye Zilong was not to be publicly attacked. Criticisms of him were to be submitted privately, in writing.

Li Yinqiao's woman friend was not to be mentioned. The situation was delicate. Wang Dongxing was worried about the repercussions if her abortion in Guangzhou should become known. Too much face would be lost. Wang feared another suicide attempt.

The criticisms of Li Yinqiao began in late October and lasted for two months, and the meetings were held for two or three hours each day. We usually met while Mao was asleep, when the staff was freed of its obligations to him. With the struggle sessions confined to Mao's hours of sleep, few knew of his role in the internal rectification campaign. But Mao used his bodyguards to orchestrate the entire performance, getting daily reports and coaching them on what to say. Thus his bodyguard Xiao Tian told of Li Yinqiao's shopping in Shanghai and complained that Li had failed in his responsibilities to Mao. He wondered out loud where the money for Li's purchases in Shanghai had come from.

Mobilizing the staff against Li Yinqiao was easy. His enemies were numerous and quick to be roused against his intimidating, arbitrary behavior. But the most damning allegations never came to the surface. Everyone was worried about saving his face. I, too, confined my criticisms to the more general abuses of privilege of which we were all in one way or another guilty—the luxury of our accommodations when traveling, the extravagance of our food, the free services, the ready access to scarce luxury goods. I remained silent on the question of the abortion in Guangzhou.

But the movement had unintended effects. While Ye Zilong was supposed to be immune to public criticism, details of his privileges leaked out—the house in Tianjin, for instance, and his participation in what his detractors called an "eat-and-drink small group" of top-ranking cadres who regularly indulged in extravagant feasts. Ye Zilong was nervous throughout the proceedings.

Wang Dongxing became an overnight hero within Zhongnanhai for daring to challenge such well-entrenched and powerful men, and his popularity soared. Zhou Enlai and Liu Shaoqi were pleased.

The denouement was Mao's. The occasion was his sixty-seventh birthday, December 26, 1960.

Two days earlier, Wang Dongxing had presented Mao with the results of his investigations. Several longtime members of Mao's staff, Wang reported, had ignored the suffering of the masses and become a privileged elite. The whole nation was suffering, Wang said, and these staff members threw lavish banquets, eating and drinking extravagantly without paying, using their privileges to buy fancy consumer goods not available in ordinary markets. They were giving everyone in Group One a bad name.

Ye Zilong, Li Yinqiao, Wang Jingxian, Lin Ke, confidential secretary Gao Zhi, head nurse Wu Xujun, and Wang Dongxing were all present at the birthday celebration. I was in Guangzhou with Jiang Qing, but Wang Dongxing told me the story later.

Because the Chairman was still not eating meat, the dinner was simple. Midway through the meal, Mao began telling a story from the Warring States period (403–221 B.C.) about Suqin's visit to his friend Zhang Yi, the prime minister of the kingdom of Qin. Suqin was in great economic difficulty and hoped Zhang Yi could find him a job. Zhang Yi put him up in an elegant guesthouse, much like the modern-day Beijing Hotel, Mao said, and made certain his guest was well entertained. But he never met with Suqin. After two months of indolent luxury, when he had still not seen the minister, Suqin returned home, convinced that he had fallen out of favor with his friend.

Upon his return, he found his house repaired and refurbished. His kitchen was stocked to overflowing with food. "Prime Minister Zhang Yi did not see you because he thought you could accomplish great deeds elsewhere," the prime minister's deputy explained. "He is sending you on a diplomatic mission. He wants you to visit six other kingdoms to convince them not to attack our kingdom of Qin." Suqin accepted his diplomatic mission with gratitude and accomplished it successfully, saving the kingdom of Qin from attack.

Mao was sending his staff on a diplomatic mission, too. "Even good friends should not live off each other," he said. "Everyone has to depend on himself, so all of us can work together to achieve great deeds. Our country is experiencing great difficulty. There is a serious shortage of food. People are starving." He wanted his friends to labor at the lower levels. By sharing the lives of the common folk, they could better understand their difficulties. Afterward, they could tell him what they learned.

Not everyone at the dinner was expected to go. Wang Dongxing, of course, would stay. But Mao wanted Ye Zilong, Li Yinqiao, Wang Jingxian, and Lin Ke to go, and confidential secretary Gao Zhi and bodyguard Feng Yaosong as well. This was his way of being fair. The rightists—Ye Zilong and Li Yinqiao—would go with the centrist Wang Jingxian and the leftist Lin Ke.

Mao wavered between Shandong and Henan as possible destinations. Both provinces, like Anhui, had vigorously pursued the Great Leap Forward, and both were now in bad shape. But Henan's economic situation was not as bad as Shandong's, he thought. The group would not starve in Xinyang in Henan province. Mao had just received a report from Xinyang county blaming counterrevolutionaries and feudal elements for the economic difficulties there. Still unable to confront the reality of how bad the situation was or why, Mao believed that counterrevolutionaries were undermining production. He saw himself as a modern-day Zhang Yi, sending his friends on a diplomatic mission, using his associates to stave off further attacks by counterrevolutionary enemies. He wanted them to go to Xinyang. "Go there," he encouraged them. "If the assignment becomes too hard for you, come back. Don't worry. No one will die."

Mao was a marvelous actor. He was getting rid of key members of his staff, consigning them to hardship and suffering, but even as he fired them, he still wanted their loyalty. So he pretended that they were friends and that he was taking this step against his will, because he needed their help.

His friends could almost believe him. They were grateful and moved by his demonstration of concern. But still they did not want to go. They tried to delay their departure, hoping to pass the Chinese New Year in Beijing. Mao ordered them gone by the end of December. He wanted them on their way.

Before they left, Wang Dongxing managed to add another of his enemies to the list—Luo Daorang, the man who had escorted me around "Labor University" in 1949. During Wang's exile, Luo had taken over temporarily as acting director of the Central Bureau of Guards and had maneuvered to prevent Wang's return to the post. Wang had been waiting to take his revenge. Luo became the victim of his own bad joke. "So many in Group One are being sent down for reform. When will the rest of us have our chance?" Luo quipped to Wang Dongxing as the arrangements were being made.

It was a costly wisecrack. "I'll talk to the Chairman and see if you can go now," Wang responded, pretending not to see the humor. Mao sent Luo, too.

With Ye Zilong and Li Yinqiao in exile, Wang's control of Group One was complete. One of Li Yinqiao's deputies, Zhang Xianpeng, was elevated to Li's old position as deputy chief of Mao's bodyguards. Mao Weizhong and Tian Chou came in as new deputy directors of the Central Bureau of Guards. Wang's confidant, Wu Jianhua, became chief of the bureau's administrative office, and Xu Tao's wife, Wu Xujun, was brought in as Mao's full-time nurse, reporting daily to Wang Dongxing and keeping him intimately informed of Mao's activities.

While he was consolidating his power within Group One, Wang Dongxing was also using the campaign against Peng Dehuai to regain control over the Central Bureau of Guards and its subordinate agency, the Central Garrison Corps—the more than two thousand well-trained and well-equipped soldiers charged both with providing external security for Mao and the other top leaders and with protecting the party's key facilities. Because most of the cadres within these two organizations had been appointed while Peng Dehuai was in power, Wang could argue that they sympathized with Peng and were rightists. Arguing that Mao had to be protected from such untrustworthy types, Wang Dongxing transferred the entire squadron, placing his own loyalists in key positions in the Central Bureau of Guards and retaining his close allies Zhang Yaoci and Yang Dezhong as the commander and political commissar of the Central Garrison Corps.

Despite his growing power, Wang could never completely win his battle against corruption, although he held the problem in check. Early in 1961, shortly after Wang's sweeping purges, Mao stopped in Changsha for several days and met with Liu Shaoqi and Zhou Enlai on his train. Newly appointed Hunan first party secretary Zhang Pinghua and his provincial public security chief were responsible for protecting the three leaders as they met. (Zhang had been appointed to this post after Mao had purged Zhou Xiaozhou, the moderate leader who had been so reluctant to introduce double-cropping into Mao's home province and who had overtly sided with Peng Dehuai at the Lushan conference.) It was customary for the expenses of Mao and his entourage to be charged to the central authorities, and Wang Dongxing ordinarily signed off on the bill. Wang was presented with the bill for Mao's stay just as we were leaving and was surprised to see two thousand chickens charged to the Chairman's account. The figure had to be wrong. Hunan was better off than many other provinces, but the famine was at its height and chickens, always a luxury in China, were almost impossible to find. Mao's entourage could not possibly have eaten two thousand chickens during the few days we were there. Besides, neither Mao nor his staff were eating meat. Zhang Pinghua agreed that the bill was a mistake. Perhaps the figure was twenty chickens, surely not two thousand.

But two thousand was the correct figure. Fifteen thousand militiamen had been called in to stand guard over the Chairman's train. The weather was cold and the soldiers were also suffering during the famine. The provincial public security chief had extravagantly ordered two thousand chickens to feed the stoic soldiers. The soldiers were ordinary people and should not have had the special privileges that even Mao had given up. The provincial authorities ought never to have ordered the chickens and they should have paid, but feeding chickens to the soldiers, they must have reasoned, was the least the Chairman could do in gratitude for their service. Like Ye Zilong and Li Yinqiao, the Hunan leadership was also taking advantage of Mao. Wang Dongxing approved the bill, but he was furious.

With Wang Dongxing's reorganization accomplished, he was in complete control of Group One, the Central Bureau of Guards, and the Central Garrison Corps—the three key units within Zhongnanhai. Under his direction, the Central Garrison Corps gradually expanded in size and in the scope of its activities. Wang Dongxing's own power grew commensurately, making him a key player in Beijing's palace wars. When the Cultural Revolution began some six years later and Mao needed paramilitary units to go into key factories and universities as his personal representatives, he turned to Wang Dongxing, further enhancing Wang's power.

In the meantime, Wang turned his attention to Mao. The dances that had previously been scheduled once a week on Saturdays were now held twice a week, on Wednesday as well as Saturday. He expanded the number of bands and "cultural work troupes" providing entertainment at the parties and simultaneously increased the range of diversions available to Mao. With Wang's return, the air force, the Beijing Military Region, the General Political Department of the People's Liberation Army, the Second Artillery Corps, and the Railway Construction Corps all provided troupes—bands, singing groups, dancers—performing for Mao's pleasure. In the Great Hall of the People, which had opened on National Day 1959, the opulent Room 118, originally the Beijing Room, was set aside especially for Mao, and some of the young female attendants there and from other rooms in the Great Hall of the People also served his pleasure. He no longer needed intermediaries to make the arrangements. Exposed so often to so many young women, Mao made the arrangements himself. He was sixty-seven years old. In a September 1961 meeting with Field Marshal Montgomery, Mao acknowledged for the first time the theoretical possibility of his death—suggesting that he could die from an assassin's bullet, a plane crash, a train accident, drowning or, just possibly, disease. But Mao's sexual appetite was increasing with age. He barely felt the absence of Ye Zilong and Li Yinqiao.

44

While Wang Dongxing was preoccupied with consolidating his power in Beijing, I was in Guangzhou engaged in my own personal struggle. I had gone to the southern city in late December 1960 at Jiang Qing's request. The Chairman's wife was spending the winter there, and her usual complaints continued. She was ill, she said, and troubled by light, noise, and drafts. Her nurses, attendants, and bodyguards were of little help, and she complained about them constantly. She needed my services.

But her demands on me had become excessive. Even Mao had become suspicious. Rumors began circulating again within Group One, fueled by Ye Zilong and Li Yinqiao, that Jiang Qing and I were "good." "Let the two of them stick together," Mao had responded sarcastically when he heard that Jiang Qing wanted me to join her in Guangzhou. He encouraged me to go.

I did not want to go. Jiang Qing's physical ailments were imaginary, and I had no way to solve her psychological problems. Her staff was miserably unhappy, but my efforts at mediation had little effect. Being with the Chairman's wife made me extremely uncomfortable. I knew Mao was suspicious, and I did not want to give the rumors credence.

But I had no choice. The Chairman ordered me to Guangzhou. He even sent me off in a special air force plane.

When I arrived at the villa where Jiang Qing always stayed in Guangzhou's Islet guesthouse, her nurses and guards rushed out to meet me, already complaining. The Chairman's wife was not sick, they insisted. The proof of her health was in her activities. Guangdong party secretary Tao Zhu was holding frequent dancing parties, and Jiang Qing was always belle of the ball. All the top leaders of the province joined the festivities. Everyone, from the highest provincial leaders down to her bodyguards and attendants, had to dance with Jiang Qing at least once, and she could dance for three or four hours with no sign of fatigue—and then watch movies, too. How could she be sick?

But when I saw her, Jiang Qing insisted she was sick. Her nurses and attendants, she said, were rude and inattentive, disrespectful, and lax in their duties. She was clearly irritated when I told her that I would give her a checkup and return right away to Beijing. "I just don't understand that doctor," she complained later to one of her nurses. "He comes to Guangzhou, tries to get away with doing a slipshod job, and then wants to run back to Beijing. Who does he think he is?"

Not wanting to anger her further, I decided not to rush the checkup or mention my wish to leave. I would bide my time waiting for Jiang Qing to bring up the question.

The Chairman's wife was lonely, in desperate need of companionship, and she had chosen me as her companion. Life in Guangzhou should have been idyllic. Every day was a holiday for Jiang Qing, who had nothing but leisure time. We quickly settled into a routine. With dancing parties or movies every evening, Jiang Qing would sleep very late, rising only at around ten or eleven in the morning. After eating and dressing, she would begin her activities at twelve or one. At two or three she would take a nap, waking again at four or five in the afternoon. We would go for a walk together then or watch a movie, and then it was time for dinner. We ate separately, but I shared Jiang Qing's life of splendor. The famine was getting worse, but we never knew it on our protected little island in Guangzhou. I ate extremely well.

Days thus passed idly by. On December 26, the same day Mao was in Beijing announcing the exile of Ye Zilong and Li Yinqiao, we celebrated the Chairman's birthday at a banquet hosted by Guangdong party secretary Tao Zhu. New Year's Day came and went. Our surroundings were beautiful and life was comfortable, but I was painfully bored and ill at ease, and I could see that the Chairman's wife, for all her privilege and luxury, was profoundly unhappy.

Mao's philandering was becoming more blatant, and Jiang Qing was very insecure. But as I listened to her talk, I came to realize there were other reasons for her unhappiness. Jiang Qing had political ambitions. Many thought that was why she had pursued Mao so actively in Yanan. But her efforts to attain power had been thwarted.

One way to deny her power was to make sure her party rank was low enough that it conferred no authority. Party officials were all assigned grades. One was the highest rank, reserved for Mao and the top five party secretaries. The next highest ranks ran from two through six. Other high-ranking cadres were placed in grades seven to thirteen, middle-ranking cadres in grades fourteen to seventeen, and lower-level cadres in ranks eighteen to twenty-five. Jiang Qing was a grade nine, but Ye Zilong and Wang Dongxing were assigned the higher grade of seven. She complained about this to me one day, pointing out that she and I were just the same, ordinary members of the Chairman's staff, and accusing Yang Shangkun of arbitrarily making her a nine.

Mao himself had agreed to Jiang Qing's rank. Her talent did not match her ambitions. She had no skills and would accept direction only from Mao. Bad-tempered and fond of lecturing everyone, she got along with no one. No one wanted to take orders from such a woman.

Jiang Qing's imaginary illnesses were linked to her thwarted ambitions. Her neurasthenia was political. Were she ever to become well, she would have to work, and if she had to work, her rank as grade nine commanded neither power nor respect. But as Mao's wife, without work, people kowtowed before her—not because they respected or liked or even wanted to serve her but because she was the Chairman's wife. The fawning and flattery would stop were she ever assigned an official job. The many enemies she had made with her sharp tongue and nasty temper would scorn her.

She needed to be sick, I finally understood, because illness was the only way she could dominate others. And she needed Mao to believe that she was sick, because otherwise he might ask her to work, and that would make Ye Zilong and Wang Dongxing her superiors.

After I had been in enforced indolence for three weeks, Jiang Qing called me to her living room. Motioning for me to sit, she pointed out that I had been there for several weeks without doing a thing. "What do you have in mind?" she wanted to know.

"I have been waiting for you to tell me when you want the checkup," I responded.

"There is something else I want to discuss with you," she said.

I steeled myself.

"The Chairman is in good health and has said himself that he does not need a doctor with him all the time. But I am in poor health," she said. "Since Dr. Xu Tao left, I have not had a personal physician. I want you to serve as my doctor. You can still take care of the Chairman when he needs you."

Jiang Qing's proposal was my greatest fear come true. I had agreed to serve as her physician when she and the Chairman were together. Now she wanted me to stay with her all the time, treating Mao only when he was ill. This I did not want to do.

Her offer was no surprise. I had suspected there was something behind the invitation to join her in Guangzhou. I had already prepared my response.

I told her that my superiors had assigned me to work for the Chairman and that working for her was not the assignment given me by the party. My superiors had not given me orders to work for her. Nor had the Chairman told me of the change. I pointed out that I thought changing jobs would be unwise.

Jiang Qing had already spoken to Mao, however, and he had agreed. She was willing to talk to my superiors. No problem.

"I still think we should give this matter some further thought, Comrade Jiang Qing," I continued. "It is really not a good idea to change my job this way."

Jiang Qing was becoming tense. "And why is it not a good idea?" she wanted to know, her voice rising. "Is the Chairman the only person you respect? You look down on me, don't you?" Jiang Qing had always feared that I admired her husband while scorning her.

What I feared, though, was the gossip. If I were officially appointed her doctor, the palace rumors would be confirmed and our affair would become fact. "It is not a question of looking down on anyone," I countered. "As a physician, of course I will treat any patient I am asked. But I'm afraid that if we do it your way, people will talk. What they say might not reflect well on you or the Chairman."

Suddenly, she stood up and glared at me. "What are you talking about? What does not reflect well on us?"

"It's just gossip," I responded. "There is no use talking about it."

Jiang Qing was becoming extremely agitated. "Doctor, I have always treated you well," she said. "If you have something to say, then say it. Speak out!"

"If you insist, Comrade Jiang Qing, then I will say it. Since I returned to Group One at the end of 1959, there have been rumors. Some people have said that you are too nice to me, that there is something 'special' between us. Someone has even told this baseless rumor to the Chairman. He responded by saying, 'Let the two stick together.' Comrade Jiang Qing, this is the reason I do not think your idea is a good one."

She turned quiet. "Who said this?" she asked, her voice strained.

"Let it go. It doesn't matter."

"Don't be silly, Doctor. I have been nice to you because I know it is not easy to find a doctor for the Chairman. He likes you, and I have been easy on you because of this. Now someone is spreading a rumor. Who is it?"

"If you insist, I will tell you. It is Ye Zilong and Li Yinqiao." I had no qualms about telling the Chairman's wife who was spreading the rumors. I was furious with both Ye and Li. They thought that if they told Mao, I would be forced to quit.

Jiang Qing gave up her plan and made a tearful phone call to Mao. I returned to Beijing a couple of days later, on January 12, 1961, by special air force plane. "Don't ever tell anyone," Jiang Qing warned me when I went to take my leave.

The situation in Beijing had become visibly worse. There were almost no people on the streets, and those who were, were thin and listless. People were staying at home to conserve energy. When my family celebrated the New Year a couple of weeks later, we had only a thin porridge of rice and vegetables. Ordinarily, we would have stuffed ourselves with all sorts of delicacies—meat and fish and dumplings. The lunar New Year is the one day of the year that Chinese families everywhere traditionally gorge themselves. This year, there was nothing.

I waited before talking with Mao. The Ninth Plenum of the Eighth Central Committee was to begin two days after my return, and I knew he was busy with that. The plenum would finally start to confront the dark side that Mao had so wanted to ignore. Mao was still depressed and spending more time in bed. To this day, ruthless though he was, I believe Mao launched the Great Leap Forward to bring good to China. The problem was that he had no modern education and no idea of what the modern world was or how China might join it. The twentieth century was marching forward and Mao was stuck in the nineteenth, unable to lead his country. Now he was in retreat, trying to figure out what to do.

The plenum was a blow to Mao. The participants set the restoration of agricultural production as the party's most vital task. With so many people starving, Mao's dream of rapid industrialization was empty. People had to have food in their stomachs first.

I met with the Chairman on January 18, just after the meetings had concluded, and told him about my conversations with Jiang Qing and the rumors about our special relationship. I told him that I had kept quiet for a long time but that I thought Ye Zilong and Li Yinqiao were trying to insult the Chairman, not me. "What is their evidence of a special relationship? Why have they been saying this?" I asked. In fact, I was also angry with Mao, who had also fostered the gossip. Telling him the rumors was an insult to him, too, a subtle slap in his face.

Mao listened attentively until I finished, his eyes narrowing as I talked. Jiang Qing had already told him the story. "Don't worry, I understand everything," he said. "Forget the whole thing. Who can say he has never said anything behind another's back?" It was only then that Mao told me that Ye Zilong and Li Yinqiao had been demoted and would be leaving soon for Henan. Even Wang Dongxing had not told me yet.

The Central Bureau of Health dispatched several other physicians to examine Jiang Qing in Guangzhou—Ji Suhua, the president of Beijing Hospital, Xue Bangqi, the president of Shanghai's East China Hospital, and Su Zonghua, the president of the Shanghai Psychiatric Hospital, who was both a psychiatrist and a neurologist. She kept them waiting for six weeks, until Mao arrived with Wang Dongxing and me in late February.

The doctors felt greatly honored to be called upon to treat Jiang Qing, but they had already been away from their posts for too long and were anxious to finish their work. "They take themselves too seriously," Jiang Qing quipped when I explained that they hoped to carry out the exam as soon as possible.

Finally, she agreed that each doctor could examine her on a separate day and that she would take a day of rest between each exam, so the process was spread over six days. Dr. Ji Suhua, the surgeon, and internist Xue Bangqi took little more than an hour each to complete their work. Only Su Zonghua's neurological cum psychiatric exam took much time. Jiang Qing had been told Su was examining her for possible neurological, rather than psychiatric, problems. She was cagey and successfully evaded any question that might give the doctor real insight into her psychological problems.

I met with Jiang Qing soon after the exams. She wanted to know what kind of disease the doctors had found.

I told her the doctors found nothing significantly abnormal.

"Your health continues to improve. They would like to meet with you to discuss their findings," I said.

But Jiang Qing did not want the doctors to say there was nothing significantly wrong. She did not want to meet with the doctors and demanded a written report instead. And she did not want the Chairman to be told anything about the checkup. She wanted Mao to believe she was still sick.

A tug-of-war ensued. The doctors' new report contained only minor revisions of an earlier one. It concluded that Jiang Qing's recovery from cervical cancer was progressing, alluded to her chronic neurasthenia, and recommended that she continue her activities—watching movies, dancing, listening to music, and photography. But Wang Dongxing opposed any report suggesting that Jiang Qing was ill. He did not want the doctors to legitimize her indolence by suggesting movies and dancing as a cure for nonexistent maladies.

I, too, ran afoul of the physicians. I had been present and agreed when the Central Bureau of Health instructed them to take good care of Jiang Qing and to treat her health problems seriously. Later, in exasperation, I backtracked, telling them it was pointless to try to accommodate her every whim and urging them to report frankly that her health was good. The doctors were extremely conscientious and knew nothing of how badly Jiang Qing treated people. But my patience had already been tried, and Wang Dongxing's hostility toward Mao's wife only fed my own growing bitterness.

The doctors' report satisfied no one. "What is this?" Jiang Qing demanded as soon as she had read it. "These people are totally irresponsible. What do they think they are doing?" She returned it to them as unacceptable and dismissed them.

Guangdong party secretary Tao Zhu hosted a farewell banquet to thank the doctors for their services. They knew that Jiang Qing was unhappy with their report but had no idea how vengeful and vicious she would be. All three men would suffer miserably during the Cultural Revolution. Ji Suhua was imprisoned for years and so badly beaten that he lost his mind. When he was finally released at the end of the Cultural Revolution, his brain seemed to have atrophied. He was never able to function again and died shortly thereafter. Xue Bangqi was also the object of numerous criticism and struggle sessions. He survived the Cultural Revolution only to die of a heart attack at its end.

Psychiatrist Su Zonghua suffered the most. He was imprisoned for his alleged anti-party, anti–Jiang Qing activities and was badly beaten while incarcerated. He wrote me several letters from prison, reminding me how seriously he had taken his assignment to treat Comrade Jiang Qing and how conscientious he had been. I wrote the Shanghai Psychiatric Hospital attesting to his innocence but never received a reply. Su committed suicide shortly thereafter, while he was still in jail. He could no longer bear the torture.

After the doctors left, I was the only outlet for Jiang's fury at not being declared ill. Our relations continued to deteriorate. She began telling people that I had changed, and accused me of turning against her. As proof, she cited an instance in 1958 when I had helped her out of a distasteful obligation by telling Mao that she was sick. Now I was no longer willing to make excuses for her.

She saw my change in attitude as the result of the shifting balance of power within Group One. I no longer needed her protection, she said. With Wang Dongxing in exile and Ye Zilong and Li Yinqiao in power, I had had to rely on her for support. Now Ye and Li had been sent away, and my friend Wang Dongxing had returned to rule Group One with an iron hand. With Wang Dongxing protecting me, Jiang Qing reasoned, I could afford to slight her. She thought I looked down on her, but she also assumed that my adulation for the Chairman continued unabated.

Jiang Qing had misinterpreted me, however. It is true that with Wang Dongxing back in power my life within Group One had become easier, and I certainly did not like Jiang Qing—her decadent life of luxury and leisure, her pretending to be ill when her health was as good as mine, her constant bossing and pushing people around, her incessant, impossible demands. She was as bad as the evil landlords of an earlier era whom the party vociferously attacked. But I had grown to hate the hypocrisy around me, the communist leaders' public carping against the corrupt bourgeois life-style of their predecessors, the touting of their high and lofty communist moral principles, while they themselves were living lives of luxury as the masses suffered and toiled and died. My hopes and dreams, my visions of Mao and of the new, good society, were shattered for good.

Jiang Qing was wrong in assuming that I still revered Mao. My adulation of him had dissipated, too. What lofty moral principles did he follow? He had cast aside Peng Dehuai, one of the country's great revolutionary leaders, a man loyal to the communist cause and devoted to the good of China, as if he were garbage, and he was gathering young women around him like the most degenerate of ancient emperors. And the Chinese people? The Communist party had taken "the people" and praised them to the sky while these very people were being oppressed and exploited, forced to endure every hardship, accept every insult, merely to survive. "The people" were nothing but a vast multitude of faceless, helpless slaves. This was the "new society," the communists' "new world." Jiang Qing was right that I was disgusted with her. But I was disgusted with her husband, too, with all of Group One. "New China" had become corrupt.

45

Depressed over the agricultural crisis and angry with the party elite, upon whom he was less able now to work his will, Mao was in temporary eclipse, spending most of his time in bed. The Spring Lotus Chamber in Zhongnanhai was renovated and refurbished, and while construction was under way, the twice-weekly dances continued in Huairen Hall. When the renovation was complete, a room just off the dance floor was furnished with a huge bed so Mao could rest. I was still attending Mao's dances and could see him taking young dance partners into the room to "rest" with him. (It was at about this time that the Beijing Room in the Great Hall of the People was renamed Room 118 and turned over to Mao for his private use. The suite was the most opulent I had ever seen, its furnishings and chandeliers surpassing those in the palaces of the Kremlin.)

To be brought into the service of Mao was, for the young women who were chosen, an incomparable honor, beyond their most extravagant dreams. Many women refused his advances, but they were usually older and relatively well educated. Many of his nurses, for instance, believed that personal involvement with the Chairman would have violated their professional ethics. Those who agreed were elated by the opportunity. Everyone who worked for Mao was carefully screened, and the young women were no exception. Careful screening guaranteed that the young women would be filled with awe, admiration, and wonder for the Chairman. All were the offspring of impoverished peasants, from families who owed their lives to the Communist party, for whom Mao was their messiah and savior.

Liu, for instance, had been a beggar as a child. When her father died and left them destitute, mother and daughter had taken to the streets to beg. Liu was only eight or nine when the Communist party came to power and she was chosen to train with the air force's Cultural Work Troupe. The Communist party saved her.

Another young woman, a member of the Railway Corps' Cultural Work Troupe, was the orphaned daughter of "revolutionary martyrs." Her parents, both party members, had died for the communist cause. The young woman never graduated from primary school, but the party rescued her, too, when she was only a child by training her as a dancer for the railroad's cultural troupe.

To have been rescued by the party was already sufficient good luck for such young women. To be called to the Chairman was the greatest experience of their lives. For most Chinese, a mere glimpse of Mao standing impassively atop Tiananmen was a coveted opportunity, the most uplifting, exciting, exhilarating experience they would know. The privileged few who actually got to shake his hand would go for weeks without washing, as friends and acquaintances came from miles around to touch the hand that had touched the hand of Mao and thus to partake of a transcendent, almost mystical experience. During the Cultural Revolution, even the mangoes Mao presented to the workers became sacred objects, worshiped on altars, and a sip of the water in which a bit of one such mango had been boiled was drunk as a magic elixir. Imagine, then, what it meant for a young girl to be called into Mao's chambers to serve his pleasure!

They never loved Mao in the conventional sense. They loved him rather as their great leader, their teacher and savior, and most knew the liaison would be temporary. They were all very young when they began serving Mao—in their late teens and early twenties—and usually unmarried. When Mao tired of them and the honor was over, they married young, uneducated men with peasant pasts.

But for the duration of the relationship, Mao expected the same loyalty from these young women that he demanded from everyone else, and they needed his permission to marry, which he usually gave only after he had cast them aside. Some of them, not understanding the terms of the relationship, married without his permission during the long intervals between being called before him. Sometimes Mao renewed the relationship nonetheless. Mao never fully understood how the young women viewed him, not making the same distinctions between himself as their great leader and savior and himself as a man. "The Chairman is such an interesting person," one young woman told me one day. "But he cannot tell the difference between one's love of him as the leader and love of him as a man. Isn't that funny?"

The young women stood in the same awe of Mao's sexual prowess as they did of his political leadership. At sixty-seven, Mao was past his original projection for the age at which sexual activity stops but, curiously, only then did his complaints of impotence cease altogether. It was then that he became an adherent of Daoist sexual practices,* which gave him an excuse to pursue sex not only for pleasure but to extend his life. He was happiest and most satisfied with several young women simultaneously sharing his bed. He encouraged his sexual partners to introduce him to others for shared orgies, allegedly in the interest of his longevity and strength.

Mao's claim that Daoist sexual practices were a means of keeping him healthy were nothing more than an excuse for his own sexual appetite, but I could not avoid knowing of them. His paramours, ever ready for a call from the imperial chambers, were so proud to serve the Chairman that some were uninhibited in talking about those experiences with me. They never did anything to hide their relationship. Young but uneducated, they turned to me as a doctor and senior member of Mao's staff. Mao often gave them the Daoist sex manual, *Classic of the Plain Girl's Secret Way,* and asked them to read it in preparation for their trysts. The text, written in classical Chinese, was difficult to read and there were many ideographs the young women did not understand. They would question me about the meaning, and over the years, I learned the Daoist text well. The young women appreciated what they learned and what the Chairman taught. "He is great at everything—simply intoxicating," one of the young women confessed to me one day, referring to Mao's sexual prowess.

Mao's sexual activity was not confined to women. The young males who served as his attendants were invariably handsome and strong, and one of their responsibilities was to administer a nightly massage as an additional aid to sleep. Mao insisted that his groin be

*The Daoist prescription for longevity requires men to supplement their declining *yang*—the male essence that is the source of strength, power, and longevity—with *yin shui*—the water of *yin,* or vaginal secretions—of young women. Because *yang* is considered essential to health and power, it cannot be dissipated. Thus, when engaged in coitus, the male rarely ejaculates, drawing strength instead from the secretions of his female partners. The more *yin shui* is absorbed, the more male essence is strengthened. Frequent coition is therefore necessary. For an authoritative account of Daoist sexual practices, including translations of many of the texts, see Douglas Wile, *Art of the Bedchamber: The Chinese Sexual Yoga Classics Including Women's Solo Meditation Texts* (Albany: State University of New York Press, 1992).

massaged, too, a practice I became aware of only in 1960, when one of the guards refused to oblige him. "This is a job for a woman, not me," he told me just before he left. Later, in 1964, I witnessed a similar incident on Mao's train. As his guard was preparing him for sleep, Mao grabbed the young man and began fondling him, trying to pull the man into bed with him. For a while I took such behavior as evidence of a homosexual strain, but later I concluded that it was simply an insatiable appetite for any form of sex. In traditional times young men, often effeminate and pretty, played the female roles in Chinese operas, and many were brought into the sexual service of wealthy merchants and officials. Both *The Dream of the Red Chamber* and *The Golden Lotus,* China's classic pornographic novel and another of Mao's favorites, contain stories of such liaisons. Catamites are part of Chinese tradition.

Mao's bodyguards, though, were neither homosexual nor actors, and the presence of so many attractive young women often caused problems for them. In imperial times, the chastity of concubines had been guaranteed by a prohibition against any males, except for the emperor himself and his eunuchs, passing the night within the walls of the Forbidden City. But Mao's bodyguards were not eunuchs. They were young, healthy, handsome rural youth, often woefully naive before being fully initiated into Mao's inner circle. Confronted with frequent temptations, some of them succumbed.

One young bodyguard who overstepped the bounds paid a heavy price. When one of Mao's girlfriends came into the duty office one night to count out the Chairman's sleeping pills, the young bodyguard began cooing praises of her soft, tender skin and even dared to fondle her on the behind.

"*Liumang*," she screeched, using the catchall epithet that translates, politely, as "scoundrel." She ran immediately to Mao, who summoned Wang Dongxing.

"What do you think you're doing, trying to pull teeth from the tiger's mouth?" Wang, rushing to the scene, yelled when he saw the young guard.

The guard waited in terror as Mao and Wang Dongxing conferred. "This is awful," he kept lamenting, pacing the floor as his fate hung in the balance. Mao ordered Wang to confiscate the bodyguard's handgun and cart him off to jail. Wang demurred, taking the gun but rescuing the guard from prison, sending him instead to work for the public security bureau in a coastal town.

Other young bodyguards got into trouble without having sought it.

One morning at about four o'clock I was awakened by another of Mao's guards, a naive nineteen-year-old: Something terrible had happened, the young man was saying to me in desperation, shaking me awake.

We were in Shanghai, in the elegant old Jinjiang Hotel in the heart of the former French quarter, where Mao always occupied one of the top floors. The entire hotel had been cleared for his use. Mao's usual group of young women was along, and his favorite of the moment was sharing his bed that night.

The guard had gone to add some hot water to the Chairman's tea and unwittingly walked in on Mao and the young woman. He was new to the Chairman's personal entourage and had yet to be initiated into the details of Mao's personal life. He said he did not know that the young woman was there. He had not even seen her directly, spotting her instead through the gap in the silk screen that was always placed just beyond the entrance to Mao's room, affording him a measure of privacy even with an open door. "Just as I walked in, she fell out of bed onto the floor. She was completely naked! I was so scared I just ran away. What should I do?" He was convinced that the young woman had fallen out of bed in fright over seeing him.

I sat up in bed, fully awake, and urged the guard to calm down. "Tell me, did the Chairman see you?"

"I don't know," he responded. "I ran out the second I saw her."

I was worried. Mao's paranoia was growing and his moods were unpredictable. I had no idea what he would do if he found out his guard had seen him.

The guard began crying, panicked. "I'm new here," he said. "Nobody told me when to go into the Chairman's room. I've just been feeling my way. I didn't know this kind of thing was going on." He wanted me to testify on behalf of his innocence.

I assured him that I would but cautioned him that he had to be more discreet in the future and make certain before entering that no women were in Mao's room. "The Chairman did not call for you, and you should not go in unless he does. Otherwise, he'll think you're spying," I said.

The guard wanted to resign from Group One immediately.

But he had to go back to the Chairman. He was on duty, and regulations required the bodyguards to stay by Mao's side.

Mao and the young woman were yelling at each other when the guard returned. He hovered at the door, incredulous, convinced the argument was about him. But Mao saw him there and invited him in.

The woman was wailing, and Mao wanted the guard to witness the scene. He soon found out what had happened.

The guard had entered Mao's bedchamber just at the onset of an argument between the Chairman and the woman. She had met a young man she wanted to marry, but Mao would not agree. The more she insisted, the more adamant Mao became. The woman finally became so angry that she accused Mao of being a corrupt bourgeois woman-izer, using her for his own sexual pleasures. Mao was so furious that he pushed her out of the bed. It was at this moment that the guard entered the room. The two had been so immersed in their argument they had not even known he was there.

Wang Dongxing was brought in, and Mao insisted that a staff meeting be called immediately to criticize the young woman. Wang Dongxing was instructed to organize the session.

The young woman's special relationship with Mao made her fear-less. She said that if a meeting was called, she would tell the truth about her relationship with the Chairman and accuse him of being a bour-geois womanizer. Wang was in a quandary. He had to call a meeting. Mao had ordered it. But if the young woman was not placated, she would tell her side of the story. Wang's efforts to protect the Chairman from himself would be shattered. Wang called on me for help.

I talked to the woman, trying to find a way for both Mao and her to save face and persuade her to keep her peace and protect the Chairman's reputation. No good would be served if she made her accusations public. She was still tearful and angry, but after much discussion she agreed to make a self-criticism before the staff, saying she was wrong to be rude to Chairman Mao.

Mao accepted her self-criticism. His face had been saved. But little good came to the young woman. Mao still refused to allow her to marry. Only in 1966, after the Cultural Revolution began, did she finally get married. The relationship was never so ardent after that, and Mao turned his attention to another young woman, a member of the Railway Corps, whom he had met at one of the Zhongnanhai dancing parties.

The new object of Mao's affection would spend the whole night in his bedroom and would often move in with Mao when Jiang Qing was out of town, sleeping with him when he slept and waiting on him when he was awake—serving him meals and tea, sponging him down with hot washcloths. Mao began taking her with him on trips, and the two stayed together, their relationship obvious to the local security forces and hotel attendants who ought not to have known. The young woman was delighted. "What kind of life is it anyway, half in the dark and half in the open?" she asked me.

She became proud to the point of arrogance of the honor Mao conferred upon her, convinced that to be chosen as Mao's woman made her better and more privileged than anyone else. She lost all sense of Mao's need for privacy, doing everything she could to flaunt her special relationship.

But Wang Dongxing's job was to protect Mao from his own indiscretions. He had to prevent Mao's private life from becoming public. His staff and the confidential secretaries were expected to be discreet. But no one outside Group One could be expected to stay silent. Wang did not want to risk the Chairman's reputation. He wanted the woman to stay in a separate room when they traveled.

But he could not say so to Mao for fear of irritating the Chairman. He used an unsophisticated nineteen-year-old bodyguard as his sacrificial lamb, instructing him to make the suggestion to Mao. The guard did and Mao, remarkably, agreed, sending his female companion pouting off to a nearby chamber. But Mao was so perturbed with the young guard that he had him fired and transferred out of Zhongnanhai.

The young woman introduced Mao to other women. Her relationship with the Chairman became a family affair, for she arranged for him to indulge himself with some of her female relatives. He was disappointed with one, a member of an opera troupe who was no longer so young or pretty, but his dalliance with the woman's sister was more successful.

In December 1961 Mao invited me to join him, the young woman, her sister, and her sister's husband, a military officer, for a banquet in the villa where we were staying in Wuxi. As we ate the delectable meal, there was not a hint of what would follow. The scene was idyllic, the air fragrant with the scent of plum trees. It had just snowed, and was still misty. The place was famous for its delicious fish, and the whole area is renowned for its teas and silks. Broad-leaved mulberry trees that feed the silkworms grow in abundance there, too.

It did not matter to Mao that the woman's sister was married. Nor did the cuckolded husband feel disgraced. Indeed, he considered it an honor to offer his wife to the Chairman—and a stepping-stone to military promotions. At the end of the dinner, Mao sent the husband home and spent the next three days with the woman and her sister, interrupting his activities only long enough to meet with Shanghai mayor Ke Qingshi and Anhui's Zeng Xisheng.

Even Wang Dongxing was outraged at the affair. "If [the girls'] mother were still alive, the Chairman would have her, too," Wang snapped. His greatest opprobrium was reserved not for Mao but for the military officer and cuckolded husband. "He sold his own wife," Wang said.

Wang saw Mao's sexual adventures as a fight against death. The Chairman is getting on in age, he said to me one day. He wondered whether a fear of death was leading Mao to grab as many young women as he could.

Most of Mao's women had been innocent young girls when they first came to him. Over the years, I saw the same phenomenon repeated. After being brought to Mao's bed, they would become corrupted. Mao's sexual demands and his own character were one source of the corruption. His power was another. Rather than being humbled by Mao, the women became arrogant. Uneducated, unskilled, with no great futures, their association with Mao was their sole distinction. And what a claim it was! They became demanding, supercilious, using their association with Mao to assert their superiority over others. In time, when the Cultural Revolution began, some of the young women Mao had cast aside even used their special relationship with the Chairman to grab power for themselves.

Watching so many innocent young women become corrupted through association with Mao, I began to sense that Jiang Qing's life had followed a similar path. Maybe she really had been kind in Yanan when she first married Mao. Maybe he had corrupted her as well.

With so much sexual activity, venereal disease was practically inevitable. One young woman contracted trichomonas vaginalis, thus starting a chain. The young dancers in her cultural troupe often shared each others' clothes, and I suspect that the woman contracted the disease from wearing another dancer's underwear. Trichomonas vaginalis is not, strictly speaking, a venereal disease, but an infected woman transmits the disease through intercourse to her male partners. They in turn can pass the disease on to other females. The disease usually produces considerable distress to the woman but is ordinarily asymptomatic in the male, who thus becomes a carrier without knowing it. Once one of Mao's partners became infected, he quickly contracted the disease as well, and soon it had spread. He sent the infected women to me for treatment.

The young women were proud to be infected. The illness, transmitted by Mao, was a badge of honor, testimony to their close relations with the Chairman. They were proud, too, to receive treatment from me. As the Chairman's doctor, I had access to the best and most modern medicines, imported from the West, and they considered it a privilege to be treated with the Flagyl I prescribed.

But treating Mao's women did not solve the problem. Because Mao was the carrier, the epidemic could be stopped only if he received treatment himself. I wanted him to halt his sexual activities until the drugs had done their work.

The Chairman scoffed at my suggestion, saying that doctors always exaggerate things. I explained that he was a carrier of disease, passing it on to others even though he himself was experiencing no ill effects. "If it's not hurting me," he said, "then it doesn't matter. Why are you getting so excited about it?"

I insisted, wondering what would happen if Jiang Qing were to become infected.

Mao found my question amusing. "That'll never happen," he said. Mao's sexual relations with his wife had long since ceased. "I told her a long time ago that I'm too old—can't do it anymore," he said with a wave of the hand and a smile on his face.

I suggested that he should at least allow himself to be washed and cleaned. Mao still received only nightly rubdowns with hot towels. He never actually bathed. His genitals were never cleaned. But Mao refused to bathe. "I wash myself inside the bodies of my women," he retorted.

I was nauseated. Mao's sexual indulgences, his Daoist delusions, his sullying of so many naive and innocent young women, were almost more than I could bear.

But I had to find a way to prevent the disease from spreading further. At a minimum, I could make certain that the bedding and towels in the guesthouses where Mao stayed were sterilized. But the staff at the guesthouses considered it an insult to the Chairman to sterilize his bedding, and I could not explain the problem to them without revealing Mao's secret.

I spoke privately to the staff in Group One, who were already aware of the problem, and urged them to use their own towels. And I instructed them how to sterilize Mao's bedding and towels without the Chairman's knowledge.

But Mao remained a carrier the rest of his life.

46

Women became even more important to Mao after one of them discovered the secret bugging devices. It happened not long after Chinese New Year, in February 1961, when we were en route to Guangzhou on Mao's special train.

Wang Dongxing seemed to know from the beginning that the trip would bring trouble. More women than usual were accompanying Mao. "When you put two women together, they are noisier than a gong," Wang said to me just after we had set out.

In addition to the female train attendants, the young confidential clerk who was so open about her liaison with Mao was there, and so was the woman with whom Mao had quarreled because she wanted to get married. I was startled to see a teacher I knew well there, too, and even more shocked to learn of her longtime liaison with Mao. The kind and honest young teacher had met Mao at one of his dances, and the two had struck up a relationship then. She had never been further from Beijing than the Fragrant Hills, and Mao had invited her along to show her the world.

The wife of a high-ranking military official, a dark-skinned, depressed-looking woman of about forty, was also there. She was said to have known Mao in Yanan. He had sent her off to the Soviet Union when their romance faltered and later arranged for her to marry the military official. Jiang Qing had long known about the romance and vengefully wanted the woman's husband demoted. But the man was a close associate of Peng Dehuai's, and so long as Peng remained minister of defense, the military official was protected. But when Peng was purged in 1959, that protection was gone, and Jiang Qing had begun pressuring Lin Biao to take action against the official. The wife, obviously anxious and unhappy, had come to persuade Mao to intercede on her husband's behalf.

Mao called her into his compartment several times while we were traveling, and on the first night after our arrival in Hangzhou I could not help but notice that she spent several hours there. Just after she left his room, though, she disappeared. One of the other women became worried and asked me to help find her. The woman was not found until early the next morning. She and Mao had quarreled, and she had spent the night huddled on a rock by the lake, crying. Mao sent her back to Beijing that day.

After a few days in Hangzhou, we headed west by train toward Wuhan, stopping briefly so Mao could meet with Zhang Pinghua, Hunan's first party secretary.

The meeting took place on the train, and Mao was late.

He was lingering in his compartment with the female teacher while Zhang and his deputy, Wang Yanchun, waited in the adjacent reception car. Wang was so rooted in his peasant ways that he squatted rather than sit on the sofa. When Mao finally emerged, I joined the teacher and several of his other female companions for a stroll outside the train. The young technician responsible for secretly recording Mao's conversations, joined us in our meanderings.

"I heard you talking today," the young technician suddenly said to the teacher, interrupting our idle chatter.

"What do you mean you heard me talking?" she responded. "Talking about what?"

"When the Chairman was getting ready to meet Zhang Pinghua. You told him to hurry up and put on his clothes."

The young woman blanched. "What else did you hear?" she asked quietly.

"I heard everything," he answered, teasing.

The woman was stunned. She turned and bolted for the train as the rest of us followed quickly behind. The other women were also distressed. If he had heard one conversation with Mao, surely he had heard others as well.

Mao's meetings were concluding as we returned to the train, and the teacher went immediately to his compartment, demanding to speak with him. She reported the entire conversation with the technician.

Mao was livid. He had never suspected the bugging. The revelation came as a shock. He called Wang Dongxing into his compartment, where the two stayed behind closed doors in intense conversation for an hour. Wang, so recently returned from exile, said he did not know about the bugging devices, either. When he emerged from the meeting, he ordered the train to proceed immediately, at top speed, to Wuhan.

As the train sped north, Wang called the technician and Mao's confidential secretary to meet with him, informing them that the Chairman wanted to know who had ordered the bugging. Wang claimed that since this was the first trip he had taken with the Chairman since his return, he simply took all the staff members who ordinarily accompanied the Chairman, including the recording technician. Wang began interrogating the young men and told the technician that Mao had ordered his arrest.

But Wang did not arrest the technician. "You have no place to run," he told him. But he demanded to know who had ordered the bugging.

The confidential secretary pleaded ignorance. He said the bugging had started when Ye Zilong was in charge. Ye was the man to consult. But Ye was away doing labor reform.

The technician also claimed not to know. He was just doing his job, he said, acting under orders from "the leadership."

"And did the leadership order you to record the Chairman's private conversations, too?" Wang Dongxing demanded, glaring at the young technician. "Don't you have anything better to do? Why were you looking for trouble? Why didn't you tell Chairman you wanted to record his talks? You recorded all sorts of things you never should have. What am I supposed to tell Chairman?"

The young man was speechless.

By the time our train reached Wuhan and we had settled into the Plum Garden guesthouse, it was four o'clock in the morning. Wang Dongxing roused a local electrician and went immediately to remove all the bugging equipment from the train. I went to bed.

When I woke that afternoon, the bugging equipment—recording machines and tapes, speakers and wires—had been put on display in the conference room, and the staff was gathered around examining the paraphernalia. The Plum Garden guesthouse had also been bugged, and that equipment was on display, too. Mao ordered photographs taken as evidence, with Wang Dongxing, Kang Yimin, the secretary and the technician standing behind the table.

Kang Yimin, the deputy director of the Office of Confidential Secretaries who had worked just under Ye Zilong, had come from the General Office in Zhongnanhai to discuss the matter with Wang

Dongxing. Kang was a simple, honest, but uneducated man, and he and Wang quickly came to blows. Kang knew that the real decision to record the Chairman's conversations had come from higher up than Ye Zilong. Bugging the Chairman was far too serious a matter to be decided by Ye. Why they—or I—ever thought it could be gotten away with, I will never understand.

Confronted with Mao's discovery and not wanting to bring unknown higher levels into the dispute, Kang wanted Wang Dongxing to find some convincing way to explain the whole thing away. But Wang was determined to find out where the order had originated. Mao wanted an investigation, and Wang Dongxing was determined to conduct it.

In the end, though, the two men compromised. Wang Dongxing agreed to tell Mao that the bugging had been ordered to provide material for a party history.

Mao was infuriated. "So they're already compiling a black report against me, like Khrushchev?" he bellowed. A "party history" based on bugging his private conversations could only be used against him, and nothing bothered him more than the possibility of the type of attack Khrushchev had launched against Stalin. The attack against Stalin had also been full of damaging personal detail, and Mao did not want the details of his own personal life recorded on tape.

But it was not these revelations he most feared. His private life was an open secret among the party elite. His greatest fear was the potential threat to his power. Mao's frequent travel to other parts of China, where he met alone with local leaders, was part of his political strategy, a tactic designed to leap over the cumbersome bureaucratic machinery of the party and state and to maintain direct contact with local-level leaders. He did not want the central authority to know what he said to the provincial and local-level leaders. His role as the source of all policy would be diminished were representatives to carry his words back to Beijing, where central leaders could devise policy based on his conversations outside the capital. Mao wanted the central authorities to be more directly dependent on and loyal to him. If they knew what he said when traveling, they could pay lip service to their loyalty without having to be dependent. That was what he was trying to avoid.

He ordered Wang Dongxing to burn the tapes immediately. "Don't leave a single one," he commanded. "I don't want them providing material for any black report." Faced with Mao's fury, the technician confessed that other places, including the guesthouse in Hangzhou that we had just left, were also bugged. Mao ordered

Wang to dispatch a team to remove that equipment and destroy those tapes, too.

Several people lost their jobs as a result of the incident. Ye Zilong's lieutenant Kany Yimin and Mao's confidential secretary were both fired. Kang went to work in the People's Bank. The latter was transferred to the Second Ministry of Machine Building and was replaced by Xu Yefu, the confidential secretary who had earlier lost his job when he talked openly about Li Yinqiao's accusation that Jiang Qing was running away to Hangzhou to avoid being criticized. The witless technician whose teasing of Mao's girlfriend had precipitated the discovery, was sent to Shaanxi for labor reform.

Mao never believed that the underlings who lost their jobs in 1961 were the real culprits. "They don't understand what this is all about," he said. "They don't know anything."

Mao, like Kang Yimin, believed that the orders to listen in on his conversations could have come only from leaders at the highest level. The Ministry of Public Security would have to be involved, too. Mao was convinced that they had been spying on him as part of a plot. His growing belief that there was a conspiracy against him within the highest ranks of the party dates from here. The differences between Mao and the other party leaders were still hidden, but the rift that would explode with the Cultural Revolution was quietly widening. Mao was biding his time.

Mao was unnerved by the bugging incident. Ordinarily suspicious, he had still never imagined that secret recording devices had been picking up his every word, that tapes of his conversations were being sent back to the central secretariat in Beijing. Nearly as shocking to Mao was the behavior of his personal staff. He assumed that his inner circle, in whom he had placed his trust, who had served him most loyally and longest, had been part of the plot. He knew we were aware that his conversations were being recorded and sent to the central secretariat. But we had kept it a secret. Mao became more wary of his staff following this episode. His faith in our loyalty began to decline. He came to trust women far more than men, dismissing his male attendants and surrounding himself with women. His young women came to serve as his personal attendants and trusted confidantes.

Mao's increasing wariness of me dates to this episode, too. When he asked, "Any news?" as he did every time we met, he wanted me to tell him everything I knew. Failure to disclose everything could be taken as evidence of a plot. His suspiciousness began to take deeper hold, and Mao never fully trusted me again.

47

Our stay in Wuhan was brief. We continued south by train, the tension mounting as we went. We were on our way to Guangzhou. Mao had called a political work conference. All the highest leaders would attend—Liu Shaoqi, Zhu De, Chen Yun. Mao was suspicious of everyone now, and security arrangements were tight. With the famine continuing and disagreements within the party growing, the political situation was unstable.

Guangzhou continued to be a particularly difficult security problem since sabotage was a real threat. Infiltration from nearby Hong Kong was relatively easy, and if word of the upcoming meeting was leaked, spies could make their way into the city, and anything was possible. A foreign assassin might even try to murder Mao or other top leaders. A year before, at the enlarged politburo meeting in Shanghai, the Ministry of Public Security had discovered that Taiwan intelligence had learned of the meeting in advance. Mayor Ke Qingshi, assuming an internal leak, had directed a full-scale investigation of everyone involved with the meeting, checking mail, phone calls, telegrams, and all outside contacts. Only later did the Ministry of Public Security and the central authority's Department of Investigation realize that Taiwan had merely deduced the meeting from the increased air traffic into Shanghai.

Guangdong's first party secretary, Tao Zhu, was visibly nervous. Immediately after our arrival, he called a meeting to map out stringent security measures. Minister of public security Xie Fuzhi and Wang

Dongxing, acting as both vice-minister of public security and the man responsible for the leaders' safety, were in charge, and the leaders and staff of the Guangdong bureau of public security all attended. I participated, too. I was in charge of coordinating health care for the conference participants.

Following the security discussions, I convened a meeting with local health officials to work out plans for servicing the conference participants' medical needs. In the midst of discussions with the president of Guangzhou People's Hospital, I received an urgent phone call. It was Jiang Qing's nurse. Jiang was very upset, she said, and urged me to hurry there immediately. Jiang Qing's neuroses were once more disrupting vital national business. I was forced to leave the meeting to find out what was wrong.

I walked into Jiang Qing's villa at the Islet guesthouse to discover her staff huddled together. The nurses were crying, and the male guards and attendants were tense. "It's really bad this time," said Sun Yong, the security officer in charge.

The evening before, when Jiang Qing stepped into the hot bath drawn for her by her nurse, she had suddenly cried out in pain, accusing the nurse of trying to scald her with boiling water. Then she accused the nurse of tampering with her sleeping pills. Someone, she insisted, was trying to poison her. As the senior supervisor of her nursing staff, I was responsible and the ultimate blame rested with me.

I tried to calm down the staff, assuring them that I understood their difficulties and knew they were doing their best. I promised that the party would protect them from Jiang Qing. Then I went to see the Chairman's wife.

"Just what kind of nurses have you appointed for me, Doctor?" she demanded when I walked in, throwing a washcloth down on the table. "Just what is it you are trying to do?"

I sat down opposite her. "What is it?" I asked.

"What is it? What happened? You don't know what happened?" she responded incredulously.

I explained that I had been at a meeting.

Jiang Qing told the story I had just heard, accusing the nurse of deliberately scalding her with boiling water and of tampering with her sleeping pills. "There is some sort of ghost in here," Jiang Qing said. She suspected a conspiracy. Someone, she thought, wanted her dead.

I tried to explain. The water might have been too hot for her comfort, but it could not have been boiling. The tap water was never boiled, and besides, the nurse had tested it first without being scalded herself.

"So you think I'm lying?" Jiang Qing retorted. "And what about the sleeping pills? The color of the pills has changed. The old ones were red. The ones yesterday were pink. What about that?"

I had not meant to suggest that she was lying, I told her. I was only saying that the water might have been hot but that it could not have been boiling. I explained that her sleeping pills were imported from Hong Kong and that because they were bought at different times, the colors might be different, too. I assured her that her medicine had gone through stringent certification. Nothing could be wrong with it. It could not be poison. Beijing Hospital had screened and sealed it, then sent it to Guangzhou. It was unsealed only by Xiao Zeng and Xiao Li, two nurses who had been thoroughly investigated by the Central Bureau of Guards and the Central Bureau of Health. They had absolutely no political problems. Otherwise, they would never be allowed to work for Jiang Qing. "There may be some shortcomings in their work, but there is no ghost inside," I said. "If there were a plot, then even the Central Bureau of Guards and the Central Bureau of Health would have to be involved. That's just not possible."

But Jiang Qing accused me of trying to cover up for them. "Your attitude is wrong. I'm not going to argue with you anymore," she said.

Jiang Qing ordered me to get Wang Dongxing immediately.

I was furious at the absurdity of Jiang Qing's charges. She was accusing me of being involved in a conspiracy to poison her.

Wang Dongxing was unusually conciliatory and did his best to soothe her.

"You are vice-minister of public security and director of the Central Bureau of Guards," Jiang Qing began. "You are in charge of everything that happens around the Chairman. May I ask you one question, please?"

"Of course, Comrade Jiang Qing."

"When the people you supervise perform services for others, what kind of attitude should they have?"

Wang Dongxing was still smiling. "Comrade Jiang Qing, is there a problem? I think we can work it out. We just need a little patience."

"Oh, for heaven's sake," Jiang retorted. "Okay, I will tell you slowly. But that doctor of yours opposes me every time I speak. How am I supposed to be patient?"

I interrupted her, trying to tell my side of the story. But before I had said three words, Jiang Qing cut me off. "Shut up. Don't say anything else," she warned. Then she repeated the story of the boiling water and the poisoned pills to Wang Dongxing. "Shouldn't I criticize my nurses when they do something wrong?" she wanted to know.

"Shouldn't I expect some sympathy from the doctor when I tell him my problems? But all I get is a lecture. He was shouting at me. He didn't treat me like a patient. What kind of attitude is this? Do you really think he is serving the people wholeheartedly?"

When she paused, I again tried to tell my side of the story. Again, she interrupted me. "Medical workers are supposed to show concern for their patients, not debate them. This doctor is downright arrogant. Is this some form of psychological torture?"

I tried again. "Comrade Jiang Qing . . ."

But she would not let me speak. "Stop trying to debate me," she yelled. "Stop arguing with me!"

I had had enough. I stood up. "We are supposed to be having a meeting here," I said, "and I believe everyone has a right to speak. If you don't want me to talk, fine. I don't see why I should stay." I walked out of her room, slamming the door behind me. I decided to quit.

"See? Do you see?" I heard her say as I was leaving. "He dares to act like that even in front of a vice-minister!"

I walked around the grounds trying to calm myself down. Then I realized that I had to see Mao immediately. He would side with the first person who spoke to him. If Mao believed the nurses were trying to harm Jiang Qing, even poison her, the ultimate responsibility was mine. I could be in serious trouble, imprisoned or even executed. I wanted to tell him my story before Jiang Qing had a chance to tell her distorted version. But her guard, Sun Yong, found me before I had a chance to reach Mao. Comrade Jiang Qing and Vice-Minister Wang Dongxing wanted to see me immediately.

"You're being dismissed from your job and confined to your room," Jiang Qing told me when I entered her room.

"Good," I responded, and turned around to leave.

I was happy to be dismissed. I only resented being confined to my room. I went straight to Mao.

"Chairman," I began. It was two or three in the afternoon by then, and Mao had just wakened. He was still lying in bed, his eyes half closed, about to drink the tea his bodyguard, Xiao Zhang, had just brought.

"Any news?" he replied, repeating his usual greeting.

"The news is that Jiang Qing has dismissed me and ordered me confined to my room."

"*Zheme lihai?*" he responded, taking a deep drag on his cigarette. "That bad? What happened?"

I told the story from beginning to end, starting with the difficulties she had created over her physical exam several months previously and how angry she had been with the results. I ended by assuring Mao that the sleeping pills she was taking were exactly the same as his.

He continued smoking in silence after I had finished. "Jiang Qing is unreasonable," he finally said. "You have told me everything. It's all right. Don't tell anyone else about this. I'll talk to Jiang Qing. In the meantime, though, why don't you stay away from here for a few days? Don't make any appearances. We still have to do something to save her face. Tell the nurses not to be afraid of her. She's just a paper tiger."

Jiang Qing was on her way in to see Mao just as I left.

I stayed away for three days. When Mao and Jiang Qing went with Tao Zhu to see the famous porcelain works in Foshan county, I watched a movie with Zhu De—*High Noon.* I loved it. Gary Cooper was my favorite actor.

Jiang Qing was eager to see me punished, but Mao had clearly instructed her to make peace. The day after their return from Foshan, she called me in to see her. "I know the Chairman has full confidence in your medical skills," she said. "But that is no reason for you to be so arrogant. I must admit that I was impatient. Last night the Chairman asked me to tell you to relax. You can rest assured about your job. Let's forget about this. Let's look toward the future." She handed me a copy of *Internal Reference.* Mao had marked an article he wanted me to read. "The Chairman wants you to pay more attention to important national issues," she said.

48

In March 1961, the most important issue facing China was the nation-wide famine then claiming the lives of millions of peasants. The purpose of the expanded politburo work conference in Guangzhou was to review agricultural policy. Mao had spent much of February absorbed in formulating a workable agricultural program and planned to submit a draft of his plan to the work conference for review.

The article Mao wanted me to read was about an innovation in agricultural organization that Anhui had introduced to cope with the crisis. Anhui, traditionally one of China's poorest provinces, had been devastated by the famine. In the beginning, Anhui party secretary Zeng Xisheng had been an ultra-radical supporter of the Great Leap Forward, and he had introduced Mao to the backyard steel furnaces. By early 1961, some 10 million Anhui peasants were on the verge of starvation, and millions died in the ensuing months. Hundreds of thousands, those with sufficient energy, were fleeing in search of food. Zeng Xisheng's enthusiasm for the Great Leap Forward had dissipated, and he was now desperately trying to restore agricultural production. He had begun distributing small plots of communal land to individual peasants, who agreed to farm the land in return for paying the commune a specified portion of their crop. The peasants did not actually own the land, so Zeng could claim that the system was still "socialist," and therefore, he hoped, acceptable to Mao.

Zeng Xisheng believed Mao supported him when he began introducing the new policy after the Shanghai meetings in January 1960, more than a year earlier. Mao had spoken well of the field responsibility system then, and Zeng Xisheng had interpreted his words as encouragement. The initial results of the new policy had been positive. Farming their assigned land, responsible for its output, peasants could clearly see the relationship between their efforts, what the land produced, and their income. Agricultural production in Anhui was on the upswing.

Mao's draft proposal to the Guangzhou conference mentioned neither Zeng's new field responsibility system nor other similar forms of household contract production that were being introduced in other parts of China. But after Zeng Xisheng spoke at the meeting on March 15, Mao again seemed to warm to the idea. "If we do it right," he said after hearing Zeng's presentation, "we can increase national grain production by a billion *jin.** Our lives would be easier then." Zeng again interpreted Mao's comments as approval.

In fact, controversy over the policy was about to split the Communist party apart.

Ke Qingshi, the Shanghai mayor and now also chief of the politburo's East China region, led the battle against Zeng. Ke was still a close follower of Mao and no friend of Zeng Xisheng. He believed in socialism for the sake of socialism. As head of the East China region, Ke Qingshi should have been overseeing work in Anhui, and he felt slighted that Zeng had introduced the new responsibility system without consulting him first. He would soon become the most vocal spokesman for retaining a collective system whatever the cost.

The convictions of the central leadership were not yet clear at the Guangzhou meetings. But their proclivities were. It was in March 1961 that I first heard Deng Xiaoping, speaking in support of Zeng's proposal, make what was to become the most famous and notorious statement of his political career: "I don't care if it's a white cat or a black cat," he said. "It's a good cat so long as it catches mice." Call it capitalist or socialist, Deng's overriding goal was to raise agricultural production and end the famine.

Liu Shaoqi, always less forceful than Deng, his language less colorful, came to his position more gradually. But even in Guangzhou, he was inclined to permit experiments in household production.

The Guangzhou meetings did not settle the issue. Party leaders wanted more firsthand information on what was happening in the countryside before deciding how the problems could best be solved. Mao's draft regulations on work in the people's communes (the so-

---

*A *jin,* or catty, is 1.1 pounds.

called 60 points) were approved without reference to Zeng's new inno-
vations, but the draft status of the proposal meant that changes could
be introduced later. The country's top leaders decided to go to the
rural areas themselves to investigate, and agreed to reconvene in May
to report on what they had learned. Liu Shaoqi, Zhou Enlai, Zhu De,
and Deng Xiaoping left for the countryside immediately. The public
facade of unity had been maintained.

But behind the scenes the party was seething with tension, torn by
increasingly insidious clashes of personality and ideology and Mao's
growing willingness to promote his sycophantic followers regardless of
their abilities or skills.

I sensed from the moment I read the article about household
contract production that Zeng Xisheng's policy would bring trouble.
On the surface, the policy made excellent sense. If distributing land
directly to the peasants was the most effective way to increase agricultural production, then clearly that policy was best for China. Agriculture was the lifeline of the country. Millions were dying of hunger. We
had to eat. The majority of the country's leaders had chosen the
socialist road because they believed that only socialism could overcome poverty, increase the living standard of the vast majority of
Chinese people, and make China rich and powerful again. This is why
I supported socialism—not for socialism's sake but rather as a means
to an end. Faced with a severe agricultural crisis, many party leaders
believed that returning farming responsibility to individual peasant
households would cause production to increase. When agricultural
production did go up, support for the experiment grew.

The problem with Zeng's policy was that it smacked of private
farming, which was not socialist. The party was being divided by its
members' different perceptions of what socialism meant and what was
best for the country. Mao believed in socialism for the sake of socialism. His highest ideal was not wealth or production but collective
ownership, life in common, equality, a primitive form of sharing.
Whether socialism would increase the living standard of the Chinese
people was one of Mao's concerns but not the main one. He knew that
the peasants wanted above all to own their own land. "What we want,
though," Mao said, "is socialism. We are facing difficulties in agricultural production now, so we have to make concessions to the peasants.
But this is not the direction we should take in the future."

Nor did it matter to him that household farming seemed more
effective than the commune in increasing agricultural output. He was
stubborn. "Some people," he said, quoting an old Chinese saying,

"don't give up their convictions until they see the Yellow River and have no other place to retreat. I don't give up my convictions even when I see the Yellow River." Mao would not give up.

When the leadership reconvened in Beijing in May and June 1961, the country was in serious trouble. The people were visibly thinner, their faces grayer, their bodies more swollen from malnutrition. The streets were emptier. People were staying at home. They had no energy to work or to go outside. The first wave of urban transfers had begun. Unable to supply the cities with food, the party was sending some 10 million urban residents from all over the country to rural areas—a way of minimizing the possibility of urban unrest and of bringing the hungry closer to potential supplies of food.

The news from the leaders' fact-finding visits to the countryside left little cause for optimism. The situation in the rural areas was bad. The convictions of the party leadership were becoming more firm. The adamantly pragmatic Chen Yun, silent during the meetings in March, was the most vocal of Mao's dissenters. "The peasants are doing nothing now but complain," he reported. "They are saying that under Chiang Kai-shek they 'suffered' but had plenty to eat. Under Mao Zedong everything is 'great' but they eat only porridge. All we have to do is give the peasants their own land. Then everyone will have plenty to eat." Chen Yun wanted to disband the communes altogether and return the land to the peasants.

Mao's 60-point draft on commune organization was revised again. The public dining halls, already abandoned in many parts of the countryside, were officially dismantled, and the leadership decided to send another 10 million urban residents to the countryside in 1962. Output targets for industry, steel production in particular, were scaled back dramatically. But the communes remained intact, and the public unity of the party was maintained.

In the summer of 1961, Mao returned to his mountain retreat in Lushan, the site of the disastrous meeting in 1959 when Peng Dehuai wrote his letter of criticism and Mao forced the defense chief's dismissal. Mao wanted to convene another meeting. This time there would be an agenda, focusing on the readjustment of the national plan for agriculture and industry, and Mao would tolerate no disruptions.

Mao still had supporters when the meetings convened in August 1961. Ke Qingshi could always be counted on to follow the Chairman's lead. Lin Biao, too, was vocal in his admiration. In May, Lin had ordered the army's nationally circulated newspaper, *Liberation Army*

Daily, to print a short aphorism from Chairman Mao on the front page of every edition. The military commander was leading a new campaign within the army to study Mao's thought, taking every opportunity to declare that "the thought of Mao Zedong is the highest manifestation of Marxism-Leninism" and to encourage the entire population to "read Chairman Mao's books, listen to Chairman Mao's words, and be Chairman Mao's good soldiers." But his admiration for the Chairman seemed to me less a matter of genuine conviction than a stepping-stone to power.

Wang Renzhong, the Hubei party secretary, also supported Mao. He was by then an unthinking sycophant. Peng Dehuai seemed to reverse himself, criticizing the household contract system and arguing that the collective economy ought to contribute the dominant share of the national income.

Zhou Enlai and Zhu De were silent on the issue of rural collectives. Both had angered Mao over collectivization and did not want to irritate him again. Tao Zhu, Guangdong's first party secretary and newly promoted head of the central-south region, wavered, generally favoring household contract production but suggesting that only 30 percent of collectively held land be distributed to households. "This way people won't starve to death," Tao said. "If this is capitalism, then I prefer capitalism. Do we really want everyone to be poor under socialism?"

Liu Shaoqi was moving more firmly in the direction of contracting agricultural production to individual households. "We have to go into maximum retreat in both industry and agriculture," he said. "Anything that lifts the peasants' spirit is good. We can't say that one method is best to the exclusion of all others. We need to adopt the system of household contracts and individualized farming."

Deng Xiaoping still did not care whether cats were black or white, declaring his support for whatever system would increase agricultural output. To continue collective farming, he thought, was pointless. When Ke Qingshi criticized Zeng Xisheng's description of the benefits of contract farming, Deng rebuffed him. "It's too early for the East China region to reach that conclusion," Deng snapped.

Mao disagreed. I thought he would be ruthless. In 1960, Mao had invited me to join him for a meeting with the colorful, wiry British field marshal Bernard Montgomery. Montgomery had accused Mao of being a tyrant, and when he arrived at the entrance to Yinian Hall in Zhongnanhai, wearing a bright red shirt, Mao shook Montgomery's hand and asked whether he minded shaking hands with an aggressor. "If you cannot push everything else aside and fight ruthlessly for your goal," he had told Montgomery, "then you will not reach it. You have to know exactly what you want and then ruthlessly remove every obstacle standing in your way."

I had expected him to be ruthless in Lushan, urging his own view upon a recalcitrant party elite. But he was not. He rarely even attended the meetings, following them instead through the written reports that were presented to him each evening. He met once in private with Anhui's Zeng Xisheng, cautioning him further against private farming, but there were no great outbursts of ire.

Mao was still in retreat, in part from necessity and in part by his own strategic calculations. Withholding his final judgment, permitting voice to other views, he was once more allowing the snakes to come out of their holes. His enemies' views were solidifying. The battle lines were being drawn.

But I knew Mao was furious with the party leadership. One night in the midst of the meeting, while we were studying English, he suddenly said, "All the good party members are dead. The only ones left are a bunch of zombies."

I was astounded. Only with the outbreak of the Cultural Revolution five years later would I know for certain who those "zombies" were and realize that he would be happy to see them dead, too.

49

Mao did not attend most of the meetings in Lushan where the party debated about how to cope with the disaster as peasants still starved by the millions. Mao never admitted that he was in disgrace, never openly acknowledged that the Great Leap Forward had failed, and he still resented being reminded of the catastrophe his policies had caused. But his withdrawal from public life was the behavior of a man in disgrace.

He no longer spoke of meeting and mingling with the masses, no longer sought the limelight, though I am certain he felt the Chinese people still adulated him. His life depended on the admiration of others. He craved affection and acclaim. As his disgrace within the party grew, so did his hunger for approval. Lin Biao's campaign to study the thoughts of Mao was one way to feed this craving. His women were another. They adored him, worshiped him. He needed his women more, and he needed more of them, because he had lost so much face.

Jiang Qing joined Mao in Lushan, staying with him in the old Chiang Kai-shek villa. Her presence was an impediment to his liaisons. There were dancing parties every night, and Mao's dancing partners were many, but Jiang Qing was there, too.

He mollified Jiang Qing with a poem. It bothered her that her husband wrote poetry for other women—a paean to his first wife, Yang Kaihui, and another to a more recent liaison—but that she herself had never been the subject of her husband's verse. When she presented Mao with some of the magnificent photographs she had taken in Lushan—she spent much of her time there pursuing her hobby and had become a genuinely skilled photographer—he granted her wish and inscribed one of the best with a poem:

> At bluegreen twilight I see the rough pines
> serene under the rioting clouds.
> The cave of the gods was born in heaven,
> a vast wind-ray beauty on the dangerous peak.

Jiang Qing was delighted. She showed Mao's poem to everyone she met and was inspired to compose her own poem in praise of herself. Entitled, "On Self," it was embarrassingly inept and immodest:

> Overlooking the river a soaring peak
> Its face obscured in mists
> Mostly it is not beheld
> Just occasionally its majesty is revealed.

The "soaring peak" was a play on the characters that made up Jiang Qing's name, and she was claiming that others unjustly prevented her grandeur from shining through. Jiang Qing wanted everyone to think she was a woman of great talent victimized by circumstances. During the Cultural Revolution she would make her poetry a rallying cry on her behalf.

Having satisfied Jiang Qing with a poem, Mao withdrew, like an emperor, to his private world. I joined him every day just after he woke, and we would swim together in the reservoir next to the comfortable, modern new villa the Jiangxi provincial committee had constructed for him, even as the peasants went hungry, after the meetings in 1959. He used the building for the many clandestine meetings he wanted to keep hidden from his wife and the party elite, retreating to it after his swim. His favorite during this visit was a young nurse from the Lushan sanatorium, whose acquaintance he had first made during the Lushan meetings in 1959.

Sometimes, in an effort to escape from the prying eyes of Jiang Qing and others, Mao would take me and a few women down the mountain to the Yangtze River town of Jiujiang. There they would swim in the river and cavort at the guesthouse. But the summer heat would soon become oppressive, and we would wend our way back up to the "soaring peaks."

It was while we were in Lushan during that summer of 1961 that Mao invited his second wife, He Zizhen, to visit.

Sometime that spring or early summer, He Zizhen had written a letter to Mao warning him of trouble. "You should pay close attention to the people around you," she wrote. "Some of them might belong to the Wang Ming faction and try to do you harm." Wang Ming, the leader of the Bolshevik faction of returned students who had challenged Mao in the early 1930s, right after Mao and He Zizhen were married, had long been in disgrace and had spent the 1950s in the Soviet Union. He posed no threat to Mao. He Zizhen's mind had gone sometime after she and Mao were separated. They never got a formal divorce. When Mao lost interest in He, shortly after their arrival in Yanan in 1935, after she had become one of a handful of women to complete the Long March, she had gone, or been sent, to the Soviet Union, passing the difficult war years there together with her daughter, Li Min, and Mao's sons—Mao Anying and Mao Anqing. Soviet psychiatrists had diagnosed her as schizophrenic, and her psychological problems had continued after her return to China. Mao had set her up in a comfortable house in Shanghai at government expense, but she had never returned to normal.

Mao wrote, assuring his former wife that the Wang Ming faction was no longer a threat and that he had sent some of them down for reform and others away to study. Don't worry. Take good care of yourself, he reassured her. "Whenever you can, try to take a look at our socialist construction work."

Now he wanted to see her.

Mao arranged for the director of the Shanghai public security bureau to send He Zizhen a carton of foreign-made "555" cigarettes and one thousand *yuan,* and asked the public-security personnel to accompany her to Lushan. The Shanghai officials used He Zizhen's younger brother, an officer in the garrison command there, as an intermediary.

She arrived during the party meetings, and I went with Mao to receive her in the new villa.

He Zizhen was elderly by then. Her hair was silver-gray and she walked with the unsteady gait of the aged. But her pallid face burst with delight as soon as she saw Mao.

Mao rose immediately and walked toward her, taking her hands into his, and escorting her to a chair as He Zizhen's eyes filled with tears.

He gave her a little hug and said with a smile, "Did you get my letter? Did you receive the money?" He was good to her, as gentle and kind as I had ever seen him.

"Yes, I received your letter and also the money," she said.

Mao wanted to know more about her life and about the medical treatment she was receiving. Her voice was barely audible, and after the brief flash of recognition her words became incoherent. She seemed flushed with excitement, but her face had gone blank. Mao invited her to have dinner with him, but she refused.

"All right," Mao said soothingly. "We have seen each other now, but you haven't talked much, have you? After you go back, listen to your doctor and take good care of yourself. We'll see each other again."

And then she was gone.

For a long while after she left, I remained with Mao as he sat silently, smoking cigarette after cigarette, overcome with what I took to be melancholy. I had never seen him in such a mood. I sensed in him a great sorrow over He Zizhen.

Finally, he spoke. He was barely audible. "She is so old. And so sick."

He turned to me. "This Dr. Su Zonghua, the one who treated Jiang Qing last time in Guangzhou, is he the same doctor who has been treating He Zizhen?"

I said that he was.

"And what is her illness called after all?"

"It is called schizophrenia."

"What is schizophrenia?"

"It is a condition in which the mind cannot correctly relate to reality. Its cause is not yet clearly understood, and the drugs used to treat it have not proven very effective."

"Is it the same illness that Mao Anqing has?"

I told him that it was and reminded him that Mao Anqing was under treatment in Dalian.

Mao said that probably neither of them could be cured and that there was nothing we could do.

I could only nod in agreement.

In 1962, in Shanghai, I saw him in a similar mood when he brought the woman with whom he had had his first sexual experience as a teenager to visit. Some fifty years had passed, and the woman was old and gray. Mao gave her two thousand *yuan* and sent her home. "How she has changed," he said.

To my knowledge, Jiang Qing never knew about either meeting.

50

Nineteen sixty-two was a political turning point for Mao. In January, when he convened another expanded Central Committee work conference to discuss the continuing disaster, his support within the party was at its lowest. Seven thousand cadres attended—party and military officials from the regional bureaus, provinces, cities, prefectures, and counties, together with managers of industry and mining—so the event has been known ever since as the 7,000 cadres' conference. The participants were not the select party elite who made the decisions about how the country would be run but the cadres responsible for implementing higher-level decisions in their local areas. In Beijing, they ate good food, stayed in good hotels, and were well entertained at night. The leadership wanted their support.

Liu Shaoqi was in control, but he consulted Mao about the speech he was preparing for the 7,000 cadres' conference. Mao said he did not want to see it. He wanted the meeting to be "democratic," he said. The participants would be encouraged to present their own opinions, based on their experiences in their own jurisdictions, and the draft of Liu's speech would then be revised on the basis of what the participants had said.

But Mao was not prepared for Liu's speech. Liu refused to accept Mao's official explanation that the country's economic disasters had been caused by the weather. "Natural disasters hit only one region of the country," he argued in his address in the Great Hall of the People. "Man-made disasters strike the whole country. We must remember this lesson." He wanted to bring back the leaders who had been purged for opposing the "left adventurism" of the Great Leap Forward—the local cadres who had been supporters of the more balanced view of Peng Dehuai. He was making preparations to exonerate them.

I knew the Chairman was furious. "He's not using the class stand-point," Mao complained to me right after the meeting. "He's not addressing the question of whether we are going the capitalist road or the socialist road. He talks about natural disasters versus man-made disasters. This kind of talk is a disaster in itself."

But Liu Shaoqi's viewpoint was widely shared. The party was badly divided. So bleak was the situation in China, there was so little agreement on vital issues, that the meetings went on for more than a month, as one disillusioned local official after another railed against the troubles facing the country and the policies that had brought us there.

But the meeting was cathartic. Mao, as usual, rarely attended. While administrators from all over the country met nearby to pour out their complaints, Mao spent most of his time in the Great Hall of the People's Room 118, ensconced on his extra-large bed, "resting" with the young women assembled there for his pleasure, reading the daily transcripts of the proceedings that were taking place in the same building.

With Mao in retreat, the basic-level cadres were able at last to end the pretensions of the Great Leap Forward, to confront the stark reality of the economic disaster. The local-level cadres had been under tremendous pressure throughout the Great Leap. The slogan of the day, "Go all-out, aim high, achieve better and faster results," had pushed them to set ever higher and more impossible production targets, and they risked being labeled rightists or worse and losing their jobs if they kept the targets low or failed to fulfill the ones they set. They had lied and cheated when the targets proved impossible to meet, and with pressure still coming from the top, they were being blamed for much that went wrong. The 7,000 cadres' conference was their oppor-tunity to pour forth their complaints against the party leadership. A giddy euphoria set in as they got to speak their minds.

The complaints were never directed against Mao. They were focused instead on the policies of the Great Leap Forward. But every-one knew the policies were Mao's. To criticize the policies was to criticize Mao.

Mao did not like what he was reading in the daily transcripts. "They complain all day long and get to watch plays at night. They eat three full meals a day—and fart. That's what Marxism-Leninism means to them," he said to me one day. Required by protocol to be on hand around the clock, I was spending a boring month pacing the corridors of the Great Hall, listening to gossip, and reading in my office just adjacent to Mao's suite.

Finally, as the criticisms continued, Mao was forced to admit that at least some of the responsibility for the disaster was his. No one, so far as I knew, ever directly suggested to Mao that he offer a self-criticism. It was part of his political strategy.

Mao was loath to admit his mistakes. His was a life with no regrets. In 1960, I had heard him tell Britain's colorful Field Marshal Montgomery that he had "done a lot of stupid things and made a lot of mistakes," but to ranking party leaders or the people of China, Mao was psychologically incapable of admitting that the catastrophe besetting the country had anything to do with him. His self-criticism was the first Mao had made since coming to power in 1949. "For all errors directly or indirectly attributable to the central authority, I am responsible," he said in his speech on January 30, 1962, "because I am Chairman of the central authority." But Mao never said concretely what his mistakes had been, and he quickly countered by making certain that others took responsibility, too. "I don't mean that others should try to evade their responsibilities," he said. "Indeed, many others also have a share of the responsibility. But I should be the first person to assume responsibility for the errors." Then he began attacking the household contract agricultural system.

I am convinced Mao never really believed he had done anything wrong. But in retrospect I can see his fear even then that he was losing control of the party and China. He intended to remain the center, the nucleus, of the nation even as he retreated to the second line. Giving Liu Shaoqi the position of chairman had been a test of his loyalty, and by 1962 and the 7,000 cadres' conference, Mao was becoming convinced that Liu was less than loyal. The country had two chairmen, two centers, two nuclei, and that Mao could not accept. Thus he "took responsibility" for the disasters only to reassert his position at the center, not because he believed he had done anything wrong.

Lin Biao was one of the few supporters Mao had left, and the most vocal. Lin's speech followed directly after Mao's. "The thoughts of the Chairman are always correct," he said. "If we encounter any problem, any difficulty, it is because we have not followed the instructions of the Chairman closely enough, because we ignored or circumscribed the Chairman's advice."

I was sitting behind the stage, hidden by a curtain, during Lin's speech. "What a good speech Vice-Chairman Lin has made," Mao said to me afterward. "Lin Biao's words are always so clear and direct. They are simply superb! Why can't the other party leaders be so perceptive?" I knew then that Mao's self-criticism had been staged, that he had not been sincere in admitting his "mistakes." But even then I was skeptical of Lin. He had been out of the limelight so long, without major responsibilities and so uninvolved in the country's affairs, that his speech seemed insincere. Almost everyone involved in administering the party and the state was dissatisfied with Mao and the Great Leap Forward. Lin Biao had ulterior motives.

Hua Guofeng, the former party secretary of Xiangtan prefecture in Mao's native Hunan, whom I had first met in 1959, was more sincere and less sycophantic than Lin, but his refusal to criticize Mao won the Chairman's appreciation. At the 7,000 cadres' conference, Hua pointed out again, as he had the year before, that "after our great undertakings of 1958, 1959, and 1960, the people have lost weight, the cattle have lost weight, even the land has lost weight. We cannot try for great undertakings anymore." But at this meeting, Hua coupled that observation with a bow toward Mao. "If we want to overcome the difficulties in our rural areas," he said, "we must insist on going the socialist road and not on adopting the household contract system or individualized farming. Otherwise we will come to a dead end."

"Hua Guofeng is an honest man," Mao had said to me after the meetings in January 1962. "He's a lot better than many of our national leaders." With the purge of Zhou Xiaozhou and his supporters in Hunan and the promotion of Zhang Pinghua to first party secretary, several provincial-level slots had been freed. Hua Guofeng was promoted to head the party secretariat in Hunan, in charge of day-to-day affairs of the province. Mao liked what he did there.

The retreat from the Great Leap Forward continued after the 7,000 cadres' conference and so did the centrifugal force tearing the party asunder. Party and state operated increasingly independent of Mao. The communes were finally restructured, cut back in scale, with production organized at a smaller, more manageable level, equivalent to the small-scale collectives of 1956. Industrial targets were lowered again. The whole economy was to be restructured, and the leftist line of the Great Leap Forward continued to be roundly criticized.

In February and March, when the State Commission on Science and Technology convened a meeting of scientists in Guangzhou, there was even a movement to exonerate the intellectuals, despite Mao's known antagonism to them. The country's scientists and intellectuals had never recovered from the anti-rightist campaign of 1957, when hundreds of thousands had been fired, demoted, or sent to do labor reform. A pall of depression continued to hang over the intellectual community. Even those who had not suffered direct political persecution existed in a perpetual state of fear, afraid to speak out, often unable to work in their chosen profession or forced to attend so many political meetings that their capacity to work had suffered. Vice-Premier Chen Yi's speech at the science-and-technology conference set a new tone. "There is something other people won't dare to say, but I will," he declared to the embattled intellectuals. "China needs intellectuals, needs scientists. For all these years, they have been unfairly treated. They should be restored to the position they deserve." His words were a direct affront to Mao, but he gave the intellectuals new hope that their services were needed and their contributions appreciated.

At the same meeting, Zhou Enlai's keynote speech, "On the Question of Intellectuals," further reversed the anti-intellectual trend that had prevailed since the anti-rightist campaign. Zhou told the group that in socialist China most of them could be counted as members of the laboring class and therefore friends of socialism, and he argued that "to destroy superstition does not mean to destroy science." Destroying superstition, in fact, meant relying on scientists. He urged scientists and intellectuals to become actively, wholeheartedly involved in the nation's development effort.

The scientists were as happy about their meeting as the local-level officials had been about the 7,000 cadres' conference, and they easily succumbed to Zhou's flattery. In speech after speech, they poured forth their gratitude for the concern the party was showing them. The "rightists" were particularly elated. Their labels might soon be removed. They might be called back to respectable work again.

Zhou knew, as did his audience, that Mao had led the 1957 attack against intellectuals, asserting that professors were ignorant and calling upon the workers and peasants to cast off their "superstitious" inferiority complex. Zhou would never speak without the approval of Mao. His speech was the official word of a representative of the party center. Both Mao and the politburo had approved his speech in advance.

But reading the transcripts of the meeting after the fact, Mao was unhappy with the tone of the conference. "There's something I would like to ask," he said to me sarcastically one night after reading the report. "Who makes history—the workers and peasants, the laboring people—or someone else?" Mao remained convinced that only the workers and peasants, not scientists and intellectuals, made history. Peasant rebellions had been the driving force of Chinese history.

Shortly after the meetings where Zhou Enlai's liberal, conciliatory views had been so well received, Mao decided to call another, less public, meeting to discuss the position of intellectuals in Chinese society. No longer able to work his will through normal bureaucratic channels, he was beginning to marshal his forces behind the scenes, formulating his strategy and mustering support for a later counter-attack. Quietly, unobtrusively, he began mobilizing people sympathetic to his views. One of these was Chen Boda, Mao's leading political secretary and editor in chief of the party's theoretical journal, *Red Flag*. Chen Boda, Mao had decided, was the party's leading Marxist theoretician. "No revolution can proceed without a theory," Mao said to me. "Chen Boda is one of the very few theoreticians our party has."

Chen Boda was no theorist, but he had written well and extravagantly in praise of the Great Leap Forward. Quoting Marx that one day under communism is equal to twenty years under capitalism, Chen Boda had asserted that with the Great Leap Forward, the dawn of Chinese communism had arrived. So rapidly was China progressing, Chen suggested, that China was accomplishing in one day what took twenty years to accomplish under capitalism. China had been transformed. Communism was around the corner.

Confronted two years later with the massive starvation during the Great Leap Forward, Chen dismissed the millions of deaths. "This is an unavoidable phenomenon in our forward march," he declared. No wonder Mao liked this mean, petty, and ambitious man. In one simple sentence, he absolved Mao of responsibility for one of the greatest catastrophes the country had ever faced—a catastrophe for which Mao's policies were directly responsible.

Mao turned to Chen in 1962 for help in steering the country back to the left. It was Chen Boda who organized the meeting to reassert the true Maoist view of intellectuals. Mao addressed the meeting, and the message he delivered was at obvious odds with Zhou Enlai's earlier speech. "Intellectuals work in offices," Mao said. "They live well, eat well, dress well. They don't walk very much. This is why they often catch colds." Mao wanted the nation's college students, university faculty, and administrators to spend five months doing manual labor in factories and the rural areas—a move that intellectuals were sure to see as yet another form of punishment. Mao wanted them to participate in class struggle and learn about revolution.

"Things are getting complicated now," Mao continued. "Some people are talking about a household contract system, which is really nothing but a revival of capitalism. We have governed this country for all these years, but we are still able to control only two thirds of our society. One third remains in the hands of our enemy or sympathizers of our enemy. The enemy can buy people off, not to mention all those comrades who have married the daughters of landlords."

I had no idea what Mao was talking about, but his hostility to intellectuals and to other ranking leaders was too obvious for me to ignore. When the Cultural Revolution began several years later and Jiang Qing came to power, she labeled the science-and-technology meeting chaired by Chen Yi and Zhou Enlai a "black conference," accusing "certain" party leaders—meaning Zhou and Chen—of having kowtowed to bourgeois intellectuals by removing their bourgeois hats and replacing them with "the hat of the laboring class."

Liu Shaoqi's work also continued to be at odds with Mao. Liu was working to bring the victims of Mao's 1959 purges back into the service of the country. Within the party, it was a popular move. During the 7,000 cadres' conference—quietly, behind the scenes, and unknown to me at the time—people had begun raising the issue of Peng Dehuai. This purge had been unfair, they were saying. They were beginning to compare Peng Dehuai to Hai Rui, the upright Ming dynasty official purged by the emperor for his sound advice and wise criticism—the official Mao claimed to admire.

Liu Shaoqi may well have agreed. By April, the central secretariat, under Liu's direction, had issued a set of guidelines for rehabilitating people who had been purged for supporting Peng Dehuai and criticizing the Great Leap Forward. Called "On the Reevaluation of the Work of Party Cadres and Party Members," the guidelines would exonerate at least 70 percent of the accused cadres. Only the purge of Peng Dehuai would not be reconsidered. Even Liu Shaoqi would not override Mao on the case of Peng.

Liu did not ask Mao's approval for the process of rehabilitation, nor did An Ziwen, the director of the party's Organization Department and thus the person in charge of political rehabilitations. Mao got hold of a copy of the guidelines nonetheless. He gave me the document to read. "It seems this An Ziwen never reports his work to the central authority," Mao said, "so the comrades at the center know nothing about the activities of the Organization Department. He is blocking information from reaching us, setting up an independent kingdom. They are exerting pressure on me, don't you think?"

Tian Jiaying told me that when An Ziwen learned of Mao's criticism, he was furious. "The center? Who is the center?" he asked. "There are a number of leading comrades in Beijing—Liu Shaoqi, Deng Xiaoping, Peng Zhen. They are in charge of day-to-day administration of the party. When I report to them, am I not reporting to the center?"

Chen Yun was another ranking party leader who was clearly at odds with Mao. Chen was a vice-chairman of the party, nominally at the pinnacle of power, but his relations with Mao had long been strained and he had little influence. Mao viewed him as something of a rightist, and the two rarely met. With the agricultural disasters of the early 1960s, Chen Yun was convinced that the only solution was a dissolution of the communes and a return of land to the peasants, and after the 7,000 cadres' conference, he was put in charge of directing the party's economic and financial work. When he submitted a report detailing his suggestions for managing the crisis and turning land back to the peasants, Mao refused to approve it. This "paints a very dark picture," he wrote in the margins, "showing not one trace of light. This man, Chen Yun, came from a small businessman's background. He cannot get rid of his bourgeois character. He leans consistently to the right."

For the party chairman to accuse one of the vice-chairmen, the man in charge of the economy, of having a bourgeois character and leaning consistently to the right was incendiary. Chen Yun was much higher in the party hierarchy than Peng Dehuai. Mao's accusation could split the party apart. So inflammatory were Mao's words, so damaging to Chen Yun, so dangerous to party unity, that Tian Jiaying took the unprecedented step of ordering Lin Ke, who had recently returned from exile, not to forward the document with Mao's comments to the central secretariat. If it had been forwarded, the document could be used in future attacks against Chen Yun.

Tian had no authority to stop such an important transmission, but he admired Chen Yun and agreed with his judgment. He did not want to foster a split at the highest levels of the party. Lin Ke hid the document under his mattress. It was not transmitted to the top.

Someone—I never knew who—must have told Chen Yun what Mao had written because Chen immediately retreated to Suzhou to recover from an "illness" that could only have been political. Chen was never dismissed from his post, nor was he ever directly attacked. But never again during Mao's lifetime did he play an active role in politics. Not until 1980, after the Cultural Revolution and Mao's death, did Chen Yun return to the political stage. Ironically, having retreated when he learned of Mao's critique, he was spared many of the agonies of the Cultural Revolution. Because he was not working then, the attacks against him were mild compared to what others suffered.

The purloined document attacking Chen Yun was recovered in

1964. Xu Yefu, a rival of Lin Ke's, who had returned as Mao's confidential secretary after the discovery of the bugging devices, knew about the incident and had Lin's apartment searched while Lin was away on a trip with Mao. The hidden document was found, and Xu Yefu forwarded it to the central secretariat and reported the case to both Mao and Wang Dongxing. Lin Ke was dismissed from Group One for good. No one replaced him. Xu Yefu became Mao's exclusive confidential secretary. Tian Jiaying escaped censure at the time. But when the Cultural Revolution began, he was the first of Mao's staff to be attacked.

Seeing the plight of my friend Lin Ke and listening to the vicious attacks against him, I was doubly grateful that I had not accepted Mao's offer to serve as his secretary. Had I agreed, I would have been attacked, too.

Wang Dongxing thought me overly sensitive when I told him of my suspicions that Mao was growing increasingly disenchanted with the top leadership of the party. "We aren't the Communist party of the Soviet Union," he insisted. "The Chinese Communist party is united." But I was listening carefully to Mao. The situation was tense.

51

Mao had reached his Yellow River. He was determined to push on. In the summer of 1962, he emerged from his retreat. When he told me he would call two major party conferences in the upcoming months, I knew that his counteroffensive was about to begin. What I did not know was who would be attacked first.

The first party conference, held in Beidaihe on August 6, was a relatively small gathering of leaders at the rank of provincial first party secretary, minister, and above. Mao delivered a speech called "Classes, the Situation, and the Contradiction." Mao had spent much of his time in retreat formulating his theoretical justification, in Marxist terms, of the attacks he was about to launch against his own party. He could not simply purge the leaders he did not like. He did not have the power. Like all Chinese leaders, he needed Marxist morality to justify his actions. By relying on Marxist morality, he could mobilize the masses against the leaders he wanted to purge.

His justification was the argument that classes do not disappear with the introduction of socialism. Even after the collectivization of property, classes continue to exist, Mao said, and class struggle persists. Contradictions between the bourgeoisie and the proletariat, between the capitalist road and the socialist road, continue too, he said, and so does class struggle.

With the Tenth Plenum of the party's Eighth Central Committee that met the following month, in September 1962, Mao's theoretical justification for his counterattack was further refined. Not only do classes and class struggle continue to exist, Mao asserted, but the battle between the proletariat and the bourgeoisie will be protracted and sometimes severe. "In the historical period from the proletarian revolution to the proletarian dictatorship, and in the transitional period from capitalism to communism, which may last several decades or longer, a class struggle between the proletariat and the bourgeois classes, a struggle between the capitalist road and the socialist road, still exists," he said. China was facing a danger of capitalist restoration that had to be fought through relentless class struggle.

Still later he would argue that the party itself had become a haven for capitalists. Members of the bourgeoisie were right in the party ranks.

His two speeches were filled with invective, and his attacks were wide-ranging. He lashed out against intellectuals, further reversing the conciliatory stance of Zhou Enlai and Chen Yi. A union between intellectuals and workers is premature, Mao asserted. "The party has not yet properly educated the intellectuals. The bourgeois spirit hangs like a ghost over their heads. They are vacillating."

He struck out against Peng Dehuai, too. Peng had submitted a lengthy appeal for his political rehabilitation, professing his support for the people's communes and asserting that he had never formed an anti-party group or colluded with the Soviet Union. Instead of accepting Peng's appeal, Mao escalated the charges, accusing him now of having colluded not only with the Soviet Union but with all reactionary forces of the world, including even, he implied, the United States. Peng, Mao said, had been trying to conduct a worldwide counterrevolutionary, anti-communist chorus. There would be no reversal of verdicts on Peng Dehuai or those who had sympathized with his views. Exoneration of the enemy was out of the question.

Then he turned his opprobrium against the Panchen Lama of Tibet, denouncing him as "an enemy of our class." Tibet's chief spiritual leader, the Dalai Lama, had fled to India in 1959 when negotiations between the central Chinese government and Tibetan leaders had broken down and many Tibetans had rioted. A crackdown had followed, and the Panchen Lama, ordinarily subservient to Beijing, was now arguing that Beijing's so-called "democratic reforms" had moved too far to the left. He hoped that the ultraleftist trend in Tibet could be corrected.

Li Weihan, the director of the party's United Front, who had supported the Panchen Lama's views, was next to come under Mao's gun. Mao denounced him as a "capitulationist," accusing him of kowtowing to the Tibetan lords and criticizing him for promoting unity between intellectuals and workers. Li Weihan was dismissed from his position. The Panchen Lama was spared, but attacks against him continued. During the Cultural Revolution, the Panchen Lama spent nearly ten years under house arrest.

Wang Jingxian, head of the central party offices responsible for liaison with foreign Communist parties, had suggested improving ties with the Soviet Union and Eastern Europe while reducing economic aid to communist parties seeking the liberation of Asia, Africa, and Latin America. Wang was stripped of his power, accused by Mao of being a revisionist. Wang remained in his post, but his substantive responsibilities were transferred to deputy director Zhao Yimin.

Mao saw the system of contracting production to rural households as an example of the persistence of capitalism and ordered the practice halted. Advocates of the policy were capitalists and had to be purged. He attacked Deng Zihui and Liao Luyan, the two men responsible for the national direction of agriculture. Deng Zihui, director of the party's Rural Work Department and the man who had been encouraging a more moderate approach to agriculture since I joined Group One in the mid-1950s, was accused of being a veteran rightist of ten years' standing. Liao Luyan, the minister of agriculture under the State Council, who had argued that the mess of the Great Leap had more to do with policy than weather, was labeled a revisionist.

Anhui's Zeng Xisheng was among the first of the local leaders to be purged, just after the meetings concluded. The province's successful agricultural experiments were brought to an end, and agricultural production in the already poor and suffering countryside plunged further still.

Ge Man, the party secretary of Linxia prefecture, in Gansu province—a rival with Anhui for the dubious honor of poorest province in China—was next on Mao's list. Ge Man had introduced the contract responsibility system into Linxia prefecture and the results had been good. Agricultural production had increased. Gansu provincial party secretary Wang Feng, attributing the widespread hunger and poverty in Gansu to the formation of people's communes, fully supported Ge Man in his experiments. Mao accused both men of being "capitalist roaders," but only prefectural chief Ge Man was purged in 1962. Wang Feng did not lose his position until August 1966. When the Cultural Revolution began, he was among the first three people to be labeled by Mao as "counterrevolutionary revisionists." Ge Man suffered renewed attack at the same time and committed suicide.

The autumn of 1962 was a turning point for Mao and the party. Mao's insistence that classes persisted even under socialism effectively silenced the voices of reason, voices of potential dissent. The spirit of openness and daring that had characterized the 7,000 cadres' conference was reversed. Those who had the good of the country at heart, who believed that agricultural production would best be served by taking responsibility for agricultural management out of the hands of the collectives and the cadres and giving it back to the peasants, dared not push their views. Mao's arguments about classes and class contradictions provided the theoretical underpinnings for all the purges that followed, culminating, in 1966, with his Great Proletarian Cultural Revolution. To disagree with the Chairman was to risk becoming a counterrevolutionary and a "capitalist roader," and for Mao there was no greater crime.

The purges continued after the September 1962 Tenth Plenum, and the man Mao put in charge was Kang Sheng.

Kang Sheng was a longtime party member and had been with Mao in Yanan. Indeed, it was said that Kang Sheng had sponsored Jiang Qing's membership in the party and arranged for her to go to Yanan, where she met and married Mao. Kang Sheng and Jiang Qing were both from Shandong province and their close relationship went back long before the revolution of 1949.

I first met Kang Sheng in 1958. He had not been actively involved in politics after 1949. He had been hospitalized sometime around the communist takeover and was not released until the beginning of the Great Leap Forward, when he became one of its most vocal supporters. My friends, doctors responsible for his treatment at Beijing Hospital, told me he was suffering from schizophrenia, and I do not know why he was finally released. My contact with him was minimal—and strained. I saw him visit Mao occasionally, but their meetings were always private, and Kang Sheng never indulged in the same small talk, the easy give-and-take, of other leaders who visited the Chairman from time to time.

He and Jiang Qing became particularly close after 1966, during the Cultural Revolution, and they occasionally asked me to join them to watch Jiang Qing's favorite American movies. Jiang Qing was always solicitous and respectful of Kang, more solicitous than I ever saw her with anyone else. She asked his opinion on everything and took his answers to heart. She called him Kang Lao, one of the most respectful and affectionate forms of address available in the Chinese language. He was the only person to whom she ever accorded such an honor.

I usually tried to avoid Kang Sheng, sensing in him some deeper evil that I could never fully explain. He had the look of deceit about him. Even his photographs, I think, convey an air of evil. I associated him with the dark side of the party, with all the dirty work that had to be done, delving into people's pasts, finding new enemies, suggesting new targets for attack. I did not want to be part of that, nor would Mao have wanted me to be. There was much that I never knew.

Kang's political activities picked up after the Tenth Plenum. When Mao attacked Vice-Premier Xi Zhongxun, accusing him of supporting the rehabilitation of Gao Gang and of being anti-party, he put Kang Sheng in charge of investigating "the Xi Zhongxun anti-party plot." Kang Sheng's investigations implicated more than three hundred cadres from the party, government, and military, including Central Committee member Jia Tuofu, Ma Wenrui, the minister of labor under the State Council, and Bai Jian, vice-minister of the State Council's first ministry of machine building.

I knew Xi Zhongxun well, and the charges against him and his supporters were fabricated. But Kang Sheng's job was to depose and destroy his fellow party members, and his continuing "investigations" of ranking party leaders in the early 1960s laid the groundwork for the attacks of the Cultural Revolution to come. Many casualties followed immediately in the wake of the Tenth Plenum. Vice-Premier Xi Zhongxun was sent down to Henan and later put under house arrest. He remained in political disgrace until 1980. Many of the three hundred people falsely implicated suffered similar fates.

Mao also began trying to reassert control over agriculture following the Tenth Plenum, halting the trend toward private farming and trying to prevent what he saw as a capitalist resurgence. The process was slow, and the question of what had gone wrong with the Great Leap Forward was forgotten. Not until May 1963, at a meeting of the politburo and secretaries of the regional bureaus in Hangzhou, was Mao victorious. It was then that his draft "Resolution on Certain Problems of Rural Work at the Present Time" was discussed and passed. The resolution asserted that both feudal and capitalist forces were attempting to stage a comeback in the Chinese countryside, leading to sharp class struggle in the rural areas. Mao's solution to the problems was to launch what he called a "socialist education campaign" in the Chinese countryside. Class enemies had to be properly identified and brought to task, and local cadres and peasants had to be educated in socialism and class struggle.

From the protective bubble of Group One, I still knew little about what was going on in the Chinese countryside—except that the Great

Leap had been a catastrophe and recovery from the famine was slow. I did not understand Mao's socialist education campaign. Sitting on the train after the May 1963 Hangzhou meetings, talking to Wang Dongxing and Lin Ke, just before he left Group One for good, I questioned the policy. Just when communes were successfully restructured and peasants seemed to be getting back into a more reasonable routine, Mao wanted to stir things up again, I pointed out. He was calling on teams of urban cadres to go down to the villages to check into the economic and financial conditions of the people's communes. The presumption was that many of the local cadres had become corrupt during the famine. The city teams would both get a firsthand understanding of the hardships in the villages and act as outside investigators into cadre corruption in financial accounting, food distribution, property divisions, and the system of how commune members were paid.

Lillian was sent to join one of the first teams sent to the countryside, so the campaign had an immediate personal impact on me. With Lillian gone, I was left to take care of our two sons—John in junior high school and Erchong in kindergarten. But I had no way to care for two children. I was with Mao almost around the clock. And what if he decided to travel?

And what sense did it make to send Lillian, the daughter of a landlord, to conduct "socialist education"? Not only was she not a member of the Communist party, her family was considered the class enemy. What use could she be investigating and educating fellow class enemies?

But when I tried to intervene on her behalf, the director of the Institute of West Asian and African Studies at the Chinese Academy of Social Sciences, where she was a research fellow, told me that Lillian was being sent to the countryside precisely because of her "bad" class background. Witnessing how others like her were being reformed, she could be reformed herself. And everyone has a family, he told me. If people were exempted from the campaign just because they had no one to take care of their children, there would be no way to conduct the campaign. The central authority had ordered the campaign. Everyone had to cooperate, regardless of the difficulties.

Lillian left for the countryside in late September 1963.

I complained to Wang Dongxing. "Our leaders require us to work hard day and night," I told him, knowing he considered himself my leader, "and then they show no concern for our own personal difficulties. This is no way to treat people."

Wang asked the Central Bureau of Health to intervene, explaining confidentially to Lillian's boss that I was Chairman Mao's doctor. She was allowed to return immediately.

Liu Shaoqi was also having problems with Mao's socialist education campaign. Liu took it upon himself to revise Mao's original resolution on rural problems, proposing instead his own guidelines, "Regulations on Some Specific Policies in the Socialist Education Movement in Rural Areas (Draft)." When a Central Committee work conference met in September 1963 to discuss Liu's proposal, Mao was clearly upset, accusing Liu of trying to undermine his efforts to promote class struggle. I think, though, that what really bothered Mao was less the specific content of Liu's September proposal—what came to be called the Second Ten Points—than the fact that Liu had made the proposal at all. What angered Mao was that Liu Shaoqi had dared to revise Mao's document. Mao, after all, was always right. His original resolution, he was certain, laid out the country's rural problems in such clear and convincing terms that any revision could only muddy the waters.

Above all, Mao resented Liu's assertion of his own authority. In revising Mao's resolution, Liu was once again asserting control over the center. Mao considered himself, and himself alone, the center. There could not be two centers.

Mao grew angrier with Liu Shaoqi in 1964, when Liu sent his wife, Wang Guangmei, to head one of the work teams investigating the situation in Taoyuan (Peach Garden) production brigade in Hebei province. To send Wang Guangmei to the countryside was appropriate. Mao wanted cadres from Beijing to do this. What Mao resented was the fanfare that accompanied Wang Guangmei's departure and that upon her return she reported her experiences and observations to a huge gathering of cadres and thus became a model for all other work teams to follow. Mao did not like Liu giving power to his wife and was not pleased that both of them were upstaging him. Even then, difficult though it was to believe and much though I hoped it was not true, I sensed that Mao's real targets were people like Liu Shaoqi and Deng Xiaoping. For the time being he continued his usual practice of purging lesser figures while leaving the top leadership intact.

Ironically, while he was criticizing Liu for allowing his wife to participate in politics, Jiang Qing had been given new political responsibilities.

52

Jiang Qing had made her first public appearance on September 29, 1962, two days after the close of the Tenth Plenum. The occasion was a meeting with the wife of Indonesia's president Sukarno, and a photograph of the event, the first of Mao's wife ever published, appeared in the *People's Daily* the next day. As Mao shook hands with Mrs. Sukarno, Jiang Qing, dressed in a neat Western-style suit, stood between them, smiling broadly, while Zhou Enlai's wife, Deng Yingchao, hovered in the background. The *People's Daily* had already published several photographs of Liu Shaoqi's wife, Wang Guangmei. In his ceremonial position as head of the republic, Liu Shaoqi had been on hand to greet Mrs. Sukarno when she arrived at the airport. Wang had accompanied her husband, the wife of one head of state greeting the wife of another.

Jiang Qing's public appearance aroused widespread public attention. It was a violation of the longstanding prohibition against her involvement in politics, but as with Wang Guangmei, protocol demanded her presence. In fact, Jiang's appearance presaged an active political role. The world of Chinese culture and arts was about to fall under her hand, and culture and art would become the stage from which the Great Proletarian Cultural Revolution was launched.

Jiang Qing's new activities made my life easier at first. The more involved in politics she became, the more her hypochondria and neurasthenia eased. I was called less frequently to deal with her complaints or to mediate disputes between her and her nurses.

But Jiang Qing still had a vendetta against me, and political power gave her a new means to try to settle scores. My first brush with the new Jiang Qing came in early 1963.

I had learned that the renowned Beijing Opera Theater had been performing a newly revised version of *Red Plum*. I had found the opera thrilling in my youth, and now it was being staged with a new title, *Li Huiniang*. Prominent figures in the worlds of art and literature, including Tian Han, one of the country's leading playwrights, had written articles praising the opera for its depiction of the rebellion and revenge of an exploited woman. Liao Mosha, the director of Beijing's United Front Department, writing under the pen name Fan Xing, also praised the opera, arguing that there was nothing wrong with plays about ghosts.

I had last seen *Red Plum* as a child, and my memory of the story was fuzzy. What I remembered most was the scene in which a beautiful female ghost returns to earth, dancing gracefully across the stage in a diaphanous white silk gown. Long a fan of Beijing opera, I wanted to see the new production. But working with Mao left me no time to do so.

Then, coincidentally, Mao began talking about opera with me one night. He did not like operas about beautiful young females, he said. He preferred operas featuring middle-aged men. But I remembered that *Li Huiniang* had both beautiful females and middle-aged men. I thought that Mao, too, might enjoy the scene where the beautiful young actress seems to float across the stage. I suggested that he see it.

He agreed. "Let's have it performed at Huairen Hall here in Zhongnanhai," he said. "That way we all can see it. Tell Wang Dongxing to make the arrangements."

The performance became a special event within Zhongnanhai. Because Mao himself had requested the opera, all the other top leaders attended, too. Even Lillian joined us.

Midway into the performance, sitting just behind Mao, I realized I had made a terrible mistake. I had not remembered the story at all. The turning point in the opera comes when Song dynasty premier Jia Shidao, then an old man, is watching a song-and-dance performance from a boat on Hangzhou's West Lake, Mao's favorite retreat. Jia's many young concubines are gathered round. As they watch, the beautiful Li Huiniang, one of Jia's favorite concubines, spots a dashing young scholar and blurts out in spontaneous admiration: "What a handsome man!" she says, loudly enough for Jia Shidao to hear. Jia is so infuriated with the young woman's lapse in loyalty that he has his favorite concubine executed. The scene I had remembered was the concubine returning from the dead—a beautiful ghost seeking revenge on the man who had been both her lover and executioner.

Just at the point when the beautiful concubine cried out in admiration for the younger man, Mao's demeanor changed. Aside from his occasional outbursts of temper he rarely allowed himself overt displays of displeasure. But I had learned to read his changes in mood—the slight frown, the raised eyebrow, the stiffening of his body. I realized that I had unwittingly insulted him. The scene had struck too close to home, to Mao's own philandering and to his young women. It recalled Mao's refusal to allow one of them to marry the young man she loved and her accusations that he was a bourgeois womanizer.

At the opera's conclusion, when the performers took their curtain call, Mao stood up, sulky and glum, offering only three or four desultory claps and leaving without his usual friendly greetings and thanks to the performers. He was silent as we walked back. My intention to please him had been a terrible failure. I knew he would be angry with me, and I knew that eventually he would find a way to vent it.

Shortly afterward, Shanghai's leading newspaper, *Wen Hui Bao,* began printing articles criticizing both the man who had written the opera and Liao Mosha, arguing that the play was ideologically incorrect and suggesting that the problems had something to do with class struggle. Then the government banned any further staging of operas or plays that had anything to do with ghosts, and Mao began criticizing the Ministry of Culture for failing to give proper guidance to theatrical works, calling it a ministry "for the monarch and court officials, for talented young men, beautiful women, and dead foreigners." Suddenly an opera that I had seen as innocuous but beautiful was becoming a major political and ideological issue, a manifestation of the continuing class struggle that was part of Mao's new interpretation of China.

Several months went by and still I had not been implicated. Then Wang Dongxing came to see me. "We're in big trouble," he said. "Jiang Qing thinks *Li Huiniang* is a very bad opera, a big poisonous weed. It talks about ghosts. It praises superstition." Jiang Qing knew that Mao had not asked to see the opera himself but that someone had suggested it to him. She knew that none of the other top leaders, or Mao's political secretary Chen Boda, had made the suggestion. She knew that whoever did was both very close to the Chairman and a follower of Beijing opera. She knew that I was the only opera buff among Mao's inner circle and that Mao and I often talked about our mutual hobby. Only I could have made the suggestion. But she never mentioned my name.

Mao protected me, not out of friendship, but because he still needed me to serve as his doctor. When Jiang Qing asked him who had suggested the opera, he claimed not to remember. Wang Dongxing protected me, too, saying that he didn't know who made the suggestion and that he had merely been following orders when he arranged to have it performed. Besides, he knew nothing about opera—what was good and what was bad.

But Jiang Qing insisted on knowing and told Wang Dongxing to find out. "She has a bone to pick with you," Wang warned me. "She wants you out of here. She's been looking for an excuse for a long time, and now she's found one." Jiang Qing, he told me, was not going to let this go easily. She wanted to have me labeled a rightist.

Finally, Wang Dongxing and I decided to talk to Mao and suggest that we tell Jiang Qing that he decided to see the opera after reading Tian Han's article praising it. Mao agreed, and Wang Dongxing gave the article to Jiang Qing to read.

The Chairman's wife was delighted, but our plan was a disaster for Tian Han, for she now had an excuse to attack him. "So it's those people in literature and the arts who were behind it," she said to me after Wang had shown her the article. "Fine. Let the bastards come out so we can grab them. They can't get away with it." She was going to Shanghai. She and Ke Qingshi had become allies and they were going to work with Ke's cronies on a strategy of attack.

But she had to try one last time to coax me out of my hole.

"You saw *Li Huiniang* when it was performed here, didn't you?" she asked me casually, just before she left for Shanghai. "How did you like it?"

"The opera has been around for a long time," I replied. "It's a fantasy. It's similar to the revolutionary opera *White-Haired Girl.* They are both about young girls who are exploited by landlords."

She thought my theory strange and wondered how the two operas were alike.

I told her that they were both stories about oppressed females trying to get revenge. The white-haired girl is still alive but she is tortured so much she looks like a ghost. Li Huiniang becomes a ghost after she dies of torture.

But Jiang Qing thought I was talking nonsense. "Those two stories are completely different," she said. "Talking about ghosts promotes superstition. It's not good for the common people."

"But opera is art," I tried to explain. "The ghost is fantasy. Shakespeare's *Hamlet* has a ghost. It's not superstitious."

Jiang Qing did not agree. To her, ghosts were both superstitious and somehow a manifestation of class conflict. Shakespeare was both dead and English, and the plays of a long-dead foreigner were neither an accurate representation of reality nor progressive. "Just because Shakespeare's plays have ghosts doesn't mean we have to have ghosts, too," she said. "The Chairman has discovered many problems in literature and art that indicate serious class conflict. You had better pay attention to my words."

I was too conservative for Jiang Qing, still unable to escape the influence of my own bourgeois background. If I persisted in arguing with her, I knew she would have me labeled a rightist. The possibility was sobering. I was forty-three years old and already my hair had turned white from the anxiety of maneuvering within Group One. I had grown thin. But I had to survive, and self-interest required me to remain silent.

Jiang Qing left for Shanghai, where she relished her new role as overseer of culture. Ke Qingshi, loyal to Mao, was anxious to do his bidding and to assist Jiang Qing. He introduced her to Zhang Chunqiao, head of Shanghai propaganda. She had a busy schedule, visiting theaters, opera houses, dance troupes, and musical bands. "I am just a plain soldier, a sentry of the Chairman patrolling on the ideological battlefront," she would tell everyone she met. "I am keeping watch and will report what I find to the Chairman."

What she found, not surprisingly, was a world corrupted by capitalism, riddled with evil influences from the past.

On December 12, 1963, Mao asked me to read one of the results of Jiang Qing's investigations into Chinese culture—an article directed by Ke Qingshi called "Conclusive Report on the Revolutionary Changes in Plays and Operas in Shanghai." Mao had written comments on the document. "Take a look," he said. "We have established a socialist foundation in our economy, but the superstructure—literature and art—has not changed so much. Dead people are still in control of literature and the arts. We should not belittle our achievements in film, plays, folk songs, art, and novels. But problems still exist, and those problems are especially serious in the field of theater. We have to study this problem. Even party members are enthusiastically promoting feudal and capitalist art but ignoring socialist art. This is absurd."

Several months later, Mao turned his attack directly against the All China Federation of Literature and Art. "For the last fifteen years, the organizations and magazines under their control have not been carrying out the party's policy," he said. "They still act like overlords, shying away from close contact with the workers, peasants, and soldiers. They don't reflect the socialist revolution. They're moving in the direction of revisionism. If these organizations are not thoroughly reformed, one day they will become like the Hungarian Petöfi Club." When young Hungarian workers established the Petöfi Club in 1954 to advocate greater freedom and democracy, the government waited two years before decimating them in the crackdown of 1956. Mao was planning his own crackdown on dissidents within China.

53

It may not have been accidental that Mao introduced Jiang Qing to the political stage just as his private life was taking a different turn. Less than a month after Jiang Qing made her public debut, Mao was smitten by Zhang Yufeng, the woman who would later become his closest female companion. I had first seen them together in Changsha, Hunan, at an evening dance party arranged in Mao's honor by the new provincial party chief, Zhang Pinghua. The stewardesses on the train, including Zhang Yufeng, were invited, too, and after a few dances, Mao led her away by the hand, sending the other young women who had accompanied him to the party back to the train. Mao stayed in Changsha for another two days, and when the train journey resumed had Zhang transferred from the staff dining car to become an attendent in his own compartment.

Mao was not monogamous. Several women surrounded him whenever Jiang Qing was gone, and he never stayed with one for more than a few days at a time. He alternated as we traveled between the train and his villas, and in his villas, he would be joined by other females from his entourage. That fall of 1962, two confidential clerks were his favorites. In Shanghai, the two women joined him at the western suburbs (Xijiao) guesthouse—the magnificent complex of villas that Ke Qingshi had had constructed for Mao and other top leaders in the early 1960s, in the midst of the economic disasters. Set amid rolling fields crisscrossed by running brooks, the property had once belonged to a Shanghai industrialist. The lovely Japanese house the man had built for his Japanese concubine was still there. One of the new buildings was Mao's residence and the other his place of recreation, with a dance hall. Mao's pattern in Shanghai, though, was to spend most of his waking hours in the newly refurbished Jinjiang Club downtown, in the center of the old French quarter. Shortly after he woke in the afternoon, we would go there in his bulletproof Soviet-made ZIS, where he would peruse the documents that came to him daily and play with the young women until well after midnight, returning to the western suburbs through deserted, darkened streets at about two or three in the morning.

I always accompanied Mao to the Jinjiang Club, and so did the two young clerks, sitting together in the last of Mao's three-car cavalcade. Jiang Qing was also in Shanghai then, but she stayed behind in the villa and was asleep when the Chairman returned. Their schedules were so different that they rarely saw each other. By now, Jiang Qing must have known the truth about her husband's behavior. He returned to his villa only as a way of saving his wife's face. I had come to believe that Mao and his wife had reached some sort of understanding that in return for a public role as Mao's wife and a renewed pledge not to leave or divorce her, Jiang Qing agreed not to interfere with the growing number of young women around her husband. Mao had every reason to trust his wife politically. Without her husband she was nothing. And Jiang Qing could at last fulfill her political ambitions.

Years would pass before Zhang Yufeng established herself as Mao's most important confidante. He did not fully trust her at first. Zhang was from Mudanjiang county, in Manchuria's Heilongjiang province, where her "father" was a railway worker. But that area had been occupied by the Japanese in the 1930s, and Zhang Yufeng once told Mao that she had been born, in 1944, of a liaison between her mother and a Japanese dentist for whom her mother worked as a servant. Believing that Zhang Yufeng was half-Japanese, Mao also suspected that she was a Japanese spy. I never did know the full story behind Zhang Yufeng's parentage, but Mao's trust was long in coming.

My own relationship with Zhang Yufeng was rocky almost from the start. Our first minor altercation took place just after the Hangzhou meetings in May 1963 where Mao began pushing the socialist education campaign in the countryside. We were on the train back to Beijing when Mao called me into his compartment.

He was in bed, wearing nothing but his robe, and Zhang Yufeng was standing close beside him. Mao pointed to the left side of his chest and complained of an ache. "I don't feel well," he said.

There was a bright red pimple the size of a rice grain on Mao's left chest, but his temperature was normal and the nearby lymph nodes showed no sign of infection.

"Did he get it from scratching?" I asked. Mao had a long history of itchy skin and often scratched and pinched himself so hard that the skin broke. He often asked his attendants to scratch him, too. I suspected that this was how the infection had begun.

With her back to Mao, Zhang Yufeng winked at me, letting me know that the pimple had been scratched.

The problem was minor. I applied an antiseptic ointment and covered it with sterile gauze. "It will be fine soon," I assured Mao. "You don't need any medicine or a shot." But I told him the spot must not be touched. I advised applying a hot compress. Mao refused.

That evening, he called me to his compartment again. The gauze had disappeared and the pimple had ruptured and grown to the size of a soybean. Clearly, someone had squeezed it. The surrounding tissue was red and hard. A pink line extended from the small wound to his left armpit, and his lymph nodes were swollen. He was running a fever.

Mao resisted when I insisted on giving him a shot of penicillin. He wanted me to cut out the pimple instead. But it was too early for an incision. To drain the pus would make matters worse. But I convinced him to take some U.S.-made tetracycline capsules and told both him and Zhang Yufeng not to touch the spot again.

I was worried. Mao claimed that Zhang Yufeng had squeezed the pimple for him, and the infection was spreading. I could not trust either of them to leave the spot alone, and I was afraid that the infection might worsen. I called Shi Shuhan, the director of the Central Bureau of Health, in Beijing. Shi too was worried, and immediately informed Zhou Enlai of Mao's condition. Zhou wanted to dispatch other physicians to help me treat the Chairman.

Another doctor was hardly necessary from a medical perspective, but Wang Dongxing insisted that the problem was more than medical and accused me of being inflexible and naive. "You told the Chairman not to squeeze, but he squeezed anyway. He may ignore you again now. Let the other doctors come. They can share responsibility with you. If anything goes wrong, you can support each other. Words alone will be no defense. Believe me, this is not simply a question of medical technique."

Finally, I had to agree. I told Mao that Beijing wanted to send another doctor to treat him, too. He agreed that Ji Suhua, who ran

Beijing Hospital, could come. Dr. Ji flew immediately to Nanjing and boarded the train when we stopped.

By now, Mao's condition had worsened. The pimple had grown to a walnut-size abscess dotted with five or six spots of pus. Below the abscess was a carbuncle the size of a small peach. The lymph nodes under Mao's left armpit had swollen further.

Ji Suhua was nervous. He had never met Mao before. Mao tried to engage in his usual banter. He invited Dr. Ji to sit next to him and inquired about his name and birthplace. The doctor's surname was rare, and Mao wondered whether he had been related to a famous Qing dynasty writer and historian named Ji Luqi. Dr. Ji did not know.

"So you're just trying to be a good doctor, not paying so much attention to affairs of your clan?" Mao said, trying to put the doctor at his ease.

Dr. Ji was still nervous. His forehead was covered with perspiration and his hands were trembling. His nervousness only grew as his examination of the Chairman continued.

"Someone has squeezed this," he blurted out as soon as he looked at the abscess. Mao and Zhang Yufeng were suddenly silent.

"This is serious," Dr. Ji whispered to me when the exam was complete. We knew we would have to make an incision to drain the pus from the abscess, but the carbuncle made surgery risky. The infection could easily spread, causing potentially life-threatening septicemia. It was the most serious medical problem I had faced with Mao.

Mao's train compartment was too crowded to set up medical equipment, and I felt we should delay surgery, continue to administer tetracycline and apply hot compresses to Mao's left chest and armpit. Both Mao and Dr. Ji concurred, and we waited until the next day, when the abscess had softened somewhat, to undertake the first incision.

Our train arrived in Beijing shortly afterward. In another five days, the abscess had softened further, and a second, larger, incision was made. A large amount of pus drained out. The lymph nodes, however, did not improve, and three days later a third incision was performed on Mao's lymph nodes. Only then did Mao's recovery begin. By then it was the end of June.

By mid-July, the incisions were healing well, but the wound was still not completely closed. No one was happy with me. Jiang Qing was irritated because I would not let Mao go to Beidaihe with the top leaders. I was afraid that if Mao were to swim, the wound could become infected again, and I knew that no one could prevent Mao from swimming at Beidaihe. Jiang Qing grumbled that none of the other leaders would go without Mao. They could hardly go on vacation while Mao was still ill in Beijing. What if Mao wanted to meet with them? The whole summer, she said, was lost.

Mao, too, was upset because I had not foreseen how serious his situation would become. "Now you are telling me that everything is fine," he said after the incisions had begun to heal. "But when we were on the train, you told me that the problem was not serious and then it became serious. As a doctor, you have to anticipate both the good and the bad so you won't be caught short. First you said the incision would take only a few days to heal, and now ten days have passed and it's still not healed. You should have told me in the beginning that I could either become seriously ill or quickly recover. That way, you would have been well covered."

I promised that in the future I would be alert to both possibilities.

Zhang Yufeng was upset with me because I refused to exonerate her as the source of Mao's illness. I believed she must have squeezed the pimple without washing her hands. Mao blamed her, too, until his death. But because I was his doctor, the ultimate responsibility was mine, and I never forgave Zhang Yufeng for undermining my instructions. I never let her off the hook, and our relations were never good.

54

The first edition of the *Quotations from Chairman Mao* was published in May 1964. It was a small book, no bigger than the palm of a hand, covered in gaudy red plastic and filled with aphorisms drawn from Mao's speeches and writings. The cult of Mao had begun.

And so had a reversion from the practical, mundane demands of building a viable modern economy, as though nothing had been learned from the disasters of the Great Leap Forward. Ideological purity, not expertise, was what mattered. Lin Biao was at the forefront of the movement. He introduced the slogan of the "four firsts": Put the human factor first; political work first, ideological work first; and living ideas first.

Mao loved the adulation, returning Lin's flattery with compliments of his own. "Lin's idea of the four firsts is a great creation," Mao said. "Who said we Chinese cannot create and invent things?" Mao ordered the whole nation—schools, industry, communes—to learn from Lin Biao and the People's Liberation Army. "The merit of the Liberation Army," Mao said, "is that its political ideology is correct." The army set up political departments in work units everywhere in China to teach the thought of Mao. "Only this way can we whip up the revolutionary spirit of the tens of millions of cadres and workers in our industries, in commerce, and in agriculture," Mao said. Suddenly all of China was engaged in political study, reading Chairman Mao's works, reciting by heart the most simplistic of the Chairman's writings.

The cult of Mao was spreading to every factory and school and commune in China. The party Chairman was becoming a godhead.

Not everyone shared Lin Biao's worship of Mao or wanted to push his cult. The more pragmatic and sober-minded members of the party leadership were outspoken in their criticisms of Lin. Deng Xiaoping, then serving as secretary-general of the party Central Committee, and Lu Dingyi, the director of propaganda, insisted that Mao's little red book was both an oversimplification and a vulgarization of Marxism and Mao. To tout Mao as the greatest of all Marxist-Leninists, they argued, was to create needless divisions within the Marxist ranks.

Luo Ruiqing, then chief of the general staff and secretary-general of the Military Affairs Commission, was appalled. "If Mao Zedong's thought is really the most advanced and creative development of Marxism-Leninism, does that mean there is no room for further development of Marxism or of Mao? Is there a second most advanced? A second most creative?" Luo saw recitations from the little red book as a needless exercise in forced memorization, a silly effort to find answers to everything where answers could not be found, a separation of reality and theory.

Luo also took great exception to Lin's views on military matters. Lin Biao still believed that guerrilla tactics were the only way to fight a war and argued that ideology was more important than weapons, revolutionary ideals more important than strategy. By 1964, China's relations with onetime big brother the Soviet Union had deteriorated to the brink of war, and Lin was arguing that victory depended on imbuing soldiers with the thought of Mao Zedong. Luo Ruiqing had a different, more practical view. He thought soldiers needed weapons, too, and he wanted to train the Chinese army to fight a modern war.

Mao was not happy with leaders who objected to the cult of personality. But he was not yet able to strike out directly against them. He found other scapegoats instead. The Central Bureau of Health was one.

In the spring of 1964, as the party leadership was squabbling about the little red book, Liu Shaoqi contracted tuberculosis. Vice-minister of public health Xu Yunbei brought me the news and asked me to tell Mao so as to prepare him for the more formal written report on Liu's health that would follow.

Mao seemed neither concerned nor surprised when I told him. Indeed, a flicker of satisfaction crossed his face. "What's everyone so excited about?" he wondered. "If he's sick, then let him take a rest and have the doctors treat him. This has nothing to do with you. Don't get involved. Let other people handle it."

But Liu's illness galvanized Mao into action. Though he could not attack his rival directly, he could try to make Liu Shaoqi's life miserable. Mao issued a series of instructions concerning the health care of the highest leadership. The Ministry of Public Health was to terminate its special services to the top leaders. They would no longer have their own personal physicians. The Central Bureau of Health, responsible for ensuring that the leaders received only the most sophisticated health care, was to be abolished. Mao ordered that Beijing Hospital, which treated only the elite, be renamed Hospital for Serving Lords.

Mao had criticized the Central Bureau of Health and Beijing Hospital before. "Those lords live in luxury and comfort," he had said, referring to the life-style of the top leaders. "Medical services are always available to them. Even with the most minor health problem, they receive the greatest of care."

The Central Bureau of Health was completely unprepared for Mao's attack, and its director, Shi Shuhan, was stunned. The entire Ministry of Public Health was thrown into turmoil, and the top leaders, from Liu Shaoqi on down, were upset.

No one dared challenge the order. But no one was willing to throw the leadership to the mercies of the country's public health-care system, either. A way had to be found both to comply with Mao's command and ensure that the leaders still received their special health care.

After lengthy discussions between representatives of the Central Bureau of Health and officials of the Ministry of Public Health under the State Council, a compromise was worked out. The Central Bureau of Health would be abolished and so would the Zhongnanhai Office of Health, which was jointly administered by the Central Bureau of Health and the Central Bureau of Guards. Shi Shuhan and Huang Shuze, formerly in charge of the Central Bureau of Health, were promoted to vice-ministers of public health, but much of their concrete work, overseeing the health of the highest leaders, remained the same. Most of the personal physicians serving the top-level leaders would be appointed to head departments in Beijing Hospital on call to serve the leadership when needed. Beijing Hospital would continue to serve the party elite, though Mao's orders required the hospital to open its doors to the public. Worried about how to guarantee the safety of the leaders being treated there, afraid that "bad elements" might do the leaders in, the Ministry of Public Health had to restrict public access. Its solution was to limit public services to the staff from work units in the hospital's immediate vicinity and to make the party leadership in each of those work units responsible for guaranteeing the political reliability of the patients.

Mao, of course, still had to have his own personal physician, but the Zhongnanhai Office of Health, which was my organization, had been abolished. I was appointed deputy secretary of the Committee on Medical Science under the Ministry of Public Health and the Science and Technology Commission. The Committee on Medical Science was formed to plan and direct high-level medical research, and I worked there in the mornings, spending my afternoons and evenings at Zhongnanhai with Mao. Like everyone else, I agreed that Mao should continue to have his own private doctor. He was the Chairman and he deserved his special privileges. Only much later did I come to regard it as unfair.

One issue remained to be solved. No one in the health-care profession wanted to change the name of Beijing Hospital to the Hospital for Serving Lords. But since Mao had ordered the change, only he could rescind the order. The task of persuading him to change his mind fell to me. Xu Yunbei and Shi Shuhan insisted.

I reported to Mao the proposed abolition of both the Central Bureau of Health and the Zhongnanhai Office of Health and my appointment to the Committee on Medical Science. "Only one problem remains," I concluded, after explaining the changes in great detail. "The name Hospital for Serving Lords doesn't sound right. The hospital was built in the 1920s by the Germans. It has always been called Beijing Hospital. Can we keep the name?"

Mao did not object. "Call it Beijing Hospital then. I'm glad it's open to the common people now."

Mao's own life did not change greatly with the restructuring of the elite health-care system. Nor did Jiang Qing's. Jiang Qing, because of her "poor health," continued to be served by a team of nurses, and I remained Mao's personal physician. Even though I worked mornings for the Committee on Medical Science, my work was inseparable from Mao. Since Mao's most frequent medical complaints were bronchitis and the common cold, all my efforts were spent researching how to treat or prevent those two illnesses.

For me, the greatest personal change was that my family moved out of Zhongnanhai. With the abolition of the Office of Health, we no longer had the right to live there.

We did not move far. The abolished Central Bureau of Health vacated its space in the beautiful old-fashioned courtyard complex in Gongxian Lane where I had had my first fateful meeting with Fu

Lianzhang on my return to China in 1949. Lillian and I and our two sons were assigned a comfortable four-bedroom old-style house in the complex. The setting was magnificent. Our courtyard was full of flowers, and the milky-white tuberoses seemed to bloom year-round. We marked our arrival by planting a date tree and soon it was yielding delicious fruit. Our new location was convenient to some of our favorite spots in the city—the Longfusi food market and the bustling shopping district of Wangfujing. Beijing Normal University High School, where my elder son was studying, was close enough for him to bike to, and a chauffeur-driven car took me back and forth to Zhongnanhai. The Polish embassy was redecorating its residences at about the time we moved, so we were able to buy old furniture from there at bargain prices to decorate our new home.

I was happy to be gone from Zhongnanhai. There, faced with so many restrictions, we had been prohibited from inviting our friends and relatives to visit us. Sitting at the window of our new place, looking out over our flower-filled courtyard, I could almost forget the tragedy of having had to give up my family's ancestral home. I could even forget Mao and Group One. I loved our new home.

Mao had only one regret about his decision to abolish the Zhongnanhai Office of Health. One night at three o'clock in the morning, shortly after I had moved to my new home, he called for me, apparently not realizing that I had moved to Gongxian Lane. "I never thought I was doing myself such a disservice," he said to me the next day. So I put a bed in my office in Zhongnanhai in order to be on call at night as well. I often slept there, and occasions to be with my family continued to be rare.

Mao's relations with Liu Shaoqi and Deng Xiaoping continued to deteriorate. In January 1965, Deng Xiaoping convened a party work meeting to discuss the socialist education campaign, which was focused on eliminating corruption among rural cadres and had as its slogan the "four cleanups"—cleaning up rural accounts, properties, granaries, and work points. Mao was not feeling well when the meeting convened, and Deng suggested that he not attend. But Mao did attend and delivered a speech arguing that the problem in the countryside was a contradiction between socialism and capitalism. Liu Shaoqi interrupted Mao's talk to argue that the conflict was not only one of class but of the "four cleans" and the "four uncleans" and of contradictions both within the party and outside the party. The next day, Mao brought copies of the country's constitution and the party's regulations to the meeting and argued that according to the constitution he was a citizen with the right to speak his mind, and that as a member of the party he also had the right to speak at meetings. He said that "one of you," meaning Deng Xiaoping, had tried to prevent him from participating in the meeting and another, meaning Liu Shaoqi, would not allow him to voice his opinions.

The Third Plenary Session of the People's Congress took place from December 21, 1964, to January 4, 1965. Into the "Report on the Work of the Government," to be presented by Zhou Enlai, Mao inserted several passages of his own. These passages indicated that he still believed in the idea of the Great Leap Forward, though he now placed the idea in a different context. He stated, "We cannot take the conventional road of economic development and crawl step by step after others. We must shatter the convention, adopt as much as we can the most advanced technology, and, within a relatively short period of time, build China into a strong, modern, socialist country. This is the idea of the Great Leap. . . . One of China's great revolutionary leaders, our predecessor Sun Yat-sen, said at the beginning of this century that a great leap would take place in China."

After Chinese New Year 1965, Mao left Beijing for a trip, taking with him two female confidential clerks. He also invited Wang Hairong, the granddaughter of his cousin Wang Jifan. On the train, Mao continued to have Zhang Yufeng as his special attendant. By the time he reached Wuhan, many women surrounded Mao and eagerly competed for his favors, squabbling constantly.

One morning, Wang Hairong burst into the duty office and complained bitterly to me. "How can you let a person like Zhang Yufeng work here? She is a shameless, ill-tempered woman, and very rude to the Chairman. Last night the Chairman said to me that Zhang was driving him crazy. He is advanced in age; we can't allow Zhang Yufeng to insult him. If you don't do something about her, I'll report the matter to the Central Authority."

"Take it easy," I said. "Tell me what happened."

"I cannot take it easy. I cannot stand it that this person insults the Chairman." She walked out of the office, looking for Wang Dongxing.

At this moment, the guard Xiao Zhang came in and said, "The Chairman is angry. He says Zhang Yufeng has gone too far; he wants to have a meeting called to criticize her."

Upon hearing of this incident, Wang Dongxing said to me with annoyance, "Do we always have to wash this kind of dirty laundry? How can we call a meeting on this matter? Mao's personal relations with these women are so tangled! How can a meeting decide anything?"

Still, Mao had asked for a meeting, and so a meeting was held in his dining room in the guesthouse. Wang sat there for a moment only; then he left, asking me to preside.

Wang Hairong repeated her charges.

Zhang Yufeng responded, "When Mao and I got into a quarrel, he swore at me, even at my mother. I had to swear back."

As she was about to tell how the quarrel started, I thought it necessary to stop the meeting before she further exposed Mao's sorry relations with her. I felt that if I let her continue, Mao might come to feel—even though he had ordered this meeting himself—that some of us were trying to probe into his private life.

But Wang Hairong would not let the subject go, arguing that nothing had been settled. Unable to handle the situation, I sent for Wang Dongxing and asked him to pacify Wang Hairong. I also asked head nurse Wu Xujun to persuade Zhang Yufeng to see Mao for a self-criticism.

Wang Hairong did not like the way the matter was handled, and insisted that Wang Dongxing and I had no sense of justice. She returned, angrily, to Beijing. Zhang Yufeng was still angry, too. She asked why she had to criticize herself before Mao when it was Mao who had sworn at her and her mother. She left the guesthouse and returned to the train.

Nevertheless, things soon returned to normal.

Then Mao caught a cold, which in turn led to acute bronchitis, with fever and coughing. I treated him, and soon his fever was gone and his coughing less frequent. He developed laryngitis, however, and within two days he had lost his voice. Worried that the loss might be permanent, he kept asking me for treatment. I explained to him that it would take a while for the inflammation of the larynx to subside, but he persisted in asking for a cure.

I ordered that he be given physical therapy, but he did not like it and discontinued it after only a single session. Then I asked him to take some Chinese herb medicine, which proved very effective. He regained some of his voice within two days and was fully recovered three days after that.

Then he wanted to go swimming. Ignoring my warning against it, he said, "All your treatments, this one and that one, Chinese medicine and Western medicine—none of it does any good. My swimming treatment is still the most effective." He swam in the guesthouse pool.

After May Day 1965, Mao decided to visit Jinggangshan, on the border of the Hunan and Jiangxi provinces, where he had established a guerrilla base and launched his rebellion in 1927. We took the train to Changsha, in Hunan province, and continued our trip from there by car. Zhang Yufeng, still not entirely over her anger, refused to go.

The point of the trip to Jinggangshan was to threaten the Central Authority by implying that Mao might now reestablish a base for himself there, from which he might reorganize the party and the army if the Central Authority did not submit to his will. This trip was part of his continuing attack on his rival Liu Shaoqi.

The secretary of the Hunan provincial party committee joined Mao for the trip, but no one from Jiangxi province accompanied us, because Wang Dongxing, who had been vice-governor of the province for nearly five years when he was "sent down for reform," was familiar with the area we were visiting.

We stopped in Chalin county, Hunan, for the night. The county government vacated all its offices in order to provide quarters for us. The place was full of mosquitoes, and the insect spray we carried was for Mao's use only. The rest of us had to sleep under thick linen mosquito nets, which trapped much of the smoke from the moxa that was burned to repel the insects. I felt dizzy the next morning.

We arrived at Jinggangshan and stayed in a two-story guesthouse in Maoping, which was a hamlet with a rice field at its center. On the south side of Maoping was a store selling handicrafts; in one room was displayed a shoulder pole said to have been used by Marshal Zhu De to carry water barrels during the rebellion in the 1920s. (During the Cultural Revolution it was claimed that Lin Biao had used this pole, yet another example of the falsification of history during this period.) Jinggangshan itself was full of bamboo groves, and a small paper mill there produced a kind of white translucent paper from the bamboo. I hadn't seen this kind of paper since I was a boy.

We left Jinggangshan on May 29 and returned to Beijing in the middle of June.

Mao's dissatisfaction with Liu Shaoqi and Deng Xiaoping was reflected in his increasing disaffection with the health-care system. Soon he was lashing out against the Ministry of Public Health as well. "I want you to tell the people in the Ministry of Public Health something," he told me on June 26, 1965. "They are providing health care to only 15 percent of the people of this nation. Of these 15 percent, it's those lords in the national and local governments who receive the best care. The ministry thinks that so long as those lords are happy, its work is being done well. But the vast percentage of people in the countryside have no health care at all—no medicine, no doctors. I'm

going to write a poem dedicated to the Ministry of Public Health—
'Health care, health care, it benefits high officials; peasants, peasants,
their life and death are nobody's business.'

"The Ministry of Public Health is not serving the people," Mao
continued. "It is not the people's ministry. The ministry pays attention
only to city residents, to those masters. Let's give it a new name—the
Ministry of Urban Health, the Ministry for the Health of the Lords.
Our hospitals have all sorts of modern medical equipment and technology, but they ignore the needs of the villages. We are training doctors
to serve the urban areas. But China has 500 million peasants." Mao
wanted sweeping reforms of the health-care system, a reorientation
from the elite to the masses, from the cities to the countryside.

He wanted to reform medical education, too. "Medical students
don't need to read so many books," he insisted. The most famous
doctors of Chinese history, Hua Tao and Li Shizhen, never attended
medical school. Medical schools do not have to enroll high school
graduates. A primary-school certificate should be sufficient to begin
studying medicine. Medical skill is learned through practice. The type
of doctor we need in the villages doesn't have to be so talented," he
said. "They'd still be better than witch doctors. Besides, this is the only
type of doctor the villages can afford."

Mao also criticized the Ministry of Public Health for investing
manpower and resources in research into rare and exotic diseases,
trying to advance medical science without paying attention to the
prevention and treatment of common illnesses. "I'm not saying we
should ignore advanced medical science," Mao said, "just that only a
minor portion of our manpower and resources should be spent there.
We should devote a major portion of our resources to what the masses
need most.

"There's another thing that is really strange," Mao continued.
"Doctors always put on masks when treating patients. Are they afraid
the patients might catch a disease from them? No, I think they are
afraid of catching some disease from the patients. It seems to me that
doctors should wear masks only when they really need them. Otherwise, they create a barrier between doctor and patient."

Mao had a new proposal. He wanted to staff the urban hospitals
with newly graduated physicians, the ones with the least experience.
The better-trained, experienced senior doctors should be sent to the
countryside. "Our medical profession should concentrate its future
work on the villages."

I was astonished at Mao's broadside against the medical profession, but he instructed me to report his thoughts to the Ministry of

Public Health, so I drew up a lengthy memo of our conversation, dated June 26, 1965, and submitted it both to the ministry and to Peng Zhen, the deputy secretary to the Central Committee's secretariat. I had no idea that during the Cultural Revolution, the memo would become Mao's "June 26 directive," the basis for launching the nationwide barefoot-doctor campaign, used by the radicals to launch class struggle in the medical profession, ruining China's urban health-care system. And it hardly occurred to me that Mao would send his personal physician to the villages, too.

In the tension and confusion that accompanied the abolition and restructuring of the Central Bureau of Health, the spark that had set Mao off was deliberately forgotten. Mao ordered the end of special medical care for the top leaders immediately after learning that Liu Shaoqi had contracted tuberculosis. He had ordered me not to get involved in treating Liu Shaoqi's illness, and to this day I know nothing of how Liu was cured. But we in Group One knew that Mao's attack on the health-care system was also a disguised attack on Liu Shaoqi. "It's still too early to say that Liu Shaoqi will succeed the Chairman," Tian Jiaying concluded. "We don't really know yet. The Chairman doesn't always stand by his words. One day he says one thing, tomorrow another. Nobody can be sure what he thinks." Wang Dongxing agreed.

We kept our concerns to ourselves. I never told anyone in the Central Bureau of Health that Liu Shaoqi's illness had prompted Mao's restructuring. Those of us in Group One who had heard Mao's private quips about Liu Shaoqi never shared them with anyone beyond the inner circle. Wang Dongxing was the only person I told how worried I was.

55

At the end of June 1965, a few days after I had written the memo calling for experienced doctors to go to the countryside, Mao called me in to see him. "The class struggle in the countryside has become extremely serious," he said, "and the 'four cleanups' campaign is raging like wildfire. But everyone in Group One is still here, doing nothing. That's no good." Mao wanted Wang Dongxing to lead a team from Group One to participate in the socialist education campaign in the countryside. Wang's boss, public security minister Xie Fuzhi, was already in the countryside as leader of a team. Our turn had come.

We interpreted Mao's orders as punishment. "So what have we done this time to displease the Chairman?" Wang Dongxing wanted to know when I broke the news. Tian Jiaying and I were convinced that we were about to lose our jobs. Mao's way of overhauling his staff had always been to send them first to the countryside for "reform" and then to assign them different work. This was how Ye Zilong and Li Yinqiao had lost their jobs in the winter of 1960. We were afraid we would suffer a similar fate.

Mao wanted almost all of us in Group One to go. Only one secretary, Xu Yefu, and one attendant, Zhou Fuming, were to stay behind. Jiang Qing would not have to go, either. Her maladies had quickly returned in the face of possible hardship.

Tian Jiaying saw advantages in our leaving. The political situation in Beijing was becoming tense. None of us knew what would happen next, but we all feared that it would not be good. At least when the trouble hit, Tian reasoned, we would be out of harm's way. But none of us was happy about being sent to the countryside, and Wang Dongxing, responsible for getting us there, managed to drag his feet. Finally, Wang decided we would go to Qianshan county, in his native Jiangxi. Mao urged us to be quickly on our way.

I was worried about who would take my place while I was gone and wanted Huang Shuze, one of the vice-ministers of public health, to serve as Mao's doctor. But Mao was still fuming at both the urban health-care system and the hypochondria of his colleagues and did not want another doctor. "My health is good," he insisted. "I don't need any health care. I'm not like those lords who have their blood pressure taken and their pulse measured every time they feel the slightest discomfort. I don't want health care. I don't need Huang Shuze. Just a nurse will be enough. And she doesn't have to be from Beijing Hospital, either." Nurse Wu Xujun would accompany us. Mao wanted her replacement to come from the 301 Hospital, the leading health facility of the People's Liberation Army.

Pu Rongqing, the vice-president of the 301 Hospital, was flattered that Mao had requested one of his nurses. "Beijing Hospital has a much better health-care system," he pointed out when I went to make the arrangements. He was right. Even Pu Rongqing himself had no formal medical training. He had learned his skills as a medic with the Red Army.

Pu asked us to interview two nurses who already had experience with high-ranking military cadres. Both were quite acceptable—one quiet and reserved, the other outgoing and friendly—so we showed Mao their photographs and asked him to choose. He chose the outgoing Liu Xiaoyan. "She looks smart," he said.

Our team from Group One left for the countryside at the beginning of July.

By the time we arrived in Qianshan county, our socialist education work team was one hundred people strong. In addition to staff from the Central Bureau of Guards, the Central Garrison Corps, and the Second Artillery Corps, the Jiangxi provincial party committee also sent along its own representatives. Mao also sent his daughter Li Na, accompanied by a staff member to attend to her needs.

My relations with Li Na had been tense ever since the 7,000 cadres' conference in January 1962, when I had been called away from the Great Hall of the People to see Li Na at Peking University, where she was a student in the history department. I arrived to find Mao's daughter suffering from a severe cold and fever and being fussed over by Lu Ping, then serving simultaneously as president and party secretary of the university. The party secretary from the history department was there too, and both men were concerned. They were extremely polite, repeatedly apologizing that I had not been summoned earlier. They themselves had just learned of Li Na's illness and had called for me as soon as they knew. Li Na, though, was furious, claiming that I had not gotten there soon enough, that no one cared about her, insisting that no one would care if she died. She was inconsolable, whining and crying and complaining incessantly. Finally, I lost my temper.

"You're twenty-one years old," I snapped at her. "You're not a kid anymore. You are sick and the leaders of the university have come to see you. What more do you want? There are more than ten thousand students here at Peking University. If they all acted like you, how do you think they could run the university?"

My outburst made her angrier, and she began crying and yelling all the more, behaving like a three-year-old. She continued to scream as I forced her into my car to take her to Beijing Hospital. She was so unruly en route, yelling and screaming and fighting the whole way, that we were stopped twice by police, who thought something was wrong.

Later, when I told Mao what had happened, he was angry. "Beijing Hospital is for high-level cadres," he said. "What is Li Na doing there?"

I explained that ordinary hospitals would not admit patients suffering from colds but I had been afraid to let her return to Zhongnanhai because she might pass her cold on to him. Li Na had been admitted to Beijing Hospital because she was Mao's daughter.

Mao did not want his children to receive special privileges and told me not to send her to Beijing Hospital again. Then he wanted to know where Li Na, Li Min, and Mao Yuanxin ate when they were in Zhongnanhai. I said that Mao's chef cooked for them, and they ate in his kitchen.

Mao did not like that, either. "Tell Wang Dongxing that from now on they are not allowed to eat in my kitchen. They have to eat in the public dining room."

This new regulation did not endear me to Mao's children and nephew, and when Jiang Qing found out about it, she too was angry. I had treated her daughter rudely and deprived her of her special privileges. She wanted Mao to fire me. Mao did not, but in the end even Mao was unhappy with me. When he encouraged me to be nice to Jiang Qing and Li Na, I pointed out that Li Na was mean and nasty and impossible to please, unlike her gentler sister, Li Min. Mao did not appreciate my saying this, even though he knew it was true. Now, as if to prove that his children were getting no special privileges, he was sending Li Na with us to the countryside. Wang Dongxing had to arrange for someone to come along to take care of her.

From the beginning, our mission in Jiangxi seemed wrong. To send the privileged elite of Beijing to direct a campaign against corruption and foster class struggle in the countryside seemed absurd. We had traveled thousands of miles from Beijing to Jiangxi by train and car at government expense. We lived in guesthouses paid for by the government and ate food for which others paid. Merely getting us to the villages and keeping us there was costing the government a lot. And the experience of our group was being duplicated all over the country. Hundreds of thousands of city folk were being sent to the countryside, at great expense, to participate in this "socialist education campaign." And none of us wanted to be in the villages. We had been sent against our will.

After we arrived in Qianshan county, our work team divided into four groups, each assigned to a different village. After the failure of the Great Leap Forward, the people's communes had each been subdivided into several production brigades, which were equivalent geographically to the old rural villages. Each brigade, in turn, was further divided into production teams. Wang Shengrong, the deputy director of the Central Bureau of Guards, and I were in charge of a group sent to work in Shixi production brigade, and we were joined by two local officials—Zhang Zhenhe, a public-security official of Jiangxi's Shangrao prefecture, and the party secretary of Qianshan county. I liked both local officials enormously. They uttered not a word of complaint about the hardships we faced and remained friendly and cooperative with everyone they met.

The peasants of Shixi village were poor beyond my imagination. I had been back in China for sixteen years and with Mao for eleven of them. My job made me privy to all sorts of secret information. I knew of the famine and hunger brought on by the Great Leap Forward. I knew the countryside was poor. But these peasants were poorer than poor. Their clothes were threadbare and patched. Their food was meager and almost indigestible—unhusked rice mixed with sand and bits of gravel, topped by a few paltry vegetables. The peasants' homes were miserable, leaky huts without even rudimentary furniture, and the only roads were narrow dirt paths that turned into mud after a rain. There were no schools in the village of Shixi and I never saw any newspapers, magazines, or books. The overwhelming majority of adults in the village were illiterate, and illiteracy was being perpetuated in their children. The closest school was several *li* away, and few of the children were receiving even primary education. Our "four cleanups" team arranged to show an old film from the fifties one night. We set up the projector outside in one of the fallow fields, and peasants came from miles around. Some walked for hours from as far as fifteen miles away to see the film. It was the first movie most of them had ever seen.

But our lives, even in the countryside, were luxurious beyond the imagination of the peasants. In order to be more like them, we had cast off our city garb for the rough cotton padded jackets and pants supplied by the Central Garrison Corps, but still the villagers were envious of our outfits. Our clothes had no patches. As I was chatting one day with one of the older peasants in the village, he touched and patted my jacket. "If only I could have an overcoat like this," he said, "then I would know that communism had arrived."

We were a continual source of curiosity to the villagers. Wang Shengrong, the deputy director of the Central Bureau of Guards, who was a member of our group, was a particular source of wonder. Wang's love of food was obvious from his weight. The peasants in our team, all painfully thin, had never seen anyone so fat. Every time Wang emerged from his hut, the villagers would rush to surround him and gawk. The adults would ask him what he ate to make him so fat, and the children would run after him as though he were a creature from another planet. The villagers never learned his name. To the peasants he was always *da pangzi*—the big fat man.

According to the ideology of the day, our team was to "live, eat, sleep, and work" with the poor peasants. But the villagers were much too poor to accommodate outsiders. They were as hospitable as their circumstances allowed, offering us a dilapidated storage shed for housing. We managed to construct some wooden beds, using hay for mattresses and spreading our quilts and bedding over the hay. We set up our own kitchen, too, and because we had come to purge ourselves of special privilege and to live like peasants, we ate the same coarse food that they did—sandy rice and all.

We labored in the fields. There were twelve families in our host team, collectively farming some fifty *mu* (nine acres) of land. In addition, each family was assigned a tiny plot for growing household vegetables. There were no machines, no draft animals, and very few tools. We used our hands, our arms, our feet, every muscle and bone in our body, and the work was backbreaking, exhausting, and primitive. We were working like animals. With so little land and such primitive techniques, the harvests were meager indeed. After paying taxes to the state, the peasants had hardly anything left.

Elsewhere science and technology were progressing. But here in the backwaters of Jiangxi, Chinese agriculture had not changed for a thousand years. Talk of a Great Leap Forward was ridiculous. I could not understand why China was not exerting all its energy and intelligence to develop labor-saving agricultural machines to bring the peasants out of their degradation, backwardness, and poverty. When I confessed to Wang Dongxing that I could not understand why, sixteen years after the revolution, the peasants were still so poor, he pointed out that many other places were poorer still.

I knew he was right. Many of the young wives in Shixi village had fled their native Anhui during the height of the famine several years before, when their husbands and children died. With their new husbands in Shixi, they were making new families. The situation in Anhui had greatly improved, but the women would not go back. Life was better in Jiangxi.

In the midst of this poverty, our job was to foster class struggle. The "four cleanups" campaign required us to investigate cadre corruption within the production team, as though the place had not always been so poor, as though corruption rather than the policies of the Great Leap Forward had been responsible for the disasters of the "three bad years." The assumption was that the cadres in these impoverished teams had manipulated finances to their own advantage, had confiscated team grain for their own consumption, had allocated public property for their own use, and had cheated the peasants out of their work points.

There was corruption. That was undeniable. But to focus on corruption at the level of poor teams like this one was absurd. Our socialist education work team had no way of inspecting account books. There were no account books to inspect. The peasant responsible for bookkeeping was barely literate and would not know how to keep books. And there were really no accounts to keep. The team was so poor, and the villagers lived and worked together so closely, that everyone knew everything about everyone else. They knew what everyone had and what everyone earned and what the team produced. The local people had been living and working together for centuries. The team cadres could not have benefited from corruption even if they had tried. It was the cadres at the higher levels of the commune, and those higher still, at the level of the county and the province, who were reaping the economic rewards of corruption and graft. The higher-level cadres were the ones with the power to extract taxes from the peasants, to direct the peasants into any endeavor they wanted. They were the ones with the power to be corrupt.

The class struggle that Mao argued was still continuing with such intensity, the battle between the landlords and the poor peasants, feudalism and socialism, the bourgeoisie and the working class, was also a tragic farce. Sometime during land reform, just after the communists had taken power in this village, all the villagers had been assigned a class label. Those designated landlords or rich peasants lost all their property, and they, and every member of their families, had been placed under supervision by the village. The goal, it was said, was to reform the landlords and rich peasants, as well as their spouses and children, through hard labor. Periodically, especially on national holidays, the former landlords and rich peasants would be assembled as a group to receive a lecture from the local public-security or production-team cadres about the alleged misdeeds of their past. Whenever anything untoward occurred in the village—if a nail was found in the cattle feed, for instance—the old landlords and rich peasants were automatically suspected and hauled out for interrogation.

The hardest-working and poorest peasant in the village, a man who labored unceasingly from dawn to dusk, had been designated a landlord's son and was invariably assigned the hardest and heaviest jobs. He worked without a word of complaint. But the man, in fact, was not a landlord's son. He had been born into one of the village's poorest families, and his impoverished parents, in order to save him, had given him in adoption to a landlord. For that, he had been labeled the son of a landlord, forced to work as a coolie, deprived of all rights, and was at the beck and call of the village leaders. Among the impoverished villagers, he was the poorest and most miserable, forced to eat the least and the coarsest of rice. His clothes were cast off by others as beyond repair.

The father of another so-called landlord's son had never even owned land. But his grandfather had. The label landlord's son was hereditary, passed down from generation to generation. The abuse meted out to the son of the landlord who had owned no land was torture, from which he could not escape.

This system of labeling children for the alleged crimes of their fathers, of perpetuating the stigma generation after generation and treating the offspring like criminals, was obviously unfair. I thought surely the time had come to change the status of these people, who had already suffered so much. But my suggestions were ignored, and I was warned about the potential political consequences should my sympathies be known.

Other members of the team had told the peasants that I was Mao's doctor, but that was no protection. "You think that just because you are Chairman's doctor you can put in some good words for the son of a landlord," one of the villagers warned me one day. "But let me tell you—if anyone here reports what you have said to the government, you can get into big trouble." Speaking in defense of a landlord, even if the landlord had been unfairly labeled, was to risk being labeled oneself. This was Mao's class struggle. The innocent had been persecuted for sixteen years. Mao had said that class struggle would continue for the entire stage of socialism, which might last for fifty or a hundred years. The legacy of torture would not stop with the first generation of landlord sons but would continue to grandson and great-grandson and so on until the arrival of communism. When the Cultural Revolution began in 1966, the sons and daughters of the high-level cadres perpetuated the slogan "Dragons beget dragons; phoenixes beget phoenixes; rats beget rats." The sons and daughters of high-level party cadres were sacred, the dragons and phoenixes of Chinese mythology. The sons and daughters of the former landlords and rich peasants were no better than rats. Against this horrible abuse and injustice that permeated the countryside, I and the other members of my team were powerless.

The awful poverty afflicting the Chinese villages and the injustice of the type of class struggle I was witnessing and my helplessness before it depressed me. After sixteen years of revolution, it seemed to me that China had not progressed at all. The standard of living was terrible. The government was cruel. Life for the disenfranchised was harsh. However bad life may have been under the Guomindang, hard work and good luck had always brought rewards. Poor people with talent had a chance to rise to the top. The social and economic status of individuals and families was not set in stone generation after generation. Change for the better was always a hope.

I did learn something from my participation in the socialist education campaign, but not the lessons Mao wanted me to learn. My alienation grew. My dissatisfaction with the Communist party deepened. While high-level party cadres ate and drank and lived in luxury, the peasants in the countryside barely subsisted. They were poorer and more miserable than anything I had imagined. What good had the Communist party done? Where were the great transformations Mao's revolution had wrought? Our work team had come to the countryside to stir up class conflict. And to what avail? We would leave the village and the peasants would remain poorer than ever and the government coffers would be depleted.

My political disaffection grew, and still I remained silent.

IV

1965–1976

56

In early November 1965, after we had been in Qianshan county for three months, Wang Dongxing was summoned back to Beijing for an urgent meeting. Something important was happening, but none of us knew what. We were isolated in our villages and had little news from outside. Wang expected to return in a few days.

Weeks went by. Winter came, and the weather turned depressingly cold and rainy. Our work in the fields came to a halt. My boredom, anxiety, and alienation grew. Still Wang did not return.

Finally, at the end of December, he came back.

"You didn't expect me to be gone so long, did you?" he teased. Then he suddenly turned serious. "Something has happened." Wang Dongxing had not gone to Beijing. He had gone to Hangzhou, where Mao was staying, to meet with him.

Several of the top leaders—Beijing party chief Peng Zhen, chief of general staff Luo Ruiqing, director of the party's General Office Yang Shangkun, and director of the Propaganda Department Lu Dingyi—were in serious political trouble. The party was holding a series of secret meetings to decide how to handle their cases. Few decisions had been made.

One matter, though, had been decided. Yang Shangkun, who had first angered Mao during the Black Flag Incident and whom Mao blamed for the bugging of his train and guesthouses, had been dismissed. Wang Dongxing had been appointed to replace him. Wang would continue as head of the Central Bureau of Guards, because the position had real power. And while he never resigned from his post as vice-minister of public security, he never returned to the job. The directorship of the General Office was a much more powerful position.

"I said I was not qualified for the job," Wang told me, "and suggested Chen Boda instead. The Chairman did not agree. Then I suggested that Hu Qiaomu serve as the director of the General Office, with me serving as his deputy director. The Chairman said that Hu Qiaomu was too pedantic and ill suited to administrative work. He insisted that I take the job."

"So you've been promoted," I exclaimed. "Congratulations!"

Immediately, I wondered how the political changes would affect me. Luo Ruiqing and Yang Shangkun had given the final approval when I was brought on as Mao's doctor. If there was to be a sweeping purge of their subordinates, I might come under attack. But Wang Dongxing had been my real sponsor and continued to protect me. He was being promoted. Perhaps I would be safe. But I was uneasy. This was the most far-ranging and highest-level political shakeup since the communists had come to power, and it would surely reverberate to many levels of Chinese society.

Wang Dongxing, too, was sober. He had come back to Jiangxi not just to finish our work with the socialist education campaign but to escape the political fray. He wanted to wait out the battle until the issues had been decided. He wanted us to stay there, too. Once the purges began, subordinates would be implicated. We were safer in the countryside.

My malaise continued. I had always shied away from politics, but I had learned to stay well informed about the shifts of political wind. It was a way of staying safe. The countryside was safe for now, but I needed to know more about what was happening at the center, what Mao was thinking and what plans he had. In the village, it was difficult to figure out what was going on in Beijing.

The attack against the four party leaders was not a complete surprise to me. After the bugging incident, Mao never trusted Yang Shangkun, and while he placed real blame on leaders still higher in the hierarchy—on men like Deng Xiaoping and Liu Shaoqi—his practice was always to hit at the middle levels first.

And Mao had long been suspicious of Beijing party chief Peng Zhen. Several years earlier, he had told me that Kang Sheng suspected Peng of "anti-Mao" tendencies. In my experience with Peng, he had been completely loyal to Mao, always asking after the Chairman's health. But Kang Sheng was telling Mao that Peng Zhen had criticized the "three red banners" of Mao's Great Leap Forward, wondering how revolutionary they really were.

Lu Dingyi's political trouble was also no great surprise. As director of the Propaganda Department, Lu was in charge of literature and the arts. With Jiang Qing and Ke Qingshi on the offensive against the world of culture and with Mao supporting their attacks, Lu's political difficulties were almost inevitable.

I was best acquainted with Luo Ruiqing, having worked closely with him from the beginning of my service to Mao and from that first incident at Beidaihe when Luo had opposed Mao's swim in the turbulent sea. Luo had always put Mao's safety and protection first and was never in any real sense disloyal to him. But he did have differences of opinion with Lin Biao—and consequently with Mao.

I had known Luo Ruiqing was in political trouble since June 1964, when he organized a huge military exercise near the Ming tombs, outside of Beijing. Soldiers from both the Beijing and the Jinan military regions participated in the coordinated maneuvers, conducted under the unified command of Luo Ruiqing, Yang Yong, and Yang Dezhi. Lin Biao was invited to observe, but he refused. He did not believe in military exercises, he said.

Mao did review some of the maneuvers, but was able to twist what he saw in support of Lin Biao's line that men and ideology were more important than weapons. When a squadron of soldiers scaled a five-story building without any equipment, Mao was delighted at how much could be done without modern weapons. The maneuver, he said, was an example of how backward, underdeveloped China could overcome even the most powerful and technologically advanced of enemies, proof that China could conquer the giant enemy to the north. "The Soviet Union is a giant," Mao said to Luo after witnessing the maneuvers, "but it is not untouchable. So long as we have a method for handling the giant, nothing, no matter how big and powerful, should scare us."

But Mao knew that Luo Ruiqing was pushing for the modernization of the Chinese army, outspoken in his disdain for Lin's—and Mao's—theory of man over weapons. "Luo isn't worth the clothes on his back," Mao quipped to me one day.

I was able to learn more about Luo Ruiqing's plight from some documents, drafted by the navy and passed on by the Military Affairs Commission to Mao, that Wang Dongxing brought back. Lin Biao's wife, Ye Qun, had been campaigning against Luo Ruiqing. In November 1965, just before Wang Dongxing was called back to Beijing, she flew to Hangzhou to complain to Mao that Luo opposed her husband's slogan "Let politics take command."

Mao sided with Ye Qun. "Those who do not believe in putting politics in command and only give lip service to the idea are trying to propagate 'eclecticism,' " he had written on the document Wang gave me. "We have to beware of their position."

Air force political commissar Wu Faxian had joined with Ye Qun against Luo Ruiqing, alleging that Luo had opposed Lin Biao's appointment to replace Peng Dehuai from the beginning and was now trying to persuade Lin Biao to resign. When Lin Biao had been ill and unable to meet with Luo Ruiqing, Luo had lashed out against Lin, shouting, "If he's sick so often, how can he be responsible for anything? Let someone else take over his job. Don't stand in the way."

Luo was bothered by Ye Qun's active involvement in politics, suggesting she should spend more time caring for her chronically ill husband. If Lin's health were better, Luo said, he could devote more attention to the business of the central authority. Wu Faxian claimed that Luo Ruiqing really wanted Lin Biao to resign, saying that Luo Ruiqing had tried to prevail upon Liu Yalou, the commander in chief of the air force, to encourage Ye Qun to persuade her husband to step down. "Everyone has to step out of the political arena at some point," Luo was said to have argued, "and so does Lin Biao." Luo Ruiqing wanted Lin Biao to remove himself from his position in the Military Affairs Commission so that he, Luo Ruiqing, could take over the position himself. If Ye Qun persuaded her husband to resign, Luo promised that she would eventually be rewarded, although I never learned how.

Ye Qun and Wu Faxian did not listen to Luo Ruiqing, and Mao sided with them. Luo Ruiqing was deprived of his major military responsibilities in mid-December.

I was worried. Luo's removal was not a good omen.

Several of Wang Dongxing's comments also led me to believe that Zhou Enlai was worried, too, siding with Luo Ruiqing and wary of Lin Biao. Premier Zhou Enlai was urging Wang to return to Beijing as quickly as possible. Zhou was in charge of the daily affairs of state. As early as 1964, Zhou had complained to Wang Dongxing about the scarcity of administrative talent at the highest levels of government, saying how difficult it was to get anything done, "because we have so few capable people." Peng Zhen managed party administration; Luo Ruiqing was in charge of the army; and Zhou was responsible for the government. Zhou despaired that with such a big country there were so few people doing most of the work. Other people, he told Wang, talked a lot but did little. With Peng Zhen and Luo Ruiqing under attack, Zhou Enlai was more worried still. Getting anything done in Beijing would be all the more difficult. He urged Wang Dongxing to return to Beijing to assume his new administrative position as soon as possible. But Wang Dongxing intended for us to stay in the country-side, working in the socialist education campaign, until April 1966.

I was happy to stay. With the political situation so tense, who could predict what would happen upon my return to Beijing?

I was soon to find out. Several days after Wang Dongxing's return, as I was still trying to digest the impact of the great political uncertainties, Mao summoned me.

It was New Year's Day, 1966, and the team from Group One wanted to celebrate the holiday properly. That morning, head nurse Wu Xujun and I slogged through the mud, drenched by a chilling rain, to the village where Wang Dongxing was based. We city folk were the only ones observing the holiday. The peasants in the villages were still tied to the lunar calendar. Despite our attempts to draw them into our festivities, they insisted that their new year would not arrive for an-other six weeks. The Western calendar made no sense to them.

Wang Dongxing had ordered meat and flour for the occasion and set us to work making traditional New Year's dumplings. Some of us chopped meat and made the filling, others mixed flour and water for the dough, and the rest of us wrapped the dumplings in final prepara-tion for cooking. When we were almost done, a public-security official from Shangrao prefecture, out of breath and dripping with perspira-tion, suddenly burst into the room. He had arrived unexpectedly by jeep and was in a hurry. "No need to rush," someone joked. "There are plenty of dumplings."

The official called me, nurse Wu, and Wang Dongxing aside. "I've been trying for two hours to get you by phone," he said, "but I couldn't get through." He had been called by the Jiangxi provincial party committee at three that morning. The Chairman was ill. He was in Nanchang, the provincial capital, and wanted me and nurse Wu to go there immediately.

The drive would take eleven or twelve hours by jeep, and we had to set out immediately.

I wanted to return to Shixi to pack an overnight bag, but Wang Dongxing objected. I could buy what I needed in Nanchang, he said. The trip was secret. "If you go back, everyone will ask where you are going," he said. Wang decided to join us. He wanted to know how serious Mao's illness was and to seize the opportunity to catch up on news from Beijing. If the Chairman was not seriously ill, he would return to the village immediately.

We never got to eat the dumplings. Wang insisted on leaving immediately. We set off in the rain on the unpaved mud road, stopping for a quick bite at the Shangrao guesthouse and then creeping along at a snail's pace, slipping and sliding, the mud splashing the windshield so it was often impossible to see, until we finally reached a gravel road. From there, our speed picked up. It was midnight by the time we arrived in Nanchang.

We met first with Fang Zhichun, chairman of the Jiangxi provincial people's congress, and several other provincial party officials. "The Chairman has been here two weeks," Fang explained, "and he became ill two days ago. We thought it best to call Dr. Li."

We were escorted to the Binjiang guesthouse, where Mao and his entourage were staying. Wang Dongxing's subordinate, Central Garrison Corps commander Zhang Yaoci, was there and so was Xu Yefu, the opportunistic secretary who had managed to get rid of Lin Ke and take his place. A new chief of security guards, Qu Qiyu, was responsible for Mao's immediate personal security, and a new male attendant, Zhou Fuming, was responsible for Mao's personal needs. Several young women were there—a nurse and his two favorite confidential clerks—and so was train attendant Zhang Yufeng. Three chefs had come with him, and over a dozen armed guards. With all of Mao's previous staff now replaced, the atmosphere was completely different. I felt vaguely uncomfortable.

Mao's new personal attendant, a young man from Hangzhou named Zhou Fuming, who had cut Mao's hair a few times before joining Group One (Big Beard Wang had finally retired, with a generous pension), was the one I knew best, so he told me what had happened. Mao had celebrated his seventy-second birthday on December 26 by drinking a little wine in the afternoon and then going for a walk along the Gan River, accompanied by several of his female friends. It was windy, but Mao had felt warm and unbuttoned his shirt. Then he and Zhang Yufeng squabbled. The two were carrying on an old argument. A year earlier, Mao had discovered that Zhang Yufeng had developed a close friendship with someone on his staff. But Mao was determined to control her life. When he found out, he forced Zhang Yufeng to kneel down before him and apologize. The male staff member was expelled from Zhongnanhai and sent to Nanjing, but the episode continued to trouble the relationship between Mao and Zhang Yufeng, and another flare-up had taken place on the afternoon of Mao's birthday.

The Chairman's cold had started just afterward, and by evening he was coughing heavily and running a fever. He had refused all offers to see local Nanchang doctors, hoping to heal himself. The party leadership in Jiangxi became increasingly distressed. The Chairman's health was deteriorating and he refused all help. Finally, when he could bear the fever and discomfort no more, Mao asked for me and nurse Wu.

I went in to see him. He was lying in bed, his face flushed, his breathing labored, coughing constantly. "I've been like this for a few days already," he explained. "I thought I could stick it out, but I can't. I had to ask you to come." I was still the only doctor Mao trusted.

He had a temperature of 104 degrees, and the cold had turned into bronchitis. I suggested we give him a shot of antibiotics to treat the bronchitis and lower his fever. He agreed.

It was five o'clock in the morning before nurse Wu and I finally returned to the Nanchang guesthouse, where Wang Dongxing and a number of Jiangxi officials were waiting. We decided that if Mao's condition improved the next day, the three of us would return to the countryside that afternoon.

Wang Dongxing went with me to see Mao the next day. The antibiotics were taking effect. His temperature had gone down. But Mao was still coughing, and he wanted to continue the treatment for a few more days. He ordered Wang Dongxing back to the village, leaving me and nurse Wu to treat him.

Wang was irritated. Mao had sent us all down to eat bitterness and participate in the socialist education campaign and then report back to him on our work. But he had not asked a single question about what we were doing. Wang wondered what was going on in Mao's mind.

Wang returned to the village that evening, his question unanswered.

Mao was less accessible than before. He was surrounded by young female companions, who took turns caring for him. One was always by his side. Zhou Fuming rarely went into the Chairman's room. He would fetch Mao's food or tea from the kitchen and then hand it to one of the young women, who would serve it to Mao. Knowing that the women were intimately involved with the Chairman and not wanting to intrude into his personal affairs, I stayed in the background, trying to minister to his health without disturbing his privacy.

But I was worried about his health. His bronchitis and cough responded quickly to the antibiotics and cleared up in a matter of days. But in the course of treating his bronchitis, I realized that since I had been sent to the countryside, Mao had begun taking an extraordinary number of sleeping pills—ten times the normal dosage and enough to kill an ordinary person. Over the years, as Mao's reliance on sleeping pills continued, he had developed an amazing tolerance for barbiturates. But I had no idea where the dividing line between his tolerance and a potentially lethal dose might be. In the countryside, I could not have been held responsible had Mao overdosed on sleeping pills. In Nanchang, directly overseeing his health, I was responsible for anything that went wrong.

The number of sleeping pills Mao was taking was directly linked to the current political tension. His insomnia and politics were always linked. A couple of members of his staff told me that he had begun increasing the dosage in November 1965, after Lin Biao's wife, Ye Qun, had come to him with the news of Luo Ruiqing's opposition to her husband. On December 8, Mao had convened an enlarged meeting of the politburo standing committee in Shanghai, where he had dismissed Luo Ruiqing as chief of the general staff and appointed his deputy, General Yang Chengwu, to replace him. The meetings had lasted a week, and Mao was so tense he barely slept at all. He began downing the barbiturates in increasingly larger dosages, taking the pills even when he had no intention of going to bed.

I had to break him of this dependence.

I went to see him around midnight a week after I had come back. He was lying in bed reading a history of the later Han dynasty (A.D. 25–220). Mao read history rather than Marx when preparing for political battle, and the Han dynasty history was particularly well written and full of strategic intrigues.

"This time it looks like you do have some tricks in that medicine bag of yours," he said when I went in. "I seem to have recovered."

"It was just ordinary medicine," I responded. "But it worked."

He handed me a pamphlet and wondered if I had read it. I had come to raise the question of his sleeping pills, not to discuss politics, but I glanced at the title of the piece. I recognized it—"Commentary on the Newly Revised Historical Play *Hai Rui Dismissed from Office*." Isolated though we were in Shixi, it was one of the few things I had read. Written by Shanghai "theoretician" Yao Wenyuan and published in the November 10, 1965, issue of Shanghai's *Wen Hui Bao,* the article was a critique of a play written by Beijing vice-mayor Wu Han. The play was a paean to Hai Rui, the upright Ming dynasty official Mao had so often asked his own party officials to emulate.

The critique had puzzled me. Mao himself had promoted the traditional operas about Hai Rui. Wu Han, in addition to being a vice-mayor of Beijing, was a professor at Peking University and one of the country's leading Ming dynasty historians. Mao's longtime interest in Ming dynasty history had brought him into early contact with Wu Han. After Mao's encouragement to study history, I sometimes sat in on his chats with Wu Han. Mao had criticized an earlier work of Wu's—a biography of Ming dynasty founder Zhu Yuanzhang called *Beggar Turned Emperor*—for its historical inaccuracies, its critique of Zhu's role in the Red Turban Army, and its use of Zhu Yuanzhang to criticize the modern-day Chiang Kai-shek. In a series of remarks that would have been heresy had they come from anyone but Mao, the party chairman defended Chiang's role in history—from his northern expedition of 1926–27 to his refusal to succumb to political pressure from the United States to his insistence on the indivisibility of China. Wu Han had accepted Mao's criticisms, though, and his authorship of a play about Hai Rui seemed to agree with Mao's own call to study the example of Hai Rui. I could not understand why either Wu Han or the play were under attack.

Mao wanted to talk about the piece. He supported Yao Wen-yuan's critique, which, he said, was written on the basis of an idea of Jiang Qing and Zhang Chunqiao.

The "idea" traced back to the 7,000 cadres' conference in January 1962 where Mao had been forced to make what came to be known as his "self-criticism." Mao's dismissal of Peng Dehuai had been a frequent topic of private discussion at the 7,000 cadres' conference, and many people believed that Peng's dismissal had been unfair. People began comparing the Jiajing emperor's unfair dismissal and imprisonment of Hai Rui with Mao's dismissal of Peng Dehuai. Peng Dehuai and Hai Rui were both impeccably honest and principled officials, devoted to the welfare of their country and loyal to their leader; they pointed to shortcomings not to rebuke him but to add to his glory by improving his rule. Peng Dehuai was the modern-day Hai Rui.

The two leaders had something else in common, too. Neither accepted criticism with grace.

Jiang Qing's suspiciousness, her new political persona, and her interest in literature and the arts lent a certain predictability to her discoveries of playwrights disloyal to her husband. Maybe it was only natural for her to suspect Wu Han of disloyalty after seeing his play *Hai Rui Dismissed from Office.*

But Beijing mayor Peng Zhen, propaganda chief Lu Dingyi, and deputy propaganda chief Zhou Yang all refused her demand that a campaign be organized to criticize the play. Wu Han was their colleague and friend, a highly respected intellectual, and a man known to listen to Mao. Had he not followed Mao's suggestion to change the name of his biography of Ming dynasty founder Zhu Yuanzhang from *Beggar Turned Emperor* to *The Biography of Zhu Yuanzhang*? Had he not written *Hai Rui Dismissed from Office* in answer to Mao's call to learn from Hai Rui? The Beijing leadership had no reason to listen to Jiang Qing. She held no official position and had been forbidden since the Yanan days from participating in politics. She was looked down upon by the political elite. Actresses were traditionally despised in China, and an actress who furthered her political ambitions by manipulating a marriage with the leader was particularly deplored.

But at this turning point in his career, Mao needed Jiang Qing. Even her political ambitions were of use. She was, as she claimed, the most loyal lieutenant he had, because without Mao, Jiang Qing was no one. When Shanghai leader Ke Qingshi died suddenly in April 1965 of acute pancreatitis, his mantle was passed to the city's propaganda chief, Zhang Chunqiao, who was as anxious as his predecessor to do Mao's bidding. Zhang Chunqiao brought in his close associate Yao Wenyuan, the editor of the *Jiefang Ribao* (*Liberation Daily*), to work directly with Jiang Qing. Mao, meanwhile, withdrew and was not consulted on the contents until the final draft, just before it was published in *Wen Hui Bao*. The attack was meant to launch a campaign against both Wu Han and other supporters of Peng Dehuai. Other newspapers and magazines were expected to join in the attack.

But the Beijing media ignored Yao Wenyuan's attack. "For nineteen days after it was published in *Wen Hui Bao,* the Beijing newspapers adamantly refused to print the article," Mao told me that night. He was furious. "It was only after I sent my word that the Beijing newspapers began reprinting it. Don't you think they are awfully tough?"

I was confused. I still did not understand why Hai Rui and Wu Han were under attack. I certainly had no idea that Yao Wenyuan's article was the opening salvo of what was about to become Mao's Great Proletarian Cultural Revolution. Nor did I fully understand to whom Mao was referring when he said that "they" were awfully tough. Only after the Cultural Revolution began did I understand that "they" included head of state Liu Shaoqi and all the top leaders most closely associated with him.

I remained silent. I needed to understand Mao's position better. I promised Mao I would read Yao Wenyuan's pamphlet again.

"Yes, take another look," Mao said, handing me the article. "Then tell me what you think."

I tried to steer the conversation back to his health.

"There is something else," I began. "The number of sleeping pills Chairman is taking now is excessive, more than ten times the usual dose."

"That much?" Mao asked.

"Yes. I've been checking Chairman's medical records. Such a large dose could be harmful to Chairman's health."

"So what should we do?"

"I think we have to adjust the dosage as soon as possible." I suggested that we fill some gelatin capsules with harmless glucose, fill others with a mixture of half glucose and half barbiturate, and then mix the placebos together with his regular sleep medication. The color of the capsules would be the same, so Mao would not be able to see the difference, but the actual dosage would be cut way down. Mao agreed.

But Mao was still troubled. He wanted to talk.

"There's something about this guesthouse," he said. "It's poisonous. There's something poisonous here. I can't stay here any longer. Tell Zhang Yaoci to get ready. We're going to Wuhan."

The paranoia I had first sensed in Chengdu in 1958, when Mao suspected that his swimming pool was poisoned, was tightening its grip. Mao thought that his illness in Nanchang had come from a poison infecting the guesthouse. But the only poison was political, the intrigue and backstabbing at the highest levels of communist power.

I had to tread lightly. I passed Mao's orders on to Zhang Yaoci, telling him to get ready to move Mao and his entourage to Wuhan. Then I used the secure line to phone Shi Shuhan, who was now a vice-minister at the Ministry of Public Health, to inform him of Mao's most recent illness and explain how we had decided to handle the problem with his sleeping pills. The pharmacy at Beijing Hospital would be responsible for making the glucose-filled gelatin capsules.

Shi Shuhan was worried. He was afraid that Mao's fever might be an indication of something more serious than bronchitis—pneumonia perhaps. He wanted to tell Zhou Enlai and send a team of specialists to look at the Chairman. He urged me to cover myself by giving Mao a chest X ray. But I was certain that Mao's physical health had returned to normal. What worried me was his consumption of barbiturates and his irrational fear of poison. He was afraid of conspiracies against him, and I wanted to give him no excuse for fear. If other specialists came to examine him, if I insisted that he get an X ray, he might suspect that I was lying to him about his illness or trying to avoid responsibility or bringing in spies. If we talked to Zhou Enlai without first informing Mao, he might also suspect some sort of conspiracy. I convinced Shi Shuhan to let well enough alone.

57

We left for Wuhan that night on Mao's private train, arriving around noon the next day. The new glucose-filled capsules had already arrived from Beijing by plane and were delivered by the Office of Confidential Secretaries, together with the Chairman's daily batch of party documents. Nurse Wu and I moved into the guesthouse together with the rest of Mao's staff—attendants, confidential secretaries, and female companions.

The atmosphere of the inner court was different now. Wang Dongxing had always wanted to know all he could about what Mao was thinking and doing, but Zhang Yaoci wanted to avoid involvement. In the face of so much political tension, he was trying to protect himself by keeping his distance from Mao. He would not allow me to brief him on Mao's health, insisting that he was responsible only for the Chairman's security. If he were to know anything about Mao's health, he could be held responsible if anything went wrong.

Qu Qiyu, the section chief of security guards, on the other hand, was maneuvering to learn all he could about Mao, trying to get closer to the Chairman. He hovered around Mao's women, milking them for information, and he manipulated access to Mao, trying to make certain that nurse Wu and I would always have to go through him. I found his arrogance and pushiness distasteful.

I supervised the experiment with Mao's sleeping pills, and the method seemed to work. After five days, he was weaned of the excessively heavy dosage and back to his earlier dose. My presence was no longer needed. The time had come for nurse Wu and me to return to Shixi. I was anxious to be gone. The atmosphere in Group One was too tense, and our work with the "four cleanups" campaign was not complete.

Zhang Yaoci, however, wanted us to stay. He was still worried about the Chairman's health and was afraid of being held responsible should anything go wrong. He did not like Qu Qiyu, either. With me and nurse Wu around, he could stay informed about the Chairman without a commensurate increase in responsibility, and we served as a sort of buffer against the arrogance of Qu Qiyu.

But we had to return. I went to tell Mao, explaining that his health and dosage of sleeping pills were both back to normal and that Wu Xujun and I still had work to do for the "four cleanups" campaign. "If you need us, you can send for us and we will be back immediately," I said.

Mao did not want me to go. "The 'four cleanups' is no longer the most important matter," he said. "Something else is happening now. You should stay here. It will be good for you. I may need you to do something for me in a while."

I was shocked. The "four cleanups" campaign had been a gigantic undertaking, one of the largest since land reform, with hundreds of thousands of urban cadres being sent into villages all over the country. Now the socialist education campaign was no longer important. That explained why Mao did not want to discuss the movement with Wang Dongxing. But I was still in the dark about this new, more important undertaking.

I hesitated. Mao wanted me to stay, and he had confidence in my medical abilities. He would protect me and keep me safe if I confined my work to my medical practice with him. But the atmosphere around him was tense, and Qu Qiyu was the type of power-hungry person who liked to stir up trouble. Work in Group One would be fraught with booby traps. I was conflicted, weighing the costs of my choices. In the end, difficult though life in the countryside was, I decided it was safer politically there. I wanted to return to Shixi.

"Wu Xujun and I have nothing with us but the clothes on our backs," I explained to Mao. "It's not very convenient for us here. We have to return for our clothes."

"No problem," Mao replied. I was to tell Zhang Yaoci to have our city clothes sent from Beijing. Mao would let us know later if he thought we should go back to the countryside. As so often in my life, I had no choice but to stay.

The aura of impending change was almost palpable. Mao withdrew into his room, waited on by his female attendants, and beyond them Qu Qiyu built another impenetrable shield surrounding the Chairman. I stayed away from the duty office, visiting Mao only when he called, hovering on the periphery, wondering what was going to happen.

58

I waited for more than a month. Then on February 8, 1966, Mao allowed me to listen in on a meeting in the huge reception room of the Meiyuan guesthouse, where we were staying in Wuhan. He often encouraged his staff to listen to his conversations as a way of keeping ourselves informed. I sat apart from the participants but could overhear everything. Three members of a committee established in July 1964, the "Five-Man Group of the Cultural Revolution," had just arrived from Beijing. The committee had recently been charged with directing criticism of Wu Han's play *Hai Rui Dismissed from Office.* Its members included propaganda chief Lu Dingyi, politburo member Kang Sheng, Beijing mayor and member of the central secretariat Peng Zhen, deputy chief of propaganda Zhou Yang, and head of the *People's Daily* Wu Lengxi. Lu Dingyi, Kang Sheng, and Peng Zhen had come to meet with Mao, accompanied by Xu Liqun, another deputy of the Propaganda Department, and Hu Sheng, a deputy editor in chief of *Red Flag,* the party's monthly propaganda journal.

Mao presided. He said that last December 21, he had told Chen Boda and Kang Sheng that he thought Yao Wenyuan's article attacking *Hai Rui Dismissed from Office* was very good. But Yao Wenyuan still missed the point, which was that the Ming dynasty's Jiajing emperor dismissed Hai Rui from office and in 1959 Mao dismissed Peng Dehuai. Peng Dehuai, Mao said, is the modern-day Hai Rui.

Mao turned to Peng Zhen, the head of the five-man committee. "Is Wu Han really anti-party, anti-socialist?" he wanted to know.

Before Peng Zhen could reply, Kang Sheng interjected to say that Wu Han's play was an "anti-party, anti-socialist poisonous weed."

No one dared to contradict him.

"Of course, if there are different opinions, they should be aired," Mao said as the silence continued. He said he wanted different opinions to be expressed, so we could compare them and see clearly which was right and wrong. "You should all feel free to speak. Let different opinions be aired here."

Peng Zhen finally spoke. He wanted to defend the contents of a document he had brought with him. Entitled "An Outline Report of the Five-Man Small Group to the Center," the document argued that the issues raised in Wu Han's play were academic rather than political. "I think we should follow the Chairman's instructions, letting one hundred schools contend, one hundred flowers bloom when discussing the academic issues raised by the play," Peng said. "We need a lively discussion." The Outline Report, already agreed to by the politburo standing committee, awaited only Mao's final approval.

Lu Dingyi spoke in support of Peng Zhen, emphasizing the academic nature of the debate, arguing that labels like anti-party and anti-socialist had to be avoided. If not, he argued, there will be complete silence.

Kang Sheng said nothing after Peng Zhen and Lu Dingyi presented their views. The battle lines were clear. Kang Sheng was interpreting the Wu Han affair as an issue of class struggle and wanted open political attacks against Wu Han and his supporters. Peng Zhen and Lu Dingyi were trying to keep the conflict in check by arguing that the controversy surrounding the play was nothing more than intellectual debate.

Minutes passed and no one said anything more. Mao adjourned the meeting.

But the participants still did not know where Mao stood. Peng Zhen wondered whether he had the Chairman's approval to write and distribute an intra-party commentary.

"You people work it out," Mao responded. "I don't need to see it."

I knew immediately that trouble was in the wind. Mao was deliberately setting a trap. His refusal to review the document could only mean that he did not approve. But Peng Zhen did not understand Mao the way I did. Peng Zhen and Lu Dingyi were heading for trouble. Distribution of their Outline Report meant danger.

. . .

Four days later, on February 12, 1966, the "Outline Report of the Five-Man Small Group on the Current Academic Debate" was disseminated to the party, together with a written commentary from the "central authority." But Mao had not seen the document, and those in the central authority who had were divided. The views represented in the document were those of Peng Zhen and Lu Dingyi. Discussions of *Hai Rui Dismissed from Office,* the document said, would be strictly academic.

Mao interpreted the document as a rebuke to his views. He agreed with Kang Sheng that Wu Han's play was a "poisonous weed" and that Wu Han himself was anti-party and anti-socialist. Lu Dingyi had been in serious political trouble before the report was published, and Peng Zhen had been under suspicion. Now the two men were in still greater jeopardy. By confining the discussion to academic debate, refusing to condemn Wu Han, they risked being branded anti-party, anti-socialist themselves.

"It appears that what I said before is correct," Mao said to me the night the Outline Report was distributed. "Reactionaries don't fall down unless you hit them hard." Mao was getting ready to hit hard. Peng Zhen's document was to become notorious ever after as the infamous anti-socialist "February Outline Report." Peng Zhen was about to be toppled.

59

Mao became tense and irritable following his meeting with Peng Zhen and Lu Dingyi. The sleeping pills were of little use. He would stay awake twenty-four hours at a time, until he finally became too exhausted to continue. His eating was affected, too. He would take only one small meal a day. I upped the dosage of his sleep medicine a bit, but waited until I knew he was nearly exhausted before giving him the pills. I was anxious about the increased dosage but even more worried about the effect of so little sleep on a man his age. After a week, his eating and sleeping returned to normal, and I began to relax a bit.

Just as my immediate anxieties had eased, Zhang Yufeng came to me with a new problem. "The Chairman thinks someone was in the attic of his guesthouse last night," she said. "He's heard noises there every night since we came."

I nearly laughed. The idea was preposterous. How could anyone possibly sneak into Mao's attic? The security surrounding the Chairman was impenetrable. But Zhang Yufeng was serious. And so was Mao.

I knew no human being could possibly be hiding in the attic. But it was possible that an animal had managed to get in. Maybe the noise had come from a rat. When Mao's staff discussed the problem, one of the guards said he had noticed some footprints that might belong to a wildcat.

The guards set traps, using fish as bait, and within two days the contraptions had done their work. Two wildcats were caught—one the size of a tiny panther, the other no bigger than a large house cat. Mao's villa in Wuhan was nestled in the woods, and the house was reserved for his exclusive use and ordinarily unoccupied. The bobcats had moved in without anyone knowing.

With the dead bobcats outdoors on display for Mao and everyone in his entourage to see, I assumed the "bad guy" theory would be put to rest. But Mao's paranoia remained strong. He was still worried that someone was in the attic. He insisted we leave immediately.

Within hours after the wildcats were caught, we were on our way to Hangzhou.

Mao remained anxious even in Hangzhou, and I sensed, even in the absence of concrete information, that the political situation was tense. Shortly after we arrived, I learned that Lin Biao's wife, Ye Qun, had called from Suzhou, where she and her husband often stayed, and asked to see Mao immediately. She flew in the next day, met with Mao behind closed doors for three hours, and then flew back to Suzhou. No one else was present at their meeting, and neither Mao nor Ye Qun told anyone in Group One what they had talked about.

I had dinner with the Chairman that night. "I don't know what kind of central secretariat Deng Xiaoping thinks he is running," Mao said while we were eating. "He had questionable characters there before and he's got questionable characters with him there now. Peng Zhen is number one. His control of the Beijing Municipal Party Committee is so tight you can't poke a hole in it with a needle or force a single drop of water through. Lu Dingyi controls the Department of Propaganda like the Palace of Hell, making sure that no leftist writings pass through. And there's Luo Ruiqing, who tried to prevent implementation of 'Let politics take command' and who tries to propagate eclecticism—and Yang Shangkun, who is always so busy gathering information and passing it around." Ever since he had found out about the bugging equipment, Mao had been convinced that Yang Shangkun was a spy. "This is Deng Xiaoping's central secretariat," he concluded in exasperation.

A day or so later, Jiang Qing came to visit Mao. As she came in, I saw that the change I had noticed in 1962 was now almost complete. She walked briskly, her back straight, and I saw not the slightest sign of her old ailments. She barely acknowledged my presence, merely nodding arrogantly in my direction as she passed by. Her entourage had recently been reduced to a nurse, an attendant, and a single security guard from Shanghai. Her old complaints had completely disappeared, her nurse told me while we waited. She was no longer bothered by bright lights or noises or drafts. Her headaches were gone. There was no ringing in her ears. She no longer needed the services of a doctor.

Jiang Qing's visit with her husband was brief, and she returned to Shanghai immediately thereafter. Only after her second visit, several days later, in late February, did I learn what they had discussed.

Lin Biao and Jiang Qing were forging an alliance. The two had convened a meeting in Shanghai from February 2 to 20, 1966, to discuss the ideology of armed forces–supported literature and art. Jiang Qing had been consulting Mao about the report from that conference. Mao gave me the final document to read.

The report was pure Mao. It was an attack on Lu Dingyi, warning that since the founding of the People's Republic, "the literary field and most professors have stood as a black force trying to dominate our politics." What surprised me was not the content of the document but the new relationship between Jiang Qing and Lin Biao: Lin Biao's route to power would be through the Chairman's wife. He would win Mao's support by first winning his wife's. The device had often been used in Chinese history, but it was devious and I never trusted people who used it. By calling upon Jiang Qing to serve as a publicist for her husband, Lin Biao was also deliberately catapulting the Chairman's wife into power. I was uneasy from the start. Jiang Qing with political power could be dangerous indeed.

I had never met Lin Biao. I had never even gotten a good look at him. Following liberation, Lin Biao had held several high-level posts, but he did not work and was such a recluse that he did not even go to Tiananmen to celebrate May Day and National Day. I had been sitting backstage when I heard him speak during the 7,000 cadres' conference, so I had only glimpsed him from the rear. But he was one of the country's ten marshals and reputed to be a brilliant leader—strong, decisive, and tough. Before meeting him, I shared the general admiration for his military genius. Lin's new alliance with Jiang Qing soon gave me the opportunity to meet him.

In March 1966, just after her visit with Mao, the Chairman's wife caught cold and asked me to go to Shanghai to treat her. Mao encouraged me. "I'll be in Shanghai pretty soon," he said. "It's not good for me to stay in one place too long." His paranoia persisted. After a few days anywhere, the anxiety set in and he had to be on his way. He did not feel safe in Hangzhou, either.

Transformed by her new involvement in politics, her neurasthenia largely cured, even Jiang Qing agreed that her cold was nothing serious. But the day after I arrived in Shanghai, Lin Biao suddenly showed up, too. He had learned that Jiang Qing was sick, he said, and wanted to pay his respects.

It was then that I first saw him. What struck me most was the army uniform he wore. It was so tight it might have been glued on. He arrived in the anteroom accompanied only by his secretary and took off his heavy wool coat. He was a slight man and short, with a pale gray face and a military cap that he wore even indoors to cover his spottily bald head. He was wearing thick leather boots. Lin barely nodded in my direction and never said a word. His eyes were so black the pupils and irises were indistinguishable, and they emitted an almost spiritual gleam.

Jiang Qing ordered that they not be disturbed, and the two met for three hours behind closed doors while I talked with Lin's secretary, Li Wenpu, and learned something of Lin's habits and his past. Lin Biao and Jiang Qing had much in common. Lin, too, had been a hypochondriac, suffering from neurasthenia, so afraid of light and drafts that he never went outside. Like Jiang Qing, his recent political involvement had also given him energy. His old neuroses had disappeared. Lin Biao was a changed man. His illness, too, I surmised, had been political.

But he still got sick. I discovered that several months later, in August 1966, just as the Cultural Revolution was reaching its first frenzy. Lin Biao was gaining more and more power and Wang Dongxing was trying to enter into his own alliance with the man Mao was about to choose as his successor. Lin Biao was sick, and Wang Dongxing wanted me to go with him to visit Lin at his residence at Maojiawan.

When we were escorted into his room, Lin Biao was in bed, curled in the arms of his wife, Ye Qun, his head nestled against her bosom. Lin Biao was crying, and Ye Qun was patting him and comforting him as though he were a baby. In that one moment, my view of Lin Biao changed—from bold and brilliant military commander to troubled soul unfit to lead. Two doctors, Xu Dianyi and Wu Jieping, arrived shortly after we did, and Wang Dongxing and I accompanied Ye Qun into an anteroom while the doctors conducted their examination. They found a kidney stone in Lin Biao's urinary tract and immediately administered medication. Lin Biao quickly calmed down, but my view of Lin did not change when I learned the cause of his illness. The passage of a kidney stone through the urinary tract is excruciatingly painful, but I expected a marshal like Lin to face such pain with courage.

While we were waiting, Ye Qun told me about her husband. Lin Biao had become addicted to opium in the 1940s and later to morphine. Late in 1949, he was sent to the Soviet Union to be cured of the addiction. It had not recurred, but his behavior continued to be strange. Lin Biao was still so afraid of wind and light that he rarely went outside, often missing meetings. His fear of water was so extreme that even the sound of it would give him instant diarrhea. He would not drink liquids at all. Ye Qun made sure he received liquid by dipping steamed buns in water and feeding them to her husband. That and the water in food were the only liquids he got.

Lin Biao never used a toilet. When moving his bowels, he would use a quilt, as if it were a tent, to cover himself and would squat over a bedpan that his wife would place on his bed.

I was astonished. Lin Biao was obviously mentally unsound, but Mao was promoting him to the highest reaches of power. Soon he would be hailed as Mao's "closest comrade in arms." One day Lin Biao would be governing the entire nation.

Back at Zhongnanhai, I told Mao of Lin Biao's problems. He was expressionless, silent. But I never discussed Lin's problems with other leaders or with medical colleagues. To have revealed such privileged information about one of the country's highest leaders would have been a political crime.

I stayed in Shanghai that March after Jiang Qing recovered from her cold, and I witnessed her new political activity. One fellow leftist after another came to visit, and always the meetings took place behind closed doors, cloaked in an aura of mystery, intrigue, and conspiracy. Yao Wenyuan, the Shanghai propagandist who had written the original article attacking Wu Han's play about Hai Rui, came not long after Lin Biao, shutting himself up with the Chairman's wife. Qi Benyu, who would later become the director of the General Office's Bureau of Secretaries,* followed, and then Guan Feng, one of the ultraleft editors at *Red Flag* magazine.

Mao arrived in Shanghai on March 15. He convened an enlarged meeting of the politburo standing committee two days later, where he continued Jiang Qing's argument that the academic and educational circles were dominated by bourgeois intellectuals who had endeavored for years to quash all leftist opinion and thought. He singled out four men for particular rebuke—playwright Wu Han, the author of the increasingly controversial *Hai Rui Dismissed from Office;* Beijing his-

---

*After Wang Dongxing became director of the General Office in 1966, the Office of Confidential Secretaries and the Office of Political Secretaries were combined to form the Bureau of Secretaries.

tory professor Jian Bozan; vice-mayor of Beijing Deng Tuo; and director of the United Front Work Department of Beijing municipality
Liao Mosha. These leading intellectuals were Communist party members in appearance, Mao argued, but members of the Guomindang in
thought and behavior. He proposed launching a "Cultural Revolution" in literature, history, law, and economics. I was naive enough to
hope that this revolution would be confined to culture and that I could
stay out of the storm.

At the end of March 1966, several days after the enlarged politburo meeting and while we were still in Shanghai, Mao met several
times with Jiang Qing, Kang Sheng, and Zhang Chunqiao. He wanted
to revoke Peng Zhen's February Outline Report, he told them. It
confused the class line. He wanted the Beijing Municipal Party Committee, headed by Peng Zhen, the Propaganda Department, headed by
Lu Dingyi, and the Five-Man Small Group of the Cultural Revolution—consisting of Peng Zhen, Lu Dingyi, Kang Sheng, Zhou Yang,
and Wu Lengxi—abolished. There were too many dubious individuals
in these three organizations, he said. And he wanted the thrust of the
Cultural Revolution expanded.

Mao was pursuing a two-pronged attack. He was calling upon the
politburo standing committee to criticize leading bourgeois intellectuals. At the same time, he was going outside the standing committee and
the party hierarchy to foster a rival group centering around his closest
allies—Jiang Qing and Kang Sheng in particular—whose task was to
attack Mao's enemies within the standing committee and the central
secretariat of the party. The move was unprecedented. Never before
had Mao launched an all-out attack against such high-level officials.

But Mao persisted. In early April, we returned to Hangzhou.
There, from April 16 to 20, he convened another meeting of the enlarged politburo standing committee. At this meeting he officially expanded his attacks to include Beijing party chief Peng Zhen. By
refusing to read or comment on Peng Zhen's February Outline Report,
which had tried to limit the cultural debate to academic issues, Mao
had allowed Peng to dig his own grave. Now he openly accused him
of taking an anti-party stand and demanded the dissolution of the
Five-Man Small Group of the Cultural Revolution and the formation
of a new one. The atmosphere at the April meeting was extraordinarily
tense.

I felt unsafe. Group One was no longer the same, and I neither
knew nor trusted the new arrivals. Mao had become inaccessible
within the wall built by his new security man, Qu Qiyu. Wang Dong-

xing had still not returned to Group One, and I had not seen him since we parted in Nanchang just after New Year's Day. Without him to protect me, I was at sea.

I wanted to see Wang Dongxing at the Hangzhou meeting, to learn what he knew about the political situation and seek his advice. I wanted to encourage him to return to Group One.

Wang was meeting with Zhou Enlai when I arrived at the Xiling Hotel late one night. Zhou was tense and not happy to see me.

"Do you know what time it is?" the premier asked. "Why have you come?"

"I want to report to Comrade Wang Dongxing on the Chairman's health over the past several months," I replied.

"Why do you have to make your report so late at night?" Zhou demanded.

Wang Dongxing interjected, trying to soothe Zhou's obviously jangled nerves. "I asked him to come, Premier," he said.

"Then hurry," Zhou said to Wang Dongxing. "Comrades Kang Sheng and Chen Boda are here. We can't keep them waiting." He turned to me. "When you have finished, please return immediately to the Wangzhuang guesthouse."

I had never known Zhou Enlai to be so tense and irritable, and interpreted his mood as a sign of serious political trouble. When I asked Wang what was wrong, he refused to say. "You know enough already," he said. "It concerns the central authority. It's best for you not to ask anymore. Tell me about the Chairman's health."

I was left to guess at the seriousness of the power struggle, and I was uneasy not knowing. I reported to Wang Dongxing on Mao's health and urged him to return to us at Group One. Zhang Yaoci, I explained, was a timid man who confined himself exclusively to matters of security. He was not doing much of a job. I would not feel safe until Wang Dongxing returned.

But Wang felt excluded from Group One. He wanted to return, but he could not do so until Mao asked. However, he promised to visit the Wangzhuang guesthouse to say hello when the meetings were over.

I was nervous about my visit to the Xiling Hotel. Zhou Enlai had been too tense, and there was too much I did not know. But I did know that he had an urgent meeting with Kang Sheng and Chen Boda, two leftists who liked to stir up trouble. As a precaution, I decided to report the whole episode to Mao. If he learned about my meeting from someone else, he might think I had been acting behind his back.

"So what are they doing over there?" Mao wanted to know, a faint smile on his lips, when I told him I had met with Wang Dongxing.

I told him Zhou Enlai had wanted me to leave quickly and seemed worried that I had some ulterior motive in being there.

"It was just a visit, nothing to get upset about," Mao assured me.

My report to Mao later saved me. At the end of 1966, when the newly formed "Central Cultural Revolution Small Group" expanded the targets of the Cultural Revolution to include Wang Dongxing, an attempt was made to implicate me as well. At that time, every meeting was seen as conspiratorial and every friend, acquaintance, and colleague of an accused person was in danger of being implicated, too. A security guard remembered having seen me at the Xiling Hotel and wrote a letter to Kang Sheng, who was masterminding the attacks. He accused me of colluding with Wang Dongxing and Zhou Enlai in some sort of plot, passing some secret information on to them. Kang Sheng gave the letter to Mao.

Mao gave me the letter and asked me to pass it on to Wang Dongxing for safekeeping. "You told me about the visit," he said. Mao protected both me and Wang Dongxing. The matter was dropped.

The enlarged standing committee of the politburo met again on April 24, 1966. Mao wanted the committee to discuss a new document that Chen Boda had drafted and Mao had revised, "A Circular of the Central Committee of the Chinese Communist Party." The main purpose of the circular was to revoke Peng Zhen's February Outline Report stressing the "academic" nature of the literary debate over Hai Rui and to disband the original Five-Man Small Group of the Cultural Revolution headed by Peng Zhen. This is when the new Central Cultural Revolution Small Group was formed, under the direct supervision of the politburo's standing committee. The focus of the Cultural Revolution was shifting. The movement was not about academic issues. Mao was launching what he called a "vigorous attack" on bourgeois elements within the party, the government, and the army.

The "Circular of the Central Committee of the Chinese Communist Party" was submitted to an enlarged politburo meeting held the following month, from May 4 to 26. The circular was passed on May 16 and became the guiding light of the Cultural Revolution, known throughout China by the date on which it had been adopted—the May 16 Circular.

Mao did not attend the May meetings. We were still in Hangzhou. But when he showed me the list of members of the new Central Cultural Revolution Small Group, my heart sank. The leftist Chen Boda was the head, and Kang Sheng was adviser. Jiang Qing had been appointed first deputy director. The sycophantic Wang Renzhong and Shanghai leader Zhang Chunqiao were deputy directors. The members, Wang Li, Guan Feng, Qi Benyu, and Yao Wenyuan, were all radical leftists. The initial suggestions, Mao said, had been made by Lin Biao. Mao had added Wang Renzhong.

The appointment of Jiang Qing made me particularly uneasy. She would take great delight in finding "bourgeois elements" in the party, and now, with real power, she could use the political campaign as an excuse to do away with her many enemies. Our relationship had continued to deteriorate since 1960, and now she was in a position to make trouble for me and my family.

Mao knew Jiang Qing's vindictiveness might reverberate to me. He encouraged me to make my peace with his wife, as his nephew, Mao Yuanxin, had done. Mao Yuanxin had been locked into an ongoing battle with Jiang Qing since childhood and ordinarily did not even bother speaking when he returned to Zhongnanhai on his summer vacations. But when the Cultural Revolution began, he wrote Mao a letter of apology. He had finally realized, Yuanxin wrote, that Jiang Qing was Mao's most loyal student and he had come to regard her with deep respect.

Mao was pleased and showed the letter to Jiang Qing.

Yuanxin, then a student at the Harbin College of Military Engineering, in China's far northeast, was an astute politician. Jiang Qing responded well to her nephew's apology, taking him under her wing and molding him into her leading lieutenant. When Jiang Qing went to battle against her opponents, Mao Yuanxin would often lead the way, and he rose rapidly through the military ranks. Within a few years, he had been appointed political commissar of the Shenyang Military Region in Manchuria.

Mao was hinting that I, too, should try to win his wife's favor. But my differences with Jiang Qing were not so easily resolved. Mao Yuanxin was her husband's nephew, and Jiang Qing's own political career was furthered by forgiving him and welcoming him into her fold. But I could do nothing for her and did not want to foster the new power she had been granted. And I could never bring myself to kowtow before her. I knew it was only a matter of time before she moved against me, and I was filled with a sense of impending doom. Jiang Qing would try to do me in. I had to find protection.

60

In May 1966, right after he had stirred things up, Mao went into retreat.

"Let others stay busy with politics," he said to me a few days after the May 16 Circular had been approved. "We're going to take a rest."

This was a familiar strategy. Mao would retreat into inactivity, allowing the political movement to develop without him. It was a way of allowing the snakes—his enemies—to come out of their holes. We were going to stay in Hangzhou for a while, away from political trouble.

Mao's retreat did not sit well with the party leadership. The Cultural Revolution needed his leadership. Mao's real goals, I think, were still a mystery to most of the party elite. Liu Shaoqi and Deng Xiaoping came to Hangzhou in early June to report to Mao about the progress of the movement and to solicit his advice. "Let them handle the problems of the movement by themselves," Mao said to me after the two leaders had left. "I need a rest."

The implications of Mao's retreat were ominous. Without his direction, the party would be plunged into chaos.

Mao was in high spirits in Hangzhou and enjoyed his stay. The Zhejiang authorities organized dancing parties for him almost daily, and he often climbed the Dingjia Hill near his villa. But he was frequently pensive and taciturn, lost in his own thoughts. By mid-June he was on the move again. He wanted to go back to his native village of Shaoshan. We arrived there on June 18.

Since Mao had last visited Shaoshan, in June 1959, Tao Zhu, now first secretary of the Central-South Bureau, had constructed a new villa for the Chairman at a place called Dishui Cave. Mao had said that he wanted to retire in Shaoshan and live in a thatched-roof cottage. The villa was Tao Zhu's response.

Dishui Cave was nestled in foothills, surrounded by shrubbery and forest, and cut off from the world outside. Mao knew the area well. As a child, he had gathered firewood in the surrounding forest, and he reminisced about kowtowing before a huge rock—Grandmother Rock, he called it—on top of Big Drum Hill. He had often napped in the Tiger Resting Pavilion atop another hill.

Beijing seemed very far away from the peace and seclusion of Dishui Cave, and news was harder to come by. The confidential couriers delivered their documents only once every two or three days. I was anxious to find out what was happening in Beijing and encouraged the couriers to talk. The capital was descending into chaos. The schools had been closed, and the students had taken to the streets, rampaging through the city. No one, it seemed, could control the situation. I pressed the couriers for more details, but with the situation so tense, they were reluctant to say more.

I did learn that my old boss, Fu Lianzhang, who had urged me to return and sent me to work at "Labor University," had already become a victim of the Cultural Revolution. Fu had been forced to retire in 1958. His habit of checking up on the political activities of the leaders through expressions of concern for their health had finally proven so irritating that all the leaders wanted him gone. I had heard little about him since, but the couriers had brought Mao a letter from his former doctor.

Fu had been called out of retirement to be "struggled against" and had made an unsuccessful attempt at suicide after the attacks against him began. He wanted Mao's help. "Fu Lianzhang is a good man," Mao said to me. "He's retired, no longer involved in politics. There is no reason to struggle against him. I'll do something to protect him."

But Mao's efforts were too little and too late. Toward the end of 1966, Fu was taken forcibly from his home by a group of rebels from the army's General Logistics Department. He was never heard from again. He died during the struggles against him, and his body was never recovered.

Ten days after our arrival in Shaoshan, the heat became unbearable. We were swimming daily in the Shaoshan reservoir, but the villa at Dishui Cave had no air-conditioning, and the electric fan was no help. Mao decided to move on. We left for Wuhan on June 28.

Our access to news from Beijing was much better in Wuhan. The confidential couriers came daily, with documents, magazines, and letters. I received my first letter from Lillian in months and realized with a start that I had not been in Beijing or seen my family for more than a year—since I had accompanied Wang Dongxing and the "four cleanups" campaign work team to Shixi village, Jiangxi, in July 1965.

Following the Cultural Revolution from Wuhan, Mao thoroughly enjoyed the upheaval his movement had unleashed in Beijing. With Mao withdrawn, his enemies were showing their hands, making it easier for him to strike them down. I sensed this not only from my meetings with Mao but from a letter he wrote on July 8, 1966, to Jiang Qing in Shanghai.

Mao never really had a plan for the Cultural Revolution. But the letter to his wife revealed what he thought about it then. As Mao's suspicions about so many others around him worsened, his political faith in Jiang Qing grew.

"Every day I read documents and other materials with great interest," Mao wrote to her from our retreat in Wuhan. "Great chaos will lead to great order. The cycle appears every seven or eight years. The demons and monsters will come out by themselves. Their class character dictates it."

Mao wrote, too, about the discomfort he felt over Lin Biao's campaign of adulation. "I don't believe the few pamphlets I wrote are as magical and powerful as he says," Mao said. "It's like Old Wang saying his watermelon is sweet because he is selling it. But after he started exaggerating, the whole party and the whole nation have followed suit." Mao claimed that Lin Biao's introduction of the cult of Mao was the first time in his life he had succumbed to an opinion contrary to his own on an issue of great importance. "A person with a great reputation will find difficulty living up to it in reality," Mao wrote, quoting the Han dynasty's Li Gu. "These words apply to me exactly." Mao claimed to have protested such adulation at the April standing committee meeting in Hangzhou. But Lin Biao had paid no attention, repeating his praise in May. "So newspapers and magazines have exaggerated the importance of my writings even more, as if they were the product of a superman. I have been forced to accept his argument. I guess his intention is to beat the devil [Mao's enemies in the party] by invoking my magic powers."

Mao was neither certain that his Cultural Revolution would

achieve its goal nor convinced that socialism had come to China for good. The "rightists," he felt, might return to power, and Mao himself might be smashed to pieces. But he was convinced that his ideas would remain and that socialism would eventually be revived. No victory for the reactionaries could ever be permanent.

Mao also had a warning for Jiang Qing: "Don't let victory intoxicate you," he cautioned. "Think often of your weaknesses, shortcomings, and mistakes. I don't know how many times I have told you this. You must remember it."

Jiang Qing was so excited about the letter, despite its criticisms of her, that she wanted it printed and distributed for others to read. Mao had shared with her some of his innermost political thoughts, and she took this as a demonstration of her husband's trust. It enhanced her own legitimacy. She had already begun sharing the letter with members of the inner circle when Mao found out and had the copies recalled. I copied the letter into a notebook before returning it to the General Office's Office of Administration, and have it even now.

I have thought often of that letter in the quarter century since. To this day, even with all that has happened, I still see it as evidence that Mao was more politically prescient than even he knew. Lin Biao, whom Mao never fully trusted and whom he was using temporarily in his struggle against his other enemies in the party, did turn against him, and following Mao's death the "rightists" did return to power.

As long as Mao himself stayed away from the capital, watching the Cultural Revolution from afar, I was able to avoid involvement in the unfolding political struggle, so I was happy not to be in Beijing. Having stayed out of earlier political campaigns, I had every intention of sitting out the Cultural Revolution, too. Mao, though, was determined to have me participate.

By early July, Mao had been away from the capital for months. Beijing was in chaos. He was getting ready to return. "The situation in Beijing has become very lively," he said to me one evening. "We can't rely only on documents to learn what is going on. We need to see the situation in person. Only then can we differentiate the good people from the bad. I have to stay here for now, but you return to Beijing first and have a look. Get ready and leave tomorrow."

He wanted me to investigate the Cultural Revolution in Beijing and report my impressions to him. This was the "something" he had said he might want me to do for him when he refused to let me return to Shixi.

But the political situation in Beijing was much too complicated.

Neither the politburo nor the central secretariat was in control any longer. Even Mao's closest lieutenants were under attack. How was I, a mere doctor, a man who had so studiously avoided all involvement, to distinguish enemy from friend? "I won't be able to tell the good persons from the bad," I protested to Mao. "Whom should I talk to after I return?"

Mao instructed me to see Tao Zhu, whom I had first come to know while he was first party secretary in Guangdong province and whom Mao had just appointed adviser to the Central Cultural Revolution Small Group. He had also replaced Lu Dingyi as head of the Propaganda Department. Tao Zhu was a logical person for me to see. He was head of the Propaganda Department, and was also responsible for administering the State Council's Ministry of Public Health. "Tell him I sent you," Mao said. "Let him make arrangements for you to see how the revolutionary rebel movement is doing and to take a look at the big character posters the masses have put up. Tell me what you think after I return to Beijing."

I was skeptical. Under Mao's direct protection, I felt safe. Alone, called upon to investigate a movement I did not understand, I would be surrounded by danger. "A thousand people will die this time, I think," Mao had said to me a few weeks earlier. "Everything is turning upside down. *Wo xihuan tianxia da luan.* I love great upheavals."

I did not love great upheavals, and this one frightened me a lot. But I flew back to Beijing the following day, as Mao had ordered—the first time I had been there in more than a year.

Thus it was that I was in Beijing on July 16, 1966, when Mao took his celebrated swim in the Yangtze River. Having been swimming with Mao so many times before, I barely noticed the event. Nor did it occur to me that foreign skeptics might gasp in disbelief that a seventy-three-year-old man could swim faster and further than an Olympic champion. I knew how swiftly the Yangtze flows through Wuhan. Mao had only floated on his back, his giant belly buoying him like a balloon, carried down the river by the current. I also knew by then that Mao's swims were acts of defiance against the party leadership and a signal that the battle was about to begin.

For me, Mao's swim in the Yangtze meant that his self-enforced exile was over. He was returning to the political stage. Two days later, on July 18, he returned to Beijing. Henceforth, the Cultural Revolution would follow his direction.

61

My family had missed me greatly—especially so with the bitter political turn. Our reunion was joyful, and I shared a special dinner with my wife and two children my first night back. But Lillian was tense. I knew that she was distraught about Jiang Qing's new political role, convinced that her vindictiveness would eventually be turned against us. But something more was bothering her.

"I have some terrible news," she said that night after the children had gone to bed. She was whispering. With the advent of the Cultural Revolution, we had to whisper even in our own home.

"Tian Jiaying committed suicide," she said.

I was stunned. Tian Jiaying was one of my best friends. As one of Mao's political secretaries, he had kept me informed about politics, and we saw eye to eye on many matters. I had thought often of Tian Jiaying in recent months, particularly since learning that Chen Boda and Jiang Qing were both on the new Central Cultural Revolution Small Group. Tian and Jiang Qing had never gotten along, and Chen Boda's opportunistic support of the Great Leap Forward had brought the two men into nasty conflicts. Tian Jiaying had never supported the Great Leap Forward and had become increasingly disaffected following Mao's purge of Peng Dehuai in 1959. I had expected my friend to be in trouble. But I had never imagined that he might take his own life—and so quickly, even before the real meaning of the Cultural Revolution was clear. Many of my close friends would take their lives during the Cultural Revolution. Tian Jiaying was the first.

I was shocked, too, that no one had told me. Surely other members of Mao's staff in Hangzhou and Wuhan must have known. Why had no one told me?

Lillian knew only that a few days after the formal decision to launch a Great Proletarian Cultural Revolution on May 16, Wang Dongxing, as newly appointed director of the General Office, had talked with Tian Jiaying and then sent several staff members to take custody of his documents—a sure sign that Tian was about to be purged. The order to seize the documents of a man so highly placed would have had to come from very high up. Either Zhou Enlai or Mao himself must have issued it. That night, after the documents were seized, Tian Jiaying hanged himself.

Lillian was worried about me. Why had Mao sent me back to Beijing first, without him? She was convinced that Mao was testing me. He wanted to know what my attitude toward the Cultural Revolution would be, whose side I was on, whether I would remain loyal to him. She pleaded with me to lie low and say as little as possible. She was afraid that I, too, would soon come under attack and that I would not be able to bear the insults. She was worried that I might collapse under pressure and commit suicide.

Members of the Communist party are not allowed to commit suicide. Suicide is seen as a betrayal of the party. The family members of such traitors bear the dead man's label forever, known for the rest of their lives as the "wife of a traitor" or the "son of a traitor" and are condemned to the most despicable lives. Lillian would be fired from her job, forced into menial labor, and my whole family would be exiled. She pleaded with me that night not to take my life. "If you commit suicide, that would be the end of us all," she said.

I promised that nothing would drive me to suicide. But I knew I would be attacked. And I knew that my family would suffer, too. An attack against one member of my family would be an attack against all. There was no escape.

My mind was racing. There was only one way out. "The day they arrest or imprison me," I instructed Lillian, "you must file for divorce."

Only much later did I realize how foolish I was. Divorce could not save my family. Repeatedly during the Cultural Revolution I saw whole families go under once one of them had come under attack. Death, divorce, or separation provided no reprieve.

I prepared myself for my first test. Lillian was right: Mao had sent me back to Beijing to test my loyalty to him. The day after my return, I told Wang Dongxing that Mao had asked me to meet with Tao Zhu to learn how the Cultural Revolution was unfolding. Tao would be arriving in Beijing the next day. Wang Dongxing asked me to help with the arrangements for Tao's housing in Zhongnanhai and to join him at the airport to welcome Tao.

As we drove from the airport back to Zhongnanhai, I told Tao of the assignment Mao had given me. "No problem," Tao said. He suggested I visit Peking Union Medical College, now renamed Chinese Medical University, the next day. "I'll ask someone from the Central Cultural Revolution Small Group to go with you," he said.

I hesitated. I was ill at ease with the leftists in the group. To get myself mixed up with any of them would mean becoming more involved politically than I wanted. It might imply that I was one of them, "standing on the side of the left." For me to meet Tao Zhu was fine. Mao had set up the meeting. For me to meet with the leftists was courting danger. If I met with anyone in the group other than Tao and that person later got into trouble, I would have no protection. Mao could say that his instructions were for me to meet with Tao Zhu and no one else.

Wang Dongxing understood my dilemma instinctively and came to my defense. "The Chairman merely asked Dr. Li to talk with you, not other members of the Small Group. I don't think he should get involved with any of the others yet," he said.

Tao Zhu agreed. He suggested I accompany minister of public health Qian Xinzhong the next day when he visited Chinese Medical University. Someone from Tao Zhu's Propaganda Department would accompany us.

Chinese Medical University was in turmoil, and our arrival on the campus was a major event. Qian Xinzhong was directly responsible for the functioning of the university. The students were on strike, and big character posters attacking university officials were everywhere. I was astonished to see that one of them was an attack against the minister of public health, Qian Xinzhong himself. He was accused of being a "Guomindang remnant." Qian had once been a surgeon with the Guomindang army but had joined the communist side in 1934, after being captured during a battle in Anhui. In the past, the party had welcomed such "defectors" from the Guomindang, and Qian, to my mind, had joined the party early, during the war with Japan and before the final civil war between the nationalists and the communists. I would have thought his party credentials were impeccable. The atmosphere on the campus had the quality of a witch-hunt.

I thought of myself. Anyone outside my protective inner circle who investigated my background could make similarly irresponsible attacks, and the consequences would be terrible. My past would destroy me. I had joined the party late, well after liberation. My father had been a high-ranking official under the Guomindang, and my wife was the daughter of a landlord. The fact that I had been so thoroughly investigated and cleared in 1953 would mean nothing at all.

The students were in the auditorium, waiting for Qian's arrival, and the place was packed with highly emotional students. I could hear them shouting slogans even before we entered. I sat, unobtrusive and anonymous, in the back as Qian Xinzhong went to the stage. Comrade Xu, the representative from the Propaganda Department whom Tao Zhu had sent to accompany us, melted into the crowd and disappeared. The unruly students began shouting questions at those onstage, and I heard accusations that Qian Xinzhong and the Ministry of Public Health had served only the "lords" and ignored the health care of the masses. They were quoting Mao's important "June 26 [1965] Directive" as their justification. Suddenly I realized that this June 26 Directive was the memo Mao had asked me to write after our conversation in June 1965, just before I went to join the "four cleanups" campaign with Wang Dongxing. It was the memo I had sent to Peng Zhen and minister of public health Qian Xinzhong. The contents of my conversation with the Chairman had been transformed into Mao's June 26 Directive and were being used to attack my friend Qian Xinzhong.

I was miserable. I liked and admired Qian. Had I not forwarded Mao's criticism to the Ministry of Public Health, he might not be going through this awful verbal harassment. Of all the people in the room, only Qian himself knew that I had written the directive, that I was accompanying him there at the suggestion of Tao Zhu and, by implication, Mao. Only Qian knew that I was Mao's doctor. I left the meeting shaken, vowing never to attend another like it. And I knew that I had to avoid the possibility of ever being interrogated and having my own past exposed. Forced to answer questions about my own past and family background, I would be destroyed. Wang Dongxing, seeing me so upset, agreed.

Tao Zhu's political fortunes changed quickly. He was purged in December of that year because he was too independent from Jiang Qing and because he continued to support many leaders, including Qian Xinzhong and Hubei party chief Wang Renzhong, who had been targeted for purge. After Tao Zhu and Qian Xinzhong had been purged, Comrade Xu from the Propaganda Department, who had accompanied us to the meeting at Chinese Medical University only to melt into the crowd, suddenly reappeared to accuse me. He wrote a letter to Chen Boda, the director of the Central Cultural Revolution Small Group, charging that I had formed a close alliance with the now deposed Tao Zhu and had accompanied Qian Xinzhong to Chinese Medical University in order to defend the Ministry of Public Health. Chen Boda forwarded the letter to Mao, who in turn showed it to me.

"But you are the one who asked me to return to Beijing and see Tao Zhu," I said.

Mao smiled. "If you are being accused of forming relationships with anyone, then I guess we have to say you're pretty close to me," he said. He wanted me to write my own big character poster attacking Qian Xinzhong. I did not, but I never told Mao. Nevertheless, the Chairman saved me from being caught in the roundup of alleged Tao Zhu supporters. Others as innocent as I had no such protection.

Mao still wanted me actively involved in the Cultural Revolution. He was not going to allow me to stay on the sidelines. His test of my loyalty was relentless. Two days after his return to Beijing, he called me to his bedroom in the Chrysanthemum Fragrance Study. He wanted me and head nurse Wu Xujun to accompany his daughter Li Na to Peking University the following day. "Take a look at the big character posters, talk with the students, find out if they really are counterrevolutionaries," he said.

While Mao had been in retreat in Hangzhou and Wuhan, refusing to return to Beijing and letting Liu Shaoqi take charge of the Cultural Revolution, Liu had sent work teams into the city's universities to direct the unfolding political movement. But Mao suspected that instead of supporting the student rebellion, the work teams had been suppressing the students, condemning them as counterrevolutionaries.

I did not like the idea of accompanying Li Na. Many people had known her when she was a history student there. I was afraid that if the three of us went together, people would think that Mao was involved.

But Mao was not concerned. "So what?" he said. "It's fine if they think I'm involved. You must support the students, though."

Li Na invited several of her former schoolmates and professors to meet with us in one of the dormitory rooms. I said little as the students complained about the university authorities. Lu Ping, the president of the university, who had come to Li Na's aid when she had a cold and I came to take her to Beijing Hospital, was the object of particular opprobrium. The university party committee had suppressed their revolution, the students said, and when the work team came to replace the party committee, it too had intimidated the students, accusing the activists of being counterrevolutionary. After listening to the students' complaints, we strolled around the campus, reading the big character posters that were plastered everywhere. The whole university population seemed to be outside, and people were clustered in small groups, locked in political debate.

What was happening at Beida (Peking University) was of little interest to me, however. The real political problem was not on university campuses but in the highest ranks of the party. The leaders themselves had to find a way to resolve their differences, I thought. There was no need to involve the students.

Mao, of course, thought otherwise. He was at war with leading members of his own party, and now, even more than in 1957, he knew he could no longer rely on the party to rectify itself. Nor could he depend on the intellectuals to criticize the party. When he had called on them to "let one hundred flowers bloom, one hundred schools of thought contend," they had responded not only by attacking his enemies but by arguing against socialism and criticizing the Chairman as well. During this Cultural Revolution, he would leap over the cumbersome bureaucracy of party and state and go straight to those whom he knew revered him, and he considered the young his most reliable allies. Only the young have the courage to do battle with the old political forces, he had told me in July, while we were still in Wuhan. "We have to depend on them to start a rebellion, a revolution. Otherwise, we may not be able to overthrow those demons and monsters."

Mao had not needed me to report on the situation at Beida. He knew what was happening there. He had sent me to test my attitude toward the Cultural Revolution.

He wanted to know whether I thought condemning the students as counterrevolutionaries was correct.

"No, of course not," I answered immediately. "How could so many students be counterrevolutionaries?"

"Right," Mao responded. "That's exactly the question." I had passed my first test. Shortly thereafter, he abolished the work teams that Liu Shaoqi had set up, charging them with trying to suppress the students and their revolt.

Having returned to Beijing, Mao emerged from retreat and his role became increasingly public. On July 29, 1966, he called a meeting in the Great Hall of the People, where some ten thousand students from Beijing's colleges and middle schools came to hear the official announcement that the work teams were being disbanded. The student rebels who had been victimized were now exonerated. Liu Shaoqi and Deng Xiaoping were forced to take responsibility publicly for having dispatched the work teams in Mao's absence.

Mao did not intend to participate in the meeting. He refused to be publicly associated with the likes of Liu Shaoqi and Deng Xiaoping. But unbeknownst to either the leaders or the students, he did go to the auditorium. Just before the proceedings began, I joined him where he sat, hidden from view behind the curtain. Listening intently, Mao said nothing until Liu Shaoqi made what he called a "self-criticism."

Liu's self-criticism was much like Mao's in 1962. Liu admitted to no wrongdoing, saying only that he and his associates were "old revolutionaries facing new problems." Inexperienced, they did not yet understand how to carry out this Great Proletarian Cultural Revolution.

When Mao heard this, he snorted. "What old revolutionaries? Old counterrevolutionaries is more like it."

My heart sank. I had been deluding myself about the Cultural Revolution, and now its purpose was clear. The ultimate targets were Liu Shaoqi and Deng Xiaoping. They were the "counterrevolutionaries" Mao insisted were hidden in the party, the "party people in authority taking the capitalist road." The Cultural Revolution was a campaign to destroy them.

Zhou Enlai followed Liu Shaoqi to the podium, trying to outline for the students the meaning and goals of the Cultural Revolution. Behind the curtain, Mao stood up to leave, ready to return to Room 118, his opulent suite in the Great Hall of the People, not far from the auditorium.

Then suddenly he changed his mind. "We have to support the revolutionary masses," he said.

When Zhou Enlai finished his presentation, the curtains behind the stage parted, pulled back by several attendants, and suddenly, unexpectedly, like magic, Chairman Mao stepped through the opening and onto the stage. The crowd roared. Mao waved to the cheering audience, now thundering out its approval with rhythmic chants of "Long Live Chairman Mao! Long Live Chairman Mao!" as the Chairman himself walked back and forth across the stage, slowly waving, saying nothing, his face impassive. With the chants still echoing in our ears, Mao left the stage and walked in triumph back to Room 118, with Zhou Enlai trailing like a faithful dog behind. Mao had neither looked at Liu Shaoqi and Deng Xiaoping nor acknowledged their presence, and the two men, dazed, remained onstage. Few in the audience could have missed Mao's message. He was distancing himself from Liu and Deng.

. . .

Three days later, on August 1, Mao wrote a letter to a young student at the middle school run by Qinghua University. A group of youngsters there had formed a rebel organization they called the Red Guards, and Mao praised the organization and said that "to rebel is justified." Mao's words were reprinted in student publications and immediately became the rallying cry of young people everywhere in China. Red Guard groups began springing up in middle schools and universities throughout the country.

Then, as if to support the big character posters that had begun appearing on campuses everywhere, Mao wrote his own big character poster. Entitled "Bombard the Headquarters," its contents were quickly disseminated by the central authority. Mao argued that in the last fifty days or so, certain "comrades" at both the national and the local levels of government had taken a reactionary, bourgeois stand, enforcing the dictatorship of the bourgeoisie. They are trying, he asserted, to strike down the spectacular Great Proletarian Cultural Revolution. With Mao's blessing, the Cultural Revolution spread further as young people throughout China took to the streets to bombard their own party headquarters, certain that Mao himself supported their rebellion, assured that "to rebel is justified" and that they were good and right.

Mao continued to ignore the party bureaucracy. On August 10, 1966, he "received the masses" at the west gate of Zhongnanhai. Later, he stood atop Tiananmen to receive millions of Red Guards who had come to Beijing from all over the country. Eight times during the fall of 1966 I would stand with Mao atop Tiananmen—or sit with him in an open jeep—as he waved to the young Red Guards who had traveled from the far parts of the country to see their great leader. Lin Biao was there, too, his neurasthenia cured by his new political role. The sun shines brightest in Beijing during the fall, and the wind atop Tiananmen is strong, but Lin Biao apparently no longer feared sun or drafts. He accompanied Mao each time, smiling and waving to the crowds below.

I knew by then that the hostility to Liu Shaoqi and Deng Xiaoping I had first sensed at the Eighth Party Congress in 1956 was coming to a head, and that both were likely to be toppled. Still, for the great majority of his countrymen, the real purpose of Mao's Cultural Revolution remained unclear. In private, with only me and a few others to hear, Mao had said that Liu Shaoqi was a counterrevolutionary. In public, he was more conciliatory. When the Eleventh Plenum of the Eighth Party Congress convened from August 1 to 12, 1966, the Chairman's remarks were relatively benign. It would be monarchical if ours were the only party allowed to exist, he said, and it would be equally strange if the party were without internal factions. He even seemed willing to forgive those who had differed with him. We can't prohibit people from making mistakes, he said. We must permit them to correct their mistakes. But his words were deceptive. Mao did not really allow factions to oppose his views. Nor was he willing to forgive those who differed with him. Anyone who had previously opposed him, all those who had ever criticized him, would soon be ruthlessly purged.

The Chinese have a saying that it takes many years for a river to be covered with three feet of ice. It had taken many years for Mao to reach the point where he was able to purge his enemies, and the grudges he held often traced back to before liberation. To emerge victorious, he was willing to plunge the entire country into chaos.

62

With Mao behind them, the student rebels were unleashed to move from their schools to the streets, and the house searches of those suspected of "bourgeois" tendencies began. When the Red Guards began breaking into private homes to question the occupants and search for evidence of their antipathy toward socialism, the tranquility of my life at Gongxian Lane was shattered.

From the beginning, the elitism of the country's health-care system was a major target of the Cultural Revolution, and the leaders of the Ministry of Public Health were under continual attack. Three of the vice-ministers lived in my compound. After the house searches began, both Red Guards and staff members of Jiang Qing's Central Cultural Revolution Small Group disguising themselves as Red Guards began invading my compound, hauling out the vice-ministers and searching their homes. I was not meant to be a target, but with so much chaos—adolescents on the march, false accusations flying, and everyone under suspicion—I lived in terror of being called out for interrogation. Lillian urged me not to come home but to seek refuge in Zhongnanhai. So long as I was with Mao, the students could not drag me out.

Mao agreed. He gave me a special assignment. He wanted me and head nurse Wu Xujun to read the reports that were pouring in from all over the country, screen them, and pass the most interesting or important articles on to him. With the burst of political activity everywhere in the country, a great surge of documents was coming in, too, and Mao's regular staff could not possibly read them all.

I enjoyed my new assignment. All sorts of new information was turning up, much of which had previously been secret. Even documents and minutes from the central authority were suddenly being published by student Red Guards, and so were the records of the struggle sessions against the leaders who were coming under attack.

Reading the reports kept me informed about the movement without having to be involved. Living at Zhongnanhai and rarely returning home, I managed, temporarily, to stay safe. I felt sad that the serenity and beauty of Gongxian Lane had been so rudely shattered but was grateful for the protection of Zhongnanhai.

Then even Zhongnanhai was no longer safe. Everyone who worked there came under suspicion. Even Zhou Enlai was a target, accused by Jiang Qing and her friends of being a turncoat. The evidence came from an independent newspaper, *Shen Bao,* published in the 1930s in Shanghai, which contained a signed article by a man named Wu Hao, Zhou's underground pseudonym at the time, announcing that he had left the Communist party. I was at the indoor swimming pool when Zhou came to discuss the problem with Mao, a library copy of the original newspaper under his arm. The article was a forgery by enemies in the Guomindang, Zhou said, pointing out that he had already left Shanghai at the time of the alleged announcement and could not possibly have written it himself. Mao himself never talked to me about the incident, although I know it bothered Zhou until he died. But Mao was satisfied with Zhou's report and furious about the irresponsible behavior of his wife's colleagues Wang Li and Guan Feng.

The case of Tian Jiaying was also unsettled. He had been liked and respected by many in Zhongnanhai, and they were both grieved and shaken by his suicide. But Tian Jiaying had been branded a traitor, and all of us who had been associated with him were therefore under suspicion. Zhou Enlai, still loyal to Mao and worried that other traitors lurked even within Zhongnanhai, fearful even that some among the staff might want to do away with the Chairman, ordered Wang Dongxing to increase security and undertake new investigations to ensure the reliability of us all. Wang put one of his subordinates from the General Office, a good and reasonable man named Yu Gang, in charge. The suspects were taken away to a "study class," and the Zhongnanhai staff members were called upon to evaluate their own political conduct and to report on anyone who might have opposed

Chairman Mao, the party, or socialism. Friends and colleagues of Tian Jiaying were particularly suspect.

Within weeks, I was accused by Tian Jiaying's widow, Dong Bian. As Tian Jiaying's wife, her own loyalty to Mao and the party was automatically suspect, and she was a member of the "study class." She wanted to "draw a clear line of demarcation" between herself and her traitor of a husband, to demonstrate her loyalty to the party beyond any shadow of a doubt. Unless she could prove her loyalty, she would be forever branded the wife of a traitor. Accusing me was a way of redeeming herself and proving her devotion to the party.

Dong Bian was strong on logic but weak in evidence. She pointed out that Tian Jiaying and I had been good friends and that we often confided in each other. She had no concrete examples of my anti-party behavior, but if Tian was an anti-party element, then I, as his friend, must be too.

Another suspect, Tian Jiaying's secretary, Pang Xianzhi, also accused me, and he had real evidence. He reported on a conversation between me, Wang Dongxing, and Mao's former secretary Lin Ke one day in 1963, traveling on Mao's special train, when I had criticized Mao's policy of class struggle. I did not like his new "socialist education campaign," Pang Xianzhi said, and he quoted me as having complained that "the Chairman does not want the people to have a single moment of peace. Just as we're starting to produce enough food to feed the people, he wants to stir things up again." He also accused me of having impugned Mao's character, saying that the Chairman was a philanderer who took advantage of young women.

Pang Xianzhi had never heard me say such things. But his report was accurate. Lin Ke had reported the conversation to Tian Jiaying and Pang Xianzhi. In the witch-hunting atmosphere of the Cultural Revolution, my remarks were nothing short of counterrevolutionary. If Jiang Qing or her cronies in the Central Cultural Revolution Small Group were to find out, my arrest would be certain.

But Wang Dongxing protected me. He had no choice. Wang was already under scrutiny, his every action observed by rebels within the Central Bureau of Guards, and I was the first link in a chain that led directly to him. He had recommended me as Mao's personal physician, and if I should turn out to be a counterrevolutionary, then Wang would be a counterrevolutionary too. Moreover, Wang was present when I made my counterrevolutionary remarks, and he had not reported them, a sign that he agreed and another reason to label him counterrevolutionary. And if I were arrested and forced to confess to my crimes and report my conversations with the Chairman's staff, I would naturally implicate others. I could easily implicate Wang Dongxing. He, too, had made plenty of incriminating remarks, especially about the Chairman's private life.

Wang was cavalier. "At worst, we'll go to jail together," he said. "In prison, we can eat and live for free, and we wouldn't have to work. What's there to be afraid of?"

But Wang's power over me was now great. The two letters of accusation were in his possession, and if he turned against me and released them to Jiang Qing or her allies, I would go to jail.

Wang could not burn the letters. He was too closely watched, and burning evidence was yet another sign that one had something to hide. He kept the letters in safekeeping in his own apartment and instructed Lin Ke, then at the New China News Agency, to keep my indiscretion secret. He ordered Yu Gang, who was directing the investigations within Zhongnanhai, to warn Pang Xianzhi to stop his accusations. When May 7 Cadre Schools were established in 1967 and millions of party cadres were exiled to hard labor in rural areas, Wang sent all the remaining suspects from the "study class," including Pang Xianzhi, to Wang's native Jiangxi, where Wang and I both had our own experience in exile. Pang stayed for more than a decade, until 1978.

But only months after the accusations against me, the rebels in Wang Dongxing's own Central Bureau of Guards turned viciously against him. Posters, written by his subordinates, began appearing in Zhongnanhai saying that Wang Dongxing should be burned alive, roasted to death. The unit from which Mao's driver, Zhang Zhengji, had been drawn was particularly rebellious. Wang's house was no longer safe. The rebels might search it. He had to get rid of the documents.

Wang Dongxing took the accusatory letters to Zhou Enlai, the next link in the chain, and asked him to keep them safe. Zhou was nervous. Taking the letters was like holding burning coals in his hands, he said. He, too, was under suspicion, but he needed Wang Dongxing's protection and support. So he took the letters and locked them in his safe. They stayed there until Zhou's death in January 1976. Only then did Wang Dongxing retrieve and burn them.

The attacks against Wang Dongxing did not last for long. Mao stopped them. "The public-security system cannot be disrupted," Mao told me. Mao gave the orders to Zhou Enlai, and Zhou, in turn, ordered that none of the people working closely around Mao were to participate in revolutionary rebel activities. Mao told his driver, Zhang Zhengji, to remember that Wang's position was sacrosanct and no harm was to come to the man charged with protecting the Chairman. "Tell others what I have told you," Mao ordered. Mao's own safety was at stake, after all, and in the turmoil that he had unleashed Mao wanted to be sure that he would be protected.

Wang took the opportunity of Mao's directive to further consolidate his own power, launching a counterattack against the revolutionary rebels within the Central Bureau of Guards and sending them, too, to the May 7 Cadre School in Jiangxi. His organization must have been the only one in China both to survive the Cultural Revolution intact and to become stronger still. The party organization was such a shambles that even the politburo had ceased to function. Party leaders at every level were under attack. Many had been overthrown. Most were unable to function. The bureaucracy under the State Council, directed by Zhou Enlai, was also in chaos. With the politburo incapacitated, an ad hoc policy committee had to be formed. It consisted of the members of the Central Cultural Revolution Small Group plus Premier Zhou Enlai, minister of public security Xie Fuzhi, Lin Biao's wife, Ye Qun, and Wang Dongxing.

63

Mao needed Wang Dongxing. Wang was in charge of the Chairman's security, and Mao did not feel safe. As he moved to cast out his enemies, he grew more insecure. After discovering that the Chrysanthemum Fragrance Study, his residence in Zhongnanhai, had been bugged, he never trusted the place again and suspected that new listening devices had been planted in his absence. He wanted to move.

Shortly after his return in July 1966, we moved to his villa, Building 1, in the Jade Spring (Yuquan) Hills outside Beijing. I stayed with him there, but after a few days, he complained that the place was contaminated—poisoned, he thought. He wanted to move again.

We went to Diaoyutai, the huge estate for state guests to the west of Zhongnanhai that had once served as an imperial fishing ground. Another complex of villas had been built there, nestled among the trees and fishing ponds. The Central Cultural Revolution Small Group had set up its headquarters there, in Building 16, and Jiang Qing, Chen Boda, and several other members of the group had already moved into nearby villas. Mao moved to villa number 10. Jiang Qing was staying in villa number 11.

Then Mao began to feel insecure in Diaoyutai, too, and wanted to move again. He went to Room 118 of the Great Hall of the People, where he had often sought pleasure from the young female attendants who served him. He lived there for several months, and continued throughout his life to take refuge there. But toward the end of 1966, he moved back into Zhongnanhai—not to the Chrysanthemum Fragrance Study, where he had lived since 1950, but to the building that housed his indoor swimming pool. New rooms, more modest than his earlier quarters, were constructed, and he stayed there until weeks before he died.

Briefly, soon after his return to Beijing, goaded perhaps by the asceticism of his Cultural Revolution, Mao gave up his female companions. The Zhongnanhai dancing parties had been revived when he returned to Beijing in July, and when Jiang Qing returned from Shanghai later that month, she joined them, too. Mao still enjoyed the parties and the music from the decidedly counterrevolutionary, and therefore banned, opera *The Emperor Seduces the Barmaid.* But Jiang Qing was now the arbiter of culture, and her personal transformation was complete. Upon her return to Beijing, I was shocked to see that her style of dress had completely changed. She wore loose-fitting jackets and trousers, so baggy they might have fit Mao, and her shoes were sturdy, masculine, and flat. She was arrogant and dictatorial. She held the fate of millions in her hands and was possessed by a new and determined prudery. Dancing parties were unacceptable to her new code. By the end of August she had persuaded Mao to end them.

"I've become a monk," he told me shortly thereafter.

But in a couple of weeks the young women were back. Room 118 was Mao's primary place of pleasure, and the young women attendants from the Fujian Room and the Jiangxi Room (each of China's provinces has a "room" in the Great Hall of the People, decorated with representative artifacts) were his favorites for a while. Even when the Cultural Revolution was at its height, Tiananmen Square in an uproar and the streets outside in turmoil, Mao continued to savor the imperial life, playing with his young women inside the Great Hall of the People and within the walls of Zhongnanhai.

Many of the people who had previously been close to Mao got in trouble during the Cultural Revolution, and they turned to him for protection.

Zhang Yufeng was the first to come—in early November 1966. She appeared one afternoon at the Zhongnanhai guard gate laden with *maotai* liquor and chocolates for Mao. Since she had no direct access to the Chairman, she called his nurse, Wu Xujun, instead. Zhang was still an attendant on Mao's special train, but since he was in Beijing, the two had not met for several months. Zhang Yufeng, then in her early twenties, had already married, and she was in trouble.

The "revolutionary rebels" in Zhang Yufeng's Department of Special Transportation Services had overthrown the party secretary and taken over the department. But Zhang Yufeng was a loyal member of the party and had supported her boss and thus she herself came under attack. Her gifts for Mao were an effort to persuade him to protect her.

When Wu Xujun reported the conversation, Mao not only saw Zhang Yufeng but agreed to help. Her friendship with him was well known in the Department of Special Transportation Services, and no one doubted her when she returned to report on her meeting with the Chairman. When she told her colleagues that Chairman Mao himself had said that her boss, the party secretary, ought not to be over-thrown, her job was quickly restored. And Zhang Yufeng was safe.

One of Mao's girlfriends from the cultural work troupe of the air force, was the next to call, and again Wu Xujun met with her first. She was accompanied by two of her friends, and all three young women burst into tears when they saw Wu. They poured out their story. The Cultural Revolution had spread to the air force, too, and their work unit was divided into two factions—the rebels intent on overthrowing the existing party leadership and the "protect-the-emperor faction" determined to maintain the status quo. Loyal party members like the three young women were, naturally, supporting the existing party leadership. All of Mao's girlfriends were. The political screening that allowed them to become close to Mao required that they be loyal to the party.

When the rebels gained the ascendancy, the three young women were driven from their dormitories. By the time Wu talked to them, they had already been wandering the streets for two days, desperate.

Mao was delighted to meet with the three women. "If they don't want you, you can stay with me," he said. "They say you're protecting the emperor? Well, I'm the emperor."

They benefited greatly from their liaison with the Chairman. When Mao instructed Lin Biao's wife, Ye Qun, the director of the Cultural Revolution within the Military Affairs Commission, to call off the attacks against the three women, Ye Qun did more. She asked the commander in chief of the air force, Wu Faxian, to appoint one of them director of the new revolutionary committee of the cultural work troupe, quickly transforming her from a pariah wandering the streets to a Cultural Revolution celebrity.

The young women returned often to Zhongnanhai after that. As chaos raged outside, Mao would often withdraw for several days at a time to relax with them. During one such session, Jiang Qing suddenly arrived from Diaoyutai unannounced, sending the young women into a panic. Alerted by the head nurse, they barely had time to hide before the Chairman's wife burst into his room.

Mao called Wu Xujun in shortly after. "When other top leaders want to see me, they all have to ask my permission first. Why is Jiang Qing such an exception? Tell Wang Dongxing to make sure that the armed guards don't let her in until I give my okay." From then until Mao died, Jiang Qing had to request permission to visit her husband.

The friendship between the women and Ye Qun continued. In 1969, when one of them became pregnant, Ye Qun assumed that the baby was Mao's and arranged for her to stay in a room reserved for high-level cadres at the air force general hospital, sending her delicacies every day while she awaited the birth of her baby. When the child was a boy, Ye Qun was delighted. "What wonderful news!" Lin Biao's wife exclaimed. "The Chairman has had several sons, but some have died and one has become ill. With this baby boy, he can continue his family line." Several people commented that the child looked just like Mao.

I and Wu Xujun visited her in hospital. My work required that I maintain good relations with Mao's female companions, too. She related the story of Ye Qun's visit, assuming I shared the belief that the baby was Mao's. I kept the fact of Mao's infertility to myself.

64

By January 1967, the country was in chaos. Fighting was breaking out, and some of the combatants had guns. Party and government offices were paralyzed. Factory production was plummeting. In some places, production had stopped altogether. Transportation was breaking down. Lin Biao and Jiang Qing were leading the rebels. "Overthrow everything" and "Wage civil war" were their slogans.

Factories and schools were split in two, with groups of militant rebels leading the attacks against the party committees while party supporters—the "protect-the-emperor faction"—fought aggressively back. The party committees were often badly divided, too. Party leaders everywhere were turning against each other in order to gain power themselves.

The conservatives still had the upper hand. Party committees over the years had amassed too much power to be easily overthrown. Ideology and principle had little to do with the struggles.

Mao took the side of the rebels. He wanted the conservative party committees purged. In late January, he called in the army to support the rebel left. He did this, he told me, because the Cultural Revolution cannot succeed unless we back the leftists. The army's job was to support the leftist masses, industry, and agriculture, and to carry out the militarization of all government agencies and give military training to all high school and college students. Within months, some 2 million soldiers had been called in to "support the left."

In Beijing, Mao turned to Wang Dongxing and the troops of the

Central Garrison Corps for support. The Central Garrison Corps—known now also by its code name,* the 8341 Corps—stood outside the military chain of command. Mao had a direct line of communication with Wang Dongxing and could give orders without having to go through the cumbersome military bureaucracy of Lin Biao and the regional military commanders. But Mao did not see Wang Dongxing every day. I did. So I became part of the loop. Mao often ignored official protocol by asking me to pass his instructions on to Wang.

In the spring of 1967, I informed Wang Dongxing that Mao wanted him to send troops from the Central Garrison Corps into several factories in Beijing, beginning with Beijing Textile Factory. Wang, in turn, ordered his deputy at the Central Garrison Corps, Yang Dezhong, to establish an office for "supporting the left." The "support-the-left office" established a "military-control committee," consisting of some eighty members of the Central Garrison Corps. Responsibility for taking over Beijing Textile Factory was given to two members of the military-control commission, Long March veteran Gu Yuanxin and Central Garrison Corps political department deputy director Sun Yi. Gu and Sun soon led a team to the textile factory.

Mao would not let me sit on the sidelines. He wanted me to join the Central Garrison Corps team being dispatched to Beijing Textile Factory. I would serve as an observer and liaison—Mao's eyes and ears, he said—reporting back to the Chairman on the situation there. Other members of Group One were sent to other model factories.

I hated the assignment. It was a trap. The political situation was too complex for me to maneuver without making mistakes. I blamed Jiang Qing for the assignment. She was already accusing me of locking myself inside Zhongnanhai and refusing to get involved. Noninvolvement, which I regarded as a virtue, she saw as a vice. Mao, too, was insistent. He wanted me to participate in this Great Proletarian Cultural Revolution. Only then would he know for certain whose side I was on. It was an opportunity, he said, to transform myself through participation in the revolutionary storm.

I tried to compromise. I wanted to confine my activities to medical matters. I suggested to Mao that I form a medical team and go into the factories as head of the team. "This way we can approach the workers naturally and get the information we want," I told him. He agreed.

*During the Cultural Revolution, as many party secrets were revealed, the code name for the Central Garrison Corps was also made public. Afterward, all military units were assigned new numbers, but the Central Garrison Corps continued to be referred to popularly as the 8341 Corps.

I arrived in the factory in early July, a few weeks after the military commission.

Beijing Textile Factory was located in the eastern suburbs of the city, about a half-hour bicycle ride from Zhongnanhai, and it produced both cotton and polyester and specialized in the manufacture of underwear. The factory's greatest claim to fame was its export of women's underwear to Romania. The factory had close to one thousand workers, and they were divided into two factions. The party committee had already been overthrown, and the former party chief and his deputy had been demoted to foremen. But the struggle over which of the factions would ultimately control the plant continued. The vast majority of workers—eight hundred of the nearly one thousand—were watching the struggle from the sidelines, trying to avoid involvement. But the two hundred activists had thrown the place into turmoil. Management had completely broken down, no one was working, and fistfights were breaking out. Gu Yuanxin and Sun Yi, Wang Dongxing's representatives from the Central Garrison Corps, were nowhere close to settling the disputes. But they saw my arrival as a way to unite the two groups. They could use me to invoke the authority of Mao.

"We were sent here personally by Chairman Mao," the two Garrison Corps officers insisted to the leaders of the two factions not long after my arrival. "Chairman Mao wants the two sides united."

When the factory leaders refused to believe that the military team had been sent by Mao, I was brought out as proof. "If you don't believe us, take a look. Chairman Mao's own personal physician is with us."

The factory leaders did not believe that I was Chairman Mao's doctor. I had come quietly, incognito. Outsiders were still not supposed to know my relationship to Mao.

The military team showed the factory leaders pictures of me standing next to the Chairman while he was reviewing the Red Guards. Their skepticism was shaken. I found out later that they had someone tail me when I left the factory. When they saw my car being waved into Zhongnanhai, they concluded that I must be Chairman Mao's doctor after all. With my own position thus demonstrated, the leaders of the contending factions could believe that the military commission really had been dispatched by Chairman Mao himself. Suddenly both the rebels and the "protect-the-emperor faction" were willing to compromise and accept the mediation of the military team. Their differences were quickly settled. In September 1967, a new "revolutionary committee" was established to run the factory, and production soon got rolling again.

I had been reporting frequently to Mao. He was delighted when I told him the news. He did not believe the working class had any basic internal differences. The workers should be united, he said. So Mao wrote a note to support the workers to prove that the military commission really was under his direct control. *"Tongzhimen, nimen hao?"* Mao wrote, handing the note to me. "Comrades, how are you?"

I passed the note to Wang Dongxing, who gave it in turn to the factory's new revolutionary committee. The committee members were so ecstatic that they immediately convened a meeting of the entire factory to "present" Chairman Mao's message to the workers. I refused their offer to sit on the stage, preferring to stay invisible. When the workers learned that Chairman Mao himself had written them a note—"Comrades, how are you?"—they went wild with cheers and applause. Mao's note was posted on the bulletin board in the factory courtyard, where everyone came to look. Then the factory leaders took a photograph of the note and had it enlarged to hundreds of times its original size. The inscription was as big as a wall. The enlarged photo was hung at the entrance to the factory for everyone to see whenever they arrived for work.

The newly established revolutionary committee was declared a model committee, operating under the personal direction of Chairman Mao. Much of the credit for the factory's success went to Wang Dongxing. By the spring of 1968 five other leading factories were under Wang Dongxing's control—the New China Printing Plant, the North Lumber Yard, the Second Chemical Plant, the Nankou Motor Vehicle Plant, and the February 7 Motor Vehicle Plant. These six factories were soon known throughout the country as Chairman Mao's personally directed model factories.

Suddenly everyone wanted to jump on the 8341 Corps bandwagon and come to Beijing Textile Factory to be under the direct control of Mao. The first group to join was dominated by female attendants from the Great Hall of the People and female staff from the Zhongnanhai General Office. An attendant from Room 118 organized the young women, and both Wang Dongxing and Mao welcomed their participation. The women, dressed for the occasion in military costume, arrived at the factory with great fanfare, enthusiastically welcomed by their male comrades, who gave them a huge rally. Reporters were there to record the event for history, and both *People's Pictorial* and *Liberation Army Pictorial* ran photos of the triumphant arrival at the textile factory of the "women soldiers."

Jiang Qing was distressed when she saw the photographs, accusing the attendants from the Great Hall of the People of "disguising" themselves as soldiers. Everyone was dressing like soldiers then, including Jiang Qing. But Jiang Qing resented lowly attendants assuming the lofty position of soldier. She was quickly silenced when Wang Dongxing assured her that Mao himself had authorized the team and permitted its members to wear military uniforms.

Lin Biao's wife, Ye Qun, and chief of the general staff Huang Yongsheng were next to visit the factory and bestow their blessings on its great accomplishment as a model personally directed by Chairman Mao. They singled out Sun Yi, the deputy director of the military-control committee, for particular praise. Promising him a promotion, they invited Sun to relate the story of his successful negotiations to a meeting of the Military Affairs Commission and the headquarters of the air force. Having thus established a solid friendship with Sun Yi, Ye Qun and Huang Yongsheng began intruding into the management of the factory, sending their own representatives as permanent observers.

With the participation of Ye Qun and Huang Yongsheng, the line from Mao to the factory was no longer so straight. I thought the primary loyalty of both Wang Dongxing and Sun Yi ought to be with Mao and never trusted the "leadership" Ye Qun was bringing to the plant. I was afraid her interference might bring trouble to Wang Dongxing and Sun Yi. What if Sun Yi were to boast of his close relationship with Ye Qun and Huang Yongsheng? Would not the Chairman become suspicious?

I raised my concerns with Wang Dongxing. "Sun Yi is your subordinate, and Mao might think you're switching loyalties," I explained.

But Wang Dongxing did not agree. His power was growing as the Cultural Revolution unfolded, and he was entering into alliances with whoever would further his goal. His hatred of Jiang Qing continued unabated, and his long-term aim was to bring her down. Lin Biao was important to his long-term goals, and he took every opportunity he could to build political support with the man who was slated to become Mao's successor.

During Lin Biao's illness in August 1966, after I accompanied Wang to visit him, Wang Dongxing told me that he had made a private visit, taking the opportunity to explain the nature of his work with Mao. Convinced that Lin Biao's alliance with Jiang Qing was merely expedient, Wang also told Lin about his own ongoing conflict with the Chairman's wife. Wang seemed convinced that once Lin Biao's power was secure, he might be willing to break his alliance with Jiang.

By August, that alliance had been forged. Lin Biao promised to protect Wang should he ever be in trouble. Wang Dongxing agreed to keep Lin Biao informed of important developments around Mao.

Wang's strategy was dangerous in the extreme. "If anybody leaks this agreement, it will be disastrous," I told him.

Wang thought otherwise. "I swear I will do everything I can to bring Jiang Qing down," he insisted. "Leak? Who will leak? Not you, not me." I was the only person, so far as I know, whom Wang told about his covenant with Lin Biao. But every time I saw the effusive greetings Wang extended to Lin Biao and his wife, I felt queasy. I was always uncomfortable with Lin Biao's leadership and knew Mao's demand for loyalty was total. Wang Dongxing was playing with fire.

65

My relations with Mao had been deteriorating, too. He was suspicious of everyone and interpreted my reluctance to get politically involved as a sign of less than total loyalty to him. One did not need to side with the opposition to make Mao suspicious. Staying on the political sidelines roused his suspicions, too.

The first concrete sign of Mao's displeasure came on July 13, 1967. Mao was leaving for Wuhan that day, and for the first time since I had taken over as his doctor, he did not invite me to go. Lin Biao had suggested that one doctor from the army and another from the air force accompany him.

I was alarmed, and so was Wang Dongxing. My exclusion from the trip, he was certain, was the work of Jiang Qing. Lin Biao did not know enough to suggest that I stay behind. Jiang Qing must have made the suggestion to him, and Wang was afraid she would use the occasion of Mao's absence to destroy me.

The violence of the Cultural Revolution elsewhere continued to spread. Organizations were split. The beatings and fistfights continued, and so did the use of guns. The situation in Wuhan, where Mao had spent so much time, was particularly serious. He was going there to mediate.

Beijing was on the verge of chaos. With Mao gone, Jiang Qing would be in control, and Wang Dongxing feared that I might be kidnapped by someone on her side. He urged me not to return to the textile factory. One of her agents could grab me there. "Stay in Zhong-nanhai," he said. "If you get into trouble, come immediately to join us in Wuhan." In Zhongnanhai, at least if trouble broke out I could find a way to communicate with Wuhan.

I did stay in Zhongnanhai, but only to witness Wang Dongxing's worst fears come true. With Mao gone and Jiang Qing's group in control, even that privileged haven soon disintegrated into violence.

Head of state Liu Shaoqi was the primary object of attack. Hundreds of young student protesters began gathering outside the west gate shortly after Mao left the city, filling Fuyou Street to the west of Zhongnanhai and shouting slogans demanding the overthrow of Liu. The vermilion walls were plastered with big character posters attacking the man Mao had once declared his successor. As the afternoon wore on, the crowd grew larger, and traffic stopped altogether. That night the students set up camp outside the gate. The place was a mess with so many people, and the smell, from thousands of sweaty bodies in the heat of July, the rotten food, and the open, makeshift toilets was nauseating. I remained in Zhongnanhai, sleeping uneasily in my office, wary of what each new day might bring. Never in the history of the People's Republic had Zhongnanhai been besieged. Members of Wang Dongxing's Central Garrison Corps, responsible for protecting the leaders' compound, were standing impassively by as the crowd of protesters continued to grow. Whatever Wang Dongxing may have thought was of little consequence then. He was in Wuhan with Mao.

On July 18, the situation turned nasty. I was in my office reading the morning newspaper when a guard rushed in. Liu Shaoqi was being "struggled against" outside the State Council auditorium. I ran there immediately.

A crowd had gathered, consisting mostly of cadres from the General Office's Bureau of Secretaries. Soldiers and officers from the Central Garrison Corps were there, too, watching. No one was offering even the slightest help to Liu Shaoqi. Liu and his wife, Wang Guang-mei, were standing in the center of the crowd, being pushed and kicked and beaten by staff members from the Bureau of Secretaries. Liu's shirt had already been torn open, and a couple of buttons were missing, and people were jerking him around by the hair. When I moved closer for a better look, someone held his arms behind his back while others tried to force him to bend forward from the waist in the position known as "doing the airplane." Finally, they forced him down and pushed his face toward the ground until it was nearly touching the dirt, kicking him and slapping him in the face. Still the soldiers from the Central

Garrison Corps refused to intervene. I could not bear to watch. Liu Shaoqi was already an old man by then, almost seventy, and he was our head of state.

I left the struggle session against Liu Shaoqi and went first to the living quarters of Deng Xiaoping and his wife, Zhuo Lin, and then to see Tao Zhu and his wife, Zeng Zhi. They, too, were being struggled against, though not quite as violently. The two men and their wives were being pushed and shoved and jeered at by a crowd, but there was no kicking or beating.

Yang Dezhong was observing the attacks, too, and I asked him what had happened. The Central Cultural Revolution Small Group had announced the night before that the top leaders would be struggled against today. Yang had called Wang Dongxing as soon as he heard the announcement but had received no word from Wang since.

Wang was in a difficult position. He could not inform Mao directly of the violence in Zhongnanhai. To make such a report would be to oppose a decision of the increasingly powerful Central Cultural Revolution Small Group, and no one would dare risk criticizing the rising leftists. Besides, Wang's relations with Mao had long been strained over the question of Liu Shaoqi. Wang had accompanied Liu and his wife on their trip to Indonesia in 1963. Mao had given his formal approval and Wang had met with the Chairman afterward to report, but Mao's suspicion that Wang was too close to Liu Shaoqi remained, and Wang did not want to appear to be siding with the man Mao was determined to overthrow.

On July 21, three days after the struggle sessions against Liu, Deng, and Tao, Wang Dongxing called me. He had gone to Shanghai. Mao was there, too. An air force plane was waiting for me at the Beijing airport. I was to join them in Shanghai immediately.

Within hours, I was in Shanghai, being escorted to the western suburbs guesthouse, where Mao and his entourage were staying. Security for the Chairman had not been so tight in years. More than a hundred armed guards from the Central Garrison Corps were there, in addition to the local Shanghai security forces. Violence was everywhere now, and the safety of the Chairman was a matter of continual concern. His staff of secretaries, clerks, and couriers had also grown, and every room in the sprawling complex was filled.

Mao was suffering from one of his frequent attacks of bronchitis and had a new venereal complaint as well—genital herpes. His sexual contacts were too far-flung and my own relations with the Chairman were too strained for me to be able to identify the source. I treated it with Chinese herbal medicine and administered Ceporin for his bronchitis. I cautioned him that herpes was contagious and could spread through sexual contact, but he ignored my warnings. He did not think the problem was so bad.

The Chairman wanted to talk and asked me about the situation in Beijing. I told him that the rebels had seized Zhongnanhai and described the violent struggle sessions against Liu Shaoqi, Deng Xioping, and Tao Zhu. Mao was silent. Uncertain of my political stand, he was more reserved with me now than in the past. But his silence was also a sign of displeasure over the events in Beijing.

I saw him again that night, and he asked me to repeat my description of the situation in Zhongnanhai. "They just don't listen to me," he complained when I had finished, referring to the Central Cultural Revolution Small Group, which included his wife. Mao insisted that he had told them not to abuse the three leaders. "They ignored me," he insisted, clearly upset with the Small Group. I concluded that he had not ordered the attacks after all.

I stayed with Mao in Shanghai for close to a month. He was waiting to return to Wuhan. Mao had gone to Wuhan on July 14, but the situation was so unstable that Zhou Enlai, who was also there, feared for the Chairman's safety and persuaded him to leave. The factional struggles in Wuhan had become violent. Chen Zaidao, the Wuhan military commander who had nearly drowned when he tried to swim upstream during Mao's first dip in the Yangtze, had been under heavy attack from the opposing rebel faction, which was trying to overthrow him. Before Mao went to Wuhan to mediate, the Central Cultural Revolution Small Group had sent the ultraleftist Wang Li to negotiate a reconciliation between the contending sides, but in fact Wang Li had supported the rebels opposing Chen Zaidao. Chen Zaidao's faction was so enraged with Wang Li that they seized him and put him under arrest.

It was then that Zhou Enlai went to Wuhan to investigate the situation and to negotiate for the release of Wang Li. Then Mao arrived, staying as usual in Meiyuan guesthouse, on East Lake. Some of Chen Zaidao's supporters, still holding Wang Li in custody but determined to demonstrate their loyalty to Mao, swam to the island where Mao was staying, hoping to meet the Chairman and explain their side of the story. Mao's security guards arrested the swimmers and took them into custody.

When Mao learned what happened, he opposed the arrest of the swimmers. Even as the rebel faction accused the swimmers of plotting to bring harm to the Chairman, Mao, confident of the adulation of the masses and knowing that Chen Zaidao was still his loyal supporter, was certain the swimmers only wanted to talk. He wanted to meet with both groups and negotiate a reconciliation between them. Zhou Enlai was nervous. The disputants were armed, and Zhou wanted to put some of them under arrest. He feared for Mao's safety and urged the Chairman to leave Wuhan immediately. Zhou himself would stay behind to negotiate the reconciliation.

Mao went to Shanghai while Zhou stayed to negotiate. Through Zhou's mediation, Wang Li was finally released, and both Wang Li and Chen Zaidao were escorted to Beijing.

A month later, I flew with Mao on his return to Wuhan. Mao did not think there were any counterrevolutionaries among the two Wuhan factions, he told me as the plane was circling over the city preparing to land. "The trouble is that Wang Li provoked them into fighting. And when Zhou Enlai came to mediate the dispute, the fighting scared him to death. He forced me to flee to Shanghai in a hurry. But there aren't any counterrevolutionary factions here." Mao thought that Wang Li, Guan Feng, and Qi Benyu—three of the most provocative members of the Central Cultural Revolution Small Group—were the ones who had fomented the trouble and allowed the feuding to get out of hand.

Mao's return to Wuhan was triumphant. To prove that there were no counterrevolutionaries and no one who wanted to harm him, he rode slowly through the streets in an open jeep, with me sitting directly behind him and one hundred armed guards in civilian clothes surrounding us. Enthusiastic crowds, representing both the pro– and the anti–Chen Zaidao factions, lined the streets yelling, "Long Live Chairman Mao! Long Live Chairman Mao!" This was Mao's way of "receiving the masses of the two factions."

In Mao's absence, Beijing remained in the hands of the leftists, and Wang Li and Guan Feng turned their attacks against Mao's old colleague foreign minister Marshal Chen Yi. Chen Yi had been outspoken in his criticism of the Cultural Revolution, joining with other ranking military leaders in February 1967 to protest military involvement and challenging the excesses of the young Red Guards. In August, Wang Li and Guan Feng, with Jiang Qing's support, organized a group called the May 16 Rebels, named after the circular announcing the start of the Cultural Revolution. They seized control of Chen Yi's Foreign Ministry and later burned the offices of the British chargé d'affaires to the ground.

Mao had Wang Li and Guan Feng purged immediately upon his

return to Beijing in August. The arrest of their associate Qi Benyu took place the following January.

Wang Li, Guan Feng, and Qi Benyu were radical and provocative to be sure, but they were only scapegoats. The real power within the Central Cultural Revolution Small Group lay with Kang Sheng, Chen Boda, and Jiang Qing. They were making the decisions. Mao was clearly unhappy with Jiang Qing. One day while we were still at Meiyuan guesthouse in Wuhan and Mao was reading some short stories by Lu Xun, he suddenly looked up and began talking about one of the least likable of Lu Xun's female protagonists, a promiscuous maid named A Jin, whose many boyfriends were always making noise, getting in trouble, and picking fights. A Jin was a woman who enjoyed making trouble for others. "Ye Qun is just like A Jin," Mao said, referring to Lin Biao's wife. "So is Jiang Qing."

But even with all the trouble his wife was then making, even though he was obviously perturbed, Mao still made no move to stop her.

66

Mao also made no move to stop Jiang Qing in the spring of 1968, when she turned viciously against me.

The problem began with my wife. Kang Sheng's list of hidden counterrevolutionaries was growing, and he had decided to put Lillian on it. Lillian's past had never been secret, and Kang Sheng had no trouble discovering that she had worked for both the British and the Americans and had relatives who lived on Taiwan. Her past made her triply suspect. Had she been a spy for the British? The Americans? The Guomindang? Perhaps for all three? Kang Sheng called for a thorough investigation of her case.

Jiang Qing wanted me investigated, too. I was also a counterrevolutionary, she said, and no less suspect than my wife. My case was turned over to Wang Dongxing.

Wang naturally came to my defense, assuring both Kang Sheng and Jiang Qing that I had already been thoroughly investigated. Of course he would look into the matter again, but he was certain my problems, if any, were minor.

Jiang Qing persisted but tried a different tack. On July 1, 1968, the anniversary of the founding of the Chinese Communist party, after presiding over an evening of celebration in the Great Hall of the People, the Chairman's wife came down with a toothache. She wanted a doctor to take a look. Wang Dongxing sent for me.

I protested. Jiang Qing needed a dentist, not a doctor. Besides, how could she trust me? She had already accused me of being a counterrevolutionary when I had tried to care for her earlier. I suspected a trap. Jiang Qing's real enemies within Zhongnanhai were Wang Dongxing and Zhou Enlai, and they were her ultimate targets. To declare me a counterrevolutionary was the first step in declaring Wang and Zhou counterrevolutionary, too. Jiang Qing's nearly psychotic behavior was part of her political plot.

Jiang Qing was also Wang Dongxing's ultimate target, and he was determined, finally, to do her in. But Wang Dongxing, for now, preached reconciliation. He wanted me to find her a dentist and use the opportunity both to demonstrate my respect for the Chairman's wife and to smooth over our troubled relationship. Reluctantly, I agreed.

I asked two leading dentists from the 301 Hospital of the People's Liberation Army to move into Diaoyutai, where Jiang Qing was still living, and to prepare to work with the Chairman's wife. Jiang Qing kept them waiting six days before finally consenting to an examination. The dentists discovered that one of her teeth was loose and possibly infected. They thought it should be extracted, and Jiang Qing agreed.

The dentists wanted to give Jiang Qing a shot of antibiotics before performing the extraction and asked her nurse to test for a possible allergy. The skin test proved negative, and the nurse administered the antibiotic.

About half an hour later, Jiang Qing became hysterical. She itched all over. There was poison in that shot, she yelled. Terrified, her young nurse came running to me, pleading for my help. I examined Jiang Qing but could find nothing wrong. Her pulse and heartbeat were normal, and there was no evidence of rash or irritation on her skin. I thought a tranquilizer might help sooth her nerves, but she refused the medication and sent for Wang Dongxing instead.

"Li Zhisui tried to poison me with medicine," the Chairman's wife exploded as soon as Wang walked in. Wang asked me to leave while he met alone with Jiang Qing.

Then he met with me. Even after listening to my account of the skin test, he still thought that Jiang Qing might be having an allergic reaction. I disagreed. I had examined her skin, taken her blood pressure, listened to her heart. Everything normal. Nothing wrong.

Suddenly, I was struck by the gravity of Jiang Qing's accusations. She was charging me with deliberately trying to poison her. "I have to see the Chairman right away," I told Wang Dongxing. "I have to tell him about this."

"It won't work," Wang responded. "Jiang Qing wants me to

report to the Chairman. If you get there first, she will be all the more upset. We have asked the Chairman to come here to Diaoyutai." Wang wanted me to wait for Mao and explain my side when he came.

I waited alone in the reception room just outside Jiang Qing's living quarters. Jiang Qing's bodyguards and staff had disappeared, so frightened by her outburst that they wanted nothing to do with me.

An hour passed, and still Mao did not come. I felt like a prisoner awaiting a verdict.

Then he walked into the reception room, escorted by head nurse Wu Xujun, her hand on his arm. I rose to greet him, but he just stared at me blankly without a word, not even acknowledging my presence, walking straight into Jiang Qing's bedroom. When Wang Dongxing came out, I asked what he had told the Chairman.

"I told him that Jiang Qing wanted him to come over because she had had an allergic reaction to a shot of medicine."

I was furious. "But I told you I had examined her and that everything is normal. Why didn't you tell him that? Jiang Qing is trying to ruin me by cooking up a false case against me."

Just at that moment the door to Jiang Qing's bedroom opened and Mao walked out. Again he stared right past me as though I did not exist, leaving without saying a word.

Even Wang Dongxing was worried then. "Jiang Qing is playing tricks," he said. "She may try to send one of her people over here to kidnap you. I think it's best if you go back to the textile plant. Once you get there, don't leave. My troops from the Central Garrison Corps are there. They'll try to protect you. It might work. You may be safe."

I wanted desperately to talk to Lillian, to warn her that I might be arrested or abducted. But she was at work when I returned home, so I could only write her a note, saying that I had to leave and might be away for a while.

I hid at Beijing Textile Factory for two weeks, cut off from any news about my fate. When I could stand it no longer, I left to meet with Wang Dongxing. Only then did I learn what had happened.

Just after I had left Diaoyutai, Jiang Qing gathered all her secretaries, bodyguards, nurses, and chefs together and ordered them to sign a joint statement accusing me of attempting to poison her. Naturally, they complied. That night, Jiang Qing received a visit from Lin Biao and his wife, Ye Qun. Jiang Qing told them that I was a counterrevolutionary—that I had been a counterrevolutionary before 1949 and was a counterrevolutionary now. She gave the unused portion of her medicine to Ye Qun and asked her to have it analyzed, emphasizing (*at left*) Jinggangshan, May 1965. Dr. Li, Mao Zedong, and head nurse Wu Xujun in front of the guesthouse.

Mao Zedong being greeted by local people, Jinggangshan, May 1965. To Mao's left are Dr. Li and the local governor.

(*at left*) Meiyuan (Plum Garden) guesthouse, Wuhan, July 3, 1966. Dr. Li and Mao Zedong, shortly before Dr. Li's return to Beijing to investigate the Cultural Revolution.

Atop Tiananmen, August 1966.
Mao Zedong greets the Red Guards.
Dr. Li is just behind Mao.

(*at right*) Tiananmen Square, October 1, 1966, on the seventeenth anniversary of the founding of the People's Republic. Mao Zedong and Zhou Enlai left the balcony atop Tiananmen to join the Red Guards in the square. In front, Mao and Zhou. In the second row, Wang Dongxing is the third person from the left, Dr. Li is just behind Zhou, and head nurse Wu Xujun is beside Dr. Li. Standing directly behind Wang Dongxing are bodyguard Sun Yong and Central Garrison Corps commander Zhang Yaoci. The others are guards.

November 1966. Mao Zedong reviews the Red Guards from an open jeep. In the front seat: Wang Dongxing and driver. In the backseat: minister of public security Xie Fuzhi, Mao, Dr. Li, and bodyguard Zhou Fuming.

December 26, 1967, Mao Zedong's seventy-fourth birthday. Mao poses with members of the First Company of the Central Garrison Corps near the indoor swimming pool. Wang Dongxing is to the left of Mao, Dr. Li is to the right, head nurse Wu Xujun stands in front of Dr. Li, and Central Garrison Corps commander Zhang Yaoci is at the extreme right.

Fall of 1969, in front of Mao Zedong's special train, at Tianjin.
Clerk Sun Yulan (with glasses) and nurse Ma (with pigtail) are in
the middle of the front row. Second row, from right to left: Dr. Li,
Central Garrison Corps commander Zhang Yaoci, head nurse Wu
Xujun, and Wang Dongxing. Mao is eighth from the left. The others
are attendants, nurses, chefs, and secretaries.

Early 1972, Chinese Spring Festival, at the duty room
of the indoor swimming pool. From left to right: Dr. Hu Xudong,
Central Garrison Corps commander Zhang Yaoci, Premier Zhou
Enlai, Dr. Li, and Dr. Wu Jie.

September 1976, during the ceremony commemorating Mao's death.
Dr. Li is the second person from the left in the third row.
The others are doctors, nurses, and security officers.

December 26, 1977, at a workshop concerning the preservation of
Mao Zedong's remains. Dr. Li is seated in the foreground, on the
right. Beside him is Huang Shuze.

Early summer 1984, at the South Lake dock in Zhongnanhai.
Dr. Li and his wife, Lillian. Dr. Li's apartment was
on the third floor of the building, overlooking the lake.

repeatedly that the medicine was poisonous and that she expected the analysis to reach the same conclusion.

Ye Qun, in turn, had called Wang Dongxing. Jiang Qing, Lin Biao's wife was certain, would only be satisfied with a report that the medicine was poisonous.

Wang urged Ye Qun to have a genuine evaluation made by qualified lab technicians and to present the results to Jiang Qing just as she received them. The matter was not so simple as Jiang Qing pretended. The medicine, Wang reminded Ye Qun, had not come directly from me but from a pharmacy that was under the supervision of the Central Garrison Corps. Ultimate responsibility for the medicine rested with Wang Dongxing. According to the rules, a physician could prescribe medicine for Mao, Jiang Qing, and other top leaders, but the doctor could not actually pick up the medicine. If there was a problem, the pharmacy was responsible, not me.

Ye Qun had the medicine analyzed by the military's Academy of Medical Science. The report concluded that the medicine in the bottle corresponded with the label. No poison was discovered.

Jiang Qing was furious. When Ye Qun showed her the results, the Chairman's wife snatched both the medicine and the written report and threw them to the floor, asserting that the report had been written by some "bad element" in the Academy of Medical Science.

Ye Qun fought back, defending herself and her husband. She explained to Jiang Qing that she and Lin Biao had considered the matter of the greatest importance. Lin Biao himself had personally delivered the medicine to the president of the Academy of Medical Science. The analysis had been treated with the utmost gravity and care.

Nothing could placate Jiang Qing, and the two women parted unhappily. Ye Qun, however, had the foresight to pick up the medicine and the report and to deposit both for safekeeping with Wang Dongxing. The strains in the alliance between Jiang Qing and Lin Biao had already begun to show. Wang Dongxing was leaning to the side of Lin Biao. I was a helpless pawn in their political tug-of-war.

Jiang Qing's tooth problem persisted—although in fact it was so loose that a gentle yank would have dislodged it. Lin Biao and Zhou Enlai took responsibility for finding her doctors and dispatched Wu Jieping and Bian Zhiqiang to treat her. When she met the two new doctors, she again accused me of trying to poison her and demanded that the two men sign a statement charging me with administering poison. Wu and Bian were dumbfounded and raised the problem with

Wang Dongxing. He advised them to tell the truth. They did, defending me, and Jiang Qing sent them away.

But Jiang Qing still had the accusation from her staff. She showed the signed document to Zhou Enlai and asked Zhou to issue an order for my arrest.

Zhou waffled. I was Chairman Mao's personal physician, he pointed out. The order for my arrest would have to come from Mao. Jiang Qing urged Zhou Enlai to meet with the Chairman.

Zhou, too, consulted with Wang Dongxing. Wang suggested that Zhou Enlai explain the whole situation to Mao and ask the Chairman how to handle it. Wang himself did not want to raise the issue directly with Mao. If medicine under his jurisdiction were determined to be poisonous, Wang, too, would be implicated.

Zhou Enlai met with Mao and defended me. Because of my long association with Group One, he said, I was well known to most people in Zhongnanhai. My work might not always be satisfactory, but Zhou was convinced I would never do deliberate harm.

Some two weeks after the event, Mao finally agreed. "Li Zhisui is with me day and night," he told Zhou. "If he were counterrevolutionary, why wouldn't he harm me instead of Jiang Qing? Wouldn't it be a lot easier for him to harm me? A long time ago Jiang Qing accused the doctors and nurses of trying to harm her because she found out that some of her sleeping pills were fake. I told her that some of my sleeping pills were fake too. They were supposed to be. That way we would take fewer real ones."

But I was not fully back in Mao's favor. He did not actively intervene on my behalf, and Wang Dongxing was certain that Jiang Qing would persist in trying to get rid of me. I still was not safe. "You can't go home," he said. "She may still send someone there to abduct you. You have to stay in Beijing Textile Factory. The medic, Li, is there. If there is trouble, send him to tell me."

I stayed in the factory for more than two months, in constant fear of abduction. Jiang Qing and the Central Cultural Revolution Small Group had almost unbridled power. There was nothing to stop her, not even Mao. Mao did not always know what Jiang Qing was doing then, and she could easily direct others to abduct me and later deny responsibility, claiming not to know.

67

I was still hiding in the plant on July 27, 1968, when word came that Mao had ordered workers from his six "personally directed factories," and ones under control of the 8341 Corps, to form "worker propaganda teams" to take over Qinghua University. Mao now wanted two universities, Qinghua and Beida, to come under his "personal direction" too.

Qinghua was one of the best and most famous of the country's universities, specializing in science and engineering. Its student rebellion was almost as famous as the one at Beida. In the spring of 1966, Liu Shaoqi's wife, Wang Guangmei, had been in charge of the work team sent to direct the Cultural Revolution there. She had supported the party leadership and been opposed by the most radical and rebellious of the students. In April 1967, the students had taken revenge against Wang Guangmei when one of the leading student rebels, Kuai Dafu, led a massive struggle session against her. In 1963, Wang had met with Indonesia's President Sukarno and, as the wife of China's head of state, wore a traditional-style Chinese *qipao* and a string of pearls. This, the students said, was evidence of her decadent and bourgeois life-style. During the 1967 struggle session at Qinghua, Wang was forced to wear a tight-fitting *qipao* and a string of Ping-Pong balls around her neck as thousands of students shouted slogans calling for her downfall. The university had been ungovernable ever since. Now Mao wanted to reestablish order and was willing to do so by force.

At four o'clock that afternoon, workers from the textile factory and soldiers from the 8341 Corps would be leaving the factory for Qinghua. I did not have to join them. But I wanted to go. I wanted to see the takeover of the university myself.

Sun Yi, the deputy director of the military-control committee at Beijing Textile Factory, was in charge of the contingent from our factory. We set out by truck, 150 people in all, piled more than ten to a truck. Hundreds of trucks from other factories also converged at the Qinghua University gates, forming an occupying force thousands strong. Later reports said 30,000 people participated. At the entrance to the campus, Yang Dezhong, political commissar of the Central Garrison Corps and director of the overall operation, took charge. Jumping down from the trucks, we were organized into military formation, and at Yang's command, we began marching onto the campus. I stayed toward the back, walking with the medic, Li.

The march was orderly at first, but when we reached the building housing the physics department, the lines ahead of us suddenly stopped and commotion broke out. The students had set up barricades to stop us. Yang Dezhong ordered us to remove the barriers and continue marching forward.

Dusk had settled by then, and it was difficult to see. I could only stay in formation, following the people ahead, walking blindly. I had no idea where we were going.

Suddenly, I heard an explosion and the whole place was pandemonium. Voices were yelling that a bomb had gone off and people had been killed. The march halted again, and soon we saw three bloodied bodies being carried away.

It was now completely dark. I could see nothing. Our formation was in total disarray, but still we were moving forward. Then I heard gusts of wind. The people in front turned and began running in my direction, their hands shielding their heads. I halted in my tracks, dumbfounded, trying to figure out what was wrong, when the medic, Li, took off his jacket and put it over my head. Only then did I realize that the gusts of wind were rocks flying through the air. Rocks were flying everywhere, little nut-sized stones showering down like rain, and my fellow marchers were finally breaking ranks, running in all directions. Li grabbed hold of me and ran, too, pulling me in what he thought was the direction of the entrance gate. But he was unfamiliar with the huge campus, and it was so dark we could see nothing. By the time we finally found the gate, we had become completely separated from the marchers from our factory. We saw no one we recognized. Then a heavy rain began to fall, drenching us to the bone. We sat on the roadside in the pitch dark, in pouring rain, wondering what to do.

By then it was about four in the morning, and other marchers, equally bewildered, had begun to join us.

I saw a car pull up alongside us, and heard a voice. Suddenly, I realized that my name was being called. It was Mao's driver, Zhang Zhengji. "Hurry, he's looking for you, Dr. Li," Zhang was saying.

"Who is looking for me?" I wondered, still bewildered.

"Who else but Chairman? He's at the Great Hall of the People. He's asked the students to be there, too." I left Li behind, and Zhang Zhengji drove me to the Great Hall of the People.

Mao's aides surrounded me as I walked in, plying me with questions. "You've suffered so much, Dr. Li," they were saying. "How many rocks hit you?" I was such a mess from the rain and from running that they thought I had been wounded in the melee.

My head ached and I felt sick from hunger, fatigue, and cold, but I had not been hit by the rocks. Wu Xujun gave me some tiger balm ointment to rub into my temples for my headache. After a bowl of noodles and a painkiller, I felt much better.

Mao was waiting for me in Room 118. He was sitting on a sofa reading when I went in. He stood up as soon as he saw me and came forward to greet me. I rushed toward him. He took both my hands in his and looked at me closely before speaking. I sensed that he really did like me, despite the strains in our relationship and Jiang Qing's repeated accusations against me. "What a sorry situation you're in," he said. "You're totally soaked." I explained that the rain was heavy.

"You've had a rough time, haven't you?" he asked, knowing what an adventure I had just had. "Are you hurt? Don't cry." He had mistaken the tiger balm ointment on my face for tears.

"I'm not hurt," I said. "But three people were hurt by bombs. I don't know whether they are alive or not."

Wang Dongxing had also been there and reported that one person had been killed; the other two were expected to recover.

"Why don't you change your clothes and get some rest now?" Mao suggested. He had invited some of the leading radical student leaders—Kuai Dafu of Qinghua University, Nie Yuanzi of Beida, Tan Houlan of Beijing Normal, Han Aijing of Beijing College of Aeronautics, and Wang Dabin of Beijing College of Geology—to meet with him and with members of the Central Cultural Revolution Small Group. He invited me to join the meeting.

Mao, for now, had decided to protect me. By inviting me to join the meeting, he was signaling his intention to the Central Cultural Revolution Small Group. Lin Biao, Zhou Enlai, Kang Sheng, and Jiang Qing would all attend the meeting. Seeing me with Mao, they would know that I was still one of his people and should be left alone. Perhaps I would not be abducted after all.

Jiang Qing greeted everyone else at the meeting warmly but said nothing to me, pretending I was not even there. Mao may have exonerated me, but she had not. Her accusation that I had tried to poison her still stood. Her behavior bothered me less, however. With Mao's protection, I felt safe again, and for once I appreciated being a member of Group One.

Mao's protection was only temporary, however. I had passed his tests so far, but my loyalty was still under scrutiny and the tests would continue.

Mao's meeting with the students that day was a milestone in the Cultural Revolution. He wanted the student factions to stop fighting and unite and warned them that if they kept splitting in two, there would soon be two of every school—two Qinghuas, two Beidas, two Beijing Normal universities.

The students were a feisty bunch, and I remember Han Aijing in particular. "Both sides have been using the Chairman's words to justify their actions," he pointed out to Mao. "But the Chairman's words can be subject to different, even conflicting, interpretations. While the Chairman is alive and can settle the disputes, such problems can be resolved. But when the Chairman is no longer with us, what shall we do?"

Kang Sheng and Jiang Qing were furious. "How dare you talk such nonsense?" they demanded.

But Mao liked the question. He had alluded to the same problem in his earlier letter to Jiang Qing. "When I was young, I used to ask such questions myself," he said, "questions that others would not dare to raise. Certainly my words can be given different interpretations. It's inevitable. Look at Confucianism, Buddhism, Christianity—all these great schools of thought have broken down into factions, each one with a different interpretation of the original truth. Without different interpretations, there can be no growth or change. Stagnation will set in, and the original doctrine will die."

But Mao's meeting with the students did not achieve its goal. The students could not unite, and Mao apparently decided that his faith in the young had been misplaced. Several days later, on August 5, Mao announced he wanted to present the workers a gift of several mangoes that had been given to him by Pakistani foreign minister Mian Arshad Hussain. The gift was the signal to the country that Mao had lost faith in the feuding, factionalized students and that he was placing his hope now in the workers. Not long after, the student leaders were sent to the countryside, and millions of ordinary middle school and university students followed. They could be reformed in the countryside, Mao said. Students had to "learn from the poor and lower-middle peasants."

Mao gave the mangoes to Wang Dongxing, who divided them up, distributing one mango each to a number of leading factories in Beijing, including Beijing Textile Factory, where I was then living. The workers at the factory held a huge ceremony, rich in the recitation of Mao's words, to welcome the arrival of the mango, then sealed the fruit in wax, hoping to preserve it for posterity. The mangoes became sacred relics, objects of veneration. The wax-covered fruit was placed on an altar in the factory auditorium, and workers lined up to file past it, solemnly bowing as they walked by. No one had thought to sterilize the mango before sealing it, however, and after a few days on display, it began to show signs of rot. The revolutionary committee of the factory retrieved the rotting mango, peeled it, then boiled the flesh in a huge pot of water. Another ceremony was held, equally solemn. Mao again was greatly venerated, and the gift of the mango was lauded as evidence of the Chairman's deep concern for the workers. Then everyone in the factory filed by and each worker drank a spoonful of the water in which the sacred mango had been boiled.

After that, the revolutionary committee ordered a wax model of the original mango. The replica was duly made and placed on the altar to replace the real fruit, and workers continued to file by, their veneration for the sacred object in no apparent way diminished.

When I told Mao about the veneration being accorded his mango, he laughed. He had no problem with the mango worship and seemed delighted by the story.

68

Mao was protecting me, but I no longer saw him every day. He had no need for my medical services. I worked instead at Beijing Textile Factory, serving as a doctor for the workers and their families, reporting back to Mao every few days. The workers at Beijing Textile Factory were lucky, and so was I. The factory was peaceful, and normal production continued. Since it was one of the factories "directly administered by Mao," the contending factions had reached an early accord. "What's all this talk about the Cultural Revolution?" Mao had asked after one of my reports from the factory. "Aren't people still getting married and having babies? The Cultural Revolution is very remote from most people."

The Cultural Revolution became remote from me, too, and Mao was right that many people were trying to ignore it, hoping it would go away. But in other work units and other parts of the country, the Cultural Revolution was continuing to create turmoil, and outbreaks of violence continued. For many, the violence raging around them was impossible to ignore. Without direct intervention from the top, the feuds could not be stopped.

In October 1968, Mao called me back to Zhongnanhai. He had been bothered by a toothache for several days.

It was strange to return. Group One had completely changed. Wang Dongxing had set up new facilities for me on the third floor of his own building because Mao Yuanxin and Li Na had taken over my duty office, using it as their living quarters. None of Mao's former staff remained. Like me, everyone else had also been sent to join the military-control committees in other factories under Mao's "direct control," serving as Mao's eyes and ears. His bodyguard, Zhou Fuming, had been sent to the February 7 Locomotive Factory. Xie Jingyi, a staff member of the Bureau of Confidential Matters, was in Qinghua University, where the fundamentally uneducated young woman soon became the deputy director of the revolutionary committee there— vice-president of one of China's leading universities.

Uniformed soldiers from Wang Dongxing's 8341 Corps continued to keep guard over Mao, but what was most striking to me about the Chairman's inner circle was the number of young women about. I did not know Mao's new aides, attendants, or bodyguards, but it was clear the new replacements worshiped him, much as I had when I first went to work for him. I think the older members of his original staff suffered a similar affliction to mine: The more one knew Mao, the less he could be respected. By changing the inner circle, bringing in a fresh crop of worshipers, Mao assured himself continual adulation.

I examined the Chairman. His teeth were still coated with heavy green plaque, but I had no way of knowing what was wrong and I had no dental equipment. I tried to explain that I was not a dentist and therefore unable to make a diagnosis. I suggested that we bring in a specialist.

"You can treat me," Mao insisted. "We don't need a dentist."

I resisted, fearing that I might do him more harm than good. "Dentistry is a specialty," I explained once more. "A non-dentist like me could do more harm than good to your teeth."

Mao was silent. I knew him well enough to know that his silence was a sign of disagreement, but I felt strongly that it would be inappropriate for me to treat him.

Wang Dongxing insisted that I try. "This is the first time Chairman has asked for your help since Jiang Qing charged you with trying to poison her," he said. "Everyone on his staff but you has been replaced. It is important for you to try your best to serve him. Jiang Qing is still lurking out there, you know, trying to get you."

This was true. Jiang Qing was still trying to find a way to arrest me. When Ye Qun and Zhou Enlai refused to cooperate in her accusations of poison, she had turned to Mao's nurse, Wu Xujun. Knowing that Wu Xujun and I had worked closely together for years, Jiang Qing ordered Wu to work for her in Diaoyutai, trying all the while to persuade the nurse to sign a written statement formally accusing me of deliberately trying to harm her. An accusation from Wu, Jiang reasoned, would carry particular weight.

When Wu Xujun refused to sign, even after Jiang Qing's continual badgering, the Chairman's wife turned against her, too, accusing her of being part of an elaborate cover-up. When Jiang Qing ordered an investigation of Wu Xujun, the nurse fled to Wang Dongxing, who protected her by finding her a room in his own compound in Zhongnanhai.

I deeply appreciated the support Wu Xujun had given me and wanted to do all I could to help her. I took her with me the next time I saw Mao, hoping she could tell her side of the story. Mao was surprised to see her. The last he knew, Wu had been working in the February 7 Locomotive Plant. But he listened to her story about Jiang Qing's effort to force her to accuse me of trying to harm her. "Now I'm about to be declared a counterrevolutionary," Wu Xujun concluded.

Mao laughed. "Very good," he said. "My place is becoming a haven for counterrevolutionaries. You two counterrevolutionaries can stay here with me." Neither of us had to work for Jiang Qing anymore, he told us. Jiang Qing could find her own doctor and nurse. "Dodge her when you see her coming," he told us. "Try to avoid running into her."

I could hardly avoid Jiang Qing. Our paths within Zhongnanhai frequently crossed. She never spoke to me. She would look right past me as though I was not even there.

I tried to find a dentist for Mao. Ordinarily, I would have called someone from Beijing Hospital, but the chaos of the Cultural Revolution had spread to the hospitals, too, and Beijing Hospital was in an uproar, split into two contending factions. The head of the hospital and the party secretary had both been overthrown, and no new leadership had been appointed. To call a dentist from one faction would be taken as an indication that I, and by implication Mao, supported that faction over the other, but I had no idea which faction to support and could not afford a political mistake. Finally, I arranged to have a leading dentist from Shanghai's East China Hospital fly up to Beijing. Mao kept the man waiting for days even as I tried gently to remind the Chairman that the dentist was ready to examine his teeth.

Then Mao lost his temper. "I told you I didn't want this dentist," he yelled at me, "but you keep insisting I see him. You're trying to force me to do something I don't want to do. No wonder Jiang Qing is against you."

Those were ominous words, and unfair. I was not a dentist and could not pretend to be one. Mao did not want me to force him to do anything against his will, but he was forcing me to do something I was not able to do. He was adamant. He refused to see the dentist and insisted I treat him instead.

So I treated Mao by consulting the dentist every day on how to examine Mao and what treatment to give. I studied books on dentistry. Mao's disease was periodontic. His gums were deteriorating. He would never let me, or anyone, clean his teeth properly. The best I could do was help him rinse his mouth with antiseptic, clean out the surface food particles, and administer medicine to the site of infection. After a month, the problem was better.

Mao's malaise was not just physical. It was political, too. The party leaders who had not been purged were preparing to convene the Ninth Party Congress in April 1969, and they were badly divided. The guiding principles of the Eighth Party Congress, which had convened thirteen years before, in September 1956, had never been officially reversed. Those principles—supporting the idea of a collective leadership, promising that China would never have a cult of personality, removing Mao's thought as the country's guiding ideology, and criticizing Mao's "adventurism"—had long been anathema to Mao, and so had the men he held responsible for propagating them—Liu Shaoqi and Deng Xiaoping.

In the intervening years, Mao had maneuvered to reverse those principles, and his efforts had culminated in the Great Proletarian Cultural Revolution. As the party prepared for the Ninth Party Congress, the mere mention of collective leadership would have been a counterrevolutionary crime, and the cult of Mao was at its height. All China was wearing Mao buttons and carrying his little red book and reciting his quotations, and even the simplest transaction in a shop had to include a recitation from Mao's words. His portrait was everywhere. Tens of millions of people throughout the country began each day by bowing before a picture of Mao and asking it for their day's instructions. They ended the day by bowing again, reporting to Mao and confessing their mistakes. Every workday began and ended with collective recitations of Mao's thoughts. Chairman Mao's thought was not just the country's guiding ideology, it was its collective mantra.

And adventurism? Mao's Great Leap Forward had resulted in the worst famine in human history. We know today that at least 25 or 30 million people died.* His Cultural Revolution had plunged the country

*Some put the figure as high as 43 million.

into chaos, destroying lives, families, friendships, the whole fabric of Chinese society.

Liu Shaoqi, China's head of state, whom Mao blamed for all that he saw wrong with the Eighth Party Congress, had not only been purged but in October 1968 had been expelled from the party and subjected to gross abuse. In April 1969, I did not know where Liu was and would have been afraid to ask. Later, long after the party meeting was over, I learned that he had been shipped to Kaifeng, in October 1969, seriously ill, and died the following month, his illness untreated.

Deng Xiaoping, too, had been purged. The politburo had been decimated. Most of the provincial party leaders had lost their jobs, and governance of the provinces was now in the hands of "revolutionary committees" dominated by the military. The majority of the Central Committee elected by the Eighth Party Congress had been removed.

The Ninth Party Congress was to be the culmination of Mao's efforts over the past thirteen years. It would officially reverse the principles of the Eighth Congress and reestablish Mao as the supreme leader and his thought as the country's guiding ideology. It would formally elect a new Central Committee, which in turn would appoint the politburo. With Mao's will made official through party law, his Great Proletarian Cultural Revolution could also officially be declared successful.

As time for convocation of the party congress grew near, relations between the survivors of the purges—those who had united to throw out the old guard—grew tense. Mao appeared cool, aloof from the battle, but the alliance between Lin Biao and Jiang Qing was unraveling. Zhou Enlai, ever loyal to Mao, and anxious too about the allegations that he had been a traitor, was caught in the middle. The two dominant contending groups, one supporting Lin Biao and the other under Jiang Qing's control, were trying to pack the Central Committee and the politburo with their respective followers.

Zhou Enlai was visibly distressed. He almost never discussed political questions with me, but one evening when our paths crossed at Wang Dongxing's home, he took me aside for a private talk. He wondered what Mao was saying about the future composition of the party leadership.

"He has not said much about it," I reported honestly. "He just says he wants the Central Cultural Revolution Small Group and the ad hoc policy group to handle the question." Jiang Qing was in control of the Small Group, and because all members of that group were also members of the ad hoc policy group, she exerted considerable power over that body, too. The accusation against Zhou was coming directly from Jiang Qing, and I felt I had to warn Zhou about her vendetta against him.

"From the very beginning of the Cultural Revolution, Jiang Qing has singled you out as a target," I told him. I explained that when she said that the Cultural Revolution was a conflict between the new revolution and the old government, the "old government" could be no one else but the premier. I explained that the Chairman was very unhappy with her when she and her colleagues organized "May 16 Rebels" in the foreign ministry to oppose Zhou and foreign minister Chen Yi. "The Chairman thinks this group is counterrevolutionary and told the Central Cultural Revolution Small Group to state very clearly at a rally of ten thousand people that they do not oppose you," I said. "Jiang Qing did not agree, and I heard her talking to her colleagues Kang Sheng and Chen Boda. None of them want to hold a rally to support you. They thought a gathering of a few dozen people would do. They are still plotting against you."

Zhou was distraught. "For decades I have done everything I could to help Jiang Qing," he said. He pointed out that during the Second World War, when he was in Chongqing and Jiang Qing wanted to have a toothache treated there, he personally had flown to Yanan to take her to Chongqing. And when she had to go to the Soviet Union, both in 1949 and in 1956, Zhou had made all the arrangements.

Suddenly, Zhou's demeanor changed. "Have you told anyone else about this?" he wanted to know. I explained that Wang Dongxing knew everything and that we had often talked but that I had discussed the current political situation with no one else. Zhou relaxed a bit, urging me not to repeat our conversation.

Zhou Enlai, more than any of China's top leaders, had remained loyal to Mao—so faithful, in fact, that Lin Biao had once characterized him to Wang Dongxing as an "obedient servant." Zhou was more than loyal. He was subservient, sometimes embarrassingly so. I was present on November 10, 1966, when Mao and Zhou met to plan the seventh gathering of the Red Guards in Tiananmen Square. The crowds had grown bigger each time Mao appeared, and this time the public-security officials were projecting a crowd of 2.5 million students. The square, though, could accommodate only half a million people, and the logistics of marching so many students through were complicated. Zhou Enlai was suggesting that in addition to filling the square, the students should line Changan Avenue, the wide boulevard that runs east and west through Beijing, just in front of Tiananmen, and also some of the side streets running north above the square. Mao would ride through the streets in an open jeep, reviewing the students at the various scattered points.

As he was talking to Mao in Room 118, trying to explain his idea, Zhou got out a map and spread it on the floor, kneeling on the carpet to show Mao the direction his motorcade would take. Mao stood, smoking a cigarette, watching Zhou crawl on the floor.

For Zhou to kneel before Mao seemed to me humiliating, and I was deeply embarrassed to see a man of Zhou's stature, the premier of China, behave that way. Mao seemed to take a sardonic pleasure watching Zhou crawl before him. Nowhere were the contradictions of Mao's dictatorship more pronounced than in his relationship with Zhou. Mao demanded Zhou's absolute loyalty, and had he not received it, Zhou would no doubt have been overthrown. But because Zhou was so subservient and loyal, Mao held the premier in contempt.

Zhou was almost as obsequious before Jiang Qing. In December 1966, when Jiang Qing arrived at the door of the room in the Great Hall of the People where Zhou Enlai was conducting an important meeting, Zhou's longtime chief bodyguard, Cheng Yuangong, suggested politely that rather than interrupt the meeting, Jiang Qing might first want to eat and return when the meeting was over.

Jiang Qing was infuriated. "You, Cheng Yuangong, behave like an obedient dog before the premier but act like a wolf to me. I want you arrested." She ordered Wang Dongxing to arrest the premier's bodyguard.

Wang Dongxing refused, agreeing only to transfer Cheng to another job.

Deng Yingchao, Zhou's wife, the premier's closest confidante, intervened. "You must arrest Cheng Yuangong," she insisted to Wang. "We don't want to show any favoritism toward him."

Still Wang refused to arrest the bodyguard. "Cheng Yuangong has worked for the premier and his wife all his life," Wang said, "and they're throwing him out just to protect themselves." He finally sent Cheng off for a stint at the General Office's May 7 Cadre School to work in the fields.

Thus it was no surprise that as the power struggle between Lin Biao and Jiang Qing unfolded, Zhou Enlai threw his lot with Jiang Qing and her faction—despite all the attacks she had directed against him. Zhou was an astute politician and knew better than anyone else that despite Mao's criticisms of his wife and their growing personal estrangement, Jiang Qing was Mao's closest lieutenant. Real loyalty to Mao required siding with her as well.

Zhou's support for Jiang Qing also led to his betrayal of Wang Dongxing.

Wang Dongxing was a key person in the unfolding political struggle. As head of the 8341 Corps, which had taken over the six factories and two universities (Qinghua and Beida) that were administered in Mao's name, he had amassed considerable power and was viewed as one of Mao's closest followers. But in the conflict between Jiang Qing and Lin Biao, he was on the side of Lin Biao, both because he hated Jiang Qing and because the strains with Mao over Wang's trip to Indonesia with Liu Shaoqi continued. As the Ninth Party Congress approached, Wang Dongxing was being considered for a position on the politburo. Zhou and Wang Dongxing were also close, and Zhou initially supported Wang's appointment, assuring him that all members of the ad hoc policy group, Wang Dongxing included, would be made members of the leading group.

In the course of the deliberations, however, Wang Dongxing developed a bleeding ulcer and had to be hospitalized. Zhou Enlai invited me and nurse Wu Xujun to accompany him to break the news to Mao, asking me to explain the gravity of Wang's illness. As I was telling Mao about the dangers of a massive loss of blood, Zhou started to cry. "Wang Dongxing is such a good comrade," he said. Suddenly, nurse Wu and I also burst into tears, and the three of us sat sobbing together in front of Mao.

Mao remained impassive, the expression on his face never changing, and he never said a word. When our tears stopped, we too sat silent and embarrassed, not knowing what to do. Finally, Mao said, "If Wang is sick, get him the treatment the doctors suggest. We can do nothing else."

As we left, Mao remarked to his nurse that we had been crying over Wang as though there had been a death in our families. Our shared tears had led Mao to suspect that Zhou Enlai, Wang Dongxing, Wu Xujun, and I were not only close but something of a faction.

Wang Dongxing was not worried about Mao's suspicions. "We all work for him, not for anyone else," he said when I visited him in the hospital.

But Zhou Enlai was worried. He wanted to do nothing to rouse Mao's suspicions. Jiang Qing and Kang Sheng were adamantly opposed to Wang's appointment to the politburo and met with Zhou to persuade him to join their opposition. Zhou agreed. While Wang was still seriously ill, recovering from his ulcer, Zhou asked him to withdraw from the competition.

Wang Dongxing was incensed. "He did precisely what Jiang Qing and Kang Sheng asked him to do," he fumed at me from his bed. "The man has no sense of personal loyalty."

The two sides were forced to compromise. When the Ninth Party Congress was held in April 1969, Wang Dongxing was elected a member of the Central Committee and an alternate member of the politburo, despite Jiang Qing's objections. Lin Biao had backed Wang Dongxing, and he and his faction were in the ascendancy. Lin Biao gave the political report at the Ninth Party Congress and was officially designated Mao Zedong's "close comrade in arms and successor." Mao's thought was reinstituted as the guiding ideology of China.

Lin Biao's son, Lin Liguo, also gained power. Not long after the Ninth Party Congress, he was made deputy director of the War Department of the Air Force Command and hailed as a natural "third-generation" leader. The air force put together a collection of Lin Liguo's speeches and sent them to Mao. Within the air force, Lin Liguo's name was often mentioned right after that of his father, and calls for loyalty to the air force often included calls for loyalty to Lin Liguo, too.

My spirits plunged after that. Mao's goal of reversing the principles of the Eighth Party Congress had been achieved. It was the culmination of thirteen years of struggle. The party representatives I most respected had all been purged—more than 80 percent of the previous Central Committee was dismissed—and the newcomers were all unfamiliar to me, members of the Jiang Qing or Lin Biao factions. With their followers taking over leadership of China, I despaired for my country.

69

With Lin Biao approaching the height of his power, all China was becoming militarized. Charged with restoring order to the country, the army had taken control of government offices and work units at every level of Chinese society. The party secretaries who had once controlled China's provinces had been removed, replaced by provincial military commanders, and soldiers were in charge of the bureaucratic hierarchy from the top to the bottom, even in the villas frequented by Mao. Led by Lin Biao, the whole country was studying Mao's thought, and because the People's Liberation Army excelled in the study of Mao, everyone was learning from the army, too. Everyone wanted to bask in the glory of the military. We all wore military uniforms. Even I did. Only Mao, still insisting on the comfort of his old, baggy clothes, held out. He wore a uniform only for his rare public appearances, to show his support for the army.

Our country had two main enemies then, the Soviet Union and the United States, and in March 1969, China and the Soviet Union fought military skirmishes over Zhenbao (Treasure) Island, along the Heilongjiang border. In the months that followed, the whole country was mobilized for war. Tens of millions of people were evacuated from the cities and shipped to rural areas in a variety of guises. Cadres from both the government and the party, and intellectuals and teachers who had yet to be struggled against, were sent to do manual labor in so-called May 7 Cadre Schools. The schools were supposed to provide intellectuals with an opportunity to taste the harsh realities of rural life and to learn from the country's poor and lower-middle peasants. But the intellectuals rarely lived with the peasants. They lived in miserable circumstances in rural concentration camps, and they were forced to perform backbreaking labor from dawn to dusk, often beyond the breaking point. The real purpose of the May 7 Cadre Schools, everyone knew, was not learning but punishment. Students from middle schools and universities, the same students Mao had once called upon to rebel against the authorities, were sent "up to the mountains and down to the countryside" to be "reeducated by the poor and lower-middle peasants." As the war scare grew, others were evacuated away from the borders. In August 1969, the remaining city residents were mobilized to "dig tunnels deep" in preparation for aerial, possibly nuclear, attack. In Beijing, the underground tunnels, crisscrossing the length and breadth of the city, were to serve as air-raid shelters in which the entire population could live for weeks.

At the height of the militarization, with the war fever at its hottest, Mao presented me with a riddle. "Think about this," he said to me one day. "We have the Soviet Union to the north and the west, India to the south, and Japan to the east. If all our enemies were to unite, attacking us from the north, south, east, and west, what do you think we should do?"

Mao's assumption that we were surrounded by enemies bent on doing us in was one I shared, but I did not know how to answer his question. What should we do? I thought about his question for a day before telling the Chairman that I still could not answer.

"Think again," he said. "Beyond Japan is the United States. Didn't our ancestors counsel negotiating with faraway countries while fighting with those that are near?"

I was aghast. Our newspapers were filled with vitriolic attacks against the United States. China was offering aid to Vietnam, now struggling in its war against the United States. "How could we negotiate with the United States?" I asked, incredulous.

"The United States and the Soviet Union are different," Mao explained. "The United States never occupied Chinese territory. America's new president, Richard Nixon, is a longtime rightist, a leader of the anti-communists there. I like to deal with rightists. They say what they really think—not like the leftists, who say one thing and mean another."

Neither I nor Wang Dongxing believed Mao. The mutual antagonism between China and the United States dated to the outbreak of the Korean War, in June 1950, and the invective against the United States had never mellowed. American imperialists were accused of seeking hegemony by force in all of Asia. Capitalism, we were certain, was weak and dying, the victim of its own internal contradictions.

But Mao was serious, and China was in the process of a major foreign-policy realignment.

Nixon the rightist was also directing the United States toward a new path. The American president had already sent friendly feelers to China via Pakistani president Yahya Khan and Romania's Nicolae Ceauşescu, stating that he did not support the Soviet proposal for creating a collective Asian security system and assuring Mao that he opposed the Soviet Union's talk of a surgical strike against China's nuclear facilities. Mao's interests for China coincided with Nixon's strategy for the United States. "What collective Asian security system?" Mao had exclaimed when he learned of Nixon's assurances. "It's an Asian war system, designed to attack China." Mao was bellicose toward the Soviet Union, countering its threat with one of his own. "China's atom bombs and missiles may not be able to reach the United States," he said, "but they can easily reach the Soviet Union."

In December 1969, Premier Zhou Enlai passed on to Mao a cable from our embassy in Poland, where China and the United States had been conducting inconclusive and sometimes hostile meetings for years. At a cocktail party to mark the opening of a fashion show in Warsaw, the American ambassador to Poland had suggested another meeting with our ambassador in Warsaw. He had something of substance to discuss.

Mao showed me the cable. He was delighted. "We have been talking without saying anything for eleven years," he said. "Now we can start over again and talk seriously. Nixon must be sincere when he sends word that he is interested in talking with us."

I took the opportunity of Mao's desire for rapprochement to broach the question of renewing my subscriptions to American medical journals. With the Cultural Revolution's ban on subscriptions to American publications, I felt increasingly isolated from medical science, but Mao was getting older, and I knew that soon my responsibilities for his health would become more onerous. I wanted to learn as much as possible about medical advances. Without access to American medical journals, I explained to Mao, we had no way of learning about progress there.

"The United States is doing everything it can to get information about us," Mao responded. "Why are we so stupid to shut our eyes to what's going on abroad? Write a report listing the medical journals you want."

Mao sent my request for journals to both Zhou Enlai and Kang

Sheng. "I want them to think carefully about our relations with foreign countries," he said, "especially the United States."

China's public rhetoric attacking the United States continued undiminished and so did our support for North Vietnam in the on-going war. But behind the scenes, the rapprochement with the United States was quietly unfolding. Mao was beginning to negotiate with his archenemy from afar even as China prepared for war with our onetime big brother nearby.

70

As all of China mobilized for war and Mao talked of détente with the United States, his disaffection with the man who had just been designated his heir apparent and closest comrade in arms was growing. I first became aware of Mao's hostility toward Lin Biao during a trip south in May 1969, right after the Ninth Party Congress.

In Zhongnanhai, the growing number of soldiers surrounding Mao was not so obvious. Soldiers from Wang Dongxing's 8341 Corps had always guarded him. For me, returning to Mao's inner circle after a long absence, what was most striking was still the number of young women about. Many of them traveled with him, too, and new ones always seemed to appear wherever we were. During our trip in May 1969, visiting Wuhan, Hangzhou, and Nanchang, all the attendants in Mao's villas were young women, and female members of various provincial song-and-dance troupes kept him constant company. Two singers from one of the provincial music-and-dance troupes were particular favorites during this trip, and they both invited their sisters to join them in Mao's room. Asceticism was the public watchword of the Cultural Revolution, but the more ascetic and moralistic the party's preachings, the further the Chairman himself descended into hedonism. He was waited on constantly by a harem of young girls. It was at this time, the height of the Cultural Revolution, that Mao was sometimes in bed with three, four, even five women simultaneously.

But beyond his room, hovering close by, were the uniformed

soldiers who were responsible for Mao's safety. It was only during this trip that I was fully aware of how dramatically their numbers had increased after Mao called in the military to quell the chaos of the Cultural Revolution. Both the need to beef up Mao's security and the fact that all organizations were under military control had meant an increase in the number of soldiers.

But Mao hated being surrounded by soldiers and railed against all the uniforms around him. "Why do we have so many soldiers around here?" he kept complaining. The soldiers smothered his freedom. People in uniform, he knew, reported everything they saw to their superiors. He still hated his activities being reported to anyone. He wanted the soldiers gone.

I interpreted Mao's antagonism to the soldiers as a growing struggle with Lin Biao as well. Wang Dongxing did not agree. "Why should he worry about the soldiers?" he said when I told him of Mao's concern. "The military control committees are everywhere, and the armed forces are supporting the left. With the military in positions of leadership, of course the staff are all soldiers. The Central Bureau of Guards may be the only organization in the country not under military control, but we still wear military uniforms, too." Wang Dongxing's ordinary political acuity was failing him. He refused to connect Mao's growing hostility to uniforms to the chasm that was coming to divide Mao from Lin Biao.

A small incident in November 1969 convinced me that Mao's hostility to Lin Biao was serious. We had returned from our southern trip in late September, only to set out for Wuhan again in mid-October. In late October, a cold wave struck and the temperature in Wuhan plunged. I knew from past experience that Mao was sure to catch cold unless we turned on the heat. As usual, he refused. He would exercise to increase his resistance, he said. But I knew he would catch cold and so did Zhang Yaoci, who was then in charge of security and worried that he might be blamed if Mao became ill. Zhang called Ye Qun, hoping that she would talk to her husband and get him to suggest turning on the heat.

I was with Mao when Zhang Yaoci reported that Lin Biao had called urging the Chairman to turn on the heat. Mao was silent, feigning indifference. His disagreement was obvious, but I was hardly prepared for the outburst that followed Zhang's departure. "Why does Zhang have to report on everything that happens here? When other people [Lin Biao and Ye Qun] fart, Zhang acts like they're announcing an imperial edict!" Mao was not about to follow Lin Biao's imperial decree.

The heat in Wuhan was not turned on. By late November, with the cold settling in, Mao did catch cold, and because he also initially refused my medical treatment, the cold soon turned into acute bronchitis. Only then was he sick enough to accept my treatment and agree to turn on the heat.

Mao knew that I had encouraged him to turn on the heat and that I attributed his bronchitis to his refusal. He also knew of Jiang Qing's continual attacks against me and her repeated accusations that I had attempted to poison her. In the dog-eat-dog mood at that time, when attack was so easy and the consequences so dire, she could easily hold me responsible for Mao's illness.

Once more Mao protected me. He asked me to write a medical report on his cold and bronchitis. "I want to clear you of any responsibility for my illness," he said. "I was the one who did not want to turn on the heat."

My uneasiness about Mao's relationship with Lin Biao continued, and with it my growing conviction that Wang Dongxing's alliance with Lin Biao was becoming dangerous. I repeated my concerns and still he would not listen. Wang was loyal to Mao, but he was also intent on expanding his own power. He was quick to build bridges to anyone who could further his political ends. Wang's ties with Lin Biao had made sense as the Cultural Revolution evolved. No one was more loyal to Mao than Lin Biao, Mao's closest comrade in arms, the man who had started the campaign to study Mao's thought and who said that one of Mao's words was worth ten thousand of anyone else's. To work with Lin Biao was to work for Mao. The two were inseparable. But the situation was changing, and Wang Dongxing was uncharacteristically slow to catch on.

71

Early in 1970, gossip began circulating within Group One that one of Mao's female companions, a confidential clerk in the General Office, was having an affair with another member of Mao's staff. Wang Dongxing wanted to put an end to the relationship. He was impeccable in his own personal dealings, so faithful to his wife that the thought of straying never crossed his mind, and he never understood Mao's lust. But Mao was an exceptional man and Wang therefore granted him the right to exceptional behavior. But he was scrupulous about the behavior of Mao's staff. While we were in Wuhan, Wang decided to call a staff meeting to criticize the woman and her friend, and he wanted me to serve as chair.

I refused. I liked the young woman. Unlike many of the women around Mao, she was still naive and innocent, willing to serve Mao only because of the tremendous respect and awe with which she viewed the Chairman. I did not believe the accusations against her. She and the young man joked and laughed together, but nothing more than that. She and the man would greatly resent public accusations against them, and Mao was not likely to approve of the idea, either. But Wang Dongxing insisted. He thought I was too timid. "The worst that can happen is for you to lose your job in Group One," he told me. "You can always find work elsewhere." Having twice been exiled himself by Mao, Wang had still not completely forgiven the Chairman and was not yet certain how far Mao would go in supporting him. Much as he wanted to avoid another exile, he was always prepared for the possibility and wanted me to be ready, too.

Wang Dongxing was still my boss. I had to obey him. I called the meeting as he ordered.

The young woman was so unhappy with the criticisms that she asked two of Mao's other female friends, including Zhang Yufeng, to go with her to complain to Mao. I never learned what they said to the Chairman, but he soon let me know that I had made a colossal mistake.

"You're really not such a smart fellow, are you?" he said to me sarcastically a few days later while we were on the train from Wuhan to Hangzhou. "You meddled in things you shouldn't have. You still have a lot to learn, you know. When we get back to Beijing, I want you to organize a medical team and go to the countryside, where you can really serve the people, make contact with the people, get some education from the poor peasants. It'll do you a lot of good."

I decided to go to Heilongjiang, the province in China's far northeast, on the border with the Soviet Union. It was around Zhenbao (Treasure) Island in Heilongjiang, just along the border, that the military clashes had broken out between the two sides, and the whole population was now busy digging underground bomb shelters in preparation for war. I wanted to see how the masses, by getting ready for war, were demonstrating their great creativity. Mao agreed.

I was almost relieved to leave. Even with Mao's protection, my circumstances in Beijing had continued to decline. The rebellion within the Ministry of Public Health had heated up again in 1969, and so had the assault on my apartment compound in Gongxian Lane. One of the contending factions had cut off water and heat to the compound while rebels from the other side, in control of the ministry payroll, refused to pay anyone who had not declared himself a member of their faction. But I refused to take sides.

When the situation became unbearable, Mao had Wang Dongxing transfer my personnel files from the Ministry of Public Health to the safer Central Bureau of Guards, and I moved my family to an apartment complex a couple of blocks from Zhongnanhai that housed the staff of the General Office.

Then, not long after the announcement that cadres and intellectuals were to be shipped off to May 7 Cadre Schools, Lillian's entire office was sent to a remote area of Heilongjiang, near the Soviet border, leaving me behind and responsible for our two sons.

Lillian lived not only in miserable physical circumstances but in continual fear as well. Her bourgeois background continued to cause her problems, and when her group gathered every evening to delve into their fellows' political pasts, hers was constantly held up for criticism. We both knew that only the fact that I was Mao's doctor protected her from still greater abuse. If I lost my job, her life would disintegrate.

In Heilongjiang, I would have a chance to see Lillian and perhaps to comfort her. Even if my medical team was in a different part of the province, we would still be closer than we were with me in Beijing. Away from the political tensions of the capital, I was certain we would find ways to meet.

Heilongjiang was an appropriate site for my banishment for another reason, too. High-ranking officials of the Qing dynasty had often been exiled there in disgrace. Ningan county, known during the reign of the Manchus as Ningguta, was the place to which most exiles had been sent. I, too, felt like a man in disgrace, sent against his will into exile. So I chose Ningan county as the place for our medical work.

Wang Dongxing did not want me to go. He had other plans for me. With the Beijing Hospital still in chaos, Wang Dongxing was increasingly concerned about how to guarantee proper medical facilities for Mao and the other party elite. He decided to convert the high-ranking cadres' club at Yangfengjiadao (Bee Raising Alley), near North Lake just outside of Zhongnanhai, into an exclusive hospital, reserved solely for Mao and the country's other highest-ranking officials. Named 305 Hospital of the People's Liberation Army, the facilities were to be under direct military control. Wang wanted me to serve as president of the new hospital.

But I blamed the fiasco of my exile on him. He had directed me, against my better judgment, to organize the criticism against Mao's female companion. Mao's trust in me had already been undermined, both by my reluctance to be an activist in the Cultural Revolution and because of the repeated accusations against me by Jiang Qing and Kang Sheng. Nonetheless, I saw myself as a scapegoat. Wang Dongxing, blinded by his own antagonism to Jiang Qing, was leaning too closely to the side of Lin Biao, refusing to see that Mao no longer fully trusted either Lin Biao or Wang himself.

I had continued to warn Wang Dongxing that loyalty to Lin was not the same as loyalty to Mao, telling him of the flashes of hostility toward Lin I had detected in Mao, trying to persuade him that Mao really did demand absolute loyalty directly to him. Wang would scoff. Sophisticated though he was politically, he could not believe me. But I was certain that Mao was punishing me in lieu of Wang.

After hiring a nanny to take care of my sons, I organized a

medical team consisting of seven people—two doctors from the Beijing Hospital, a surgeon, Dr. Niu, a nurse from the newly formed 305 Hospital, a political officer named Zhang from the Central Garrison Corps, the medic Li, who had protected me during the melee at Qinghua University, and myself. We left by train on June 29, 1970, heading for Harbin, the provincial capital of Heilongjiang.

72

Wang Dongxing made certain that we began our disgrace in style. We were greeted in Harbin by officials from the Heilongjiang revolutionary committee and taken on a grand tour of the city that lasted an entire week. We inspected the well-equipped local militia unit, watching them train in preparation for the coming war with the Soviet Union. We visited the complex underground air-raid tunnels that were being constructed. We saw a number of field hospitals that had been set up on the outskirts of the city. Their medical facilities were simple and basic but sufficient for the emergencies of war. My request to take a look at Zhenbao Island itself was turned down. The skirmishes there were continuing, and local officials told us the place was too dangerous.

From Harbin, we traveled by train to the small and orderly town of Mudanjiang, where we were taken on another sight-seeing excursion. We spent the night along the beautiful Jingbo Lakes, which sit in the craters of a line of extinct volcanoes, linked like a string of pearls. It was a wild and beautiful place, still inhabited by tigers and bears. Many White Russians had fled there after the October Revolution, making a good living hunting animals for fur. Only with the coming of the Cultural Revolution in 1966 had they fled, dispersing to other parts of the world.

Finally, after ten days of sight-seeing and banquets, hosted always by high-level provincial officials, we went to Ningan by car, joined by two other doctors from Heilongjiang. My life as a "barefoot doctor" had begun.

I lived in the offices of a people's commune, sharing a room with the medic Li. Li treated me as a father and took good care of me as well. The fields that surrounded us were huge, stretching beyond the horizon, so large the eye could not see their end—completely different from the small fields and clustered villages in the south. The soil in Heilongjiang was fertile and black, planted with corn and soybeans.

The peasants' homes were different too, constructed of clay, with thatched roofs. The interiors were dominated by the *kang,* the raised brick platform bed that was the source of warmth in winter, where families ate and slept together without much regard for differences of generation or sex. Unlike most parts of the country, Heilongjiang had not suffered major deforestation, so wood was plentiful and used as fuel for the *kang,* fed by the chimney of the cooking stove that ran underneath the platform.

Ningan county was populated both by Han Chinese and ethnic Koreans, who had different customs. The homes of the Koreans were neater, thanks to a kind of painted paper they glued across their *kang*s, which made the brick platforms look clean. The Chinese threw straw on the top of the *kang,* so their homes always seemed primitive and messy. The peasants in Ningan were not as impoverished as the ones in Jiangxi, but they were still very poor. The rural areas had no doctors, and if any of the peasants needed to see a physician, they had to travel to the city. But none of them had ever even considered visiting a doctor—it cost too much money, and the doctors were too far away. The concept of modern medical care simply did not exist. One day at harvest time an old village woman put an awl through her eye. I had neither the medicine nor the equipment to treat her properly and wanted her to go to a hospital in the city. But the trip was out of the question. The possibility never even occurred to her, and my attempts to convince her failed. She could not afford it.

We were the only doctors most of the peasants had ever seen, and we traveled every day from village to village treating them, using only basic medicines and the simplest techniques. I think Mao had sent me there thinking perhaps the peasants would see me as a "bourgeois remnant" and turn against me, but the peasants were always happy to see us. Whatever help we could give was always better than anything they had received before. Two diseases predominated—tuberculosis and tapeworm. The village pigs wandered free, and they invariably had tapeworm. While fuel was plentiful, the peasants still never cooked the pork well enough to destroy the tapeworm. I enjoyed treating the common diseases of ordinary people.

But I never got to see Lillian. Because China and the Soviet Union were on the brink of war, and Heilongjiang was the place most likely to be affected, she had been transferred to a May 7 Cadre School in Henan, thousands of miles away, just before I arrived. I missed my family tremendously. It was as though some evil fate was conspiring to keep us apart. From the rare letters I received, I knew that life for Lillian and my children was difficult. Rumors were circulating about why I was in Heilongjiang. Some said I had been exiled because I had political problems. Some said I had defected to the Soviet Union or been kidnapped by the Russians. My family was very depressed by such rumors, and so was I.

But my own life in the countryside was peaceful. News from outside rarely reached us. The Cultural Revolution may have been continuing in other parts of the country, but we never knew it in Ningan.

On November 6, 1970, four months after I had arrived, I was on a medical call to one of the local villages when a jeep driven by Commander Zhong, the local military chief who had showed us around when we first arrived, roared into the tiny square. He had been looking for me for hours, riding from village to village. The General Office in Beijing had called. I had been ordered to return to Beijing immediately. The matter was urgent.

I hopped into Zhong's jeep without even returning to change clothes, leaving Zhang and Dr. Niu in charge of the medical team. We raced toward Mudanjiang, which had the only airport in the area, arriving at about nine in the evening. Commander Zhong insisted on hosting a farewell banquet in my honor. I could not refuse. Good manners required such formalities. But I was anxious to be on my way, worried about what I might find.

I arrived at the Mudanjiang airport at about eleven at night. A Soviet-made IL-62—a medium-sized four-engine propeller plane with about one hundred seats—was waiting on the tarmac. It was empty. I was the only passenger. The plane took off as soon as I was on board.

We landed at Beijing's special Xiyuan airport at a little after two in the morning, where Mao's driver, Zhang, was waiting for me. We sped along the empty, darkened streets to Zhongnanhai. I was still dressed in my winter peasant garb—quilted cotton trousers and a heavy quilted jacket—and I was perspiring heavily by the time we pulled up to Mao's residence at the swimming pool. Mao's nurse, Wu Xujun, was there to greet me.

"He's waiting for you," she said. "Go see him first. Then I'll tell you what happened."

73

Mao was sitting on his sofa, gasping for breath, his face flushed. "I'm in real trouble," he said. "I'm seriously ill. I had to call you back. You have to look at my chest X ray. Tell the head nurse to get it for you. Then tomorrow examine me and tell me what you think." We chatted for a while about my work in Ningan. I assured him that I had enjoyed being a "barefoot doctor" and that life had not been so hard. I left him as soon as I could. I wanted to see the X ray.

"Something really big has happened, President Li," Wu Xujun said as she handed me the X ray.

I was confused. President Li? Why was she calling me president?

"Your appointment as president of 305 Hospital has come through," she explained. "Chief of staff [of the PLA] Huang Yongsheng has already announced it." While I was in exile, the chiefs of the general staff, the political department, and the general logistics department of the People's Liberation Army had agreed to my appointment as president of 305 Hospital.

"And what has happened? What is this something big?" I asked Wu Xujun.

The problem was Lin Biao. The split between him and Mao was widening.

The problem had reached crisis proportions with the Second Plenum of the Ninth Congress of the party Central Committee, held in Lushan in August–September 1970, not long after I had left for Heilongjiang. Lin Biao had wanted to restore the post of chairman of state, the position Liu Shaoqi had assumed in 1959 after Mao had resigned. With Liu's purge, the position had been abolished. Lin insisted on restoring it and suggested that Mao resume the post. But he knew Mao would refuse and was maneuvering to have himself elected. Not wanting to give the appearance of lusting after power, however, he wanted others to act on his behalf.

Lin wanted Wang Dongxing on his side. As Wang told me the story, Lin's wife, Ye Qun, had contacted him before the Lushan meetings to solicit his support. She was worried that unless Lin was given some official position, such as chairman of the republic, his designation as Mao's successor would be meaningless. She also knew that Mao would not like the idea and hoped that if other leaders pressed Lin's cause, the Chairman would be forced to give it some thought.

At Lushan, Lin's closest associates—commander in chief of the air force Wu Faxian, commander in chief of the navy Li Zuopeng, and commander in chief of the general logistics department Qiu Huizuo—lobbied on his behalf, especially within the small groups that met outside the plenary sessions. Chen Boda, the former director of the Central Cultural Revolution Small Group and a member of the politburo standing committee, had also pressed Lin's case. He wrote a piece called "On Genius," praising Mao effusively and attributing China's progress to his genius, and arguing that Mao should resume the post of chairman of the republic. The tract was distributed to the small groups that were meeting by region and published as part of the Lushan conference proceedings in Bulletin Number Two of the North China group.

Many participants mistakenly assumed the bulletin reflected Mao's own views and that Mao wanted to resume the post.

But Mao categorically did not agree. Early in 1970, he had made it clear to the politburo standing committee that he would not become chairman of the republic again. Most conference participants did not know this. But if people agreed that someone should occupy the post and Mao refused, Lin Biao was the only possible choice. This was Lin Biao's strategy.

Lin Biao had made the same mistake as Liu Shaoqi, and in Mao's eyes it was an egregious crime. Lin Biao wanted two chairmen in China, and Mao would have only one. He made certain the leadership knew this by calling an enlarged meeting of the politburo standing committee on August 25, 1970. The meeting revoked Bulletin Number Two, Chen Boda was purged, and a campaign to criticize him was launched.

Wang Dongxing was one of those implicated in the affair. He had listened to the urgings of Ye Qun and spoken at Lushan in favor of Lin Biao. Mao was furious with him, accusing him of betrayal and of joining the Lin Biao camp. Intending to punish Wang without dismissing him permanently, Mao ordered Wang Dongxing temporarily relieved of his duties so he could "think over his conduct." Wang, who was still in communication with Mao, confessed everything, telling the Chairman about his conversations with Ye Qun and reporting fully on her efforts to secure Lin's appointment. Zhou Enlai, who wanted Wang permanently dismissed, had appointed Yang Dezhong to take over directorship of the Central Bureau of Guards; and Kang Sheng, acting at the behest of Zhou, had asked Wang Liangen, the director of the political department of the General Office, to take over Wang's post as director there. Zhou had made the appointments quietly, without informing Wang Dongxing.

Wang remained stoic. "I made a big mistake," he told me, "and I'm writing a report on my conduct, examining my faults behind closed doors, so to speak, just taking a break from my duties. I spoke at the conference and the Chairman got mad at me, but regretting it now won't get me anywhere." Still, he was furious with the people who had maneuvered against him—Zhou Enlai and Kang Sheng—and with Yang Dezhong and Wang Liangen, who had been slated to take over his posts. "They'll hear from me later, just wait," he told me.

Wang's "mistake" was reverberating now throughout Group One. Mao was suspicious of Wu Xujun too, accusing her of belonging to the Wang Dongxing camp and relieving her of all but the most essential nursing duties.

The young women from the cultural work troupe of the air force had been dismissed—including the one who some believed had borne Mao's child, together with her two friends. The three young women were too close to Ye Qun and Lin Biao, and Mao suspected that they had begun to serve as spies. "They were all unreliable," he told me later.

Zhang Yufeng, the attendant from Mao's train, had started waiting on him instead and moved to Zhongnanhai. Then two women from the Foreign Ministry—Wang Hairong, the director of protocol within the Foreign Ministry and later to become a vice-minister, and Tang Wensheng (Nancy Tang), deputy head of American and Oceanic Affairs and Mao's frequent English-language interpreter—came to have considerable power within the inner circle. They served as liaison between Mao and the top-ranking leadership, keeping such tight control that finally even Zhou Enlai had to go through them to see Mao.

.   .   .

Nothing final had been decided at the Lushan meetings in August-September. The power struggle within the party was continuing. With Lin Biao's power declining, Jiang Qing's was increasing. Wu Xujun told me that the deal I had long suspected had apparently become explicit at Lushan. If Jiang Qing kept quiet about his infidelities, Mao would support Jiang Qing's efforts to build her own power. And now, in November, Mao was sick, as he often was at times of political struggle, before the outcome was final.

He had started feeling sick while the meetings were still in session. As usual, his discomfort began with a cold that first settled in his chest and then turned into bronchitis. He refused to see a doctor, and his situation got worse. By late October he was so ill that Zhou Enlai insisted he get medical treatment and sent three physicians to examine him. They took a chest X ray, prescribed antibiotics, and told him he had pneumonia.

Mao's paranoia was in full bloom, and he suspected a plot. Lin Biao, he was convinced, wanted him dead. Mao's understanding of medicine had not greatly improved under my tutelage, and he was convinced that pneumonia was inevitably fatal, the result of hopelessly rotten lungs. Mao thought Lin Biao was behind the three doctors who told him he had pneumonia. Mao did not believe them.

But he did not get better, either, and finally Zhang Yufeng suggested that I be recalled from Heilongjiang. Wang Dongxing had wanted to call me back much earlier but knew that anyone he suggested would be implicated as a member of his clique.

Mao did have pneumonia. The X rays left no doubt. But I could not tell him that. If I told him that he had pneumonia, I would be accused of being a member of the Lin Biao–Wang Dongxing clique. So I told him it was his old problem—acute bronchitis, nothing too serious. A few shots of antibiotics and he would be fine.

Mao started thumping his chest with both fists when I related my diagnosis. "Lin Biao wants my lungs to rot," he said. "You just show those X rays to the doctors and see what they say now. They were really funny, those three guys. One examined me without talking at all. Another one talked incessantly but did not examine me. And still the other one put a mask over his mouth and neither talked nor examined me. If they still think it's pneumonia, then I'll stop the injections. Let's see if I die."

I consulted with the three doctors, explaining why we could not let Mao know he had pneumonia, trying to assure them that what was most important was to make certain he received appropriate treatment. They agreed, but the director of the Zhongnanhai Clinic was not happy. "We had no idea what happened in Lushan," he said. "How could we have known that politics and the Chairman's health would get all mixed up? We're really unlucky. We did exactly as Premier Zhou instructed."

Mao, though, was delighted when I told him that the doctors now agreed that he had bronchitis rather than pneumonia. He credited me with saving his life and invited me to dinner as his honored guest. My days as a "barefoot doctor" were over. He did not want me to return to Heilongjiang. "There may be something here I want you to do for me," he said. A week or so later, Wang Dongxing arranged for Lillian to return to Beijing, too. My family at last was reunited.

By December 18, 1970, Mao's health had improved sufficiently that he was able to meet with American journalist Edgar Snow, who had first interviewed the Chairman in Baoan in 1936, had written the classic bestseller *Red Star over China,* and had remained a friend of China's over all those years. "I think Snow must be working for the Central Intelligence Agency," Mao told me at the time of the visit. "We have to give him some inside information."

Believing that Snow would pass the information on to his superiors in the CIA, Mao used the meeting to further U.S.-China relations, conveying his willingness to invite Nixon or any other ranking American official to meet with him in Beijing. He also took the occasion to warn the CIA of the deeper conflict within Chinese politics. "There are three types of people who shout 'long life' to me," Mao told Snow. "The first type really means it. There aren't too many of these. The second type is just following the crowd. Most people fall into this category. The third type are those who shout the slogan but really want me to die early. Not too many people fall into this category, but there are some."

I had lived in the United States for some time before realizing that Edgar Snow was a pariah in his own country when he visited China in 1970 and that his message to the American government was delivered too late, well after direct channels between China and the United States had been established. And Snow probably never understood whom Mao was talking about when he said that some people wanted him dead even as they shouted, "Long live." Mao was referring to Lin Biao.

74

By August 1971, Mao's distrust of Lin Biao was reaching the breaking point. Xie Jingyi, the deputy director of the revolutionary committee in control of Qinghua University, had told him about a secret spy organization that Lin's son, Lin Liguo, had set up in the air force. Consisting of several units, code-named "the joint fleet," the "Shanghai small group," and the "instruction guidance brigade," the underground groups were conspiring to take power from Mao. Xie Jingyi's husband, Xiao Su, an officer on the staff of the air force headquarters, was warning Mao to be careful. The Chairman needed to shore up his own support in the military.

Lin Biao's personnel appointments had been made largely at the center. Most of his supporters were in Beijing. Mao thought the loyalty of the regional and provincial-level military commanders still rested with him. "I don't think the regional commanders will side with Lin Biao," he told me. "The People's Liberation Army won't rebel against me, will it? Anyway, if they don't want my leadership, I'll go back to Jinggangshan and start another guerrilla war."

On August 14, he decided to make sure of the regional commanders' support.

We left in his special train that day, heading south and stopping at Wuhan, Changsha, Nanchang, Hangzhou, and Shanghai, meeting secretly with party, government, and military leaders. Mao's message to all the groups was the same: At the Lushan conference, someone had been in a big hurry to take over as chairman of the republic. That person was trying to split the party and grab power for himself. The problem had still not been solved.

Mao never attacked Lin Biao by name, but the object of his accusations was unmistakable. It was well known that Mao did not like Lin's grab for power, and he had become overtly suspicious of the cult of personality Lin was pushing with such apparent enthusiasm. "There is someone who says genius appears in the world only once in several hundred years, and in China such genius has not come along in several thousand," Mao quipped. "This does not accord with reality. There is somebody who says he wants to support me, elevate me, but what he really has in mind is supporting himself, elevating himself." The "somebody" was obviously Lin Biao.

Mao was suspicious, too, of the power Ye Qun had over her husband. "I have never approved of the idea of letting one's wife be in charge of one's office," he said. "But Ye Qun is in charge of Lin Biao's office. Huang Yongsheng, Wu Faxian, Li Zuopeng, and Qiu Huizuo all have to go through her to get to Lin Biao. A person should depend on himself to do his work—reading and commenting on documents. Don't depend on secretaries. Don't give secretaries a lot of power."

There was urgency in his words. This was not only a power struggle but an attempt to do away with Mao's leadership and tear the party asunder. He held Lin Biao responsible. But he was still willing to compromise, to rely on "education" rather than force to reunite the party—"curing the illness to save the patient," he called it. "We should try to save Lin Biao. No matter who makes mistakes, we cannot disregard the necessity of unity. It doesn't look good. After I return to Beijing, I'll look up Lin Biao and his followers and ask for a talk. If they don't look for me, I'll look for them. We may be able to salvage some of them, but not others . . ."

We were away from Beijing for almost a month, arriving at the special train station in Beijing's Fengtai county at dusk on September 12, 1971. Before returning to Zhongnanhai, Mao met with the leaders of Beijing municipality and the Beijing Military Region, reiterating his concerns about Lin Biao. We arrived at Zhongnanhai at about eight in the evening. There was no particular urgency about his talks in Beijing and nothing untoward about his return.

I was still in Mao's residence at the swimming pool, helping with the details of unpacking, when Wang Dongxing received a phone call from Beidaihe. It was a little after ten at night.

The call was from Zhang Hong, a deputy commander of the Central Garrison Corps. Zhang had just received an urgent communication from Lin Biao's daughter, Lin Liheng, whom we called by her familiar name, Lin Doudou. Ye Qun and Lin Liguo had kidnapped Lin Biao and were forcing him to flee.

75

Wang Dongxing made an urgent phone call to Zhou Enlai.

Zhou left his meeting at the Great Hall of the People and went immediately to Zhongnanhai, arriving around eleven. Mao had not been told. I was there when Zhou broke the news and listened as he delivered the report.

Zhou Enlai told Mao that Lin's daughter, Lin Doudou, had phoned Zhang Hong in Beidaihe to say that her mother, Ye Qun, and her brother, Lin Liguo, had kidnapped Lin Biao and forced him into a limousine. Ye Qun, in the meantime, had called Zhou directly to say that Lin Biao needed a plane but that none was available. Zhou knew that an air force Trident was parked at the Shanhaiguan airport just outside Beidaihe, at the eastern terminus of the Great Wall, and suspected that Ye Qun's call was a ruse to cover up their impending flight. The situation was critical.

Mao's face collapsed when Zhou Enlai told him that Lin Biao had fled. But he quickly regained his composure and listened silently, his face now impassive as Zhou continued to talk. If Mao feared for his own safety, he never let it show.

Zhou suggested that Mao move immediately to the Great Hall of the People. Lin Biao's intentions were still unclear, but he had many military supporters in Beijing. If they were planning a coup, an armed attack might be imminent. The Great Hall of the People was safer and easier to protect.

Wang Dongxing arranged for a car to take Mao and Zhou to the

Great Hall of the People, and he ordered an extra battalion of soldiers from the Central Garrison Corps to stand watch there, dispersing them throughout the massive building as sentries and mobile patrols. The entire 8341 Corps was called to active duty, and all contact with the outside was shut off.

Mao and his personal entourage—Zhang Yufeng, head nurse Wu Xujun, his personal attendant Zhou Fuming, his personal secretary Xu Yefu, and I—arrived in Room 118 shortly before midnight. Wang Dongxing and Zhang Yaoci set up a command post in the adjacent room. I went back and forth between the two places as Wang Dongxing waited for the reports coming in from Beidaihe. Zhou Enlai stayed with Mao, who passed the time reading a Chinese history book, joined by the female attendants of Room 118.

At about twelve-fifty in the morning of September 13, 1971, less than an hour after we had arrived, deputy commander Zhang Hong called. Zhang and his aides had pursued Lin Biao's Red Flag limousine to the Shanhaiguan airport. They had opened fire on the armored limousine, but to no effect. The back window was bulletproof. On the way, the limousine had halted briefly, and Lin Biao's secretary, Li Wenpu, was shoved to the ground and fired upon by someone inside the limousine. Li Wenpu was later sent to the 305 Hospital with a bullet wound in his right arm, but Wang Dongxing ordered him isolated and later moved him to an unknown place.

The limousine carrying Lin Biao was too fast for their military jeep. Zhang's forces arrived at the airport just as the plane was taxiing down the runway.

Zhou Enlai suggested to Mao that they order a missile attack against the plane.

Mao refused. "Rain will fall from the skies. Widows will remarry. What can we do? Lin Biao wants to flee. Let him. Don't shoot," he said.

We waited.

There was no need to shoot. We soon learned that the plane had taken off in such haste that it had not been properly fueled. Carrying at most one ton of gasoline, the plane could not go far. Moreover, the plane had struck a fuel truck taking off, and the right landing gear had fallen off. The plane would have difficulty landing. And there was no co-pilot, navigator, or radio operator on board.

Chinese radar was tracking the plane's route, and reports on its location continued to come in to Wang Dongxing and Zhou Enlai. It was heading northwest, in the direction of the Soviet Union. Later, the official documents describing Lin's flight said that Lin's original intention was to fly south to Guangzhou to set up a separate government there. I never heard that on the morning of September 13.

At about 2:00 A.M., word came that Lin Biao's plane had left China and entered Outer Mongolian airspace. The plane had disappeared from Chinese radar. Zhou Enlai reported this to Mao.

"So we've got one more traitor," Mao said, "just like Zhang Guotao and Wang Ming."

The next big news came that afternoon, when Zhou Enlai received a message from Xu Wenyi, the Chinese ambassador to Outer Mongolia. A Chinese aircraft with nine persons on board—one woman and eight men—had crashed in the Undur Khan area of Outer Mongolia. Everyone on board had been killed.

Three days later, on September 16, the ambassador informed Zhou Enlai that dental records had positively identified Lin Biao as one of the dead. "That's what you get for running away," Mao said when he received the news.

Wang Dongxing was ecstatic over Lin Biao's death. "*Si de hao, si de hao,*" he kept repeating. "It's good that they're dead. Otherwise there would have been trouble."

Zhou Enlai was also pleased. "It's best that it ended this way," he said to me. "A major problem has been settled."

Zhou Enlai was in charge of the investigation that followed. With the revelations of Lin's conspiracy, those who had once been close to him maneuvered to distance themselves from their relationship. No one wanted to be accused of having sided with Lin Biao or been part of his plot.

Zhou Enlai had been closer to Lin than he wanted now to admit. Scrupulous about organizational hierarchy, Zhou had continued reporting directly to Lin Biao even as the strains between Mao and Lin had grown, and on matters that Mao had specifically asked to be kept secret. I knew this from my own experience. In 1970, Mao had asked me to organize some medical research into a cure for the bronchitis that was still his major health problem. Implementation of the proposal required Zhou's cooperation, but Mao did not want Lin to know. In fact, he did not want Lin to know anything about his health. He still thought that his earlier bout with pneumonia had been some sort of plot by Lin Biao and was convinced that Lin wanted him dead. He was afraid Lin Biao would try to poison him. Mao ordered me to tell Zhou not to mention the project to Lin.

When I explained this to Zhou, emphasizing how wary Mao was of Lin Biao, Zhou hesitated at first. But he agreed.

Barely a week later, Ye Qun called me, inquiring about the Chairman's health and assuring me that her husband welcomed a major nationwide research project on a cure for bronchitis. Zhou Enlai was the only person I had told, and he had obviously talked.

I went immediately to confront him. My own loyalty to Mao was at stake. If the Chairman found out that Ye Qun knew of the project, he would accuse me of telling Lin Biao and his wife.

"Yes, I reported the matter to Vice-Chairman Lin," Zhou said. "You know, everyone here belongs to an organization and works under the supervision of a superior. Vice-Chairman Lin is my superior. How could I not report this to him?"

The night of September 12, as we were waiting in the Great Hall of the People, Zhou came to me privately, claiming that he had never told Lin Biao about Mao's health. "I was alert enough not to do that," he said. It was a warning to me that when the investigations began, I was not to mention the incident to Mao. If I did and Zhou Enlai were challenged, it would be Zhou's word against mine. I would surely lose.

But if Zhou Enlai had gone out of his way to report to Lin Biao on such a trivial matter, what other secrets of Mao's had he revealed to Lin? Wang Dongxing made certain that Mao never knew. Wang and the 8341 Corps were responsible for searching Lin Biao's residence in Maojiawan after his death. They found many photographs of Zhou Enlai and his wife, Deng Yingchao, with Lin Biao and Ye Qun. The photographs could be used by Zhou's enemies to criticize him for his relationship with Lin. Wang personally delivered the pictures and other potentially damaging documents to Zhou's wife, who remained forever in his debt.

Wang also found many pictures of Jiang Qing with Lin Biao and his wife. He handed them over directly to Jiang Qing, who ordered them burned. No one was admitting to having had close relations with the man who had become a traitor.

Mao stayed hidden in the Great Hall of the People for more than a week, protected by Wang Dongxing's forces. Zhou and Wang wanted to make certain that the potential military coup had been quashed and all of Lin Biao's closest associates were arrested before Mao returned to Zhongnanhai. That Lin Biao had been part of a conspiracy against Mao was clear. The content and extent of the plot were not.

The Lin Biao affair came to be known as the 9-13 incident, after the date in September when he died, and months went by before Zhou's investigation was complete. According to the report, Lin Biao, Ye Qun, and their son, Lin Liguo, had begun planning a coup as early as March 1971, calling it the "5-7-1 project." In Chinese, "armed uprising" is pronounced the same as "5-7-1." Their goal was to apprehend, and possibly to assassinate, Mao and to seize power themselves.

The Chairman had long been suspicious of Lin Biao, and he had been warned of a conspiracy. He thought Lin wanted him dead and was afraid he might try to poison him. But I do not think Mao ever believed that Lin Biao might be plotting to assassinate him and seize power himself.

Mao's trip south to meet with regional political and military leaders was part of his political strategy, intended to solidify his own position and to gain regional support. According to the official report, Mao's talks with the military commanders were a signal to Lin that time was running out and served as the final catalyst to his plans. The talks were supposed to be secret, but the political commissar of the Wuhan Military Region, Liu Feng, had leaked their contents to the political commissar of the navy, Li Zuopeng, a leading supporter of Lin's. Li Zuopeng in turn had alerted chief of the general staff Huang Yongsheng, another of Lin's close associates. Huang Yongsheng reported the content of Mao's August talks to Lin Biao and Ye Qun, then summering in Beidaihe. They immediately began plotting Mao's assassination.

They had several plans. The air force's Fifth Armed Forces Corps could bomb Mao's special train. Commander Wang Weiguo of the air force's Fourth Armed Forces Corps could shoot Mao. Or they could blow up the oil storage facilities near the Hongqiao airport in Shanghai, where Mao's special train was expected to stop. Finally, there was a plan to plant a bomb under a railroad bridge in Shuofang, near Suzhou, and set it off just as Mao's train crossed the bridge.

I do not know whether the report detailing Lin Biao's conspiracy was accurate. Zhou Enlai, after all, had a personal stake in the outcome. I can only say what I saw when I was with Mao when the first reports came in and during the time we spent in the Great Hall of the People thereafter.

I do know that assassinating Mao was never going to be easy. Wang Dongxing and his security personnel had seen to that. So had Mao. His plans were always secret, and changed so quickly and often that even his closest security personnel were kept off guard. Lin Biao's plans never stood a chance. When Mao returned safely to Beijing, Lin Biao knew that he had lost his war with Mao. He had to take flight. He knew the fate of others whose challenges to Mao had been less direct. I did not know then—but surely Lin Biao did—that Liu Shaoqi had died in prison, from physical abuse, illness, and medical neglect.

So had many other former high-ranking leaders. Lin Biao's own death, once his plot against Mao had failed, was certain. In the end, Lin Biao ran out of time.

Lin Doudou's report that Lin Biao had been kidnapped was false. Doudou was so devoted to her father that in her eyes he could do no wrong, but her relationship with Ye Qun was so strained that she was convinced Ye was not her natural mother. The victim of her own self-delusions, Lin Doudou convinced herself that her father had been kidnapped. She could not admit that he had plotted a coup and was fleeing.

In late 1971, when the Lin Biao affair was made public, the whole country was shocked. People within the highest reaches of the party were stunned. I was. I had known of Mao's reservations about the man everyone called the Chairman's closest comrade in arms and had been aware of an intense struggle between the two men since the Lushan conference in 1970, when Lin maneuvered to try to have himself declared chairman of the republic. The Cultural Revolution was vicious and vindictive, and many people had died. But nothing had prepared me for the extent of Lin Biao's perfidy or the drama of his final flight. Friends asked me later if I had feared for my life in August and September 1971 as I traveled with Mao while Lin was plotting his death. They wondered what it was like hiding with him in the Great Hall of the People, waiting until Lin Biao was dead and the arrests had been made. I was never afraid. I did not know enough to be afraid. I was aware only of power struggles, not of attempts against Mao's life.

76

After Lin Biao's death, Mao's health took a turn for the worse. He had never fully recovered from pneumonia in November 1970, when I was called back from Heilongjiang to treat him. But his physical decline after the Lin Biao affair was dramatic. When the immediate crisis was over, the arrests had been made, and Mao knew he was safe, he became depressed. He took to his bed and lay there all day, saying and doing little. When he did get up, he seemed to have aged. His shoulders stooped, and he moved slowly. He walked with a shuffle. He could not sleep.

His blood pressure, normally 130 over 80, shot up to 180 over 100. His lower legs and feet swelled, especially at the ankles. He developed a chronic cold and cough and began spitting up heavy amounts of phlegm. His lungs were badly congested. None of the tests I ran indicated pathogenic bacteria, including the infection in his lungs. This was a sign of declining resistance. His heart was slightly enlarged and his heartbeat was irregular.

I urged him to have a thorough physical, with a chest X ray and an electrocardiogram. But Mao resisted. I suggested he take ginseng, the traditional Chinese tonic that he had often taken in the past. But Mao said he did not believe in traditional Chinese medicine. I warned him that if we did not control his recurrent lung infections, he risked heart failure. I wanted to give him a series of antibiotic injections. But he did not want shots. He would take pills. But when he felt better after taking the pills for a few days, he would stop, and no encouragement or explanation of mine could convince him to resume. The pattern kept repeating.

On November 20, 1971, little more than two months after Lin Biao's death, when the affair was still officially secret, people were shocked to see the television broadcast of Mao's meeting with the North Vietnamese premier, Pham Van Dong, in Mao's haven in the Great Hall of the People. As Mao escorted the North Vietnamese premier to the door, the cameras revealed Mao's shuffling walk. His legs, people said, looked like wobbly wooden sticks.

As always when adversity sent him to bed, Mao was thinking through a new political strategy. The party had been decimated since he launched the Cultural Revolution in the spring of 1966, more than five years before, and many high-ranking officials were dead. Others were in exile. Many who had been purged had been accused of disloyalty to Mao. But no one had been as disloyal as Mao's closest comrade in arms, and many of the leaders Mao had purged had warned him against Lin Biao, arguing that he was unfit for leadership. They had opposed the hyberbole of Lin's cult of personality, his simplistic insistence on men over machines, his opposition to modernization, his inane mouthing of slogans.

After lying in bed for nearly two months, Mao was ready for a reconciliation. He wanted the men he had purged to return.

77

Chen Yi's funeral was the first hint I had that Mao was planning to rehabilitate the men he had overthrown.

Chen Yi, the former minister of foreign affairs, died on January 6, 1972, of colon cancer. He was a feisty and outspoken man, and he had been fearless in his opposition to the excesses of the Cultural Revolution, the fanaticism of the Red Guards, and the misguided leadership of Lin Biao. In February 1967, he was one of several high-ranking leaders to speak out strongly against those excesses. At a meeting that month, vice-premiers Tan Zhenlin and Li Fuchun criticized Lin Biao, Jiang Qing, and several of their colleagues for their conduct in the Cultural Revolution. At the same time, during a meeting of the Military Affairs Commission, marshals Chen Yi, Ye Jianying, Xu Xiangqian, and Nie Rongzhen made a similar critique. On February 17, 1967, Tan Zhenlin had written a letter to the central authorities saying that he ought not have joined the struggle for revolution, should never have joined the Red Army, and should not have joined Mao's forces in Jinggangshan in the early 1930s.

His letter was forwarded to Mao. "I cannot imagine that Tan Zhenlin's thoughts have become so muddled," Mao wrote in the margins. "This is totally unexpected."

After he received the letter, Mao called several members of the Central Cultural Revolution Small Group together for his response. He agreed with Lin Biao's accusations against Tan Zhenlin, Chen Yi, and their colleagues of trying to revive the monarchy and reverse the course of the Cultural Revolution. Their attempt to stop the Cultural Revolution became known as the February Adverse Current.

With Mao's critique, Lin Biao and Jiang Qing had all the excuse they needed to launch a nationwide campaign against the men who had criticized them. A new wave of purges began. Chen Yi was forced from office. Following the purge of so many senior members of the politburo and the Military Affairs Commission, both bodies ceased to function. Decision-making powers of the politburo were handed over de facto to the Central Cultural Revolution Small Group. When Chen Yi died in early 1972, he was still in disgrace.

His funeral was scheduled for three o'clock in the afternoon of January 10 at the Babaoshan cemetery on the western edge of the city, where most of the country's revolutionary leaders were interred. Mao was not supposed to attend. He and his old comrade had never made their peace. Zhou Enlai was to preside over the ceremony instead, and Ye Jianying would deliver the eulogy. Ye sent his proposed remarks for Mao's approval. When Mao saw the sentence, true to the official line, that described Chen Yi as a man "with achievements as well as mistakes," Mao crossed out the reference to Chen's mistakes. Mao had rehabilitated his old comrade.

When Mao woke at one o'clock in the afternoon on the day of Chen Yi's funeral, he suddenly decided to participate after all. He did not even bother to dress. Hastily, he slipped on a silk robe and leather slippers and insisted that we leave immediately, ignoring our warnings about the bitter cold and gusty wind. We managed to cover him with a coat and hat, and I accompanied him as he walked stoically to his car. Wang Dongxing alerted Zhou Enlai and called ahead to Babaoshan, warning Yang Dezhong that the Chairman was on his way and urging him to see that the room was heated.

We arrived at the funeral home before most of the mourners. But Chen Yi's widow, Zhang Qian, and their children were already there, and Mao asked them to join him at the reception hall. Mao rose, helped by his attendant, when Zhang Qian entered and walked toward her with outstretched arms, taking her hands in his. Chen Yi's widow was crying. Mao blinked his eyes too. "Chen Yi was a good comrade," he said.

Several other leaders had arrived—Zhou Enlai, Ye Jianying, and Zhu De—and from over my shoulder I heard someone exclaim that the Chairman was crying. Chen Yi's comrades burst into sobs, and the wails filled the room.

But the Chairman was not crying. He was putting on a good show, blinking his eyes and making an effort to wail. His acting skills were still finely honed.

Cambodia's recently deposed prince Norodom Sihanouk was also there, and it was in his conversation with the prince that Mao signaled his desire for a reconciliation with fallen leaders. As he shook Sihanouk's hand, Mao said that his closest comrade in arms had tried to flee to the Soviet Union but died in a plane crash in Outer Mongolia instead. "That closest comrade in arms was Lin Biao, but really he opposed me. Chen Yi supported me."

Then Mao began talking about the February Adverse Current, saying that he had come to regard the "adverse current" as an attempt by Chen Yi and other faithful veteran leaders to oppose Lin Biao, Chen Boda, Wang Li, Guan Feng, and Qi Benyu—the fallen radicals of the Cultural Revolution. The "adverse current" in fact was positive.

After Chen Yi's funeral, the rehabilitations began. Yang Chengwu, the former acting chief of the general staff who had been so good to Group One during our stint of hard labor at the Ming tombs reservoir, was one of the first to be reinstated, together with Yu Lijin, former political commissar of the air force, and Fu Chongbi, the former commander of the Beijing Garrison Command. They had been dismissed by Lin Biao at a March 24, 1968, meeting of ten thousand military officers in the Great Hall of the People. "Lin Biao's accusation against them was false," Mao said. He wrote a note to Yang Chengwu and asked Wang Dongxing to deliver it. "Yang Chengwu, I understand you," Mao wrote. "The Yang, Yu, Fu case was a mistake." Their names were cleared.

Luo Ruiqing was the next to come back. "Lin Biao also falsely accused Luo Ruiqing," Mao said. "I listened to Lin and dismissed Luo. I was imprudent to listen so often to his one-sided views. I have to criticize myself."

Mao never admitted that the Cultural Revolution had been a mistake. But Lin Biao's perfidy convinced him that he needed to change his strategy. He put Zhou Enlai in charge of rehabilitating many of the leaders who had been overthrown.

78

Mao's health continued to decline. He was already sick by the time we returned to Zhongnanhai from Chen Yi's funeral. The funeral parlor at Babaoshan had been cold, and Mao had stood, increasingly uncomfortable and unsteady on his feet, throughout the entire proceedings. He was coughing when we left, and his legs were trembling. When he tried to get in his car, his legs were so shaky that I had to help put them inside. I had never seen him so weak. His health had taken a dramatic turn for the worse.

He was running a slight fever, and his lung infection had returned. I wanted to begin antibiotic injections.

Mao refused. He wanted no more shots, only pills.

But the pills did no good, and his condition worsened. His legs swelled, and his lungs became more congested. His coughing was labored, his heartbeat irregular. The Chairman was very sick. I wanted him to have a thorough physical exam and thought he should be seen by specialists.

"You just want to dump your responsibility on others," Mao responded testily. I was at a loss.

Five days later, he stopped taking the antibiotics altogether. "They're useless," he said. Still he was uncomfortable, spending all his time in bed, his sleep intermittent, his thinking disoriented.

At around noon on January 18, 1972, Wu Xujun rushed to me with an emergency. She could not find Mao's pulse.

I ran into his room. His pulse was racing, 140 beats to the minute.

I alerted Wang Dongxing and Zhou Enlai and insisted that Mao had to let the doctors examine him. We had to determine what was wrong.

Zhou agreed. I was to head a special medical team consisting of Shang Deyan, director of anesthesia at Beijing's Fuwai Hospital, Gao Rixin, director of anesthesia at Beijing Hospital, Wu Jie, the director of internal medicine at Beijing Hospital, Hu Xudong from the Zhongnanhai Clinic, and Yue Meizhong, the director of internal medicine at Xiyuan Hospital and a member of the Chinese Academy of Traditional Medicine. A number of nurses would also participate, and we agreed to ask Mao to have an electrocardiogram.

Mao did not want a team of specialists. I insisted. If he did not agree, I said, he would not recover from his illness. His condition was worsening. He was so weak and his breathing so laborious that he could not even cough. His edema had spread upward, and I was afraid his internal organs might be involved.

Finally, Mao agreed. The team administered a full physical examination and took an electrocardiogram. The results indicated that he had developed a pulmonary heart condition—congestive heart failure. Because his heart was not pumping sufficient blood, his brain was not getting enough oxygen, which was why he was constantly drowsy, unable to open his eyes, napping constantly. The electrocardiogram also revealed arrhythmia.

Mao could still speak, but he was exhausted and irritable. His sense of humor was gone. When Yue Meizhong tried to explain Mao's condition in terms of traditional Chinese medicine, Mao stopped him. "Okay, okay. Just go away and discuss this somewhere else," he insisted. As we turned to leave, he called me back. "Traditional medicine isn't going to do me any good," he told me. "Let that guy go."

Dr. Yue was over seventy years old, a famous and highly reputable doctor of traditional Chinese medicine. We could not just send him away.

Wang Dongxing and I conferred about how to remove Dr. Yue without causing him to lose face. We decided that Wang Dongxing would listen to the doctor's diagnosis and Wang in turn would consult with Dr. Yue about a minor health problem he was having. Wang somehow managed to assuage Yue's feelings.

Wu Jie, Hu Xudong, and I were in charge of Mao's treatment. We decided to give him injections of penicillin, together with oral digitalis to stimulate his heart and diuretics to relieve the edema. Mao agreed to everything but the diuretics. "Don't try everything at once," he said. "Otherwise, you have nothing left if the problem continues."

Mao still did not understand modern medicine. He had heard that

Kang Sheng was ill and wondered what medicine he was taking, He wanted to take the same thing. But following the Lin Biao affair, Kang Sheng had become clinically depressed. He stayed in his room at Diaoyutai, sitting immobile on a sofa, saying nothing. His condition was completely different from Mao's. But his doctor, a man named Gu, had told me that the only medicine Kang trusted was antibiotics. I used that information to persuade Mao to continue his antibiotic treatment and insisted that he take the other drugs, too. But Mao was delighted to hear that Kang Sheng took only antibiotics. "See, I don't need all those different drugs," he said. He stopped the digitalis after only one dose.

The antibiotics had no effect on Mao's congestive heart failure. The blood tests had indicated that his oxygen level was so dangerously low that a less robust man would have died. Mao's life was in danger.

On January 21, I spoke with Zhou Enlai again, urging him to persuade Mao to cooperate in the treatment and emphasizing the real danger to Mao's life. I also pointed out that Mao had told me he did not want Jiang Qing to interfere in his treatment and that I therefore thought it best that Jiang Qing be kept out of our discussions. Zhou agreed.

But when Zhou returned to Mao's residence at the indoor swimming pool that evening, I was shocked to see that Jiang Qing was with him. "The Chairman is seriously ill," he explained to me when Jiang Qing left the room. "If something were to happen to him, what would I say to her? She's a politburo member and Chairman's wife. Besides, everyone belongs to an organization. She and I are both politburo members. How could I not tell her?" Zhou was ever the loyal party man.

Wu Jie and Hu Xudong joined me in describing Mao's condition to Jiang Qing and Zhou Enlai. I emphasized that unless treatment were begun at once, Mao's life was in danger. Zhou questioned us in detail about our proposed treatment.

"Wasn't the Chairman in good health just a few days ago at Babaoshan?" Jiang Qing asked. "The Chairman was in good health all last year," she continued. "He is physically strong. Nothing is going to happen to him. Don't get so panicky."

But Zhou Enlai knew Mao was ill. He had been watching his decline since Lin Biao's death. He asked me to accompany him and Jiang Qing to talk with Mao. My medical expertise would be useful, he said. I could help them persuade Mao to accept treatment.

I entered first. Clad only in an open robe, Mao was sitting on his sofa, his head back, eyes closed, breathing noisily through a half-open mouth, his bare chest rising and falling with each breath. His arms and legs were sprawled motionless on the sofa, as though paralyzed, and he was pale. "Chairman," I whispered to him, standing next to the sofa. "Premier and Comrade Jiang Qing are here to see you."

We drew up chairs, sitting close to him, while Wang Dongxing and Zhang Yaoci stood outside, straining to hear what we said. Zhou shooed them away.

Mao coughed, convulsed, until he was finally able to expel the phlegm from his lungs. I reached for a spittoon as Jiang Qing handed him her handkerchief. Mao pushed his wife's hand away, using the spittoon instead. Jiang Qing and Mao had been separated for so long that she no longer knew her husband's habits. He always used a spittoon.

"What are you all doing here?" Mao demanded. "Tell me!"

Zhou glanced at Jiang Qing, who was sitting upright, silent. "We were just discussing Chairman's health," he began, "and want to report to you."

"There is nothing to report," Mao responded. "You are not doctors and don't know what is going on. You have to listen to the doctors."

Looking at Jiang Qing, Zhou continued. "Just a while ago, the three people . . ."

"What three people?" Mao demanded.

"Li Zhisui, Wu Jie, and Hu Xudong. They explained Chairman's health condition to Comrade Jiang Qing and me."

Mao's eyes had been closed. Now he opened them. "And what about my health?"

"The Chairman has caught a cold," Zhou explained. "This has led to a lung infection. The lung infection in turn has affected your heart. We believe it necessary to improve Chairman's treatment." Zhou turned to me. "Please explain the illness and your proposed treatment again to Chairman," he requested.

Mao did not let me explain. "What was that medicine you gave me?" he asked. "I've lost my appetite because of it. And you've given me so many shots my rear end aches and itches."

Jiang Qing saw her opportunity. "In 1968, Li Zhisui tried to poison me with his drugs, and you wondered why he tried to poison me and not you. 'Wouldn't it be easier to poison me than you?' you asked. Remember? Now it's clear. He is trying to harm you."

"Oh? So you've done a great deed, haven't you?" Mao said sarcastically, turning to me.

I felt as if I had been punched in the stomach. My mouth was suddenly dry. I was paralyzed with fear. Jiang Qing was accusing me of harming the Chairman, and Mao was agreeing.

"Step out of the room," Jiang Qing said to me. "You won't be playing your tricks around here anymore."

Suddenly, I was at peace. Nothing mattered anymore. I stood up. I was about to be arrested, and I knew that I would be sentenced to death for trying to harm Mao. I was resigned. The end had come at last. Walking slowly to the door, I was aware only of Zhou Enlai. He was stiff, immobilized, all color drained from his face. His hands were trembling.

Mao spoke just as I reached the door. "Don't leave," he said in a booming voice. "If there is anything to be said against you, it will be said openly." He turned to Jiang Qing. "Why talk behind someone's back?" he asked her.

I felt like a rock on the edge of a cliff that had finally fallen safely to ground. If I could defend myself, I knew I would win. I could see Zhou relaxing, too.

I began to explain to Mao what I thought was wrong. The reason he had lost his appetite, I told him, was because his weakened heart had slowed his circulation. "Your body is swollen, too, and I think it very likely that some of your internal organs, like your stomach and intestines, are also swollen and suffering from lack of oxygen. It is because of this that you don't want to eat. And the medicine is not being rapidly absorbed because of your circulation problem. This is why you feel itchy and achy where the needle went in."

But Mao was not listening. He was shaking his head, his hand tapping the sofa. "Jiang Qing, somebody took that lotus stalk you sent me and boiled it in water, and I vomited after I drank it. Your medicine is no good, either." Lotus stalk is a traditional Chinese herbal medicine, and Kang Sheng had recommended it to Jiang Qing.

I nearly laughed with joy to hear Mao snap at his wife. She was sullen, dabbing her forehead with a handkerchief, gasping.

Mao leaned his head on the sofa. "I don't think the medicine either of you gave me is any good," he said. He turned to me. "Stop all medications. Whoever wants me to take medicine, leave the room."

I was horrified. Mao was sick. Without medicine, he would die. He had to get well.

Mao turned to Zhou Enlai. "My health is too poor," he said. "I don't think I can make it. Everything depends on you now . . ."

Zhou Enlai was distraught. "No, Chairman's health problem is not serious," he interrupted. "We all depend on Chairman's leadership."

Mao shook his head weakly. "No. Cannot make it. I cannot make it. You take care of everything after my death," he said wanly. "Let's say this is my will."

Jiang Qing was aghast. Her eyes opened wide, her hands curled into fists. She was about to explode in anger.

Zhou drew his legs toward his chair and put his hands on his knees, leaning toward Mao, frozen. The chairman of the Chinese Communist party was turning leadership of the whole country—the party, government, and army—over to the premier. And he was doing it in front of his wife, who wanted control herself. I was still trembling from my ordeal and perspiring heavily. I barely understood the import of Mao's words. I think now that he was confronting his own mortality for the first time.

"It's done now," Mao finally said. "You can all go."

As we reached the duty office where Wang Dongxing and Zhang Yaoci were waiting, Jiang Qing threw her military cap on the floor. "There's a spy ring around here," she said, spitting out the words. "I'm going to have it thoroughly checked." Then she turned to Zhou Enlai. "Call a meeting of the politburo immediately, in Huairen Hall," she said, walking angrily away. I could only guess who Jiang Qing thought the spies were, but I was sure she would count me among them. Perhaps she thought Wang Dongxing was our leader.

"Comrade Dongxing," Premier Zhou said, turning to the chief of Mao's security. "Notify all members of the politburo now in Beijing. We have to meet immediately." It was nine o'clock in the evening.

79

At eleven o'clock, two hours into the politburo meeting, Wang Dong-xing summoned Wu Jie, Hu Xudong, and me to an anteroom of Huairen Hall. He had asked doctors Wu Jieping and Bian Zhiqiang to come, too. We waited in silence as the meeting continued in the adjacent room.

Then Yao Wenyuan came out. "Jiang Qing wants me to talk to you," he said. He turned to Wu Jieping and Bian Zhiqiang. "You two are not involved in treating Chairman," he said, "but perhaps you can help us assess the situation.

"Chairman's health has always been good," Yao began. "Whenever he attends a public function or receives foreign guests, our news releases always say that he looks wonderful, vigorous, that his face is ruddy and glowing with health. It's not empty talk." He showed us a photograph of the recent meeting between Mao and the North Vietnamese premier Pham Van Dong. "Look at this. Look how powerful the Chairman's handshake is. He has a cold now, nothing serious. You claim that the Chairman has a problem with his lungs and his heart. Where is your evidence? You are even talking about some so-called congestive heart failure. It's obvious that you're just making this up to disturb the public. I'm not saying you have political problems, but you're creating political confusion. You have to take responsibility for it." The photograph of Mao and the North Vietnamese premier was a still. It was impossible to see how weak he had been, and I had no way of knowing whether Yao Wenyuan had seen the television broadcast.

Yao asked us to explain. I could say nothing. He had already made up his mind. Yao turned to doctors Wu Jieping and Bian Zhiqiang. They were also silent.

"If you have nothing to say, then you can leave," Yao said. "You will be notified of the politburo's decision."

It was two o'clock in the morning by then. We returned to the swimming pool. None of us could sleep, and Wu Jie was trembling in fear. He was sixty-four years old, twelve years my senior, and had already suffered years of persecution. He had been a member of the Guomindang and president of Beijing Hospital before 1949, and when the Cultural Revolution began he had been badly beaten and confined to a "cow shed" for three years, then forced to do hard labor. He was afraid he would be arrested again.

I tried to comfort him. Everything we had done for Mao—the physical exam, our diagnosis, our treatment—had had Mao's approval. Mao was seriously ill, but not dead. He would vouch for us. What was most important was that we had never harmed him or had any intention of hurting him.

But I was worried. Mao was very sick, and without medication he would only get worse. We needed his support. And I was worried about what the politburo might do. It was hardly a fair and impartial body.

At four o'clock in the morning we were summoned back to Huairen Hall. This time we brought Mao's electrocardiogram. Any doctor could see that Mao had two serious heart conditions—ventricular extrasystol, or premature heartbeat; and cardiac ischemia, an insufficient blood supply to the heart.

While we waited, two other politburo members came out to meet with us—Marshal Ye Jianying and Vice-Premier Li Xiannian. Ye Jianying did the talking. Ye was unfailingly polite to me and always called me President Li, because I was president of the 305 Hospital.

"The politburo has asked us to talk to you again about Chairman's health," he said. "Don't be nervous. Just tell us clearly what the problem is."

I started from the beginning, describing the deterioration in Chairman's health after the Lin Biao affair and continuing to his current condition. I showed him the electrocardiogram, going over it in great detail, pointing out the problems as revealed on the chart. Ye Jianying himself had heart problems and had taken many electrocardiograms. He understood what I was trying to convey and examined the chart very carefully, listening intently to my explanation.

"It's clear he has heart problems," he finally said. "How can anyone say he does not? How can anyone say the doctors have simply invented their findings?"

Then he began asking about the meeting between Mao, me, Zhou Enlai, and Jiang Qing. I reported the conversation in detail, including Mao's apparent designation of Zhou Enlai as his successor.

Ye assured us that we had made no mistakes. "I don't see why you should assume responsibility for stopping treatment. The Chairman has ordered it. None of you has to worry. Return to the swimming pool now and start preparing for further treatment. Get the emergency equipment ready, too. From now on, I will be on duty in the swimming pool myself. If you run into problems, just let me know."

Ye turned to Li Xiannian, who had not said a word, and asked if he had any questions. Li still had nothing to say. Ye Jianying dismissed us. We returned to the swimming pool. By then it was about seven o'clock in the morning.

A great burden had been lifted from our minds. Ye Jianying had intervened on our behalf. We began discussing how best to treat the Chairman, and as our spirits rose, Wu Jie almost smiled. We had a bite to eat and went to sleep.

When I woke at three that afternoon, Ye Jianying was waiting. Wu Jie and Hu Xudong were already with him when I joined them in the reception room.

"I'm on duty now," Ye Jianying said when I came in. "Let's have a chat. President Li, you have been working for Chairman for eighteen years. We all know you very well. You must do what you think is necessary now. Don't worry about the criticisms. We all have occasional setbacks. Who can say he hasn't?"

Then he turned to Wu Jie. "Director Wu, you have been a doctor for decades. You have saved many lives. Many of those people were older than Chairman. Can you help Chairman recover now?"

Wu's response was immediate. "If Chairman allows us to treat him, we can make him well."

Ye smiled. "Good. Chairman does not want treatment now. He is angry. But when he gets over that, he'll need your help."

Then Ye Jianying turned to Hu Xudong, who, at forty years old, was twelve years my junior. "I have not met you before," he said. "You look like the youngest of the three doctors." Ye thought Hu

Xudong could do the physical work involved in treating Mao, like taking care of the oxygen tanks and the respirator.

Ye left the swimming pool at about five that evening, and the two doctors returned to the Zhongnanhai Clinic. I stayed at the swimming pool.

That evening Wang Dongxing wanted a report on Mao's condition. But I had not seen the Chairman since the night before and was reluctant to see him now. Wang agreed. "Don't rush it," he said. "Otherwise things will get worse."

Wang briefed me on the politburo meeting the night before. Jiang Qing had claimed that there was a spy ring around the Chairman and demanded that the politburo conduct an investigation. Wang Hongwen, Zhang Chunqiao, and Yao Wenyuan, her three closest supporters, agreed. A ruckus ensued. Wang Dongxing wanted to quash the investigation, but Ye Jianying had cautioned him to remain quiet. "He put his palm on my knee and pressed it, signaling me that the time was not right," Wang said. "In the meantime, Premier Zhou tried to calm everyone down, asking everyone to be patient and talk things over slowly."

Jiang Qing, though, had thrown the politburo meeting into confusion. "The Chairman is in good health," she had said, addressing Zhou. "Why are you forcing him to transfer power to you?" It was then that she had asked Yao Wenyuan to represent the politburo and meet with the doctors, sending also for Wu Jieping and Bian Zhiqiang.

But other members of the politburo, not privy to the conversation between Mao, Zhou Enlai, Jiang Qing, and me, had no idea what Jiang Qing was talking about when she said Zhou was forcing Mao to hand over power to him. Ye Jianying had asked Zhou to explain. "The Chairman is ill and has said some things," Ye responded after Zhou had reported on the meeting with Mao. "Why is everyone so excited? Why does it matter so much?" He wanted Li Xiannian to accompany him and hear the doctors' side of the story and said that he would stay on duty at the swimming pool.

But Jiang Qing did not want Ye Jianying standing vigil at the pool. "No one is supposed to be near the Chairman unless he agrees," she said. Wang then asked Ye to limit his time at the pool.

Wang Dongxing was worried about Mao's health. "No matter what, I think you have to try to get Chairman to start treatment," he told me. "We cannot delay much longer."

· · ·

Mao had just awakened when I returned to the swimming pool. With his heart trouble, he could only sleep sitting up and he had fallen asleep on his sofa. His breathing was still loud and laborious.

I went in to see him. His eyes were closed, and he was breathing rapidly, the phlegm from his lungs making a gurgling sound. His lips were gray. He still did not ask for treatment, so I left.

I ran into Xu Yefu in the reception room. He was on his way to see Wu Xujun with some documents for Mao. "Something odd just happened, Dr. Li," he said. "Jiang Qing took me and Zhang Yufeng aside to tell us that there is a spy ring around Chairman Mao. She told us to keep our eyes open and asked me to sleep in the small room next to Chairman so I can watch what is happening. I tried to explain that since I don't have any medical training I could not be of much help to Chairman. Then I talked to Director Wang Dongxing, and he told me to ignore her. Now I don't know what I'm supposed to do." I had no advice to give.

Mao's edema worsened. His neck and forehead were visibly swollen. I was growing increasingly anxious. The Chairman's illness was acute, worsening, yet nothing was being done. Zhang Yufeng was often with him, but she would also disappear for long periods. She was busy helping her parents and her sister move from Mudanjiang to Beijing, and Beijing mayor Wu De was helping her.

Ten days passed. Still Mao did not ask for treatment.

Then, on the afternoon of February 1, he called for me.

"Do you think there is any hope?" he asked. "Would you still be able to help me recover?"

"If you will let us treat you, of course there is hope," I said. Already I could feel a flood of relief. "I will do everything I can to help you."

I took his pulse. It was weak and irregular.

"What is your treatment?" Mao wanted to know.

"We still have to get rid of your lung infection, get your heart stimulated again, and do something about relieving the buildup of fluid in your body. We have to give you both shots and some oral medication."

"Still those injections?"

"If we don't use injections, there is no way to get rid of your lung infection, and the lung infection is the cause of all your other problems," I insisted.

"All right," Mao said finally. "Let's start the treatment."

I had been close to despair. Suddenly I was ecstatic, so relieved that my energy surged. I was determined to make Mao well. As time had slipped by and Mao still refused our treatment, my concern was not merely with his immediate health. For weeks I had been burdened by a fact still secret from the Chinese people. China's history was about to be transformed. President Nixon was coming to China. He was scheduled to arrive on February 21. Mao wanted to meet with him. I had three weeks to make him well. We swung into action immediately.

The origin of Nixon's visit goes back to the World Table Tennis Tournament held in Nagoya, Japan, in late March 1971. On March 14 of that year, the China National Committee on Sports debated whether to send a team to the tournament. At that time, China and Japan had no diplomatic relations. Some members of the National Committee were worried that Japanese rightists and Guomindang agents might harm our players, and many other committee members were not in favor of the expedition for a variety of reasons. Zhou Enlai, however, wanted the Chinese team to go to Japan, and wrote to Mao for his approval. Mao agreed, and told the players that they should fear neither hardship nor death. The table tennis team became the first Chinese sports team to travel abroad since the Cultural Revolution.

Toward the end of the games, several American players suggested to the Chinese team that they would like to visit China, and hoped they could be invited. This request soon came to the attention of Zhou Enlai, who passed it on to Mao with the recommendation that the American team be told that a visit might be possible at some future time—a polite rejection. Mao received Zhou's report on April 6, 1971, agreed with it, and returned it to Zhou. But at midnight of that same day, as Mao was finishing his dinner, and I had given him his sedatives, he asked head nurse Wu Xujun, in drowsy, slurred speech, to call Wang Hairong, chief of protocol at the Ministry of Foreign Affairs. He wanted to invite the American team to China right away. Mao was on the point of falling asleep when Wu repeated Mao's words to him, to confirm that she had the message right. Mao nodded and fell sound asleep.

This was the first time that China had proposed a clear and open offer of friendship to the United States. Zhou Enlai later commented, "A small ball shakes the big ball," referring to the effect that this table tennis match would have on the future of the world.

80

At first we nearly lost Mao. Immediately after he agreed to be treated, Wu Jie and Hu Xudong joined me at the swimming pool. After the confrontation with Jiang Qing several weeks before and her veiled accusation that I was a spy, I no longer wanted to work alone. This way, if anything happened to Mao, responsibility would be shared and Jiang Qing's power over me diminished. We asked Shang Deyan to bring the emergency medical equipment from the Zhongnanhai Clinic. I tested Mao for allergy to the antibiotics we wanted to administer, and when the test proved negative, we asked Wu Xujun to give Mao a shot in his left hip.

Twenty minutes later, Mao began coughing. He was weak and had no strength to expel the phlegm. The liquid caught in his throat, and suddenly he was choking, unable to breathe, gasping for breath. He collapsed.

We sat him up. Hu Xudong began pounding Mao's chest, panicked, yelling, "Chairman! Chairman!" He was pounding too hard for a man Mao's age. His ribs could have been broken, and I worried about the confusion his actions were causing the attendants who were in the room. I called the Zhongnanhai Clinic again to get the emergency equipment there immediately. We administered a number of intravenous drugs, including Gentamicin and steroids, to combat the lung infection, stimulate Mao's reflexes, and reduce the bronchial spasms.

Ten minutes passed. Shang Deyan had still not come. I ran to the clinic. Shang was waiting for a mini-van. We grabbed the equipment and ran back to Mao's room. He was still unconscious. Shang Deyan set up the suction machine and cleared Mao's throat. We administered oxygen through a mask.

Within moments, Mao opened his eyes and pulled off the mask. "What are you all doing?" he asked.

"How do you feel?" I wanted to know.

Mao said he felt as though he had been asleep. When he saw the intravenous tube in his arm, he tried to yank it out. I stopped him. "You can't take that out. If you do, we won't be able to get the medicine into your bloodstream."

"Why are there so many people in here?" he wanted to know. "I don't need so many people." The non-medical staff scurried out of the room.

Mao's collapse was the closest call we had ever had. Wang Dongxing had been alerted immediately, while Mao was still unconscious, and he in turn notified Zhou Enlai, then in a meeting at the Great Hall of the People. Zhou was so shocked that he lost control of his bladder and bowels, soiling his pants. He washed and changed his clothes before rushing to the swimming pool. Mao had recovered by then.

Zhou looked in on Mao and talked briefly with Zhang Yufeng, who had been there through most of the crisis. He was still tense when he called the medical team together and asked Wu Jie, Hu Xudong, and me to explain what had happened.

"Zhang Yufeng thinks the Chairman collapsed because of an allergic reaction to the antibiotics," he said when we finished our briefing. "You are going to have to look into that."

Shang Deyan, who had actually done the suctioning, was certain there had been no allergic reaction. "It wasn't a reaction to the shot," he insisted. "Chairman was able to breathe as soon as the phlegm was sucked out. He returned to normal immediately."

Zhou Enlai accepted our explanation but still wanted a full report. "This is a very serious matter," he emphasized, "and the politburo has not been informed." He wondered what would have happened if the rescue operations had failed and why Shang Deyan, in charge of the emergency procedures, had not been at the swimming pool when the crisis began. He was upset by the delay in getting the rescue started.

I explained that Mao had ordered Zhang Yaoci to permit only Hu Xudong, Wu Jie, and me into the swimming pool area, and he refused to have emergency equipment on hand. Our medical work would be severely hampered without the emergency equipment, and I had tried to convince Zhang Yaoci to bring it in despite Mao's objections, but he would not disobey the Chairman. I had planned to raise the question directly with Mao as soon as his condition improved. The emergency had arisen before I had a chance.

Zhou agreed that Mao's health was most important. "We'll have to rearrange the swimming pool area," he agreed. He said he would ask Wang Dongxing to install the necessary equipment.

We put Mao on a regimen of antibiotics, digitalis, and diuretics. Zhang Yufeng continued to be uncooperative and insisted on knowing exactly when the diuretics would work. I estimated that Mao would urinate about 2,000cc in approximately four hours.

Zhang Yufeng sneered. "Are you sure?"

"Nobody can be absolutely sure," I responded. "We can only say that the drug normally has this effect. The important thing now is that Chairman takes the proper dosage at the right time."

"That's not my business," Zhang Yufeng snapped. "The head nurse is responsible for the medication."

Wu Jie, not yet initiated into the inner circle, was shocked by Zhang Yufeng's behavior. "Who is this Zhang Yufeng?" he wanted to know as she stomped away. "Why is she so rude?"

I could not tell him about Mao's private life. "You'll understand after you've been here a while," I replied.

About four hours after the first dosage of diuretics, Mao passed 1800cc of urine. We were delighted. Mao was happy, too, and gathered the medical team together in his room. He wanted us to explain his illness and the course of treatment again.

"It looks like I can recover, then," he said. "America's President Nixon is coming. Have you heard the news?"

"Premier Zhou has mentioned it," I said.

Mao said that Nixon would arrive on the twenty-first of the month and wondered if he could be fully recovered by then.

"If we continue treatment, you'll have no problem meeting him," I promised.

"Good. Then let's continue the treatment."

He invited us to dinner to share some of his favorite dishes— Wuchang fish and *shuanyangrou,* the thinly sliced lamb cooked in a broth-filled pot and dipped in a rich, delicious sauce. As we were eating, Mao learned that Wu Jie was not a member of the party. Dr. Wu explained that he had belonged to the Guomindang before liberation and had therefore been prohibited from joining.

Mao laughed. "I used to be a member of the Guomindang myself," he said, referring to the period in the early 1920s when the Communist party and the Guomindang had collaborated. "What does that matter?" He turned to me. "Tell Beijing Hospital that Wu Jie will join the Communist party at my recommendation." Wu Jie became an instant member of the party.

Zhou Enlai was delighted that Mao was recovering so quickly and had his picture taken with the medical team to show his appreciation. He asked us to join him and his wife for Chinese New Year, promising to serve the traditional dumplings and a cake for dessert. As he was leaving, he reminded me of President Nixon's upcoming visit. "Make sure Chairman is well enough to see him," he said.

81

Richard Nixon arrived in Beijing on February 21, 1972. Since February 1, when Mao finally agreed to be treated, the medical team had worked around the clock to restore the Chairman's health. His condition had improved considerably. His lung infection was under control, and his heart irregularities had subsided. His edema was better, but he was still so bloated that he had to be fitted with a new suit and shoes. His throat was still swollen, and he had difficulty talking. His muscles had atrophied from weeks of immobility, so we put him on an exercise routine a week before President Nixon's arrival. He practiced sitting down and getting up, and an attendant guided him slowly around the room to get him used to walking again.

Mao was as excited as I had ever seen him the day Nixon arrived. He woke early and immediately began asking when the president was scheduled to arrive. Zhou Fuming gave him a shave and a haircut—his first in more than five months—and rubbed scented tonic into his hair. Then Mao sat on the sofa in his study to wait as frequent phone calls came in charting Nixon's progress. When he learned that Nixon's plane had just landed, he asked Wu Xujun to tell Zhou Enlai he wanted to see the president immediately. As the official host, Zhou would be accompanying Nixon everywhere. Zhou insisted that courtesy and protocol required that Nixon be given time to rest in his Diaoyutai villa before starting his formal activities. Mao did not object but reiterated his wish to meet with the president at the earliest opportunity.

Zhou hosted a luncheon for Nixon and then escorted him to

Diaoyutai. Again, Mao talked to Zhou and urged him to bring Nixon to see him.

The medical team had made extensive preparations for the meeting. The emergency medical equipment—including oxygen tanks and a respirator that Henry Kissinger had sent after his secret visit the previous July, in preparation for Nixon's visit—had to be removed from Mao's room. We dismantled Mao's hospital bed and moved the rest of the equipment into the corridor connecting Mao's study and bedroom. We had to be prepared for emergency treatment if Mao's health suddenly failed. We put the oxygen tanks in a huge lacquered trunk and hid the rest of the equipment behind big potted plants. No one could guess from a casual glance, but we were prepared to reassemble the equipment within seconds should anything go wrong. Zhou Enlai had told Nixon that Mao had been ill with bronchitis, but I do not think the president was ever fully informed of Mao's problems. Mao only explained to Nixon that he could not talk very well.

I was waiting in the entrance hall outside Mao's study when the Red Flag limousine carrying Nixon and Zhou Enlai pulled up. Nancy Tang was serving as their interpreter. President Nixon was the first member of the American entourage to enter the building, followed by Henry Kissinger. Then came Winston Lord, later to become the American ambassador to China. I was struck by how young he looked—like a twenty-year-old college student. Secretary of State Rogers was not with the delegation. Nixon wanted Kissinger to serve as his primary foreign policy spokesman, so Zhou Enlai had arranged for China's foreign affairs minister, Ji Pengfei, to meet with Rogers while Nixon and Kissinger were meeting with Mao.

As President Nixon walked in, I nodded and motioned him in the direction of Mao's study. Then I went immediately to the corridor where all the medical equipment was hidden. There was a brief flurry when a member of Nixon's security staff realized he had lost his president and radio contact with the staff in Diaoyutai. Nixon had been whisked away too quickly for them to see where he had gone. The huge indoor swimming pool had been covered over shortly after Mao's illness began, and the room had been transformed into a magnificent reception hall. But the tin roof was blocking communications. One of the Chinese interpreters assured the American Secret Service that Nixon was safe with Mao.

Sitting in the corridor just outside Mao's study, separated only by an open door, I could hear the entire conversation and was prepared to intervene if Mao suffered a relapse. The content of their talk has been reported in President Nixon's memoirs, which I later read in

Chinese translation, and it would be presumptuous of me to repeat the official version of that momentous meeting, which was scheduled to take fifteen minutes and lasted sixty-five. One part of the conversation did particularly impress me, though. Mao explained to Nixon that even though relations were better, the Chinese press would still carry articles attacking the United States, and he expected the American press to keep up its criticisms of China. The peoples of both countries were so used to the criticisms that readjusting to the new friendship would take time. And the question of Taiwan was a continuing problem.

Mao was delighted with Nixon's visit. As soon as the president left, he took off his formal clothes and changed back into his customary bathrobe. I joined him immediately to take his pulse, which remained steady and strong.

Mao wondered whether I had heard the talk.

I assured him that I had been right outside the door, listening to every word. I, too, had been excited about the visit. A new era was coming, I thought. My Western education had left me with positive impressions of the United States, and until 1949 relations between China and the United States had been good. That changed with the Korean War, but the meeting between Nixon and Mao meant that the old hostility would end and friendlier relations would begin.

Mao liked Nixon. "He speaks forthrightly—no beating around the bush, not like the leftists, who say one thing and mean another." Nixon had told Mao that the United States wanted to improve relations with China for the benefit of the United States. "That's just what he should say," Mao thought. "He is much better than those people who talk about high moral principles while engaging in sinister intrigues. Isn't it also for the benefit of China that we want to improve relations with the United States?" Mao laughed out loud at the thought. The mutual interest that brought the two countries together was the threat of the "polar bear" to China's north.

In the picture of Mao shaking hands with Nixon that was published, both were smiling broadly, and the Chinese report described Mao as energetic and glowing with health, his face flush with color. Many noted that Mao had gained weight and took that as a sign of good health, too. The American press, knowing that Mao had been ill and was having trouble speaking, speculated that the Chairman had had a stroke. But the Chinese and the Americans were both wrong. Mao had not gained weight. He was bloated by edema. He had been suffering from congestive heart failure, not a stroke.

Mao's health improved in the afterglow of his foreign policy triumph. His edema subsided, his lung infection cleared up, and his coughing stopped. He had given up smoking during his illness, and his coughing and bronchitis did not return. His spirits stayed high. My own contact with him increased, and our relations seemed to improve. I was still living in one of the changing rooms just off the old swimming pool area and was seeing the Chairman daily. Relations between China and the United States were his main topic of conversation, and I listened often to his description of their evolution. Mao believed that America's intentions in China had always been relatively benign. While Great Britain, Japan, and Russia had imperialistic designs and became deeply involved in China's internal affairs, the United States had remained aloof. Official contact between the American government and the Chinese Communist party had not begun until the 1930s, more than a decade after the party's founding, but unofficial contacts with Americans had always been friendly. Mao liked Edgar Snow, though he was certain the journalist worked for the CIA. And he greatly respected Dr. George Hatem, the Lebanese-American who had treated the communist troops, joined the party, and stayed in China after liberation to become a Chinese citizen.

The first official contact between the Communist party and the United States was made during the Second World War, Mao said, when the American government sent a military mission to Yanan. Relations with members of this so-called Dixie Mission had been good, and many of the American officers had been impressed with the Communist party's program and its aspirations for a new China. Friendly contacts had been maintained until the end of the war, when American diplomats arranged for Mao to fly to Chongqing, in August 1945, to begin peace negotiations with Chiang Kai-shek in an effort to avert civil war. Cooperation in Chongqing had been good, too, and the American diplomats continued to express admiration for the Chinese communists. With American help, the nationalists and the communists had reached an understanding, known as the October 10 agreement, about the peaceful reconstruction of China.

Franklin Roosevelt had been behind the friendly relations, Mao thought. Just as Mao believed that his own leadership was transforming Chinese history, so he believed that Roosevelt had changed the course of the United States and world politics. He admired the American leader and believed that the history of China and of U.S.-China relations would have been different had Roosevelt lived to see the communist victory.

When Harry Truman assumed the presidency after Roosevelt's

death, Mao argued, he transformed American policy toward China, supporting the Guomindang both economically and militarily and turning against the communists. Mao attributed the outbreak of China's civil war to Truman's support for the Guomindang.

Mao credited Japan with the communist victory in the civil war. If Japan had not invaded China in the 1930s, the communists and the nationalists would never have cooperated in the struggle against the Japanese aggressors, and the Communist party would have remained too weak to seize power. Japanese aggression, he asserted, was a bad thing that had been transformed into good, for which the Chinese communists should be grateful.

The world had waited nearly thirty years for the enmity between China and the United States to be resolved, and Mao believed that the new era of cooperation was of worldwide import. A chain reaction was set to go off. One by one, the nations of Europe, Africa, and Latin America would follow the American lead and establish diplomatic relations with China. China's entrance into the United Nations in October 1971 was part of that worldwide trend.

Mao believed that countries with different economic systems could still cooperate, and he looked forward to greater economic ties with capitalist countries. South Korea was an example. The capitalist South Koreans liked hot food, and socialist China produced plenty of chili peppers. Already, Mao said, China was exporting 300,000 tons of chili peppers to South Korea each year, a good arrangement.

But Mao did not predict a new era of international peace. He still saw global politics in terms of a struggle among three worlds. The "first world," to which only the United States and the Soviet Union belonged, was economically advanced, rich, and well armed with nuclear weapons. Both countries were intent on global domination, and the buildup of their military power posed constant threat of war. The "second world," including Japan, Europe, Canada, and Australia, was also rich and had some nuclear weapons, and could not remain aloof from the struggle. The "third world," populous and poor, was the victim of superpower struggles. China belonged to the third world, together with the countries of Africa, Latin America, and most of Asia. Peace, Mao believed, was temporary. Every generation would experience war.

Thus, Mao never expected relations with the United States to be smooth. Reverses and setbacks were inevitable. The next generation of world leaders would have to solve the problems that this generation had started.

Mao's analysis of world trends was right in one respect. Nixon's visit did begin a chain reaction of recognition for China. Mao had another foreign policy triumph that year when Japanese prime minister Kakuei Tanaka visited Beijing in September. Unofficial contact between China and Japan had been growing for years, and bilateral trade had steadily increased. When Japanese officials were offended because they had not been informed of the U.S.-China rapprochement in advance, Liao Chengzhi, charged with "people-to-people" diplomacy, invited Tanaka to visit.

Prime Minister Tanaka was accorded the same diplomatic courtesies as Nixon, and the outcome of his visit was a joint communiqué announcing the establishment of formal diplomatic relations between China and Japan. Mao thought his talks with Tanaka had been warmer and more intimate than his meeting with Nixon. When Tanaka tried to apologize for his country's invasion of China, Mao assured him that it was the "help" of the Japanese invasion that made the communist victory and this visit between communist and Japanese leaders possible. He confessed to Tanaka that his health was not very good, and he told the Japanese prime minister that he could not live much longer, but this was another of Mao's games. Mao still believed in his longevity but often took the opportunity to test foreign reaction to his possible death.

Mao and Tanaka had much in common. Neither had gone to college, and both had reached their positions only after struggle. Mao saw Tanaka as courageous and decisive in pushing for the establishment of diplomatic relations with China against strong opposition from the ruling Liberal Democratic party.

President Nixon and Prime Minister Tanaka had something in common, too. Both were forced to resign from office. But Mao continued to welcome them both to China and regarded them always as "old friends." The friendship with the United States never went as far as Mao would have liked. There remained the question of America's support for Taiwan, and formal diplomatic relations between China and the United States did not occur until 1979, three years after Mao's death, while Jimmy Carter was president.

82

The improvement in Mao's health was fleeting.

When his edema cleared up, it was obvious he had lost weight. Mao had dropped from his normal 180 pounds to 154, and his whole body seemed to have shrunk. His face had lost its fullness and become sharper rather than round, and his big belly had disappeared, the skin now sagging. The muscles in his hands—the right one, especially—had atrophied, and his calves were flabby and thin.

Mao thought that exercise would improve his health, but he was too weak for any vigorous activity. He could walk only slowly and with support, and his arms and legs sometimes trembled. I noticed that his production of saliva had increased, and he often drooled.

He began to complain about his eyesight. Everything looked hazy, he said, and he had to use a magnifying glass to read. We increased the magnification, but he still did not see well.

I was worried in particular about the muscular atrophy and involuntary trembling and suspected some new disease. I wanted Mao examined by both a neurologist and an ophthalmologist. But Mao did not want to see another doctor. Only after repeated urging did he finally consent to see an ophthalmologist.

We invited Zhang Xiaolou, the president of Beijing's Tongren Hospital, to examine Mao's eyes. Mao insisted that the exam be conducted in his study, and there was no room for Dr. Zhang's ophthalmological equipment. He had to conduct the examination with only an ophthalmoscope and a set of optometry lenses.

Zhang was nervous meeting Mao, as nearly everyone was, and was not sure how to proceed. Mao engaged the doctor with his usual banter, asking him about the characters that made up his name. *Xiaolou* means "small building," and Mao assured him that the Tongren Hospital would have a very large building if the doctor treated him successfully.

Zhang's examination was methodical and meticulous, and he was soon drenched in sweat. He discovered a slight corneal nebula on Mao's right eye and suspected cataracts. But he needed a more thorough examination, with more sophisticated instruments, to be certain. He suggested a further examination.

Mao was impatient. "It has already taken too much time," he complained. He did not want to be examined again.

But Zhang could not determine appropriate treatment until his diagnosis was certain. He needed to examine Mao's retina. He could not just abandon his patient.

When I could not persuade Mao to be examined again, I called Zhou Enlai to enlist his help. But Zhou had been so badly stung by Jiang Qing's accusations against him during Mao's last illness that he did not want to get involved again. He urged me to be patient and to continue reasoning with Mao.

Mao remained adamant. There was nothing I could do. Dr. Zhang was not called back.

Mao was spending most of his time with Zhang Yufeng. Since his illness in January, the two of them usually ate together, and she had now begun to control access to the Chairman, making it difficult for both Jiang Qing and other top leaders to see him. Jiang Qing came to rely on her to learn what Mao was doing and used her as a conduit for her own messages to the Chairman. Jiang Qing began courting Zhang's favor, showering her with gifts—watches, Western-style clothes, expensive fabrics—as a way of persuading the young woman to speak well of her to Mao, convince him to support her latest political moves, and persuade the Chairman to meet with his wife now and then. Zhang was accommodating, but because she did not understand politics or the factional tensions still rending the leadership asunder, her communications were often muddled.

Zhang and I never got along, and as her control over the Chairman increased, our relations grew more strained. She began giving Mao a small cup of fiery *maotai* liquor with his meals, to which I, as his doctor, objected, fearing that the high alcohol content might lead to fits of coughing. But Mao insisted that since he had given up smoking and had not drunk much in the past, a little *maotai* could not harm him now. Besides, he thought the *maotai* might help him sleep. With Zhang's influence over the Chairman growing, haggling with her about a little *maotai* seemed pointless.

Then Zhang Yufeng became pregnant. By the end of 1972, everyone in Group One knew of the pregnancy, and some speculated that Mao was the father. I knew, of course, that Mao had long since lost his reproductive capacity and that a seriously ill man approaching eighty could not possibly father a child.

Both Zhang Yaoci and Wang Dongxing wanted Zhang Yufeng to have the best medical care and asked me to make the arrangements. I thought the state-run hospital used by the Railroad Administration's special services unit, where Zhang Yufeng's treatment would be free, was fine and was reluctant to make special arrangements. But Zhang Yaoci insisted that Zhang Yufeng had told him Mao wanted her to have special care and would pay for all expenses.

I gave in and arranged for the baby to be delivered at Peking Union Medical Hospital. Knowing my own connection to Mao, the ranking administrators there naturally assumed that Zhang Yufeng was also highly connected and put her in a private room on a special ward reserved for high-level leaders. Zhang Yufeng's husband, Liu Aimin, visited his wife during her period of confinement, and so did many important people. Zhang Yaoci and Jiang Qing both came, bearing gifts, special foods, and diapers. Jiang Qing urged her to recover quickly and return to work. Zhang's younger sister, Zhang Yumei, was helping out during her period of confinement, but the sister was too young and ill-informed to serve as an intermediary between Jiang Qing and her husband. Jiang Qing needed Zhang Yufeng back for her own political ends.

Mao was not the only top leader whose health was declining. The founders of the Communist party, the survivors of the Long March, were aging. Mao was approaching eighty, and so were many of his associates.

Kang Sheng was the first of the politburo members to become ill. Kang was despised, widely regarded as sinister and cruel, and even many members of the party elite held him responsible for the deaths of innocent people. When Kang's sister-in-law, Su Mei, committed suicide in 1967, more than fifty people had been arrested and charged with her murder, including the emergency-room doctor at Beijing Hospital who had tried to save her life. The doctor was accused of putting poison in the stomach pump, and a number of Red Guards were arrested for conspiring with the doctor. The doctor was imprisoned for thirteen years before being found innocent and released. Few would miss Kang Sheng or mourn his death.

In mid-May 1972, Zhou Enlai informed me that a recent lung X ray and urinalysis indicated that Kang was probably suffering from bladder cancer. He wanted me to go with him to break the news to Mao. I hesitated, thinking Mao should not be informed until the diagnosis was certain. Zhou agreed.

A subsequent cystoscopic examination revealed that the doctors' suspicions were correct. Bladder cancer. They wanted to operate.

It was an unwritten rule that no politburo standing committee member or any member of Mao's staff could undergo major surgery without permission from the Chairman. Zhou Enlai was responsible for arranging for Kang's medical care, but Mao's approval was necessary for the surgery.

Mao refused to allow the operation. His old medical prejudices remained. Cancer—of anything but the breast—cannot be cured, he claimed. The more cancer is treated, the sooner the person will die, Mao insisted. He did not believe in telling the patient he had cancer, either, because he was certain that the anxiety of knowing would result in an earlier death. "Don't tell the patient, and don't perform surgery," were his instructions. "Then the person can live longer and still do some work."

But Kang Sheng already knew that he had cancer, and his doctors had urged immediate surgery. He was desperate.

Finally, Kang and his doctors compromised. The treatment would not be "major" and hence could be performed without Mao's permission. Rather than invasive surgery, they performed a local cauterization, going into the bladder through the urethra to remove the tumor.

Kang Sheng's plight had prompted Zhou to have a physical exam himself. He had a lung X ray and a urinalysis and urged Mao to do the same.

Mao refused the X ray. He only allowed us to do a urinalysis. He had no faith in doctors or in medicine. Medicine is good only for diseases that can be cured without intervention, he thought. If the disease is serious, the patient will die with or without medicine.

Mao's tests were normal, but Zhou's urine revealed the presence of cancerous cells.

First, Wang Dongxing and Zhang Chunqiao took the news to Mao. Mao did not believe them. He accused the doctors of looking for disease because they had nothing better to do. Doctors keep themselves busy doing nothing, he insisted. He brought me in to ask how it was possible to tell from looking at someone's urine that he had bladder cancer. Zhou looked perfectly healthy to him, Mao said.

I was finally able to convince Mao that Zhou Enlai really did have cancer and that the diagnosis had not been the figment of the bored doctors' imaginations. But Mao wanted the tests on Zhou Enlai stopped and refused to allow him to be treated. Cancer cannot be cured, he insisted, and treatment only causes pain and mental anguish and does the patient no good. "Leave the patient alone and let him live out his life happily," Mao said. "If I have cancer, I definitely will not have it treated."

He insisted we stop testing him as well. "You test here, you test there, always looking for some new disease," he said. "Who knows if the test results are accurate? You doctors just like to stir things up and you won't stop until you get everyone upset. I don't want you to run any more tests on me. A simple checkup will do."

Mao was adamant. From then on, he refused anything more than the most perfunctory exam—no electrocardiograms, no chest X rays, no blood tests.

Despite my personal feelings about Zhou, I, like many others in Zhongnanhai, was extremely concerned about his health. Zhou was exceptionally energetic, working long hours, sleeping little, managing the affairs of party and state. The party's best leaders had been purged. Aside from Zhou, only incompetents remained, and they spent most of their time in factional struggles. Zhou's responsibilities had consequently expanded, taking a great burden off Mao. No other leader had Zhou's experience and stamina. Mao was too weak and sick to take over Zhou's tasks.

Wang Dongxing was less concerned about Zhou's health. Only Mao was indispensable. The death of Zhou—the death of anyone— could not matter much so long as Mao was alive. Wang Dongxing urged me not to worry. Mao would have no difficulty managing.

By early 1973, Mao was having difficulty speaking. His voice became low and guttural, and his words were hard to understand, even for those of us who knew him well. The slightest physical activity took his breath away, and his lips would turn gray. We set up oxygen tanks in his bedroom and study and administered oxygen when he overexerted himself. Mao was no longer mobile, and because his eyesight was failing, he read less. Jiang Qing suggested that his study be set up to show films, and Mao began watching movies imported from Hong Kong, Japan, and even the United States. *Gongfu* martial arts films were his favorites.

But Mao's mind remained clear. He would not give permission for Zhou Enlai's surgery, but he would find someone to replace him. The time had come to reinstate Deng Xiaoping.

83

Mao never had the same antipathy toward Deng that he had had for Liu Shaoqi. In October 1968, at the Twelfth Plenum of the Eighth Central Committee, when Liu Shaoqi was stripped of his power and expelled from the party, Lin Biao and Jiang Qing argued for Deng's expulsion too. Mao refused. Deng was a capable administrator, a good communist, and he believed in Marxism-Leninism. Deng, Mao thought, could still be reformed. Maybe he could use Deng again.

My first inkling of Deng's possible reinstatement was at Chen Yi's funeral in January 1972. By then, the distance between Mao and me had grown, and the Chairman no longer took me into his confidence. Wang Dongxing was my primary source of important political information. But at Chen Yi's funeral, I overheard Mao talking with Chen Yi's widow, Zhang Qian. Deng Xiaoping's problem was different from Liu Shaoqi's, Mao said. Liu's "contradiction" was antagonistic. He was an "enemy of the people." Deng's problem was more benign, falling "within the ranks of the people."

Zhou's illness was one reason for bringing Deng Xiaoping back. So was the increasingly complicated political situation following the death of Lin Biao. The party leadership was divided into two contending camps. Jiang Qing and her ultraleft associates Zhang Chunqiao, Wang Hongwen, and Yao Wenyuan were on one side, and the ailing Zhou Enlai and Marshal Ye Jianying were on the other, and the Lin Biao incident was one point of disagreement.

Zhou Enlai wanted to accuse Lin Biao of ultraleftism, but Jiang

Qing wanted him declared an ultrarightist. Mao settled the debate in favor of Jiang Qing. On December 17, 1972, more than a year after Lin Biao had fled and after Zhou was diagnosed with cancer, Mao decided that Lin Biao had been "an ultrarightist and a revisionist, trying to split the party, conspiring to betray the party and the nation."

After the incident in early 1972 when Mao seemed ready to hand leadership over to Zhou and Jiang Qing responded by arguing that her husband was surrounded by a ring of spies, Mao seemed to distance himself from Zhou. He was wary that Zhou was too "right"—a revisionist. On July 4, 1973, Mao criticized Zhou Enlai for not discussing major issues with him, reporting only minor matters instead. If the situation does not change, Mao said, China will become revisionist. Five months later, in December, Mao criticized Zhou again.

Jiang Qing used Mao's growing distance from Zhou to launch a new attack on the premier—the bizarre campaign to "criticize Lin, criticize Confucius." Zhou Enlai was accused of being a modern-day Confucius.

Zhou's position was awkward. He was still loyal to Mao. In charge of day-to-day administration but under attack from Jiang Qing and her faction, he could demonstrate his loyalty only if he had explicit instructions from the Chairman. But Zhang Yufeng had become Mao's gatekeeper and made it difficult for the two to meet. Zhou used Mao's meetings with foreign leaders to catch a few words with the Chairman, but such meetings were rare, and the two had little time to chat. Zhou Enlai thus turned to his two subordinates within the Foreign Ministry, Wang Hairong and Nancy Tang, to carry messages to Mao. The two women could speak freely in front of Mao, but their position was difficult because Zhang Yufeng was nearly always with him.

As Mao and Zhou grew estranged and Jiang Qing's faction seemed on the verge of near-total control, Mao stepped in to restore balance. In March 1973, he recommended that Deng Xiaoping be brought back to take up his former position as vice-premier, and the politburo agreed. Deng's influence grew. Moreover, Mao continued to rehabilitate many veteran cadres who had been purged during the Cultural Revolution and whom Jiang Qing regarded as rightist. When the Tenth Party Congress was convened from August 24 to 28, 1973, I was so preoccupied with Mao's health that I did not recognize its political import.

Mao's anoxia—the shortage of oxygen in his body—had become increasingly severe, and in order for him to attend the meetings in the Great Hall of the People, we had to install oxygen tanks in his car, in

Room 118, at the podium where he would be talking, and in an emergency clinic we set up just under Room 118. Only when the meetings were over did I pause long enough to learn about the leadership changes that had just taken place. The membership of the newly selected Central Committee contained many rebels who had been active in the Cultural Revolution. But surprisingly, the lineup also included many old party cadres who had been purged in the early stages of the movement. Of the five party vice-chairmen, only two, Wang Hongwen and Kang Sheng, were members of the Central Cultural Revolution Small Group. Three were veteran party leaders—Zhou Enlai, Ye Jianying, and General Li Desheng. Jiang Qing and her Cultural Revolution leftists had no more power at the end of the congress than when it began. Mao had kept his wife's power in check.

Mao's political shakeup continued. In December 1973, he called a series of politburo meetings, attended by the commanders of the eight military regions as well, to work out a rotation of the military commanders. The military commanders had been in their posts for years, and with the growing power of the military under Lin Biao and the damage to central party control due to the massive purges of the Cultural Revolution, the power of the regional military commanders had grown. Mao feared they were getting too much power, pursuing their own interests, and becoming less loyal to him. His solution was to pluck them out of their power bases and rotate them to new positions.

The return of Deng Xiaoping was part of that strategy. Deng's administrative talents could bring power back to the center. "I am calling a talented leader back into service," he said at the meeting of military commanders. "He is Deng Xiaoping. We are sending out notices on his appointment as a member of the politburo and the Military Affairs Commission. The politburo deals with everything of importance—the party, the government, the army, the people, and the schools. It covers every geographic area—north, south, east, west, and center. I thought the politburo needed a secretary-general, but Deng didn't like that position. So he is being appointed chief of the general staff of the People's Liberation Army." Deng would be in control of the regional military commanders, too.

Mao knew that some people were afraid of his new chief of the general staff. "He is a man of decisiveness, who has done good deeds seventy percent of the time and bad deeds thirty percent. But the man I have called back is your old boss, and the politburo called him back, too, not I alone." Mao's health was on the decline. He could no longer attend all the politburo meetings, so Nancy Tang and Wang Hairong served as his liaison, using Zhou Enlai as their intermediary. Zhou reported to them on everything that happened there, and they ferried documents back and forth. Mao had withdrawn, but his power was undiminished.

Jiang Qing and her colleagues responded to the growing power of Deng Xiaoping by stepping up their attacks against Zhou. In early 1974, their campaign to criticize Lin Biao and Confucius went into high gear. On January 18, Mao approved Jiang Qing's report "Lin Biao and the Confucius-Mencius Way" and asked the whole nation to study it. A week later, a huge rally was held in Beijing to launch the movement. Yao Wenyuan was the principal speaker, and Jiang Qing, Chi Qun, the former propaganda head of the Central Garrison Corps and now the first party secretary of Qinghua University, and Xie Jingyi, then the deputy party secretary at Qinghua University, gave speeches attacking Zhou Enlai and other "rightist" party officials. Zhou was there, too, even though the rally was directed against him. He apologized for not having called the rally earlier and led the crowd in shouting the slogan "Learn from Comrade Jiang Qing." Wang Dongxing, who also attended, told me he thought Zhou was a coward.

Jiang Qing's "Criticize Lin, Criticize Confucius" campaign never caught on. The Chinese people had been rallied to support one political movement after another since 1949, and each movement had been more deadly and debilitating than the last. As the Cultural Revolution turned first against this enemy and then against that, as the Communist party was decimated and even the man once touted as Chairman Mao's closest comrade in arms plotted a coup against him, the people of China became fed up, disgusted. They were coming to see the political campaigns for what they really were—naked high-level power struggles that had little to do with them. Now Jiang Qing and her faction were trying to overthrow Zhou Enlai and take control of the country—the party, government, and army. But the people refused to go along. Jiang Qing's "Criticize Lin, Criticize Confucius" campaign was a flop.

Then Mao criticized Jiang Qing. On March 20, 1974, he wrote his wife to say, "It would be better for us not to see each other. For years I have advised you about many things, but you have ignored most of it. So what use is there for us to see each other? There are Marxist-Leninist books—and books by me—but you won't study them seriously. I am eighty-one years old and seriously ill, but you show hardly any concern. You now enjoy many privileges, but after my death, what are you going to do? You are also like those people who 'do not discuss major policies with me but report to me every day on trivial matters.' Think about it."

I was too busy to follow these events. My attention was focused on Mao. His health was deteriorating.

84

In July 1974, we learned that Mao was going to die.

His eyesight had continued to deteriorate, and by early 1974 he could not see a finger in front of his face. He could only tell light from dark. His speech had become so muddled that even those who knew him well could no longer understand him. It was as though he had lost control of his tongue, and he seemed unable to close his mouth. The muscular atrophy in his arms and legs was worse, especially on the right side of his body.

Mao's antipathy toward the medical profession continued, and even as I urged him to be examined by specialists, he continued to rail against doctors. Finally, he agreed to see an ophthalmologist and a team of neurologists. Zhang Yufeng had heard good reports about the ophthalmology department at Sichuan Medical College and suggested bringing in specialists from there. I was delighted. So long as Mao agreed to the exam, the rest was easy. Through the Ministry of Public Health, I invited a doctor named Fang from my alma mater, West China Union University Medical School, now renamed the Sichuan Medical College, and another named Luo, also from my alma mater and now at Sichuan Provincial Medical Hospital, to Beijing. They stayed in the 305 Hospital, seeing patients and performing operations, waiting for Mao's call.

In the meantime, two neurologists examined Mao—Huang Kewei, the director of the neurology department at the 301 Hospital, and Wang Xinde, the director of the neurology department at Beijing Hospital.

After examining Mao separately, the two doctors asked to consult with each other before discussing their conclusions with Mao. Mao asked for a written report. He did not want to see the doctors again.

I met with the two neurologists to discuss their findings. Their initial impression was that Mao had Parkinson's disease or had suffered a minor stroke. But as they discussed the test results and weighed the medical evidence, they now saw something else. They suspected that Mao had an extremely rare motor neuron disease, amyotrophic lateral sclerosis, known colloquially in the West as Lou Gehrig's disease. The illness involved the deterioration and eventual death of the motor nerve cells in the medulla and the spinal cord which control the muscles of the throat, the pharynx, the tongue, the diaphragm and intercostal muscles, the right hand, and the right leg. They wanted another medical opinion before making a final diagnosis, however, and suggested inviting Zhang Yuanchang, the director of the neurology department of the First Medical College of Shanghai, to Beijing.

Zhang Yuanchang came. After reviewing the results of the tests, he agreed with doctors Huang and Wang. Mao was suffering from amyotrophic lateral sclerosis, an illness so rare that Dr. Zhang had seen only two cases in his thirty years of clinical experience. The cause of the disease was unknown and there was no effective cure.

We discussed the prognosis. The doctors had had so little experience that they turned to foreign medical journals. Experience in the West suggested that the paralysis of Mao's right side would progress and he would become increasingly immobile. Once the disease spreads to the motor nerve cells of the throat, the pharynx, and the tongue, most patients die within two years. Mao had already reached that stage. In the final two years, as the throat, pharynx, and tongue become paralyzed, the patient experiences extreme difficulty swallowing and must be fed through a nasal tube. Otherwise, the patient runs a constant risk of choking, suffocation, and recurrent lung infections. With swallowing increasingly difficult, food and liquid often enter the trachea and lodge in the lungs, leading to infection and, often, pneumonia. In the last stages, swallowing is impossible. The diaphragm and intercostal muscles governing respiration also become paralyzed, and finally the patient is unable to breathe. With no effective cure, treatment could prolong the patient's life, but not for long. The use of a nasal tube for feeding could prevent food from lodging in the lungs. A respirator could aid breathing. Any physical activity had to be monitored carefully, because it was easy to fall and break a bone.

I was stunned. Mao's death was certain and probably only two years away. Wu Jie and Hu Xudong, still part of Mao's medical team, were also shocked. How could we write the medical report? Explaining the disease in language comprehensible to Mao and the other ranking leaders was almost impossible. And we could never tell Mao that he would die within two years.

We talked first with Wang Dongxing. But Wang knew nothing about modern medicine and could not understand what we were trying to say. He wondered how the Chairman could possibly have contracted such a bizarre disease and could not believe that Mao had only two more years to live. Mao was still able to eat and drink. The muscles of his throat were not paralyzed. He did not believe that there was a disease without a cure. He could not believe the doctors' prognosis. "After all your examinations, this is what you produced?" he asked. "This will not do. You have to do something else."

The next day, we met with Marshal Ye Jianying, using models of the human body to show him how the eyes, the brain, and the spinal cord worked. He followed our presentation closely, asking questions, examining our models intently, attempting to understand. Ye Jianying had always trusted doctors, and he understood our presentation better than most of the other leaders. Mao's eye problem, he agreed, was less serious than the motor neuron disease. If his blindness was due to cataracts, an operation might help. If the eye problem was something else and the blindness proved incurable, the worst was that Mao would no longer be able to see. But the motor nerve cell problem, he agreed, was serious. He suggested setting up medical task forces in major metropolitan areas to treat other patients with amyotrophic lateral sclerosis. We could then use the most successful procedures to treat Mao.

Then we informed Zhou Enlai. Zhou had no difficulty understanding the problem and knew immediately how serious it was. His own health was declining. He knew he needed surgery but was still waiting for Mao's approval. New tests had revealed severe hematuria (blood in the urine)—some 100cc a day—and Zhou's physicians were insisting on immediate surgery. Zhou, too, wanted the operation performed, but he was not willing to go ahead without Mao's consent. Zhou's wife, Deng Yingchao, finally intervened. Mao had been charmed by the young female lab technician Li, who was a member of our medical team and in frequent contact with the Chairman. Since she was not a doctor and therefore could not be accused of trying to scare her patient, Deng decided to ask the young woman to talk to Mao and make the case for her husband's operation. Only after talking to Li did Mao finally agree. On June 1, 1974, Zhou Enlai checked into the 305 Hospital, where urologists Wu Jieping, Xiong Rucheng, and Yu Sungting performed a simple cauterization. Knowing the severity of his own illness, Zhou had no trouble understanding that Mao was also seriously ill. He was concerned.

He wanted us to keep looking for a cure and suggested that the Chinese delegation to the United Nations in New York be asked to gather information about Western treatment for amyotrophic lateral sclerosis. When we told him that the United States had no effective treatment either, he said, "So the case is terminal."

We were all silent. No doctor wanted to say that the Chairman's death was inevitable.

"Then you must use the available time to find a way to deal with the problem. If you really cannot cure the disease, then at least you should try to prolong Chairman's life," Zhou said.

On July 17, 1974, I met with the medical team in the 305 Hospital to discuss possible treatment procedures. We needed to review everything that could go wrong during the course of Mao's illness. Each specialist was asked to outline procedures for dealing with every possible problem in his area of expertise and submit a written report detailing his plans.

Xu Yingxiang, the president of Beijing's Tongren Hospital, and his colleague Li Chunfu, the director of the ear, nose, and throat department there, joined us to discuss the effects of paralysis of the throat and pharnyx and to work out procedures for dealing with that problem. The doctors agreed with what was widely known: that the only way to prevent food or liquid from entering the trachea was to feed Mao through a nasal tube. Zhang Yuanchang, the Shanghai neurologist, was particularly concerned about paralysis of the intercostal muscles, which control breathing. We would need a respirator and had to be prepared to perform cardiopulmonary resuscitation. In the long term, respiration was the most serious problem. If Mao could not talk, he could still write, and if he could no longer swallow, we could feed him through a nasal tube. But there was no way to keep him alive if he could not breathe.

The politburo was meeting even as we were discussing the Chairman's health. I learned later that it was during this meeting that Mao lashed out against Jiang Qing, separating himself from her politically and warning her, Zhang Chunqiao, Wang Hongwen, and Yao Wen-yuan against forming a Shanghai faction of four. From warnings such as this came the later epithet Gang of Four.

The politburo meeting concluded while we were still working out our plans, and Zhang Yaoci called us shortly after to inform us that Mao had decided to take a trip. He would be leaving in two hours, and Wang Dongxing had directed that Wu Jie, Hu Xudong, and I, as well as the two ophthalmologists from Sichuan, accompany Mao. The neurologists were to return to their hospitals and await further notice.

I was aghast. Mao's condition could turn critical at any time. We had not finished our discussions, and the doctors had yet to write their reports. We had not yet decided how to handle all the possible medical emergencies. Nothing could stop Mao from leaving, but he needed a whole team of specialists along. The neurologists were critical to our work, and so was an ear, nose, and throat specialist. We needed an internist, too, plus special emergency rescue equipment and a trachial tube in case Mao had difficulty breathing. I explained this to Zhang Yaoci.

But Zhang was implacable. Mao's health was not his concern. He had his orders. "Wang Dongxing has ordered you to stop your discussions," he said. The decision about who was to accompany Mao had already been made. There was nothing Zhang could do. "We have to follow orders," he said.

Wu Jie, Hu Xudong, the two ophthalmologists, and I began packing immediately, taking as much emergency equipment as we could. We left with Mao by train for Wuhan.

We were there for two months.

Mao's condition worsened. His throat and pharynx, as we had feared, were becoming paralyzed, and swallowing was becoming more difficult. Mao could no longer swallow solids and had to be put on a semi-liquid diet—a thick broth of beef or chicken. He would lie on his left side while his attendants—usually Zhang Yufeng or Meng Jin-yun—fed him, letting the liquid slide down his throat and into the esophagus. Food occasionally spilled into his trachea, causing lung infections. But he refused medical care. He refused even to see me or the other doctors. Wu Xujun, who saw Mao occasionally, kept me informed. She, in turn, passed messages from me to Mao, urging him to let us see him and emphasizing that he needed treatment.

Mao refused.

Finally, I wrote a full medical report, spelling out his problems in great detail and using diagrams to illustrate what was wrong, and asked Zhang Yaoci to submit it to Mao. He gave it to Zhang Yufeng, who gave it to Mao. The only thing I did not reveal was the prognosis. Few doctors in China informed their patients that a disease is likely to be terminal. We believed that the anxiety such knowledge provoked could actually shorten the patient's life. With hope for recovery, the patient's life could be prolonged. Certainly, no doctor would take responsibility for telling the Chairman that his disease was fatal. But it was my job to prolong his life, and we could only do that if Mao agreed to treatment.

Mao finally met with me after reading the report. He did not like what I had said. He never liked to hear bad news about his health and always suspected a plot. He pointed out again, as he had so many times before, that doctors are too pessimistic and refuse to see the bright side. Doctors scare both their patients and themselves, he said. Mao did not believe he was seriously ill. He had had laryngitis in 1965 and was convinced that his current problem was nothing more than that. When I tried to convince him otherwise, he refused to listen. But he agreed to see the ophthalmologists.

Mao cracked his usual jokes when the ophthalmologists came, and he tried to be cordial. But his speech was so muddled that no one could understand what he was saying.

The ophthalmologists confirmed that Mao had cataracts. When Mao wondered if they had found anything else, they said they would have to remove his lenses surgically before drawing further conclusions. Mao was irritated that his questions could not be answered without surgery. When I met with him after the ophthalmologists left, he was still irritated, complaining that they could do him no good. He asked me to send them away. From then on, he refused to see any doctors—even me.

But I was still in charge of his health and would be held responsible if anything went wrong. I was becoming desperate, sleepless, unable to eat, constantly worried. I saw myself as a doctor devoted to the Chairman's health. He saw me as an enemy. I explained my dilemma to Wang Dongxing, emphasizing that the doctors Mao had brought with him were not specialists in motor neuron disease and might not be of much use in an emergency. We needed other doctors too, especially neurologists and specialists in ear, nose, and throat diseases. We also wanted an orthopedist to join the team in case Mao fell and we had to set a bone. Wang agreed only to ask the Hubei provincial revolutionary committee in Wuhan to set up an emergency rescue team. I never met the Wuhan medical team. They never came to Mao's villa and never saw the Chairman.

Many people close to Mao had difficulty believing he was ill.

When Wang Hairong and Nancy Tang accompanied Li Xiannian and Imelda Marcos, wife of the Philippine president, to visit Mao in Wuhan, they could see that Mao was having difficulty talking and often drooled, but they found his spirits still high. They were amazed when I told them that Mao was seriously ill. "Chairman is such a strange person and has such a strange disease," Nancy Tang said.

Jiang Qing remained in Beijing during Mao's stay in Wuhan. Her campaign against Zhou Enlai was giving her a new sense of power, and she had begun comparing herself to the only empress in Chinese history—the Tang dynasty's Wu Zetian, remembered by the Chinese people as an evil and wicked woman. Articles praising the empress had begun appearing in the press, and everyone knew that Jiang Qing fancied herself a modern-day Wu Zetian. In honor of her own meeting with Imelda Marcos, Jiang Qing's tailors had made several costumes fashioned after those of the empress. When she saw the elaborate imperial gowns, even Jiang Qing realized how inappropriate they were. She never wore them. What role Mao had in dissuading her, I never knew. But Wang Hairong and Nancy Tang told Mao about her gowns, and from Mao's silence I knew that he disapproved.

85

In September 1974, we left Wuhan for Changsha, the capital of Mao's home province of Hunan.

Mao wanted to swim. He was trying to treat his illness himself and thought he could build up his strength through exercise.

The doctors from Beijing, Wu Jie and Hu Xudong, were appalled. With the paralysis of his larynx and pharynx, any accidental ingestion of water could easily choke him. His limbs were atrophied and weak. There was no way Mao could swim. But the staff in Group One who had worked with Mao for years knew no one could stop him, that if anyone tried, he would become even more defiant and accuse them of trying to control him. Wang Dongxing refused to allow the doctors to raise their concerns with Mao. They had to be on hand, prepared to intervene in an emergency.

Mao went into the pool as the doctors stood ready, but the swim was soon aborted. Every time he put his face in the water, he choked and his face turned red. The guards quickly extricated him. He tried two more times in Changsha, with the same result. After that Mao never swam again. Deng Xiaoping was visiting Mao in Changsha at the time and reported to the politburo upon his return that Mao's health was fine. The Chairman had even gone for a swim.

Mao became more immobile after his aborted swim. He spent most of his time in bed, lying on his left side, because he had difficulty breathing in any other position. He developed a bedsore on his left hip as a result, and from then until his death, bedsores were a recurring problem. As soon as one healed, another would form. He developed an allergy to his sleeping pills and broke out in an itchy rash all over his body. We changed the medicine and applied an ointment to the rash, and that problem subsided.

I saw little of Mao during the two months I spent in Changsha, and he refused to see other members of the medical team at all. Wu Xujun kept me informed of his condition, and I got occasional word after he met with his visitors from Beijing. But shortly after that, Wu Xujun left Group One for good.

Mao's hostility toward doctors was heightened by news of Zhou Enlai's decline. His bladder cancer had recurred, and a second operation had been performed in August. Mao's conviction that surgery did not work was thus confirmed. "I said he should not have an operation," Mao complained, "but he insisted. So now he has to have a second one, right? I think he will have a third one, a fourth one, until he dies. When ordinary people are sick, they often let it go. After a while, the illness is gone. If it's not, that just means it can't be cured."

The political situation in Beijing was still tense. The Second Plenum of the Tenth Central Committee and the Fourth National People's Congress were both scheduled for January 1975, and both meetings would appoint new personnel. Deng's positions as vice-premier, vice-chairman of the Military Affairs Commission, chief of the PLA general staff, and politburo standing committee member had to be approved, and Jiang Qing and her group opposed them. They wanted Wang Hongwen appointed vice-chairman of the National People's Congress. As the time approached, the power struggle heated up, and both factions began sending emissaries to meet with Mao, trying to win him over.

Wang Hongwen visited Changsha on behalf of Jiang Qing and her faction. With Xu Yefu dying from lung cancer, Zhang Yufeng had taken over all his secretarial responsibilities—reading documents to Mao and screening his visits—and was maneuvering to be formally appointed Mao's confidential secretary. Wang Dongxing was reluctant to approve the appointment, but Wang Hongwen supported it and met with Zhang Yufeng frequently. He arranged for several servants to assist her, to do her laundry and cook her meals, while she served Mao. Before the arrangements were complete, Mao issued a personal edict— "Whoever is meddling in my domestic affairs, get out"—Wang Hongwen beat a hasty retreat to Beijing.

Wang Hairong and Nancy Tang arrived in Changsha on October 20, 1974, representing Zhou Enlai. Jiang Qing's most recent barrage against the premier accused him of selling out to foreigners. Zhou had been trying since before the Cultural Revolution to increase China's shipping capacity, both by promoting a domestic shipbuilding industry and by buying ships from abroad. When China launched its own Shanghai-made Fengqing ship in 1974, Jiang Qing accused the premier of betrayal for buying foreign ships. Deng Xiaoping, back on the politburo, sided with Zhou. The meeting ended in a deadlock until Mao sided with Zhou and Deng.

Formally, Zhou Enlai and Wang Hongwen were jointly responsible for the slate of appointments for the upcoming party and government meetings. The two came together to visit Mao in Changsha on December 23 to review their proposals with him. I knew little of the political machinations behind the appointments. Zhang Yufeng knew even less, but her appointment as Mao's confidential secretary had finally been approved, adding to her arrogance. When Zhou came to discuss the appointments with Mao, she accosted the premier to complain about her odious responsibilities to Mao—helping him eat, drink, bathe, and use the bathroom and putting him to sleep. "Can't you do something about it?" she demanded. Zhou was too embarrassed to reply.

When the Second Plenum of the Tenth Central Committee met in January, Deng's appointments as vice-chairman of the party and member of the politburo standing committee were made official. Later, at the Fourth National People's Congress, Zhou was reelected premier of the State Council and Deng Xiaoping was made first vice-premier. Mao needed Deng to help Zhou Enlai run the country's day-to-day affairs and insisted on his appointments. Zhou's illness made Deng Xiaoping's leadership all the more urgent. Deng took charge of day-to-day work of the Central Committee. Once more, Jiang Qing and her faction had been held in check.

86

Mao did not attend the Beijing meetings. He was still in Changsha. Wang Dongxing did not attend, either. He did not want to get embroiled in the factional disputes.

I wanted to return to Beijing. I had little to do in Changsha, but knew we were not prepared for a further deterioration in Mao's condition. The medical team in Beijing had yet to complete its plans. We needed to prepare for the medical emergency I knew we would soon confront.

Hu Xudong, Wu Jie, and I returned to Beijing in early January and organized a medical team consisting of Jiang Sichang, the director of the ear, nose, and throat department at the Liberation Army General Hospital; Zhou Guangyu, the director of surgery at Beijing Hospital, Gao Rixin, the director of anesthesiology at Beijing Hospital, and Yuan Zhaozhuan, from the dermatology department at Peking Union Medical College.

Hu Xudong accompanied the medical team to Changsha while I began briefing several top leaders, beginning with Ye Jianying, hoping to solicit their cooperation. With Mao so recalcitrant, we needed their help, and the entire politburo would soon have to be informed of Mao's problem. Marshal Ye had always been solicitous of the problems I faced with Mao. We chatted for a while, recalling the twenty-one years I had spent with Mao. Then I described Mao's condition over the last six months and explained how hampered the doctors were by Mao's refusal to see us. We talked about how to convince Mao to permit us to insert a nasal tube into his stomach for feeding. I was worried about his choking and the possibility of pneumonia if food were to get stuck in the trachea again.

Ye Jianying was encouraging. My relations with Wang Dongxing and Zhang Yaoci, with whom I was in daily contact, had become strained, however. No matter how I tried to explain the urgency of Mao's condition or how many models and diagrams I used, they still could not understand. Zhang Yaoci was particularly recalcitrant. As soon as he knew that Mao's disease was incurable, he wanted to distance himself as far as he could from involvement in his medical care. He was afraid that knowing Mao's condition would make him responsible if anything went wrong. Zhang's job was security.

Ye Jianying wanted to help. He did not think Mao would voluntarily agree to the nasal feeding, and he warned that Jiang Qing could still cause problems. He remembered the scene she had caused during Mao's illness in 1972 and believed she could turn against me again. He urged me not to be frightened and promised to come to my aid if I was attacked. He offered to help obtain medical equipment and sent similar assurances to the other members of the medical team, too.

On January 20, I met with Zhou Enlai, who was still living in a suite in the 305 Hospital. Zhou's health had taken another turn for the worse. Just before he had left for Changsha in December, the doctors had discovered blood in his stool. Knowing of the premier's scheduled visit to Mao and of the party plenum and the National People's Congress in January, they waited to tell him. The congress had concluded on January 17, and Zhou's report had called for a major redirection of the government, focused on the modernization of China. With the meetings over, Zhou was about to have a colonoscopy. The doctors suspected he had cancer of the colon.

Zhou was thin and pale, but he refused to be bedridden. He was sitting on a sofa, dressed in his usual elegant Mao suit. When I explained that I had been back for two weeks but had not wanted to bother him, he chided me for the delay. He wanted to know about the Chairman's health.

By then, Mao had left Changsha for Hangzhou, and I was scheduled to join him there the next day together with other members of his medical team. The first group had already left. In my absence, the Chairman had been persuaded to have a complete physical exam.

Zhou had also been talking to doctors about Mao. He knew the Chairman's cataracts would be easy to treat. His worry was the motor neuron disease and he wondered whether we had worked out a solution. It was still difficult for him to believe that there was no cure.

I reiterated that neither China nor the West had discovered a cure.

Zhou thought some doctors of traditional Chinese medicine should take a look. I explained that Mao did not believe in traditional Chinese medicine, and it would be almost impossible for him to take the type of medicine such doctors prescribed—herbs boiled in water, fed hot and in large quantities to the patient. Mao was choking on even small amounts of water. How could he drink large quantities of herbal medicine?

Zhou did not press the issue, asking me instead to give the Chairman his best wishes.

I left the next day with a team of twelve nurses and ten physicians—Wu Jie, two neurologists, three ophthalmologists, two radiologists, and two laboratory doctors. We would join the team of surgeons and ear, nose, and throat specialists who had gone ahead.

Mao's physical examination took four days to conduct. Regulations specified that a doctor treating a top leader could deal only with the aspect of the patient's illness relevant to his own specialty. Doctors were not allowed to consult with each other either on their diagnoses or recommended treatment. My job was always to analyze the different reports and put together a plan of treatment. The rule was designed for reasons of security rather than health and was especially counterproductive for Mao. Mao had several interrelated diseases, and consultation among the doctors was crucial to determining both the nature and severity of his illness and deciding the best course of treatment. Upon prodding, Wang Dongxing finally agreed that while the specialists would each examine Mao separately, we could meet together afterward to decide how to treat him. The ear, nose, and throat specialists and the surgeons conducted their examinations first, followed by the internists, neurologists, and ophthalmologists. Then an electrocardiogram was done, and chest and heart X rays were taken. The purpose of the heart X ray was to determine whether his heart was enlarged. An enlarged heart indicates danger of heart failure.

The results confirmed that Mao had cataracts, amyotrophic lateral sclerosis, coronary heart disease, pulmonary heart disease, an infection in the lower half of both lungs, three bullae in his left lung, bedsores on his left hip, and a shortage of oxygen in his blood (anoxia). He also had a slight fever and a severe cough. The medical team believed that a nasal tube was necessary both for feeding and for administering medications. They also recommended cataract surgery.

I was responsible for drafting the report to Mao explaining both the diagnoses and the proposed treatment. On January 27, 1975, I presented the report to Zhang Yaoci, going over the contents with him in detail and urging him to explain the document to Zhang Yufeng. Mao was blind, and Zhang was responsible for reading and explaining his reports.

At five-thirty the next morning, Zhang Yaoci woke me. The entire medical team was to meet with him and Wang Dongxing immediately. Zhang Yufeng had just delivered Mao's response to our report.

We gathered in the building where Wang Dongxing was staying. Zhang Yaoci reported. Zhang Yufeng had objected to the doctors' report. In her opinion, none of the treatment procedures we had suggested was any good. Zhang Yufeng had her own suggestion about how to treat the Chairman, and Mao had agreed. Zhang Yufeng wanted to treat Mao through infusions of glucose. Glucose injections had become a popular tonic among several top leaders during the Cultural Revolution, as had blood transfusions. After Jiang Qing heard that blood transfusions from healthy young men were a way to promote longevity, she had arranged to have young PLA soldiers donate blood for her transfusions. Reports of these treatments had reached Zhang Yufeng, who believed that glucose would both supply the necessary nutrients and treat the Chairman's illnesses as well. She wanted the infusions to begin immediately.

The medical team was stunned, silent. Wang Dongxing wanted to know what we thought. He refused to allow us to discuss the question among ourselves. Instead, he went around the room asking each member whether he agreed or disagreed with Zhang Yufeng's recommendation. If we all agreed, the infusions would begin immediately.

Incredibly, most members of the team agreed—not for medical reasons but for political ones. They had to obey the party leaders.

I was the last to be asked. I pointed out that while glucose infusions are often used in emergencies, they would be of little help to Mao and could cause complications. I was worried about the effect of such large amounts of fluid on Mao's already weakened heart. Moreover, since impurities in the glucose occasionally cause anaphylaxis, steroids would have to be added to counteract the possibility of a massive allergic reaction. We did not want to do anything to add to Mao's medical problems. Zhang Yufeng would not be responsible if anything went wrong. She was not a doctor. As head of the medical team, I would be responsible, regardless of the fact that I had disagreed with the treatment. I was adamant.

Zhang Yaoci was exasperated. Mao was still rebelling against the doctors, but at least he had agreed to Zhang Yufeng's suggestion. Now he wondered what to do.

I blamed both Zhang Yaoci and Zhang Yufeng. We all knew that

Mao would not like our prescribed treatment, and since Mao would see neither me nor any of the other doctors, responsibility for reading and interpreting the report to Mao rested with Zhang Yufeng. But Zhang Yufeng refused to talk to us, so I had urged Zhang Yaoci to explain the report to her and try to persuade her to convince Mao to follow our recommendations. She was our only intermediary, and her cooperation in his treatment was essential.

Wang Dongxing was angry with me. I was the only doctor to oppose the infusions. He insisted that I had to obey the party and warned that I would face trouble if I continued to insist on my own views.

But this was not a matter of party discipline. Doctors, not Zhang Yufeng, Wang Dongxing, Zhang Yaoci, or the party, were the experts in this case. Even Mao himself had said that when a person is sick he has to listen to the doctor.

We had reached a stalemate. Wang Dongxing instructed me to write a report to Mao explaining why I alone opposed the glucose treatment. He would leave the final decision to Mao.

I wrote the report immediately. Zhang Yaoci gave it to Zhang Yufeng, and the word from Mao came back that evening. Mao had decided against the infusions.

But my position was untenable. No one was happy with me. Without direct access to Mao, I needed all the cooperation I could get—from Zhang Yufeng in particular and from Zhang Yaoci and Wang Dongxing as well. But they were impeding Mao's medical care. Mao's condition could only worsen. And if we caved in now to their intimidation, they could continue to interfere with Mao's treatment and we doctors would be held responsible when anything went wrong.

The medical team was worried. They agreed with me medically but did not want to alienate Zhang Yufeng, Zhang Yaoci, and Wang Dongxing further. We needed their help. My survival was at stake. Since 1968, Jiang Qing had been trying to brand me a counterrevolutionary, and in 1972, when Mao was so sick, she implied that I was part of a spy ring around him. If I insisted on giving Mao proper medical treatment, refusing to give in to the arbitrary advice of Zhang Yufeng and others, I might be declared a counterrevolutionary and accused of deliberately trying to harm the Chairman. But I still stood a chance of protecting myself. If anything happened to Mao after the glucose infusions, Jiang Qing would have all the rope she needed to hang us.

I discussed the implications of our situation with Wu Jie. He thought that we should resign. We could turn our responsibilities over to another medical team. He thought that I was in trouble no matter what.

He was right. Mao's disease was incurable, and even with the best medical care, his end was certain. Mao's death was inevitable. But I could not quit. I was director of the team. Even if I wanted to quit, Wang Dongxing would not let me go. I was still convinced that our only course was to continue insisting on the best medical treatment we knew. I could not let politics interfere with my medical opinions.

Wang Dongxing was conciliatory when I talked to him alone, and he apologized for getting involved in the decision about the glucose. "I acted too rashly," he said, agreeing that it was a matter for the doctors to decide. Still, he accused me of being inflexible. He had decided that after Chinese New Year he would accompany me, the nurses, and several of the doctors back to Beijing. We would decide on the treatment procedures there. Hu Xudong, the two ear, nose, and throat specialists, the anesthesiologists, and the surgeons would stay in Hangzhou. If Mao's cataract problem could be solved, we should try to resolve that first. He suggested that we find cataract patients comparable to the Chairman in age and health and first perform operations on them. The reports of the operations could then be submitted to the Chairman, who would then decide whether he wanted the surgery performed. Wang also thought that more consideration had to be given to how to treat Mao's motor neuron disease. He was still not willing to accept the possibility that there really was no cure.

The full politburo had to be officially informed of Mao's illness. Among the top leaders, only Zhou Enlai and Ye Jianying had been briefed, and the Chinese press still described the Chairman as glowing with health, his cheeks a rosy red. Neither the Chinese people nor the high-level cadres knew anything of Mao's illness. Telling the politburo was a way of protecting both the doctors and Wang Dongxing. Jiang Qing was on the warpath against Wang Dongxing, too. She never asked Wang about her husband's health but was waiting for her opportunity to pounce if Mao died. The doctors, of course, would be blamed, and so long as Zhou Enlai, Ye Jianying, and Wang Dongxing were the only politburo members fully informed of Mao's illness and course of treatment, they too would be held responsible. Once the politburo was briefed, its members would also assume responsibility. If there really was no cure, the politburo would have to know. We needed its approval for our suggested course of treatment.

During the flight back, on February 8, Wang called me into his cabin. He knew I was angry. I explained that I was particularly per-turbed about Zhang Yufeng's suggestions about glucose infusions.

Wang was defensive. Everyone around Mao relied on Zhang Yu-feng to communicate with the Chairman. By now his speech was all but incomprehensible. Only Zhang Yufeng understood him. She had learned to read his lips. "If we dismiss her," Wang said, "how will we be able to understand Chairman?" Zhang Yufeng was there to stay. Her ability to understand his speech gave her remarkable power.

87

The politburo meeting was scheduled for February 15, 1975.

I met with Zhou Enlai in the 305 Hospital the night before, briefing him on the results of our latest tests on Mao and telling him about the controversy over the glucose infusions. Zhou's health was so precarious that I suggested he not come to the meeting.

But he wanted to be there. The politburo was about to learn the full extent of Mao's illness. He wondered if I was ready to deliver my report and warned me to be fully prepared for Jiang Qing's hostile questions. He thought it best not to mention disagreements over the glucose. The situation was complicated enough.

The medical team arrived at the Great Hall of the People at a little after two o'clock in the afternoon on February 15. The politburo was already in session. Wang Dongxing came out to discuss our presentation. I explained that we would begin with my description of the general state of Mao's health. Then Wu Jie would describe the problems with his heart and lungs and Huang Kewei would describe the amyotrophic lateral sclerosis. Zhang Xiaolou would explain the cataract problem, and Li Xuande would present X rays, further detailing Mao's heart and lung condition. All of us had diagrams, charts, and models as visual aids. I would close the discussion by detailing the team's suggested course of treatment.

Wang reiterated the importance of the meeting, pointing out that Zhou Enlai was attending despite the gravity of his illness and encouraging us to speak loudly since Deng Xiaoping was hard of hearing and would be learning about Mao's illness for the first time.

When we entered the conference room, Zhou Enlai, Deng Xiaoping, and Ye Jianying were seated at the center of a long conference table, flanked by the other members of the politburo. The medical team was asked to sit at the opposite end of the table. I felt that we were on trial.

We had discussed Mao's case so many times that the presentation went smoothly. We presented all the medical facts, including the statistical survival rate for other patients suffering from amyotrophic lateral sclerosis, letting the politburo members draw their own conclusions about Mao's own life expectancy. No one directly referred to his death. When Huang Kewei began trying to explain amyotrophic lateral sclerosis, most of the politburo members were confused.

Jiang Qing led the questioners. "You say this is a rare disease," she said. "How did Chairman get it? What is your evidence?"

We had no answers to many of Jiang Qing's questions. No one knew what caused motor neuron disease. Huang Kewei was patient, answering every question thoroughly, spending two hours drawing on every analogy he could to make his point. When his audience did not understand his explanation of paralysis of the diaphragm and intercostal muscles, Huang likened the muscles to pork-chop meat. Yao Wenyuan rebuked him for being disrespectful of the Chairman.

Huang panicked at the reprimand, stammered, and was unable to continue.

Zhou Enlai intervened, lauding the doctors for their thoroughness and thanking us all for our work. He suggested that we now discuss treatment.

I was responsible for reporting. I explained that we could operate on the cataracts but first wanted to test the possible procedures on other patients similar in age and health to the Chairman. I raised the question of nasal feeding, arguing how important it was to supply Mao with nutrients.

Jiang Qing interrupted again. "A nasal feeding means inserting a tube into the stomach," she said. "I know this procedure, and it is very painful. Does this mean you want to torture the Chairman?"

Deng Xiaoping interjected by pointing out that one of the old revolutionary marshals, Liu Bocheng, had been on nasal feeding for a long time. He wondered whether Mao had agreed to the procedure.

I said that he had not.

Deng urged us not to force Mao into anything, saying we should explain the situation to him patiently, waiting for his agreement before inserting the tube. Like most of the other top leaders, he too had difficulty believing there was no cure for the motor neuron disease, but he urged us to do all we could to control the symptoms and arrest its progress. He urged caution, too, in treating the cataracts and hoped we would learn as much as we could about how an eye operation would affect Mao's heart and motor neuron disease. He urged us to do our best and put Wang Dongxing in charge of procuring whatever equipment and medicine we might need. "The party wishes to thank you," he said finally.

Zhou Enlai echoed Deng's thanks, and Deng repeated once more, "The party wishes to thank you," before we were dismissed. The other members of the politburo had no reaction at all. By remaining silent, they absolved themselves of responsibility for Mao. Nevertheless the words of thanks were comforting, particularly after Jiang Qing's hostility, and we left the meeting considerably relieved. The underlying fear remained, however. We knew that if any member of the politburo concluded that we had done anything wrong, the gratitude would cease and the attacks against us would begin. And any of us could be removed from the team at any time if we were ever deemed politically suspect.

That March, not long after the politburo meeting, Jiang Qing and her Shanghai friends Zhang Chunqiao and Yao Wenyuan launched yet another campaign against Deng Xiaoping and other veteran leaders. This time they cited "empiricism," meaning experience as opposed to theory, as the target of attack, and Yao Wenyuan listed empiricism as the principal enemy in an article called "On the Social Foundation of the Lin Biao Anti-Party Group." It was an attack against the old Long March leaders, most of whom were peasants with little education but much political experience and who were then being rehabilitated in growing numbers. Their legitimacy was tied to their age, their experience, and their sacrifice and stamina during the Long March. Jiang Qing, Zhang Chunqiao, and Yao Wenyuan were decades younger than the Long March generation, and they were seen as party intellectuals, educated but with limited practical experience. The terms of the high-level power struggles were growing increasingly arcane, and few ordinary Chinese could have understood what the new campaign was about. It was a struggle between the younger cadres who had been promoted in the wake of the Cultural Revolution purges and the purged veterans who were returning to power. The ailing Zhou Enlai and the newly reinstated Deng Xiaoping were the primary targets.

Mao's health now prevented him from day-to-day involvement in his wife's continuing struggle for power, but when he learned of the attacks on empiricism, he lashed out against them. In April, he declared that dogmatism was just as bad as empiricism, because both were deviations from Marxism-Leninism and therefore revisionist. Jiang Qing and her faction were the dogmatists, and Mao was now chastising them.

At a politburo meeting of May 3, 1975, Mao went further. He dictated a note to Zhang Yufeng, who gave it to emissaries Nancy Tang and Wang Hairong. "You detest only empiricism, not dogmatism," he told the group, directing his comments at Jiang Qing and her faction. He said the Wang Ming faction had dominated the party for four years by holding high the banner of the Comintern to intimidate the Chinese Communist party and strike down those who did not agree. "You should all believe in Marxism-Leninism, not revisionism. Be united, not split. Be aboveboard, not involved in plots and intrigues. Don't form a Gang of Four. . . . As I see it, those who criticize empiricism are themselves believers in empiricism."

After Mao's criticisms, Deng Xiaoping presided over politburo meetings. While Wang Dongxing told me that Deng often criticized Jiang Qing and her associates, and he clearly won the battle over empiricism, Deng never attempted to have Mao's wife and her faction purged, though Jiang Qing's goal was always to get rid of him. Wang was amazed that Deng did not use his new power to get rid of her.

Deng was clever, and so was Zhou Enlai. Both men knew that despite Mao's criticisms of his wife and her associates, he intended only to limit their power, not to quash it. When Kang Sheng, bedridden with cancer, learned that Mao was displeased with his wife, he mistakenly assumed that the Chairman was prepared to see her overthrown. As he had throughout his life, he began inventing charges, claiming that Jiang Qing and Zhang Chunqiao had betrayed the party in the 1930s and even claiming to have witnesses who would testify that they were traitors. Kang met with Nancy Tang and Wang Hairong, who were Mao's liaison to the politburo, and asked them to tell Mao. But the two women first met with Zhou Enlai. They told me that Zhou had warned them not to be rash, that while Mao had criticized his wife and her associates, he had no intention of striking them down. Kang was using the two women. If they had informed Mao of Kang Sheng's charges and Mao chose to protect his wife, Kang could deny having made the allegations. Nancy Tang and Wang Hairong would be the victims. They never told Mao.

Deng Xiaoping continued to tread lightly, claiming to follow Mao's instructions—study ideology and oppose revisionism, work for stability and unity, and improve the economy. But the attacks from Jiang Qing and her associates continued. Mao Yuanxin often served as their spokesman and warned the Chairman that Deng Xiaoping was attempting to negate the Cultural Revolution, that he never mentioned its accomplishments and rarely criticized the revisionist line of Liu Shaoqi. Wang Dongxing believed that under Mao Yuanxin's influence, Mao was becoming uneasy about Deng. Mao was easily persuaded of others' ill intent. That is why it was so important in any dispute to get to see him first. As Mao Yuanxin's influence over Mao grew, that of Nancy Tang and Wang Hairong declined. By September 1975, the two women had lost their special access to the Chairman, and Mao Yuanxin took over as Mao's liaison with the politburo. From then on, Deng Xiaoping was under continual attack, and the political situation grew increasingly tense.

Following our presentation to the politburo meeting in February, we had invited two more ophthalmologists to join the medical team— Tang Youzhi and Gao Peizhi, of Beijing's Guanganmen Hospital. The two doctors were trained in both Western and traditional Chinese medicine and could contribute to our deliberations about what technique would be best for Mao. The team of ophthalmologists was having difficulty deciding how to treat Mao's cataracts. The two doctors from Guanganmen Hospital recommended the less intrusive traditional Chinese method, which took only a few minutes and involved manipulation of a special needle, to push aside the turbid lens without removing it. Since this procedure was less of a shock to the system than the Western-style cataract removal, Tang and Gao preferred it.

I also favored the less intrusive technique, fearing potential complications of even a mild shock to Mao's system. The main objection of the Western-trained ophthalmologists was that the procedure would not actually remove Mao's turbid lens, so another procedure might be necessary in the future. They were less concerned than I about the possible effects of the Western technique on Mao's overall health.

The doctors were at an impasse. We decided to follow the politburo's advice and experiment on forty elderly cataract patients with heart problems. Officials of Beijing municipality found the patients, all of whom were elderly peasant men, without families, living in the countryside. They were in need of cataract surgery but were too poor to afford it. No one ever told them they were part of an experiment on behalf of the Chairman. We put them up in the General Office's guesthouse. Half the group would receive the traditional treatment and the other half would undergo the Western-style extraction. After the operations, we would submit a report to Mao, who would decide which type of procedure he preferred.

Mao was still in Hangzhou, under the care of Hu Xudong. Zhang Yufeng finally had had her way. Beaten down, Dr. Hu relented and began administering 800cc to 1000cc daily of a 5 percent glucose solution, to which he added a considerable dosage of steroids. But he was worried about the effect it would have on Mao and called both me and Wu Jie several times for consultation. I continued to object to the use of glucose, and since I was not in Hangzhou to observe and no blood or urine tests were being done to test the effects, neither I nor Wu Jie could offer any advice.

When he returned to Beijing in late April, Mao was still taking the glucose. I advised Hu Xudong to take a blood test and use the results to persuade Mao that he needed to stop the intravenous feedings. Wu Jie agreed. We were both afraid of possible complications if the glucose feedings went on too long.

Zhang Yufeng insisted on the infusions. Hu Xudong compromised by reducing the feedings to once every other day.

In mid-May, Zhang Yufeng read a report in *Reference Materials* that two Chinese doctors had successfully treated the heart disease of a high-ranking Romanian leader. She wanted the two doctors on our team. When Zhu Xianyi, the president of Tianjin Medical College, and Tao Huanle, from the department of internal medicine at Beijing Hospital, returned from Bucharest, I invited them to join us.

But the Romanian leader had been suffering from subacute bacterial endocarditis—a bacterial infection of the heart—and his disease had been cured with antibiotics. Mao's problems were different. The two new members of the team were no better able to advise us than the heart specialists we already had. But Mao wanted to meet them.

On June 10, I took the two men in to meet with the Chairman. As we entered the room, Zhang Yufeng and Mao were having an argument. Mao began gesticulating angrily when he saw us, but none of us could understand what he was saying. Only Zhang Yufeng knew that he was demanding that she explain why they were quarreling.

Two days earlier, Mao had become angry with Zhang Yufeng when he wanted her to read documents to him and she could not be found. When Zhang came back, Mao had scribbled on a piece of paper, "Zhang Yufeng, get out."

Zhang had fought back, yelling that she would get out and cursing that if Mao did not let her go, he would become a dog. Mao was still furious. "I have a bad temper," he said, "but Zhang's is even worse. She swore at me."

Zhang complained that she did not know why the doctors had to hear the whole story, and the two doctors, meeting the Chairman for the first time, were dumbfounded. But Mao still wanted to hear about their treatment of the Romanian leader. The doctors assured the Chairman that his problems were completely different from the Romanian's, but Mao wanted them to join our team anyway.

When I encouraged the doctors to join us, they demurred. They were impressed with the quality of the doctors already serving Mao and thought we had enough doctors to set up a hospital. They had no additional contribution to make. Mao was already being served by the best physicians in China.

Wu Jie agreed. We already had enough experts. But I wanted Zhu Xianyi and Tao Huanle to stay. The more reputable doctors we had, the less the likelihood we could later be declared counterrevolutionary. But we had to maintain a united front. We had to consider our recommendations carefully and do all we could to reach unanimous conclusions. If Zhang Yufeng or Jiang Qing and her cronies ever heard we had differences, they could play us off against each other and accuse one side or the other of being counterrevolutionary. Many of the doctors were politically inexperienced and had no idea that disagreements among us could lead to later political attacks. Wu Jie did understand, however, and we worked together to convey our strategy to the team. The entire medical staff had to agree on Mao's treatment. If one or more doctors disagreed, we would discuss the issue further. But once the decision was made, we had to stand united. We added another member—Xu Delong, the director of neurology at Huashan Hospital in Shanghai, who had been conducting experimental treatments in Shanghai of patients with amyotrophic lateral sclerosis.

88

By the end of July, our operations on elderly cataract patients were complete, and the findings were submitted to Mao. He decided on the traditional Chinese method. He said it would be safe, less painful, and quicker.

The operation was to be performed in the old swimming pool area, converted now to a huge reception hall. We draped off an area for the operating room. Doctors Tang Youzhi and Gao Peizhi would perform the surgery. Zhou Enlai and Deng Xiaoping came to observe the proceedings.

Mao was nervous, but the two doctors explained what they were about to do in full detail. Finally, the Chairman relaxed enough to crack a joke, saying that in the Yuan dynasty (A.D. 1279–1368), the poet Sadula had written, "Looking southeast toward Wu [Jiangsu province] and Chu [Hubei province], nothing fills my eyes." After this surgery, Mao said, his eyes would be filled.

The operation on Mao's right eye took only twelve minutes, and when it was over the eye was covered with gauze. Mao agreed that if the surgery was successful, he would ask the doctors to perform the same procedure on his left eye in two months.

Ten days later, the gauze was removed. Mao was excited. "I can see sky and sun again," he said, "but not very well." The doctors explained that while they had pushed aside the turbid lens, they had done nothing else to restore his eyesight. They suggested that glasses would improve the Chairman's vision. Mao wanted glasses but refused to have any more eye exams. We brought him glasses in several different strengths before he finally settled on a pair that worked. Afterward, he was able to read official documents himself.

By mid-October 1975, when Mao was supposed to have his second cataract operation, the political situation was almost unbearably tense. Jiang Qing's campaign against Deng Xiaoping continued, and Wang Dongxing believed her goal was not only to have him overthrown but executed, too. Her own access to Mao was limited, but she used Mao Yuanxin and Zhang Yufeng to convey her messages. No one, not even Wang Dongxing, knew what Mao was thinking, and I had few opportunities to see him. We did know that Mao was restless and irritable, and Wang was worried about doing anything that might provoke Mao's anger and lead to the dismissal of Deng. He did not want us to raise the issue of another cataract operation, nor would he allow us to propose further treatment for Mao's motor neuron disease.

The high-level party struggle was considered top secret, and I was not allowed to discuss it with my fellow doctors. I could only say that Mao was too busy for the cataract operation and that we could only continue our present treatment without trying anything new.

Medical ethics and Chinese politics collided. The doctors took their responsibilities for Mao's health seriously and were reluctant to stand back just because Mao was busy. Wang Dongxing was concerned that their attitude would further irritate Mao and thus upset the political balance, so he ordered most of the doctors back to their hospitals. Only Hu Xudong, two ear, nose, and throat specialists, and one anesthesiologist were asked to remain in Zhongnanhai to be available in case of emergency. I was still living in the General Office's guesthouse, where I had supervised the experiments in cataract surgery.

In late October, Mao turned sharply worse. He began coughing up large amounts of phlegm, panting heavily, and his production of urine declined drastically, to less than 500cc a day. He was still not letting me in to see him, and I learned of his condition only from the nurses. But the decline in his output of urine indicated a serious condition of the heart, lungs, and kidneys. At this point, I did think glucose injections were necessary and ordered the nurses to administer them. I wanted the doctors to examine him.

Wang Dongxing called the doctors back immediately, and Tao Huanle, the director of internal medicine at Beijing Hospital, moved into Zhongnanhai.

The situation was nerve-racking, and Hu Xudong, who had originally ordered the glucose infusions for Mao, was particularly anxious. He no longer wanted to be part of the team, but he had no way to escape. One night, after taking a sleeping pill, he dropped a burning cigarette butt on his quilt. The quilt ignited, causing considerable damage to his room and burning his windpipe severely. Hu Xudong was taken to Beijing Hospital, where he stayed until after Mao's death, successfully escaping responsibility for treating the Chairman.

With Hu Xudong's departure, I moved back to Zhongnanhai. I wanted the three neurologists there too, to keep a close watch on Mao. Zhang Yaoci would not agree. Zhang Yufeng thought the doctors were useless, and Zhang Yaoci would do nothing to cross her.

That Zhang Yufeng should have such power over Mao's health was preposterous. The Chairman was seriously ill, and we needed the specialists in case of emergency. I told Zhang Yaoci that I would write a request that the doctors be brought to Zhongnanhai and wanted a written reply from him denying it. Only then did Zhang Yaoci relent and raise the matter with Wang Dongxing. Wang ordered the three doctors to Zhongnanhai.

Mao and Zhang Yufeng began watching movies from Taiwan and Hong Kong in his study, and a screening room was set up in the old swimming pool area for the staff of Group One. The doctors were often invited to watch, and sometimes it was impossible to refuse. Zhang Yaoci wanted everyone there. It would not look good for the staff of Group One to watch movies without the doctors when the Chairman was so seriously ill. Often the movies ran until two or three in the morning.

The campaign against Deng Xiaoping was picking up. In August, the deputy secretary of the revolutionary committee at Qinghua University, Liu Bing, had written a letter to Mao criticizing the party secretary of the revolutionary committee, Chi Qun, and another deputy secretary of the revolutionary committee, Xie Jingyi, for being arbitrary in their work and leading lives of decadence. Liu Bing gave the letter to Deng Xiaoping and asked him to forward it to Mao. Deng, in turn, gave the letter to the Bureau of Secretaries, which gave it to Mao.

Mao defended Chi Qun and Xie Jingyi, saying that the two had firmly carried out his revolutionary line. Later, Mao used the letter to attack Deng Xiaoping. He saw Liu Bing's letter as an attack against himself and accused Deng Xiaoping of siding with Liu Bing. The Qinghua incident, Mao said, was not an isolated event but a reflection of the two-line struggle that the Cultural Revolution had apparently not solved.

In October, Mao had begun meeting with Mao Yuanxin to put his views of Deng Xiaoping on record. The talks were secret, their content available only to high-ranking party officials, and they were highly critical of Deng. He accused senior party officials of retreating from revolution to protect their vested interests—nice houses, cars, drivers, servants, and high salaries—and he argued that a new bourgeois class had grown up within the party. They should be the target of the new socialist revolution. Mao reiterated his support of the Cultural Revolution, criticizing it only because the movement had overthrown everything at once and become an all-out civil war. He criticized Deng Xiaoping by name for not caring about class struggle and for saying that any cat whether black or white was good so long as it caught mice. Deng was one of those party members who had joined the new party bourgeoisie. Deng refused to listen to instructions or report to his superiors and did not consult with the politburo, the State Council, or Mao. Deng thought political campaigns had hurt the party's veteran cadres, and Mao wondered what Deng thought about the campaigns against Chen Duxiu, Peng Dehuai, Liu Shaoqi, and Lin Biao. Deng had said that the Cultural Revolution hurt students because they had not been allowed to study, but Mao accused Deng of not studying Marxism-Leninism. Mao did not believe that Deng would never attempt to reverse the verdicts of the Cultural Revolution and said the reason Deng did not talk to others was because everyone was afraid of him.

Mao thought Deng's leadership style was a major problem. But he still thought Deng could be reformed. He was not willing to overthrow him yet.

Another campaign was launched—against rightists and against reversing the verdicts of the Cultural Revolution. Deng Xiaoping was the main target.

Mao was by then so weak that he had great difficulty standing, and the paralysis of his right side was becoming more pronounced. He needed oxygen to breathe. He refused to be fed through a nasal tube, and his weight continued to drop. His attendants fed him a liquid diet of sticky chicken broth that they dripped into his esophagus while he lay on his left side. His whole appearance had changed. Only his black hair was the same.

Mao needed nutrients, and the medical team decided he should be fed intravenous solutions of amino acids imported from the United States and Japan. Zhang Yufeng objected. "The doctors are always asking the patient to take more medicine," she said. "Why don't they try it out on themselves first?"

Wu Jie and Tao Huanle were shocked. They had spent their professional lives treating high-level cadres at Beijing Hospital, but no one had ever asked them to try out the medicine first. They wondered whether they would have to undergo surgery if their new patient ever needed an operation.

In the end, I was the only one to receive the amino acid infusion. The imported solution was expensive, and our supplies were limited. They had to be reserved for the Chairman.

89

Zhou Enlai was dying. Mao never visited him in the hospital. The Chairman was too sick. But at the end of November 1975, Mao asked me to visit Zhou. The premier was still in the 305 Hospital, and I met with his doctors first. Zhou had cancer of the bladder, colon, and lung. Strangely, the cancers were independent of each other, not the result of metastasis.

Zhou was thin and shrunken, but he was still handsome. His neatly combed black hair had only a touch of gray, and he was wearing his usual Mao suit. Zhou refused to be confined to his bed. I met him in the reception area of his hospital suite. He seemed sad.

I told the premier that the Chairman was concerned about his health. Zhou wondered how Mao was doing and asked again whether we had found a cure for his amyotrophic lateral sclerosis. I briefed him on the Chairman's health, ignoring his question about a cure. Zhou asked me to extend his thanks and good wishes to Mao. "It appears I cannot make it," he said. "Take good care of Chairman." When I said goodbye and offered my hand at around 7:00 P.M. on November 29, he was too weak to lift his hand. That was the last time I saw him.

Zhou Enlai died on January 8, 1976.

There was little reaction in Group One. Even Wang Dongxing was silent. We had all known that Zhou was dying, and Jiang Qing opposed the premier to the end. For me, his death was hardly unexpected. What worried me most was the power struggle to follow. Jiang

Qing and her faction were winning. The attacks against Deng Xiao-ping continued, and while he had not been formally removed from power, he was no longer allowed to work. Mao himself was dying.

Many of the doctors on Mao's medical team had also treated Zhou, and they wanted to visit the 305 Hospital to pay their last respects. When I presented their request to Zhang Yaoci, his response was swift and stern. The doctors were not permitted to go, and no one was to wear the black armband of mourning. When I questioned the decision, Zhang became adamant. He was following orders, he said, and did not know the reason behind them. He cautioned the doctors that we would be in trouble if we asked again.

Inside Group One, life continued as usual. The staff still watched movies in the old swimming pool area each night. As Chinese New Year approached, Zhang Yufeng wanted to celebrate. She suggested that Zhang Yaoci set off firecrackers outside Mao's residence. Zhang was happy to please her, but when the firecrackers began exploding, the area suddenly swarmed with guards and soldiers from the Central Garrison Corps. Zhongnanhai had long had a ban against firecrackers. They sounded too much like gunfire and made security more difficult. Zhang Yaoci had failed to tell the security forces his plan. Many onlookers were also drawn to the scene, and a rumor began circulating that the Chairman was celebrating Zhou's death with firecrackers.

People began speculating uneasily about who would replace Zhou. With Jiang Qing's faction on the ascendancy and Deng Xiao-ping under attack, many presumed that Wang Hongwen would be named the new premier. But to everyone's surprise, Mao recom-mended that Hua Guofeng be made acting premier and first vice-chairman of the party. The politburo, meeting on January 21 and 28, accepted his appointment. The formal announcement was made on February 3, 1976.

Like many people, I was stunned. But I thought the appointment was a smart move. So did Wang Dongxing. The Chairman's mind was still clear. The appointment was an affront to Jiang Qing and her cronies. The top-level leaders were split between the veteran Long March cadres (the empiricists) and the younger radicals, whom Mao had accused of dogmatism. Mao did not want to hand over leadership to either side. So he made a man who belonged to neither group premier. Few people had ever heard of Hua Guofeng, the man who once ran Xiangtan prefecture in Mao's home province and had moved on to become first party secretary in Hunan. He was what we called a

'38 cadre—a man who had joined the revolutionary movement in 1938, just after the start of the War of Resistance against Japan. Wang Dongxing was pleased with the choice. Hua was an experienced and dependable leader and a modest, amiable man. The problem was that Hua would soon be made a new target of Jiang Qing and her associates. He was definitely not one of them.

Instead, the attacks against Deng Xiaoping picked up. In early March, transcripts of Mao's talks with his nephew in which he attacked Deng Xiaoping were distributed within the party. I sympathized with Deng. He was an able, astute administrator and probably the only leader capable of leading the country once Zhou and Mao were gone.

Many people found Mao's criticisms unfair. And people resented that Zhou Enlai had not been properly mourned. Beginning in mid-March, knowing that the Qing Ming festival for honoring the dead would be celebrated on April 4, the citizens of Beijing began going to the Monument to the Revolutionary Heroes in Tiananmen Square to place mourning wreaths for Zhou. The movement was spontaneous, and the crowds grew larger by the day. The country had not witnessed such an outpouring of popular sentiment since before the communists came to power in 1949.

I sympathized with the movement and was impressed by the courage of the citizens of Beijing. We all knew that the demonstrators were doing more than mourning the death of Zhou. They were also protesting against Jiang Qing and her radical faction and showing support for Deng Xiaoping. I wanted to go to the square, both to show my sympathy and to see for myself what was happening, but Wang Dongxing and Zhang Yaoci warned me to stay away. Plainclothes police were everywhere, and if my photograph ever appeared in their files, I would have a lot of explaining to do. If I had to go there on business, they said, I should make certain the curtains on my car were drawn.

Toward the end of March, I used a visit to Beijing Hospital on business for Mao as an excuse to go. The square was filled with tens of thousands of people singing, making speeches, and reading poems. The mourning wreaths stretched from the Monument to the Revolutionary Heroes in the center of the square all the way to Changan Avenue just in front of the Gate of Heavenly Peace, and thousands of banners were flapping in the breeze. It was an impressive and moving sight. My driver was grateful for a chance to witness the event. His superiors had warned him, too, against going. He would have liked to stay longer and take a closer look, but I thought it better to go back.

Later I learned that our license plate had been recorded. The police did not investigate, because the car was registered to the Central Bureau of Guards.

Day after day the crowds returned, both mourning and angry. Jiang Qing and her associates were coming under particular attack. On the evening of April 4, the holiday of Qing Ming, the crowds swelled to the hundreds of thousands. The politburo met to decide what to do. Its members concluded that the peaceful demonstrations were part of a deliberate, planned counterrevolutionary movement. Mao did not attend the meeting. Mao Yuanxin served as his liaison. When Mao Yuanxin gave the Chairman a written report summarizing the politburo deliberations, Mao concurred. That night, the order was given to remove the wreaths, banners, and posters from the square and to begin arresting the counterrevolutionaries.

The next day, April 5, the situation turned violent. Angry demonstrators began clashing with the militiamen, police, and soldiers from the People's Liberation Army. Reinforcements were brought in, and by nine o'clock that night, ten thousand militiamen, three thousand policemen, and five battalions of security forces had sealed off the square, beating and arresting the demonstrators who remained inside.

Jiang Qing spent the whole day in the Great Hall of the People, at the western edge of the square, observing the crowd through binoculars. I was in the reception room at the old swimming pool at eleven that night when she came to tell Mao about the successful suppression of the "counterrevolutionaries"—a great victory for her faction. I have no idea what she said to Mao. But I thought the Tiananmen demonstrations were a genuine mass movement, not the "small handful" of counterrevolutionaries that Jiang Qing and her gang accused them of being. Mao had always said that force should not be used against the masses. Now the masses had become the enemy.

Jiang Qing left Mao's room triumphant and invited us to join her to celebrate with *maotai,* peanuts, and roast pork. "We are victorious," she said, offering a toast. "Bottoms up. I will become a bludgeon, ready to strike." It was an unpleasant experience, and I was very upset.

The politburo met again on the morning of April 6, after the mass arrests. Thirty thousand militiamen were ordered to patrol the square and its environs, and nine battalions of soldiers were called to stand ready. Again Mao Yuanxin conveyed the decision to his uncle, and Mao concurred.

The next day, Mao Yuanxin gave Mao the articles from the *People's Daily* condemning the counterrevolutionary incident. Wang Dongxing told me what happened. Mao believed that the incident was counterrevolutionary. It had taken place in Tiananmen Square, in the heart of the nation's capital. Buildings and vehicles had been burned, and fights had broken out. Deng Xiaoping had been behind the incident, Mao said. He had to be dismissed from all his positions in both the party and government, retaining only his party membership. Mao wanted Hua Guofeng to become the permanent premier and first vice-chairman of the party. Mao Yuanxin conveyed Mao's recommendations to another meeting of the politburo. The politburo agreed, and the announcement was made over the People's Broadcasting Station. Deng Xiaoping had been purged again, and Hua Guofeng had permanently replaced Zhou Enlai.

That evening, Wang Dongxing presided over a meeting of Group One and the medical team. We met in the reception room at the old swimming pool. Wang Dongxing announced the politburo decision and distributed a document about the campaign to criticize Deng Xiaoping and oppose his efforts to "reverse the verdicts" of the Cultural Revolution. When the meeting was over, he asked me, Zhang Yaoci, and several of the security officers to stay behind. He warned us to be careful and to watch our words, and he instructed me to pass the message on to the other doctors on the team. The doctors were from several different hospitals, and Wang did not know them well, either personally or politically. Wang had been a supporter of Deng Xiaoping, and he too stood to lose now that Deng had been overthrown. I understood his warning as an effort to keep us silent about his relationship with the deposed leader.

The doctors were not talking politics, though. Their attention was focused on Mao. He still refused our efforts to examine him and would not allow any tests. Our only measure of his health was the urine samples the nurses provided us, and we had brought in sophisticated equipment from the 305 Hospital to help with our analyses. We were able to increase Mao's output of urine from 500cc to 800cc a day, but with such limited access to him, our efforts on behalf of the Chairman were limited.

90

On May 11, 1976, Tao Huanle and I were on duty at the swimming pool when Yu Yaju, one of the best and most experienced nurses on the medical team, rushed in. Mao was perspiring heavily and gasping for air, she told us. We ran to the Chairman's study. Zhang Yufeng stopped us. We insisted, suspecting that Mao had suffered a heart attack. We did not wait for permission to see him.

Mao was conscious but lethargic and made no objections as we began our work. We immediately performed an electrocardiogram and began emergency treatment. A single phone call to Zhongnanhai's Building H, where the medical team was housed, alerted other members of the team, who were there in moments. Mao had suffered a heart attack, a myocardial infarction—a small area of his heart muscle had died from insufficient oxygen. He was still experiencing ventricular extrasystol, or arrythmic heartbeat. Meng Jinyun and Li Lingshi, two women serving as nurses, told us that Mao's attack had begun shortly after his meeting with Laotian prime minister Kaysone Phomvihane, while he was in the midst of an argument with Zhang Yufeng.

Hua Guofeng, Wang Hongwen, and Zhang Chunqiao had been notified immediately and rushed to the swimming pool while we were giving Mao emergency treatment. When the Chairman's condition stabilized, we briefed them. His condition was critical. The three politburo members agreed that Mao needed complete rest. The Foreign Ministry was to inform Chinese embassies throughout the world that Mao would no longer be receiving foreign visitors.

We were concerned that Mao's argument with Zhang Yufeng had precipitated the heart attack, so Hua Guofeng told her that the Chairman was very old and ill and urged her to be patient with him. Zhang Yufeng was irritated. Wang Hongwen stepped in to persuade her. "Xiao Zhang, please take good care of Chairman. We will be grateful to you," he said.

Hua designated four politburo members—himself, Wang Hongwen, Zhang Chunqiao, and Wang Dongxing—to supervise the doctors, and we were told to inform Hua immediately in the event of emergency. Zhang Chunqiao suggested that the policy of sending Mao politburo documents be revised. Mao had continued to receive and review all politburo decisions despite his declining health, and his concurrence had been necessary for implementation. Hua Guofeng, Zhang Chunqiao, and Wang Hongwen agreed that henceforth the flow of documents would be slowed. The politburo would decide case by case whether to send its decisions to Mao. The Chairman needed rest. For the first time, Mao's control over the politburo was slipping. His power was declining. Jiang Qing's faction would dominate.

We were successful in stabilizing Mao immediately after his heart attack, but his condition continued to deteriorate. The arrythmia continued, and his urine output dropped to 500cc a day. The paralysis of his throat had progressed to the point that he was getting very little liquid and few nutrients. His attendants continued to feed him thick broths of chicken or beef but could get only small quantities down.

On May 15, the medical team held an urgent meeting with the politburo team in charge of our work. We pointed out that Mao was not getting sufficient liquid or nutrients, and his precarious condition demanded that we begin feeding him through a nasal tube.

Wang Hongwen wondered whether Mao was still receiving the glucose infusions. He was, but we could not administer sufficient quantities without overburdening his heart. Zhang Chunqiao argued that no one could force Mao to have the nasal tube put in. He would have to be persuaded, and Zhang Yufeng was the only one who could do this. Zhang Yufeng was called to the meeting. Hua Guofeng wanted her to listen to the doctors' assessment so she could talk to Mao.

Zhang Yufeng refused to come. She was too busy tending the Chairman, she said, and she was not a doctor. Attending the meeting would do her no good. The politburo members were at an impasse. Finally, Wang Hongwen said that he would talk to her.

At the end of the meeting, Hua Guofeng asked to see the nasal tube and had us explain how it worked. He thought that if the four politburo members in charge of Mao's health tested it on themselves, they could persuade the Chairman to use it. Hua, Wang Hongwen, Wang Dongxing, and Zhang Chunqiao agreed to return the next day. The doctors would insert the tube in each of them, and they could explain the procedure to Mao. Everyone in Group One agreed to test the nasal tube, too. Mao's personal staff could also try to persuade him.

Just after the meeting broke up, Wang Hongwen approached me. He had found a new medicine for Mao—ground pearls. He already had them—the best pearls that Shanghai could provide—and they had been ground. He wanted me to administer them to Mao.

I stalled. We had experimented on other patients to determine which cataract treatment would be best for Mao. I suggested we put together groups in Shanghai and Beijing and test the effects of ground pearls. Wang Dongxing chided me, accusing me of not trusting Wang Hongwen, a vice-chairman of the party. But I never carried out the experiments, and Mao never received the ground pearls.

Of the four politburo members who agreed to test the nasal tube, only Hua Guofeng actually did. The others—Wang Hongwen, Wang Dongxing, and Zhang Chunqiao—made excuses. Wang Dongxing had used a nasal tube during an earlier operation for ulcers. Wang Hongwen and Zhang Chunqiao were busy with meetings.

Hua Guofeng found the procedure a bit uncomfortable. He felt nauseated as the tube was inserted into the nostril and through his throat, but he felt no pain. He was prepared to describe the experience to Mao. Zhang Yufeng was the only member of Group One not to try. "I'm not sick," she said, "so what good would it do to try? Besides, even if I do try, Chairman may still not agree."

Zhang Yufeng was right. Mao still did not agree. He refused to let us run any tests, but he let us take his pulse.

On the night of May 30, Mao suddenly began perspiring heavily again and lost consciousness. The doctors were called immediately, and as we were reviving him, we quickly inserted a nasal tube into his stomach. He regained consciousness immediately, before we had time to run an electrocardiogram, and he quickly yanked out the tube we had just put in. When one of the doctors tried to stop him, Mao shook his fist at him. He ordered the doctors out.

I stayed behind. We still did not know why he had fainted, though I suspected either hypoglycemia from lack of nutrients or another myocardial infarction. I wanted to do a blood test. He finally agreed to allow us to prick his ear to get a small drop of blood—not enough for a sophisticated test. We could only do a blood sugar count, which was low. The results told us little about his condition.

I insisted that he have an electrocardiogram. We needed to determine whether he had suffered another heart attack. After much persuasion, he allowed us to attach an electrode to his chest that we connected to a radio-controlled electrocardiograph in the reception area. Three heart specialists would take turns monitoring his heart from the reception area, prepared to intervene in an emergency.

Our battles over movies continued. I insisted that the movies, sometimes two a day, were not good for Mao's health, not only because he had to get out of bed to watch them but because some provided more excitement than I thought he needed—graphic rape scenes in films about the Japanese invasion, for instance. Others, like *The Sound of Music* and *Love Story,* were not objectionable, but I was still afraid that moving him around too much would put undue strain on his heart.

Zhang Yufeng wanted Mao to watch movies. Jiang Qing did not, though for reasons different from mine. She thought the light would hurt Mao's eyes and that the air would become foul. She asked her husband to stop watching them.

Wang Dongxing was in favor of movies, less because he thought they were good for Mao than because he was opposed to Jiang Qing. Wang gathered all the doctors together and asked us to write a report in favor of continuing them. The Chairman is sick, he argued, and needs some recreation. Is he not even allowed to watch movies?

When I reported that the doctors agreed that Mao should rest and that the movies were more excitement than his heart could bear, Wang Dongxing was annoyed. Wu Jie was worried that Wang and I were on the verge of blows. He warned me that we could not afford to offend Wang further. We needed his support to do our work. The doctors lost the argument. Mao and Zhang Yufeng continued watching movies.

Mao was restless. After lying in bed for a while, he would feel warm. His attendants would help him move to his sofa, but after sitting awhile, he would want to go back to bed. Jiang Qing suggested bringing in a second bed, so Mao could go back and forth between them. We brought in another bed. Mao was too weak to move by himself. Several people had to help him, and I was always worried that he might fall and break a bone.

On June 26, Mao was more restless and irritable than usual, continually moving back and forth between his two beds. I suspected that he was about to take another turn for the worse. That evening, Tao Huanle and I tried to encourage Zhang Yufeng to keep the Chairman quiet. His arrythmia persisted and his heart was severely short of blood. We were afraid of another myocardial infarction. Zhang Yu-feng refused to listen, arguing that the Chairman was not behaving any differently than usual. "Nothing will happen," she insisted. "I don't think it's that serious."

At seven that evening, Mao took his sleeping pills and was lying in bed. But he was still restless. He moved first to his other bed and then to the sofa. Ten minutes later, he wanted to get back into bed. His heart was being monitored on a screen outside his room. Suddenly, the electrocardiograph registered another myocardial infarction.

Tao Huanle and I rushed in to begin emergency treatment, followed shortly thereafter by Hua Guofeng, Wang Hongwen, Zhang Chunqiao, Wang Dongxing, and the entire medical team. This myocardial infarction was much more severe than the last, affecting a larger area of the heart. We worked until four o'clock the next morning, when Mao's blood pressure finally began to stabilize. We had inserted the feeding tube again, and this time Mao did not pull it out.

We upped the number of medical personnel on duty and worked out a schedule for shifts. Twenty-four nurses began working around the clock, with eight nurses on duty in three eight-hour shifts. The doctors also divided into three shifts, with five doctors per shift, including one to monitor the electrocardiograph. The four politburo members divided into two shifts. Hua Guofeng and Zhang Chunqiao took the day shift, from noon to midnight. Wang Hongwen and Wang Dongxing were on duty from midnight to noon. I supervised all the shifts and briefed the politburo members on Mao's condition the previous twelve hours at the beginning of each one.

Jiang Qing, still living at Diaoyutai, moved back into Zhongnan-hai, staying at the Spring Lotus Chamber, which had been refurbished and modernized in 1974. She had no responsibility for supervising Mao's treatment and dropped in only occasionally to take a look at her husband.

Zhang Yaoci, at Zhang Yufeng's suggestion, wanted to place the nurses under her supervision while I supervised the doctors. The nurses worked most closely with Mao, and since Zhang Yufeng was always there too, she thought she was best able to supervise them. I insisted that the nurses had to follow the doctors' orders, without interference from Zhang. Zhang Yaoci decided not to press Zhang Yufeng's case.

Zhang Yaoci also wanted the doctors to take custody of Mao's medicine. But the regulations had always specified that doctors could only prescribe medicine and not administer it. As a matter of security, we were not allowed direct access to it, nor were we allowed to administer it. The nurses gave Mao his medicine. I insisted on sticking to the rules. If anything went wrong, who would be held responsible?

My relationship with Zhang Yaoci took a nosedive over this disagreement, and we had a heated argument. He accused me of disobeying the "organization"—him—and said it was only because of the Chairman that he bothered to put up with me at all. I pointed out that security regulations that had been in effect for decades prohibited me from following his orders. From then until Mao's death we often argued, and I suspected that when Mao was gone, he would find a way to retaliate.

91

On July 17, 1976, Hua Guofeng called the medical team to a politburo meeting being held in the reception room in the old swimming pool. Three weeks had passed since Mao's second myocardial infarction, and his condition had stabilized. But his life was still in danger. His lung infections continued; his kidney function was poor; and he was still at risk for another heart attack. We presented a detailed report to the politburo, and I emphasized the precariousness of Mao's condition.

When we finished our report, Jiang Qing wanted to know why, if Mao had already suffered two myocardial infarctions, he might still have another one. She accused us again of exaggerating the gravity of Mao's condition in order to escape responsibility for our inability to treat him. She insisted that Mao just had a case of bronchitis, that his lungs had been good, and that he had never before had kidney problems. "You make everything sound so awful," she said. "I think you have not been properly reformed. In bourgeois society, doctors are the masters and nurses the servants. That is why Chairman says we should accept only a third of what doctors say."

The medical team was stunned. The nurses lowered their heads in embarrassment.

Hua Guofeng defended us, pointing out that the doctors were working very hard, doing their best to carry out their duties. He, Wang Dongxing, Wang Hongwen, and Zhang Chunqiao had been on duty, in shifts, around the clock supervising our work. He understood what we were doing and was pleased that three weeks had passed without further medical emergency. He wanted us to work doubly hard, to prepare for all possible emergencies and be ready to treat whatever new problem might arise. "We don't understand medicine," he said, "so we have to ask you to provide Chairman with the best possible medical care. The party center is grateful to you."

We were thankful for Hua's support, but everyone on the medical team was concerned about Jiang Qing's accusations. By saying we had not yet been reformed and were behaving like doctors in bourgeois society, she was implying that we were counterrevolutionary, for which we could pay a heavy price. Our medical explanations meant nothing to her. The case of Stalin's doctors weighed heavily on all our minds.

After the meeting, during Wang Dongxing's shift, I spoke to him about our concerns. He, too, was worried. "Jiang Qing is becoming increasingly arrogant," he said. "She's always criticizing someone during politburo meetings." Earlier in the month, at a State Council planning meeting, she had attacked Hua Guofeng. Hua himself was having a hard time with Jiang Qing. Wang Dongxing wondered what I thought about getting rid of her now, while Mao was sick.

I was cautious. Mao was ill, but he was still alive and very alert. His mind was clear. He was blind in his left eye, but he saw well with the right one. Nothing of importance could be kept from him, and it was impossible to get rid of Jiang Qing without his consent. He would never agree to the purge of his wife. "You have to wait until he dies," I told Wang.

"It will be very difficult after Chairman's death," Wang said.

"Not necessarily," I replied.

Wang told me that he and Hua Guofeng had already talked about arresting Jiang Qing. Hua was not certain they would be able to seize her and was afraid that if she escaped, her enemies would be in serious trouble. Wang Dongxing said he had told Hua that he would go to the ends of the earth to get rid of Jiang Qing.

Wang Hongwen came in as our conversation was ending. I briefed him on the Chairman's condition and went to look in on Mao.

In the next few days, Mao's condition improved somewhat. His heart regained some strength, and the medicines and nutrients he was receiving through the tube in his stomach were having some effect.

On the night of July 27–28, I had stayed in the swimming pool area for several hours after giving my usual briefing when Wang Dongxing and Wang Hongwen began their midnight shift. I returned to my room in Building H sometime before three o'clock in the morning. I ordinarily slept in my cubbyhole off the old swimming pool, but the ordeal with Mao was exhausting me, and I could sleep better in Building H.

I was just drifting off to sleep when I was jolted awake by a violent shaking. The whole building was trembling. Outside my window, the sky was a brilliant red. It was an earthquake. The other doctors and nurses were running into the courtyard outside and were calling me to join them. But I was too tired. I stayed in bed. Then my telephone rang. Wang Dongxing was yelling at me from the other end of the line. "Hurry! This is a huge earthquake. Why aren't you here yet?"

I rounded up the medical staff and we ran to Mao's study.

Yu Yaju, Li Lingshi, Meng Jinyun, and Zhang Yufeng had been with Mao when the earthquake struck. His bed had been dangerously shaken, the whole building had trembled, and the rattling of the tin roof over the old swimming pool had been fearsomely loud. Some of the boards covering the swimming pool had been pried loose. Mao was awake and alert, and after wondering aloud what was happening, he knew that an earthquake had struck. Wang Dongxing and Wang Hongwen were conferring. Mao had to be moved, and they were trying to decide on the safest place. Wang Hongwen suggested the Gong Garden villa in western Beijing, built for Mao under Zhou Enlai's instructions in early 1972. But Mao never liked Gong Garden and had refused to stay there. Wang Dongxing suggested Building 202, constructed in 1974 and meant to be earthquake-proof. The building was just south of the swimming pool and connected to it by a corridor. When I told Mao we thought he should move to the safer Building 202, he agreed. We immediately wheeled him on his hospital bed through the corridor to the new building, and the medical staff moved all the equipment. Mao's new room was much larger, and it accommodated our medical equipment easily. The work of the medical team was easier there.

In the midst of a heavy rainfall the evening after the first earthquake, a second one struck. But Building 202 was so well constructed we barely felt it.

Mao's condition had stabilized, but he was still critically ill. The medical team was working around the clock. In the aftermath of the earthquake, Zhang Yufeng started the movies again. Mao was too ill to watch, but Wang Hongwen had imported a new projector and a wide-screen television from Hong Kong. They claimed they were screening the movies—often two a day—for Mao, for when he was well enough to watch. Zhang Yaoci would often join Zhang Yufeng and the entire staff of Group One, and they were sometimes not around when we needed them. When Jiang Qing stopped by to look in on her husband, they would quickly hide the equipment. To the medical team, it seemed that Mao's staff was relaxing and having fun while we were working ourselves to exhaustion. The behavior of Group One was bad for the medical team's morale, and I raised the issue with Wang Dongxing. Wang was not concerned. "They watch movies. You doctors treat your patient. You don't interfere with each other. What's wrong with that?" But the movie watching did interfere with our work. One time they took away the extension cord on Mao's feeding tube so they could plug in their equipment. When I complained to Zhang Yaoci, he said that while the medical team had lots to do, the staff of Group One did not. He was going to have a bell installed so we could call when we needed them.

Jiang Qing was another source of interference. She was still pushing the campaign against Deng Xiaoping and would sometimes bring us documents about it. She wanted the doctors on duty to rewrite the documents in characters large enough for the Chairman to read. When I protested that the doctors were consumed by their work with Mao, she pointed out that the Chairman's condition was stable. "Let him read some documents to make him feel better," she said. Hua Guofeng and Wang Dongxing tried to persuade her not to bring more documents, but she refused to listen.

Jiang Qing was afraid she might be suffering from some of Mao's diseases. She wanted his medical team to conduct a series of examinations on her. I pleaded on behalf of the exhausted and overburdened doctors, but Wang Dongxing and Zhang Yaoci supported her request, so the doctors ran a series of tests. She was perfectly healthy. Wang Dongxing thought Jiang's request was a ploy. She would want her own team of doctors after Mao's death and was using the examinations to decide whom she liked best.

On August 28, before she left for an inspection tour that included a visit to her favorite Dazhai brigade, Jiang Qing asked me to appoint two doctors from Mao's medical team to accompany her, claiming that there were so many doctors around the Chairman that surely a couple would not be missed. She relented only after I protested that each doctor had a specific assignment and our ability to treat the Chairman would be affected if anyone left.

Mao was becoming fretful again. He could breathe only while lying on his left side, and the tremors in his hands and feet were continuous and pronounced. His arrythmia grew more severe. We changed his medication and his condition improved somewhat, but his health was still precarious.

At five o'clock in the afternoon of September 2, Mao suffered another myocardial infarction, far more severe than the previous two and affecting a much larger area of his heart. His body was giving out. We began emergency treatment immediately. X rays indicated that his lung infection had worsened, and his urine output dropped to less than 300cc a day.

Mao was awake and alert throughout the crisis and asked several times whether he was in danger. His condition continued to fluctuate and his life hung in the balance, but I assured him we were confident he would recover. I had to reassure him. No one wanted to tell the Chairman that he could die at any moment.

Three days later, on September 5, Mao's condition was still critical, and Hua Guofeng called Jiang Qing back from her trip. She spent only a few moments in Building 202 before returning to her own residence in the Spring Lotus Chamber. She was tired, she said, and she did not ask how her husband was doing. The doctors could not understand her callousness. Wang Dongxing found it quite understandable. Mao was the last obstacle to Jiang Qing's absolute power. She was waiting for him to die.

On the afternoon of September 7, Mao took a turn for the worse. His death, we all knew, was imminent. Jiang Qing came to Building 202 when she learned the news. Mao had just fallen asleep and needed the rest, but she insisted on rubbing his back and moving his limbs, and she sprinkled powder on his body. We protested that the Chairman should not be moved and that the dust from the powder was not good for his lungs, but she instructed the nurses on duty to follow her example later. Then she met with the medical team, shaking hands with each of us in turn and repeating to everyone, "You should be happy now." Her behavior was so bizarre that only later did I realize she must have meant that we should be happy because Mao would soon be dead and she would be in power.

She returned that evening, looking for a document she had brought to Mao earlier. We were so busy treating the Chairman that no one offered to help, and she flared up, saying that someone had stolen the papers.

The next morning, September 8, she came again. She wanted us to change Mao's sleeping position, claiming that he had been lying too long on his left side. The doctor on duty objected, knowing that he could breathe only on his left side, but she had him moved nonetheless. Mao's breathing stopped, and his face turned blue. Jiang Qing left the room while we put him on a respirator and performed cardiopulmonary resuscitation. The Chairman revived, and Hua Guofeng urged Jiang Qing not to interfere further with the doctors' work.

But there was no longer anything we could do. At ten minutes past midnight on September 9, 1976, Mao's heart stopped beating and the electrocardiograph went flat. The Chairman was dead.

V

The Aftermath

92

The power struggle began immediately.

I moved to the Great Hall of the People while Mao's body lay there in state, maintaining an office in the Henan room. As deputy head of the task force responsible for the permanent preservation of Mao's body, I had to supervise its care. Wang Dongxing was also staying in the Great Hall, responsible for security. Outside of Zhongnanhai, I was cut off from my direct sources of information, and so was Wang Dongxing, but Hua Guofeng was keeping Wang informed, and he in turn came often to report to me.

I learned that politburo opinion had turned quickly against Jiang Qing and her associates. While Mao was alive, Jiang Qing had been accorded the greatest respect. When she walked into a meeting, everyone would stand and the room would fall silent. She would be offered the best seat, and people hung on her every word. No one dared argue with her. As the politburo began meeting after Mao's death, however, the deference stopped. No one paid any attention when she came into the room. People continued chatting or reading documents, and no one bothered to stand or offer her a chair. When she spoke, no one listened, and the other leaders often talked among themselves while Jiang Qing tried to get their attention. The atmosphere within the politburo had been transformed.

My own situation was still precarious. Jiang Qing had heard that I did not believe Mao's body could be permanently preserved, and both she and Mao Yuanxin withdrew themselves from involvement in the funeral arrangements and efforts at preservation. If Mao's body could not be preserved, she could claim not to have been involved and could turn against those who were. Wang Dongxing was convinced this was part of Jiang's plot against Hua Guofeng. She would hold him responsible if the preservation did not work.

But she would hold me responsible, too. I was the deputy chairman of the preservation committee, but Liu Xiangping, the minister of public health and chairman of the committee, was a close associate of Jiang Qing's. Jiang Qing's wrath would be directed at me. My own fate had not yet been decided, and I remained tense.

At midnight on September 23, and again at four o'clock in the afternoon of September 25, Jiang Qing visited the medical team in Zhongnanhai. Mao's funeral had been held a week before, but his doctors and nurses had still not been allowed to return to their hospitals. Jiang Qing wanted to invite us all to join her in studying the *Selected Works of Mao Zedong,* claiming that most of his post–World War Two writings were actually hers.

Jiang Qing was aware that politburo opinion was turning against her. She talked about Zhang Xueliang, the general who had kidnapped Chiang Kai-shek in 1936 and forced the wartime reconciliation between the nationalists and communists. Chiang had put Zhang Xueliang under house arrest after his own release and had taken the general with him to Taiwan, where his house arrest continued. The general, Jiang Qing said, was allowed to go to restaurants, movies, and church, but the only person to whom he was allowed to talk was his lifelong female companion, Miss Zhao Si. "What kind of life is that?" Jiang Qing wondered, claiming already to have prepared herself for exile.

But Jiang Qing claimed to have a way of handling the "revisionists" within the highest ranks of the party. "I have found a way to knock them down," she told the doctors. "It's just that I can't tell you about it."

That night, September 25, I told Wang Dongxing what Jiang Qing had said.

He was concerned. He knew that Jiang Qing's supporters were distributing guns and ammunition to the militia in Shanghai, and the party secretary of Qinghua University, Chi Qun, was working closely with Mao Yuanxin. Chi Qun was a member of Wang Dongxing's Central Garrison Corps—Qinghua University was under military rule—and he was organizing the Beijing militia. Wang had received word that Mao Yuanxin, as political commissar of the Shenyang Military Region, was organizing an armored troop division to move on

Beijing. "This may be Jiang Qing's way of knocking down her opponents," Wang said. He feared a coup d'état and thought Jiang Qing's allies were likely to move soon.

Wang Dongxing was prepared to launch a countercoup. Hua Guofeng had wanted to move slowly against Jiang Qing and her faction, Wang told me, fearing that he did not yet have enough power within the party and knowing that he did not control the army. But when reports began coming in that the militia in Shanghai and Beijing were being armed and Mao Yuanxin was preparing to move in troops from the northeast, Wang persuaded Mao's successor that they could not wait much longer. Hua had raised the issue with Marshal Ye Jianying. He agreed to take control of the military. The arrests would take place inside Zhongnanhai by Wang Dongxing's Central Garrison Corps, and Ye Jianying would enlist the support of Beijing garrison commander Wu Zhong shortly before the arrests began. Yao Wenyuan's bodyguards came from the Beijing garrison rather than Wang Dongxing's 8341 Corps, so their cooperation would be necessary in Yao's arrest.

Wang warned me that I was to tell no one, be extremely careful, and make every effort to behave normally. "If Jiang Qing asks you to do anything, do it," he said. He warned me not to visit his office. If he had anything more to communicate, he would find me.

I was nervous about the impending showdown, but I knew it would succeed. Wang Dongxing's forces had complete control over Zhongnanhai. No other troops were allowed entrance. Wang was smart and decisive, and I knew he would carry it off.

The members of the medical staff were preparing to return to their own hospitals, but permission for their release had still not been granted. Before they left, they wanted to have their picture taken with Hua Guofeng, Wang Hongwen, Zhang Chunqiao, and Wang Dongxing—the four politburo members who had kept watch over Mao in the last months of his life and with whom they had worked closely. Wang Dongxing agreed, but was still not ready to release them and asked them to stand by.

Several days passed, and my tension was growing. At eleven o'clock on the morning of October 4, Zhang Yufeng came to Building H, where the medical staff was staying, and told us to meet Jiang Qing after lunch at Coal Hill, just north of the Forbidden City. Coal Hill had been closed to ordinary people during the Cultural Revolution, but Jiang Qing went there often. We were going to pick apples and then go to the famous Fangshan Restaurant in Beihai Park to study the *Selected Works* of Mao.

In half an hour, we had collected a dozen baskets of fruit. Jiang Qing did not join us until later, in time to enjoy our apples and invite us to join her at the restaurant to study Chairman Mao. She had originally thought of holding the meeting on October 9, she said, but she had heard the medical team was about to be dispersed and wanted to get us together before we left. She was still trying to decide whom to choose for her medical team and wanted the doctors and nurses to talk, but no one knew what to say. She accused us of being too reserved and told us about her meeting the day before at the February 7 Truck Factory. The workers there had been so talkative they wanted to keep going even after their shifts. "The revisionists could never get the workers so excited, could they?" she asked. We still did not know what to say.

She began by comparing Deng Xiaoping to the Ming dynasty's Wu Sangui (1612–1678), who had turned China over to the control of the Manchus. Deng had also sold out to foreign countries, she said, citing the export of oil and textiles. Deng, it seemed, had allowed the sale of plain cotton cloth. Jiang Qing thought there was a lot more money to be made by selling textiles that had already been dyed. Then she accused the deposed vice-premier of torturing Mao while he was ill, sending him documents to read when his eyesight was bad. She also said that Deng had accused Mao of behaving like the aging Stalin. "There are still a few clowns hopping around now," she said. "Let them hop. Their days are numbered."

I suspected that Jiang Qing and her allies were on the verge of attempting a coup.

After we returned to Zhongnanhai, Wang Dongxing asked us to gather at the Purple Light (Ziguang) Pavilion for the group photo he had promised. Hua Guofeng invited Jiang Qing to join us and told her the politburo would be meeting afterward. Jiang Qing had been irritated about the meeting, wondering why she had not been informed earlier and complaining that Hua had not even told her what would be on the agenda.

We had our group photo taken. The entire medical team, the staff of Group One, and Mao's security guards stood with Hua Guofeng, Wang Hongwen, Zhang Chunqiao, Jiang Qing, and Wang Dongxing. Wang Dongxing took me aside immediately after and asked me to visit him that night.

I went to his home at 11:00 P.M. and briefed him on our afternoon conversation with Jiang Qing. He was convinced that Jiang Qing and her allies were getting ready to move and that his countermove could not be delayed. The longer Wang and his forces waited, the greater the possibility of a leak. By then it was early on the morning of October 5. Hua Guofeng had called a meeting of the politburo for ten o'clock on the night of October 6. They would convene at Jade Spring Hills, in the northwest suburbs. The politburo still had not been informed that Wang Dongxing, Hua Guofeng, and Ye Jianying planned to arrest Jiang Qing and her closest associates. The arrests would take place shortly before the politburo meeting was scheduled to begin. After the arrests, Wang, Hua Guofeng, and Ye Jianying would go to Jade Spring Hills and present the waiting politburo with a *fait accompli* and ask for their approval. Whoever did not agree would also be put under arrest. Wang asked me to send the medical team members back to their hospitals. Only three or four doctors were to remain. When the arrests occurred, he wanted as few people in Zhongnanhai as possible.

It was already three o'clock in the morning when our meeting concluded, and the medical staff had already turned in for the night. I would send them back the next day.

But at nine the next morning, before I had a chance to meet with them, Zhang Yufeng came to tell us that Jiang Qing wanted to go apple picking again. We were to go at once to Coal Hill.

We went immediately and had been picking apples for two hours when Jiang Qing arrived. She picked a few apples, too, before inviting us to join her for lunch at the Fangshan Restaurant, renowned for its imperial-style cuisine. Then she led us again in studying Mao's works.

Wang Dongxing called me, annoyed, in the middle of our study session, and I had to explain that Jiang Qing had ordered us to join her before I had a chance to send the medical staff away. He ordered me to send the nurses back to their hospitals immediately. The doctors and Jiang Qing were to report immediately to the State Council building, where we would again report on the events leading to Mao's death. The report we had made to the entire politburo on September 22 had been interrupted. Now the four politburo members overseeing Mao's care, plus Jiang Qing, would listen to the report again. The meeting, I am convinced, was a ruse, an attempt by Hua Guofeng to maintain an air of normalcy and feigned respect for the very people he was about to arrest.

As the meeting at the State Council began, Jiang Qing wondered why she had not been notified earlier. Hua explained that he wanted the assembled politburo members to hear the report about Mao's death before presenting it formally to the full politburo again. The meeting proceeded under strictest security. None of the secretarial staff, the security guards, or the attendants were permitted into the room.

Hua began the meeting by pointing out that twenty-six days had passed since the Chairman's death but the politburo had still not heard the formal report of the events leading to his death and the measures taken to prevent it. He wanted the five politburo members who had been most closely involved with Mao's medical care to hear the doctors' briefing. The five politburo members would then write their own report, sign it, and present it for approval to the full politburo.

I read from the same report I had tried to present on September 22. Before I was finished, Jiang Qing interrupted. "Comrade Guofeng, I don't feel well," she said. "Fortunately, the four of you who were on duty at the swimming pool are here. I have to leave."

She began walking unsteadily toward the door, as though drunk, and I called the attendants outside to assist her. But they had strict instructions not to enter. As I stood up to help her out, I saw Wang Dongxing look at me and shake his head. By then it was too late. Jiang Qing was faking illness, and Wang was irritated with me for assisting her. Later he told me Hua Guofeng suspected that I was still courting favor with Jiang Qing, and both men were irritated with me for helping her. I convinced Wang Dongxing that I was merely acting "normally," just as he had instructed, and he finally agreed that I had behaved properly, giving her no cause for suspicion.

I finished reading my report, and no questions were raised.

Zhang Yufeng arrived just as the meeting was concluding. Jiang Qing wanted the doctors to return to the Fangshan Restaurant. We had not finished studying Chairman Mao's works. The meeting was adjourned.

On the morning of October 6, I and the remaining doctors on the medical team were reviewing Mao's medical records, preparing to revise our report to the politburo, when Zhang Yaoci interrupted. Jiang Qing wanted her picture taken with the entire medical team. I was reluctant to comply. The nurses had returned to their hospitals, and the few doctors remaining behind were busy. I asked Zhang to check with Wang Dongxing, but Wang was still asleep. I suggested that he contact the nurses himself, but he refused. I contacted the Ministry of Public Health, who arranged for the nurses to return to Zhongnanhai. We had our picture taken with Jiang Qing, and the nurses were sent back again. Later, the picture was taken as evidence that the nurses were Jiang Qing's supporters, and Zhang Yaoci refused to admit that he had ordered the photograph. Only when Wang Dongxing intervened were the nurses cleared.

That night Hua Guofeng called an eight o'clock meeting for the politburo members most closely associated with the publication of Mao's works—Zhang Chunqiao, Yao Wenyuan, Wang Hongwen, and Jiang Qing. The meeting was to be held in Zhongnanhai's Huairen Hall. The members were told that they would first discuss plans for publishing the fifth volume of the Chairman's works and then join the entire politburo at Jade Spring Hills to present their proposal to them.

Hua Guofeng and Ye Jianying arrived in Huairen Hall well before the meeting was scheduled, together with Wang Dongxing and officers from the Central Garrison Corps. Wang hid in an adjacent room.

Zhang Chunqiao was the first to arrive. His security guards and secretaries were ordered to stay outside. When he walked into the conference room, Hua Guofeng announced his arrest. Zhang Chunqiao did not resist.

Wang Hongwen arrived shortly thereafter. When Hua announced his arrest, Wang struggled briefly and was quickly subdued by Wang Dongxing's officers. When the brief fight was over, Wang Hongwen nearly collapsed and had to be held up.

By ten o'clock, when Yao Wenyuan had still not arrived, Wang Dongxing ordered a combined force of officers from the Central Garrison Corps and the Beijing garrison command to arrest him in his home.

Jiang Qing did not come, either. She was still in her quarters in the Spring Lotus Chamber. Zhang Yaoci led a squadron of Central Garrison Corps soldiers to arrest her in her home. When Zhang announced the arrest, she said, "You too! I have long anticipated this day."

I was in my room in Building H when the arrests were carried out. Zhongnanhai was quiet, and there were no obvious signs that anything was amiss. Only the next morning did one of my friends in the Central Garrison Corps inform me that the arrests had taken place. Mao Yuanxin was also arrested, as well as Qinghua first secretary of the revolutionary committee Chi Qun, deputy secretary Xie Jingyi, and many other supporters of Jiang Qing.

Wang Dongxing's forces took the Gang of Four to the same underground complex where Mao's body lay, where they were put in isolation and guarded by soldiers of the 8341 Corps. As soon as the arrests were carried out, Hua Guofeng, Wang Dongxing, and Ye Jianying went to Jade Spring Hills to inform the waiting politburo. They all agreed.

The news was still secret, but I returned home the next day. It was the first time in over a year that I had slept in my own bed. When I told

Lillian that Jiang Qing and her faction were under arrest, she was stunned but delighted. She thought our long ordeal was over and that our life could begin again.

But I could still not relax. The woman I had long despised was in prison, but other members of the politburo, like Xu Shiyou, were still convinced that Mao had been murdered, and our medical report had not been approved. I had made other powerful enemies, too. Zhang Yaoci had told me clearly that if not for Mao, he would get rid of me. Now Mao was dead. Although Wang Dongxing had taken me into his confidence to tell me that the arrest of Jiang Qing and her allies was imminent, my relations with him, too, had become strained. With the Chairman dead and the Gang of Four under arrest, Wang's power had increased. He no longer needed me. Lillian and I and our two sons celebrated the overthrow of the Gang of Four with a Beijing duck dinner in the famous Hongbin Restaurant on Changan Avenue. But I still feared for my safety.

A year later, toward the end of 1977, a new campaign was launched. Leading cadres were being sent for reform to May 7 Cadre Schools. I was still president of the 305 Hospital and hence its leading cadre. Zhang Yaoci got his revenge. When he suggested that the hospital's leading cadre should be reformed through hard labor, I had no way to refuse, and Wang Dongxing did not intervene on my behalf. I was sent to the countryside of Jiangxi to do heavy labor. I was fifty-seven years old.

I stayed for more than a year, living and working as a peasant.

In Beijing, the power struggle continued. In December 1978, after Deng Xiaoping's return to power, Zhang Yaoci and Wang Dongxing were purged. Deng had never forgiven the Central Garrison Corps for not protecting him during the Cultural Revolution, and he never returned to live in Zhongnanhai. With the purge of Zhang and Wang, the way was clear for my return to Beijing. I went home in January 1979 and resumed my position as president of the 305 Hospital.

But there were rumors. I had been too close to Wang Dongxing. I was pressured to denounce him, to tell what I knew of his past. If Wang Dongxing had been guilty of political crimes, so was I.

Then Mao's role in Chinese history grew controversial, and I had been too close to Mao. If Mao had made mistakes, so had I. Some people said his doctor had had too great an influence on Mao. Mao's detractors could accuse the doctors of doing too much to save the Chairman, and his supporters could accuse us of doing too little.

The power struggles continued and the questions surrounding

Mao's death remained unsettled. The leaders who had supervised the medical team—Hua Guofeng, Wang Dongxing, Wang Hongwen, and Zhang Chunqiao—were purged, and no one was left to vouch for our efforts. In December 1979, I wrote a letter to Deng Xiaoping asking to be relieved of my duties at the 305 Hospital. I could do nothing there, and I was very unhappy. I was given a sinecure. I became the deputy vice-president of the Chinese Medical Association.

With Deng's new "open door" policy, I was given several opportunities to travel abroad. Thus there was nothing very unusual in the summer of 1988 when I requested permission to visit my two sons in the United States. Zhao Ziyang was general secretary of the Communist party then, and China had never been more open. But, really, my permission to leave was a fluke. Had the proper authorities been informed, my request would not have been granted.

I came to the United States for Lillian. Our years of tribulation had taken their toll. In February 1988, her health had begun to fail, and the treatment she was receiving in China was doing little good. That August, I brought her and our granddaughter, Lili, to join our two sons and their wives in Chicago. We hoped that with advanced medical care in the United States, Lillian's life could be saved. But the medical treatment failed. Lillian died on January 12, 1989, of chronic renal failure.

Friends in China had often suggested that I write about my life with Mao. Tian Jiaying, knowing that I kept a diary, had suggested it as early as 1960. In 1977, when Ye Jianying visited me at the 305 Hospital, he too encouraged me to write. He thought that after twenty-two years at Mao's side, I had a contribution to make to our understanding of history. After that, many newspaper and magazine editors urged me to write. Always, I refused. I could not write the truth in China, and I did not want to tell lies.

Lillian finally convinced me to write. In her last days in the hospital, before she slipped into a coma, she urged me to write this book as a record for our children, grandchildren, and the generations to follow and as a history of life in Mao's imperial court. I have paid for this book with my life. My dream of becoming a neurosurgeon never came to pass, and my hopes for a new China were dashed. My family life was destroyed, and now Lillian is dead. In 1990, when the Central Bureau of Guards wrote requesting to take over my apartment, I did not agree. In 1992, they did confiscate my home, however. I wrote letters of protest to Yang Shangkun (then president of the republic), Yang Dezhong (director of the Central Bureau of Guards), Chen Mingzhang (the minister of health), and Jiang Zemin (head of the Communist party). I have received no answer. I devoted my professional life to Mao and China, but now I am stateless and homeless, unwelcome in my own country. I write this book in great sorrow for Lillian and for everyone who cherishes freedom. I want it to serve as a reminder of the terrible human consequences of Mao's dictatorship and of how good and talented people living under his regime were forced to violate their consciences and sacrifice their ideals in order to survive.

NOTES

BY ANNE F. THURSTON

3   After 1973, Mao was never photographed standing up or walking, since he had to be physically assisted. Chinese sources record another meeting, on May 27, 1976, between Mao and Pakistani prime minister Bhutto.

7   Chinese sources say that Mao's arranged marriage took place in 1908, that the young woman moved into the Mao family house, and that she died in 1910. Reports on whether the marriage was consummated differ.

21   Much of what Mao said during this trip was circulated to ranking officials after the flight of Lin Biao.

27   Chen Xilian was closely associated with Hua Guofeng and also had ties to Mao Yuanxin and members of the Gang of Four. He was forced to resign in February 1980, after Deng Xiaoping's return to power.

37   Peking Union Medical College was founded in 1904 by six Western churches. The Rockefeller Foundation support began in 1914. Shanghai's Fudan University was moved to Chongqing during the war.

40   According to Bo Yibo, there were only sixty thousand "higher-level" intellectuals in China in 1949.

46   At that time, cadres were divided into four ranks in terms of the size of the pot in which their food was cooked. Top leaders ate out of the smallest pot, and the food was cooked for them and their families by chefs. High-ranking cadres had small pots, but their food was not as

good and the chefs not as skilled. Middle-level cadres, like Dr. Li, ate food cooked in medium-sized pots, and lower-ranking cadres ate food cooked in huge pots, which served large numbers of people, and the food was coarse.

49   One of the reasons Wang Dongxing may have been in charge of the photographers was the suspicion with which cameras were viewed. Cameras imported from the West were frequently inspected for fear that foreign spies had hidden secret weapons inside, and the explosion of a flashbulb during a picture-taking session with Liu Shaoqi and Zhou Enlai once created great security concerns.

53   An additional concern was the sudden death from a cerebral hemorrhage of Ren Bishi, the fifth ranking member of the party elite. It was also at this point that each of China's top leaders was assigned a personal physician.

56   The Chinese continue to assert that the United States used germ warfare in Korea, and the United States continues to deny it.

56   Other reports say Mao and Yang Kaihui had three sons, one of whom died when they went to Shanghai after their mother's execution.

58   Wang Hebin, who served as Mao's physician prior to Dr. Li, reports that Mao once gave him some letters from Anqing in which Mao's son describes his mind being occupied by a little person who was always prodding him to do things he ought not do. Anqing wrote that he could not control or hide from the little person, which made him uneasy, but without him, Mao Anqing felt lonely. After the episode described here, Mao Anqing was diagnosed by Chen Xueshi. The psychiatric profession was nearly decimated under the communists, and Chen later spent many years in jail. Dr. Li does not know what drugs were used to treat Mao's son or other high-ranking patients. ECT, however, was never used. Wang Hebin says that Mao Anqing was sent for treatment to the Soviet Union for several years after this incident.

60   Several other doctors had treated Mao prior to 1954, including Fu Lianzhang, Chen Binghui, Zhong Fuchang, and Zhou Yisheng prior to 1949, and Wang Hebin, Zhou Zezhao, and Xu Tao after the establishment of the People's Republic.

62   The word Chen Zongying used to describe Jiang Qing was *saojian-huo,* meaning both "flirtatious" and "base."

68   Mao had been studying English on and off since he was a youth. In 1912, he had entered a Western-style business school but had to withdraw after a month because most of the courses were in English. Some believe his ineptitude with foreign languages is one of the reasons he never studied abroad.

69   Mao's love of fatty pork is well known, and he is said to have believed such food necessary for the functioning of his brain. Both his earlier doctor, Xu Tao, and his wife, Jiang Qing, had clashed with Mao over his eating habits, and the clash with his wife is said to have led to their eating separately.

70   Yudin is the coauthor of *A Concise Philosophical Dictionary,* also published in Chinese, and recognized as an authoritative expositor of Stalin's thought. The Soviet Union began publishing criticisms of Mao's "On Contradiction" and "On Practice" in 1953, the same year Yudin came to serve as the Soviet ambassador to China. While Mao welcomed the arrival of Yudin, some Chinese later believed that he was sent to learn more about Mao's philosophy in order to criticize it.

72   Some sources say He Zizhen had six children, one of whom was delivered during the course of the Long March. Of the six, only one was male. Only Li Min is known to have survived. Two of the children were given to peasant families and never found again. The others died.

72   Given the deprivations of the Long March, it is almost impossible to believe that Fu Lianzhang had a chicken every day. Fu's biographer says he was born in 1894, a year after Mao.

72   Mao's insomnia, beginning at least in 1927, is well documented in Chinese sources. Some people attribute it to the rigors of guerrilla warfare, which often required nighttime activities and made any regular schedule impossible. In addition, Mao is known to have lost sleep at times of political struggle. Others' memoirs say that his bodyguards were forbidden from waking him once he fell asleep, and they counted the number of hours he slept by the week rather than the day. Rarely was he said to have slept more than thirty hours a week.

77   At least since the communists established their guerrilla base in Yanan in the mid-1930s, Mao was always given the best residence available. His cave in Yanan is said to have been the most comfortable.

81   Another source says Fu Lianzhang's daughter and son-in-law were killed sometime after the beginning of the Long March in 1934. Fu's physician son-in-law, Chen Binghui, is said to have treated Mao in 1932. The fact that Fu and his family were well off financially and lived a comfortable life was one source for the charge that they were "anti-Bolshevik." Fu Lianzhang was saved through the help of Mao and Zhang Wentian, but his relatives were not.

83   Reports have Mao playing mah-jongg as early as 1927.

90   Big Beard Wang's confession is not the only reason the campaign was stopped. Many were falsely accused.

93   Mao had begun hosting dancing parties in the mid-1930s in Yanan, where Ye Zilong had organized the participation of young women and a band of amateur musicians from his section of confidential secretaries.

94   Mao himself agreed in 1953 that the cultural work troupe should not be set up so close on the heels of the "three-anti" campaign against corruption, waste, and bureaucratism, but it was still not disbanded.

103   The unretouched photos of Mao smiling clearly reveal his blackened teeth.

104   The Berkeley *Wellness Letter* of September 1992 notes recent ads of a "famous Romanian anti-aging formula" that will "make you younger overnight" and describes the alleged wonder drug as pro-caine (trade name Novocain). The report says that a Dr. Anna Aslan experimented with the drug in Bucharest in the 1940s. No studies have ever shown the drug to live up to its claims.
       Here and elsewhere, the Western reader will notice the absence of informed consent in Chinese medical practice. The notion is relatively new in the United States as well.

105   In a September 1961 meeting with Field Marshal Montgomery, Mao talked about his death and possible successor. Before the meeting, he told Xiong Xianghui that even Qin Shihangdi had not been able to find the elixir of long life and said that such an elixir was nonsense.

107   Mao's bowel habits have been written about by others who were close to him. It is said that in Jinggangshan Mao's wife, He Zizhen, used her fingers to clean out Mao's bowels and later learned how to administer enemas. During the civil war against the nationalists, Mao refused to use a lavatory, and his bodyguards would accompany him to the fields, dig a hole where he could empty his bowels, then cover the hole with dirt. It is said that during the Long March, Mao's bowel movements were a source of inspiration to his soldiers.

110   Here and elsewhere, Dr. Li uses the term *depression* in the popular rather than strictly medical sense, since he was not trained in psychiatry. The Chinese perception of mental illness has changed since Mao's death, and psychological counseling clinics have been set up in many Chinese cities.

116   Scholars of this period describe a much more complicated interaction between the Comintern and the Chinese Communist party, and many are more charitable to Wang Ming than to Mao. Similarly, Soviet help to the Chinese communist cause, while not extensive, was greater than Mao was willing to recognize.

117   Almost 90 percent of the munitions used by China during the Korean War were bought from the Soviet Union. The Chinese borrowed more than $1.3 billion from the Soviets in order to buy them.

118   Zhu De joined Zhang Guotao, who later split with Mao, during part of the Long March.

120   Edgar Snow's account appears in *The Long Revolution* (New York: Vintage, 1971), p. 175.

121   Traditional Chinese folk belief posits that the fate of a sibling who lives after another sibling has died becomes stronger, as though the living take on the strength and power the deceased would have possessed had he lived.

125   Khrushchev remembers the crudity of Mao's language in asserting that China could produce more people, and he and other Soviet leaders were apparently horrified at his callousness with respect to human life. See *Khrushchev Remembers,* translated and edited by Strobe Talbott (Boston: Little, Brown, 1974), p. 255.

130   One Chinese account asserts that Mao never flew after 1955–56. Dr. Li, however, can remember thirteen occasions after then that he flew with Mao.

132   Jiang Qing was also involved in the decision to build the pool. Mao's own account of the incident says he offered to pay 50,000 *yuan* for the construction.

148   Mao's tailor was a French-trained fashion designer named Wang Ziqing; his Leimeng Dress Shop was on Beijing's busiest shopping street, Wangfujing.

152   Wang Hebin, who served as Mao's doctor from August 1949 to October 1953, had been trained in medicine in Yanan. After leaving his post with Mao, he went to the Soviet Union for further study, returning to work for a while in Beijing Hospital. At Mao's death, he was working in Taiyuan, Shanxi.

157   Under Mao's prodding, the Chinese had upped the 1957 production targets for both grain and steel. Grain yield would increase from 300 to 500 million tons, and steel production from 18 million to 30 million tons. That Mao's plan was adventurist can be seen in the fact that in 1984, the year that produced the largest harvest in China's history, grain yield was only 400 million tons; steel production only reached 30 million tons in 1983.

167   From *The Poems of Mao Tse-tung,* translation, introduction, and notes by Willis Barnstone, in collaboration with Ko Ching-po (New York: Harper & Row, 1972), pp. 85–87.

    Some have read Mao's poem, with its reference to death, as an indication of his knowing he did not have much longer to live, and thus not that much time to build his "great walls" and establish himself as a modern-day Qin Shihangdi. The "storms and waves" have been seen as the impediments to his plans put up by Khrushchev's attack on Stalin and his own colleagues' commitment to a slower approach.

175   Some sources say Wang Guangmei was Liu's fifth wife. We have only been able to confirm that she was the third.

180   Bo Yibo says the first time he heard Mao talk about retreating to the second line was in the summer of 1954.

197   Again, Dr. Li is using the term *depression* in the popular sense, not in the psychiatric meaning of clinical depression. The timing may be off here. Mao was quite active between November 1956 and May 1957, giving speeches in January, February, and March 1957 and traveling to several cities in March. Mao also had a series of meetings with intellectuals and leaders of the "democratic parties" in April. It seems more likely that Mao's depression began in May or June 1956, when the criticisms of his "adventurism" began, and that it lasted until November, when he began implementing his own counterattack. He may have become depressed again in May 1957, when the criticisms of the Communist party became virulent.

215   In 1956, Yale-in-China Medical School was renamed Hunan Medical College. Today it is Hunan Medical University.

221   Reports saying that Dr. Li shared a room with Mao's interpreter, Li Yueran, are mistaken.

224   Mao's inspiration for asserting that China would overtake Great Britain within fifteen years may have been Khrushchev's boast that the USSR would overtake the United States within the same period. Dr. Li did not, however, hear Khrushchev's speech. The term *Great Leap Forward* was first publicly used by Zhou Enlai in a speech in the summer of 1957, and the *People's Daily* called for a Great Leap Forward on November 13 of that year, before Mao's return from Moscow.

225   Khrushchev's recollections of Mao during the 1957 meetings in Moscow can be found in *Khrushchev Remembers, op. cit.,* pp. 250–257.

229   Chen Yi, then a vice-premier and the Chinese foreign minister, is said to have made similar complaints against Jiang Qing, saying that in order to satisfy her demands for silence he had had to take off his shoes and walk around in bare feet.

229   Chen Boda had been criticized by Mao for suggesting that the contradiction between the proletariat and the bourgeoisie had been solved and saying that the main contradiction was between China's economic and cultural development and the people's demands.

230 Bo Yibo had opposed Mao's "adventurism" in 1956 and had rejected the call to achieve "greater, faster, better and more economical results." When Mao began his counterattack in September 1957, Bo Yibo was one of those criticized. Mao accused him of leaning to the right.

233 The poem is by Yu Xin, who lived in the period of the Northern and Southern dynasty, A.D. 513–581.

235 Mao had begun using the phrase "greater, faster, and more economical results" in late 1955 and early 1956.

245 Li Dongye was appointed minister of metallurgy, and Liu Huafeng became the secretary-general of the party's Organization Department. He Zai first became a section chief of the Organization Department and later its secretary-general.

248 The original photograph, which appeared in the *People's Daily* on May 26, 1958, showed Beijing mayor Peng Zhen standing near Mao. When Peng was purged during the Cultural Revolution, he was airbrushed out of the picture.

261 Khrushchev's description of the 1958 visit can be found in *Khrushchev Remembers, op. cit.,* pp. 258–261.

263 For a fuller explanation of the genesis of people's communes, see Roderick MacFarquhar, *The Origins of the Cultural Revolution 2: The Great Leap Forward 1958–1960* (New York: Columbia University Press, 1983), pp. 77–88.

264 Mao is no doubt referring to Jack Belden's *China Shakes the World,* first published in 1949 and republished in 1970 (New York: Monthly Review Press, 1970).

266 While Mao cautioned Dr. Li that the trip was secret, the Chairman was trailed by numerous reporters and officials, and the trip soon became a great media event.

282 Zhou Enlai's capacity for alcohol was well known in China, and he suffered throughout his life from frequent nosebleeds.

290 Other reports from China indicate that Mao visited steel factories in the northeast in February 1958, but Dr. Li remembers this trip taking place in the winter of 1958–59.

302 Film clips taken of Mao during his second visit to Shaoshan show that a tombstone was added.

334 The Chinese for "sticking together like glue" is *ni xingying bu li, ru jiao si ji*—your body and shadow won't separate, like glue, like paint.

343 In fact, Xinyang had been devastated by the famine.

351 Grain yield went from 200 million tons in 1958 to 170 million in 1959, 143 million in 1960, and 147 million in 1961. Not until 1966 did grain yield exceed the amount for 1957.

366   Some of the scholars who have read this account doubt that Mao's quarters could have been bugged without his permission. Dr. Li is reporting on what he actually saw and heard, which led him to believe that Mao did not know.

379   Mao met Montgomery again in 1961. He invited the field marshal to swim with him in the Yangtze, but indigestion prevented Montgomery from joining Mao.

382   See Barnstone, *The Poems of Mao Tse-tung, op. cit.,* p. 103.

382   One Chinese source puts the meeting with He Zizhen in 1959. Another agrees that it was in 1961.

385   The 7,000 cadres' conference took place from January 11 to February 7, 1962.

388   Chinese sources say Mao first met Hua Guofeng in 1955.

389   Dr. Li may be referring here to a meeting in early March on theater and the arts.

395   Li Weihan's memoirs say he was dismissed in December 1964, although Mao's criticisms of him began in 1962. Wang Jingxian was not dismissed until March 1966. Deng Zihui was dismissed when the Rural Works Department was abolished in November 1962.

396   One Chinese source says that Wang Feng was dismissed in November 1966.

397   The Chinese definition of schizophrenia is clearly much broader than that given in the *Diagnostic and Statistical Manual of the American Psychiatric Association,* used in the West. The psychiatric profession was nearly devastated after 1949, and there were few practicing psychiatrists.

400   Wang Guangmei's report was given in July 1964 to the Hebei provincial party committee and in September 1964 to the party Central Committee. While Jiang Qing began making public appearances in 1962, Mao did not criticize Wang Guangmei until 1964.

402   The *People's Daily* reports a public performance of *Li Huiniang* as early as August 1961, together with favorable reviews, including one by Liao Mosha. In March 1963, the party Central Committee circulated a directive forbidding performances of operas about ghosts, and in May 1963, Liao Mosha's laudatory review of *Li Huiniang* was publicly criticized.

405   Jiang Qing's cooperation with Ke Qingshi began as early as 1962.

416   Beijing Normal University High School is one of the finest in the city, reserved for the best students, many of whom are children of intellectuals and the political elite. Dr. Li's housing was also far superior to that of other doctors at the time, many of whom lived with extended families in very cramped quarters.

420   The rural practice of turning to folk healers such as shamans and spirit mediums for medical help was criticized as superstitious by the communists. Few rural Chinese would agree with the connotation of "witch doctor."

433   Yang Shangkun was officially removed as director of the General Office in November 1965. Luo Ruiqing was officially removed in December 1965. They were both removed from their positions on the Central Committee secretariat in May 1966.

443   Mao's fear of poison may be more reasonable than appears. The one time I stayed in a villa once reserved for Mao, the most striking thing, beyond the size of the rooms and their opulence, was the peculiar odor, so strong that sleep was difficult. A Chinese friend who visited another of Mao's villas also remarked on the strange odor. Most of Mao's haunts were in the hot and humid south and they were left unused when Mao was not there, sometimes for years. I can only conclude that they became mildewed in his absence. Others have pointed out that peasants, who spend most of their time outdoors and live in relatively primitive housing, often find adjustment to the indoors difficult and fear the stifling atmosphere.

448   There are differing interpretations of Peng Zhen's behavior over this incident. Some believe that he understood Mao's feelings from the beginning and decided to resist him.

451   Ye Qun apparently made two visits to Mao, one in November 1965, which Dr. Li did not witness, and the second in early 1966, described here.

453   Lin Biao's baldness was probably the result of favus of the scalp that he contracted as a youth.

460   Fu Lianzhang died in March 1968.

462   Some in the West believe that Mao's letter to Jiang Qing, published in China after Lin Biao's demise, was a forgery. Dr. Li does not concur. Other sources not only believe the letter to have been real but say that Mao showed the letter to Zhou Enlai, who in turn informed Lin Biao. In any case, the letter was later published and is available in English in *Issues and Studies,* January 1973.

465   Chinese sources say that Wang Dongxing sent Wang Li and Qi Benyu to seize Tian Jiaying's documents on the afternoon of May 22 and that the search continued into the night. Tian is reported to have committed suicide early in the morning of May 23.

466   Tao Zhu was appointed executive secretary of the central secretariat on May 23, 1966. Other sources indicate he had arrived in Beijing on June 4 and left for Hangzhou on June 9. His return to Beijing described here is some six weeks after his central-level appointments.

470   Other sources suggest a different order of speakers. One source suggests the order was Li Xuefeng, Deng Xiaoping, Zhou Enlai, Liu Shaoqi. Another suggests it was Li Xuefeng, Liu Shaoqi, Deng Xiaoping, Zhou Enlai. Dr. Li remembers the second order as the accurate one.

478   Kang Sheng lived in Building 8; Chen Boda lived in Building 15.

482   The figure of 2 million soldiers called out to "support the left" is confirmed by Zhou Enlai in a conversation with Edgar Snow. See Snow, *The Long Revolution,* op. cit., p. 103.

483   Military units in China are given secret code names. Many Chinese believe that the number assigned to the Central Garrison Corps—8341—was assigned on the basis of the prediction by a fortune-teller, who said that Mao would live to be eighty-three years old, which he did, and lead the Chinese Communist party for forty-one years (dating from 1935), which he also did. There is, so far as I know, no evidence to support the story.

483   According to Chinese sources, Wang Dongxing's troops arrived at Beijing Textile Factory on June 26, 1967.

486   The picture appears in *People's Pictorial,* No. 4, 1968. The revolutionary committee is reported to have been established on September 19, 1967.

492   Many in the West believe that the "May 16 Rebels" never existed. Dr. Li was not acquainted with the group, only with the accusations against it. Chen Yi was overthrown, however, and the British offices were burned.

501   This meeting was reported in the West at the time and is widely seen as a turning point in Mao's relations with radical students.

529   No one, including Chen Boda and Wang Dongxing, openly argued that Lin Biao should assume the chairmanship, though the implication was clear. The open argument focused on whether the chairmanship should be reestablished. While Lin and his supporters argued that the chairmanship should be reinstated and that Mao should assume the position, he also knew that Mao would not. If the position were reinstated and Mao did not assume it, Lin Biao was the only logical choice.

532   There is no evidence to suggest that Mao was correct in assuming that Snow was a member of the CIA. Snow's version of this interview with Mao can be found in his *The Long Revolution, op. cit.,* pp. 169–172.

576   Deng Xiaoping returned to Beijing in February 1973 and made his first public appearance in April. In August 1973, Deng was formally reinstated on the Central Committee and in December was appointed a member of both the politburo and the Military Affairs

Commission. Deng's new positions were not formally confirmed until the Second Plenum of the Tenth Party Central Committee, in January 1975, when he was appointed a member of the politburo standing committee and vice-chairman of the party.

577 Some sources attribute the idea of rotating the regional military commanders to Deng Xiaoping.

583 Despite Chinese attempts to gather information on how amyotrophic lateral sclerosis is treated in the United States, no foreign doctor ever examined Mao.

636 Wang Dongxing's purge was not official until February 1980, when he was forced to resign as a vice-chairman of the party and member of the politburo standing committee.

CHRONOLOGY

1949 Communists take over Beijing in January. Zhisui Li returns there in June at the invitation of Fu Lianzhang and begins work in the medical clinic at "Labor University." People's Republic of China (PRC) is established on October 1. Mao leaves for Moscow.

1950 Mao and the General Office move to Zhongnanhai. Zhisui Li is put in charge of the Zhongnanhai health clinic. The new government begins carrying out land reform and enters the Korean War.

1952 China carries out the "three-anti" campaign, against corruption, waste, and bureaucratism. Zhisui Li treats Mao's son Mao Anqing and meets Jiang Qing. Dr. Li is voted a model worker and is admitted into the Communist party.

1953 Korean War is concluded. China begins introducing agricultural cooperatives.

1954 Wang Dongxing appoints Dr. Li to serve as Mao's personal physician. Zhongnanhai carries out a purge of counterrevolutionaries, and many doctors are dismissed.

1955 Zhisui Li meets Mao Zedong and is invited to join him for May Day celebrations atop Tiananmen. Dr. Li administers his first physical examination of Mao. Many cooperatives that had been amalgamated into larger collectives are abolished by Deng Zihui, to Mao's great consternation. Mao begins writing *Socialist Upsurge in China's Countryside*.

1956 Khrushchev denounces Stalin in February, and Mao is angry with both Khrushchev and Chinese leaders who had suggested supporting Khrushchev. Mao swims in the Pearl, Xiang, and Yangtze rivers and launches the

100 Flowers movement, calling on intellectuals to criticize the party, following the Eighth Party Congress. Jiang Qing leaves for the Soviet Union, and Dr. Li leaves Mao's service to study neurology.

1957 Jiang Qing returns from the Soviet Union. Dr. Li is called back to Mao. The anti-rightist campaign is launched in June. Dr. Li goes with Mao to Moscow.

1958 Party rectification continues in Zhongnanhai with the Black Flag Incident. Mao launches the Great Leap Forward. Khrushchev makes a secret visit in July and August. Rural people's communes are formed, the movement to establish backyard steel furnaces spreads, and Mao orders the shelling of Quemoy and Matsu.

1959 Widespread food shortages plunge China into famine. Mao's train and villas are secretly bugged, and Peng Dehuai writes a letter to Mao criticizing the Great Leap Forward, for which he is purged. Lin Biao is appointed to succeed Peng as minister of defense, and Dr. Li is hospitalized with ulcers. Mao resigns as chairman of the republic.

1960 Famine continues. Wang Dongxing returns to Group One.

1961 Famine continues. Party leadership begins remedial measures as Mao retreats, apparently depressed, seeking solace in female companionship. Female companion reveals that Mao's train is bugged, leading to numerous dismissals.

1962 Liu Shaoqi blames the famine on man-made disasters. Communes are restructured. Mao's support within the party wanes. Lin Biao praises Mao. Mao begins counterattack by arguing that classes continue to exist even under socialism. Kang Sheng is put in charge of purging the party, and Jiang Qing makes her first public appearance. Socialist education campaign begins.

1963 Jiang Qing begins criticizing capitalist influences in art and culture. Socialist education campaign in the countryside continues.

1964 First edition of the "little red book" of Mao's quotations is published as Lin Biao pushes the cult of Mao. Mao abolishes the Bureau of Health, and Dr. Li moves out of Zhongnanhai.

1965 Deng Xiaoping convenes meeting aimed at eliminating corruption among rural cadres, while Mao argues that the contradiction in the countryside is between socialism and capitalism. Dr. Li prepares report of Mao's criticisms of the medical profession calling for doctors to work in the countryside. Mao sends Dr. Li and Wang Dongxing to participate in the socialist education campaign in rural Jiangxi. Yang Shangkun is dismissed as director of the General Office and replaced by Wang Dongxing.

1966 Dr. Li returns to Mao's service. Literary attacks continue, and members of the Beijing party committee are purged. Jiang Qing and Lin Biao form an alliance. Central Cultural Revolution Small Group is formed. Mao Zedong swims in the Yangtze and returns to Beijing to launch the Great Proletarian Cultural Revolution, greeting millions of Red Guards in Tiananmen Square. Purges continue. Country begins descent into turmoil.

1967   Fighting breaks out in many parts of China as result of the Cultural Revolution. Mao puts Wang Dongxing and the Central Garrison Corps in charge of restoring order to factories and universities in Beijing. Dr. Li's relations with Jiang Qing and Mao deteriorate. Head of state Liu Shaoqi, party secretary-general Deng Xiaoping, and propaganda chief Tao Zhu are "struggled against" inside Zhongnanhai.

1968   Jiang Qing accuses Dr. Li of trying to poison her. Mao expresses discontent with student rebels and calls upon worker, peasant, and soldier teams to take over factories and schools. Liu Shaoqi is expelled from the party.

1969   Ninth Party Congress is held in April, officially reversing many of the principles of the Eighth Party Congress. Mao is enshrined as the supreme leader and "Mao Zedong Thought" is made the country's guiding ideology. Lin Biao is designated Mao's successor and "closest comrade in arms." Skirmishes between the Soviet Union and China break out on the northeast border. China is mobilized for war. Mao begins talking about negotiating with the United States and expresses dissatisfaction with Lin Biao.

1970   Dr. Li is sent into exile in Heilongjiang in June. Second Plenum of the Ninth Party Congress is held in August-September, and Lin Biao maneuvers to reinstate the position of chairman of state and to have himself appointed to succeed Liu Shaoqi. Mao objects. Dr. Li returns to Zhongnanhai in November. Mao is seriously ill with pneumonia, and Mao blames his illness on Lin Biao. Mao meets with Edgar Snow in December and says he is willing to invite Nixon or any other high-ranking American official to meet with him in Beijing.

1971   Mao's distrust of Lin Biao continues. Kissinger makes a secret visit to Beijing in July. In August and September, Mao tours the country, meeting with regional commanders to shore up support against Lin. Mao returns to Beijing on September 12. Lin Biao, with his wife and son, flee by plane, heading toward the Soviet Union. Plane crashes in Outer Mongolia and all on board are killed. Mao's health takes a turn for the worse.

1972   Mao becomes seriously ill in January and refuses medical treatment, suggesting privately that Zhou Enlai should succeed him. Medical treatment finally begins on February 1. Nixon arrives on February 21 and meets Mao Zedong. Joint communiqué is signed in Shanghai. Zhou Enlai and Kang Sheng are diagnosed with cancer. Mao begins rehabilitating purged party officials.

1973   Deng Xiaoping returns to Beijing, referred to as vice-premier. Zhou Enlai comes under attack by Jiang Qing and her faction. Mao begins to have difficulty speaking.

1974   Jiang Qing continues attacks against Zhou Enlai. Mao criticizes his wife, saying it would be better for them not to see each other. Mao's health continues to deteriorate, and in July he is diagnosed as having amyotrophic lateral sclerosis.

1975   Deng Xiaoping is formally instated as a vice-chairman of the party. Mao's health continues to deteriorate while many refuse to believe he is ill. Doctors face interference in treating him. Politburo is formally informed of his illness. Zhou Enlai's health declines.

1976   Zhou Enlai dies on January 8. Massive popular demonstrations take place in Tiananmen Square in April. Deng Xiaoping is purged again, and Hua Guofeng is appointed to succeed Zhou. Mao suffers heart attacks in May and June. Zhu De dies in July, and Beijing is hit by a major earthquake on the night of July 27–28. Mao dies on September 9. Xu Shiyou accuses Jiang Qing and Mao's medical staff of poisoning him. Jiang Qing and three of her allies are arrested as the Gang of Four on the night of October 6.

1977   Dr. Li is sent to Jiangxi for labor reform.

1978   Deng Xiaoping returns to power.

1979   Dr. Li returns to Beijing and is criticized for his relationship with Wang Dongxing.

1980   Dr. Li is appointed deputy vice-president of the Chinese Medical Association. Wang Dongxing is removed from all party and state posts.

1988   Dr. Li and his wife, Lillian, arrive in the United States.

BIOGRAPHICAL SKETCHES

Bo Yibo (1908–):   Born in Dingxiang, Shaanxi. Joined the Chinese Communist party (CCP) in 1925. Finance minister 1949–53, vice-chairman of the State Planning Commission 1954–56, chairman, State Economic Commission 1956–66, and vice-premier 1956–66. Persecuted during the Cultural Revolution, but survived to become senior statesman after 1978.

Chen Boda (1904–89):   Born in Huian, Fujian. Entered Moscow's Sun Yat-sen University in 1927. Served as one of Mao's political secretaries. Editor in chief *Red Flag,* 1958–66, member Politburo standing committee 1966–70. Rose to great power during the Cultural Revolution, but fell from grace in 1970.

Chen Xilian (1913–??):   Born in Huangan, Hubei. Joined the CCP in 1930. Commander of the People's Liberation Army (PLA) Artillery Corps 1950–59. Commander of Shenyang Military Region 1959–73 and first party secretary of Liaoning province 1971–73. Became commander of Beijing Military Region in 1974 and a vice-premier in 1975. A close associate of Mao's nephew, Mao Yuanxin. His relations with the Gang of Four led to his resignation in 1980.

Chen Yi (1901–72):   Born in Lezhi, Sichuan. Joined the CCP in France in 1923. One of China's ten marshals. Mayor of Shanghai 1949–58, becoming vice-premier in 1954 and foreign minister in 1958. Persecuted during the Cultural Revolution. Died of cancer in 1972.

Chen Yun (1905–):   Born in Jingpu, Jiangsu. Joined the CCP in 1925. Vice-premier 1949–72. Became vice-chairman of the CCP Central Committee in 1956 and one of the top seven leaders of the CCP. Went into obscurity in the late 1950s due to his lukewarm support of the Great Leap Forward. Reemerged in 1978 as vice-chairman of CCP Central Committee to become influential senior statesman.

Chen Zaidao (1908–93):   Born in Macheng, Hubei. Joined the CCP guerrilla forces in 1927. Commander of Wuhan Military Region 1954–67. Criticized during the Cultural Revolution.

Deng Tuo (1912–66):   Born in Fuzhou, Fujian province. Became director of Beijing municipal Propaganda Department in 1951 and was director and chief editor of *People's Daily* 1950–58. Accused of being "anti-party" in 1966 and purged; committed suicide in 1966.

Deng Xiaoping (1904–   ):   Born in Guangan, Sichuan. Went to study in France in 1920 and joined the CCP in 1924. Appointed vice-premier in 1952, becoming secretary-general of the party and member of politburo standing committee in 1956. Purged at the beginning of Cultural Revolution and rehabilitated in 1973. Purged again in 1976. Since 1978, has been the paramount leader of China.

Deng Zihui (1896–1972):   Born in Longyan, Fujian. Became leader of guerrilla base in western Fujian in 1920s. Director of Rural Work Department under the CCP Central Committee in 1953. Appointed vice-premier in 1954, but was criticized as a "right conservative" by Mao in summer 1955, after which his Rural Work Department was dissolved.

Fu Lianzhang (aka Nelson Fu) (1894–1968):   Born in Changding, Fujian. Baptized a Christian and trained as medical doctor at a Christian medical school. Known as "the Christian doctor." Treated Mao and other party leaders in Jiangxi soviet in early 1930s and participated in Long March 1934–35. Vice-minister of public health in 1952, in charge of top leaders' health care. Forced to retire in late 1950s. Tortured to death during the Cultural Revolution in 1968.

Gao Gang (1905–54):   Born in Hengshan, Shaanxi. One of the founders of the CCP's northwest guerrilla base. Secretary of Northeast Bureau (Manchuria) 1945–54 and a vice-chairman of the central government 1949–54. After being accused of forming an anti-party alliance with Rao Shushi, was purged, and committed suicide in 1954.

Guo Moruo (1892–1978):   Born in Leshan, Sichuan. Joined the CCP in 1927. Trained in medicine, he became a well-known scholar and writer. Befriended Mao during the Chongqing negotiations in 1945. Vice-premier, 1949–54, chairman of the Federation of Literary and Art Circles, 1949–66, and president of Chinese Academy of Sciences, 1949–78.

George Hatem (1910–88):   A Lebanese-American and a graduate of Geneva Medical School. Went to China to practice medicine in 1933. Went to Yanan in 1936. Joined the CCP and became a Chinese citizen in 1950. Died in Beijing.

He Zizhen (born He Guiyuan) (1909–84):   Born in Yongxing, Jiangxi. Joined the CCP in 1926. Married Mao in Jiangxi in 1928 and bore him six (?) children.

Only Li Min survives. Participated in the Long March 1934–35. In 1937, left Yanan to receive medical treatment in the Soviet Union, returning in August 1947. Never formally divorced from Mao, she lived in Shanghai after 1949.

Hu Qiaomu (1912–92):   Born in Yancheng, Jiangsu. Joined the CCP in 1935. Educated at Qinghua University. Became one of Mao's political secretaries in 1945. Deputy director of the Department of Propaganda 1950–66, and editor of Mao's selected works. Politically inactive after 1961 because of ill health, he reemerged as party's leading ideologue after Mao's death.

Hua Guofeng (1921–):   Born in Jiaocheng, Shaanxi. Joined the CCP in 1940. Became party secretary of Xiangtan prefecture, Hunan, where Mao's native village of Shaoshan is located. First met Mao in 1955. Became first party secretary of Hunan in 1970. Appointed to the politburo in 1973. In 1976 became premier and first vice-chairman of the CCP, designated by Mao as his successor. In overall charge of the arrest of the Gang of Four, became party chairman and chairman of the Military Affairs Commission after Mao's death. By 1981, had been dismissed from all three important posts, remaining only a member of the CCP Central Committee.

Huang Jing (born Yu Qiwei) (1911–58):   Born in Shaoxing, Zhejiang. Joined the CCP in 1932. Jiang Qing's common-law husband in early 1930s. First party secretary of Tianjin in the early 1950s and later the minister of First Ministry of Machine Industry and chairman of the State Technological Commission. Criticized by Mao in 1958 and died the same year.

Jiang Nanxiang (1910–88):   Born in Shaoxing, Zhejiang. Educated at Qinghua University, where he joined the CCP in 1933. In 1949, appointed deputy secretary of the New Democratic Youth League (later the Communist Youth League) and later president of Qinghua University. Became vice-minister of education in 1960 and minister of higher education in 1965. Purged in 1966 during Cultural Revolution.

Jiang Qing (aka Li Jinhai, Li Yunhe, and Lan Ping) (1913–91):   Born in Zhucheng, Shandong. Common-law wife of Huang Qing in early 1930s. Shanghai actress in mid-1930s. Married playwright Tang Na in 1936. Went to Yanan in August 1937. Became Mao's fourth wife in November 1938. It is widely believed that the CCP politburo agreed to the marriage only on the condition that Jiang Qing not appear publicly as Mao's wife and that she refrain from politics. Had one daughter with Mao, Li Na. Came to political prominence during the Cultural Revolution. After Mao's death, arrested as the leading member of the Gang of Four and sentenced to death, with a two-year stay of execution. Her sentence was reduced to life imprisonment in 1983. Committed suicide in 1991.

Kang Sheng (1898–1975):   Born in Jiaonan, Shandong. Met Jiang Qing in 1918. Joined CCP in 1925. Spearheaded party rectification movement in Yanan in 1945. Entered Beijing Hospital in 1950; said to be diagnosed as schizophrenic. Politically active again during the Great Leap Forward in 1958.

Became adviser of the Central Cultural Revolution Small Group and member of the politburo in 1966 and masterminded many purges of high-ranking CCP members during the Cultural Revolution. Died of bladder cancer.

Ke Qingshi (1900–65): Born in Wuhu, Anhui. Visited Russia in 1922. Party secretary of Jiangsu province (1952–55) and Nanjing municipality (1950–52), becoming party secretary of Shanghai in 1955. Closely associated with Mao, became a politburo member in 1958 and vice-premier in 1965. Died of acute pancreatitis in 1965.

Li Min (1936–): Born in Yanan. The only surviving offspring of Mao and He Zizhen. In 1940, joined her mother in the Soviet Union and lived there until they returned to China in 1947. After 1949, lived in Mao's Zhongnanhai compound. Studied at Beijing Normal University. Married Kong Linhua in 1959 and had a son the next year. Appointed a member of the Chinese People's Political Consultative Conference in 1979.

Li Na (1940–): Born in Yanan. The daughter and only child of Mao Zedong and Jiang Qing. Studied history at Peking University 1959–65. Married in early 1970s, had a son, but later divorced. In 1974–75, appointed party secretary of Pinggu county outside Beijing and later became a vice-party secretary of Beijing. After her mother was arrested as one of the Gang of Four, was dismissed from her post and lived in difficult circumstances. Later she was given a job with the Bureau of Secretaries in the General Office. Married Wang Jingqing, former bodyguard of Liu Shaoqi, in 1985.

Li Xiannian (1909–92): Born in Hongan, Hubei. Joined the CCP in 1927. Served as vice-premier (1954–80) and finance minister (1954–75). From 1983 to 1988, was president of the People's Republic of China (PRC).

Li Yinqiao (1927–): Born in Anping, Hebei. Joined the communist revolution in 1938. Served as Zhou Enlai's bodyguard before becoming Mao's in 1947. Married Han Guixin in 1948. Became Mao's deputy chief bodyguard in 1952 and chief bodyguard in 1956. In 1962, after a year in the countryside, left to work in Tianjin. Became deputy director of the Bureau of Management of the Great Hall of the People.

Li Yunlu (?–1988): Jiang Qing's older half-sister (sharing the same father, but with a different mother). Married to Wang Keming. Supported Jiang Qing when Jiang was a child. Joined Jiang Qing in 1948 and later moved to Mao's compound in Zhongnanhai to take care of Li Na. Moved with her son to Qinghua University at the beginning of the Cultural Revolution in 1966.

Lin Biao (1907–71): Born in Huanggang, Hubei. Joined the CCP in 1925. One of China's ten marshals. Replaced Peng Dehuai as defense minister in 1959. Designated Mao's successor in 1969. In September 1971, after allegedly plotting a coup against Mao, fled by plane. The plane crashed in Outer Mongolia, en route to the Soviet Union, and everyone on board was killed.

Lin Ke (c. 1925–): A graduate of Yenching University and one of Mao's political secretaries, serving under Tian Jiaying, from the early 1950s until 1963.

Liu Shaoqi (1898–1969): Born in Ningxiang, Hunan. Joined CCP in 1921 in Moscow and studied at Moscow's University of the Toilers of the East 1921–22. Worked in the underground movement in the late 1930s. Urged the party to study "Mao Zedong Thought" in 1942. Became second only to Mao in the CCP from 1943 to the Cultural Revolution in 1966. Chairman of PRC 1959–67. Persecuted during the Cultural Revolution and died in prison in 1969, his illness untreated. Officially rehabilitated (posthumously) in 1980.

Lu Dingyi (1906–): Born in Wuxi, Jiangsu. Joined the CCP in 1925. Director of Propaganda Department of CCP Central Committee 1954–66, vice-premier 1959–66, and minister of culture 1965–66. Purged and persecuted during the Cultural Revolution.

Luo Daorang (c. 1915–1969): An overseas Chinese from Thailand who returned to China and went to Yanan early in the anti-Japanese War (1937–45). Deputy director of the General Office's Office of Administration after 1949 and acting director of the Bureau of Bodyguards in 1956. Sent to the countryside by Wang Dongxing in 1961 and appointed party secretary of Zhanjiang, Guangdong, in 1962. Persecuted to death during the Cultural Revolution.

Luo Ruiqing (1906–78): Born in Nanchong, Sichuan. Joined the CCP in 1929. Became the minister of public security in 1949 and directed security arrangements for Mao. Became chief of the PLA's General Staff in 1959. Purged in 1965, before the start of the Cultural Revolution. Rehabilitated in 1975. Died after surgery in West Germany.

Mao Anqing (1923–): Mao's second son by Yang Kaihui. Suffered severe beating by a policeman in Shanghai in the 1930s. Diagnosed as schizophrenic in the early 1950s. Married the sister of Mao Anying's widow in 1962. The two had a son in 1970.

Mao Anying (1922–50): Mao's eldest son by Yang Kaihui. Sent to Shanghai after mother's death and lived as a street urchin. Found and sent to study in the Soviet Union in 1936. Served in Korea as a Russian translator for Peng Dehuai, commander-in-chief of Chinese army. Killed in an American bombing attack in November 1950.

Mao Yuanxin (1941–): Son of Mao's brother, Mao Zemin, who was executed in Xinjiang in 1943. In 1950, after Mao Yuanxin's mother remarried, was entrusted to Mao Zedong and moved to Mao's Zhongnanhai compound. Studied at Harbin Military Engineering College. Became the party secretary of Liaoning province in 1973 and the political commissar of Shenyang Military Region in 1974. In 1975, served as Mao's liaison with the politburo. Arrested with the Gang of Four and sentenced to seventeen years in prison.

Mao Zedong (1893–1976): Born in Shaoshan village, Xiangtan prefecture, Hunan. Founding member of the CCP in 1921. Paramount leader of the CCP from 1935 until his death in 1976.

Mao Zemin (1896–1943): Born in Shaoshan village, Xiangtan prefecture, Hunan. Younger brother of Mao Zedong. Joined the CCP in 1922. Worked with Xinjiang warlord Sheng Shicai, who had Mao Zemin arrested and killed in 1943, after Sheng turned against the CCP. Mao Yuanxin is the son of Mao Zemin's third wife.

Peng Dehuai (1898–1974): Born in Xiangtan, Hunan. Joined the CCP in 1928. One of China's ten marshals. Vice-premier 1954–65 and defense minister 1954–59. Criticized Mao's Great Leap Forward in 1959 and was thereafter purged. Imprisoned in 1966 and died in prison in 1974.

Peng Zhen (1902–): Born in Quwu, Shaanxi. Joined the CCP in 1923. Appointed first party secretary of Beijing Municipality in 1949. Politburo member 1945–66. Close associate of Liu Shaoqi, first politburo member victim of Cultural Revolution, 1966. Peng survived the Cultural Revolution to become senior statesman after Mao's death.

Rao Shushi (1903–75): Born in Linchuan, Jiangxi. Joined the CCP in mid-1920s. First secretary East China Bureau 1949–52, and director of Organization Department of CCP Central Committee in 1952. Purged in 1954 after being accused of conspiring with Gao Gang in an anti-party alliance. Died in prison.

Ren Bishi (1904–50): Born in Xiangyin, Hunan. Joined the CCP in 1922. Educated in Moscow at University of the Toilers of the East, 1921–24; secretary of the secretariat of the CCP Central Committee, 1945–50. Fifth ranking party leader in 1949. Married to Chen Zongying. Died of cerebral hemorrhage in 1950.

Song Qingling (1893–1981): Born in Shanghai. Older sister of Song Meiling (Madame Chiang Kai-shek). Married Sun Yat-sen in 1914. Supported the CCP and became vice-chairman of PRC in 1949.

Sun Yat-sen (1866–1925): Physician and founder of the Guomindang, widely credited with having led the movement that overthrew the Qing dynasty in 1911 and established a new republic. Unable to maintain national power after collapse of the Qing, he turned to Soviet advisers for organizational assistance.

Nancy Tang (c. 1940–): Born in Brooklyn, New York, where her father ran a Chinese newspaper. Returned to China and attended the Chinese Foreign Languages Institute before the Cultural Revolution. Served as Mao's English-language interpreter and later as liaison between Mao and the politburo.

Tao Zhu (1908–69): Born in Qiyang, Hunan. Joined the CCP in 1926. Became the first party secretary of Guangdong province in 1953, first secretary of Central-South Bureau in 1961, and a vice-premier in 1965. Rose to fourth place in the party hierarchy in 1966 but was purged several months later. Under house arrest from January 1967 to October 1969, when he died of cancer. Rehabilitated posthumously in 1978.

Tian Jiaying (c. 1922–1966): Largely self-educated, became one of Mao's political secretaries in the late 1940s, a position he retained after the communists came to power. Under suspicion at the onset of the Cultural Revolution, committed suicide in May 1966.

Wang Dongxing (1916–): Born in Yiyang, Jiangxi. Joined the CCP's guerrilla force in mid-1920s. Became Mao's bodyguard in 1947. In 1949, he became director of the bodyguards under the General Office and a vice-minister of the Public Security Ministry, also serving as Mao's chief bodyguard and in charge of the bodyguards for all the top leaders. Became director of the General Office in 1966. Helped direct the arrest of the Gang of Four after Mao's death in 1976 but was deprived of all his posts in 1980.

Wang Guangmei (1921–): Born in Beijing. Graduated from Beijing's Furen University, founded by Catholic missionaries. In 1946, became an English interpreter for the CCP and went to Yanan. Became Liu Shaoqi's third (?) wife in 1948. Imprisoned for the duration of the Cultural Revolution, returning at its conclusion to become a vice-president of the Chinese Academy of Social Sciences.

Wang Hairong (c. 1940–) Mao Zedong's grand-niece and a graduate of the Foreign Languages Institute, becoming liaison between Mao and the politburo in the 1970s.

Wang Hebin (1924–): Born in Hebei province. Joined the communist revolution in 1938. Served as Mao's personal physician from August 1949 to September 1953.

Wang Hongwen (1935–92): Born in Changchun, Jilin. A security official at Shanghai No. 17 Cotton Mill in 1966. Rose to power during the Cultural Revolution. Was appointed vice-chairman of the CCP Central Committee in August 1973. In 1976, was arrested as a member of the Gang of Four and sentenced to life imprisonment. Died of liver disease in 1992.

Wang Ming (1904–74): Born in Liuan, Anhui. Joined the CCP in 1925. A graduate of Moscow's Sun Yat-sen University, returned to China in 1930. With the help of the Soviet Union, became a dominant figure in the CCP and the head of the Wang Ming faction of "twenty-eight-and-a-half Bolsheviks." Clashed with Mao; his own position in the party declined as Mao's importance grew. Returned to the Soviet Union for medical reasons in 1956, staying there until his death in 1974.

Wang Renzhong (1917–92): Born in Jiang, Hebei. Joined the CCP in Jiangxi soviet area in 1933. First secretary Wuhan municipality 1949–54, first secretary Hubei province 1954–66, and political commissar of Wuhan Military Region 1963–67. An important figure early in the Cultural Revolution. Later became ill and moved to Guangzhou. Returned to influence following Mao's death in 1976.

Wu Xujun (c. 1933–): Orphaned as a child; trained as a nurse in the Guomindang's Defense Medical College prior to 1949. Moved to Beijing after graduating from nursing school and became head nurse at the Zhongnanhai

Clinic. Appointed by Wang Dongxing in 1960 to be Mao's head nurse. Left Mao's service in 1974.

Wu Yunfu (1904–69): Born in Leiyang, Hunan. Joined the CCP in 1926. Director of administration under Yang Shangkun's General Office and a vice-minister of public health after 1949. Persecuted to death in 1969.

Xie Fuzhi (1909–1972): Born in Hongan, Hubei. Joined the Communist party in 1931. First party secretary of Yunnan province 1955–59, becoming the minister of public security in 1959, succeeding Luo Ruiqing. After 1969, politburo member and vice-premier 1965–72. Died in 1972, but in 1980 was posthumously expelled from the CCP for his activities during the Cultural Revolution.

Xu Shiyou (1906–85): Born in Xin, Henan. A monk trained in martial arts, joined the CCP in 1927. Commander of Nanjing Military Region 1954–74 and commander of the Guangzhou Military Region 1974–80. Appointed to the politburo in 1969 as a balance to Lin Biao's military power. Died in 1985.

Xu Tao (c. 1927–): Born in Beijing; graduated from Beijing Medical College in 1949. Served as Mao's personal physician 1953–54 and later became Jiang Qing's doctor. His wife, Wu Xujun, was Mao's head nurse.

Yang Kaihui (1901–1930): Born in Changsha, Hunan. Married Mao Zedong in winter 1920 and bore him three sons: Mao Anying, Mao Anqing, and Mao Anlong (Anlong died in Shanghai in the mid-1930s). Was arrested and executed in late 1930 for refusing to denounce her revolutionary husband.

Yang Shangkun (1907–): Born in Tongnan, Sichuan. Joined the CCP in 1926. Studied at Moscow's Sun Yat-sen University, becoming the half (because he was so young) of Wang Ming's faction of "twenty-eight-and-a-half Bolsheviks." Served as director of CCP's General Office 1948–65. Purged in late 1965; survived the Cultural Revolution to become vice-chairman of the Military Affairs Commission and president of the PRC.

Yao Wenyuan (1931–): Born in Zhuji, Zhejiang. Worked at the Policy Research Institute of the Shanghai party committee. Member of the Central Cultural Revolution Small Group. Appointed to politburo in 1969, in charge of ideology. Arrested as member of the Gang of Four and sentenced to twenty years' imprisonment.

Ye Jianying (1897–1986): Born in Meixian, Guangdang. Joined the CCP in 1924. One of China's ten marshals. The party secretary of Guangzhou municipality 1950–54; politburo member 1966; politburo standing committee member 1973–85. A leading figure in arresting the Gang of Four. Died in 1986.

Ye Qun (c. 1920–1971): Joined the CCP in Yanan; second wife of Lin Biao. Member Central Cultural Revolution Small Group. Appointed to the politburo in 1969. Died in plane crash in 1971 while fleeing with her husband to the Soviet Union.

Ye Zilong (c. 1915–): Born in Hunan. Joined the Communist army in 1930 and began working as Mao's personal secretary in 1936, a post he held until he fell out of favor in late 1961. Arrested during the Cultural Revolution. Became vice-mayor of Beijing municipality in 1979.

Zhang Chunqiao (1917–): Born in Juye, Shandong. Joined the CCP in 1938. Became chief editor of *Liberation Daily,* the mouthpiece of the Shanghai party committee in 1951, director of Shanghai propaganda department in 1963, and secretary of Shanghai party committee in 1967. Became deputy head of Central Cultural Revolution Small Group in 1966, politburo member in 1969, and member of the politburo standing committee in 1973. He was director of the General Political Department of the PLA and a vice-premier in 1975. Arrested as a member of the Gang of Four in 1976; sentenced to death, with a two-year reprieve. In 1983 his death sentence was reduced to life imprisonment.

Zhang Yufeng (1944–): Born in Mudanjiang, Heilongjiang. Met Mao in 1960 while serving as an attendant on Mao's special train and later became his constant companion. Was formally appointed Mao's confidential secretary in 1974, retaining that position until Mao's death.

Zhang Yaoci (c. 1915–): Born in Yiyang, Jiangxi. Participated in the Long March. From the same town as Wang Dongxing; served as commander of the Central Garrison Corps while Wang Dongxing was the party secretary there. One of the men responsible for Mao's security.

Zhou Enlai (1898–1976): Born in Huaian, Jiangsu. Went to France to study in early 1920s and joined the CCP in 1922. Premier of PRC 1949–76. Member politburo standing committee 1956–76.

Zhu De (1886–1976): Born in Yilong, Sichuan. Joined the CCP in 1922. Commander-in-chief of the Red Army in 1930s. One of China's ten marshals. Vice head of state of the central government 1949–59. Member politburo standing committee 1956–76.

INDEX